KT-393-999

THE
REAL
COUNTIES
OF
BRITAIN

THE REAL COUNTIES OF BRITAIN

RUSSELL GRANT

MAPPING BY

Ordnance Survey

Virgin

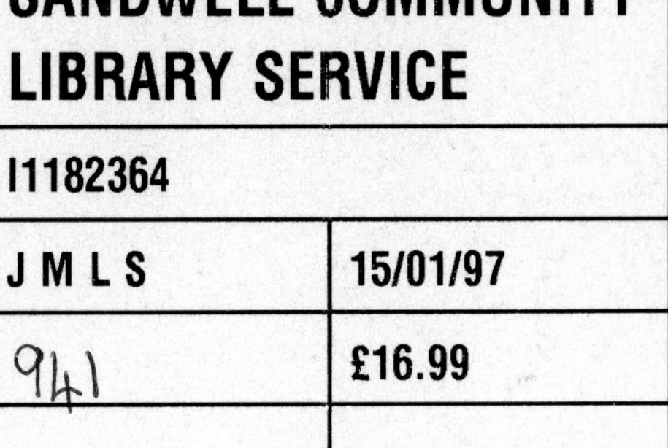

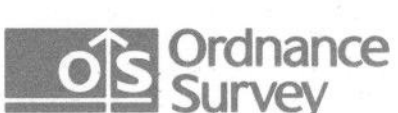

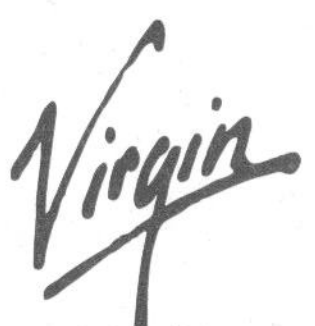

"To the Commissioners of the Review of Local Government, The Minister of State for the Environment and the Ministers of State for Scotland and Wales who had the chance in 1992, 1993, 1994 and 1995 to enrich and elevate Britain's County heritage and blew it."

First published in 1996 by Virgin Books,
an imprint of Virgin Publishing Ltd
332 Ladbroke Grove, London W10 5AH

A catalogue record for this book is available from the British Library

ISBN:1 85227 479 4
Printed in Italy

- Project Manager/Editor: James Harrison
- Designed by Edward Kinsey
- Contributors: Robin Neillands, Michael Leech, Tim Ware, Nia Williams, Keith Howell.
- For Virgin Publishing: Carolyn Price
- Heraldic Shields by Marie Lynskey.

Mapping produced by Ordnance Survey. The representation of the real county boundaries is as accurate as the information available and the mapping allows.

For the source material of the county boundaries – The Royal Geographical Society.

Publisher's Notes:
The information for each county's local government is correct as at 1 July 1996. There are still some Local Goverment Commission recommendations that are subject to Acts of Parliaments.

A directive from the Association of British Counties says that a detached part of one county – which is an island completely cut off from its parent county and surrounded geographically by another – is within the geographical bounds of the county it lies in.

CONTENTS

THE REAL COUNTIES OF WALES

THE REAL COUNTIES OF SCOTLAND

INTRODUCTION

BEFORE YOU EMBARK on finding your true roots and to which Real County you belong, read this.

The role of the County in this country enjoyed a thousand years of singular simplicity. Then in 1889 it became a would-be maze, and from 1965 a Byzantine labyrinth, as successive governments and local government commissions complicated what was once very easy to understand.

Between 1965 and the present day, yes the day you are reading this book, the County of your birth has become overwhelmed by confusion due to the disregard for history, geography and local identity mostly by politicians and journalists alike who really neither know nor, in many cases, care about your county heritage. This was vividly illustrated in the 1990's local government review and subsequent upheaval but before I go on let me face you with the facts.

THE REAL COUNTY: or Geographical County

Essentially the Real County is a creation of nature; hills, rivers, mountains, streams provided its boundaries because geography shaped it and history defined it. The name County comes from the Norman French – *comté* – on a par with the term 'shire' coined by the Saxons – meaning a portion or *sheared* off piece of land. The Real County was founded way back in time; some counties such as Kent, Essex and Middlesex are over 1,000 years old. By the time of the Norman Conquest in 1066 most English counties were formed, only six were created after.

To help I have devised an easy way of knowing whether a county's origin is from an ancient tribe or territory, or an area gathered around one central strategic or fortified town by using the suffix 'shire' for the latter. Without the 'shire' tag your county is likely to have developed from an ancient clan or kingdom.

In Wales six counties date from the 13th century whilst the remaining seven (including Monmouthshire) were created by the 1536 Act of Union under Tudor King Henry VIII. In the book I have given the Welsh name in conjunction with its English counterpart.

In Scotland the counties, or sheriffdoms and shires to give them their proper description, had their origins in numerous historic districts and parishes. Many of these historic divisions have given their ancient names to the Real Counties that superseded them, I have included both titles. It wasn't until as late as around 1800 that 32 became the accepted number of Real Scottish Counties – Ross and Cromarty, Orkney and Shetland counting as one. Up until then Scotland was a jigsaw of frequently changing and complex divisions and subdivisions with the Parish being the only available subdivision in most of the kingdom. Puzzling? Not nearly as puzzling as what follows...

THE ADMINISTRATIVE COUNTY: for Local Government purposes only

It's now the county maze twists and turns. Not immediately though for the Administrative County or County Council began life as an Act of Parliament – in 1888 for England and Wales, in 1889 for Scotland – hewn out of the boundaries of the Real County for one sole purpose: Local Government of the Real County nothing more. In many cases the two mirrored each other with the same name, boundaries and identity. But there were fundamental differences that meant *they were not the same.* One was created from natural geography and the other devised by an Act of Parliament to be called *an administrative county* to differentiate it from the real county it served. Important point because the Administrative County is an Act of Parliament and therefore only a subsequent Act can change it or abolish it. This is not so with the Real County, a natural and historic unit which needed no Government to create it therefore no Government can destroy it, as a letter from Prime Minister Margaret Thatcher's Environment Department confirmed to me.

THE JUDICIAL COUNTY ... yet another county

There are also judicial counties for legal purposes which didn't necessarily have the same boundaries as either the real or administrative county, which is why the 1888-89 Local Government Acts made the distinction between the different types of counties from the very beginning.

THE CEREMONIAL COUNTY: just when you thought it was safe…

One of the idiosyncrasies dreamed up by the 1990's Local Government Review was a Ceremonial County. These were specifically devised to take account of the abolition of certain county councils such as Avon, Humberside and Cleveland. This weak attempt to please emphasised more than anything how ridiculous it was in the 1960s and 1970s to make the administrative county synonymous with the ceremonial county. Quite obviously the real county is the county people look to for their ceremony, pageantry and pomp and is the natural domain for any Lord Lieutenant or County Sheriff.

Take County Durham for instance – and this is just one example: the 1990's Review makes it clear that the Ceremonial County of Durham will be administrative Durham – Durham County Council – the districts of Hartlepool and Stockton north of the River Tees. So far so good. But it *excludes* Sunderland, Gateshead and South Tyneside all in County Durham. But because the 1990's Local Government Review only covered the so-called Shire Counties, the Metropolitan Boroughs of the real County Durham couldn't be provided for and included within their own Durham home. So the new Ceremonial County of Durham doesn't include or represent well over half-a-million people in County Durham! It goes to show how chaotic our county structure has become, making a nonsense of the last Local Government Review and its ill-thought-out recommendations.

COUNTY CHANGES: sad, bad, and dangerous

The Real County had always been given priority, precedence and pride of place. So what went wrong? Step forward Ted Heath and the so-called swinging 60s as that is when the seeds of confusion were sown and the public's perception of the county map of Britain would never be the same again. In the 30 years between 1965 and 1997 people have lost their local identity as local government reorganization introduced the one-tier, or unitary, authority (one council looking after one area) and the two-tier (*two councils* looking after one area) administration. For example when Middlesex County Council was abolished in 1965 the County of Middlesex was *not* abolished, because they are two totally different entities. Besides, the erstwhile Middlesex County Council only administered two thirds of real Middlesex anyway!

Are you now more *au fait* about the chasmic difference between the two types of Counties? If so let me throw in a fifth county to really confuse you.

THE POST COUNTY …or your home address.

The Post County was devised by the Royal Mail for one good reason: to deliver your post efficiently and speedily to your address. It adds to general county confusion because its boundaries can be based on *either* the Real County *or* the administrative county, or even both, for the Post Office is a law unto itself. Now even this is changing for with the development of technology *the postcode has come to represent the County.* One Royal Mail executive confessed to me that soon an address will only require a name and postcode. That's already the case in five home counties who have had part of their territory turned into 'London' post districts for over a 100 years.

The Post County carries with it the power of everyday awareness and the popular identification of where most people believe they they are from. To the average person the post county is where they live and therefore where they belong…but it ain't necessarily so.

So the Post County does not necessarily conform to either the real county or the administrative county. Take Wraysbury in Buckinghamshire, administered by Berkshire County Council until 1997 and postally served by Middlesex through Staines and a Twickenham postcode! But having to write Middlesex in a Wraysbury address is anathema to some. No matter how much you point out it is *only for faster mail service and delivery* it is not acceptable to many residents who refuse to and make matters worse by writing Berkshire, an administration that will not exist, and not even Buckinghamshire their Real County whose administration does!

Their reasons range from higher insurance premiums to blatant snobbery but ultimately it is ignorance of the facts – if any County should be written in Wraysbury's address it should be Buckinghamshire.

MEDIA – spreading the county myth.
The Media feed on information but if authoritative maps, gazetteers or books are not available then how can they get town-and-county locations right? Though some of the fault lies in education some of it also stems from journalistic laziness or lack of local knowledge. The BBC used to have a policy which said a place should be located where it is popularly said to be.But that` assumes the reporter on the ground knows where he or she is: and I have come across journalists who haven't a clue and pass on their mis-information.

A news editor at the BBC, when asked why he didn't give places an accurate county location as when "Bolton, Lancashire" is described as '"Bolton, near Manchester"', replied that it was because people in Scotland wouldn't know where it was; and nor were they ever likely to know with that daft approach.

Then there are some irrational people who believe a County doesn't exist if it doesn't have a County Council. What abject nonsense ! County Councils weren't invented until 1888-89 and under that criterion, therefore, Yorkshire never existed as there has never been a Yorkshire County Council. It also means that counties such as Westmorland or Inverness-shire don't exist as they do not have a County Council either. Until the media get it right, people will get it wrong.

MAPMAKERS: Planning a route through the maze
It's a little known fact that the excellent Ordnance Survey are governed by an historic Act of Parliament which decrees they can only publish administrative units on their maps. And as most other mapmakers base themselves on Ordnance Survey, no modern maps show the boundaries of the Real County. For visitors to Britain it was impossible, until this book, to find an up-to-date map which depicts the Real County.

MEMBERS OF PARLIAMENT: British County heritage in their hands
A classic case of not knowing or not caring about our Counties, I know not which, was perpetrated by the loony Local Government Commission of the 1990s. It began with Premier Major at a Conservative party conference using cricket – the bastion of county identity – as his battle cry *'can you imagine [Yorkshire's] Len Hutton going into bat for Humberside?'* he said…urging that public opinion must be taken into account when it came to local identity. But why did a Prime Minister say this? According to previous national government statements whatever happened in local government would not undermine the role or status of the Real County. But obviously it had for the Prime Minister to say what he said! Enter the Association of British Counties formed by myself from Middlesex, Michael Bradford from Yorkshire and Val Andrews from Berkshire to campaign for the Real County to be recognised 'officially' using the Government's own statement :*'the new county boundaries are administrative areas, and will not alter the traditional boundaries of counties, nor is it intended that the loyalties of people living in them will change, despite the different names adopted by the new administrative counties'* as its fundamental principle.

The early 1990s Local Government Commission was a farce, a folly, contradictory and inconsistent: a nonsense as politicians would say. In Yorkshire and Lincolnshire it abolished Humberside but didn't take the ex-Metropolitan County Councils in the West Riding into consideration at all. They axed Berkshire County Council to give the County of Berkshire one tier local government in one part and two tier in the rest. It kept the two tier system for Lancashire County Council except for Blackpool and Blackburn which became single tier and opted out of the Lancashire CC, Wales and Scotland were given unitary authorities with little public consultation. The rest of this sorry state of affairs can be found under the local government headings for each county.

I attended a meeting in Staines, Middlesex, where Spelthorne Borough had campaigned vociferously to go it alone. A meeting with local groups, employers and interested parties was arranged to meet with the nine commissioners: two were present, a third was just leaving and six never turned up. Everybody at the Thames Lodge Hotel – Shepperton Studios, the British Airport Authority, British Airways, Chamber of Commerce every person, company and organisation present – supported Spelthorne's case for leaving Surrey County Council. However, the Local Government Commission suggested the 90,000 population of Spelthorne was too small for it to govern itself, completely disregarding what the people wanted. and government guidelines stating that size was not to be a prerogative. John Selwyn Gummer, the Environment Minister who could and should have rejected the recommendation, didn't. Rutland with around 30,000 *was* given unitary status leading to spurious headlines that Rutland was back – though it had never gone away!

The whole 1990's commission was a good opportunity wasted, it was a chance to give the Real County back its full ceremonial role and cultural integrity. As a result of this mess Lord Lieutenants were returned to some Real Counties but not others, two tier systems now operate in some areas, one tier in others, and in some counties both!. All the 1990's Local Government reorganisation did was to create greater confusion. I do find it strange that when so many MPs complain about losing British sovereignty to Europe they cannot even protect their own British County heritage back home!

WHAT THEY DON'T TELL YOU AT WESTMINSTER

Finally to illustrate how little some politicians know about our Counties read this. A government minister burbling on about Midlothian in the House of Commons in 1996 was asked by an opposition Scottish MP to name any town in that fair County. His response was silence, not even its greatest city Edinburgh passed his lips – the clue being the football club or the novel, *Heart of Midlothian*. Not only could he *not* name a Midlothian town, but he made a smart-Alec comment about a political hot potato *he* called 'the *East* Lothian question', when it was actually the *West* Lothian question! Contrast, a group of Middlesex MPs led by Sir Michael Shersby laid down an early day motion in 1991 which declared '*this house confirms that the County of Middlesex exists*'. So they've got the power if they choose to use it.

SO WHERE ARE WE EXACTLY?

People talk about the Real County in terms of 'turning the clock back' or how your County 'used to be' or the 'old' County meaning non-existent. The Lord Lieutenant, a crown appointment dating back to Tudor times should represent the Real County but due to political blunders they do in some and not in others. Politicians declare they cannot abolish what Parliament never created and the Real County was created long before MPs took their seats but do the public understand this? No! Therefore all these assurances are useless until Parliament passes legislation to preserve and conserve the special identity of the Real County.

To the ordinary person their *real* County pride, love and loyalty are based upon the history and heritage of a unique place that has been built over the centuries. Now this book, the only one of its kind available, will enable you to rediscover your true County roots, and see where you *really* belong.

THE REAL COUNTIES OF BRITAIN describes and illustrates the unchanging history and geography, boundaries and places of over a thousand years of our lands. When you hear of people or politicians talking about bringing back Pembrokeshire, Clackmannanshire or the East Riding of Yorkshire, tell them you cannot bring back something that has never gone and our Real Counties are here to stay, they are a part of your birthright.

You will find surprises, I am certain. I have been amazed by how much I have unearthed, and it is an ongoing process. Every day I receive more news in my post, putting right further misconceptions. Remember also that this book is just a taster of each of the counties that make up the table of Britain. There is a full banquet to come with a series of individual county titles in the serving hatch! So please support *your* Real County. You can start this in a practical way by writing to me with an stamped addressed envelope at:
The Association of British Counties (ABC)
c/o PO Box 5757, Royal Lytham St Anne's,
Lancashire.FY8 2TE.

THE REAL COUNTIES OF BRITAIN are alive and well – they haven't changed, they are not dead; dormant maybe, but just waiting for you to rediscover them and breathe fresh life into them.

Russell Grant, Staines, Middlesex. 1996.

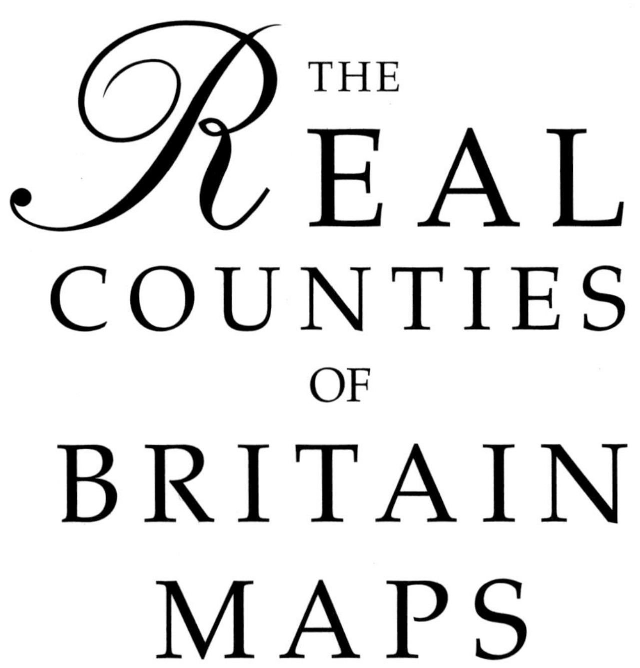
THE
REAL
COUNTIES
OF
BRITAIN
MAPS

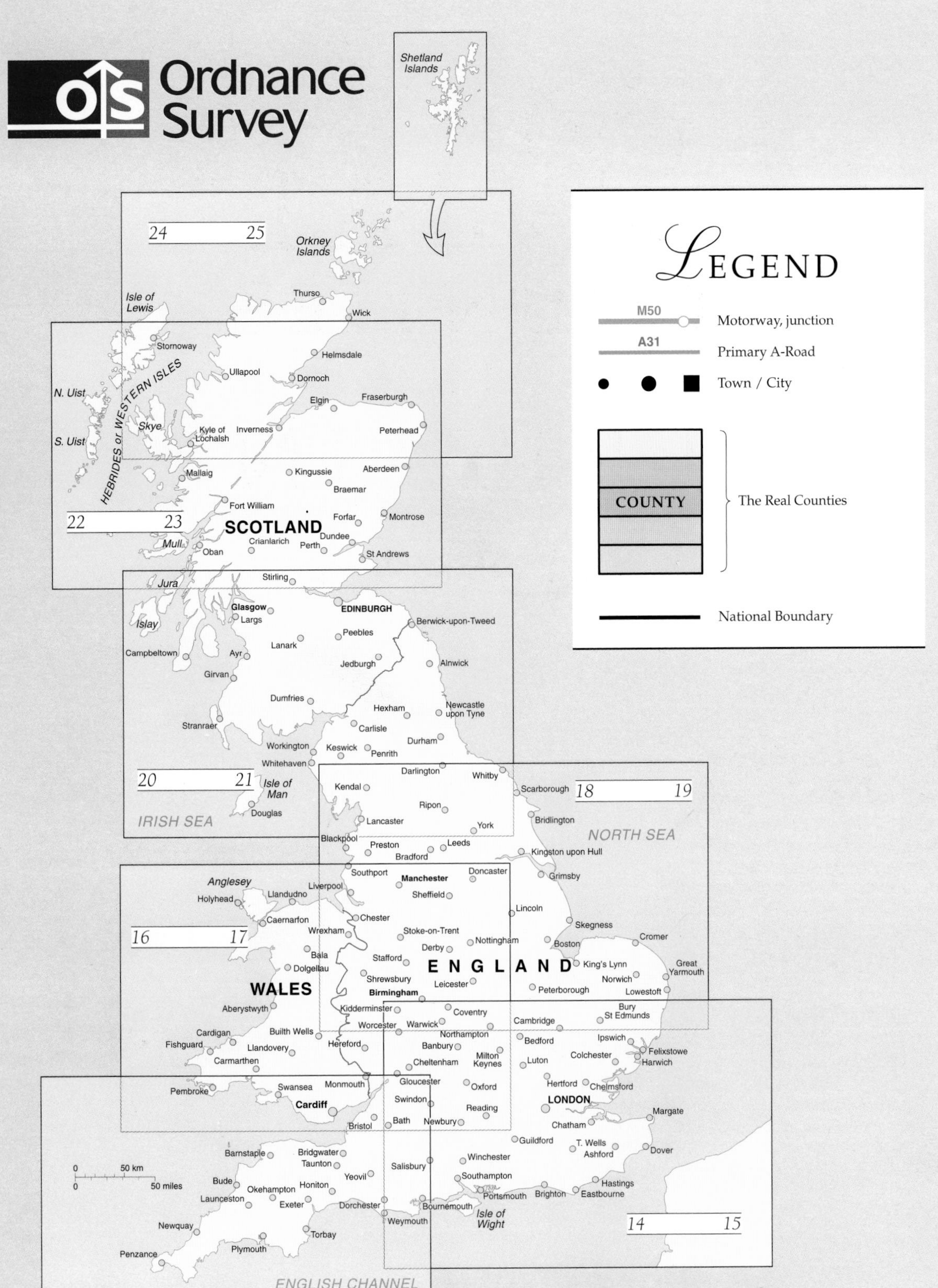

Ordnance Survey
LEGEND
M50
Motorway, junction
A31
Primary A-Road
Town / City
COUNTY
The Real Counties
National Boundary
Shetland Islands
Orkney Islands
24
25
22
23
20
21
18
19
16
17
14
15
12
13
Isle of Lewis
Stornoway
N. Uist
S. Uist
HEBRIDES or WESTERN ISLES
Skye
Thurso
Wick
Helmsdale
Ullapool
Dornoch
Elgin
Fraserburgh
Kyle of Lochalsh
Inverness
Peterhead
Mallaig
Kingussie
Aberdeen
Braemar
Fort William
SCOTLAND
Forfar
Montrose
Mull
Oban
Crianlarich
Dundee
Perth
St Andrews
Jura
Stirling
Glasgow
Largs
EDINBURGH
Islay
Berwick-upon-Tweed
Peebles
Lanark
Campbeltown
Ayr
Jedburgh
Alnwick
Girvan
Dumfries
Newcastle upon Tyne
Hexham
Stranraer
Carlisle
Durham
Workington
Keswick
Penrith
Whitehaven
Darlington
Whitby
Isle of Man
Kendal
Scarborough
Douglas
Ripon
IRISH SEA
Lancaster
Bridlington
York
NORTH SEA
Blackpool
Preston
Leeds
Bradford
Kingston upon Hull
Southport
Doncaster
Manchester
Grimsby
Anglesey
Liverpool
Holyhead
Llandudno
Sheffield
Lincoln
Caernarfon
Chester
Skegness
Wrexham
Stoke-on-Trent
Cromer
Derby
Nottingham
Boston
Bala
Stafford
ENGLAND
King's Lynn
Great Yarmouth
Dolgellau
Norwich
Shrewsbury
Leicester
WALES
Birmingham
Peterborough
Lowestoft
Aberystwyth
Kidderminster
Coventry
Bury St Edmunds
Worcester
Warwick
Cambridge
Cardigan
Builth Wells
Northampton
Fishguard
Hereford
Bedford
Ipswich
Llandovery
Banbury
Milton Keynes
Felixstowe
Carmarthen
Cheltenham
Luton
Colchester
Harwich
Gloucester
Oxford
Hertford
Chelmsford
Pembroke
Swansea
Monmouth
Swindon
LONDON
Cardiff
Reading
Margate
Bristol
Bath
Newbury
Chatham
Guildford
T. Wells
Ashford
Dover
Barnstaple
Bridgwater
Taunton
Winchester
0
50 km
50 miles
Salisbury
Yeovil
Southampton
Bude
Okehampton
Honiton
Portsmouth
Brighton
Hastings
Eastbourne
Launceston
Exeter
Dorchester
Bournemouth
Isle of Wight
Newquay
Weymouth
Torbay
Penzance
Plymouth
ENGLISH CHANNEL
MiniScale
Customised Mapping
© Crown copyright 1996
(01703) 792083

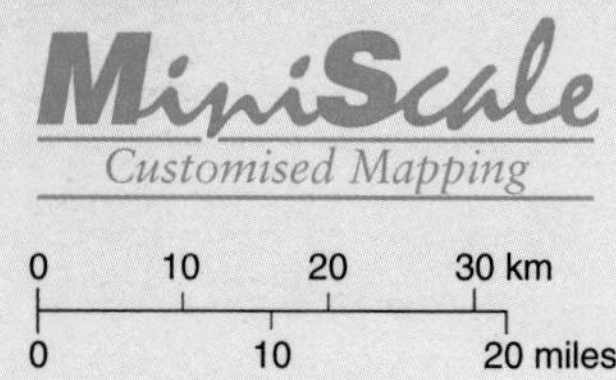

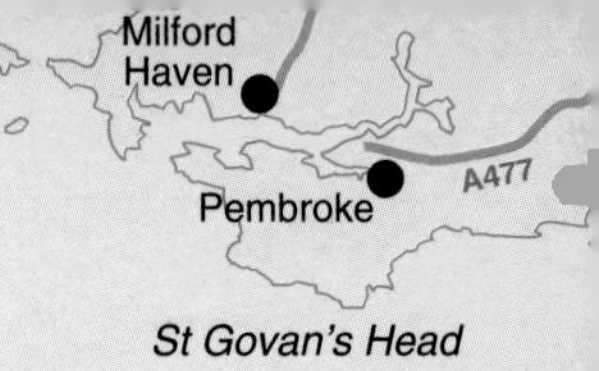

Lundy

ATLANTIC OCEAN

Hartlan

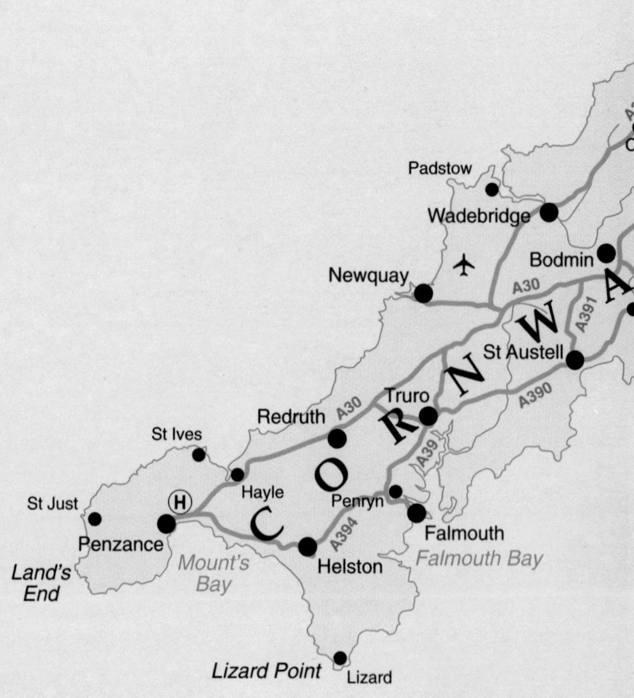

Isles of Scilly
Tresco
St Martin's
Bryher
St Mary's
St Agnes

ENGLISH CHANNEL

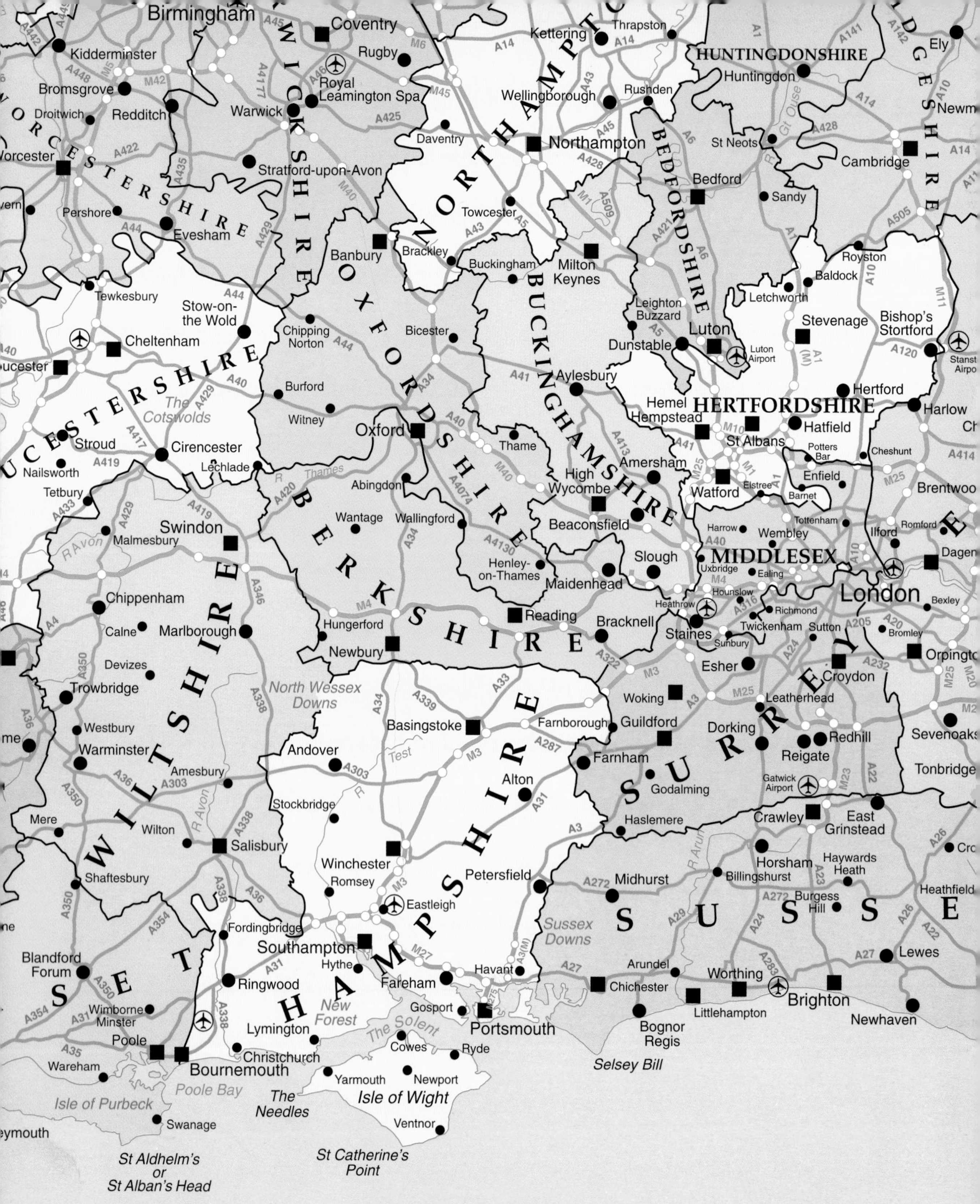

ENGLISH CHANNEL

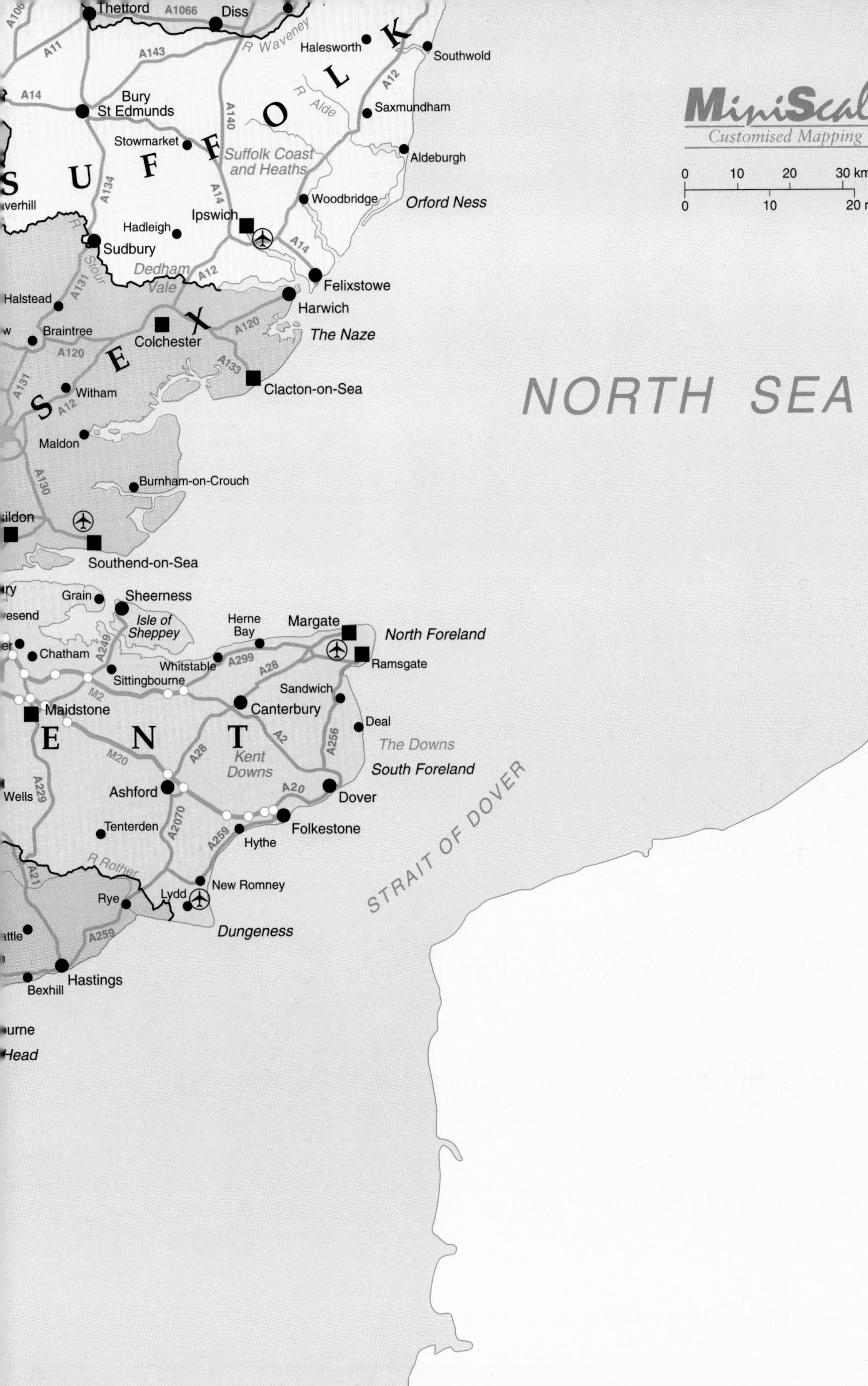

MiniScale
Customised Mapping
0 10 20 30 km
0 10 20 miles
NORTH SEA
STRAIT OF DOVER
SUFFOLK
ESSEX
KENT
Thetford
Diss
Halesworth
Southwold
Bury St Edmunds
Saxmundham
Stowmarket
Suffolk Coast and Heaths
Aldeburgh
Woodbridge
Orford Ness
Ipswich
Hadleigh
Sudbury
Dedham Vale
Felixstowe
Harwich
Halstead
Braintree
Colchester
The Naze
Clacton-on-Sea
Witham
Maldon
Burnham-on-Crouch
Southend-on-Sea
Grain
Sheerness
Isle of Sheppey
Herne Bay
Margate
North Foreland
Chatham
Whitstable
Ramsgate
Sittingbourne
Sandwich
Maidstone
Canterbury
Deal
The Downs
Kent Downs
South Foreland
Ashford
Dover
Tenterden
Folkestone
Hythe
New Romney
Rye
Lydd
Dungeness
Hastings
Bexhill
R Waveney
R Alde
R Stour
R Rother
A1066
A11
A143
A14
A12
A140
A134
A131
A120
A133
A130
A249
A299
A28
M2
M20
A2
A256
A20
A229
A2070
A259
A21

MiniScale
Customised Mapping
0 10 20 30 km
0 10 20 miles
Amlwch
Holyhead
Anglesey
ANGLESEY
A5
Menai Bridge
Bangor
A55
Conwy
Llandudno
Colwyn Bay
Abergele
Afon Conwy
A470
Llanrwst
Caernarfon
Caernarfon Bay
A487
CAERNARFONSHIRE
Betws-y-Coed
Nefyn
Porthmadog
Ffestiniog
Snowdonia
Pwllheli
Lleyn
Abersoch
Harlech
A470
A494
MERIONETH
Dolgellau
Barmouth
A487
A470
Tywyn
A489
Machynlleth
CARDIGAN BAY
A487
Aberystwyth
A44
CARDIGANSHIRE
CAMBRIAN
Rhayader
ST GEORGE'S CHANNEL
Aberaeron
New Quay
Tregaron
Afon Teifi
A487
Lampeter
Llanwrtyd Wells
A483
Cardigan
Newcastle Emlyn
Pembrokeshire Coast
Fishguard
A40
CARMARTHENSHIRE
Llandovery
A40
St David's Head
St David's
PEMBROKESHIRE
CARMARTHEN
Carmarthen
A40
Afon Tywi
Llandeilo
St Brides Bay
A40
Haverfordwest
Narberth
St Clears
A48
A483
Milford Haven
Carmarthen Bay
Pembroke
A477
Tenby
Llanelli
M4
A465
Neath
R Loughor
Swansea
Port Talbot
St Govan's Head
Gower
GLAMORGA
Worms Head
Swansea Bay
M4
Bridgend
Porthcawl

CHESHIRE
DERBYSHIRE
NOTTINGHAMSHIRE
STAFFORDSHIRE
SHROPSHIRE
LEICESTERSHIRE
WARWICKSHIRE
WORCESTERSHIRE
HEREFORDSHIRE
NORTHAMPTON
GLOUCESTERSHIRE
OXFORDSHIRE
BUCKINGHAMSHI
BERKSHIRE
MONMOUTHSHIRE
Pt of FLINT
Southport
Chorley
Bolton
Bury
Rochdale
Huddersfield
Thorne
Skelmersdale
Ormskirk
Formby
Holmfirth
Barnsley
Maghull
Wigan
Oldham
Doncaster
Bootle
Manchester
Liverpool
Wallasey
St Helens
Glossop
Rotherham
Bawtry
Birkenhead
Warrington
Stockport
Peak
Sheffield
Gainsbo
Runcorn
Worksop
Retford
Holywell
R Dee
Knutsford
Northwich
Macclesfield
Buxton
Chesterfield
Queensferry
Chester
Middlewich
Bakewell
Mold
Congleton
Matlock
Mansfield
Newark-on-Trent
Ruthin
Crewe
Leek
Alfreton
Wrexham
Nantwich
Stoke-on-Trent
Ashbourne
Ripley
Llangollen
Nottingham
Whitchurch
Market Drayton
Stone
Uttoxeter
Derby
Ellesmere
Oswestry
E Midlands Airport
Burton upon Trent
Stafford
Rugeley
Loughborough
Melton Mowbray
Llanfyllin
Newport
Ashby-de-la-Zouch
Coalville
Cannock
Lichfield
Welshpool
Shrewsbury
Telford
Tamworth
Leicester
Oakha
Much Wenlock
Wolverhampton
Walsall
Wigston
Hinckley
Church Stretton
Bridgnorth
Dudley
Nuneaton
Market Harborough
Newtown
Shropshire Hills
Stourbridge
R Severn
Birmingham
Coventry
Corby
R Welland
Ludlow
Kidderminster
Rugby
Kettering
Knighton
Bromsgrove
Royal Leamington Spa
Wellingborough
NORSHIRE
Droitwich
Redditch
Warwick
Llandrindod Wells
Leominster
Daventry
Northampton
Kington
Worcester
Stratford-upon-Avon
Builth Wells
Great Malvern
Pershore
Towcester
Evesham
Banbury
Brackley
Buckingham
Milton Keynes
Hereford
Ledbury
Wye Valley
R Wye
Tewkesbury
Stow-on-the Wold
Ross-on-Wye
Chipping Norton
Bicester
Cheltenham
Gloucester
Aylesbury
Abergavenny
Burford
Monmouth
The Cotswolds
Witney
Ebbw Vale
Oxford
Thame
Stroud
Cirencester
Pontypool
Usk
Nailsworth
Lechlade
R Thames
High Wycombe
Cwmbran
Chepstow
Tetbury
Abingdon
R Severn
Caerphilly
Wantage
Wallingford
Beaconsfield
Swindon
Newport
R Avon
Malmesbury
Henley-on-Thames
Maidenhead
Yate
Avonmouth
Cardiff
Chippenham
Reading
Clevedon
Bristol
Hungerford
Penarth
Calne
Marlborough
Newbury
Barry
Devizes
M6
M61
M62
M58
M57
M56
M53
M63
M1
M18
A1(M)
M180
M54
M42
M69
M5
M50
M40
M4
M48
M49
M32
M45
A570
A565
A580
A57
A628
A616
A629
A6102
A635
A638
A630
A631
A156
A159
A533
A556
A537
A523
A619
A60
A614
A617
A38
A46
A17
A54
A34
A536
A530
A49
A51
A534
A41
A494
A483
A495
A5
A53
A442
A52
A50
A515
A610
A453
A607
A606
A518
A449
A458
A454
A461
A444
A47
A6003
A427
A14
A43
A456
A448
A4177
A425
A428
A509
A489
A44
A422
A435
A429
A465
A479
A40
A48
A417
A419
A433
A403
A420
A4074
A4130
A413
A346
A4
A322
A48(M)
A6
A1
A45

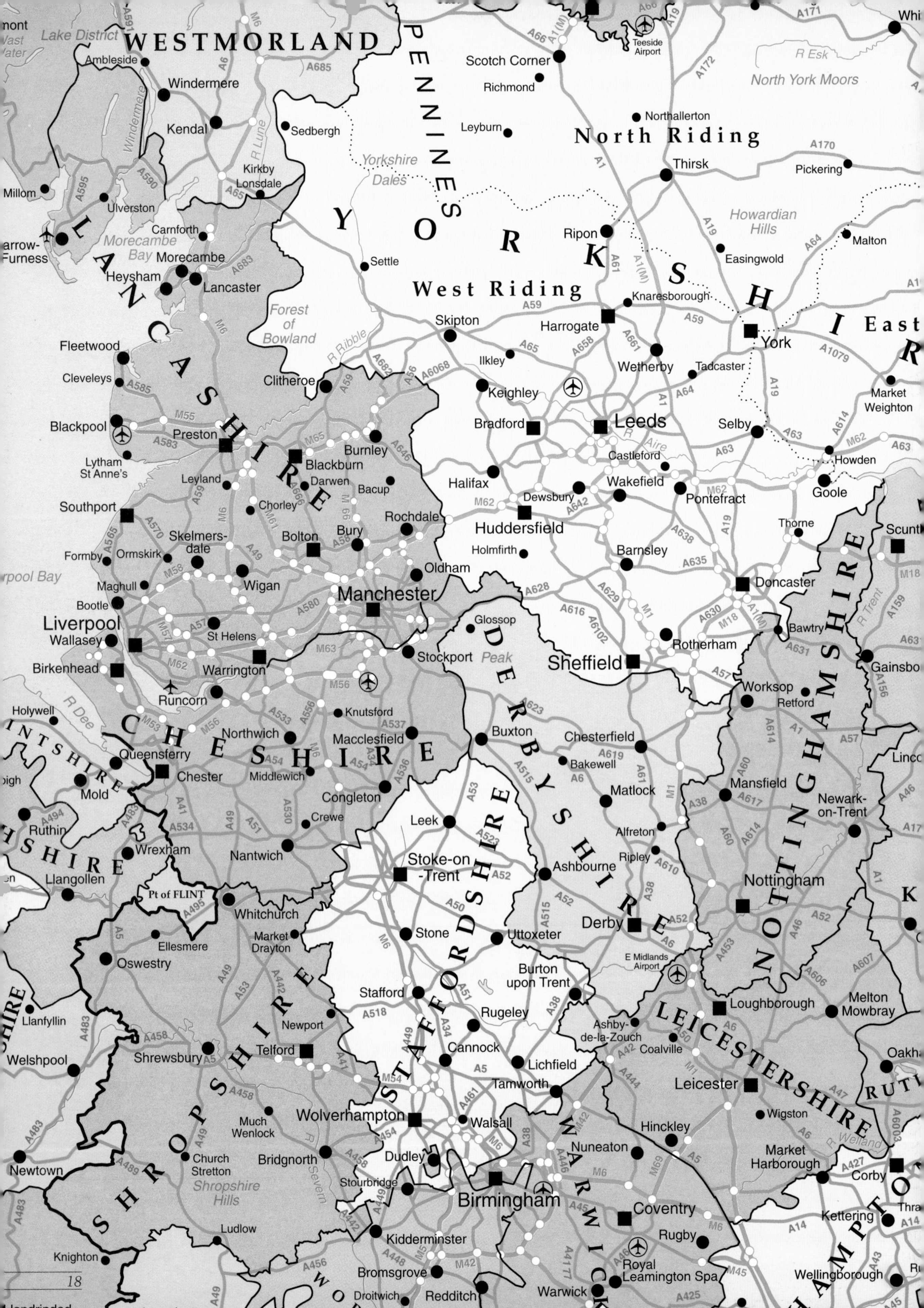

WESTMORLAND
Lake District
PENNINES
YORKSHIRE
North Riding
West Riding
East Riding
North York Moors
Howardian Hills
Yorkshire Dales
Forest of Bowland
LANCASHIRE
Morecambe Bay
CHESHIRE
DERBYSHIRE
Peak
NOTTINGHAMSHIRE
STAFFORDSHIRE
SHROPSHIRE
Shropshire Hills
LEICESTERSHIRE
WARWICK
Pt of FLINT
Ambleside
Windermere
Kendal
Sedbergh
Kirkby Lonsdale
Millom
Ulverston
Barrow-in-Furness
Carnforth
Morecambe
Heysham
Lancaster
Fleetwood
Cleveleys
Blackpool
Lytham St Anne's
Preston
Leyland
Blackburn
Darwen
Burnley
Bacup
Chorley
Southport
Formby
Ormskirk
Skelmersdale
Wigan
Bolton
Bury
Rochdale
Oldham
Maghull
Bootle
Liverpool
Wallasey
Birkenhead
St Helens
Warrington
Manchester
Stockport
Runcorn
Holywell
Northwich
Knutsford
Macclesfield
Queensferry
Chester
Mold
Middlewich
Congleton
Crewe
Nantwich
Ruthin
Wrexham
Llangollen
Whitchurch
Ellesmere
Oswestry
Market Drayton
Llanfyllin
Newport
Welshpool
Shrewsbury
Telford
Much Wenlock
Church Stretton
Bridgnorth
Newtown
Ludlow
Knighton
Clitheroe
Settle
Skipton
Ilkley
Keighley
Bradford
Halifax
Huddersfield
Dewsbury
Holmfirth
Leeds
Castleford
Wakefield
Pontefract
Barnsley
Doncaster
Rotherham
Sheffield
Harrogate
Knaresborough
Wetherby
Tadcaster
York
Selby
Goole
Howden
Thorne
Market Weighton
Malton
Pickering
Easingwold
Ripon
Thirsk
Northallerton
Scotch Corner
Richmond
Leyburn
Teeside Airport
Glossop
Buxton
Chesterfield
Bakewell
Matlock
Alfreton
Ripley
Ashbourne
Derby
Leek
Stoke-on-Trent
Stone
Uttoxeter
Stafford
Rugeley
Burton upon Trent
Cannock
Lichfield
Tamworth
Wolverhampton
Walsall
Dudley
Stourbridge
Birmingham
Kidderminster
Bromsgrove
Droitwich
Redditch
Nuneaton
Coventry
Rugby
Royal Leamington Spa
Warwick
Hinckley
Leicester
Coalville
Ashby-de-la-Zouch
Loughborough
E Midlands Airport
Nottingham
Mansfield
Worksop
Retford
Bawtry
Gainsborough
Newark-on-Trent
Melton Mowbray
Wigston
Market Harborough
Corby
Kettering
Wellingborough
Oakham
Scunthorpe
R Esk
R Lune
R Ribble
R Aire
R Dee
R Severn
R Trent
R Welland
Liverpool Bay

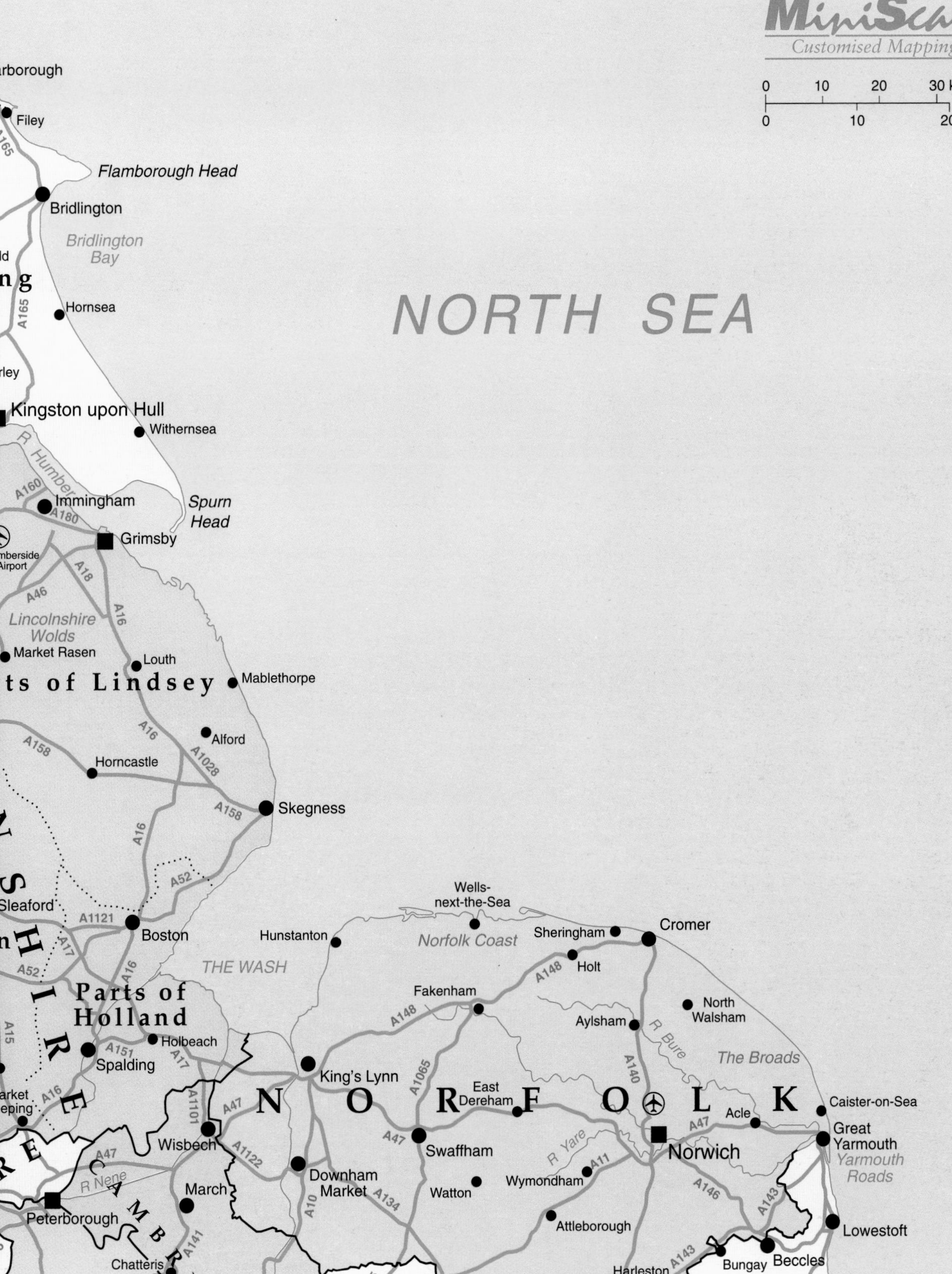

MiniScale
Customised Mapping
0 10 20 30 km
0 10 20 miles
NORTH SEA
carborough
Filey
A165
Flamborough Head
Bridlington
Bridlington Bay
Hornsea
Kingston upon Hull
Withernsea
R Humber
A160
Immingham
A180
Spurn Head
Grimsby
Humberside Airport
A18
A46
A16
Lincolnshire Wolds
Market Rasen
Louth
rts of Lindsey
Mablethorpe
Alford
A158
Horncastle
A1028
Skegness
A52
Sleaford
A1121
Boston
A17
THE WASH
Parts of Holland
Holbeach
A151
Spalding
A15
Market Deeping
Hunstanton
Wells-next-the-Sea
Norfolk Coast
Sheringham
Cromer
Holt
A148
Fakenham
North Walsham
Aylsham
R Bure
The Broads
A140
King's Lynn
A1065
East Dereham
NORFOLK
Caister-on-Sea
Acle
A47
Great Yarmouth
Yarmouth Roads
Norwich
R Yare
A11
Wymondham
Swaffham
Watton
Downham Market
A134
A10
A146
A143
Lowestoft
Attleborough
Wisbech
A1101
A1122
R Nene
March
Peterborough
CAMBRIDGESHIRE
Chatteris
A141
A142
Ely
Thetford
A1066
Diss
Harleston
Bungay
Beccles
R Waveney
Halesworth
Southwold
A12
R Alde
Saxmundham
HUNTINGDONSHIRE
Huntingdon
A1
A14
Newmarket
Bury St Edmunds

ARGYLLSHIRE
Colonsay
Scalasaig
JURA
Jura
Sound of Jura
Lochgilphead
Knapdale
Loch Fyne
Kyles of Bute
Dunoon
Loch Long
Argyll
Loch Lomond
DUNBARTONSHIRE
STIRLINGSHIRE
River Forth
Dunblane
Alloa
Stirling
Part of DUNBARTONSHIRE
Kilsyth
Falkirk
Dumbarton
Greenock
Cumbernauld
Bathgate
RENFREWSHIRE
Paisley
Glasgow
Airdrie
Motherwell
East Kilbride
Hamilton
Strathaven
Lanark
LANARKSHIRE
Port Askaig
ISLAY
Laggan Bay
Port Ellen
Tarbert
Kennacraig
Claonaig
Rothesay
Island of Bute
Firth of Clyde
Largs
Gigha Island
Lochranza
BUTESHIRE
Ardrossan
ISLE OF ARRAN
Brodick
Lamlash
Kilbrannan Sound
Irvine
Kilmarnock
Troon
Prestwick
Ayr
Cumnock
Campbeltown
NORTH CHANNEL
Mull of Kintyre
Maybole
Girvan
AYRSHIRE
Sanquhar
DUMF
R Nith
Ballantrae
Galloway
New Galloway
Dumfries
Loch Ryan
KIRKCUDBRIGHTSHIRE
Nith Estuary
Newton Stewart
Stranraer
Castle Douglas
Dalbeattie
Gatehouse of Fleet
Wigtown
Portpatrick
WIGTOWNSHIRE
Fleet Valley
Kirkcudbright
Luce Bay
Whithorn
Drummore
Burrow Head
Mull of Galloway
Workington
Whitehaven
Egremo
Point of Ayre
Ramsey Bay
Ramsey
ISLE OF MAN
Peel
Douglas
Port Erin
Castletown
R Clyde
A91
M9
M80
A811
A82
A80
M73
M8
A8
A78
A736
A77
A71
A76
A70
M74
A721
A74(M)
A83
A75

MiniScale
Customised Mapping
0 10 20 30 km
0 10 20 miles
NORTH SEA
Glenrothes
Leven
Pittenweem
Kirkcaldy
unfermline
A921
Firth of Forth
North Berwick
Edinburgh
Dunbar
A90
A1
East Linton
Tranent
Haddington
EAST LOTHIAN
A720
St Abb's Head
gston
Dalkeith
Eyemouth
A1
OLOTHIAN
Penicuik
A68
A7
A703
A702
Duns
BERWICKSHIRE
Berwick-upon-Tweed
A697
Greenlaw
Lauder
Holy Island
Peebles
Coldstream
A72
Galashiels
Northumberland
Coast
Innerleithen
Melrose
Kelso
Upper
Tweeddale
R Tweed
Selkirk
A68
Wooler
PEEBLESSHIRE
SELKIRKSHIRE
Eildon &
Leaderfoot
ROXBURGHSHIRE
A697
Jedburgh
Alnwick
Hawick
A7
Amble
offat
A1
A1068
River Annan
SSHIRE
A68
Kielder Water
Morpeth
Ashington
Langholm
A696
Bedlington
Lockerbie
Blyth
A1
A189
A68
A74(M)
NORTHUMBERLAND
Newcastle
upon Tyne
Tynemouth
Longtown
A19
South Shields
Annan
Gretna
A74
A7
A69
Hexham
A689
Brampton
River Tyne
Corbridge
Gateshead
A1
Sunderland
Carlisle
A69
Consett
A692
Chester-
le-Street
Seaham
Wigton
A596
A595
M6
R Eden
Alston
A691
Durham
Peterlee
A19
MBERLAND
DURHAM
A167
A1(M)
Hartlepool
ermouth
Crook
Penrith
Bishop Auckland
A689
A689
A68
Redcar
Appleby-in-
Westmorland
Newton
Aycliffe
Stockton-
on-Tees
A66
Keswick
A688
Middlesbrough
Brough
A66
Barnard
Castle
Darlington
Guisborough
A591
A171
Whitb
M6
A66
A1(M)
A66
A19
Lake District
WESTMORLAND
Teeside
Airport
THE PENNINES
Ambleside
A6
A685
Scotch Corner
R Esk
A172
North York Moors
Richmond
A171
Windermere
Windermere
Northallerton
Kendal
Sedbergh
Leyburn
North Riding
R Lune
A170
A1
A590
Kirkby
Lonsdale
Yorkshire
Dales
Thirsk
Pickering
A595
lom
A65
Ulverston
Howardian
Hills
Carnforth
A19
Ripon
row-
rness
Morecambe
Bay
Morecambe
Malton
YORKSHIRE
A683
Easingwold
A64
LANC
Heysham
Settle
A61
A1(M)
Lancaster
A166
West Riding
Knaresborough
Forest
of
Bowland
A59
A59
M6
Skipton
Harrogate
Ribble
York
Fleetwood
East

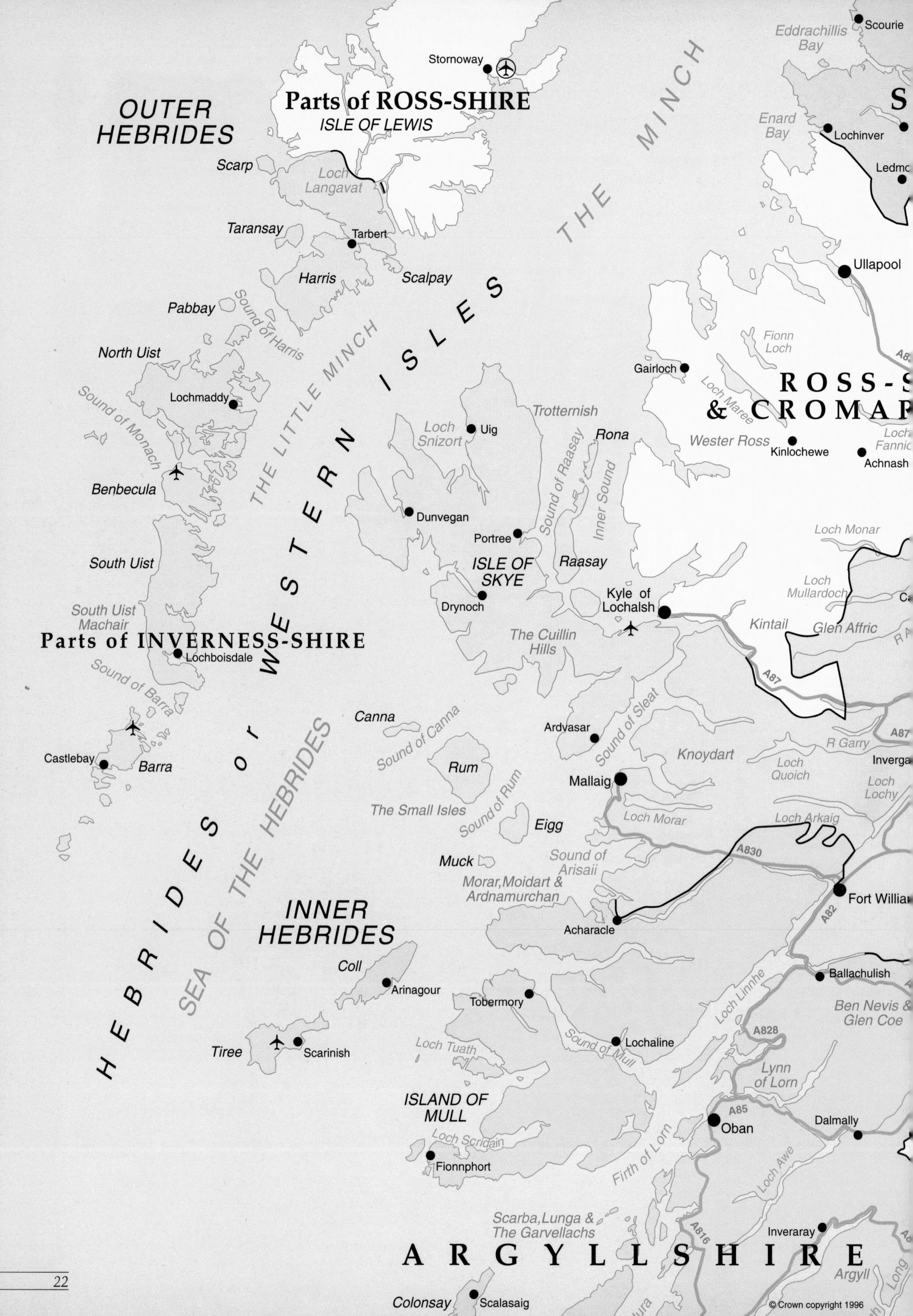

OUTER HEBRIDES
Parts of ROSS-SHIRE
ISLE OF LEWIS
Stornoway
Scarp
Loch Langavat
Taransay
Tarbert
Harris
Scalpay
Pabbay
Sound of Harris
North Uist
Lochmaddy
Sound of Monach
Benbecula
South Uist
South Uist Machair
Parts of INVERNESS-SHIRE
Lochboisdale
Sound of Barra
Castlebay
Barra
THE MINCH
THE LITTLE MINCH
WESTERN ISLES
HEBRIDES or
SEA OF THE HEBRIDES
Loch Snizort
Uig
Trotternish
Rona
Sound of Raasay
Inner Sound
Dunvegan
Portree
ISLE OF SKYE
Raasay
Drynoch
Kyle of Lochalsh
The Cuillin Hills
Canna
Sound of Canna
Rum
The Small Isles
Sound of Rum
Eigg
Muck
Ardvasar
Sound of Sleat
Mallaig
Knoydart
Loch Morar
Sound of Arisaig
Morar, Moidart & Ardnamurchan
INNER HEBRIDES
Acharacle
Coll
Arinagour
Tobermory
Tiree
Scarinish
Loch Tuath
Sound of Mull
Lochaline
ISLAND OF MULL
Loch Scridain
Fionnphort
Firth of Lorn
Scarba, Lunga & The Garvellachs
ARGYLLSHIRE
Colonsay
Scalasaig
Jura
Scourie
Eddrachillis Bay
Enard Bay
Lochinver
Ullapool
Fionn Loch
Gairloch
Loch Maree
ROSS-S
& CROMAR
Wester Ross
Kinlochewe
Achnash
Loch Monar
Loch Mullardoch
Kintail
Glen Affric
A87
R Garry
Loch Quoich
Loch Lochy
Loch Arkaig
A830
Fort William
A82
Ballachulish
Loch Linnhe
Ben Nevis & Glen Coe
A828
Lynn of Lorn
A85
Oban
Dalmally
Loch Awe
A816
Inveraray
Argyll

MiniScale
Customised Mapping
0 10 20 30 km
0 10 20 miles
HERLAND
CAITH
Altnaharra
Loch Naver
R Naver
River Thurso
Lybster
A99
A9
Helmsdale
Loch Shin
Lairg
Golspie
Dornoch Firth
Bonar Bridge
Dornoch
Tain
MORAY FIRTH
Alness
Cromarty Firth
Cromarty
Dingwall
Fortrose
Nairn
Inverness
A82
A96
NAIRNSHIRE
Lossiemouth
Elgin
Forres
MORAYSHIRE
A941
Charlestown of Aberlour
Spey Bay
Buckie
A98
Portsoy
Banff
Kinnaird Head
Fraserburgh
A90
Peterhead
A952
BANFFSHIRE
Keith
Dufftown
Turriff
Huntly
Ellon
Oldmeldrum
Inverurie
Alford
Kintore
Aberdeen
ABERDEENSHIRE
Grantown -on-Spey
Carrbridge
A95
River Spey
Loch Ness
Invermoriston
Aviemore
Glen More
The Cairngorm Mountains
Kingussie
Newtonmore
A86
A889
INVERNESS-SHIRE
Aboyne
Ballater
River Dee
Banchory
A93
Braemar
Deeside & Lochnagar
KINCARDINESHIRE
Stonehaven
Loch Ericht
GRAMPIAN MOUNTAINS
Inverbervie
Laurencekirk
A92
Blair Atholl
Loch Rannoch & Glen Lyon
R Tummel
Loch Rannoch
Loch Tummel
Pitlochry
ANGUS
Brechin
Montrose
Kirriemuir
Forfar
Aberfeldy
R Lyon
Blairgowrie
Coupar Angus
R Tay
Arbroath
Carnoustie
Dundee
Killin
Loch Tay
PERTHSHIRE
Newport-on-Tay
Lochearnhead
L Earn
Perth
A85
Crieff
R Earn
M90
St Andrews Bay
St Andrews
Cupar
A91
Loch Katrine
Auchterarder
Auchtermuchty
Falkland
Fife Ness
Crail
FIFE
A915
Callander
A84
KINROSS-SHIRE
CLACKMANNANSHIRE
Dunblane
Kinross
Pittenweem
Leven
Glenrothes
River Forth
A811
Alloa
Stirling
Kirkcaldy

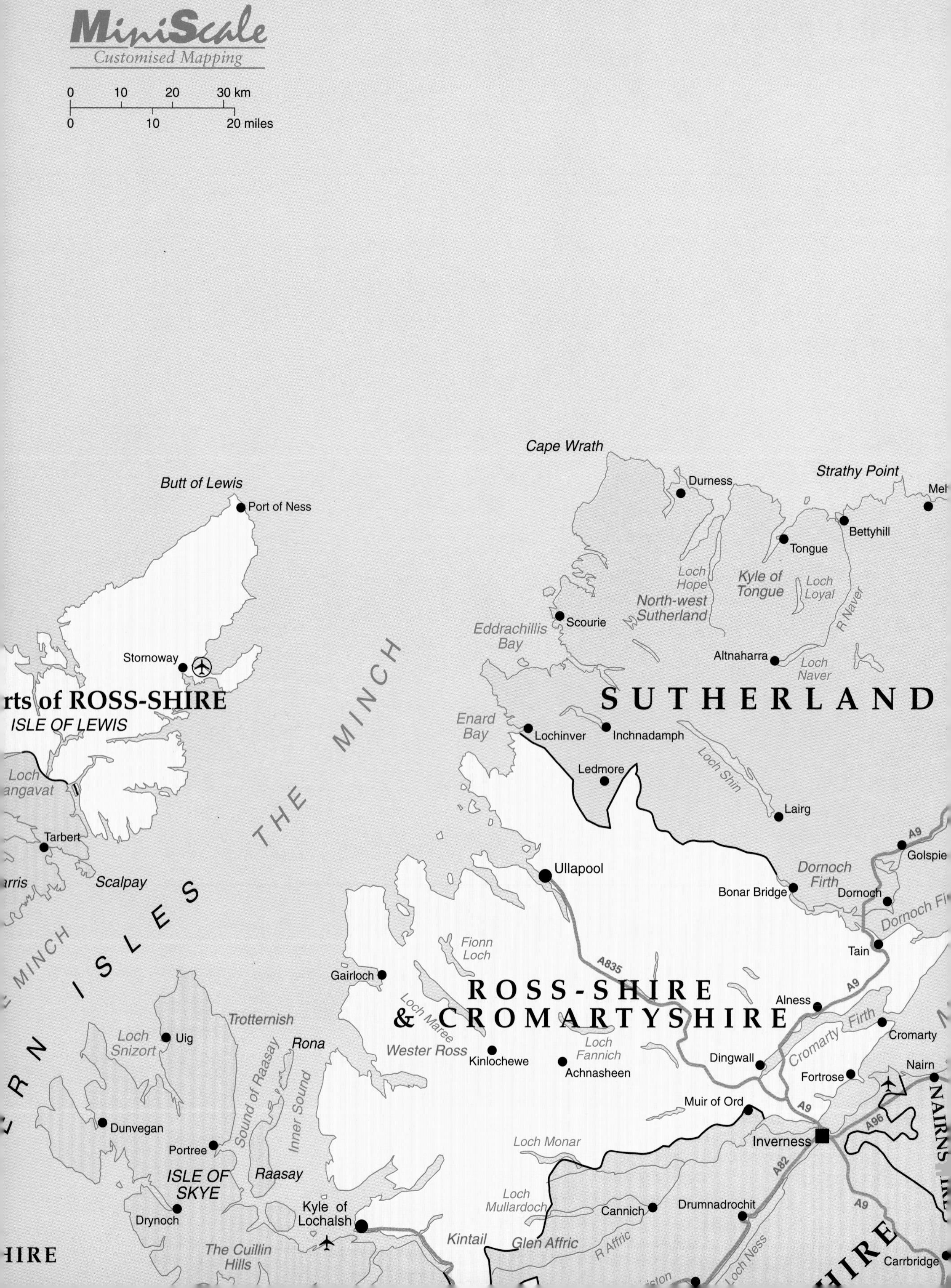

Cape Wrath
Butt of Lewis
Port of Ness
Durness
Strathy Point
Mel
Bettyhill
Tongue
Loch Hope
Kyle of Tongue
Loch Loyal
North-west Sutherland
R Naver
Scourie
Eddrachillis Bay
Stornoway
Altnaharra
Loch Naver
THE MINCH
SUTHERLAND
rts of ROSS-SHIRE
ISLE OF LEWIS
Enard Bay
Lochinver
Inchnadamph
Loch Shin
Ledmore
Loch angavat
Lairg
Tarbert
A9
Golspie
arris
Scalpay
Ullapool
Dornoch Firth
Bonar Bridge
Dornoch
Dornoch Fi
ISLES
MINCH
Fionn Loch
Tain
A835
Gairloch
ROSS-SHIRE & CROMARTYSHIRE
Alness
Loch Maree
Trotternish
Cromarty Firth
Cromarty
Loch Snizort
Uig
Rona
Wester Ross
Kinlochewe
Loch Fannich
Achnasheen
Dingwall
Fortrose
Nairn
Sound of Raasay
Inner Sound
Muir of Ord
A9
A96
Dunvegan
Loch Monar
Inverness
Portree
NAIRNS
A82
ISLE OF SKYE
Raasay
Loch Mullardoch
Kyle of Lochalsh
Cannich
Drumnadrochit
A9
Drynoch
Kintail
Glen Affric
R Affric
HIRE
The Cuillin Hills
Loch Ness
HIRE
Carrbridge

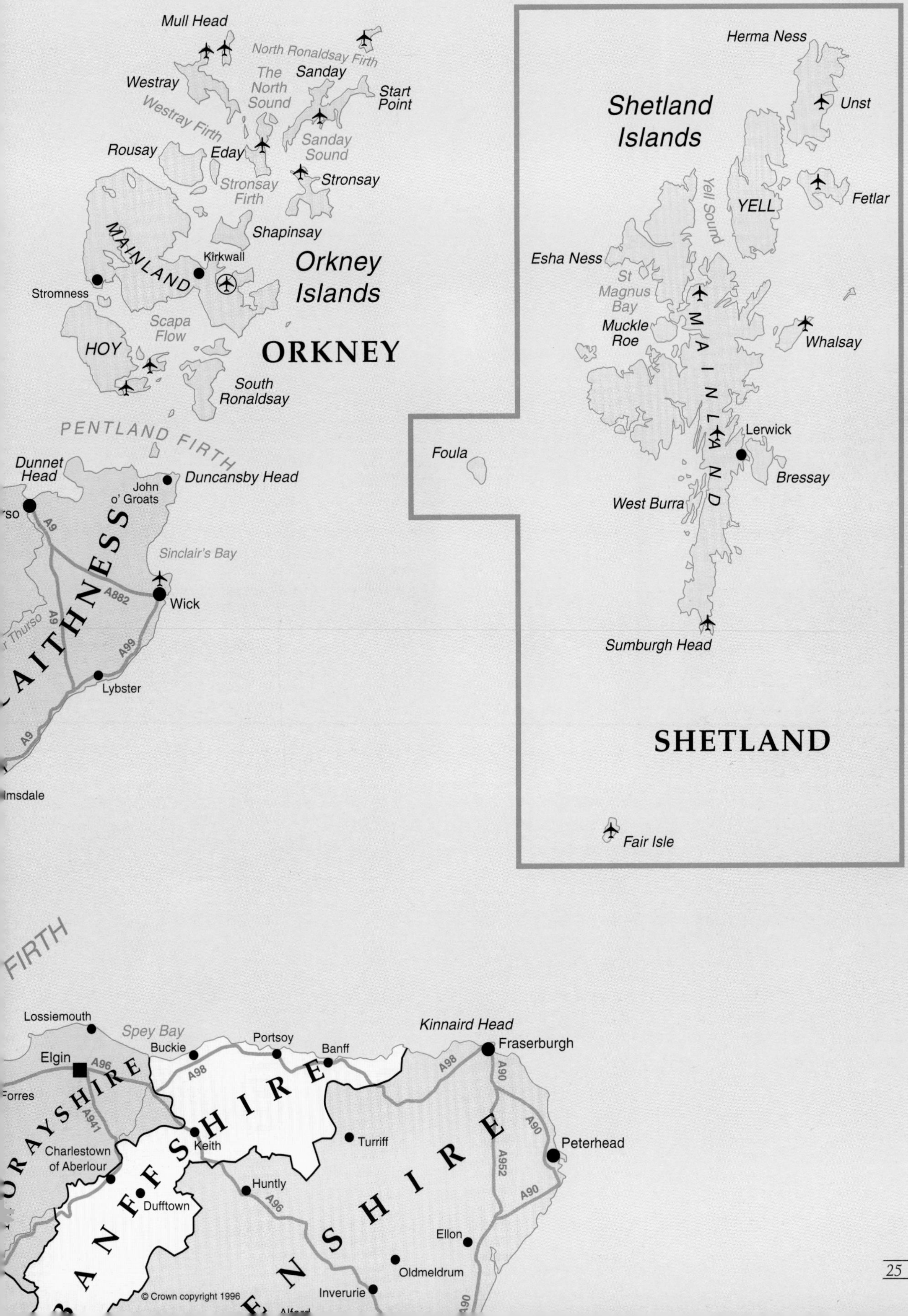

Mull Head
North Ronaldsay Firth
Westray
The North Sound
Sanday
Start Point
Westray Firth
Rousay
Eday
Sanday Sound
Stronsay
Stronsay Firth
Shapinsay
MAINLAND
Kirkwall
Stromness
Orkney Islands
Scapa Flow
HOY
ORKNEY
South Ronaldsay
PENTLAND FIRTH
Dunnet Head
Duncansby Head
John o' Groats
rso
A9
CAITHNESS
Sinclair's Bay
A882
Wick
r Thurso
A9
A99
Lybster
A9
lmsdale

Shetland Islands
Herma Ness
Unst
Yell Sound
YELL
Fetlar
Esha Ness
St Magnus Bay
Muckle Roe
MAINLAND
Whalsay
Lerwick
Foula
Bressay
West Burra
Sumburgh Head
SHETLAND
Fair Isle

FIRTH

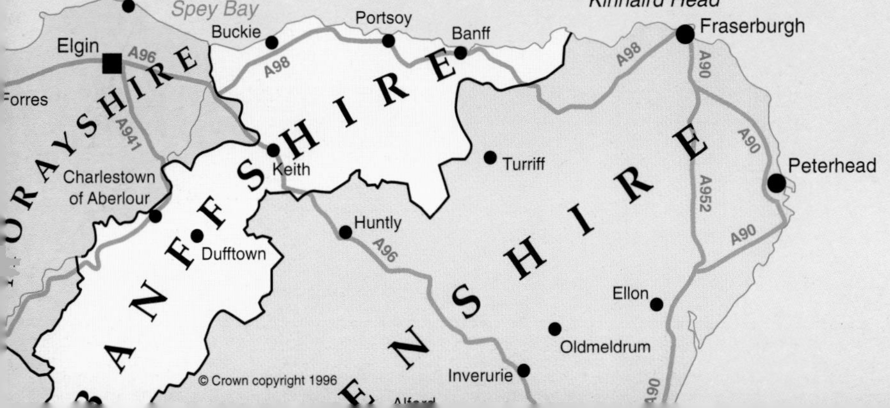

Rising Sun Hotel
THE REAL
ENGLISH COUNTIES

BEDFORDSHIRE

THE COUNTY LANDSCAPE

◆ The county stretches across the plain of the Ouse to the Chiltern Hills and most of the land is rich clay, which is why it has always been a great wheat-growing area.

◆ The county rises and falls in a series of gentle hills and valleys, from a flat, clay plain in the north through a belt of sandy hills stretching from Woburn to Sandy to a higher ridge of chalk downs in the south of the county, where the highest point of 801 feet is reached.

◆ Although Bunyan chose to translate the Chiltern Hills of the county into the "Delectable Mountains" for his epic *Pilgrim's Progress*, a more sardonic local adage merely states that "Bedfordshire is a brickworks in the middle of a cabbage patch".

FAMOUS NAMES

◆ Liberal Democrat leader Paddy Ashdown went to Bedford Boarding School.

◆ John Bunyan the Nonconformist thinker and novelist, wrote Pilgrims Progress, while in Bedford Jail.

◆Comic poet John Hegley grew up in Luton.

HATS AND CATS! Bedfordshire has Luton with its once-famous straw hat-making and straw-plaiting industries and it is also home to the roaming lions at Woburn Abbey's Safari Park – the largest drive-through, safari park reserve in Britain – and Whipsnade Zoo high on the Chilterns. And what about Leighton Buzzard? What a wonderful name! (It owes that to a certain Norman baron called Leighton de Buzzard.)

TOWNS AND VILLAGES

In early times Bedfordshire was bisected by two great and historic roads – Watling Street, connecting northern and southern England, and the Icknield Way, linking East Anglia and the West. Since the 1960s, the former has been replaced by the M1 artery, but the nearby county town of Bedford, in spite of the proximity of various industries, still retains some of its quiet residential atmosphere as it snuggles into a bend of the River Ouse. It also boasts one of the largest Italian colonies in Britain.

Its most famous son, the 17th-century Nonconformist preacher and author of *The Pilgrim's Progress*, John Bunyan, is commemorated by a statue at the foot of the town's High Street. The site of the jail where he was imprisoned for his Nonconformist beliefs is now marked only by a plaque, but the library and museum contain many mementoes and examples of his writings.

His birthplace in the nearby village of Elstow, two miles south, also retains many of its associations, including the font in which he was baptized and the church bells which he rang.

Elsewhere agriculture and market-gardening, and brick-making are still prominent. Cardington, whose colossal hangars housed the great airships built during World War 1, has recently benefited from a small resurgence in this form of transport, but in the intervening years became more familiar as a preliminary induction centre for thousands of conscripts to the Royal Air Force.

The county boasts several

WOBURN ABBEY *Park wildlife includes the white rhino and 11 species of deer.*

distinguished landmarks, including Luton Hoo, the Rupert Adam stately home of the Wernher family, which houses a renowned collection of tapestries, porcelain, paintings and Fabergé jewellery. It has also featured as the setting for more than 30 major films and television productions as a result of its proximity to London and the British film studios. They include *Oliver!*, *Never Say Never Again*, *Inspector Morse*, and Britain's box-office blockbuster of the 1990s, *Four Weddings And A Funeral*. The mansion is run by a charity and is open to the public.

Woburn Abbey, built on the site of a Cistercian foundation, has since the 16th century been the home of the Russell family, later to be elevated to the Dukedom of Bedford. A popular attraction with the visiting public, the Abbey has no fewer than 14 state apartments with many Canalettos, Rembrandts and Gainsboroughs, but the main feature is the collection of rare animals in the 3,000-acre park. Wildlife also pulls in the crowds at Whipsnade Zoo Park, an offshoot of the London Zoological Society of Regent's Park, in Middlesex, and where a number of major breeding programmes are being successfully undertaken amongst the 136 species housed here, while keen horticulturalists are attracted to Wrest Park, a series of formal gardens whose layout represents the results of a hundred and fifty years of garden design.

LOCAL HISTORY

Following the Roman occupation, the Bedford 'shire' became part of the county of the Middle Angles, before being incorporated into the kingdom of Mercia, whose monarch, Offa, was buried there. During the 11th century it became a separate shire, with its baronetcy awarded to the Beauchamp family. Their decision to side with Empress Matilda in her struggle against Stephen resulted in Bedford Castle being besieged several times.

A Bedford canon was at the root of the tragic quarrel between Henry II and Thomas à Becket, Archbishop of Canterbury. The canon was accused of causing the death of a knight, but was acquitted. The King's judiciary ordered a retrial, but the canon refused to appear, and his action was supported by Becket. The ensuing dispute led to Becket's eventual murder.

During the Civil War, the county roughly divided its support between the king and the Parliament and as a result was the scene of numerous skirmishes, sequestration and the plundering of estates. Some unsuccessful negotiations took place between the two sides while Charles 1 was at Woburn and the Parliamentary leaders at Bedford.

COUNTY FACTS

Origin of name: Anglo-Saxon, Beda's Ford, or the river crossing.
Name first recorded: 1011 as Bedanfordscir.
County Town: BEDFORD
A clean, brisk town on the river Ouse dating back to Anglo-Saxon time and subject to many Danish raids.
Other Towns:
LUTON Linked to motor manufacture and general engineering, although its football team is still known as 'The Hatters'. The airport was made famous by a TV commercial.
AMPTHILL Well-preserved little town, where, in the 16th century, Catherine of Aragon resided after being put aside by Henry VIII.
BIGGLESWADE Market-gardening centre on the river Ivel with a fine 14th-century bridge with three-pointed arches and two great flour mills beside it.
DUNSTABLE Originally a royal market town established by Henry I, now a shopping centre with some noted Victorian and ancient buildings.
FLITWICK Charming thatched cottages around a typical English village green beside the river Flit.
HOUGHTON REGIS Has a small Iron Age fort of note called Maiden Bower.
LEIGHTON BUZZARD Ancient and historic town thought to be the Lygeanburg of Saxon Chroniclers.
SANDY Another market-gardening centre in an attractive rural setting with the rivers Ivel and Ouse. The RSPB headquarters are near here.
SHILLINGTON Has the remains of an ancient round barrow named Knocking Knoll: a British chieftain is said to be buried there with his treasure chest and knocks to be let out of the barrow.
◆ Barton-in-the-Clay ◆Cranfield ◆ Eaton Socon ◆ Henlow ◆ Kempston ◆ Potton ◆ Shefford ◆ Stotfold ◆ Toddington
Main rivers: Flit, Ouse, Ivel, Hiz, Ouzel, Lea.
Highest point: Dunstable Down at 801 feet.

Bedfordshire's local government: Bedfordshire has two-tier structure excluding Luton which only has one – Luton District Council. For the rest Bedfordshire County Council sits on one level and three district councils, Bedford, Mid-Bedfordshire and South Bedfordshire, on the second. Bedfordshire's Eaton Socon comes under both Huntingdonshire District and Cambridgeshire County Councils. Ickleford and Gaddesden are Bedfordshire detached in Hertfordshire served by that county and Ickleford by North Hertfordshire District and Gaddesden by Dacorum District Councils.

COUNTY CALENDAR

◆ May Day Celebrations – Ickwell Green. The village has a permanent maypole.
◆ Good Friday: Dunstable Downs & Pascombe Pit Orange Rolling. Believed to be symbolic of the stone being rolled away from the door of Christ's tomb.
◆Gliding events on Dunstable Downs.

BERKSHIRE

WINDSOR CASTLE *Viewed from the Thames with the Round Tower, or Keep, built by Edward III.*

THE COUNTY LANDSCAPE

◆ Berkshire is a keystone in the heartland of Southern England, with the River Thames as its northern border. The country goes from the sand and gravel and flat fertile fields of the Thames Valley, where sudden heights like Windsor rise above loops of the Thames, to the Chiltern Hills, mixed with heathland and expanding beyond Reading to chalk uplands, the Berkshire Downs and high grasslands around Lambourn.

◆ A range of chalk hills just south of the Thames form the northern boundary to the Vale of the White Horse.

◆ If the Ridgeway is the oldest track, then the winding Thames is the watery highway of Berkshire.

◆ The restored Kennet and Avon Canal runs from Reading through west Berkshire.

◆ From the north you progress to chalk hills in the west, then the edge of Cotswold country. It's ultimate English countryside, simple and pleasurable. Though it has highways rushing though it it is yet veined with country roads and tiny leafy lanes, ducking and curving, gemmed with lovely settlements (notable are Boxford, Cookham, East Garston, Hurley and Sonning). In fact pretty villages are scattered throughout this still-essentially rural county providing a sight for sore eyes.

ROYAL BERKSHIRE IS its proud appellation, and – sure enough – it begins at the doorstep of London with Windsor, home of kings, queens and castle. In fact the grand profile of Windsor Castle is quite unmissable as you approach it off the M4, a long grey line of turrets and towers that is quite stunning. The other facet of Berkshire aside from royalty is the more olde-worlde aspects around Newbury and Thatcham with pretty villages hidden in the rolling hills of the Berkshire Downs.

TOWNS AND VILLAGES

As you approach Windsor, silhouetted from the motorway are the spiky spirelets of that most perfect of royal churches, St George's Chapel. The interior is an ordered succession of delicate fan vaulting in the uniquely English late Gothic style. Within the castle walls are closes, courts, gardens, grace-and-favour houses and wide terraces looking over treetops across the river towards Eton and its college (over the border in Buckinghamshire), painted by Canaletto. There's a changing of the guard every day outside the royal apartments. (Apart from Donnington Castle, near Newbury, Windsor is the only important medieval fortress in the county.) Windsor Great Park laps the town with parkland, offering walkers and riders alike fine views of the castle. Windsor's interesting buildings include Christopher Wren's classical 17th-century town hall with its pillars that do not touch the first-floor ceiling – to prove the architect's point that his design did not need their support.

To the west and caught in a loop of the Thames is Maidenhead.

Here, in a town that was once an important stop on the coach run (on which the smart and fashionable travelled to Bath), you will find the high brick spans of Brunel's rail bridge. In a riverside house the Reitlinger Bequest offers fascinating Oriental, European and African sculpture and pottery. Nearby Shottesbrooke and Warfield have fine churches, Ascot, Bracknell and Sunningdale conjure up visions of royal races, opulent suburban residences and green golf courses.

Don't be put off by red-brick development around Reading. It is a very old town and had a famous abbey, until Henry VIII suppressed the religious institutions and left it in ruins. Britain's 'silicon valley' is forgotten once you've pierced the outer rim of development, for the county town has old commercial buildings, busy streets and narrow, glassed-over Victorian shopping arcades.

To the west is Pangbourne, and riverside Streatley with a wonderful old cheese shop. Newbury has long held links with the wool cloth trade – it has an Old Cloth Hall, now a museum. Turn north to Abingdon, Berkshire's old capital with a fine county hall, numerous almshouses, a long, many-arched bridge over water and flat fields, and remains of a fifteenth-century abbey gateway.

The edge of the county is high and grassy downland dedicated to horses – for here is a set of racing studs and breeding centres around Lambourn.

LOCAL HISTORY

The airy heights of the North Berkshire downs are notable for ancient remains – 26 Bronze Age burial sites and one Neolithic long chamber are to be found near Lambourn. Some still stand high in dramatic profile, others are slowly vanishing into the turf, but they give a distinctive mystical air to the far west of this county. The University of Reading museums have collections of rural life and Greek and Egyptian works, while the town museum has Roman pieces from excavations at nearby Silchester.

Warfield's St Michael's, a gothic and Early English church, has a Green Man – a pagan figure – carved on a sedilia, a set of stone priests' seats. More visible signs of ancient art are the outlined chalk figures on the hills, including the famous White Horse at Uffington. The 85-mile Ridgeway Path, a prehistoric trade route (which ran on chalk hills to avoid marshes and low-lying forests from Devon to the North Sea) runs pass Britain's best-known chalk hill figure and site of an Iron Age hill-fort. Berkshire's royal connection goes back further than the building of Windsor Castle: the Saxon king Alfred the Great was born at Wantage in AD849 and his statue stands in the market place.

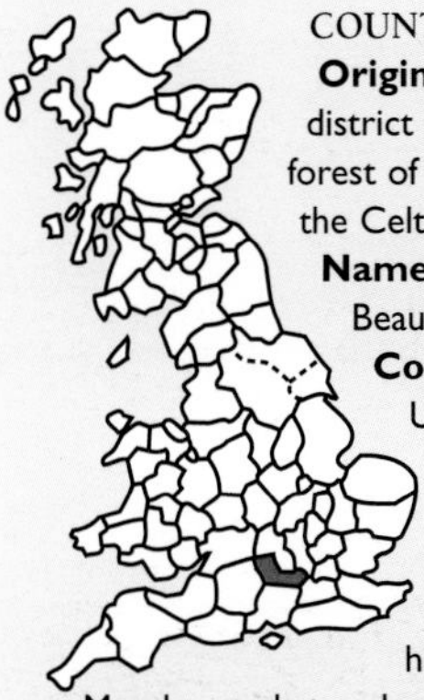

COUNTY FACTS

Origin of name: A wooded hill district originating from the great forest of birch trees called Bearroc, the Celtic word for 'hilly'.

Name first recorded: 860 as Beaurrucsir

County Town: READING Unprepossessing, but worth exploring along the Thames and Kennet rivers.

Other Towns:

ABINGDON Attractive and historic, a Thameside gem. Monday market under the old County Hall arches.

DIDCOT Good for GWR steam enthusiasts. The power station dominates and it has open days in summer.

HARWELL Also dominated by the Atomic Energy Research stack but retaining an olde-worlde charm with 14th- to 18th-century buildings.

HUNGERFORD By the river, with its clustering boats and ducks, is pleasant with a clutter ofantique shops.

LAMBOURN Fine Georgian cottages and almshouses.

MAIDENHEAD Riverside town with pub-lined towpath.

NEWBURY Notorious by-pass. Fine almhouses, a cloth museum and horse-drawn barge trips.

WANTAGE Has a set of almshouses and paving stones made of sheep bones. King Alfred, he of the burnt cakes, was born here.

WINDSOR Glorious gardens – particularly in spring. Savill and Valley Gardens are both open to the public.

◆ Botley ◆ Cholsey ◆ Crowthorne ◆ Faringdon ◆ Kennington ◆ Sandhurst ◆ Shrivenham ◆ Sutton Courtenay ◆ Thatcham ◆ Wallingford ◆ Wokingham (historically Wiltshire detached)

County rivers: Thames, Kennet, Blackwater, Lambourn, Ock, Lodden.

Highest point: Wadbury Hill at 974 feet.

Berkshire's local government: There are five unitary districts governing the major part of Berkshire: Bracknell Forest, Newbury, Reading, Windsor & Maidenhead, Wokingham. The rest of the County of Berkshire is administered by a two-tier system provided by the Vale of White Horse and South Oxfordshire Districts along with Oxfordshire County Council. The two detached parts of Berkshire in Oxfordshire at Langford and Shilton come under that County Council and West Oxfordshire District Council.

FAMOUS NAMES

◆ 'New lad' Nick Hornby developed his love of soccer (*Fever Pitch*) and music (*High Fidelity*) in Maidenhead.

◆ Kenneth Graham's immortal *The Wind in the Willows* roves along the Thames Valley.

◆ Spoon-bender Uri Geller lives in a mansion in Sonning-on-Thames.

COUNTY CALENDAR

◆ Mid-July: Swan Upping, the annual recording of the sovereign's swans on the Thames, at Windsor.

◆ Mid-August: Regatta at Hurley.

◆ Mid-September: Regatta at Cookham.

◆ Mid-June: Royal Ascot horseracing – renowned as much for its ladies' hats as its high racing standards.

BUCKINGHAMSHIRE

THE COUNTY LANDSCAPE

◆ An early 7th-century manuscript bewailed the solitude and desolation of the Chiltern Hills which comprise much of the county, and whose steep contours were for many centuries a barrier to communication, but the seemingly inexorable expansion of London has drastically changed all that.

◆ In the north and east of the county lie a series of gently rising sandy hills, below which is the fertile Vale of Aylesbury (famous for the intensive rearing of the local ducks).

◆ To the south is the long, chalk ridge of the heavily wooded Chiltern Hills, leading to the noted stretch of woodland known as Burnham Beeches in the extreme south.

◆ The River Thames forms the southern boundary of the county with Berkshire and the River Colne forming the border on the south-east with Middlesex. To the east are Hertfordshire and Bedfordshire. Northamptonshire lies to the north, and Oxfordshire to the west.

EXPLORING LOVELY LITTLE villages around Princes Risborough, browsing round the antique shops of Amersham or spending a day out under the leafy canopy of beautiful Burnham Beeches, you think Buckinghamshire is everything an English county should be. Yet this is not just *the* day-out county from the 'burbs – it's also where many west Middlesex folk settle. The south side of the county below Aylesbury is archetypal home counties exuding prosperity and richness. Mind you, it is also the site of Slough, subject of John Betjeman's biting

> *"Come friendly bombs, and fall on Slough*
> *It isn't fit for humans now,*
> *There isn't grass to graze a cow . . ."*

and now there is Milton Keynes in the north which is fascinating because the cows are concrete and the towns that make up the modern planned city – Wolverton, Stony Stratford, Bletchley, Newport Pagnell et al – are ferocious in their local identities. This is the home of the Open University, where those who cannot spare the time or the finance for full-time study can gain a degree. At the top of the county in the north, at Olney with its famous Shrove Tuesday pancake race, is where Buckinghamshire becomes a Midland county.

HAMBLEDON *Historic village nestled in the valley of the Chilterns.*

TOWNS AND VILLAGES

The otherwise sleepy former county town of Buckingham, with its higgledy-piggledy streets extending around a Georgian town hall, exhibits a lively atmosphere partly thanks to the presence of the students from the University of Buckingham, the country's only private university. In contrast Aylesbury, now the county town, has seen much of its previous historic character swamped by modern industrial development and insensitive concrete structures, although some of its half-timbered houses and the large market square still survive.

Wendover, near the high point (852 feet) of the Chilterns, has also retained some similar buildings but the two most architecturally satisfying towns are Amersham and West Wycombe. The high street of the former boasts a number of handsome 17th- and 18th-century houses, almshouses, a market and a graceful town hall. The latter, situated in a narrow valley, has a parish church dating back to the 13th century, an imposing Guildhall and Market hall of the 18th century, and an art gallery and museum whose contents reflect the importance of the furniture-making industry of the area. This was based on the abundant supplies of good timber from the famous beechwoods which are a feature of the area. The town itself, which dates from the 15th to the 18th century, is now owned by the National Trust which has undertaken to preserve its character.

The new town of Milton Keynes incorporates 13 former villages and now extends over nearly 50 square miles. Intended as a high-tech 20th-century metropolis, and designed for the convenience of motorists, with pedestrians and cyclists separated from the cars by a network of footpaths and subways, it has yet to live up to its original promise. A third of the city still awaits development and only the central shopping area displays the original noble intentions of gridform streets and cleanliness.

Life in the small town of Eton revolves around the College – that world-famous establishment for the education of princes, future politicians and pop stars' sons. Visit during term-time and you will find the town awash with boys in tail coats and stiff Eton collars. The school chapel is noted for its exquisite fan-vaulted roof.

The two major film studios established at Pinewood, Iver Heath, and Denham have both had a major impact on the county, with many famous films being made within their facilities and at nearby locations, such as the roads around Pinewood, which doubled for the Sussex roads in the venerable comedy *Genevieve*. The Black Park country park near Pinewood, with its exotic plants and foliage, served as a discreet replacement for authentic South American scenery in the film *The Mission*. The popular children's film *Chitty Chitty Bang Bang* was filmed on location at Turville, near High Wycombe, and at Iver.

LOCAL HISTORY

Prior to the Roman invasion, the region was inhabited by the Catuvellauni tribe, and in AD571 was part of the kingdom of Wessex. Its people were converted to Christianity by Saint Birin. By the ninth century, the area was part of the Danelaw, but in the early 10th century the Danes were defeated by Edward the Elder at Bledlow Hill.

During the Civil War, Buckinghamshire strongly

COUNTY FACTS

Origin of name: The farm of Bucca's people.

Name first recorded: 1016 as Buccinghamscir.

Motto: *Vestigia nulla retrorsum* ("No backward step").

County Town:

AYLESBURY Has a lovely cobbled Market Square dominated by a Victorian clock tower. Home to the famed Aylesbury ducklings.

Other Towns:

BEACONSFIELD Although much developed recently, has kept its red-brick Georgian high street buildings, but is better known for Bekonscot, the oldest model village in the world.

BUCKINGHAM Once created the county town by Alfred in 886, this is a delight to wander through with its steep narrow streets.

BURNHAM Its claim to fame is the forest of Burnham Beeches – a famous beauty spot.

CHALFONT ST GILES Pretty village with a John Milton museum.

ETON Has the famous ivy-covered buildings of Eton College – the second oldest public school in the country, founded in 1440.

GRENDON UNDERWOOD Village with Shakespeare associations.

HIGH WYCOMBE Has paper- and postage stamp-making heritage.

JORDANS Long assotiated with early Quakers. Grave of William Penn of Pennsylvania fame.

MARLOW Charming Thames-side town boasts a suspension bridge built in 1831 by the same architect who linked Buda to Pest in Hungary!

PRINCES RISBOROUGH Olde-worlde town with gabled and herringbone houses.

SLOUGH High-rise offices dominate this industrial centre. Sir William Hershel gained his first view of Uranus from his garden on the town's outskirts.

◆ Chalfont St Peter ◆ Chesham ◆ Colnbrook (shared with Middlesex) ◆ Datchet ◆ Farnham Royal ◆ Gerrard's Cross ◆ Linslade ◆ Wraysbury

Main rivers: Ouse, Ray, Thames, Colne, Chess, Wyte, Lovat, Lyde.

Highest point: Coombe Hill, Wendover at 852 feet.

Buckinghamshire's local government: A two tier system with a Buckinghamshire County Council for part of the county and four districts of Aylesbury Vale, Chiltern, South Buckinghamshire and Wycombe. The County is topped and tailed by two single unitary authorities - Milton Keynes District in the north and Slough District in the South. Buckinghamshire's Eton, Datchet, Horton and Wraysbury are ruled by the Berkshire based unitary authority of Windsor & Maidenhead. Linslade is administered by two-tier Bedfordshire County and South Bedfordshire District Councils. Caversfield is detached Buckingshire in Oxfordshire governed by Oxfordshire County Council and Cherwell District Council.

FAMOUS NAMES

◆ The countryside around Stoke Poges provided the inspiration for Thomas Gray's *Elegy In A Country Churchyard* while he was spending a summer at his mother's home there.

◆ The father of the poet John Milton retired to live at Horton in 1632, and his son spent six years there after leaving Cambridge, during which time he produced a number of works. When the Great Plague of London struck in 1666, he went to reside at Chalfont St Giles to escape possible infection.

◆ The 19th-century prime minister Benjamin Disraeli grew up at Bradenham Manor. Later in life, he and his wife purchased Hughenden Manor near High Wycombe, where he lived until his death.

◆ Hugh Grant and Andie MacDowell had their first night of passion at the Crown Hotel, Amersham, in the film *Four Weddings And A Funeral.*

◆ The jazz bandleader, composer and saxophonist John Dankworth and his wife, singer Cleo Laine, live at Wavendon where they have established an arts centre in the Stables adjoining their home. A number of major musical events and concerts are held throughout the year.

◆ Sir John and Lady Mills live at Denham.

COUNTY CALENDAR

◆ Shrove Tuesday: Pancake Day Race – Olney. One of Britain's oldest, dating back to 1445. Only ladies residing permanently in the town and wearing aprons, skirts and scarves are eligible to enter.

◆ May: Mayor's Weighing-in Ceremony – High Wycombe. Marks the appointment of the new mayor and mayoress.

◆ Sunday nearest St. Peter's Day: Hay Strewing Ceremony – St. Peter's Church, Wingrave. Hay is strewn in the aisles.

◆ November 11: Firing The Poppers – Fenny Stratford.

◆ February: Festival of the Arts – Milton Keynes.

◆ 4th week in July: Festival of Flowers – Hartwell House, Aylesbury.

◆ May/July: Wavendon Festival – Wavendon.

◆ September: Woburn Festival.

◆ End of September: High Wycombe Fair.

◆ November: Chesham Arts Festival.

◆ November: Buckingham Festival of Music, Arts & Drama.

◆ August/September: Buckinghamshire County Show – Aylesbury (September)

◆ Mid-June: Marlow Regatta.

◆ 3rd week in August: Lavingdon Show.–

supported the Parliamentary cause, and 30 of the men associated with the trial and execution of Charles I were connected with the county. Buckinghamshire boasts some splendid mansions and manor houses, some of which date back to Tudor times. The latter include the pink brick Dorney Court, whose gardens are claimed to have produced the first pineapple ever grown in the country. Chenies Manor, which has been owned by the Russell family since the 16th century, incorporates one wing built to accommodate Henry VIII and his court. A contemporary building is Claydon House, where Florence Nightingale was a frequent visitor.

More imposing are the mansion and landscaped gardens at Stowe, built for the dukes of Buckinghamshire during the 17th and 18th century, and where the skills of Vanbrugh, Robert Adam, Grinling Gibbons and William Kent were given full scope. The rakish activities of the notorious Hell-Fire Club, founded by Sir Francis Dashwood, were conducted in the Palladian setting of West Wycombe Park, which was built during the same century.

Overlooking the Thames at Cookham Reach is Cliveden, the former country home of the Astor family and now an hotel, which in the 1930s was a centre for political intrigue, and three decades later the scene of a notorious preliminary encounter in what was to become known as the Profumo scandal which subsequently resulted in the collapse of the Conservative government.

Waddesdon Manor is a 19th-century French-style mansion, built for Baron de Rothschild, and now housing a superb collection of Sèvres porcelain, together with furniture and paintings of the period. The building featured in the British television series *Howard's Way.*

Finally, tucked away near Kimble lies Chequers – the manor house that was given to the nation after World War I for the benefit of the prime ministers of the United Kingdom.

COOMBE HILL
From the top – where an obelisk marks "the wars in South Africa" – you can see for miles on a clear day.

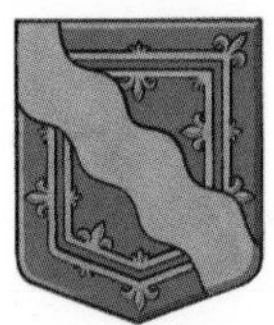

CAMBRIDGESHIRE

CAMBRIDGE *Quiet flows the Cam under the Bridge of Sighs linking two buildings of St John's College.*

IF NORFOLK IS flat, Cambridgeshire is flatter. This large spread of agricultural land shaped like a frying pan lies south of the Wash. Out of this flat fenland rises the beautiful huge Gothic glory of Ely Cathedral, but the pride of the county must be Cambridge.

TOWNS AND VILLAGES

Everybody seems to be on bikes in the glorious city of Cambridge. This university city only a little less old than Oxford sits securely in the middle of the southern part of the county. Set around quiet quadrangles, several of the ancient and beautiful colleges have gardens along the placid River Cam. Here the wide grassy banks of the Backs furnish an idyllic setting for those who like to picnic by the waterside, or drift along in a punt. The town itself is a long straggle of venerable buildings, some supremely fine such as King's Chapel, every Christmas the heart-stopping scene of the Festival of Nine Lessons and Carols. To walk through the quadrangles, a mellow parade of English architectural styles, is to enter another era.

It's a delight to discover the old town too and wander in the narrow lanes off the King's Parade, and along Magdalen Street where there are groups of medieval houses. The Fitzwilliam

THE COUNTY LANDSCAPE

◆ It is part of the Fen country, a bowl of dark alluvial soil that is rich and fertile. Indeed this prime agricultural land was once regularly flooded and the Isle of Ely rising above its marshy surroundings was often marooned in water. The fens evolved over thousands of years from ancient forests to a lonely expanse of marsh as the sea flooded the land and the rivers drained it in a perpetual see-saw process. The fens are now home to numerous wading and waterbirds as well as rare plants, and the country appeals to those who like the solitude of the watery scene.

◆ The county is at its flattest in the north around Wisbech and the Isle of Ely. The slow-moving River Ouse cuts across the county and provides a dividing line between north and south. The country around Cambridge is relieved with some hills, such as the Gogmagog range southeast of the city, although most are hardly more than undulations on a pleasant grassy plain.

COUNTY FACTS

Origin of name: Originally called Grantebridge (the bridge over the river Granta, one of the sources of the Cam). The Norman name was Cantebruge (the Cam was first called the Cante). Cam is also a Celtic word ascribed to rivers and meaning crooked or winding.

Name first recorded: 1010 as Grantabrycgscir.

County Motto: *Per undas, per agros* ("Through waves, through fields").

County Town: CAMBRIDGE A jewel of a city: dignified and spacious with beautiful college buildings and bridges.

Other Towns:

BURWELL Once a centre for barge-building and turf-making, this large village has attractive windmills and a fine church with an interior of clunch – hard East Anglian chalk.

CHATTERIS An ancient manor house stands on the site of a Benedictine nunnery built in 980 by Alfwen the niece of King Edgar in this town with a Domesday lineage.

ELY Has a Quay area – a reminder of its 'inland port' status before the Fens were drained. The 14th-century octagonal central tower of the cathedral, which replaced a square one destroyed by fire, took only 26 years to complete – that is fast for those days! It remains a marvel of 400 tons of masonry.

GAMLINGAY Mellow redbrick almhouses date from the year of the Great Plague (1665). A 15th century church also survives.

MELBOURNE A fine tithe barn, splendid Norman church and yew-lined avenues. Hard to imagine that the touring holiday originated from here, but Thomas Cook was indeed born here in 1808.

SAWSTON Has a claim to fame of sorts by being the first village college to open in 1930.

SOHAM Five miles from Ely across the causeway a splendid 7th-century abbey was established a few years before Ely (and not rebuilt after the Danes destroyed it).

WISBECH Prosperous fruit and flower-growing area with an ancient castle and beautiful merchant houses.

WHITTLESEY Domesday entry, Roman roads and now Peterborough's eastern dormitory town.

◆ Cottenham ◆ Fulbourn ◆ Girton

◆ Great Shelford ◆ Histon ◆ Littleport ◆ March

County rivers Cam, Ouse, Nene.

Highest point Great Chishill at 480 feet.

Cambridgeshire's local government: The County of Cambridgeshire comes under a two-tier administration: Cambridgeshire County Council at the top level and four District Councils called Cambridge, East Cambridgeshire, Fenland and South Cambridgeshire. Thorney has Peterborough unitary council as its service provider.

Museum, a Victorian porticoed palazzo on Trumpington Street, is world famous for its collection of treasures.

March, a centre of rail and road, is an open and often windswept town. It stands on the Old Course of the River Nene and possesses a particularly fine perpendicular church. The beamed interior of the majestically named St Wendreda is lovely, thick-clustered with wide-winged wooden angels.

Ely appears like an actor on a stage, a vision on a sudden rise in the flat fens, for the small city is dramatically crowned with a vast cathedral of several periods. It is best known for its Norman work, however – this great church's unique silhouette gives it the local name of the Ship of the Fens. As you approach it from a distance over the flat fenland and this huge vision appears you can understand why. The cathedral's fabulous Lantern, supported almost magically by vaults of vast beams of English oak, replaced a tower that tumbled down in 1322. The Lady Chapel is particularly elegant, though its lacy sculpture was scarred by Cromwell's puritanical followers. Around the cathedral are gardens. In the town are many pleasing buildings of several dates and a walk along Waterside gives fine views.

Wisbech was once much closer to the sea, which made it rich as a port. Hence the money to build, on both banks of its broad River Nene waterfront, some of the handsomest brick Georgian houses in the country – look for the deservedly renowned Peckover House. There's also a large old church.

South of Ely, in a lonely world of its own, the isolated Wicken Fen remains a fascinating repository of rare plants and bird species. It is a unique and ancient undrained bog. The nearby village has some typical charming houses. Villages in Cambridgeshire vary architecturally; some are simple and homely while others have quite palatial brick houses, often lining wide main streets. Most are low-lying so it's the tall church towers and wide-armed windmills that stand out, though these white-painted wooden monuments to an industrial age, once vital, are no longer used.

The Isle of Ely, the part of the county north of the east-west divide of the Ouse – and once an administrative county on its own – is a grey-green misted land of wide horizons, scattered with small fenland settlements consisting of small tile-roof cottages. Yet they are not without a great deal of interest: Thorney appears a lonely place surrounded by thousands of acres of reclaimed fen, but there are two ruined churches here of considerable architectural interest and a pair of fine 17th-century houses. Others include Haddenham, sitting unusually high in this flat country, with large brick houses; Leverington, with a 17th-century dovecote nearby, a centre of fine houses including an Elizabethan hall; handsome Whittlesey with its manor, 17th-century inn and medieval church; and the amusingly named Friday Bridge.

The stretch of Cambridgeshire south of the Ouse is pleasingly rural, with fat brick farms set in wide spreading fields. Close to Cambridge cluster the villages of Madingley with a post mill, half-timbered houses and an Elizabethan hall where Charles 1 hid, Trumpington with its medieval church containing a 13th-century brass reputed to be one of the oldest in England, and Haslingfield with yet another medieval church possessing a fine pulpit.

Swaffham Prior has twin churches and both it and Swaffham Bulbeck have lovely old houses – thatched cottages and a picturesque Tudor manor at the former, 17th- and 18th-century houses at the latter, one a moated farm, another a romantic house fashioned from the walls of Anglesey Abbey. Babraham sports a Norman towered church with a vivid John Piper window within and at Balsham the church has old brasses and medieval carved misericordes. Isleham church is a grand one with many treasures – brasses, misericordes and statues of knights, while the hammerbeam roof is a cloud of winged angels. Conington church has a Grinling Gibbons carving, intricate leaves, swags and fruit in soft limewood. At Longstanton the Hatton family are buried at All Saints and their crest, a golden hind, became the emblem of the buccaneering Sir Francis Drake.

LOCAL HISTORY

Wandlebury is a circular earthwork fort on the Gogmagog Hills. The original enclosed settlement dates from the early Iron Age. The Romans set to work to drain the fens, building great dykes and causeways. After they left, the area slipped back to marshland until the 17th century when perhaps as many as 700 windmills were at work draining the fens. The steam pump speeded up the process and the windmills declined. At Stretham there is a remarkable and very large village cross dating from the 1400s. and you can see a scoop-wheel machine, a rare survival of one of the engines used to reclaim the land by draining fens in the early 19th century.

Cambridge was a market town in the Middle Ages, standing on a spot where the Roman Road from Colchester to Chester crossed the river Cam. Around 1284 a band of students and teachers from Oxford founded a college that was to become the pride of the county. In addition to the cathedral, Ely has several fine ecclesiastical buildings with the King's School dating from the 15th century.

ELY Towering above the flat fenland.

FAMOUS NAMES

◆ Hereward the Wake fought bravely at Thorney and holed up in a final stand against the invading Normans at Ely. As 'the last of the English' he made the Capital of the Fens famous.

◆ The poet Rupert Brooke put Grantchester on the literary map with a line about the church clock and its indication of tea-time 'and is there honey still for tea?' The rectory is now home to novelist Jeffrey Archer and his wife Mary.

◆ Cambridge has had many famous residents. For many years the novelist E. M. Forster (*Howards End* and *A Passage to India*) lived quietly on his own in a Cambridge college. The Cambridge Footlights have provided stars from Jonathan Miller and Alan Bennett to Stephen Fry and Hugh Laurie. Comic author Tom Sharpe, who gave us the marvellous *Porterhouse Blue,* lives in Cambridge.

◆ While visiting his wayward student son, the future Edward VII, at Madingley, the Prince Consort fell ill and died shortly after at Windsor. It's said Queen Victoria never forgave the son whose transgressions unwittingly caused Prince Albert's death.

◆ The landscape designer Capability Brown, who changed the face of English gardens 200 years ago when he satisfied the current vogue for a 'natural' look was born and is buried at Fenstanton.

COUNTY CALENDAR

◆ The history of aviation is enhanced with regular events at the open air museum at Duxford.

◆ Many events all year, in and around the Cambridge colleges. In vacations visitors can stay cheaply in college rooms.

◆ The annual spring boat race between Cambridge and Oxford is held on the River Thames, between Putney and Mortlake, but the Cam has regular boating events too.

Cheshire

THE COUNTY LANDSCAPE

◆ From the Wirral, a wedge of silted land between the rivers Dee and Mersey, the ancient boundaries of Cheshire swing up into a corner of the Peak District, some 60 miles to the west, and swoop down towards the Midlands, taking in rich farming land, manor houses and churches, mill towns and moors.

◆ In the south of the county is rich red marl on which grows some of the best pasture in Britain, so this is good dairy farming country – and in 1759 noted for its cheese "esteemed to be best in England".

◆ The river Weaver in the southeast runs through what were once the largest salt fields in the kingdom. Nantwich, Northwich and Middlewich made up the Salt Wiches. Hollows caused by subsidence of salt subsequently filled with water and formed small lakes called flashes.

◆ Macclesfield Forest is a wild, hilly area some 1,800 feet above sea level.

◆ In the northwest the islands of Hilbre, Little Eye and Middle Eye, off the Wirral, are quiet havens for birdlife; in the northeast the 18-mile Gritstone Trail passes hills of the tough sandstone rock known as Millstone Grits, on its route from Lyme Park to the Staffordshire border.

BRING OUT THE red white and blue – not the Union Jack but crumbly Cheshire cheese of course and the three colours it comes in. I'm rather partial to the blue . . . it's enough to bring a broad grin to your face – like the Cheshire Cat! Seriously though, you need to be on best behaviour here especially in sophisticated Chester as it's quite posh, I always think: posh and pastoral. For sheer contrast to this Surrey-of-the-north vision you can always detour to the industrial Mersey shipbuilding region of Birkenhead (the Mersey Estuary is almost a mile across here) or the railway sidings at Crewe if you are a rail buff complete with anorak, notepad, packed lunch and carrier bag.

TOWNS AND VILLAGES

Multi-storey shopping takes on a new meaning in Chester, the handsome city where history is laid out before your eyes. The foundations of its two-mile town walls were laid by the Romans, who chose this site for the major fortress and port of Deva, on the shore of the Dee. In the Middle Ages 19 wealthy City Guilds and Companies set up shop here, and proof of the prosperity of those years can be seen in the astounding half-timbered buildings of the medieval centre. And this is where the 'high-rise' shopping comes in: in the Rows, two tiers of shops are reached by steps leading to covered galleries that were probably first built in the 13th century (though the present buildings are Tudor and Stuart). Some of the ground-floor doors are actually below ground-level, having stayed put while the pavements were raised over the years. The façades are graced with projecting windows and fine timberwork, and there are exquisite carvings on Bishop's Lloyd's House, where Adam and Eve cover their nakedness watched by the serpent, and a wealth of other scenes and characters are worked into the wood panels. There are more intriguing carvings in the choirstalls of Chester Cathedral, which stands on the site of an 8th-century college for canons. Here, under elaborate spired canopies, the panels are crowded with demons, animals and stories, including the tale of St Werburgh, who tamed and released a flock of wild geese wreaking havoc on the land.

Along the old Roman route through the fortress, Eastgate is now a busy street lined with Victorian buildings and spanned by the 18th-century gate that replaced the original arch erected by the Romans. In 1897 the ornate red, white, blue and gold clocktower, with its legs of lacy ironwork,

LITTLE MORETON HALL *A 16th-century half-timbered jewel.*

was set on top of the gate to celebrate Queen Victoria's Diamond Jubilee.

Fans of magpie architecture can have a field day in Cheshire, and will probably head for Nantwich, on the banks of the river Weaver. The Elizabethan houses that line its narrow streets were hastily built after 1583 to replace the wooden town that burned to the ground in the Great Fire of that year. After the 20-day blaze Nantwich was little more than a smouldering heap around its 14th-century parish church, St Mary's, whose octagonal tower and gruesome gargoyles survived, being made of stone. Good Queen Bess heard of the disaster and came up trumps, providing £2,000 and a supply of wood from Delamere Forest. The grateful residents expressed their thanks with a plaque on the High Street, acknowledging that Her Majesty 'hath put her helping hand to bild this towne again'.

Down on the southeast slope of Cheshire, near the Staffordshire border, is the crème de la crème of black-and-white Britain. Little Moreton Hall is a spectacular three-storey manor house, each floor jutting over the one below. Its crooked walls, covered with dizzying half-timber patterns and intricate carved mouldings, lean out around the courtyard and knot garden and over the rectangular moat; and inside are painted murals, a spiral staircase and Elizabethan plasterwork. This was the showpiece of the Moreton family, who (luckily for us) couldn't afford to follow the fashion of the day and cover their home with later improvements – because they were Royalist and Catholic at the wrong time, and had to pay hefty fines to the anti-Royalist, Puritan Commonwealth.

LOCAL HISTORY

The people of Cheshire put up a fierce fight against their Roman occupiers, but by AD79 the imperial troops had taken charge and their fleet was moored at the fortified port of Deva. After the Romans had withdrawn a few hundred years later, waves of new invaders settled in the area. By the 7th century the Saxons had arrived. During this era two beautifully carved stone crosses – one 16 feet tall, the other 11 feet – were raised in Sandbach, now a small town off the M6, its name immortalized in the motorway services station. More incursions, by Vikings and then by Normans, met with more resistance: Cheshire saw much fighting, being a strategically placed county on the border with the inaccessible highlands of Wales. In fact, this was such an important area that its nobles were virtually independent of the king for centuries. The earls of Chester held their own parliaments and Richard II even declared Cheshire a principality in its own right.

COUNTY FACTS

Origin of name: Chester means the camp or fort. The Britons originally called it Legacchestir, meaning the camp of the legions. This was then shortened to Chester, a corruption of the Latin word *castra.*

Name first recorded: 980 as Legeceasterscir.

County Town:
CHESTER An ancient city with a long and impressive history and some of the finest half-timbered buildings in the world.

Other Towns:
BIRKENHEAD Prosperous port founded by Vikings, who called it Birken Haven. Remains of 12th Century Priory. Imposing Williamson Art Gallery.
GRAPPENHALL Nice village whose Church has a grinning Cheshire cat on its tower!
HALTON Ruined 11th century castle, attractive Castle Inn, and Chesshyre Library with many rare volumes, plus glorious views over to Wales and Lancashire.
HOYLAKE Comfortable residential and seaside resort with a 4-mile promenade and famous Royal Liverpool Golf Club links. Once, it was a mere hamlet from which people set off for Ireland.
KNUTSFORD Olde-worlde atmosphere still around with good hotels and guest houses.
MACCLESFIELD Mentioned in the Domesday Book. Once the leading silk-manufacturing town in England with a legacy of 18th- and early 19th-century mills.
NANTWICH Famed for its brine baths with medicinal qualities. The leather trade flourished here and its streets were said to be paved with scraps of leather.
NEW BRIGHTON The promenade here is Liverpool's answer to the seaside.
STOCKPORT Its bridge over the Mersey was blown up in 1745 to prevent a rebel army marching from Scotland into the centre of the kingdom. Grew rich on silk, cotton, textiles and engineering. Captured by Prince Rupert in the Civil War.
◆ Altrincham ◆ Bebington ◆ Bromborough
◆ Crewe ◆ Dukinfield ◆ Hale ◆ Heswell ◆ Hyde
◆ Neston ◆ Sale ◆ Wallasey ◆ Wilmslow ◆ Winsford

County rivers: Dee, Mersey, Weaver, Dane.
Highest point: Black Hill at 1,908 feet.

Cheshire's local government: Cheshire County Council governs about half of the County of Cheshire under a two-tier system with six district councils: Chester, Crewe & Nantwich, Congleton, Ellesmere Port & Neston, Macclesfield and Vale Royal. Then there are five unitary councils shared with Lancashire – Halton, Manchester, Tameside, Trafford and Warrington – and two wholly Cheshire – Stockport and Wirral. Tintwistle is two-tier administered by Derbyshire County and High Peak District Councils.

FAMOUS NAMES

◆ Elizabeth Cleghorn Stevenson lived in the little town of Knutsford and has left her legacy in a memorial tower: as Mrs Gaskell she described the area in her 19th-century novels *Cranford* and *Ruth*.
◆ Footballer Joe Mercer, who led Manchester City to the FA Cup in 1969 and the League and European Cups in 1970, was born in Ellesmere Port in 1914.
◆ Glenda Jackson, actress and MP, hails from Birkenhead, also the birthplace of *Keeping Up Appearances* actress Patricia Routledge.
◆ Actor Ronald Pickup was born in Chester in 1941.
◆ Lyme Park, a lovely Elizabethan mansion in Disley, doubled as Pemberley for the 1995 BBC adaptation of Jane Austen's *Pride and Prejudice*.
◆ Granada TV's 1979 screen version of Evelyn Waugh's novel *Brideshead Revisited* was partly set at Tatton Park, a Georgian house in Knutsford.
◆ TV soap *Hollyoaks* is set and filmed in Chester.
◆ Outspoken cricketer Ian Botham was born in Heswall in 1955. He went to Milford School.

COUNTY CALENDAR

◆ Saturday nearest 25 January: the people of Nantwich recall their 1644 defeat of the Royalist army with a re-enactment on Holly Holy Day.
◆ June–July: every five years Chester holds its famous series of Mystery Plays.
◆ June: Cheshire County Show at Knutsford.
◆ June: Woodford Air Show near Cheadles Hulme.
◆ World Worm-charming championships near Nantwich, in June!
◆ Events at Tatton Park near Knutsford and Arley Hall near Northwich - including outdoor music.

In the relative calm of the Tudor period, Cheshire's townspeople and merchants were free to build their grand houses and elaborate churches, but in the 17th century trouble hit again, as the Civil War ripped the county apart. Nantwich was the only anti-Royalist town in the county, but it managed to defeat a detachment of the king's troops after six weeks of battle, and turned the church into a makeshift prison for the surviving Cavaliers.

Industry brought Cheshire its later wealth – in salt, silk, shipping and cotton. The Wiches (Middlewich, Northwich and Nantwich) were the salt-producing area – salt pits were worked in Roman times. From the 17th century, mines were dug to extract the salt which is not yet exhausted.

One of the few water-powered cotton mills still standing is the 18th-century Quarry Bank Mill in Styal, founded by benevolent employer Samuel Greg, who provided a school, cottages, food and a church for his workforce. This was a tradition continued by William Hesketh Lever, who invented the sweet-smelling Sunlight soap in the 1850s and built a model village, Port Sunlight, for his workers on the Mersey shore of the Wirral, south of Birkenhead.

At the base of the peninsula, further south along the Mersey, a group of ambitious tradesmen from Ellesmere had built a harbour in the 1790s – Ellesmere Port – as the gateway to their new Shropshire Union Canal, linking the river with their Midlands factories. The success of this new transport system brought a trail of warehouses, quays and mills along the route. Nowadays the port is a museum to the maritime trade of that exciting era that changed the face of British industrial life.

Near the village of Goostrey, east of the M6, a new age of discovery and technology has its working monument: Jodrell Bank, a 3,200-ton radio telescope as big as St Paul's Cathedral, but steerable. Built in 1957, this vast, 250-foot bowl sits on steel girders mounted on rails and looks up at the sky, listening for cosmic signals and picking up the information that tells the experts of Manchester University in Lancashire what's going on in outer space.

BIRKENHEAD DOCKS *The industrial face of the county.*

CORNWALL *KERNOW*

ST. MICHAEL'S MOUNT *At high tide this famous site in Marazion Bay can only be reached by boat.*

CROSS THE ELEGANT span of the Tamar bridge from Devon into Cornwall and you enter not just another county but another country. Cornwall is very different from the rest of England: it is separate, a kingdom of its own, called Kernow, and you feel it as you cross the Tamar. So there is a claim to be made that the bridge – and not Land's End – is England's final frontier. No wonder the Cornish are proud to assert that, I would be too.

England was created by the Romans, but Cornwall (like Wales) by the Celts. At Land's End, the granite mass of the Penwith Peninsula tumbles into the sea at a place steeped in ancient lore and legend unmatched anywhere else in England. But the county also harbours softer contours. On the southern fringes of Bodmin Moor, the scenery is verdant, pastoral and gentle, as it is on the Roseland peninsula, on the sheltered south coast. Other parts are more lonely and bleak, but just as lovely in their own way. Most people visit Cornwall in search of a suntan – the first family holiday I ever had was on the Lizard – but when you tire of the beaches, there is good sightseeing.

TOWNS AND VILLAGES

Cornwall has several outstanding towns and villages, and Truro not least for its Georgian streets and buildings – Lemon Street contains some of the best examples of Georgian architecture in

THE COUNTY LANDSCAPE

◆ Cornwall, in the far west of England, cuts down from Devon on its coast like a large piece of cake, sloping from north to south. The spine of the county – the watershed – is in the north, with the principal rivers – the Tamar and the Fowey, the Fal and the Helford – running to the south coast.

◆ Within the county's boundaries, there is a wealth of contrast. The north coast comprises a series of magnificent cliffs and headlands, backed by a high plateau of good agricultural land. The south coast is softer and greener, with tidal estuaries providing an abundance of bird life, the exception being the rugged Lizard peninsula, almost entirely surrounded by sea, whose exposed position results in it taking a severe battering from the Atlantic in winter. Inland, the scenery is again full of contrast – the barren, somewhat desolate landscape of the mining areas very different to the wild, boggy Bodmin Moor. The further west you travel, the fewer the trees – an exposed land which helps explain Cornwall's dependence on stone for building.

COUNTY FACTS

Origin of name: The Welsh in Cornavia. From the Latin *Cornu* meaning horn. West of the Dunnoii (Devon) was the Corneu to the Britons – the land of horn. The second syllable comes from the Old English 'wahl' meaning foreign, as that was how the English called the Britons or the Welsh.

Name first recorded: 891 as Cornwalam.

County Motto: "One and all".

COUNTY TOWN: TRURO Has a strong sense of identity: it only acquired city status in 1877 (until then, Cornwall was administered from Exeter).

Other Towns:

BODMIN Was officially the county capital (the assizes were there) and the largest town in the Middle Ages. St Petroc's Church, the largest in the county, had a spire until lightning removed it in 1699.

BUDE A popular holiday resort with a magnificent cliffy coastline. Head for the Summerleaze beach which is so wide that when the tide is out a sea-water swimming pool is created near the cliffs.

FALMOUTH A wonderful natural harbour and an attractive town, as well as being a good jumping off point for exploring the county's splendours.

FOWEY Quintessential Cornish port and worth a stroll around at any time of the year. The 15-century church of St Fimbarrus is at the centre of the town.

LAUNCESTON County capital until 1838 crowned on a hill with castle ruins. Good trout rivers nearby.

LOSTWITHIEL Built to a medieval grid plan and with interesting old buildings, such as the 13th-century parish church spire, sloping down to the Fowey.

MOUSEHOLE Picture postcard port (pronounced 'Mouzell') with an almost all-embracing granite breakwater. Once pilchards were fished, now mackerel. In 1595 a squadron of Spanish galleons appeared off the village and 200 soldiers landed here and burnt the port and pillaged. On a lighter note Nicola Bayley's *The Mousehole Cat* is a delightful children's tale and animated film based on the port.

NEWLYN Busy fishing port. Shark-fishing trips available.

PADSTOW Picturesque holiday town with Atlantic rollers providing good surfing. Narrow mainly unspoilt streets converge on a semi-circle of buildings round the quay.

PENZANCE A seaside town with splendid views across Mounts Bay to St Michael's Mount.

REDRUTH Famous back in the 1850s as a copper-producing town. The simple granite mine-buildings scattered through the town bear a passing resemblance to the Methodist chapels in the area. John Wesley was known to preach in these parts.

ST AUSTELL Centre of the Cornish Riviera and with a number of impressive buildings, such as the Italianate Town Hall.

ST IVES Colourful stone cottages, twisting narrow lanes, fine sandy beaches and picture-postcard prettiness attract both artists and tourists.

ST JUST-IN-PENWITH Victorian town with best concentration of abandoned mining engine-houses in Cornwall creating a strange and evocative landscape.

Britain – and its distinctive, triple-spired cathedral. The cathedral was built on the site of the 16th-century St Mary's parish church and was only completed in 1910. It's best seen either travelling in by train from the east, or on a boat trip up the Truro river from Falmouth, the walls of the great building rising above you like granite cliffs, the highest tower pointing 250 feet into the frequently windy Cornish sky. While you're in Truro, pay a visit to the County Museum and Art Gallery in River Street, which contains a famous painting of a Cornish giant by Sir Godfrey Kneller.

But the true character of Cornwall is to be found on its rocky, wave-lashed coast. The county has more than 300 miles of coastline and in any resort along the north and south shores you're likely to encounter the county's most famous gastronomic offering, the pasty – meat and potato (often turnip or swede but never peas) encased in half-moon shaped pastry. The pasty is held together by the thick ridge of pastry on the side. Cornwall also boasts excellent seafood including a local speciality of marinated pilchards. Star-gazy pie is a traditional fish pie in which the heads of pilchards, mackerel or herring protrude through the pastry lid – perhaps for the more hardy gourmets.

The Cornish Riviera, as it is justifiably known, includes picture-postcard fishing villages such as St Mawes and Mevagissey. Pilchards, mackerel, herring, lobster and crabs were once brought into Cornwall's little harbours and sent off again to all parts of the land and even to Europe. Today you won't find any pirates in Penzance – just a seaside town with the port where the steamer sets sail for the Scilly

PADSTOW'S *Annual May Day Obby 'Oss parade through the streets.*

Isles, 40 miles away, beyond Land's End. Like much of the rest of Cornwall, the climate is so mild here that palm trees and other tropical plants thrive in the Morrab Gardens near the seafront.

Beyond Penzance, Newlyn's old cottages climbing up a steep hill are lovely and steeped in an ambiance which, 100 years ago, attracted artists like Frank Bramley, Dame Laura Knight and Stanhope Forbes. St Ives also wooed first artists and then tourists – both lured by the cluster of colourful stone cottages which seem to fall over each other in the narrow twisting lanes. The silent stacks in the vicinity of St Just are testament to Cornwall's almost defunct tin mining industry, but large greyish-white cones or pyramids glistening in the sun advertise that at least the china clay industry lives on in and around St Austell. The mounds are composed of sand and waste from the clay pits. The greater part of this clay is not used for the making of china but for the glazing and finishing of paper.

Along the north coast, where the Atlantic rollers provide some of the finest surfing conditions in Europe, are more holiday towns, notably Newquay. The 'new' quay dates from the 16th century, when it was found necessary to find a replacement harbour for the then-prosperous nearby fishing village of Towan Blystra. The town's livelihood then depended on pilchards, but tourism replaced it with the arrival of the railways in 1876. Farther along the coast, Padstow is another labyrinthine, picturesque town of crooked streets leading down to an attractive harbour.

LOCAL HISTORY

Prehistoric man left an indelible mark on Cornwall. The county fairly creaks and groans under the weight of the activities of Neolithic Man, who arrived around 5,000 years ago. In the far west of the county, the durability of the local stone – granite – means that you don't have to look too hard to discover megalithic tombs and stone circles, such as the Merry Maidens near Lamorna Cove.

Moving on a few thousand years, much of Celtic legend dates from the Dark Ages. High on Bodmin Moor, the mystic water of Dozmary Pool is supposed to be the place where Sir Bedivere may have flung King Arthur's sword, to have it caught by an arm rising from the depths.

Right up to Tudor times few Cornishmen spoke or understood English. Their language was that of the Celt (similar to Wales) and the language still exists in the place-names: Cornwall is sometimes called 'the land of tre, pol and pen' ('tre' is home, 'pol' an inlet and 'pen' a headland).

In 1337 Edward III created the Duchy of Cornwall out of

ST NEOT Is one of Bodmin Moor's prettiest villages with a 15-century church containing some of the most impressive stained glass windows in the country.
SALTASH Seen from Devon across the Tamar this port once resembled a medieval town with grey and white houses one above the other on the hillside; now it is more a surburb of Plymouth, but that does not detract form the impressive Royal Albert Bridge spanning the river at a height of 100 feet. This was the minimum height set down by the Admiralty to Isambard Brunel. His triumph, completed in 1859, is 2,240 feet long and has 19 arches. It is best viewed from the quay where you can compare it with the road bridge. The town is far older than Plymouth:
"Saltash was a borough town
When Plymouth was a furzy down."
It was incorporated in the 12t century.
TINTAGEL Holiday town with Arthurian attractions including the ruins of Tintagel castle dating from c.1145 with bracing coastal views. Visit the Old Post Office.
◆ Callington ◆ Camborne ◆ Gunnislake ◆ Hayle ◆ Looe ◆ Marazion ◆ Mevagissey ◆ Penryn ◆ Perranporth ◆ Porthleven ◆ St Blazey ◆ Stratton ◆ Torpoint ◆ Wadebridge
County rivers: Tamar (forming the border with Devon), Camel, Fal, Fowey, Truro, Kenwyn, Allen.
Highest point: Brown Willy at 1,375 feet.

Cornwall's local government: A two-tier local government administration split between Cornwall County Council and the six Districts of Caradon, Carrick, Kerrier, Penwith, Restormel and the lion's share of North Cornwall bar the two Devon parishes of North Petherwin and Werrington.

FAMOUS NAMES

◆ In front of Penzance's Market House stands a statue of Sir Humphrey Davy, a Cornishman of genius who is best remembered as the inventor of the miner's safety lamp.
◆ Sir John Betjeman, poet and television personality, was born in Cornwall and lived for many years on the north coast, in a house overlooking the golf course at Trebetherick, near Wadebridge. He is buried in the church by the beach at Trebetherick.
◆ The late William Golding, Nobel Prize winner, was born near Newquay.
◆ Writer D. M. Thomas still lives in Truro, the town where he was born and grew up.
◆ Author Daphne du Maurier spent a third of her life beside the Fowey estuary, first at Bodinnick and later at nearby Menabilly, where she completed *My Cousin Rachel* and *The King's General.*
◆ A large part of The Beatles' *Magical Mystery Tour* – a 50-minute made-for-television fantasy coach tour – took place in Bodmin, Watergate Bay, Holywell and Newquay in 1967.
◆ Prime Minister Harold Wilson found his earthly heaven in the Scilly Isles.
◆ The popular and famous TV series *Poldark* was filmed in the county.
◆ Sir Humphry Davy, who devised the safety lamp for miners, was born in Penzance in 1778.
◆ John Couch Adams, discoverer of the planet Neptune, went to school in Saltash.

COUNTY CALENDAR

◆ Shrove Tuesday Hurling at St Colomb Major: hurling was a traditional local sport played with a wooden ball encased in silver. The goals were two miles apart! It often resulted in bruises, broken bones and even pitched battles. Today there is a gentler reminder of the time-honoured sport.

◆ On May Day is the annual Obby 'Oss festival in Padstow. A man dressed as a horse is led through the streets and there is dancing in the Market Square.

◆ May: the day of the Furry Dance – the traditional floral dancing day performed through the decorated hilly streets of Helston.

◆ Throughout the summer, a floral dance is performed every week in Boscastle.

◆ Late May to mid September: Minack Theatre Summer Festival – drama at this spectacular cliff-top open–air theatre at Porthcurno, near Penzance.

◆ Early June: the Royal Cornwall Show is a large agricultural show at Wadebridge.

◆ Late August: Bude Jazz Festival, more than 150 sessions and four street parades during the one-week festival.

◆ Mid October: Lowender Peran festival of Celtic music and dance, various venues around Perranporth.

◆ The Tate Gallery at St Ives has modern art exhibitions throughout the year (and is worth a visit anyway for its postmodern architecture, café and views). The 'visitors' comments' book' is worth a peek.

◆ Early May: the Great Cornwall Balloon Festival is a free hot air balloon extravaganza leaving from St Austell and Newquay.

◆ Celtic nations are rugby-mad and Cornwall is no exception: Camborne-Redruth sees some superb club rugby, and Cornwall can swell supporters' ranks by 50,000 when they reach the County Final at Twickenham in Middlesex!

the original Norman earldom and Lostwithiel became the centre of Duchy administration. Wander around Lostwithiel today and the Duchy connections become apparent: in the ruined Restormel Castle, some of whose walls date back to 1100, in the guildhall, donated by the Earl of Mount Edgcumbe, and the sophisticated and elaborate spire of the church, a throwback to Brittany or Gascony, with which the Duchy had trading connections. I adore the ruins at Mount Edgcumbe, it is the crowning beauty of the majestic Plymouth Sound.

Mount Edgcumbe was held for the king in the English Civil War until 1645, and the county played a prominent part in that civil war. When hostilities began in 1642, the county generally supported the Royalist cause and Cromwell's Parliamentary army was defeated on the peninsula between Lostwithiel and Fowey. But the war's outcome was determined by the New Model Army under Fairfax and Cromwell and in summer of 1646 the Royalist strongholds in Cornwall capitulated.

A mile up the River Fowey from Restormel lies Respryn Bridge and, up on a hill to the west, the grounds of Lanhydrock, a 17th-century country house later blended with Victorian splendour after a fire almost destroyed it in 1881. Set in superb woods and parkland, the house offers great views of the river. Lanhydrock was built in the early 1600s by Richard Robartes, a banker and merchant from Truro, and remained in the family for three centuries until 1953, when it was bequeathed to the National Trust. It remains arguably the finest house in Cornwall.

WHEAL COATES TIN MINE *A reminder of bygone days on the Atlantic Coast.*

But the history of this county is really about fishing and mining – industries which have both provided a living for Cornishmen for centuries. Tin mining began in the Middle Ages and, along with copper mining, was at its height in the 18th and 19th centuries. One of the most famous mines was the 12,199 feet deep Dolcoath mine near Camborne, which produced both copper and tin until early this century. Both industries are now in decline, but a new money-earner – tourism – is taking over.

CUMBERLAND

DERWENTWATER *Looking back to the hustle and bustle of Keswick in the northeast corner of this small, oval-shaped lake.*

THIS IS QUINTESSENTIAL Lakeland: a region of outstanding beauty but sorely tested by tourists – which is why I prefer it in winter. Cumberland lies in the far northwest of England with a large share of the stunning lakes and dales. In its own way it has a kind of Cornish Land's End feel about it: the people are more akin to the Celts than the Lancastrians with whom they rub shoulders; the clue is in Cumberland's name!

TOWNS AND VILLAGES

The ancient capital of Carlisle long faced attacks from the north and it remains a border town on the edge of England with many aspects of Scottish confrontation still evident in its fortified fastness. The impressive walls are now embedded in grass. Of course you can't omit the castle where Mary Queen of Scots visited and then was held prisoner (Queen Mary's Tower still stands) and the cathedral, both made of the local rufous sandstone. A great treasure is the spread of 14th-century stained glass in the cathedral's famously fine large east window. There's

THE COUNTY LANDSCAPE

◆ A high, often bleak land of moors and high fells, sheep-dotted and resounding with the lonely cry of the curlew, Cumberland shares the northern edge of England on the west, while Northumberland takes the east. In both these English counties the often harsh and heathery uplands fold into the splendid scenery and softness of the Scottish Border country, while the barrier between the two is the northern spine of the Pennines.

◆ Cumberland enfolds in its high mountain terrain of mossed and grassy hills, sculpted by glaciers in a long-ago Ice Age, the jewel-bright lakes of the Lake District, and with Westmorland to the south the county completes this spectacular area.

◆ Along the western edge of the county, part from the valley of the Eden and the Solway Plain, the hills nearly abut the sea, a narrow strip of coastal land faces the often stormy water and is made up of long stony strands with viewpoints from prominent capes such as St Bee's Head.

COUNTY FACTS

Origin of name: The name comes from the same sources as Cymru, the Ancient Briton's name for Wales. The Angles knew this name but pronounced it Cumbri.

Name first recorded: 945 as Cumbriland.

County Town: CARLISLE A cheerful place, well laid out with a wide central market, a medieval guildhall, a lively museum of local history and the pretty Jacobean-style Tullie House with formal gardens.

Other Towns:

ALSTON Some 900 feet up in the Pennines and reputedly the highest market town in England – two passes leading to the town rise to 2,000 feet. It's often the first English town to have snow each year.

BRAMPTON On the River Irthing with Naworth Castle set in a splendid park.

COCKERMOUTH A Georgian feel but also remains of the town's industrial past – a 17th-century windmill, old cotton mill and tannery buildings. Mary Queen of Scots was imprisoned in the castle in 1568.

KESWICK Pleasant and popular Lake District centre with largely Victorian feeling and striking Moot Hall.

MARYPORT At the mouth of the Ellen river at Solway Firth with harbour, sands, and bathing, and Roman stations on the nearby cliffs. It took its name from where Mary Queen of Scots landed as she fled from Scotland.

PENRITH A chief road and rail centre and market town for the district; nearby 12th-century Brougham Castle is the most extensive surviving example of military architecture in the county.

SELLAFIELD Near to the town of Egremont and known in those parts for its nuclear reprocessing plant, parts of which can be visited on guided tours from the Sellafield Visitors Centre.

SILLOTH Small port on the Solway Firth with sands and good bathing, and on a clear day you see Criffell Hill in Kirkcudbrightshire.

WETHERAL Very attractive village above the Eden river with ancient priory gatehouse looking towards Corby Castle and local caves.

WHITEHAVEN Seaport and coal-mining town with sand at low tide (some mines extend miles into the sea).

WIGTON A market town that once boasted a three-day fair where heavy Clydesdale horses (bred in the neighbourhood) changed hands.

WORKINGTON Industrial iron and steel town.

◆ Aspatria ◆ Cleator Moor ◆ Egremont ◆Frizington ◆ Millom ◆ St Bees ◆ Seaton

County rivers: Eden, Derwent, Esk, Duddon.

Highest point: Scafell Pike at 3,210 feet is the highest mountain in England.

Cumberland's local government: A two tier system prevails in Cumberland. It is called Cumbria County Council on one level and below it are four districts – Allerdale, Carlisle, Copeland and Eden which is shared with the County of Westmorland.

also a unique painted ceiling. Part of this compact and atmospheric cathedral is the chapel of the famed Border Regiment.

That great Roman stone-built barrier against savage northern tribes, the Emperor Hadrian's Wall, ran through Carlisle before ending on the long grey shore of the Solway Firth at Bowness-on-Solway. It drives on in the other direction up over lonely fells and along the River Irthing to cross Northumberland's border, north east of Brampton.

North of Carlisle, and towards the border, the largest settlement is Longtown, a place where main roads meet. This was pirate country not so long ago, the domain of the cattle rustlers, roving bands of thieves known as reivers. The museum in Carlisle has a gallery telling the story and background of these violent men, and their small fortified castles can still be seen here among the frowning fells.

In romantically wild and heathery hill country to the east of the old coach road, now the A6, are several typical villages, their grey stone cottages clinging close to the earth as if rooted in it. Some have notable churches: Wetheral, which is gothic and has river-bank cells where a saint once lived, Armathwaite, recovered from ruin, Kirkoswald, with its separate tower, and Great Salkeld, with a Norman building.

Penrith, a small contained town with a medieval church and Norman tower, is on the border with Westmorland. As you progress west from here you are in the unforgettable country of the northern Lakes. There are ancient stone bridges, such as the pack horse one at Ashness. Here the settlements are small, yet often hill-perched and picturesque.

As it rains a lot, the green-blue slatey walls have weathered, slate-tiled roofs and are mossed; while satisfying stone cottages stand in walled gardens awash with flowers in spring and summer. They in their turn are framed with lush pastures, and sometimes almost hidden against the misted grey-green hills which rise to lofty heights as they roll on towards the sea.

Roads are narrow and sometimes hard to navigate here, but the ascent is always worth the effort with plunging views over the dry stone walls. These lovely mountains are the haunt of many sheep, a local breed being the Herdwick with its white face. The hills often carry fleecy yet rainbearing clouds on their shoulders, and enfold in their sudden steep valleys the spectacular lakes that give the whole district its name. Each has its devotees, each name has a magical ring and each depth of blue-black water shows different sides and colours in different weathers. In short, as any lover of Lakeland will tell you, every brilliant stretch of water has a character all its own.

The main town here is Keswick, a busy centre at the head of Derwentwater, belted to the southeast by the Borrowdale Fells. To the north is Cockermouth, where William Wordsworth and his sister Dorothy were born in a house that can be visited. The town has a 12th-century castle with dungeons and views of the wild fells to the north. When spring comes to Cumberland the lines of Wordsworth's most famous poem come alive again as the Lakeland valleys glow with the gold of massed daffodils.

Yet there are also poor but proud workers' towns with small and plain terraces of houses that betray a hard life away from the hilly farmland of the interior. A chain of settlements along the sea includes Maryport and Workington, all the way down to Drigg and Millom, the latter's Norman church containing alabaster statues. Whitehaven is a well-planned and handsome little town, while St Bees church was once part of a nunnery. At Muncaster Castle by Ravenglass, the castellated mansion is still a family home with tapestries, paintings and antiques, set in fine gardens that feature shrubs, notably the showy rhododendron.

Local delicacies include Cumberland rum butter made with dark brown sugar, grated nutmeg, butter, icing sugar and of course rum. It's delicious with unsweetened biscuits at tea time! But it's the long coiled Cumberland sausage highly flavoured with herbs and spices that springs to mind, as well as the cold sauce for meats made from redcurrant jelly flavoured with orange, lemon and port and known as – yes! – Cumberland Sauce.

FAMOUS NAMES

- John Peel's name echoes in the wild north lands of Cumberland – he is the famous red-jacketed huntsman of '*D'ye ken John Peel with his coat so gay.*' – *not* the disc jockey of the same name!
- The name of novelist Sir Walter Scott calls up his Scottish homeland, but he also has associations here. He used Naworth Castle as a setting for *The Lay of the Last Minstrel* and he was married in Carlisle Cathedral.
- The poet William Wordsworth is closely associated with Cumberland, having been born in Cockermouth
- Radio and TV presenter Melvyn Bragg was born in Carlisle and went to school in Wigton.

COUNTY CALENDAR

- Keswick Jazz Festival takes place each May with over 40 leading British and international bands delivering high-quality jazz. There is also a fine street parade.
- Carlisle Castle is host to many English Heritage events, often costumed battles and displays of falconry, as well as musical and theatre events.
- Lanercost Priory has special events all the year round.
- Regular boating events and races on the lakes.
- Mid-June has a Victorian flavour at Silloth Green with its Victorian fair including charity and craft market, vintage vehicles, funfair and flower festival.
- September sees the annual Crab Fair and World Gurney Championships at Egremont.

LOCAL HISTORY

There are marks of ancient occupation from the Bronze Age fort of Carrock Fell to the stone circles of Castlerigg with more than 40 standing stones and the oval-shaped site of Long Meg and her Daughters. At a site south of Penrith is King Arthur's Round Table, an embanked circle of the Neolithic period, as is the nearby Mayburgh. There are many Roman remains. Most famous of these is Hadrian's Wall. Much of this stone girdle defending Rome's British dominion can be walked, even though it has been plundered for building material – not an uncommon practice before ancient monuments were appreciated.

ALSTON *Snow comes early in this high-altitude town.*

DERBYSHIRE

THE COUNTY LANDSCAPE

◆ The northernmost county of the English Midlands, Derbyshire shares with Yorkshire, Staffordshire and Cheshire the majestic limestone scenery of the Peak District; the National Park created in 1951 has been described as a massive rockery garden, 30 miles long and 20 miles at its widest point.

◆ A spur of the Pennines lies to the northwest of the county. This long range of hills runs for 150 miles from the Scottish border to the Peak District of Derbyshire.

◆ The hilly county rises steadily in the northeast, to the border with the West Riding of Yorkshire, where the heather and peat moorlands lie on a bed of millstone grit, flanking the central area of limestone laid down millions of years ago. The latter gives rise to the spectacular limestone caverns. Towards the east and the Nottinghamshire border are the economically important coal seams which, in the past, have been much exploited.

◆ Further south is the moorland country, divided by gorges or dales, with Dove Dale reputed to be the most beautiful.

THE NORTH OF the county is the high Peak District, the land of mountain, moor and plain, of lonely meres and murmuring streams, while the feel of the towns is summed up by places like the elegant spa town of Buxton, and Ashbourne, and Bakewell. Southern Derbyshire used to be busy, active, lively and industrial. Here were the grim pitheads and smoking chimneys, yet not so far away some of the best known stately homes in the land. The combination of grit and grace means Derbyshire has just about everything . . . except a seaside!

TOWNS AND VILLAGES

The county town and borough of Derby, on the River Derwent, developed as an important route focus at the foot of the Pennines. In Anglo-Saxon times it was known as Northwothige, but under the Danes as Deoraby, from which its present name is derived. In 1977 it was granted city status but, with its centre now a mass of shopping malls, holds little of interest for visitors apart from the Arboretum, its oldest park which contains a monument to the car-maker Henry Royce. The early industrial growth of the town in the 18th century was initially helped by a canal network, and later it became a major rail centre. Rail, aircraft and motor manufacturing (including the famous Rolls-Royce marque) of various types are still very important to its prosperity. Silk spinning by machine was introduced in 1719 from Italy, and many local people were once involved in the manufacture of silk hosiery, lace and cotton, and a number of factories making yarn, fabric and clothes are still prominent. Perhaps its best-known product is its high-grade porcelain. After a visit by George III in 1773, the town was granted a patent to mark its china with a crown, and the local product became known as Crown Derby. In 1890 Queen Victoria amended this to Royal Crown Derby.

BUXTON *The Octagon in the Pavilion Gardens is a Victorian concert hall.*

The spa town of Buxton is a real treat. The Romans in AD79 were the first to take advantage of the famous spring which gushes 1,500 gallons of water an hour at a constant temperature of 28 degrees centigrade. Its reputation became famous over succeeding generations, and even during her period in captivity Mary, Queen of Scots, was allowed to come here to take the waters as part of her treatment for rheumatism. The town enjoyed its hey-day towards the end of the 18th century when the fifth Duke of Devonshire decided to try and make it a rival to Bath and Cheltenham. Although his plan didn't succeed, Lower Buxton still has some graceful buildings from this period. The thermal baths closed in 1972 and, apart from a French-owned bottling plant, only a few local people still make the effort to fill their bottles at St Ann's Well on The Crescent. The 1,000-seater Opera House nearby is the main venue for the annual Buxton Opera Festival each July, and Poole's Cavern, a mile south of the town, offers an alternative to the town's manmade architectural sights; the quite remarkable stalactite and stalagmite formations in a series of large chambers.

There are a number of other limestone caverns in the county open to guided tours, especially in the area around Castleton. The substantial Peak Cavern once provided sufficient room for a small village and a rope factory which provided rigging for Drake's *Golden Hind* and many other famous ships of bygone years; while the nearby Speedwell Cavern contains the Bottomless Pit, where 40,000 tons of mining rubble were dumped without visibly raising the water level. Two other caves are the world's only source of sparkling fluorspar, used in ornaments and jewellery. The Blue John Cavern and the Treak Cliff Cavern, both near Speedwell, are open to the public

Another major above-ground attraction is The Palace of the Peak, alias Chatsworth House, the seat of the Devonshire family. A vast Palladian mansion built by the fourth Duke between 1687 and 1707, it's set in a spacious deer park, with gardens landscaped by Capability Brown. The house is crammed with a priceless collection of books, furniture and paintings including works by Rembrandt and Reynolds. Chatsworth annually boosts its business by staging a brass band festival, an angling fair, show jumping and horse trials. More than half a million people visit it each year; the current Duchess of Devonshire calls it 'a town'. Chatsworth featured in the 1972 film *Lady Caroline Lamb* (who was a niece of the fifth Duke), which starred actress Sarah Miles. (She was badly injured falling from a horse during the two week location filming there.)

Haddon Hall, near Matlock, is one of the finest medieval manor houses in England which passed from its original Norman owners, the Avenells, into the hands of the Vernon family and then, by marriage, to the Dukes of Rutland. The

COUNTY FACTS

Origin of name: Formerly known as Northworthy, meaning "North Enclosure" in English. It was renamed Deoraby by the Danes from the concentration of deer, possibly in some sort of enclosure. Derby therefore means deer village or village with a deer park or enclosure.

Name first recorded: 1049.

Motto: *Bene consulendo* ("By good counsel").

County Town:

DERBY The product of the industrial revolution and designated a city in 1977. The museum of the Royal Crown Derby Porcelain Company houses a treasure trove of Crown Derby. Famous for Rolls-Royce engines. The cathedral was built in 1725.

Other Towns:

ASHBOURNE Gateway to Dove Dale and looking much as Charles I saw it when he attended a service in the church here with its 215-foot spire after defeat at Naseby in 1645. The recipe for a distinctive local gingerbread is said to have come from French prisoners billeted here during the Napoleonic Wars and has been passed down from Ashbourne baker to baker ever since. Nice with Ashbourne water!

BAKEWELL Busy cattle market town and largest of the Peak District National Park. Beautiful 12th-century church and fine five-arched medieval bridge.

BUXTON The highest town in England and perfect base for exploring the moors and dales. The Duke of Devonshire built the Crescent and Pump Rooms opposite the town's hot springs. Join the locals and fill your own bottle with spa water from St Ann's Well.

CHESTERFIELD centre for the county's coal and iron, but best known for its 238-foot twisted spire on top of All Saints' Church which is nearly 8 feet out of true and is visible for many miles around.

MATLOCK Amidst romantic scenery a River Derwent spa town with a great hydro centre built during the 19th century at Matlock Bank. Nearby Hall Leys Gardens stretch along the river.

◆ Alfreton ◆ Belper ◆ Bolsover ◆ Chapel-en-le-Frith ◆ Clay Cross ◆ Dronfield ◆ Eckington ◆ Glossop ◆ Hadfield ◆ Heanor ◆ Ilkeston ◆ Killamarsh ◆ Long Eaton ◆ Mickleover ◆ New Mills ◆ Ripley ◆ Sandiacre ◆ Shirebrook ◆ South Normanton ◆ Staveley ◆ Swadlincote ◆ Whaley Bridge

County Rivers: Derwent, Dove, Trent, Wye.

Highest point: Kinder Scout at 2,088 feet.

Derbyshire's Local Government: The County of Derbyshire is governed by a two tier system with Derbyshire County Council in part control of the whole county bar Derby itself! There are seven district councils on the second level – Amber Valley, Bolsover, Chesterfield, Derbyshire Dales, High Peak, North East Derbyshire and South Derbyshire. The City of Derby has its own unitary council where Derbyshire County Council has no jurisdiction! Measham is a detached part of Derbyshire within Leicestershire controlled by that County's council and the District Council of North West Leicestershire.

FAMOUS NAMES

◆ The ancestress of the Dukes of Devonshire and of Portland, Bess of Hardwick was born at the Hall around 1527. After marrying, and burying, four wealthy husbands, at the age of 70, she returned to supervise the construction of a new Hall over the next seven years. Her initials, six feet high, are visible on the parapets of the towers.

◆ The lexicographer Dr Samuel Johnson was married to Mrs Elizabeth Porter at Derby in July 1735.

◆ Thomas Hobbes, the philosopher, was employed as a tutor and secretary to members of the Devonshire family from 1610, but died at Hardwick Hall in 1679 at the ripe old age of 91.

◆ Florence Nightingale, the founder of modern nursing training, was the daughter of a Derbyshire gentleman and although born in Florence, spent much of her early childhood at Lea Hirst, near Crich.

◆ Sir Osbert and Dame Edith Sitwell lived at Renishaw Hall, near Eckington.

◆ The novelist George Eliot set her first novel *Adam Bede* in Derbyshire, although changing the names of the towns and local places referred to in the plot.

COUNTY CALENDAR

◆ Shrove Tuesday: Shrovetide Football – Ashbourne. Two teams, the Up'ards born north of the Henmore stream and the Down'ards from the south bank, battle in a game akin to rugby but with a minimum of rules. Royal Derbyshire stuff.

◆ Shrove Tuesday: Winster Pancake Races – Winster.

◆ Easter: Egg Rolling – Bunkers Hill, Derby. Traditional custom symbolizing the rolling away of the rock at the entrance to Christ's tomb.

◆ April/October: Barmote Courts – Wirksworth and Eyam. The oldest industrial courts in England, dealing with matters relating to lead mining and ownership of mines.

◆ May: Chatsworth Angling Fair.

◆ Late June: Well Dressing Ceremonies – Bakewell. As a thanksgiving for the supply of pure water, panels are erected around village wells. These are lavishly decorated with leaves, mosses and flowers pressed into the clay surface to form pictures, usually with a biblical theme. Also at Wirksworth (4th week of May), Monyash (1st week of June), Hope, Tideswell, Buxton and Youlgrave (3rd or 4th week of June).

◆ Late July: Clipping the Church – Burbage, near Buxton. Ceremony dating back to Roman times. Parishioners encircle the building holding hands as an affectionate embrace or "clipping" of the edifice.

◆ August to October: Venetian Nights – Matlock. A spectacular illuminated event, rivalling the Blackpool illuminations, on the River Derwent and its banks as it passes through Derwent Gardens, displaying lighted tableaux and river craft.

◆ Last Sunday in August: Plague Memorial Service – Eyam.

◆ April/May: Buxton Music Festival – Buxton.

◆ July to early August: Buxton Shakespeare Festival.

◆ March: Clay Cross Fair – Clay Cross.

◆ 4th week in May: Derbyshire County Show – Elvaston Park, Derby .

◆ August: Bakewell Show.

hall fell into disrepair but has been fully restored this century, and provided the setting for Franco Zeffirelli's 1995 film of *Jane Eyre*.

The town of Bakewell, two miles north and on the banks of the River Wye, is noted primarily for the Bakewell Pudding, more commonly known as the mass-manufactured tart, an almond-flavoured Victorian confection as the result of a culinary mishap after a cook maladroitly confused a recipe for strawberry tart.

LOCAL HISTORY

There are numerous Bronze Age remains scattered across the Peak District, relics of the Beaker folk who penetrated the region. The Romans did not tame the wild peaks and only forayed into the high hills for lead. Their roads passed along either side of the Pennines. But they were the first to make use of the lowland areas, which eventually became part of the kingdom of Mercia. William de Peveril, the natural son of William the Conqueror, built a castle named Peak, near Castleton.

William de Ferrers, the Earl of Derby, fought on the side of the barons against Henry III, but was forced to flee after being defeated at Chesterfield. He took refuge in the local church but was betrayed by a local girl whose lover had been killed in the battle. He was imprisoned at Windsor. Mary, Queen of Scots, was held prisoner at Chatsworth and Wingfield Manor where her jailor was George Talbot, the Earl of Shrewsbury. He later arranged for her execution.

The pretty village of Eyam, eight miles north, earned the epithet 'the plague village' in 1666 after three-quarters of its population of 350 had died from bubonic plague, apparently transmitted by fleas contained in a package of cloth brought from London. The epidemic was stopped from spreading by a self-imposed quarantine organized by the local rector, William Mompesson, whose grave, along with those others who died in the plague, stands in the local churchyard. Among these are the Riley Graves where a mother buried her husband, three sons and three daughters over a space of eight days in August 1666.

William Cavendish, the Duke of Devonshire, was instrumental in bringing William of Orange to England. He and his fellow conspirators laid their plans in the 'plotting parlours' of an inn on Whittington Moor.

The inhabitants of Derbyshire have played their part in social insurrection. They supported the views expressed by Dr Sacheverell in his assize sermon in 1710 against the effects of the Glorious Revolution of 1688, and in the 1800s the Luddite movement against industrial mechanization caused great damage to the new weaving machines.

DEVON

LESS MYSTERIOUS THAN its near neighbours Cornwall and Somerset, Devon is historic, heraldic and wonderfully scenic. It is not as assertive as Cornwall, not as courageous nor Celtic, and has a rather comely English flavour. Whether your choice is the red, rolling countryside of east Devon – home to some of the richest pastureland in Britain – the beaches in and around Torbay, or the dark, brooding hills of Dartmoor, the largest expanse of wilderness in southern Britain, this county can really stretch your imagination. Great care has been taken to preserve the underdeveloped stretches of countryside and, despite abundant commercialism, there are still pockets of genuine tranquillity in the inland villages and quiet coves on the glorious coastline.

THE COUNTY LANDSCAPE

- ◆ Few counties in England can match the scenic variety of Devon. Lying between the Bristol and English channels, it has two contrasting coastlines with some spectacular countryside in between.
- ◆ The north coast, like Cornwall's, is fairly rocky with superbly wooded cliffs and, here and there, picturesque villages like Clovelly, where, in summer, donkeys still transport children down to the steep main street past whitewashed thatched cottages. Other resorts like Ilfracombe and and Lynmouth are sheltered by the treeless tableland of Exmoor.
- ◆ The south coast is altogether softer and the climate balmier – palm trees thrive in Torbay and the South Hams. A deeply indented coastline welcomes the sea well into the heart of the county.
- ◆ Inland, Devon is dominated by the massive granite peaks of Dartmoor, which reach more than 2,000 feet in the north near Okehampton. It is a bleak and wild gorse-and-heather upland. The old red sandstone plateau of Exmoor.gives rise to the River Exe which flows right across the county to the south coast, entering the sea near Exeter.

TOWNS AND VILLAGES

Exeter, once the curse of motorists as they headed west for their summer hols, is now more by-passed by the M5 than its once-notorious by-pass ever was. It's a rich county town, its central, historic heart easy to explore on foot. No other place in Devon has a greater variety of fine buildings: a cathedral, mansions, cottages, guild halls and schools. The cathedral is a massively impressive 13th-century building with two Norman towers and a magnificent west front covered with intricately carved figures: it's almost worth visiting Exeter for that sight alone. Just opposite the cathedral, in the Close, is Mol's Coffee House, a building of obscure origin on three floors, the first of which is fronted entirely by a large double bay-window.

An appealing aspect of Exeter – and indeed the whole of Devon – is the proximity to water. The River Exe is only a five-minute walk from the High Street and at the Exeter Maritime Museum on the Quay you can inspect craft gathered from all over the world.

Near Exmouth is the extraordinary Gothic folly called A La Ronde. It was created in the 1790s by two cousins, Jane and Mary Parminter who, inspired by

BRIXHAM *On the broad sweep of Tor Bay. In 1850 there were 300 trawlers here.*

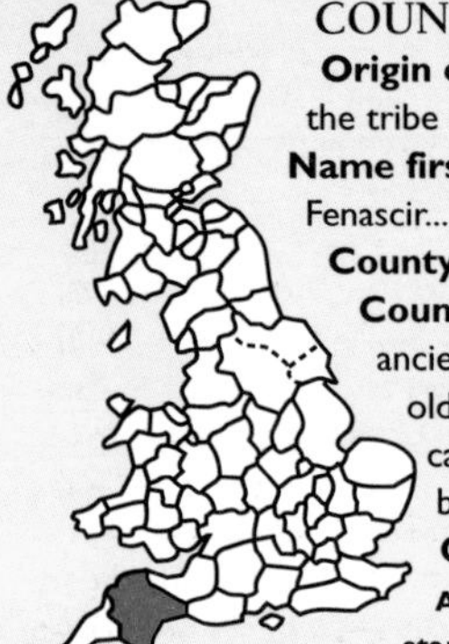

COUNTY FACTS

Origin of name: The district of the tribe of Dumnonii.

Name first recorded: 851 as Dev Fenascir...

County motto: "One and All."

County Town: **EXETER** An ancient city, one of Britain's oldest towns with a beautiful cathedral spared from the bombs of World War II.

Other Towns:

AXMINSTER Carpet making started here in 1755 with an eye to Turkish designs.

BARNSTAPLE Georgian-flavoured town, the largest in north Devon. Wool making and wharfs once made this a prosperous merchants' port.

BIDEFORD Has literary (Charles Kingsley's *Westward Ho!*) and wartime (Armada) connections and is a quiet place off-season.

BOVEY TRACEY A small pleasant hillside town with a fine mainly 15th-century church.

CHAGFORD Once a centre both of the tin and wool trade. Nearby is Castle Drogo, the 20th-century 'medieval' home of grocery magnate Julius Drewe, deesigned by Lutyens.

DARTMOUTH Crusade ships anchored here en route to the Holy Land. This naval town's formidable 15th century castle could rake the estuary with cannon shot and the river could be closed off with a massive chain.

their European Grand Tour, decided to build a sixteen-sided house based on the Byzantine basilica of San Vitale in Ravenna. The end result is full of mementoes of their tour.

Farther along the coast, between Dawlish and Brixham, vivid blue seas and golden beaches come together to form what is known as the English Riviera, with cosy resorts as comforting as clotted cream teas. With palm trees dotting the water's edge, and brightly-coloured yachts idling in the harbours, there is a touch of the Mediterranean about this stretch of coastline – even if the climate may not be quite so reliable.

Farther west still are smaller, picturesque spots like Dartmouth and Salcombe, and Plymouth, home of Sir Francis Drake and departure point for the colonization of the New World. Without a doubt Plymouth is one of my all-time favourite British cities: when you walk up the Hoe and look out at the vista to Cornwall, that has to be one of the most beautiful sights ever seen.

When the coastal towns and resorts seem too crowded to handle, head for Devon's pristine interior. You could try Exmoor – Lorna Doone Country – which straddles the Somerset border and is within easy reach of North Devon

LYNMOUTH *Site of the 1952 flood disaster, it is still an idyllic seaside village of thatched roofs, roses and cream teas.*

resorts like Lynton, Lynmouth, Ilfracombe, Barnstaple, and the Charles Kingsley's novelly-named Westward Ho! Or you could try the great granite upland of Dartmoor, where towering tors rise above barren bogland and racing clouds send sinister shadows skimming across the heather. The afore-mentioned Lynton and Lynmouth are twin villages, the first by the sea and the second almost vertically above it and together they present a fine sample of Exmoor countryside: wooded ravines, moorland rivers, cascading waters (which flooded Lynmouth with water and boulders in 1952) and cliffs nearly 1,000 feet high.

LOCAL HISTORY

Every schoolboy knows that the Pilgrim Fathers set out to colonize the New World from Plymouth, Devon's largest city. What is not quite so well known is that prehistoric man played his part in the development of the county. Dartmoor was once populated by Bronze and Iron Age farmers. Innumerable burial chambers, stone circles and standing stones point to evidence of Dartmoor's heavily populated past.

The Romans briefly established a base in Exeter and, after their withdrawal, Alfred the Great refounded the city. By the time of the Norman Conquest, this was one of England's greatest centres of population and the county continued to grow in importance during the Middle Ages, when the expansion of the wool trade sustained the city. Later the county became a focus for worldwide exploration, first by Sir Francis Drake and Sir Walter Raleigh, both born in Devon, and later by the Pilgrim Fathers, who set sail from Plymouth in the *Mayflower* and reached Plymouth Rock, Massachusetts, in 1620.

A full-size replica of the *Golden Hind,* the ship in which Drake circumnavigated the globe, is moored on the quayside at Brixham, while in Plymouth there's a statue of him on the Hoe close to the spot where he played his famous game of bowls before joining the battle against the Spanish Armada.

Later, in the Civil War, Salcombe Castle was the last place to hold out for Charles I and Sir Edmund Fortescue was permitted to march away with arms and colours flying as a tribute to his courage in defence. In the 17th and 18th centuries, Devon prospered on the back of schooner trade to the West Indies, but it needed courage again during the Second World War, when Hitler's bombs rained down on the city, the Devonport dockyards being the target. Much of the city was destroyed, but nothing can destroy the views from the Hoe and the Drake statue stands as lasting testament to Devon's proud seafaring past.

ILFRACOMBE Is the largest seaside resort in north Devon and once the fourth port of Britain. Varied countryside with cliffs and farmed hills.
NEWTON ABBOT Busy market town with fine local potteries and local cider companies.
PLYMOUTH By far the largest southwest town after Bristol. The Barbican is an attractive small urban area and site of the original town as Drake knew it: and the Hoe has outstanding coastal views.
SIDMOUTH Once a most fashionable 19th-century resort with Regency-style seaside architecture with its creams and whites and mass of wrought-iron balconies.
TORQUAY Quiet fishing village 'discovered' during the Napoleonic Wars and favoured by European royalty well before the *Hello!* era. Grand and glamorous. Nearby Kent's Cavern, a reminder of an earlier Ice Age.
◆ Ashburton ◆ Budleigh Salterton ◆ Crediton ◆ Cullompton ◆ Devonport ◆ Exmouth ◆ Great Torrington ◆ Honiton ◆ Kingsbridge ◆ Okehampton ◆ Paignton ◆ South Molton ◆ Tavistock ◆ Totnes
County rivers: Devon has more rivers than most counties including the Plym, Lyd, Tavy ('the little water'), Bovey, Dart, Avon, Teign, Exe, Taw, Tamar ('the greater water' bordering with Cornwall), Yealm.
Highest point: High Willihays at 2,039 feet.

Devon's local government: Two-tier administration exists throughout the County of Devon apart from a single-tier government for the councils of Plymouth and the towns of Brixham, Paignton and Torquay known collectively as Torbay. Devon County Council is therefore restricted to the rest of Devon and shares power with the eight district councils of East Devon, Exeter, Mid Devon, West Devon, North Devon, South Hams, Teignbridge and Torridge. A small part of Devon, namely the parishes of North Petherwin and Werrington, are administered by Cornwall County and North Cornwall District Councils.

FAMOUS NAMES

◆ The Beatles' film *Magical Mystery Tour* (1967) was filmed partly in Teignmouth and Plymouth.
◆ The television personality Noel Edmunds has a house in the South Hams, on the south coast of Devon.
◆ Saltram House, the National Trust property just outside Plymouth at Plympton, was used as a backdrop for the Oscar-winning film version of Jane Austen's *Sense and Sensibility.*
◆ Dartmoor was supposedly the place where Sir Hugo Baskerville was killed by a phantom hound in Sir Arthur Conan Doyle's classic tale *The Hound of the Baskervilles.*
◆ Ted Hughes, the Poet Laureate, lives at Barnstaple.
◆ Pop singer Elkie Brooks has a home in North Devon.
◆ Radio and television personality Angela Rippon lives on the edge of Dartmoor.

COUNTY CALENDAR

◆ Mid May: The Devon County Show at Westpoint near Exeter with livestock parade, leisure exhibition, food and drink marquee.
◆ September: The centuries-old Widecombe Fair on Dartmoor, once attended by Tom Cobleigh and friends.
◆ July/August: Teignmouth Regatta and Tor Bay Fortnight.
◆ Late May-early June: English Riviera Dance Festival of modern, ballroom, disco and Latin American dancing in Torquay.

DORSET

THE COUNTY LANDSCAPE

- A narrow, broken ridge of chalky hills in the south roughly follows the coast, the easterly ridge being known as the Purbeck Hills. Further north, a region of sandy heathland (Hardy's Egdon Heath), extends from the Hampshire border to the centre of the county, and another range of chalky downs runs eastwards towards Salisbury Plain in Wiltshire.
- Central Dorset is traversed by the wide, rolling expanse of Blackmore Vale, and in the north is the densely wooded chalk mass of Cranborne Chase, shared with Wiltshire. Portland Bill is a rocky peninsula extending south into the channel, connected to the mainland by the long pebble ridge known as Chesil Bank. The rolling hills of the interior are archetypically English, green and gently undulating, but Dorset's 75 mile-long shore is full of unusual coastal scenery, such as Chesil Beach and Portland Bill.
- The Isle of Purbeck is not actually an island, but a promontory of low hills and heathland jutting out below Poole Harbour, giving it the appearance of an island.

POOLE POTTERY *Distinctive ceramics.*

DORSET HAS BEEN my 'on location' home for many a television appearance. I filmed the old BBC show *The Goodies* at Beaminster and the classic *Canterbury Tales* at Milton Abbas. And, of course, Meryl Streep enacted one of cinema's most famous scenes on the Cobb, Lyme Regis, in *The French Lieutenant's Woman*. I have a vivid recollection of walking along the front at Weymouth, watching the ferries sail to Normandy, when I was staying at Wyke Regis with my showbiz friend Marian Davies.

TOWNS AND VILLAGES

Dorset's heart beats at a leisurely rate. Dorchester, the county town (Casterbridge in Hardy's novels), is still predominantly a market town - in many respects little changed from the days when Hardy cycled its streets in search of inspiration for his novels. His statue now stands on High West Street.

Down on the coast, Poole is one of the most continental towns in Britain. It has a wonderfully balmy climate and in the harbour – the largest natural harbour in western Europe – the forest of yacht masts and pavement cafés give you the impression you could be in Le Touquet or Sainte-Maxime – a far cry from the days

DURDLE DOOR *The sea has carved a 'door'. in the headland.*

when Poole was a favoured base for buccaneers and smugglers. In 1747 smugglers boldly raided the Customs House, departing with a rich cargo of tea.

From Poole's promontory satellite town of Sandbanks you look out across just a few hundred yards of water to where, at Studland, the Isle of Purbeck throws an embracing arm around the harbour mouth. In the harbour itself, Brownsea Island is 500 acres of woodland and heath run by the National Trust; a boy scout's paradise.

To the west are family resorts like Wareham, the comfortable old town of Bridport and West Bay, its fishing village outlet to the sea, and Lyme Regis, where Jane Austen would go when sea bathing was all the rage. Gourmets will be pleased to know that restaurants in the coastal towns and villages make a speciality of lobster – fishing is still an important industry here – and afterwards they will be able to enjoy Blue Vinny, a very strong Dorset cheese similar to Stilton.

Inland, the countryside curls and folds in great swathes of quintessentially Wessex landscape – wild and rugged downland, interspersed by pleasant wrinkles of greenery. Here you'll find the most euphonious collection of place names in England – Cerne Abbas (where the giant is cut into the hillside) and Piddletrenthide, Fifehead Magdalen and Gussage All Saints, Winterbourne Whitechurch and the delightful Droop. But in Dorset you carry on until you drop as there's so much to see.

Sturminster Newton, Blandford Forum and Wimborne Minster are towns as beautiful as they sound, and in the charming hilltop town of Shaftesbury the cobbled, cottage-lined Gold Hill has frequently been used as a backdrop to films and television commercials. Sherborne is a splendid base for exploring the ancient trackways and defensive earthworks of west Dorset.

LOCAL HISTORY

Stone Age man has left his mark on Dorset. The 115-acre site at Maiden Castle is among the most significant in Britain. It was first developed about 2400BC by a Stone Age farming community and subsequently used also in the Bronze and Iron ages. But the ancient Britons' sling stones were no match for the Romans and Maiden Castle fell in a bloody battle in AD43. Thirty-seven years later the Romans founded Dorchester – Durnovaria – and many Roman remains have been found in the town and the surrounding area, such as at Maumbury Rings, where vast gladiatorial contests were once held.

These gruesome traditions continued into the Middle Ages when the gladiators were replaced by bear-baiting

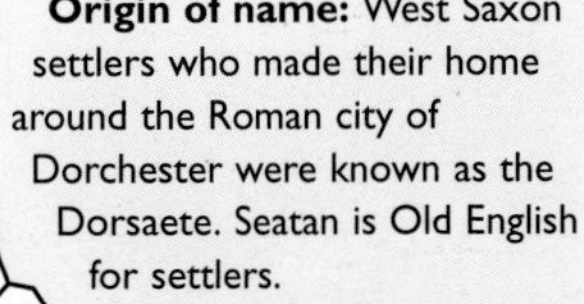

COUNTY FACTS

Origin of name: West Saxon settlers who made their home around the Roman city of Dorchester were known as the Dorsaete. Seatan is Old English for settlers.

Name first recorded: 940 as Doseteschire.

County Town:
DORCHESTER Lively market town. The local museum is a must for Hardy fanatics.

Other Towns:

ABBOTSBURY Part of 11th century Abbey still remains. Famous swannery and sub-tropical gardens.

BLANDFORD FORUM The most handsome and uniform Georgian red-brick and stone town centre by the Bastard Brothers.

BRIDPORT Once famous for its marine rope-making, now an attractive old town. The wide pavements are said to have been for twisting the lengths of hemp.

GILLINGHAM Historic town where Edmund Ironside defeated Canute's army in 1016. Royal manor of Plantagenet kings and hunting lodge King John's Palace; the moat still survives.

LYME REGIS Scarily steep and winding road drops you into this predominantly late-Georgian seaside town.

POOLE Sunny resort – tear yourself away from the harbour to see the largest Bronze Age canoe found in Britain, in the Town House museum.

PORTLAND Famous for its prison, its military bases and its quarries, source of the stone for so many great buildings – including St Paul's Cathedral.

SHAFTESBURY Market town of Saxon origin. Don't miss the museum and its display of buttons for which the town was once famous.

SHERBORNE A gem of a Dorset town historically and architecturally, with two castles and an abbey with a superb fan-vaulted roof. Cheap Street (cheap means market) has a row of Tudor tenements.

SWANAGE Medieval fishing village along spectacular cliff-lined coast that became a fashionable seaside resort with the coming of the railway.

WEYMOUTH Port with a good-looking seafront with late-Georgian terraces along the Esplanade.

WIMBORNE MINSTER Friendly and intimate small town with unusual twin-towered church, many old inns and hotels and excellent local museum.

◆ Ferndown ◆ Wool

Main rivers: Axe, Frome, Stour.

Highest point: Pilsden Pen at 909 feet.

Dorset's local government: Most of the County of Dorset is two-tiered: Dorset County Council on one level and five district councils called East Dorset, North Dorset, Purbeck, West Dorset and Weymouth & Portland on the other. Poole is governed by its own unitary authority. Chardstock, Dalwood and Stockland are Dorset detached in Devon controlled by Devon County and East Devon Councils, while Wambrook is Dorset detached in Somerset administered by Somerset County and South Somerset District Councils.

MILTON ABBAS *An 18th-century village of almost identical thatched cottages built by James Damer, later Earl of Dorchester.*

FAMOUS NAMES

◆ Thomas Hardy, outstanding English writer, was born at Upper Brockhampton, near Dorchester, and lived most of his life in Dorset.

◆ Lyme Regis's most famous resident is John Fowles, author of *The French Lieutenant's Woman.*

◆ Sherborne School, a traditional Anglican public school, has been used as a film location many times. *The Browning Version* (1951, 1994), *Goodbye Mr Chips* (1969), and *The Guinea Pig* (1948) were all made here. Although it is a working school, it is possible to see around the grounds.

COUNTY CALENDAR

◆ May 13: Garland Day in Abbotsbury. Garlands were once thrown into the sea to ensure a good fishing catch.

◆ Early June: Wimborne Folk Festival at Wimborne Minster.

◆ June: Pitchfork Rebellion pageants, to commemorate the landing of the Duke of Monmouth in 1685, in Lyme Regis.

◆ Late June/July: Swanage Festival of the Arts.

◆ July: Thomas Hardy conference, based in Dorchester, with lectures, barn dances, guided tours around Hardy Country, coach trips to Higher Brockhampton.

◆ Late August: The Great Dorset Steam Fair, one of the world's largest, is held at Tarrant Hinton, Blandford Forum.

◆ August: Dorset County Fair, Dorchester.

◆ September: Dorchester Agricultural Show.

and public executions – the notorious Judge Jeffreys once sentenced 292 men to death in Dorchester. Seventy-four of them were hung, drawn and quartered and their heads stuck on pikes throughout the county. Corfe Castle is a monument to centuries of feuding and cruelty dating back to 978, when the 18-year-old Edward the Martyr was murdered on the orders of his step-mother Queen Aelfthryth.

In happier times, British monarchs took a shine to Dorset. Edward I put the royal into Lyme Regis, the county's most westerly town, way back in 1284. George III's passion for bathing – some say it was an early symptom of his eventual madness – led to him becoming the first monarch to plunge into the sea, at Weymouth in 1789. He set a trend. Georgians headed for Weymouth in large numbers and the town is still a thriving holiday resort and Cross Channel ferry port today.

Dorset achieved another cause célèbre in 1834 when six men from the village of Tolpuddle were sentenced to be transported for banding together to form the first trade union – the Friendly Society of Agricultural Labourers. The Tolpuddle Martyrs maintained they needed a small wage increase on the grounds that their families were starving and after a public outcry they were pardoned. Their story is told in the room in Tolpuddle in which they were tried, now a museum.

DURHAM

DURHAM *Aerial view of the city and its magnificent cathedral perched on a rock, encircled by a loop in the River Wear.*

THIS LAND OF princes and bishops is now only a small part of what was once a huge swathe of stern and harsh north land known as the Palatinate. Throughout history its great families held considerable power as they defended the northern borders, their strength evidenced by the craggy castles beading its shore and crowning its countryside. Even in ruin, these citadels are unmissable in their commanding positions, especially when they are dramatically outlined against the sea by rocky coast or small sandy bay.

TOWNS AND VILLAGES

The adjectives 'startling' and 'stunning' could be applied equally to Durham Cathedral and Gateshead's Metro Centre (dripping with history and shopping). County Durham has plenty of both. Encircled by a deep loop of the River Wear, Durham presents a resounding silhouette to the visitor with cathedral, castle, chimneys and housetops clustering along a sudden high outcrop; an impressive sight at any time of day. The great Norman cathedral with its three towers is stern and strong, yet it has remarkable carving and stonework and the Galilee porch at the west end is an exotic surprise. Scots prisoners, held in the nave in the 17th century, damaged effigies so the cathedral has few memorials but the marching line of great round stone columns, incised with Romanesque decorations, is impressive. There are

THE COUNTY LANDSCAPE

◆ A hilly, sea-facing county, compact yet often rugged, and ranged around its castled capital, Durham. The county lies between two great rivers, the Tyne and the Tees, and extends inland to Yorkshire and east to the sea. Along its eastern coast industrial towns often of ancient origin and sandy shores face the grey North Sea. Many high cliffs and islands dot the coastline and Beacon Hill, owned by the National Trust, is the highest point on the Durham coast. Inland the county smooths into the long, straggling valley of the Tees with extensive stone-walled fields, and wide moors above.

◆ There are vivid contrasts within the county, with the bleak and rugged Pennines and sheep-rearing farmland of west Durham akin to the north Yorkshire moors, while the industrial, chemically-based south-east has a nuclear landscape and the mining areas of Easington and Peterlee with their big wheels signposting mine shafts to remind us that this was where the Industrial Revolution had its perhaps biggest impact. Jarrow, South Shields and Sunderland to the northeast are metropolitan areas with a great shipbuilding tradition.

◆ The landscape is based on limestone in the west, then a clay plain with sandstone outcrops such as the one at Durham jutting up. There's a lead mining centre at Killhope.

COUNTY FACTS

Origin of name: From the Saxon word Dunholme, *dun* meaning a hill and *holme* referring to an island in a river (the rocky outcrop where Durham Cathedral now stands). The Normans changed it to Duresme, which was corrupted to Durham. Bishops ruled this area until 1836 so the suffix 'shire' was never added: it is County Durham, not Durhamshire.

Name first recorded: 1000 as Dunholme.

County Town: DURHAM Is splendidly set cathedral and university city overlooking a loop in the River Wear. Student influence on restaurants and arts.

Other Towns

BARNARD CASTLE Fine medieval bridge, old houses and nearby French château-style Bowes Museum.

BILLINGHAM Friendly people, a theatre and a football club with the name Sinfonia FC (who can claim that?).

BLAYDON The Blaydon Races are immortalized in the words of the eponymous local folk song.

DARLINGTON Synonymous with the first railway in the country and a fascinating museum to match.

HARTLEPOOL Still has bits of medieval town wall. In the docks is HMS *Warrior*, the world's earliest iron-hulled battleship, and now a floating museum.

JARROW The word 'march' springs to mind but in the depths of this grimy town is a lovely 7th-century church where the Venerable Bede sought solace.

STOCKTON-ON-TEES Is famous for its open-air market started in 1310 in the broadest high street in England.

SUNDERLAND Shares with its neighbour Jarrow a shipbuilding heritage, and it became a city in 1992. Nearby Roker's St Andrew's Church (1906) is an Arts and Crafts design with William Morris tapestries.

WASHINGTON George Washington's ancestral home, Washington Old Hall, is open in summer.

◆ Birtley ◆ Boldon ◆ Brandon ◆ Consett ◆ Easington ◆ Felling ◆ Ferryhill ◆ Hebburn ◆ Hetton-le-Hole ◆ Houghton-le-Spring ◆ Newton Aycliffe ◆ Peterlee ◆ Ryton ◆ Seaham ◆ Shildon ◆ South Shields ◆ Spennymoor ◆ Stanley

County rivers: Wear, Tees. Fine fishing along the fast-flowing rivers and at reservoirs at Balderhead, Burnhope, Selset, Weskerley and Tunstall.

Highest point: Burnhope Seat at 2,452 feet.

Durham's local government: Durham County Council only administers about three-quarters of County Durham and it shares that honour with the seven district councils of Chester-le-Street, Derwentside, Durham City, Easington, Sedgefield, Teesdale and Wear Valley. All of which adds up to a two-tier system. The rest of the County has three unitary councils at Darlington, Hartlepool and part of Stockton-on-Tees (shared with the North Riding of Yorkshire). There are three unitary metropolitan boroughs of Gateshead, South Tyneside and Sunderland in northeast Durham.

cloisters and a monks' dormitory as well as a famous library and an exhibition of the diocesan treasures gleams gold and silver against sombre stone.

Throughout the town the houses are of 17th- and 18th-century date and there are two old bridges which have carried traffic for centuries. In contrast the most recent bridge, an elegant one called the Kingsgate Footway, was built in the 1960s and earned architectural awards. The castle still has much decorative stonework including a magnificently carved triple-arched Romanesque entry. Inside you can find rows of Romanesque windows and a chapel with fantastic beasts on its capitals. The entrance gateway is original though enhanced with mock-Gothic windows. Tours of the castle are conducted by enthusiastic University of Durham students who reside here. Out of term time you can actually stay in student rooms and have bed and breakfast at the castle.

There's a stone-flagged market place and all through the city little passages cut steeply down to the river's edge below. Mustard is now being made here again and there's a shop selling it beside the covered market place. The fiery condiment was originally made in Durham, and only later was taken away to Norfolk.

North from the county town, the northern border faces across the Tyne; Gateshead is its centre of communications across the deep river valley to Newcastle in Northumberland. To the west at Gibside, near Whickham, a fine house – now a ruin – possesses in Gibside Chapel a notable 18th-century mausoleum.

In Sunderland, Durham has its own Newcastle for it was once a seat of learning and in a previous incarnation, when it was known as Wearmouth, it had a monastery of considerable importance. Flanking Durham north and south are two major towns: Chester-le-Street, which has a set of statues of the ancestors of Lord Lumley, and Bishop Auckland, which is the country seat of the Bishop of Durham. Auckland Castle contains a suite of impressive state rooms. Nearby is Escomb, now the picturesque home ground for Durham County Cricket Club since being elected as a First Class County in 1992.

Stockton and Darlington resound in the history of rail travel, and the former appropriately has a rail museum marking with its site the first-ever passenger train ticket office in the kingdom. Darlington is a handsome town, with a fine high-spired church and a Victorian atmosphere. Along the valley of the Tees large village greens are common, and there is one at pretty Gainford with its Georgian houses. The village of Stanhope has a massive tree fossil in its churchyard. Reckoned to be millions of years old, it was found in a quarry. Stanhope is a walking centre for the upper River Wear valley and the North Pennines moors.

Best of all is Barnard Castle, with a wide main street studded with fascinating shops and houses, shadowed by ruined medieval fortifications. One of its inns claims a Dickens link and the novelist certainly researched *Nicholas Nickleby* here. The impressive French-style château on the outskirts is the famed Bowes Museum. It has fine furniture and paintings, and would be a jewel in any major town.

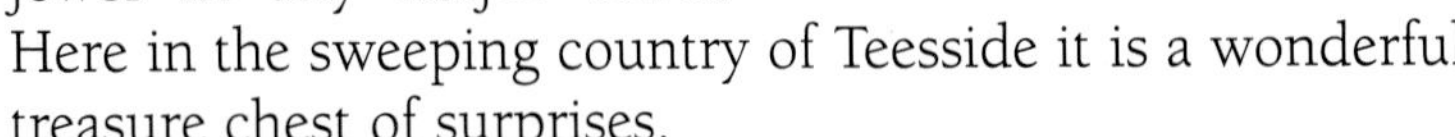

Here in the sweeping country of Teesside it is a wonderful treasure chest of surprises.

DURHAM *Miners take to the streets for their annual Gala Parade.*

LOCAL HISTORY

Legend says that a dairymaid lost her cow on the heights of Durham's rock and found it entangled in bushes. The monks bearing the body of St Cuthbert, having fled Danish raids on Holy Island, saw this as a sign and constructed a shrine and the first Saxon cathedral. It's more probable that, like William the Conqueror – who almost a century later built the castle – the monks knew an easily defended site when they saw one.

Durham resounds with history. Raby Castle with its nine towers rests on a Saxon manor given to St Cuthbert by King Canute in about 1030. Most of the castle seen today was built by the Neville family of Warwick Castle fame. Cicely Neville, the Rose of Raby, was born here, married Richard Duke of York and bore two kings: Edward IV and Richard III. The monks who had fled Lindisfarne eventually founded Durham and left there the bones of St Cuthbert, in the cathedral floor, covered by the single word 'Cuthbertus'.

For six centuries it became a place of pilgrimage until Henry VIII had it ransacked. St Cuthbert's bones were eventually returned to lie behind the lovely altar screen. Fast forward to the 18th century and the quiet hills of this county witnessed a complete upheaval with the introduction of steam-driven machinery and the harnessing of its coal, iron, the rivers and fine deep-water harbours.

Durham's local government (cont.)
government changes of the 1990s: an official ceremonial county, which on the surface seems admirable until you realize it only includes the area of Durham County Council, Hartlepool District with those parts of Stockton north of the River Tees, but *excludes* Gateshead, South Shields and Sunderland, all in County Durham. Not only is this ridiculous, it underlines the lack of understanding of what a county is and means. A prominent part of Durham detached in Northumberland, stretching from Cornhill to Tweedmouth over to Holy Island, and a further area from Bedlington to North Blyth is administered by Northumberland County Council with Berwick-on-Tweed Council as the second tier for the former and Wansbeck Council for the latter. Crayke Castle is Durham detached in Yorkshire under the control of North Yorkshire County and Hambleton District Councils.

FAMOUS NAMES

- ◆ The Venerable Bede, known as the father of English, lived at Jarrow and lies in Durham cathedral.
- ◆ During any coronation the Bishop of Durham holds the right hand of the new monarch, underlining the importance of the post.
- ◆ Paul Gascoigne, footballer, is Dunston Federation Brewery's most famous fan!

COUNTY CALENDAR

- ◆ Early April: Gateshead Spring Flower Show has an impressive array of flower displays, demonstrations and trade stands.
- ◆ July: Durham Miners' Gala in the county town.
- ◆ Mid July: Durham Regatta has various competitive races in eights, fours and pairs and sculls along the river Wear.
- ◆ August: Darlington Agricultural Show.

ESSEX

THE COUNTY LANDSCAPE

◆ The western part of the county is part of the clay based bowl around London, where it touches the Eastern suburbs of the capital. Here Essex is urban and is dotted with sleeper towns and railway lines stretching along the Thames and up to the North East.

◆ Fairly level in the middle with few heights except as sudden hills (such as at Colchester) Essex flattens its yielding clay plain even more on the fringes of its indented coastline. It changes to tidal mud as it goes east towards the North Sea and south to the Thames estuary. Here are slow flowing tidal water courses and bays where shallow inlets make a mysterious coastline of shadowy beauty.

◆ Stretching along the Thames estuary the scrubby marshland and wide mud flats with underlying silt means the coast encourages all sorts of wading and shore birds

◆ The northern half of the county has expanses of high exposed land enfolding handsome villages with plastered and painted houses, set on wide main streets. Along the border with Suffolk is prime agricultural land, rich and lush, and the scenery is mostly wide fields with prosperous farms, broken with coppices and fine big trees.

IT MAY NOT be obvious but this can be a county of ravishing scenery. Some is quite dramatic and comes as quite a surprise. Spend an evening on the mist-haunted Blackwater, for instance, cut off from the busy thoroughfares of the rest of the county, and you find yourself in quiet, reflective Essex, where white- and pastel-painted houses are often constructed of clapboard, very much an Essex style. From the clay lands that yielded much of the Agricultural Revolution as well as sweet-smelling roses, sweet peas, and saffron (not to mention sugar beet), through the planned new towns and chaotic sprawl of metropolitan Essex with its Fords, football clubs and factories churning out jam, sugar, beer and boots, there appear to be many real Essexes.

TOWNS AND VILLAGES

So real Essex could be in the coastal resorts or in the London sprawl but is more likely to be tucked in between the two. Essex runs a gamut of settlements from the clone-like conurbations near London such as Romford, Leyton, Walthamstow and Ilford (but also Epping and 13th-century Waltham Abbey) to the most romantic thatched and half-timbered villages deep in landscape that is often very beautiful and varied. To find the real Essex you will need to get away from main roads and into the countryside proper, not far off, yet a world away from the hurry of the high road.

CLACTON *Essex seaside with Punch and Judy on the beach.*

Colchester is an old and fascinating town set high on a ridge. It was a port and important city under the Romans and preserves many traces of those days from an entrance gate to bits of a theatre which can be glimpsed just by the Norman castle. This was an army headquarters and the strength of the town can be gauged from the vast Roman foundations of a temple and the fort where Boadicea herded the luckless Roman residents at the height of her success. The city has crooked lanes lined with old buildings and rows of pleasant Georgian houses mounting up to the town centre, while a number of earlier cottages are grouped above the old walls. You get a fine view from these over to the abbey porch of St John whose abbot refused to give up his church and was beheaded at the entry.

Along the coast the resorts include Leigh-on-Sea with its cockle boats, Clacton and Frinton. In the northwest are Braintree with its frescoed town hall, and attractive Dunmow, once famous

LEIGH-ON-SEA *Still famous for cockles – a Cockney teatime treat.*

for crocus flower flavouring and dyes, and later for hollyhocks and even an Ealing comedy. Thaxted has a handsome high-spired church beside an ancient wooden guildhall, while Halstead on the Colne has a Queen Anne house where Alexander Pope visited. West of here is a cluster of splendid typical villages – Finchingfield, Great Sampford, Great Bardfield and Wethersfield.

There are comic names too: Ugley actually comes from the Old English originator – one Ugca, who called the village after himself. Others are Weeley, Wixoe on the Suffolk border, Moze (it means marshy place and as a salt, panning place was recorded in the Domesday Book), Rotten End with a cluster of fine old houses beside Wethersfield air base, and Stansted Mountfitchet. This name comes from a Norman knight who was given almost 50 manors here, a pretty place divided by a highway with a noble church and a brick windmill.

Maldon makes sea salt from its flats. The oysters of Colchester were famous, first consumed by the Romans – Pliny, the Roman historian and scientist, records that the shellfish were one of the few good things about cold and clouded Britain!

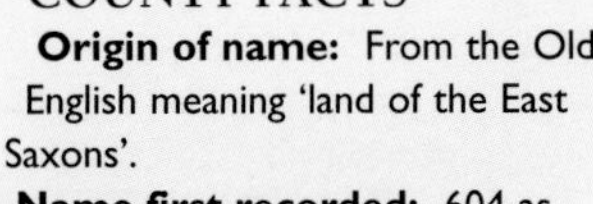

COUNTY FACTS

Origin of name: From the Old English meaning 'land of the East Saxons'.

Name first recorded: 604 as East Seaxe.

County Town: CHELMSFORD Its railway viaduct is a true monument to Victorian daring and engineering genius. It took over 10 million bricks to build!

Other Towns:

BARKING A 7th-century description has it as a town of fishermen whose boats, called smacks, lie at the mouth of a creek and take fish up to Billingsgate.

BASILDON Political heartbeat of Thatcherism and media barometer of Conservative fortunes.

CASTLE HEDINGHAM Is a pretty village with an ancient inn, the Bell.

COLCHESTER A museum 'must-see ' and fine zoo; look out for oysters to eat. Oh, and Roman ruins!

DAGENHAM Has the famous Ford factory (one of the largest car plants in Europe).

EPPING TOWN On the edge of a famous forest.

HARWICH Historic port and North Sea ferry terminal with the country's first purpose-built cinema (1911) still flickering.

MALDON A small town rich with centuries of British history.

SAFFRON WALDEN The saffron crocus gave this town its name (and its fortune until the 1700s; 30,000 flowers made one pound of spice for dye, medicine, perfume and flavouring). A pattern of medieval streets and merchant houses reflect this old wealth.

SOUTHEND-ON-SEA Funfairs, candy floss, one-arm bandits on the seafront. Hidden behind that is a resort favoured by the Prince Regent and some fine Regency traces are still left over.

STANSTED MOUNTFITCHET Commonly known as Stansted, home to London's third airport and wildlife park.

TILBURY The docks, opened in the 1880s, are the largest in the country and now handle timber, grain and general cargo bound for Britain.

TIPTREE Near Witham, is famous for fruit-preserving and jam- and marmalade-making industries.

◆ Brentwood ◆ East and West Ham ◆ Harlow ◆ Hornchurch ◆ Wanstead ◆ Woodford ◆ Witham

County rivers: Stour, Blackwater, Lea Colne, Chelmer, Crouch, Roding.

Highest point: High Wood near Langley at 480 feet.

Essex's local government: The County of Essex has two-tier local government for a large part of its territory, with Essex County Council and 12 District Councils providing the local services: they are Basildon, Braintree, Brentwood, Castle Point, Chelmsford, Colchester, Epping Forest, Harlow, Maldon, Rochford, Tendring and Uttlesford. There are seven unitary councils where Essex County Council has NO authority: Barking & Dagenham, Havering, Newham, Redbridge, Thurrock, Southend-on-Sea and Waltham Forest.

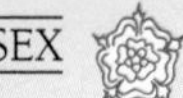

FAMOUS NAMES

◆ Boadicea, or Boudicca, queen of the Iceni tribe of East Anglia, rose against the Romans and swept down onto the stronghold of Colchester.

◆ The Earl of Essex, Queen Elizabeth's last love and a dashing if irresponsible courtier, was portrayed by Erroll Flynn in the famous film *Elizabeth and Essex*.

◆ One of the favourites of Charles II, Nell Gwyn, was among a motley company that performed *The Merry Wives of Windsor* in Boreham Hall.

◆ 'Darling Daisy', the mistress of the Prince of Wales (later Edward VII) became Countess of Warwick, and is remembered in Little Easton Church.

◆ John Fowles, author of *The Magus* and *The French Lieutenant's Woman* was born in Leigh-on-Sea in 1926.

◆ Colchester schoolboys Damon Albarn and Graham Coxton shared a teenage obsession with innovative pop music and went on to form the four-piece band that spearheaded Britpop – Blur.

◆ Gustav Holst composed *The Planets* in Essex.

◆ TV Alf Garnett (Warren Mitchell) was a fanatical West Ham fan.

COUNTY CALENDAR

◆ Mid February: Visit the Primrose Festival at Pass Nurseries at Marks Tey, which features up to a quarter of a million bloomin' primroses.

◆ End of March: Clacton's traditional ale and jazz weekend makes for a heady mixture.

◆ Fighter Meet at North Weald Airfield in Epping is Europe's premier fighter aircraft airshow; not for those of a sensitive disposition.

◆ Sailing events along the Blackwater estuary.

◆ Regular events through English Heritage at Audley End House from craft and country shows to sheepdog demonstrations and teddy bears' picnics.

◆ June/July: Harwich shows off with concerts, exhibitions, folk dancing and other entertainments.

◆ June: Essex County Show at Chelmsford.

LOCAL HISTORY

Colchester is the ancient Roman Camulodunum, where Cunobelin was king, later to be the inspiration for the Shakespeare play *Cymbeline*. It was the most important Roman garrison town in the country. Because the conquerors decided to make Colchester their capital, Essex became the most Romanized part of Britain with excellent roads such as Stane Street, Icknield Street and the Via Devana. All roads led to Colchester (rather than London) in those days and the town also received the first written record of any British city, from the pen of Tacitus.

This became the land of the East Saxons, the kingdom being founded in about AD527. Slowly the area converted to Christianity, largely due to Bishop Cedd, who in Tilbury arranged the first mission to the East Saxons. One of the country's architectural treasures lies in the simple church at Greensted-juxta-Ongar. An example of forest art or wood craftsmanship depending on your point of view, St Andrew's Church – the only surviving example of a wooden Anglo-Saxon church – is made of split oaks dating from AD850. The carpenter's marks are still visible on the solid oak walls.

The residential area of Hornchurch has a bull's head with horns over a window, a pagan symbol annexed by the 'horned church'. Castle Hedingham has a church with a double hammerbeam roof, a 12th-century rarity. It also has one of the finest Norman castle keeps in the country.

At Billericay there is the Mayflower Hall in which the Pilgrim Fathers met before they set off on their voyage to America in 1620. None of the Billericay group survived the epidemic that struck the settlers while moored off Plymouth, Massachusetts.

In 1826 the Courtauld family established a silk factory at Halstead and it remains one of the best sights of the town, with an imposing white weather-boarded frontage on the River Colne. Finally at Writtle, near Chelmsford, Marconi sent out his first broadcasts and developed his electronic industry. The village green here is framed by some delightful buildings ranging from the 1500s to the 1900s, so again Essex revels in its contrast of rural and industrial.

THURROCK *A different kind of Essex experience – Lakeside Shopping Centre.*

GLOUCESTERSHIRE

CLIFTON SUSPENSION BRIDGE Where Gloucestershire links across to Somerset.

WHEN I LIVED in Monmouthshire, which borders with Gloucestershire, I was often drawn to the Forest of Dean, once full of oak trees and then coalmines and ironworks. This is royal ancient woodland and to me it has the presence of a Tudor chase. The prettiest of its settlements, Coleford, is a treat, and nearby is Cinderford, the main town of this unchanged land. Go further across and you are in the gentle uplands of the Cotswolds where time seems to stand still as in the lovely-sounding Moreton-in-the Marsh, Bourton-on-the-Water and Wotton-under-Edge.

TOWNS AND VILLAGES

Everywhere from market towns to straggling villages large ornamented stone churches rise, embellished by the medieval rich in a public display of prosperity. Gloucester's cathedral, the brightest jewel among them, used artists imported from London to elevate it to the status of a modern marvel. In the spacious and fertile countryside imposing manors and solid farmhouses greet the gaze. From many points of view Gloucester's countryside is splendid, but alas, Gloucester city is another story.

To imagine the county town as it once was perhaps you should pick up a children's book – Beatrix Potter's *The Tailor of Gloucester*. Written and illustrated before the city was modernized its charming watercolours still give an air of an ancient and magical Gloucester, cluttered with old buildings along narrow streets.

THE COUNTY LANDSCAPE

◆ Gloucestershire is the essence of England. Its lovely hills, verdant valleys and deep grassed pastures have an air that's unique. Its views, such as Birdlip, are spectacular. The county is set with small towns and pretty villages, often constructed and roofed with golden Cotswold stone.

◆ This county shares with Oxfordshire the splendour of a part of Britain renowned for its beauty – the Cotswold Hills.

◆ The Cotswolds are actually chalk hills, the bare bones lightly soil covered and furred with fine grass. Once the sludge of prehistoric shelled creatures at the bottom of an ancient sea these hills were long ago folded and forced up under enormous pressure to form the familiar heights, rising in soft blue outline and giving the county its romantic and rural appeal. Aside from estates with planned parkland there are many great gardens here.

◆ On its farthest, and some say wildest edges to the west, Gloucestershire embraces the Bristol Channel. Part of the county, the Forest of Dean, is actually across what might otherwise be its border, the lordly River Severn.

◆ The River Avon forms one of several waterways that made Bristol such an important inland port. The city that grew rich on rum and sugar is still thriving today on its links with communications, computing and finance. This attractive, hilly, cathedral city has its own museum, but the surviving Norman, 16th-century and Georgian buildings provide enough outdoor history to satisfy the most demanding sightseer, as do Bristol's two great engineering monuments: Brunel's SS *Great Britain* and the Clifton Suspension Bridge.

◆ Theatre-lovers should check out Britain's oldest working theatre, the delightful Georgian Theatre Royal. Bristol is also home to the most vibrant nightlife, music and club scene in the West Country. More sedate visitors can relax at nearby seaside resorts or explore the surrounding rolling countryside.

◆ The first Severn Bridge connecting England and Wales was built between Aust in Gloucestershire and Beachley in Monmouthshire. A second Severn bridge was opened futher downstream in 1996.

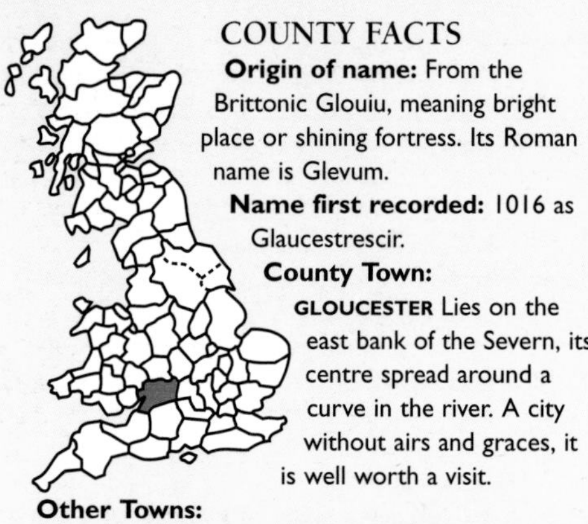

COUNTY FACTS

Origin of name: From the Brittonic Glouiu, meaning bright place or shining fortress. Its Roman name is Glevum.

Name first recorded: 1016 as Glaucestrescir.

County Town:

GLOUCESTER Lies on the east bank of the Severn, its centre spread around a curve in the river. A city without airs and graces, it is well worth a visit.

Other Towns:

BRISTOL (Shared with Somerset) Still an inland port with a canal opened in 1837 connecting the city's docks with the Severn taking ships up to 1,000 tons. The best city panorama is from the top of the 105-foot Cabot Tower, which commemorates John Cabot's voyage to America.

CHELTENHAM Boasts not one but two famous colleges (one for boys one for girls).

CHIPPING CAMPDEN Fine gabled stone houses advertise a wealthy wool industry with the 14th-century Woolstaplers Hall and medieval wool church.

CIRENCESTER Capital of the Cotswolds.

LYDNEY Roman remains and strong royal connections.

NAILSWORTH Charming Cotswold town built in a chasm.

STOW-ON-THE-WOLD Highest hill top town in the Cotswolds. The very large market square has stocks and a 14th-century cross.

STROUD At the forefront of England's broadcloth industry thanks to steam and canals. Billiard table baize cloth is still used to cover the world's tables.

TEWKESBURY Timber-framed buildings predominate in this pleasing town with one of the finest Norman structures in the country: Tewkesbury Abbey. A decisive War of the Roses battle was fought here.

◆ Almondsbury ◆ Avonmouth ◆ Chipping Sodbury ◆ Dursley ◆ Kingswood ◆ Mangotsfield ◆ Shirehampton ◆ Stonehouse ◆ Thornbury ◆ Yate

County Rivers: Severn, Windrush, Coln, Leadon.

Highest point: Cleeve Hill near Cheltenham at 1,083 feet (nearest place to London over 1,000 feet).

Gloucestershire's local government: Two tier government provides the services for the northern part of Gloucestershire with two single tier authorities controlling its southern part. Gloucestershire County Council and the six district councils of Cotswold, Cheltenham, Forest of Dean, Gloucester, Stroud and Tewkesbury provide services for the north. The South Gloucestershire unitary council and that part of the City of Bristol unitary authority north of the River Avon administer the south of the County. There are three detatched parts of Gloucestershire in Worcestershire, Kemerton is under Worcestershire County and Wychavon Councils in Wiltshire. Tidling Corner is under Wiltshire County and North Wiltshire Councils. in Oxfordshire, Shennington is under Oxfordshire County and Cherwell Councils: in Warwickshire, Little Compton and Sutton-under-Brailes are under Warwickshire County and Stratford upon Avon Councils.

Much of this was swept away under barbaric development, so there's little left to see. The few exceptions include the grouped half-timbered houses of Bishop Hooper's Lodging, now a local and regimental museum. The atmosphere of the old city is partially recaptured in the cathedral close. This amazing building with its fabled stained glass, beckoning bells (a carillon of ten with a huge medieval one) in its tower is not to be missed. One of the score of great English medieval cathedrals, its cloisters are miracles of the peculiarly English architectural style known as fan vaulting. There are tomb effigies of Edward II and Robert, the son of William the Conqueror. A mile from the centre of Gloucester engineers will be intrigued with Thomas Telford's single arch crossing the Severn at Over Bridge.

Cheltenham was laid out in the early 19th century with fine restrained terraces of typical late Georgian houses. It became Cheltenham Spa when saline springs were found in 1716. The city guards its elegance well, though intrusions into the Regency splendour of the Parade have been made. Nevertheless the broad prospect from the foot of the town up to the white facade of the Queen's Hotel will still delight. Don't miss an exploration of squares, like Montpellier, and Georgian buildings such as the Pittville Pump Room and the Montpellier Rotunda.

Cirencester's Roman origins can be explored in its intriguing Corinium Museum. There is a vast market place (where once wool was traded, as well as markets for corn and cheese). The town is dominated by beetling hedges of yew that surround Cirencester Park, stately home of the Bathursts. The church of St John the Baptist is a particularly fine one, with an impressive tower and Perpendicular stone tracery. Within are many treasures, stained glass, monuments and fan vaulting. There are lots of nice shops here and coaching inns to stay at too.

Famous settlements include golden Stow-on-the-Wold in its meandering river valley, with an Elizabethan mansion looming above it; Upper Slaughter Manor, which gains its name from a Saxon word for 'a muddy place'; Painswick, with its clipped yew trees in its churchyard and Fairford, which has famous sets of stained glass, misericordes and sculptures on the outside of its large church.

Northwest of Tetbury, with its Georgian church containing large candelabra and box pews, is Chavenage, a medieval manor. A chilling story recounts that every Lord of Chavenage who dies in the house is carried off by a coach driven by a headless man – as the ghostly equipage and its black horse pass through the entryway it bursts into flames.

Tewkesbury is a delightful compact town with half-timbered inns and an abbey. Stroud has early 19th-century Subscription Rooms, which contain the local art gallery. Between Gloucester and Bristol, Berkeley Castle is a striking medieval pile, buttressed and turreted, replete with splendid period furniture and silver. Below the castle walls are dungeons where King Edward II was hideously done to death with a red hot poker. As a relief from this horror, take a stroll along the castle's airy terraces beside wide herbaceous borders.

Nearby is Badminton (home of the Duke of Beaufort and of several horse events). In its palatial entrance hall the game of badminton was invented. Opposite the gates is a house known and mentioned by Jane Austen – Petty France, now a well recommended country hotel of the same name; it retains a genial Austen air. In this part of the county look for Westonbirt, an historic arboretum offering peaceful walks among its notable trees, and Slimbridge Wildfowl Trust. Open year round and founded by the late Sir Peter Scott, ornithologist and wildlife painter, it is home to hundreds of water and wading birds and there are usually impressive flocks to be seen from hides dotted around the preserve.

Close to the west, and to the county of Monmouthshire, Clearwell Castle is an early example of a large Gothic Revival house.

LOCAL HISTORY

There is an elaborate Neolithic burial mound at Notgrove, one called Hetty Pegler's Tump near Nailsworth and another which contained 31 skeletons at Belas Knap. Roman remains are extensive: Ermine Street, Icknield Way and Acman Street all passed through the county. Corinium Dobunorum (Cirencester) was one of the most important Roman cities and there's a well-preserved amphitheatre just outside the town. There are fine mosaics at Woodchester Roman Villa, and a large bath-house and tesselated pavements can be seen at the Roman villa of Great Witcombe. Chedworth Villa south of Cheltenham is a particularly well-preserved Roman site.

The massive 8th-century earthwork of King Offa's Dyke rims the western edge of the county and once defined the kingdom of Mercia. It was after the kingdom failed and fell apart in 910 that Gloucestershire was established.

In 1373 Edward III decreed the City and County of Bristol "was a County by itself and separated (from the) Counties of Gloucester and Somerset and in all things exempt . . . (to be) called the County of Bristol for ever". In 1996 Bristol was made a separate ceremonial County.

FAMOUS NAMES

◆ Laurie Lee, the author of *Cider with Rosie*, a loving tale of growing up in Gloucestershire, lived in Sladd.
◆ Royalty has often favoured the county and the Prince of Wales has a country house at Highgrove.
◆ King Edward I I was homosexual but had the misfortune to be married to a scheming and vicious wife who with her lover arranged his murder by red-hot poker at Berkeley Castle.
◆ The sixth wife of Henry VI I I, Queen Katherine Parr, who survived the rotund Tudor monarch, died and is buried at Sudeley Castle. Ruined in the Civil War this spectacular castle was restored almost two centuries later.
◆ The late Dennis Potter spent his formative years in a stone cottage in Berry Hill in the Forest of Dean (as recalled in *The Singing Detective*).
◆ Two blockbusting female authors hail from the county: village Aga-saga author Joanna Trollope and polo'n'sex scribe Jilly Cooper.

COUNTY CALENDAR

◆ May: Horse trials at Badminton.
◆ September: 14th-century ceremony Clipping the Yews at Painswick.
◆ July: modern music festival, Cheltenham
◆ October: literary festival, Cheltenham.
◆ March: Cheltenham Races – National Hunt Festival attracts 40,000 people on each of the 3 days it is held. Other meetings take place in December, January, March, April and November.
◆ Late July/early August: Gloucestershire Country Fair at Gloucester Park.

THE FOREST OF DEAN *The Dean Road – an ancient thoroughfare.*

HAMPSHIRE

SOUTHAMPTONSHIRE

THE COUNTY LANDSCAPE

◆ Few counties in Britain offer quite such scenic variation as Hampshire. There is the Hampshire of the chalk downs, the rolling hills punctuated by sheep and skylark. The North Downs slope towards Aldershot while the South Downs rise to their highest point near Petersfield at Butser Hill. Much of the country in between is rich fertile agricultural farmland.

◆ Different again is the Hampshire of the water meadows, the chalk streams of rivers like the Test providing some of the finest fly fishing in Britain.

◆ In the west of the county, the meadows give way to the New Forest, deeply wooded with oak, birch and beech and inhabited by wild ponies roam.

◆ The Hampshire coast offers variety, too: pine trees and steep ravines, known as chines, can be found in Bournemouth, the county's largest holiday town, but in the east the coastline is characterized by the deep-water estuaries of the Hamble and Beaulieu rivers.

◆ At the head of Southampton Water, the Isle of Wight's most important feature is the chalk ridge which runs in a dog's leg from the jagged points of the Needles in the west to the dazzling white Culver Cliff in the east.

◆ The Isle of Wight is about 22 miles long by some 13 miles wide and is an English landscape in miniature.. There are prominent chalk cliffs at The Needles, a multi-coloured beach at Alum Bay, dramatic chines such at Blackgang, rolling downs in the hinterland, and a very mild climate to suit sailors, swimmers and sunbathers alike.

BEAULIEU *Montagu's home since 1538*

PORTSMOUTH *Nelson's flagship HMS Victory on which he died at Trafalgar.*

BABBLING BROOKS, LAZY streams, watercress beds... the Hampshire hinterland is quintessential rural England. Follow the chalk rivers of the Test or Itchen, or the enchanting estuaries of the Beaulieu or Hamble, and you enter the great natural harbours of Hampshire at, say, Southampton, or Portsmouth with its naval splendour of the *Mary Rose* and HMS *Victory* jostling for premier historical position. Hampshire is very naval: but the army are also strongly based here, at Aldershot. This county beats the military drum that Britain marches to.

TOWNS AND VILLAGES

Hampshire's political hub may have changed since the days of King Alfred, but Winchester is still the county's most interesting town. The old capital of Wessex retains a rare dignity and beauty, found particularly in the Norman cathedral. Winchester has had a cathedral since the 7th century. The present building is one of the largest in Europe – 556 feet long – and buried here are the remains of King Canute, as well as more modern luminaries like Izaak Walton. Winchester doesn't just have a magnificent cathedral, it's full of beautiful Georgian and Queen Anne buildings – and good eating places. Gone are the days of 'Hampshire Hog' – pork and pudding – when pundits could pronounce…'as the hogs are never put into styes, but supplied with plenty of acorns, the bacon is by far the best in England.'

Should it rain during your visit, blame it on St Swithun, a Bishop of Winchester in Saxon times, who requested his body be buried outside the cathedral 'where the rain of heaven might fall on him'. But, according to legend, the authorities decreed otherwise. The body was to be brought back into the cathedral, but before work could begin it rained for 40 days and nights.

Beyond Winchester, Hampshire unfolds in the glorious English countryside of rolling hills and green fields, rivers curving gently through water meadows on which plump cattle graze through villages with thatched cottages and honeysuckle around the door. Stockbridge, once a stopping point for drovers heading east to the great cattle fairs of Sussex and Kent, offers some of the best fly fishing in the land. Hambledon will forever be the cradle of cricket – the game having started on Broadhalfpenny Down. The Hambledon team were once so strong that they could take on an England XI for a purse of 1,000 guineas – and still win. Today the talents of Hambledon XI may be more modest, but they can still quench their thirst after the game – as no doubt their predecessors did – at the nearby Bat and Ball Inn.

Hampshire's cricket team now plays most of its home games at Southampton, which has long since been the county's most important commercial centre. The Romans had a military port here and the Pilgrim Fathers set sail for the New World from Southampton in 1620 before putting in at Plymouth, but it was the days of the great ocean voyages across the Atlantic which secured the city's success. Southampton has several good museums – including the Spitfire Museum in Albert Road South – but, as a place to visit, it cannot match Portsmouth, a few miles along away along the coast.

Portsmouth – Pompey to the Royal Navy and followers of the football team – is still a city where you're scarcely ever out of sight of the sea. Situated on an island, Portsmouth seems to be invaded in every nook and cranny by the sea. There's the great sight of Nelson's *Victory* in dry dock near the entrance to the Royal Dockyard. Also on view here is the *Mary Rose,* Henry VIII's warship which was raised from the sea bed in 1982. Next door, Southsea is a pleasing resort with a sandy beach, amusement complex, gardens and promenade from which you can view the countless

COUNTY FACTS

Origin of name: A homm or hamm was, in Old English, a water meadow and the county has its fair share of these. The original name for Southampton was Hamtun or Homtun meaning the farm on the river land.

Name first recorded: 755 as Hamtunscir.

County Town:

WINCHESTER History, heritage and high street shopping come together in near-perfect harmony.

Other Towns:

ALTON Fine Georgian houses, antique shops and local history museum.

BASINGSTOKE A market and trading town long before the arrival of glass and steel office blocks, dual carriageways and the 1,000 roundabouts.

BOURNEMOUTH Parks, public gardens, retirement homes, language schools and miles of beach.

CHRISTCHURCH Reputedly has the longest parish church in England with fine views from its Saxon tower; also the ignoble site of John Major's walloping by-election rebuff in 1993.

COWES England's top yachting centre.

EMSWORTH Picturesque harbour and an ancient port famed for its oyster fisheries and yacht building.

LYMINGTON Seaside resort and ferry town pleasantly situated upon a hill with fine views across the Solent.

NEWPORT Isle of Wight capital with old quays of once-thriving inland port on Medina river.

PETERSFIELD Wool-trade town full of attractive old houses with lively market.

PORTSMOUTH Naval tradition and museums abound.

RINGWOOD A large and well built town lying low in the Avon valley. Its name derives from *Regnewood* which signifies the wood of the *regni* (the ancient inhabitants called *regni* by the Romans).

RYDE Souvenir-shops and bunting advertise this seaside resort worth visiting by ferry across the Solent if just to take the 'tube' along the pier.

SOUTHAMPTON A unique tidal system once made this Britain's premier passenger port for the grand, great Cunard liners 'The Queens'.

VENTNOR Perched precariously on the Isle of Wight's west coast, with Gothic Victorian holiday homes, lush botanical gardens and a History of Smuggling Museum.

◆ Andover ◆ Eastleigh ◆ Fareham ◆ Farnborough ◆ Fleet ◆ Gosport ◆ Havant ◆ Shanklin ◆ Waterlooville

County rivers: Meon, Test, Itchen, Hamble, Beaulieu, Avon.

Highest point: Pilot Hill at 938 feet.

Hampshire's local government: The County of Hampshire is a combination of two-tier and unitary authorities, with Hampshire County Council on one level and the 12 Districts of Basingstoke & Deane, Christchurch, East Hampshire, Eastleigh, Fareham, Gosport, Hart, Havant, New Forest, Rushmoor, Test Valley, Winchester on the other. By the way, Dorset NOT Hampshire County Council is the top level in Christchurch!

Hampshire's local government (cont.):
Bournemouth, the Isle of Wight, Portsmouth and Southampton are single unitary councils with no Hampshire County Council control. Hampshire detached in Sussex is a very long narrow strip stretching from Camelsdale down to near Midhurst and is two-tier, administered by West Sussex County and Chichester Councils.
Special note: In 1996 the Isle of Wight tried to break away from the United Kingdom and declare itself a tax haven on the lines of the Isle of Man, Jersey or Guernsey.

FAMOUS NAMES

- Devotees of Jane Austen will know that Britain's great 19th-century writer was born in the village of Steventon, near Alton, lived much of her life in Sawton and is buried in Winchester Cathedral.
- The house and garden where Richard Wilson and Annette Crosby's elderly antics in *One Foot in the Grave* take place are in Bournemouth.
- Many celebrities gravitate to the Isle of Wight, including Mark King, a member of the 80s stadium-filling funky pop group Level 42, who lives in Wootton.
- Location filming for ITV's popular *Ruth Rendell Mysteries* series, featuring George Baker as the country detective Inspector Wexford, took place mainly in Romsey. Other location spots included Winchester College, the King's Theatre in Southsea and Southampton University.
- Charles Dickens was born in 1812 in Portsmouth, where there is a museum dedicated to him.
- Actor Jeremy Irons was born in Cowes.
- Composer Andrew Lloyd Webber lives in a grand manor house at Sydmonton.

comings and goings of ships through Southampton Water.

It is this narrow stretch of water which separates Hampshire major from Hampshire minor, the Isle of Wight, which was first adopted as a holiday island by the Victorians, who were attracted by its safe bathing and enviable sunshine record. A mere 23 miles from east to west and 13 miles from north to south, it still retains something of a Victorian air in its leisurely resorts like Sandown and Ryde; picturesque villages like Brighstone and Godshill, on a steep hill and with a cluster of thatched cottages surrounding the 15th-century church; and the sailing centre of Cowes, where the plimsoll and sweater set gather each August for Cowes Week.

Back on the mainland, the Hamble river, on the eastern side of Southampton water, is another popular sailing centre – as is Beaulieu, where Lord Montagu's Motor Museum is more visited than the adjoining abbey, which was built by Henry VIII. But even more synonymous with Hampshire is the New Forest which, almost 1,000 years ago, became a royal hunting preserve for William the Conqueror. The forest covers more than 90,000 acres, two thirds of which are open to the public, beeches, oaks and birches providing a richness of colour which is rare in Britain. In the vast woodlands deer, ponies and donkeys run wild and, for adventurous walkers, there's a chance of coming across one of the 22 lost Saxon villages which, according to legend, lie buried beneath the thick undergrowth.

NEW FOREST *Ponies graze through 90,000 acres of forest glades and heathland.*

LOCAL HISTORY

Few of our counties are so representative of the broad span of English history as Hampshire. The country's rich and varied history can be traced here from Neolithic man, through the Celts and Romans, to the Tudors, Stuarts and indeed all the eras of the last millennium. The county's chalk uplands mask Celtic barrows. After Vespasian's capture of the Isle of Wight in AD43, the Romans turned their attention to what is now Hampshire proper, establishing a military port at Clausentum (Bitterne Manor, on the outskirts of Southampton).

Inland, they marched all over the chalk hills and created a Roman encampment at Silchester, in the north east of the county on the Berkshire border. The shape of the defences and the oval amphitheatre can be traced to this day. Under the Romans, Winchester (Venta Belgarum) was the fifth largest town in Britain, but it was really Alfred the Great who put Winchester on the map.

Alfred made Winchester capital of Wessex and for the next two centuries it ranked alongside London as the most important town in Britain – its status confirmed by William the Conqueror's coronation in both cities. Of Winchester's historic castle of Alfred's time, only the Great Hall remains – and the brightly-painted King Arthur's Round Table, which experts now say was made in the 14th century but still well worth gazing at. Winchester is a marvellous city to visit containing, as it does, buildings of every era from the 12th century to the present day. Romsey, another town with Roman connections, is similarly rich in fine buildings, notably the the 10th century Abbey Church, which still contains traces of its Saxon origins. Nearby is the old Mountbatten home of Broadlands, a magnificent 18th century mansion set in a fine park which once belonged to the statesman Lord Palmeston.

The 18th and 19th centuries – the years of great colonial expansion – saw Hampshire prospering from its maritime connections. Because it was close to plentiful supplies of oak from the New Forest (in fact Hampshire then had more wood than any other county in England), Bucklers Hard became a great shipbuilding centre. At the height of its prosperity, in the 18th century, it employed 4,000 men and built 40 of the ships which fought under Nelson in the Napoleonic wars. Echoes of this shipbuilding have long since faded but the area is beautiful if you seek solitude and scenic walks.

In the 19th century, the Isle of Wight became an island fit for royalty, literally, when in 1845 Queen Victoria decided to built herself a Palladian-style retreat there. Osborne House was, in fact, the place where England's longest serving monarch died in 1901.

Across the Solent, another queen, Bournemouth 'the queen of resorts' was also developed by the Victorians. In 1810 a Lewis Tregonwell built a holiday house here (part of which is in the Royal Exeter Hotel) and a Dr Granville recommended its mild climate as a curative. By 1840 a marina and the laying of pines began to transform this open heathland into a premier resort with six miles of super sandy beaches backed by steeply rising cliffs. Today it has an elderly, genteel image that is not wholly deserved.

***BOURNEMOUTH** Deck chairs await.*

COUNTY CALENDAR

- Spring Bank Holiday Monday: The Aldershot Horse Show, one of the largest in the south.
- Late June/early July: Bournemouth Musicmakers Festival with bands, choirs and orchestras from around the world.
- Romsey holds a carnival in July and an agricultural show in September.
- July: Royal Isle of Wight County Show, Cowes.
- August: Cowes Week yachting festival, Isle of Wight. The island is surrounded by sailboats – a sight not to be missed, especially if there is no wind!
- Early September: Farnborough International Air Show for those who can't get enough of low-flying engine roaring displays.
- Beginning of September: The Beaulieu International Autojumble, the largest jumble sale in Europe of items connected with motoring and road transport, is also held at the National Motor Museum. With its monorail and nearby country pile, this is well worth a visit at anytime.
- August: The Hampshire County Show takes place at the Royal Victoria Country Park.

*H*EREFORDSHIRE

THE COUNTY LANDSCAPE

◆ Herefordshire is a gentle county of low green hills, hedgerows and hop yards, orchards and woodlands. Its rich soil was formed from old sandstone and not only produces the glorious fruit of the county but also provides splendid pasture for the great herds of cattle for which Hereford is famous.

◆ From the Black Mountains, in the west, where sheep and cattle graze on the slopes, and the ridges begin their steady ascent into Wales, the county extends across central lowlands to the steep Malvern Hills, lying along the Severn Plain in the east. To the south are the Gloucestershire Cotswolds; to the north, the borderlands of Shropshire.

◆ Flowing through the county is the glorious River Wye, wandering in wide loops on its course from Plynlimon to Chepstow, and at its most dramatic at Symonds Yat, where it passes through a deep gorge protected by soaring, forested cliffs. Here, at the northern point of the Forest of Dean, Yat Rock sits 400 feet above the water and provides a safe home for the noble peregrine falcon.

YOU MIGHT THINK New York is the 'Big Apple' but this county really deserves the appellation. This is real gob-smacking cider country. Mouth-watering perry is also brewed here from locally grown pears. So in this county for most seasons of the year the hillsides and hedges are vibrant with blossoms of all kinds. The cool, clear Wye river cuts through the county and offers up its famous salmon (perhaps to go with the cider!). If you are very lucky, you may catch a local using a coracle on some stretches of the Wye. A tub-like boat made of wicker work, it is very similar to that used by ancient Britons.

TOWNS AND VILLAGES

The great cathedral of Hereford is one of few clues to this friendly city's exalted past. Already a bishop's see by AD676, the flourishing community became capital of the mighty Anglo-Saxon kingdom of Mercia, producing its own currency and standing fast against the hostile Welsh. A section of the walls built to fortify the town against their attacks still survives near the 15th-century Wye Bridge. Even the cathedral, a 12th-century masterpiece of soaring, delicate stonework that towers over the banks of the river, has a security-conscious past: its ancient Chained Library uses iron shackles attached to the 1,500 books to remind readers that there's no borrowing allowed. Once part of the cathedral itself, the collection is now being moved to a heritage centre next door, along with the famous *Mappa Mundi*, a 13th-century view of the world by cleric Richard of Haldingham. He was a cartographer with a vivid imagination, and what he lacked in first-hand experience was made up for with biblical inspiration: the Garden of Eden takes centre stage, and beasts and demons inhabit the countries around the world's edge.

SYMOND'S YAT *View from the Yat (meaning gap or gate) over the River Wye.*

There's an amazing little church at Kilpeck, eight miles southwest of Hereford. The Church of St Mary and St David was built in 1135 for Oliver de Marlemond, who had returned to the country from a pilgrimage to Spain with his head full of the exotic designs he'd seen en route. He was so impressed, in fact, that he brought along a company of French builders to show the English how it should be done. The result was this frenzy of carvings and decorations, most of which have nothing to do with the scriptures at all: there are Viking gargoyles and dragons and dogs and rabbits and virtually anything except the standard religious motifs.

Church-hunters will find plenty of other curiosities in this county, including the thatched Arts and Crafts building at Brockhampton; the huge, squat 14th-century belltowers of Pembridge and Yarpole, standing apart from the main churches and made of sturdy oak; and the half-timber tower of Vowchurch in the Golden Valley on the River Dore, some four miles upriver from the tranquil Cistercian Dore Abbey, a rare survivor of the Dissolution. Golden Valley is as lovely as its name suggests, but this gold is a mistranslation rather than a description. When the Normans heard the Welsh talk about the *dwr* (water) of the area they took it for *d'or,* golden; the name stuck and made the transition into Anglo-Saxon.

The sight of Ross-on-Wye's graceful church spire, rising above the tumble of houses on a high sandstone cliff above the river, is one of the real delights of rural England. The little town captures many hearts, but no one has ever repaid it as fully as John Kyrle, the 17th-century benefactor. He saw to it that the shaky church spire was made sound and laid out the clifftop Prospect Gardens, with their stunning views across the river and hills; and he introduced a public water supply. His good works were the subject of his contemporary, Alexander Pope's *Moral Essays on the Uses of Riches*, and earned him Pope's title of 'The Man of Ross'.

Among all the great medieval architecture of this county, one building stands out as a bit of a fraud. Eastnor Castle, near Ledbury, is a picture-book towered and turreted fortress straight from the Middle Ages – except that it was actually put there in 1812 as an extravagant family home, complete with deer park and lake and all the interior decoration suited to rich tastes: Italianate furniture and fine art, tapestries and, of course, knights' armour.

LOCAL HISTORY

Hillforts sprang up in Herefordshire after the arrival of the Iron Age in about 900BC. About 30,000 people settled in the county in communities of several hundred: the biggest was at 120-acre Credenhill, near Hereford. When the Romans arrived they replaced the hillforts with their own military bases, villas (including Britain's biggest, at

COUNTY FACTS

Origin of name: Comes from the Old English for army ford, that is one wide enough for an army to cross.

Name first recorded: c. 1038 as Herefordscir.

County Motto: *Pulchra Terra Dei Donum* ("This Fair Land is the Gift of God").

County Town:

HEREFORD A commanding position over the Wye, and home to Bulmer's cider. It's said that all the cattle in America decend from one original Herefordshire bull. Bull? Well that's what they say.

Other Towns:

BROMYARD The county's smallest market town with a number of half-timbered houses. Charles I sheltered at Tower Hill House in 1644.

GOODRICH Fashionable village nestling in the Wye Valley with ruined castle that dates way back, one time home of the Earls of Shrewsbury and Earls and Dukes of Kent. Dismantled in the Civil War, the view from its keep across to the Malvern Hills and Welsh Mountains is a sheer deleight.

KINGTON Unpretentious old border market town with a 17th-century school built of stone. The nearby gardens of Hergest Croft are well worth a detour.

LEDBURY A classic border market town, with its timber-framed Tudor and Stuart buildings crowding the streets – especially impressive in the cobbled Church Lane, which leads into the High Street and its black-and-white Market House on oak stilts. Another detached belltower can be found in this attractive town – a 200-foot construction belonging to the parish church, St Michael and All Angels.

LEOMINSTER Pronounced Lemster. Once-thriving wool and leather town with some fine timber-framed buildings and a 17th-century Town Hall.

ROSS-ON-WYE Was made a free borough by Henry III and is a main centre for cattle and cider. It has two distinctive main streets both about 1/2 mile long that cross each other in the middle.

WEOBLEY Was an important medieval borough and is still a sizeable village today. Eye-catching old houses line the main streets and the church has an elegant spire capping the church's very tall tower.

◆ Kingstone ◆ Leintwardine
◆ Lugwardine ◆ Whitchurch

County Rivers: Wye, Frome, Lugg, Teme.

Highest point: In the Black Mountains at 2,306 feet.

Herefordshire's Local Government: The County of Herefordshire is administered by a single-tier Herefordshire County Council. Rochford is Herefordshire detached in Worcestershire in a two-tier structure with Worcestershire County and Malvern Hills District Councils. Fwthog is Herefordshire detached in Monmouthshire under that County's unitary council. Litton is Herefordshire in Radnorshire administered by Powys unitary council. Farlow is Herefordshire detached in Shropshire under a two-tier system of Shropshire County Council and Bridgnorth District Council.

FAMOUS NAMES

◆ Comedy actress Beryl Reid was born in Hereford in 1936 and went on to fame in films such as *The Killing of Sister George* in 1968 and *No Sex Please, We're British* in 1973.

◆ Symonds Yat provided a magnificent backdrop for scenes in the film *Shadowlands*, the true story of CS Lewis and his relationship with Joy Gresham, starring Sir Anthony Hopkins and Debra Winger.

COUNTY CALENDAR

◆ April: Ross-on-Wye celebrates the good old-fashioned pint in style with its Real Ale Festival.

◆ Early May: Spring fever hits Hereford with the arrival of the May Fair, a riot of crafts, song and dance from the High Town to the Wye Bridge.

◆ June: Herefordshire shares the Three Counties Show, which is held in Great Malvern in Worcestershire, with the counties of Gloucestershire and Worcestershire.

◆ July: the market town of Bromyard, at the foot of the Bromyard Downs, hosts the annual Much Marcle Steam Gala of machinery from the past.

◆ Mid–Late August: Hereford takes its turn every three years to host the Three Choirs Festival, held since 1715 and performed by the choirs of Gloucester, Worcester and Hereford cathedrals. The city will next host the event in 1997.

◆ September: Bromyard's streets are filled with music for the annual autumn Folk Festival.

◆ October: it's harvest time and the gathering-in of hops is celebrated at Ledbury's annual Hop Fair, and in a host of other events in Big Apple Country.

Bishopstone) and a walled town of their own at Kenchester.

Herefordshire's next big part in history was during the 7th and 8th centuries, when the Mercian king Offa built his dyke to mark his boundary and endowed Hereford Cathedral. By King Canute's time, in the 11th century, the county had its name and Hereford had powerful earls – who would include Harold Godwineson, the short-lived King of England who lost his eye and his life in the Battle of Hastings.

After the Norman Conquest the lands straddling the Welsh border became battlegrounds for the ambitious Marcher Lords; their increasing resentment of crown power eventually led to the execution of Edward II's favourite Hugh le Despenser at Hereford.

Industry never made a huge impact on the county, except in the Wye Valley, where the special 'trow', or cargo boat, carried iron, corn, wood and cider to Bristol, and iron-smelting and paper-making were established by the Tudor age. The short wool of the Ryeland sheep made Leominster a prosperous wool-making centre and funded wonderfully carved buildings such as the 17th-century old Town Hall, now known as Grange Court.

The county's hop yards and apple orchards helped to slake the nation's thirst – and still do, 400 years on. Hops became profitable when the English switched from ale to beer in the 16th century; and the apple trees that flourished in the southeast's moist, clay soils produce Slack-my-Girdle, Handsome Maud, Leather Coat and other well-named crops to be pulped in the mills and transformed into cider.

HEREFORD *Hereford Cathedral's 14th-century tower reflected in the River Wye.*

Poor roads and a marginal position meant that the heavy development of the Industrial Revolution passed Herefordshire by. The stagecoach and the railway did eventually provide links between Hereford and London, the north and Wales; but this has stayed a county of villages and churches, rather than cities and factories – a beautiful corner of unspoilt Britain.

HERTFORDSHIRE

HERTFORDSHIRE is one of the counties of my childhood, with many early visits on the Green Line buses – and how very very far away it seemed from our house in Middlesex to the likes of Hemel Hempstead, St Albans, Watford and 'Ricky' – Rickmansworth. As a youngster that border may have been only a matter of miles but to my imagination it was the edge of my small world. Welwyn and Hertford and everything in the south of this county I think of as a 'home' county, but go to Hitchin and Stevenage and Letchworth and it is more like East Anglia – an entirely different feel. The essayist Charles Lamb called the county a 'homely' place – and certainly no similar-sized county has so many lovely country houses that were for generations family homes, though now, sadly, many are hotels or conference centres.

TOWNS AND VILLAGES

Though Hertfordshire up until the early part of this century was renowned as an agricultural county, the malign influence of London meant that much of its arable land has now been subsumed into the commuter belt, and modern industries like pharmaceuticals, chemicals, light engineering and electronics are now prominent. The county town of Hertford, on the River Lea, has an 18th-century Shire Hall designed by Robert Adam, and several fine buildings along Fore Street. The remains of the old Norman castle where King John of France was imprisoned in 1359 include the motte and a gatehouse.

Now almost joined to Hertford is Ware, the limit of John Gilpin's ride in William Cowper's famous poem, which has reverted to its old character since the opening of a new bypass. The Priory, once a 15th-century Franciscan foundation and with 17th- and 18th- century additions, now houses council offices. Ware was the base of the famous Bluecoat School for boys and girls of Christ's Hospital, which transferred to Sussex in 1985. The original school buildings and a row of 17th- century

THE COUNTY LANDSCAPE

- The west and northwest of the county is hilly, and forms part of the chalk ridge of the Chiltern Hills. Several rivers flow southeast and go to supply London and the Home Counties. At one time large mills with their iconoclastic water-wheels stood on the river banks.
- South of the Chilterns, the land is gently undulating, with some more low hills along the Middlesex border running in parallel with the Grimsdyke, an old Saxon earthwork. The eastern part of the county is flat (like Cambridgeshire and Essex which it borders).
- The fertile soil produces fruit, vegetables and lavender. It also contains a high proportion of flints, some of which have been used in local buildings.
- The Hertfordshire & Middlesex Wildlife Trust based in St Albans work to protect land forms and natural habitats and create nature walks in woodland and other green areas within two counties where flora and fauna are smitten by environmentally choking suburbia. In 1994 I was privileged to open one of the Wildlife Trust's nature walks at Pond Wood.

AYOT ST LAWRENCE *Shaw's Corner – the Victorian home of playwright GB Shaw.*

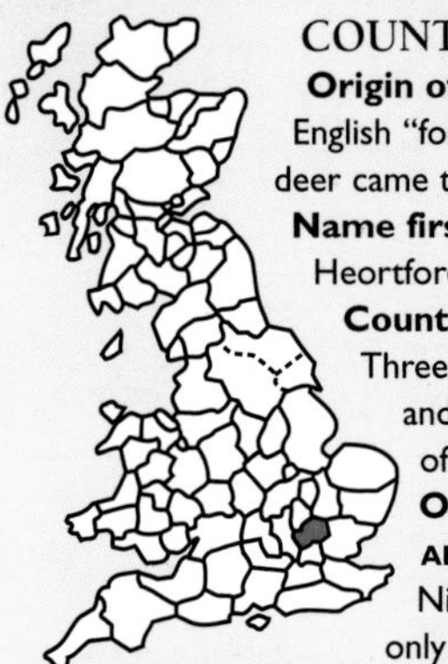

COUNTY FACTS

Origin of name: From the Old English "ford where hart, stag or deer came to drink".

Name first recorded: 866 as Heortfordscir.

County Town: **HERTFORD** Three rivers, the Lea, Beane and Rib, meet at the centre of this pretty old town.

Other Towns:

ABBOTS LANGLEY where Nicholas Breakspear, the only British Pope (Adrian IV, 1154-59) was born in nearby Bedmond.

BARNET Half in Middlesex and half in Hertfordshire, it was conferred a charter by King John and is known as Chipping Barnet.

BERKHAMSTEAD Situated on the Grand Union Canal with its old churches and inns, the town is a lovely place for a picnic and a country day out.

BISHOP'S STORTFORD A hilly town, with a mixture of medieval and Victorian buildings.

BOREHAMWOOD Those famous film studios where the BBC now makes *Eastenders*.

HATFIELD The church has a window by the Pre-Raphaelite artist Edward Burne-Jones.

HEMEL HEMPSTEAD a rather concrete town but with a delightful high street rising in a gentle curve towards the church.

HITCHIN has the remains of a prehistoric hill fort called Ravensburgh Castle.

ST ALBANS You'll find a pleasant blend of the medieval and the modern in this cathedral town.

TRING famous now for its reservoirs which attract black tern, crested grebe and many other wildfowl.

WATFORD originally Watlingford as the Roman Watling Street crossed the nearby Colne river. An 18th-century description mentions the river making the town impassable and the "very long street which is extremely dirty in the winter".

WELWYN GARDEN CITY One of the first artificially planned towns begun by one Ebenezer Howard and completed by the New Towns Act of 1946, officially designated a New Town in 1948. Residents refer to the new town as Welwyn.

◆ Bushey ◆ Cheshunt ◆ Chorleywood ◆Elstree (partly in Middlesex) ◆ Harpenden ◆ London Colney ◆ Oxhey ◆ Radlett ◆ Royston ◆ Sawbridgeworth ◆ Totteridge ◆ Tring ◆ Wheathampstead

County Rivers: Lea, Colne, Stort, Ivel, Rib, Mimram.

Highest point: Nar Hastoe village at 803 feet.

Hertfordshire's local government: Administered by two-tier local government except for one tiny part under the control of the unitary borough of Barnet – shared with Middlesex. Hertfordshire County Council represents the top level and the ten Districts of Broxbourne, East Hertfordshire, Dacorum, Hertsmere, North Hertfordshire, St Alban's, Stevenage, Three Rivers, Watford, Welwyn-Hatfield the bottom. Coleshill is Hertfordshire detached in Buckinghamshire and controlled by that County's and Chiltern District Councils.

cottages used by the boys and their 'nurses' can be seen in East Street.

On the outskirts of the village of Perry Green the former studio (open by appointment) of the sculptor Henry Moore stands amid an open-air exhibition of his work.

St Albans, situated on a hill on the left bank of the River Ver, has suffered from its proximity to the M25, M1 and A1(M) motorways but its old town still retains numerous items of interest dating back to its early history as the Roman town of Verulamium. It takes its present name from a Roman soldier who was converted to Christianity here and subsequently martyred. His remains were found when King Offa of Mercia founded a Benedictine abbey here in AD793, and which after the Dissolution became the parish church. This abbey church was raised to the status of a cathedral in 1872. Originally of Norman construction, the west end was extended in 1214-35, the monk's choir was added in 1235-60 and the Lady Chapel in 1308-26. The west front and transepts were remodelled by Lord Grimthorpe towards the end of the last century. With a total length of 556 feet, the cathedral is the second largest in England, exceeded only by Winchester.

Close by the cathedral, across the abbey gardens is the Fighting Cocks Inn, said to be the oldest in Britain. On the opposite bank of the River Ver are the remains of *Verulamium*, founded about AD45, which became the only municipium in Britain and the third largest town in the country. The ruins subsequently provided the building material for the abbey. Finds from the site can be viewed in the Verulamium Museum.

Seven miles east of St Albans, outside the old market town of Hatfield, stands the imposing early 17th-century Jacobean mansion of Hatfield House (open to visitors), with its beautiful gardens containing great mulberry trees and hornbeams. It was built by Robert Cecil, who demolished three wings of the old Tudor bishops' palace (one wing still survives), in 1607–12. Henry VIII had used the old palace as a country retreat. Elizabeth I was kept confined here by her half-sister Mary before her accession to the English throne, and is said to have been sitting beneath a tree in the garden when a messenger brought her the news of Mary's death. Memorabilia on view include a pair of Elizabeth's silk stockings, along with a curious pedigree which traces her descent from Adam and Eve, via Noah and King Lear.

The small village of Ayot St Lawrence is in one of the most pleasant parts of the county. Its fame rests on its association with the playwright and critic George Bernard Shaw who lived in the house, Shaw's Corner, up until his death in

1950. Now owned by the National Trust, it has been left in its original state and visitors can view the cramped garden shed, equipped with a telephone and mounted on a revolving base to follow the sun, where Shaw used to write.

Knebworth House was begun in 1492 by Sir Robert Lytton, but the exterior was redecorated in Gothic style by Sir Edward Bulmer-Lytton in 1843. It is better known among music fans for its year-on-year classic open-air rock and jazz festivals featuring veteran and venerable artists like Pink Floyd, Elton John, Paul McCartney, Phil Collins, Ella Fitzgerald and Sir Cliff Richard.

LOCAL HISTORY

The bones of wolf and hippopotamus found on the flat marshlands of the county tell of prehistoric times while later on beside the River Lea King Arthur is said to have checked the advance of heathen invaders from over the sea when they sailed up to Ware. And the New river by Ware has a fascinating history. It was recorded that during the reign of James I, water was conveyed from this river along a 36-mile channel – a canal really, not more than 10 feet wide, originally of stone and brick – to a basin at Islington in Middlesex, where it went on via wooden and lead pipes to feed the thirsty mouths of the metropolis.

Meanwhile back in AD61 the Roman city of Verulamium (St Albans) had quiet courtyards and gardens with beautiful theatres and temples but Queen Boudicca put a swift end to that when, as leader of the East Anglian tribe of the Iceni, she attacked in her revolt against the Romans and massacred the hapless inhabitants. It was rebuilt and destroyed again by the Saxons in about AD500, and soon afterwards the bones of the first Christian martyr, St Alban, were found and an abbey church erected in his honour.

A major battle was fought in AD896 between the Saxon King Alfred the Great and the Danes in the area around Watford. The death toll was substantial but Alfred secured the victory.

Bishop's Stortford was originally Storteford (meaning a ford on the River Stort) in the Domesday Book of 1086, but then was owned by the Bishops of London, hence its present name.

During the 14th century the peasants and townspeople of St Albans rose in revolt, seeking a charter of rights. The uprising was suppressed by Richard II in person, and a prominent rebel priest John Ball was hung, drawn and quartered. Other participants were pardoned. The Rye House plot, an abortive attempt to murder Charles II, was planned at Rye House, on the River Lea in 1683.

FAMOUS NAMES

◆ The philosopher Sir Francis Bacon lived at Gorhambury House at St Albans.

◆ The Cecils of Hatfield House were prominent ministers of state to both Elizabeth I and James I.

◆ Glittering and outrageous pop icon Elton John is the former chairman of Watford Football Club.

◆ Cecil Rhodes, the builder of the British Empire, was born at Bishop's Stortford in 1853.

◆ William Lamb (Lord Melbourne) lived at Brocket Hall near Welwyn. He was Prime Minister during the reign of Queen Victoria, and the husband of the notorious Lady Caroline Lamb.

◆ Queen Elizabeth, the Queen Mother, was born at St Paul's Waldenbury, near Hitchin.

◆ The noted music critic, writer, broadcaster and saxophonist Benny Green lives at King's Langley.

COUNTY CALENDAR

◆ Boxing Day: St Alban's Mummers – St Albans. An ancient Christmas custom in which men and women exchange clothes and visit houses. From this activity emerged mumming plays which still survive here.

◆ Mid-June: Bovingdon Revels – Bovingdon.

◆ June: Croxley Revels – Croxley. A festive celebration with music and dancing.

◆ 3rd & 4th week in July: Barnet Festival – Barnet.

◆ 3rd week September: Aylett's Dahlia Festival – Aylett's Nurseries, St Albans.

◆ Early April & September: Hatfield Fair – Hatfield.

◆ September: Stevenage Fair – Stevenage.

◆ 3rd week in July: Flower Festival – Hemel Hempstead.

◆ October: Music Festival – Bishop's Stortford.

◆ 4th week in May: Hertfordshire County Show – Redbourn.

***ST ALBANS** The West Front of the ancient Abbey.*

HUNTINGDONSHIRE

THE COUNTY LANDSCAPE

◆ Huntingdonshire is mostly a low plain sinking into fenland in the east. It is drained by the River Ouse which is a beautiful river though prone to flooding. Its dense reed beds attract many wading birds. The land bordering the River Ouse in the south comprises fertile meadows.

◆ The centre and west of the county is a mixture of mostly open farming country and some woodland. It is gently undulating country with good clay soil. In the north-east the well-drained Fenland provides good grazing land. This is almost all dairy country.

◆ William Cobbett eulogized the country between Huntingdon and Godmanchester as "the most beautiful scene and by far the most beautiful meadows that I ever saw in my life".

DRIVE UP THE A1 to Peterborough and your eyes if not your nose will lead you to Stilton – yes, this the home of Britain's most famous blue-veined cheese. Actually if truth be told the cheese used to be sold here but was originally made at Wymondham in Norfolk, but that doesn't have the same ring about it does it? This is also hunting country and some wag once suggested that fox-hunting was its chief industry. Once upon a time the upland part of the county was indeed a forest and well adapted for the hunting whence the county took its name. Today the county is more associated with the growing and processing of sugar-beet.

TOWNS AND VILLAGES

The small county town of Huntingdon was the birthplace of Oliver Cromwell, and the grammar school, which both he and the diarist Samuel Pepys attended, is now occupied by the Cromwell Museum. The west end of the building incorporates a 12th-century Hospital of St John. The house in which the Lord Protector was born still stands in the High Street and is marked with a plaque, while the birthplace of Pepys stands near a roundabout, a mile outside the town at the village of Brampton, and is open to the public by written arrangement.

Godmanchester, on the banks of the Great Ouse, was originally a Roman settlement established on Ermine Street. Its cobblestone church dates from the 13th century, but has a 17th-century tower and 15th century misericords. The 14th-century bridge crossing the River Ouse was reputedly built simultaneously from both banks, but without sufficient consultation, so that it is visibly misaligned in the centre. The medieval causeway has some pleasing houses and a Chinese Bridge which leads to islands in the river.

GODMANCHESTER *The Chinese Bridge was built in 1827.*

Although the rapid industrial expansion of Peterborough in Northamptonshire with its engineering and agri-business, has led to many north Huntingdonshire villages being absorbed into its suburbs, there are still one or two which exhibit a special charm.

Yaxley is especially pretty and still maintains its independence from the encroaching city, with timbered buildings and brick and tile cottages, along with a church which has a tall Perpendicular steeple, medieval wall paintings and a 15th-century chancel screen. Old Fletton, although now an untidy suburb, has some Saxon carvings that were possibly removed from the monastery at Peterborough at the time of the Dissolution. The village is also noted for the pale bricks which have been made here since the 1880s.

LOCAL HISTORY

Flag Fen is the only place in the country where you can see the timbers of a Bronze Age village. The site was discovered in 1982 and was a defensive man-made island built in the marshes from over a million timbers.

After the Danes invaded the region in AD870, they were eventually expelled by Edward the Elder in AD921. Oswald, Archbishop of York began the building of Ramsey Abbey in AD967 and it was consecrated in AD974. It was once one of England's richest abbeys. A ploughman subsequently discovered a body in a field at the aptly named village of Slepe, and then, in a dream, had the revelation that these were the remains of St Ivo, a Persian archbishop who had preached the Gospel in England. The relics were conveyed to Ramsey Abbey, where a number of miracles were later attributed to their presence. As a result, the name of the village of Slepe was changed to St Ives. The Earldom of Huntingdon fell to Scottish kings for a while and Stuart monarchs often visited the shire.

The final battle of the Civil War took place at St Neots in July, 1648. The Parliamentary forces, under Colonel Scroop, defeated the Royalists, led by the Earl of Holland, and they were forced to flee. During the Napoleonic Wars, a substantial number of French prisoners were confined at the village of Norman Cross.

Prior to the draining of the Fenland in the northeast during the 17th century, other major activities included turf-cutting, reed-cutting for thatch and for the manufacture of horse-collars. Saltpetre – a white crystalline salty substance used as constituent of gunpowder and in preserving meat – was also made during the 17th century, with lace-making and straw-plaiting following on during the next hundred years.

Huntingdonshire was also particularly noteworthy in the great days of the coaching age of the 1700s to the mid-1800s, since all northbound traffic from London passed through the shire, and the two major roads from York met at the Wheatsheaf Inn at Alconbury, later to become the site of a major airbase.

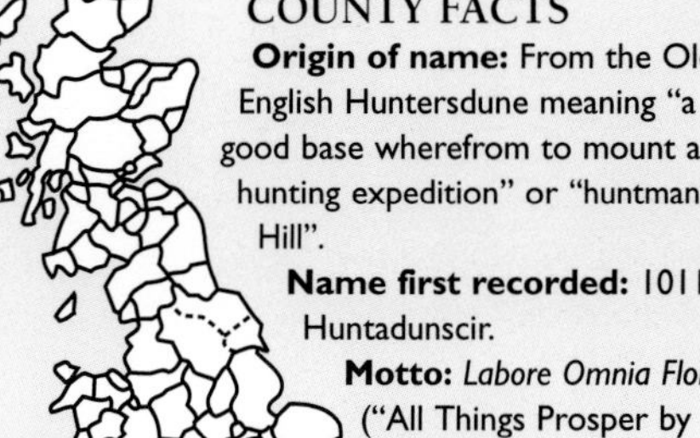

COUNTY FACTS

Origin of name: From the Old English Huntersdune meaning "a good base wherefrom to mount a hunting expedition" or "huntman's Hill".

Name first recorded: 1011 as Huntadunscir.

Motto: *Labore Omnia Florent* ("All Things Prosper by Industry").

County Town: HUNTINGDON Attractive town of Roman origins.

Other Towns:
GODMANCHESTER Once a Roman military station, nowadays a treasure-trove of architectural styles including Island Hall, a mid-18th-century mansion.
HEMINGFORD GREY Pretty village with church beside the River Ouse with a 12th-century moated mansion.
KIMBOLTON The castle was Catherine of Aragon's last home and is now a public school. It was originally a medieval mansion, later rebuilt by Sir John Vanbrugh.
ST IVES A medieval chapel survives in the centre of a six-arched 15th-century bridge over the Great Ouse.
ST NEOTS Ancient market town with fascinating old inns and a market square beside the Ouse.
◆ Alwalton ◆Buckden ◆ Ramsey ◆ Sawtrey ◆ Stukeley ◆ Warboys

County Rivers: Nene, Ouse, Kym.
Highest point: Near Covington at 256 feet.

Huntingdonshire's Local Government: The County of Huntingdonshire is served by a two-tier structure provided by Cambridgeshire County Council and Huntingdonshire district council. The Huntingdonshire villages of Old Fletton, Orton Longueville, Orton Waterville, Water Newton, Woodston and Stanground are governed by single-tier Peterborough Council. Everton and Gibraltar are detached Huntingdonshire in Bedfordshire and administered by that County's council and Mid-Bedfordshire District Council.

FAMOUS NAMES

◆ Tory Prime Minister John Major represents the constituents of Huntingdon.
◆ Oliver Cromwell represented Huntingdon in parliament, becoming Lord Protector of the Commonwealth after the execution of Charles I.
◆ Archetypal Welsh actress Ruth 'Hi-de-hi' Madoc lives in Huntingdon.
◆ Robin Hood was known as Earl of Huntingdon.

COUNTY CALENDAR

◆ Whitsun: Dicing For Bibles – St Ives. Bibles are given to twelve boys and girls of "good report".
◆ 4th week in April: National Pig Fair – Alwalton.
◆ June: Ruth Madoc Golf Tournament, Old Nene Golf Club, Ramsey.
◆ Mid-July & mid-November: Huntingdon Fair – Huntingdon.
◆ August: St Neots Carnival – St Neots.
◆ Late July: Tilbrook Country Fayre – Kimbolton.
◆ East of England Show at Stanground.

KENT

THE COUNTY LANDSCAPE

◆ Kent is crowded with orchards, plantations of soft fruits, fields of vegetables and market gardens, taking advantage of the good earth. It was once famous for hop-growing there are some still to be seen. Vines have been reintroduced and there are vineyards dotted amidst the rich pastureland from which comes Kentish wine.

◆ Along Thameside to the north, this part of Kent is a place of river fogs and unvisited atmospheric promontories beloved of Dickens when described in *Great Expectations*. In the south the Downs rear chalky outlines, their heights covered in short grass, the valleys between often steep indentations. These softly rounded chalk hills break off, literally, at the Channel to form the famous White Cliffs, especially around Dover.

◆ Occupying the southwestern corner is a surprising spread of flat marshland beneath the downs where the country drops off in a dramatic escarpment. Once flooded, this is the lonely and romantic Romney Marsh. Although western Kent is heavily populated all the county retains patches of ancient heathland along with pockets of old woods.

THERE'S SO MUCH crammed into Kent, from the glorious architecture of Greenwich to the hop-drying conical-shaped oast-houses that dot this 'Garden of England'. It is of course a cliché, but Kent's long-time tag is a true one. With so much poured into this county, it's not surprising perhaps that Kent is a county of confrontations. In its western fringes it is suburban, beyond the tidal Medway and its clutter of boats east Kent is surprisingly rural and undiscovered, even if it has long been the highway between Continental Europe and London, and then there are the archetypal seaside towns such as Herne Bay and Margate. The Medway in fact forms a neat dividing line between west and east, and even distinguishes the 'Men of Kent': that is, the natives who live west of the Medway are known as Kentish men (probably of Anglo-Saxon origin) and those who live east are called the Men of Kent (of Jutish ancestry).

TOWNS AND VILLAGES

The range of sights, for a medium-sized county, is quite enormous. Once in the county proper, and especially as travellers venture away from the fringes of London to Kentish suburbs such as Bromley and Bexley, with its Tudor Hall Place, whether by train, car, bicycle, or even on foot (Kent is excellent walking country) they will find a plethora of riches.

APPLE-PICKING *Still a 'hands-on' labour-intensive job in the county.*

The border with Sussex has many villages and is studded with crowded commuter towns such as Sevenoaks, Tonbridge, Paddock Wood and Tunbridge Wells. At the top of Sevenoaks is an 18th-century enclave and the entrance to Knole, one of the great country houses of England, a mansion reputed to have 365 rooms, seven courtyards and dozens of staircases. It's surrounded by a large park with deer, always open and maintained by the National Trust. Nearby Penshurst has a lych gate with a house above it and imposing Penshurst Place, a medieval castle with an ancient Great Hall and terraced parterres described by Ben Johnson 400 years ago.

There are spa springs in the centre of town at Royal Tunbridge Wells where you can taste the chalybeate water. In the middle of the town is a large common and abutting it is the famous Pantiles, a busy space with flagged terraces and old-fashioned shops.

South of here you come to the wide flat spaces of the Romney Marsh, with hidden villages and wide views to the sea. Sheep fatten on the salt marshes, which are home to many birds and tiny secretive communities. At its southern point is New Romney with a big and ancient church. Romney is at one end of a resuscitated miniature railway line, the Romney, Hythe and Dymchurch Railway. Hythe is an old town on a hill with a curious pyramid of skulls in the church crypt. On flat land towards the sea is the Military Canal, designed to protect army supply lines in the event of a Napoleonic invasion. Nearby at Port Lympne is Studford Castle, standing above Lemanis, the Roman fortification of the Saxon shore. The castle grounds are now a zoo for endangered species.

In the western part of the county many pleasant villages can be found. At Lullingstone is a Roman villa and a Queen Anne red-brick house and garden where silk for royal gowns was made. At Ightham is a rare example of a lovely medieval manor house islanded in a moat, busy with waterfowl. Owned by the National Trust, Ightham Mote can be visited and you can actually stay in one of the cottages in the splendid gardens. Hever has a fine house and Italian garden; Headcorn is charming with a wide main street and ancient wooden houses; and Pluckley is an estate village where all the houses have distinctive arched windows. Near charming Tenterden with its broad greens is Sissinghurst, where Vita Sackville-West made a most famous garden and south towards the sea at Smallhythe, once a harbour, Dame Ellen Terry lived in an ancient house that now houses theatrical memorabilia.

The Medway valley cuts the county almost in two and here are workaday communities known as the Medway Towns. Old centres include the county town of Maidstone with fine medieval buildings, while Rochester has exposed town walls, bricked high street and half-timbered houses, and a gaunt Norman castle on a mound which can be explored (until 200 years ago it possessed interior floors and walls, as Dover's citadel still does). Rochester's cathedral should not be missed: the second oldest in the country, it has many Norman and Early English features. The outline of the original Saxon cathedral is indicated with stones set in the floor.

East from here is the now industrial Isle of Sheppey, and

COUNTY FACTS

Origin of name: Greek and Roman writers referred to Kention, and Kent has the distinction of being the oldest recorded county name in Britain still in use. Its Celtic root *canto* means an edge or rim which is apt for the county's geographical position. The Romans called the inhabitants *Cantii* and their kingdom the land of the *Cantii*. Kent became the first of the dominant Anglo-Saxon England kingdoms. Celtic "caint" could mean "open country".

Name first recorded: 55BC.

County Motto: *Invicta* ("Unconquered").

County Town: MAIDSTONE Kent's bustling major agricultural,commercial and administrative centre has the almost fairy-tale Leeds Castle close by.

Other Towns:

CANTERBURY (Derived from Saxon for the city of the people of Kent) was the first town on Roman Watling Street and in the 6th century St Augustine founded the noble gothic pile.

CHATHAM Founded by Henry VIII and a base for the Royal Navy until 1984: the Dockyard is now an 80-acre tourist attraction.

DOVER Complete with castle this ancient cinque port and its legendary White Cliffs are the epitome of English patriotism. Premier cross-channel port with international cruise liners and a £10m passenger terminal.

FOLKESTONE Started as a fishing village later a Georgian resort but now gateway to the Chunnel and the 'Channel Tunnel Experience'.

GREENWICH Home of the famous 0° of longitude, the Observatory, the Cutty Sark, The National Maritime Museum and Millennium Celebrations.

RAMSGATE Handsome resort and working port with Victorian emphasis and a touch of class.

ROCHESTER Birthplace of Charles Dickens. Most of his last book, the unfinished *Edwin Drood*, was set here.

SEVENOAKS Became one-oak thanks to the Great Storm of 1987. Luckily, the Royal Oak Hotel in the High Street refers to only a single oak in its name.

TUNBRIDGE WELLS Prosperous Regency spa town known for its 'Royal' and 'disgusted of'. Famous Pantiles have colonnaded promenade.

WHITSTABLE Silt and salty waters made it famed for its oysters from Roman times, but pollution ended this culinary connection. Today it is still a very pleasant north Kent coast resort.

◆ Blackheath ◆ Catford ◆ Charlton
◆ Dartford ◆ Deptford ◆ Eltham ◆ Erith
◆ Gillingham ◆ Gravesend ◆ Hythe ◆ Lewisham
◆ Margate ◆ Northfleet ◆ Orpington ◆ Plumstead
◆ Sidcup ◆ Sittingbourne ◆ Sydenham ◆ Woolwich

County rivers: Darent, Medway, Great Stour, Little Stour.

Highest point: North Downs at 800 feet.

Kent's local government: The County of Kent is administered by a two-tier structure throughout the majority of the County by Kent County Council and the 12 District Councils of Ashford, Canterbury, Dartford, Dover, Gravesham, Maidstone, Sevenoaks, Shepway, Swale, Thanet, Tonbridge & Malling and Tunbridge Wells. There are five unitary councils at Bexley, Bromley, Gillingham & Rochester, Greenwich and Lewisham which Kent County Council doesn't cover. North Woolwich is Kent detached in Essex under the auspice of Newham unitary borough.

FAMOUS NAMES

◆ The Queen Mother is often in residence at Walmer Castle where Her Majesty is Warden of the Cinque Ports. Sir Winston Churchill held the office too, and resided at Chartwell near Westerham where he found peace in painting.

◆ Jane Austen, author of *Pride and Prejudice* and *Sense and Sensibility,* often visited Kent. She set parts of novels in places from Ramsgate to Godmersham.

◆ Much of *Nicholas Nickleby, David Copperfield* and other early works written in Kent by Charles Dickens, set scenes in such towns as Broadstairs. He lived until his death near Rochester there is an intriguing Dickens Museum and ornate chalet.

◆ *Absolutely Fabulous* TV star Joanna Lumley once lived at the old rectory at Goodnestone, near Wingham. This is a fine example of an estate village with ornate Victorian cottages grouped round an old inn like a country calendar picture.

◆ Rudolf Nureyev danced in a house in Sandwich where Susan Hampshire once resided.

◆ Gloria Hunniford lives in Sevenoaks.

the scattered low-lying islands of the Medway estuary. Ashford is a market and railway centre and nearby is Jacobean Godinton Park with topiary gardens. Chilham is a picturesque hilltop village with a castle by Inigo Jones. To the east is Canterbury and its lofty cathedral that is the seat of the Archbishop, its three commanding towers surrounded by many ecclesiastical buildings and walled gardens. Christopher Marlowe, a contemporary of Shakespeare, was born here and the theatre is named after him. South of the city towards the port of Folkestone, enchanting countryside is laced with tiny lanes that take you back to another age as they thread through isolated villages and past farmyards. A drive along the Alkham or Elham valleys will give an introduction to these beautiful natural features.

This part of the county stretches an indented coast along the edge of England, between the Channel and the River Thames. The Kent coastline from Dartford all the way round to Dymchurch varies from cliff to muddy strand. There is a chain of interesting towns from Deal to Dungeness, from Whitstable to Walmer – all differing enormously, yet most offering at least something to see and to do. Some, like Faversham, are Tudor surprises while others, such as Margate (a raffish seaside resort, with a fairground and amusements, yet also a 200-year-old theatre and Georgian squares), are well known. Dover is a busy port, yet also has terraces of fine classical revival houses facing its beach. Kent's seaside towns go from medieval (Sandwich) to Victorian (Broadstairs.) Many are rich with a profusion of history, architecture and folklore.

ROCHESTER *Sweeps – brushed up and ready.*

LOCAL HISTORY

Near Chatham with its maritime exhibits is Kit's Coty House, a prehistoric cromlach – that is, a structure built of three huge slabs of stone capped with a fourth. A road nearby has the reputation of being haunted and this part of Kent is particularly rich in ghost tales.

Kent is rich in Roman remains. Rutuplæ, the present Richborough, was once the Porta Britannica, the foothold established by Julius Caesar. His actual landing is marked by a stone near the wide arc of Pegwell Bay, a nature reserve. Through a noble, pale, marble arch towering above the surrounding estuary waters, two emperors came to their northern dominions and legions marched along Watling Street towards London. The Roman Painted House and the Pharos – or lighthouse – at Dover are

FOLKESTONE *Eurostar cutting a swathe through the 'Garden of England'.*

notable. At the Roman camp of Reculver, stone fortifications remain, and the Norman church, destroyed by an 18th-century divine has only the twin towers standing above the sea; they are still used as markers for mariners in the Thames estuary.

On the edge of marshes that once were the sea floor of the wide Wantsume Channel – making the Isle of Thanet separate and navigable until the end of the medieval era – is Minster, with an ancient abbey founded in AD670 which claims to be the oldest inhabited building in England.

The name Cinque Ports comes from *cinque portus* meaning 'five havens'. Actually they number more than five, especially when many minor ones or 'Limbs' are added. (Most of these are now high and dry, far from the sea.) These towns, some in Sussex, all have fascinating histories and marked walks for discovery. The home of the Warden of the Cinque Ports, a title held by many famous people, is a noble one: it's the Tudor castle at Walmer where once the Duke of Wellington resided in retirement. With sea views from its terraces and a magnificent garden with ancient yews, Walmer is managed by English Heritage and makes a marvellous outing.

West of Tonbridge, Hever Castle is where the unfortunate Anne Boleyn, second wife of Henry VIII, grew up, and where Anne of Cleeves, his fourth wife, lived after they divorced – she was less unfortunate, divorce being preferable, presumably, to beheading.

COUNTY CALENDAR

◆ Many sporting events include horse racing at Folkestone and an annual county fair at Detling.

◆ Annual Cider and Apple Fair in Kent.

◆ Regular events, theatre, storytelling and re-created military and battle scenes are put on by English Heritage at Dover, Deal and Walmer Castles. At Richborough Castle there are re-creations of the Roman life at Rutupaie.

◆ Heritage Centres at Tunbridge Wells (A Day at the Wells), Dover (White Cliffs Experience) and Canterbury (The Canterbury Tales) are open all year. Rochester has a lively Dickensian Festival every spring.

◆ Early March: The Dover Film Festival

◆ Early April: A celebration of Easter at superb Leeds Castle. Occasional outdoor classical concert with a famous orchestra and conductor with, yes, fireworks and even cannon!

◆ Early May: Rochester Sweeps Festival is a traditional festival with processions, dancing, ceilidhs, craft fairs and music.

◆ End of May to early June: Ramsgate Spring Festival is a festival of dance, classical music, drama, pageantry and the obligatory fireworks.

◆ End of May to early June: Festival of Dover is a summer version of Ramsgate's spring festival.

◆ End of May to early June: Rochester resurfaces for its world-famous festival with displays, competitions and street entertainment all connected with Dickens.

◆ Mid June: Biggin Hill International Air Fair is a five-hour display with a large exhibition area and ground-floor events too.

◆ Mid June: Broadstairs has a greater claim to fame with Dickens and hosts a festival with Dickensian garden party, country fair and a play.

◆ Kent County Show is at Maidstone each July.

LANCASHIRE

THE COUNTY LANDSCAPE

◆ Between the mountains of the Lake District and the point where the river Mersey separates it from Cheshire, this is arguably the most varied of the north-western counties. There is splendid scenery here with lofty mountain peaks and bare moorland, beautiful rivers and fast-flowing streams.

◆ In Northwest England, the main county (excluding Furness) has clearly defined geographical boundaries. To the north, it is marked by the high fells of the Lake District; to the east by the Pennines; to the south by the River Mersey; and to the west by a long and irregular coastline on the Irish Sea, broken into two unequal parts by Morecambe Bay. Off the coast at Barrow is Walney Island. The Mersey forms the boundary between this county and Cheshire for some distance.

◆ The scenery is mountainous in the north, hilly in the east, and low-lying in the south on the border with Cheshire. But there is also a good deal of fertile farmland, particularly in the Fylde and in the southwest of the county.

◆ Furness is the peninsula jutting down in the northwest, separated from the main part of Lancashire by the stretching sands of Morecambe Bay. It is bordered by Westmorland and Cumberland to its north and west.

COUNTY CALENDAR

◆ Easter: In the town of Bacup, Coconut Dancers, 'Nutters', perform a traditional dance with wooden cups attached to their hands, waists and knees. On Easter Monday, the ancient custom of Egg Rolling takes place in Preston.

◆ June: Hornby village Festival.

◆ July: St Helen's Show at Sherdley Park.

◆ July: At the Manchester Show at Platt Fields, there is a flower show, military tattoo and show jumping.

◆ End of July: Royal Lancashire Show at Chorley.

◆ August: Southport Flower Show, one of the largest in the country, is held at the end of the month.

◆ Late August: Blackpool Illuminations are turned on.

◆ August Bank Holiday: Lancaster hosts the Georgian Legacy Festival and one of the highlights is the National Sedan Chair Carrying Competition.

◆ September: The Greater Manchester Marathon is held on the first Sunday of the month.

BLACKPOOL *Seven million tourists a year flock to this famous 518-foot tower.*

THE FAMILIAR NAMES of Lytham St Anne's, Blackpool, Southport, Cleveleys and Morecambe conjure up seaside jollity. Lancashire north of the sands, as they say locally, lies Barrow in Furness nudging up to the beautiful Lake District – and Lancashire can even lay claim to part of it as Coniston Water is pure 'Red Rose'.And south? Well, the roll call of hard-grafting towns says it all: Manchester, Liverpool, Bolton, Salford, Wigan, Warrington, Widnes, St Helens and Oldham. It also pleased me to hear Matthew Lorenzo on GMTV refer to the Liverpool vs Manchester United soccer match as the 'Lancashire derby'. It's a fact that not many people realize these great cities lie in the county, and some may even recall the familiar battle cry in the 1970s of 'MANCS IS LANCS!'

TOWNS AND VILLAGES

Historic towns, picture-postcard villages, seaside resorts great and small and, of course, workmanlike industrial centres, this county is a microcosm of England itself. The industrial tradition grew up, 200 years ago, first on cotton and then on coal-mining, chemicals and engineering. Lancashire has a good record for caring for its many old buildings – the peel towers of the north and bewildering array of fortified houses, farms and even churches are reminders that the county has constantly been the target of invaders.

Southwards, the image of Lancashire is of a county of heavily-industrialized and Lowry-inspired names like Accrington, Ashton-under-Lyne, Burnley, Bootle, Rochdale, Widnes and Wigan that sound like a roll-call from the football or rugby league. They do exist and while they may not be the most picturesque towns in this county, they do have a past of which they are rightly proud. In the 1990s, civic pride rules. Once-blackened buildings are being scrubbed clean and, as industry declines, attention is being given to attracting new business – tourism, something Lancashire is brilliant at!

Wigan, immortalized in George Orwell's *The Road to Wigan Pier*, has been the butt of many music hall jokes, like its famous son George Formby, but it has had the last laugh by creating, out of a complex of former mill buildings overlooking a canal, one of the most imaginative of the new breed of heritage centres. At the heart of Wigan Pier is *The Way We Were* exhibition, which contains a vivid re-creation of a coal pit.

The rival cities of Manchester and Liverpool are both contained within the county's boundaries, and have also been quick to put industrial dereliction to positive use. Liverpool's defunct docks are now given over to cafés, restaurants, boutiques and the like; while in Manchester you can take a canal-side amble through the centre of the city (despite the devastation of the IRA 1996 bombing), stopping off to pay homage to the Coronation Street set at the Granada Studios, pop into the City Art Gallery to feast your eyes on works by Gainsborough, Hogarth, Reynolds and others, or visit Old Trafford to see Manchester United footballers or Lancashire's or England's cricketers in action.

Urban Lancashire has its appeal, but so, too, does rural Lancashire. At its northern boundary, the county meets the high fells of the Lake District in a series of spectacular peaks. South of here, the River Ribble rolls through a marvellously scenic stretch of countryside, passing within a stone's throw of delightful Clitheroe, the most northern of the cotton mill towns, dominated by its Norman castle

COUNTY FACTS

Origin of name: From the Brittonic/Anglo-Saxon meaning 'the Roman fort on the River Lane'. The local English population often called any Roman settlement 'ceaster' – hence Lune-ceaster which became Lancaster.

Name first recorded: 1127 as Loncastra.

County Motto: *In Concilio Consilium* ("In Counsel is Wisdom").

County Town: **LANCASTER**

The town fairly creaks and groans under the weight of its formidable history and some of its oldest buildings are still in use. The castle is used partly as a crown court and prison and the Shire Hall, which has a collection of coats of arms dating from the 12th century, can also be visited.

Other Towns:

BARROW-IN-FURNESS Capital of a beautiful area with the ruins of Furness Abbey once the most powerful around lying in a wooded vale. The town is a succession of terraced house dominated by the once all-menacing Trident nuclear submarines.

BLACKBURN Another of Lancashire's key cotton weaving centres with the Lewis Textile Museum to prove it. Modern engineering is the main industry.

BOLTON Busy industrial town and cotton-spinning centre with many old mills converted to other industries. Ye Old Man and Scythe inn situated in Church Gate has Civil War connections and is an attractive pub to visit. William Lever, son of a Bolton grocer was born here and went on to soapmaking and the beginnings of Port Sunlight and Unilever.

BURY A Roman station, Saxon fort and baronial castle at Castle Croft shows this was an important place before King Cotton made its name for the town.

LIVERPOOL Beatles' fans may head for Mathews Street site of the Cavern Club, or try the Magical History Tour. Take a ferry across Mersey to get glorious views of the waterfront or shop at Albert Docks. There is so much on offer in this city which vividly reflects the later history of England.

MANCHESTER The Castleford area boasts a fine industrial museum on the site of the world's oldest passenger railway station. The G-Mex Exhibition Centre and club scene is the modern face of the city.

OLDHAM History has it that this was a textile town in Charles I's day and of course it then developed into one of the great Lancashire contributors that put the Great in Britain. Its Town Hall cost £4,000 in 1840!

PRESTON Lancashire County Council's administrative centre. North End FC once a major footballing force now famed for its unique Tom Finney Stand opened in 1995. Fine museums and an art gallery.

SALFORD After cotton came rubber and waterproofing industries and considerable replanning. The Quays are a reminder of its links to Manchester to which it is more or less joined. A new Lowry Art Gallery and Albert Finney Theatre have opened here.

ST HELENS Began its development as an industrial town in the 1600s with coal-mining, and in 1773 glass making was introduced. There have been four different churches on the site of the current one.

WARRINGTON Equidistant between Manchester and Liverpool but with an identity of its own, designated a new town in 1968 and now a communications centre.
◆ Crosby ◆ Formby ◆ Grange over Sands

County rivers: The major rivers are the Mersey, Ribble and Lune, all of which flow westwards into the Irish Sea. Also the Calder, Hodder and Wyre.
Highest point: The Old Man of Coniston at 2,633 feet.

Lancashire's local government: The County of Lancashire has a complicated administrative map. Lancashire County Council only caters for about half of the County of Lancashire which is shared on a two-tier basis with 12 District Councils, namely Burnley, Chorley, Fylde, Hyndburn, Lancaster, Pendle, Preston, Ribble Valley, Rossendale, South Ribble, West Lancashire and Wyre. Blackpool and Blackburn are unitary councils where Lancashire County Council has no place. Lancashire North of the Sands known as Furness is two-tiered with Cumbria County Council, Barrow in Furness District and South Lakeland District Councils (shared with the Counties of Westmorland and Yorkshire) providing the services. In the south, a number of unitary metropolitan authorities cut a swathe across Lancashire's boundary with Cheshire where the Metropolitan Boroughs of Halton, Manchester, Tameside, Trafford and Warrington actually provide services for parts of both Counties. Todmorden (partly in Yorkshire) comes under Calderdale council. Bolton, Bury, Knowsley, Liverpool, Oldham, Rochdale, St Helens, Salford, Sefton, Wigan are unitary councils solely to administer Lancashire lands.

***LIVERPOOL** The Insurance Building & Liver Birds.*

perched on a lonely outcrop of limestone. To the east of Clitheroe, looming on the horizon like a huge hump-backed whale, is Pendle Hill which, in the 17th century, was supposed to have been inhabited by witches. It is also according to local folklore a weather predictor

"If Pendle Hill do wear a hood,
Be sure the day will ne'er do good."

In 1612, the witch-finder Thomas Potts was sent north and the most celebrated witches – the Demdikes and the Chattoxes – confessed and were sentenced to death in Lancaster jail.

You can't come to Lancashire without trying the legendary Lancashire hotpot or Morecambe Bay shrimps. This is also a county for cakes: the Nelson and Eccles' offerings come crammed full of currants, while from near Preston the over-sweet but popular Goosnargh cake is a tasty treat. Annie's Garden Restaurant at the Wyevale on Preston New Road, Westby-with-Plumpton or The Priory at Scorton both offer a healthy variety of hearty Lancashire fayre.

Lancaster, the town that gave its name to a dynasty as well as a county, is also worth a visit, perhaps as a stopping point on the way to the coast. It is a grey, rich, leaden city and I like its 'out-on-its-own' feel.

West of Lancaster, Morecambe, may be famous for its shrimps and bay, but it's also a thriving holiday resort in its own right, complete with an oceanarium, in which dolphins frolic for the benefit of visitors, and even a Wild West theme park. To the south the fertile Fylde – the name comes from the Old English word *gefilde*, meaning a plain – is one big flourishing market garden. In summer, townies heading for the coast can halt their car at roadside stalls for tomatoes or whatever happens to be in season.

As a Fylde coast base Blackpool offers a razzmatazz which is hard to match. With its seven-mile-long promenade, famous Pleasure Beach and amusement arcades, Blackpool is ideal for those in search of family fun. For a quieter respite try leafy – Lytham-St-Anne's, or pop over to floral Southport. Fleetwood, facing into Morecambe Bay at the mouth of the River Wyre, is a fishing port and an excellent place to sample the local seafood or 'Freeport' shopping.

Inland from here on the Preston-Blackburn road is Samlesbury, home to the military wing of British Aerospace and its magnificent 1530 Tudor 'Old Hall' with a glorious great hall constructed of massive and elegantly carved oak timbers: it is open to the public.

Preston itself should not be by-passed as it is a popular shopping centre with a large and busy market.

LOCAL HISTORY

Long before the rise of the House of Lancaster, Lancashire played a significant role in the history of England. The Romans passed this way, building a fort at Bremetennacum, the remains of which can still be seen at Ribchester, near Preston. The fells and moorland have always been sparsely populated, but Angles settled in the valleys and in the 7th century Lancashire was part of the Kingdom of Northumbria. Later hardy Norse farmers, descendants of the Viking invaders, established their thwaites – clearings – on the high moorlands. Once the Normans occupied Britain, the land passed into the hands of local barons. In the north of the county, the Forest of Bowland which rolls into Yorkshire – not a woodland, but a royal hunting ground – was controlled by the baron Robert de Lacy.

The House of Lancaster came to prominence in 1399, providing the kings of England for 62 years until Henry VI was deposed during the Wars of the Roses. The Reformation was not generally accepted in Lancashire and many of the local clergy remained loyal to Catholicism. Later, in the Civil War, Lancashire Royalists were roundly defeated at the Battle of Preston in 1648, and in 1715 a large contingent of Lancastrians joined the Scots army to proclaim the Pretender King at Lancaster, but the rebellion was soon put down.

Lancashire will forever be remembered for the leading part it played in the Industrial Revolution. Flemish weavers had brought their skills to Lancashire as early as the 14th century and they were followed in the 17th century by French Protestants fleeing persecution. But it was inventions such as Kay's Fly Shuttle, Hargreave's Spinning Jenny and Crompton's Mule during the Industrial Revolution that really accelerated the cotton industry's expansion. Iron ore was produced at Furness to make mill engines and the local coalfield provided the fuel to power them. Raw cotton was imported through the booming port of Liverpool (later joined by Manchester following the building of the Manchester Ship Canal) and processed in towns such as Bolton, Bury, Rochdale and Stalybridge (partly in Cheshire), where the spinning, weaving and bleaching were carried out.

As well as being an important cotton manufacturing town, Rochdale was also the birthplace of the Co-operative Movement. The depression of the early 19th century prompted a group of locals to set up their own co-operative shop in 1844, with the idea of dividing the surplus for the benefit of all. They formed the Rochdale Society of Equitable Pioneers and the original shop is now a museum.

FAMOUS NAMES

◆ Liverpool will forever be remembered for its popular music connections from the war years to the 90s rave scene. All four members of the Beatles were born in Liverpool, as were 60s singers Frankie Vaughan, Cilla Black and Gerry Marsden (Gerry and the Pacemakers). The 80s saw the likes of bedsit favourites The Smiths and Echo and The Bunnymen and New Order (resurrected in the 90s).

◆ The Manchester dance scene produced the Happy Mondays since transformed into Black Grape, and another band Oasis have crafted two of the best pop albums of the 90s. Take That burst on the scene here also in the 90s and disappeared to reappear in solo guises. Mark Owen lives at Leck.

◆ Gracie Fields was a native of Rochdale and museum honouring her is to be built in the town.

◆ Lisa Stansfield, the international pop star, is related to Gracie Fields, and like her famous relative comes from Rochdale.

◆ The town of Preston, 'Proud Preston', has many famous sons (and daughters). Sir Richard Arkright, a prominent figure in the Industrial Revolution, was born in the town and the house in which he developed his water frame in 1768 survives on Stoneygate.

◆ Other natives of Preston include the 18th century painter Arthur Devis and poets Francis Thompson and Robert Service. The opera singer Kathleen Ferrier was born three miles southeast of the town at Higher Walton.

◆ Children's author Beatrix Potter lived on the county's northern border at Hill Top Farm, near Sawrey, until her death in 1943.

◆ Writer John Ruskin, after whom the Oxford college is named, bought a house in Coniston in 1871 and retired there in 1884. He died in 1900 and is buried in the churchyard at Coniston.

◆ The Manchester aviators Captain John Alcock and Lieutenant Arthur Whitten Brown made the first non-stop crossing of the Atlantic by air in 1919, flying from St John, Newfoundland, to Clifden, Ireland.

◆ The long-running ITV soap *Coronation Street* is shot almost entirely on location in a specially built set at the Granada studios in Manchester. The set forms part of a studio tour along with *Russell Grant's World of Astrology* and *Sherlock Holmes's Baker Street.*

◆ The film version of Noel Coward's *Brief Encounter*, directed by David Lean, was shot on location at Carnforth station.

◆ *Brookside,* Channel 4's soap is shot and set in Liverpool.

◆ Albert Finney, recently resurrected in Dennis Potter's bequest plays, was born in Salford.

◆ Stan Laurel (he the tall thin one) was born at Ulverston, which now houses the Laurel and Hardy Museum.

◆ Ukelele-playing comedian with the toothy grin George Formby was born in Wigan and was hugely popular in the music halls and cinemas of the region.

◆ Josef Lock, Irish tenor and subject of the movie *Hear My Song* lived in Lytham St Annes.

◆ Errol Flynn, Clark Gable and Johnny Weissmuller were stationed in Warrington during the Second World War and drove to Royal Lytham to play golf.

◆ Dame Thora Hird comes from Morecambe.

LEICESTERSHIRE

***ASHBY-DE-LA-ZOUCH** Remains of the castle – originally a Norman manor house – include a magnificent 14th-century tower.*

THE COUNTY LANDSCAPE

◆ A largely agricultural county, with some centres of industry, but wide and open land, well watered and once heavily wooded. It is now a scatter of close-packed fertile fields, where the forests used to provide hunting.

◆ Foxes are still plentiful though, and the county is a stronghold of fox hunting with famous hunts such as the Quorn, the Belvoir and the Cottesmore meeting regularly in the winter season in the upper tongue of Leicestershire. Here in the valley of the River Eye and the Vale of Belvoir the famous Wolds mix open pastures and coverts for the foxes to breed.

◆ Cattle country, of the very best, composes the stretch of greensward of southern Leicestershire. There have been cattle markets for many centuries here, and the cows themselves wade in deep grassy fields between the county town and Market Harborough, where lanes and gated roads give this area a sense of rural backwater. The Grand Union Canal winds through south Leicestershire.

RIGHT IN THE HEART of England, Leicestershire lies farther from the sea than any other county. It has always been a cultural crossroads – this is now most obvious if you drive past the topsy-turvy shops along Leicester's Narborough Road selling silk bales, rice and other wares of the Indian subcontinent. The original immigrants arrived during the 1950s to bolster Leicester's textiles and footwear industries. Not far away, the countryside still preserves its agricultural base of wheat and root crops and, of course, sheep as you pass mouth-watering-sounding places like Ashby-de-la-Zouch, and Melton Mowbray as well as Market Bosworth with its War of the Roses history centre.

TOWNS AND VILLAGES

Leicester sits in the centre of this green heartland of England. The cathedral's attractive churchyard is a popular meeting place. Hosiery, boots and shoes and light engineering are Leicester's trades. Unfortunately the city has retained little of its great past. Roman remains can be seen in the Jewry Wall Museum (wall paintings and mosaics) and at Jewry Wall itself, a large fragment of the facade of a Roman bath and exercise hall. The handsome 15th-century guildhall with its slated roof and half timbering seems almost like a child's toy left behind in a welter of modernization and development. It has a well-preserved interior with a beamed medieval hall, as well as old police cells. There's a ruined castle, a gateway now a military museum, and a museum of old aspects of the city, the Newarke Houses Museum. Belgrave Hall with its gardens has a collection of agricultural implements.

The Grand Union Canal runs from Leicester to Market Harborough, dipping into long tunnels and carried up a hill by the prodigious staircase of locks at Foxton. This village is at the bottom of the flight of locks, arranged in two tiers of five locks each, built in 1811. Once busy with commercial traffic, the canal is now a strip of nature park with footways along the towpaths.

The River Welland runs through Market Harborough and past Medbourne, with a cluster of attractive villages nearby – Horningfold is an estate village in nostalgic period style, and Hallaton is attractive with its Norman towered church, old houses and unusual market cross. North from Billesdon Coplow, a high hill, are fine views towards Rutland. The village itself has a 17th-century schoolhouse. West is pretty Great Glen with its green and nearby country paths raised against flooding on the Wistow plain, with Fleckney, a typical terraced industrial village, nearby, and the brick-built Willoughby Waterlees.

Though Stanford-on-Avon is in Northamptonshire, Stanford Hall lies over the river (which is the boundary) in Leicestershire. Approached by a tree-lined avenue, this fine William and Mary house has collections of costumes, antiques, old cars and aeroplanes within.

Northwest of Leicester is open country towards the county of Rutland and Melton Mowbray, a hunting town where the history of the sport is well preserved. It's probably more famous as the home of pork pies and Stilton cheese. Here also are the famous Wolds, with pretty villages such as Waltham on the Wolds (with a large smock mill, now unfortunately sailless), Croxton Kerrial – stone-built, with excavated abbey ruins and monks' fish ponds – and Bottesford, where the earls of Rutland are buried (Grinling Gibbons monuments in the church). The earls (now dukes) have as their home the hill-perched Belvoir Castle, near the village. This vast and grandiose house is a fake castle, an exercise in Victorian romanticism, but it does have an older core dating back to the 11th century, and many treasures, particularly tapestries and paintings, in its staterooms. Fine views are afforded from the castle terraces over three counties.

COUNTY FACTS

Origin of name: Leicester is an English corruption of the Latin "a fort on the river Leire". The 12th-century writer William of Malmesbury referred to the Leire as the Legra.

Name first recorded: 1087 as Laegreceastrescir.

Motto: For'ard, For'ard.

County Town:

LEICESTER With a large Asian population, the town has many restaurants, shops and markets reviving life in the central city. Henry III was defied by Simon de Montfort – the first Earl of Leicester – in a successful 13th-century uprising and is commemorated with a huge auditorium, the de Montfort Hall.

Other Towns:

ASHBY-DE-LA-ZOUCH The name derives from old English aese = ash and the Scandinavian byr = habitation, given by Breton nobleman Alain de la Souche. Pleasant town with wide market street. The nearby castle remains were made famous by Sir Walter Scott in his *Ivanhoe*.

CASTLE DONINGTON A power station does not detract from the popular boating and picnic areas along the Trent. Some lovely timber-framed houses.

COALVILLE Centre of the county's mining industry.

LOUGHBOROUGH Famous 1960s college that has a reputation for producing athletics champions.

LUTTERWORTH Once an important stage coach stop, it has half-timbered houses and an old bridge over the River Swift. The church contains a memorial to John Wycliffe, the 14th-century religious reformer.

MARKET BOSWORTH More village than town, with a famous Hall reminiscent of Hampton Court. Close by is the battlefield of Bosworth which ended the War of the Roses in 1485. An excellent joint battle centre and walk exists.

MARKET HARBOROUGH A prosperous town, with Georgian buildings and a famed grammar school, a 17th-century timbered building raised above the pavement on pillars. There are coaching inns, notably the Swan with its prominent sign. This is the place where liberty bodices were invented.

MELTON MOWBRAY A pleasant old market town with lots of parkland by the river. There are 18th-century houses and ancient almshouses near the fine church.

◆ Barrow upon Sour ◆ Barwell ◆ Birstall ◆ Blaby ◆ Earl Shilton ◆ Enderby ◆ Hinckley ◆ Kegworth ◆ Oadby ◆ Shepshed ◆ Wigston.

Main rivers: Soar, Wreake.

Highest point: Bardon Hill at 912 feet.

Leicestershire's local government: Apart from the City of Leicester a two-tier local government system provides the rest of the County of Leicestershire with its public services through the Leicestershire County Council and seven District Councils of Blaby, Charnwood, Harborough, Hinckley & Bosworth, Melton, North-West Leicestershire and Oadby & Wigston. The City of Leicester is controlled by a single unitary council over which Leicestershire County Council has no power.

FAMOUS NAMES

◆ Simon de Montfort was the man who put the city of Leicester on the map, seven centuries ago.

◆ Lady Jane Grey, the tragic nine-days queen executed by Mary Tudor, lived part of her short life at Bradgate House in Charnwood Forest near Leicester. The grand house is in ruins, but the parkland is open for walks in its woods, hills, and open heathland.

◆ John Wycliffe made the first English translation of the Bible at Lutterworth.

◆ Film director Stephen Frears (*Dangerous Liaisons, My Beautiful Laundrette, The Snapper*) was born in Leicester.

◆ Gary Lineker, gentleman footballer and one of our better exports to Japan, hails from Leicestershire.

◆ Carribean cook Rustie Lee is Leicester City FC's hostess at home matches.

COUNTY CALENDAR

◆ April: National Folk Music Festival, Loughborough.

◆ Easter Monday: Bottle kicking, in which three villages compete to push casks filled with beer over a stream, and a pie sharing ceremony, the "hare pie scramble", at Hallaton.

◆ May Day: Leicestershire County Show at Dishley Grange.

◆ August: Agricultural show at Ashby-de-la-Zouch.

◆ August: Jousting Tournament, Belvoir Castle.

◆ October–November: Amateur athletics at Loughborough, and a festival and fair.

◆ Flat racing near Leicester at Oadby.

◆ End of July: British Motorcycle Grand Prix at Castle Donington.

◆ End of August: Leicester International Air Display at Leicester Aeroclub.

Loughborough lies west of Melton Mowbray and is famous as the largest bell foundry in Europe. The casting foundry of John Taylor was established here in the 19th century and has made bells for carillons and churches around the world. Across Charnwood Forest and its high point, Bardon Hill, as the crow flies is Market Bosworth, recorded in the Domesday Book, but best known for the Battle of Bosworth with the battle site a mile away. A nearby stone pyramid houses a well (Dick's Well) from which the doomed Richard III drank before the fateful battle.

Ashby-de-la-Zouch commemorates the La Souch Breton family who gained this pleasing town after the Norman Conquest. It has castle ruins and Tudor and Georgian houses along its main street, as well as an imposing terrace of Regency houses from the time Ashby was being developed as a spa. Next to the justly famous Palladian building Staunton Harold Hall with its fine grounds is a rarity, a church built in the Cromwellian period where men and women are divided by the central aisle.

LOCAL HISTORY

Charnwood Forest, Beacon Hill and other sites provided places for Bronze Age settlements. East of Leicester at Billesdon is a set of Iron Age earthworks. There is an Iron Age fort at Breedon on the Hill. Burrough Hill is a large hill fort of the Iron Age overlooking the route from Leicester to Stamford. The Romans developed the fortified town of Ratae Coritanorum, modern-day Leicester, on the Fosse Way, the military road running from Lincoln to Cirencester, and Emperor Hadrian kitted it out with an impressive array of public buildings. Waltham on the Wolds also has Roman pavements and a later Saxon settlement. Near the village of Sutton Cheney is Bosworth Field, where 500 years ago the Tudor dynasty was established when Richard III was killed. Henry Tudor took the crown, found under a thorn bush, and the Wars of the Roses finally ended when the white rose of York was vanquished.

CHARNWOOD FOREST *Most trees have been felled in this 15,000-acre forest.*

LINCOLNSHIRE

LINCOLN *The soaring spires of the county town's cathedral were completed in 1280.*

I HAVE AN impression of Lincoln that I shall never forget: I was driving up from Sleaford and all I could take in was the vast flatness when suddenly there was this pimple on the horizon and on top of the pimple was Lincoln. It was a stunning prospect from a distance. So the county may be flat but it is not dull, and it remains one of the least-known parts of Britain.

TOWNS AND VILLAGES

Aside from the main towns of Lincoln, Boston, Grimsby, Grantham, Louth, Stamford and Scunthorpe, this is a county of very small places. Most Lincolnshire settlements are tiny, and neatly grouped around a church and a manor house. The county is dominated by the county town, the noble city of Lincoln itself, standing on and around its surprisingly high and commanding hill. This is crowned with one of the country's finest and least-known cathedrals. Lincoln is an unselfconscious and antique place that sharp-eyed diarist John Evelyn called a 'confused town, long, uneven, steep and rugged', and so it remains. Built on the income from wool and cloth (Lincoln Green was a famous colour), the cathedral with its three towers is to be seen from all over the city. The third largest in the country, it is constructed of local limestone and Purbeck marble. It took more than 80 years

THE COUNTY LANDSCAPE

◆ Lincolnshire spreads from the flat shores of the North Sea westward to the Midlands and north to Yorkshire. It's undulating and in places flat, especially where it joins with the Fens and the Wash in the South. But it actually has a high central chalk ridge, the Lincolnshire Edge upon which Lincoln itself perches.

◆ The middle is ultimate farm country. Under big skies a vast open countryside broods, with vast fields and small villages. The whole county remains rural, even feudal, for if any county can claim the title, Lincolnshire is Olde England. (Although these flat fields made ideal airfields in 1940!)

◆ It is an isolated county, remaining bypassed by new connections, and by most main roads; its rail lines lead to nowhere else but points in the county. It has little heavy industry and that is up in the north in such towns as Scunthorpe and the fishing port of Grimsby towards the coast from Skegness to the Humber, all sand, mud and marsh. Otherwise wool and fine cloth have been its making. The local stone, a warm golden limestone, is used extensively in old Lincoln and some Lindsey and Kesteven villages.

◆ A dividing line runs from the Nottinghamshire border through Lincoln and angling southeast to the western coast of the Wash. It demarcates Kesteven and Holland to the south and the larger slab of Lindsey in the north. Here are the Wolds, while at the edge the sea regularly erodes the chalk; the resulting plateau of marshy clay now provides excellent beef grazing. Holland is drained fen and the land produces good cereal and sugar beet crops. Flowers too, for the bulbfields are famous. Kesteven has hills and woods with scattered villages.

◆ The city of Lincoln hugs the western border and is nowhere near the centre of its county (that is probably occupied by the Wolds village of Baumber, a pleasing place on the banks of the River Bain). From its point on its ridge of the Wolds on a clear day the towers of Lincoln can be seen. You will need to make a genuine effort to visit this straggling capital city.

◆ Like Yorkshire's Ridings the County of Lincolnshire has three ancient Divisions known as Holland, Kesteven and Lindsey.

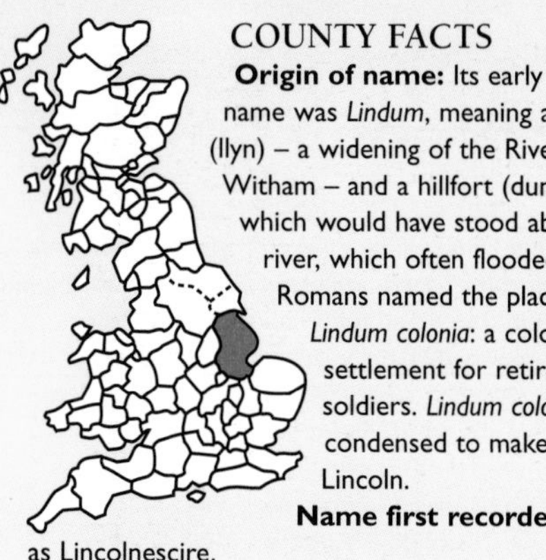

COUNTY FACTS

Origin of name: Its early Briton name was *Lindum*, meaning a lake (llyn) – a widening of the River Witham – and a hillfort (dun), which would have stood above the river, which often flooded. The Romans named the place *Lindum colonia*: a colony or settlement for retired soldiers. *Lindum colonia* was condensed to make Lincoln.

Name first recorded: 1016 as Lincolnescire.

County Motto: *Perseverance vincit* ("Perseverance succeeds").

County Town: LINCOLN A charming city running the full pageant of English history.

Other Towns:

BOSTON A vast church with a tower reminiscent of others in the Low Countries, the Boston Stump can be seen for miles. There are good medieval buildings and a 15th-century guildhall, though the town is a shadow of the busy port it once was long ago.

BOURNE With a considerable claim on history, Bourne sits beside the Carr Dyke, a great Roman drainage scheme, and the bulb-growing centre.

CLEETHORPES Once a sleepy fishing village, then a million visitors a year were attracted to its three miles of sand, beautiful boating lake, Marineland and Winter Gardens.

GAINSBOROUGH King Alfred married Ealswith and Canute's father, Sweyn, died at Thornock Park. The Old Hall is a fine late medieval country house.

GRANTHAM St Wulfram's Church's 281-foot spire is a landmark for many miles around this coaching inn town. Margaret Thatcher was born here.

GRIMSBY Once the greatest fishing port in England.

HOLBEACH Near the Wash, this is a place to stop and explore the famous local Fenland churches.

LOUTH With fine Georgian houses and a market, its stone spired-church looming above the marshes is a centre to explore the Wolds.

Mablethorpe Small holiday resort with a splendid beach on which to take in the invigorating sea air sweeping in.

SCUNTHORPE Evolved from a group of small villages including Brumby, Crosby, Ashby and Frodingham into a large industrial town. At one time it belted out ingot steel and pig iron.

SPALDING Commercial bulb growing centre with a Dutch ambience and the air full of perfume in the spring.

STAMFORD History-packed stone-built town. Burghley House founded in 1575 by Sir William Cecil.

◆ Barton-on-Humber ◆ Brigg ◆ Broughton ◆ Crowle ◆ Epworth ◆ Humberton ◆ Immingham ◆ Mablethorpe ◆ North Hykeham ◆ Sleaford

Highest point: Normanby-le-Wold at 584 feet.

County rivers: Trent, Welland, Ancholme, Witham, Brant, Glen, Bain, Steeping.

to build and apart from some Norman work is mostly in a satisfyingly grand Early English style. It is a truly magnificent building, its famous arcaded west front and exterior balanced and harmonious. Old Lincoln clustered on its hill has many fine buildings and the visitor can spend hours exploring the houses ranked around the Minster Yard, or Close. There are ancient archways too, one a Roman gateway which is still used, the Newport Arch, and the medieval Stonebow, while High Bridge is set on a Norman foundation arch over the river and still carries half-timbered houses along one side; a once common practice, this is now a rare survival.

South of Lincoln is Cranwell with its RAF college, and Grantham, which has pleasing old inns from its days as a coaching stop on the Great North Road. On its Castlegate a 14th-century house and garden open on the river and Sedgwick Meadows, both belonging to the National Trust. Near here, set in a fine park, is a spectacular brick Restoration house, Belton, with plasterwork ceilings and wood carving within. Ancaster provided much of Lincoln's stone.

On the very southern edge of the county keeping Peterborough at bay is Market Deeping, which along with the other Deepings gets its name from being in the flood plain of the Welland. Grey and gold stone Stamford, with its coaching inn, the George, is one of the county's loveliest towns. It is a remarkable mixture of pleasing architecture from bow-windowed shops to Queen Anne mansions. It is often used for TV films, notably BBC's *Middlemarch* in 1995.

To the east in flat fen lands are Dutch influenced places, often with typical brick gabled houses. Tattersall Castle is a landmark in two senses – it can be seen for miles and is an early example of a brick-built fortified house. Spalding, in Lincolnshire's ancient division called Holland, has the River Welland like a Dutch tree-lined canal running through it, and it also has the spring beauty of a coat of many colours as millions of bulbs blossom. The other product is the more prosaic sugar beet.

Local clay means extensive use of brick, as at Tattersall where there is a moated castle, church, school and almshouses. Head north and you come to Donington, a farming centre with a cobbled market and houses with pantiled roofs. The church is a landmark, but it has to give preference to the one at Boston.

The Wolds are chalk hills cut with valleys and wooded with beeches. Notable Wold villages are Old Bolingbroke, Tealby and Wold Newton. Nearby Lincoln's seaside coast is dotted with old-fashioned seaside resorts from Cleethorpes and Mablethorpe to Skegness. Grimsby and nearby Immingham are busy ports. The former is famous for its fish, some of which is smoked here. One of the biggest fish merchants in Grimsby was Russell Grant, a great guy (with a great name) whom I had the pleasure of meeting on a BBC programme.

Lincolnshire sausages are also famous, and so is the local pork and beef. Many of its potatoes go to crisp factories.

SPALDING *Daffodils stretch as far as the eye can see in spring..*

LOCAL HISTORY

Lincoln is very ancient, going back to pre-Roman times when it was a Celtic settlement. Later, on the top of the same hill, the Romans built their city and called it *Lindum Colonia*. Since its founding, the city has seen many historic events including numerous visits from medieval monarchs. Appropriately, the town retains many buildings from that epoch. It was also a Saxon city in the Kingdom of Mercia.and had a line of its own kings from Anglo-Saxon times. On a street climbing the hill is The Jew's House (home of Aaron the Jew, a money-lender whose loans to Henry II accounted for half the king's income). You will also find the Guildhall, Pottergate with its red-brick façades, a museum, an art gallery and the City Library with mementos of Tennyson. There are also large parks and an arboretum.

Viking days are recalled with place names – the ending *by* is Danish for a village and *thorpe* was a farm. You can walk along the towpath of the Fossdyke Navigation Canal, which was first excavated by the Romans. There is a Roman camp at Ancaster. Bits of the Roman wall exist around Lincoln and in the Eastgate Hotel's garden the foundation of the east gate is exposed. At Kesteven's chief town, Sleaford, there is an Iron Age village.

The Pilgrim Fathers made their first departure to Holland in 1609 from Humber Bank. In Boston they are remembered in Fydell House; sailing from Southampton in 1630 they gave the great New England city its name. The museum in Lincoln's Broadgate is part of the Greyfriars monastery, and contains many prehistoric and Roman antiquities.

Lincolnshire's local government: The County of Lincolnshire is governed by two tiers of local government: Lincolnshire County Council at the top and 7 Districts: Boston, East Lindsey, Lincoln, North Kesteven, South Holland, South Kesteven, West Lindsey. There are two unitary authorities, North Lincolnshire and North-East Lincolnshire, which rule themselves and have *no* links with the Lincolnshire County Council.

FAMOUS NAMES

- ◆ Margaret Thatcher, the longest-serving Prime Minister of the 20th century, was born at Grantham.
- ◆ John Wesley, founder of Methodism, was born at Epworth.
- ◆ The poet Alfred Lord Tennyson came from Somersby.
- ◆ Sir Isaac Newton formed the first local scientific society at Spalding and was born in Woolsthorpe.
- ◆ Daniel Lambert the heaviest man in the country died at Stamford weighing 739 pounds!

COUNTY CALENDAR

- ◆ Regular race meetings at Lincoln, where racing dates back nearly 400 years, and cricket on the Lindum.
- ◆ Mid-May: Festivals in the Fenland bulb fields in spring draw thousands of viewers. Spalding Flower Parade and Springsfield County Fair make up Britain's biggest and best flower festival with a stupendous flower parade.
- ◆ June: Lincolnshire Show in Scampton.
- ◆ September: Burghley Park horse trials.

MIDDLESEX

THE COUNTY LANDSCAPE

◆ One of the smallest counties – only 22 miles long by 14 in breadth and not more than about 90 square miles – but having the City of London (as well as Westminster) it is easily the most important and richest.

◆ It also takes in the greatest river in the country. The Thames starts its 215-mile journey from the Cotswolds and empties just beyond Middlesex between Kent and Essex. It waters the southern border with Surrey while the river Colne forms the western boundary with Buckinghamshire; and the River Lea divides the county from Essex in the east.

◆ Mainly flat, especially near the Thames, but higher ground lies to the north with the so-called northern heights reaching to 400 feet at Highgate. Fertile meadows and gardens have always been a feature of this county.

◆ The scenery is most appealing around the Colne Valley in the west while Harrow-on-the-Hill provides a notable viewpoint with the likes of Wembley Stadium and the ever-changing high rises along the Great West Road and Western Avenue.

COUNTY CALENDAR

◆ 16 May: Middlesex Day parades and events countywide. Commemorating the Middlesex regiment's famous battle against Napoleon in the Peninsular War when "the Diehards" held the French Army at bay.

◆ January to March: International Rugby at Twickenham.

◆ April to September: Middlesex County Cricket Club matches at Lord's, St.John's Wood and Uxbridge.

◆ 3rd weekend in June: Middlesex County Show at Middlesex County Showground, Uxbridge.

◆ All year round: Soccer internationals and cup finals at Wembley.

◆ October: Middlesex County Sports Awards Twickenham.

◆ May: Chelsea Flower Show.

◆ July: British Rose Festival Hampton Court

◆ April: The University Boat Race alongside the Middlesex and Surrey banks of the Thames

◆ August Bank Holiday: Notting Hill Carnival, a vibrant Caribbean celebration.

◆ 1st Wednesday after Whitsun: Pinner Fair.

◆ August: Harrow Show.

◆ September. Barnet Fair.

◆ May: Middlesex Rugby Sevens at Twickenham.

◆ Mid-June: The Fleadh Music Festival at Finsbury Park has a Celtic ring to it.

HARROW-ON-THE-HILL *St Mary's Church and the famous Harrow School.*

IF YOU BELIEVE in fairy tales then you'll believe in the wicked fable that Middlesex doesn't exist, that it's only a 'postal' county. As this is my home county we're talking about I naturally get very incensed about this fallacy. But of course it does exist and it is as real as any of the other 85 counties in this book, if not more so. By real I mean it never changes, it's been the same county since it was named 'the land of the Middle Saxons' way back in time. So let's dispel this myth once and for all as we explore this small but full-of-surprises county.

TOWNS AND VILLAGES

Harefield in the northwest border, where I was raised, is known the world over as the greatest heart hospital in the world. Once called 'the Switzerland of Middlesex' as the air was so pure it still retains its villagey identity with green and pond but it's the beautiful church of St Mary's surrounded by yew in a hidden dell that steals the honours. Take the road to Ickenham past the little hamlet of Newyear's Green through verdant Middlesex meadows and find the medieval church of St Giles with its unusual wooden spire opposite the original village pump. Not far away, the important town of Ruislip has St Martin's church the last resting place for radio's *Mrs Dale*, Jessie Matthews. Wood from the Middlesex woods round Ruislip was used for work on the Tower of London, Windsor Castle and Westminster Palace. Also close to Ruislip is the Polish war memorial by RAF Northolt where vanquished European nations sent their men to carry on the fight against tyranny from Middlesex airfields. Now Prime Ministers and diplomats take off to wage a different kind war in Europe.

The A40 takes you towards the historic Middlesex military town of Uxbridge, with its RAF base. During the Battle of Britain fighter squadrons for the hard-fought southeast were controlled from here. The RAF station is still very much at the heart of the town. It is Middlesex CCC's country venue and the centre for the County Show. Farther along there is the domesday village of Hillingdon, where I was born, with its greenclad church of St John the Baptist where my mum and dad were wed and I was christened. Perhaps of more genuine historic interest is nearby Swakeleys, a glorious H-shaped Jacobean mansion built between 1629 and 1638. Samuel Pepys visited Robert Vyner, a Lord Mayor of London, here in 1665.

Back on the Shepherds Bush Road just by Hayes, an early Saxon settlement, lies the lovely church of St Mary's. Along with Harefield's it was one of Sir John Betjeman's favourite Middlesex churches and here you can capture the atmosphere of olde worlde Middlesaxia. Further en route is Southall, still Middlesex's oldest thriving horse market, and now as much a bazaar for rice and spice as Asian immigrants from the 1950s have made it their home. At Hanwell, the first identity crisis confronts the visitor for postally Middlesex becomes a series of numbers – W7 starts here – but it is no less Middlesex for all its postal digits.

The 'ings' as in Ealing and other Middlesex place names are peculiarly frequent in this little county and mean the 'tribe of'; hence Ealing, Gilla's people. Ealing, the first-ever Middlesex borough, is known as the 'Queen of the Suburbs' with its modern shopping malls and evocative town hall. It was here that comic relief first began at the world-famous film studios just off the Broadway, where

COUNTY FACTS

Origin of name: From the Old English meaning the territory of the Middle Saxons (between Essex, Wessex and Sussex).

Name first recorded: 704 as Middleseaxan.

County Town:

BRENTFORD Important strategic position made it the centre of military and transport activity. Boston Manor house given by Elizabeth I to the Earl of Leicester. Brentford was never a seat of administration but the centre of polling in the county.

ACTON A one-time 18th-century spa town which went through a regeneration of the town centre in the 1990s. It saw Civil War activity.

BLACKWALL The most easterly village of Middlesex. From here the Virginia Settlers under Captain John Smith set sail in 1606 to found the first permanent colony in America.

BUSHY AND HAMPTON COURT PARK Bushy has a superb avenue of horse chestnut trees with sheep and deer. Hampton Court Park is adjacent to Cardinal Wolsey's Palace. The southern part is now a golf course but most well-known is its world-famous maze.

CAMDEN TOWN Populous town which Charles Dickens, who lived there as a boy, described in *Dombey and Son* as "frowsy fields, and cow-houses, and dunghills and dust-heaps". The one-time HQ for TVAM with its infamous Egg Cup house is now the studios for VH1 and MTV Europe.

CHARING CROSS Area known as the mapmaker's final destination as from here all mileage to and from London is arrived at. Originally a tiny hamlet called Charing, Edward I's wife Eleanor rested here on her way to Westminster Abbey. Where

WEMBLEY *The twin towers.*

GOLDHAWK ROAD W12 Pie 'n' eels 'n' mash floating in parsley sauce!

her coffin rested the king ordered a cross to be built.

CHISWICK The place to live if you're a beer-drinking media person! Fuller's brewery is based in the town as are many BBC workers. Chiswick House is an exceptional villa based on Palladio's Villa Rotunda in Vicenza. The Beatles shot some of *Help!* here. Hogarth's House, the artist's country retreat, is just round the corner.

CLERKENWELL Was the centre for the Justices of the Peace.

COLNBROOK: A village half in Buckinghamshire and half in Middlesex, called Ridsworth locally. The first ever Cox's Orange Pippin Apple was grown in Middlesex in 1845, at the hamlet of Poyle.

CRANFORD A Domesday village once called 'the prettiest village in Middlesex'. It now has one of the only two surviving cages in Middlesex which housed offenders overnight before their appearance in front of the magistrate. Cranford Park is a popular but somewhat desecrated beauty spot.

EDGWARE One of Middlesex's most important market towns with the first settlement on Brockley Hill just north of the modern town centre. The Romans named this settlement *Sulloniacae* on Watling Street. It was in AD978 that Edgware was first mentioned. Henry II confirmed a gift of land to the Priory of St Bartholomew's and then King John ordered that the Countess of Salisbury could keep the manor of Edgware on the death of the Earl.

EDMONTON An important Middlesex town and parish and centre of the Edmonton Hundred, an ancient division of Middlesex. The Bell was once a popular resort and it was here that John Gilpin by William Cowper took his wife on their wedding anniversary: 'Tomorrow is our wedding day, And we will then repair, Unto the Bell at Edmonton, All in a chaise and pair.' Charles and Mary Lamb lived at Bay Cottage, Church Street. John Keats served his apprenticeship to Thomas Hammond the surgeon also in Church Street.

FULHAM A fashionable Thameside town with Fulham Palace the one-time residence of the Bishops of London until 1973. The football club has attracted many famous names like Jimmy Hill and Tommy Trinder and just to rub it in Chelsea FC home at Stamford Bridge is actually in Fulham!

GOLDERS GREEN Theatrical town famous for its Hippodrome theatre and the Anna Pavlova Russian Ballet Festival at Ivy House. Its cemetery has seen Sir Henry Irving, WS Gilbert, Tommy Handley,

Sid James, Kenneth Williams et al 'carried on' famously. Now it's a centre for the BBC. In fact the BBC dominates this corner of Middlesex. Many of its employees who live in Ealing, Acton and Chiswick are picked up by buses from Uxbridge and spilled out at Shepherd's Bush Green – the end of the line – to pursue their careers in television at the studios on Wood Lane.

The Uxbridge Road takes you through the heart of west Middlesex towards Shepherd's Bush – Entertainment City. This colourful one-time hamlet of Middlesex described by historian Faulkner in 1839 as a 'pleasant village' is now a focal point for recreation. The BBC TV centre is in Wood Lane, the new centre for BBC 2 and Radio is next door at White City where the 1908 stadium once stood. The 1914 Market draws people from all over the world to sample its wares. The Bush Theatre is a major fringe company taking over the tradition of theatre in the town from the old Shepherd's Bush Empire. At the Bush take a break to savour a Middlesex delicacy at the Goldhawk Road end of the market – pie 'n' eels 'n'mash floating around in a green parsley sauce with the pie crust made from eel fat!

Think of any of what-you-might-call famous London place names and chances are they are part of Middlesex: how about Hammersmith or exclusive Holland Park – with its Jacobean mansion – Notting Hill, Bayswater and Marble Arch, the monument which stands where many a Middlesex ne'er-do-well was executed at Tyburn? Hyde Park is in Middlesex as well. Move off down Park Lane past the Duke of Wellington's Apsley House and you can see the rooftops of Buckingham Palace. Pass the monarch's home and carry on to Parliament Square, Westminster, where you will find the Middlesex Guildhall – where the county's government was dispensed until 1965 – opposite the Commons. The coat of arms and sculptures still bedazzle and bring a lump to the throat of all true Middlesaxons.

From Westminster and its fabulous Abbey it's all points east – the City and Docklands – still in Middlesex. Following the River Lea, the border with Essex, you pass Channel 4's *Big Breakfast* canal-side house and another television connection comes with Alexandra Palace where the first BBC broadcast was ever made in 1936, now the centre for many an antique fair.

Edgware was settled by the Romans at Brockley Hill and

was an important Middlesex town, being the last stopping place on ancient Watling Street for travellers from the city to the north. Nearby Finchley was the haunt of highwaymen and at Hendon the Welsh Harp marks the place where the only truly Middlesex river, the Brent, has its source. Close-by Wembley is both a Middlesex town and landmark famous all over the world for its stadium built for the British Empire Exhibition in 1924–25. First recorded in 825, it is an ancient Middlesex settlement. Arthur Lucan, known as Old Mother Riley, lived in the town. Look from one of the twin towers of Wembley, the home of English soccer, and you can see over to Hampstead; from the heath itself, one of the last vestiges of the great Middlesex forest, view St John's Wood and the home of Middlesex cricket at Lord's. Talking of high places, Harrow on the Hill with its world famous school is an imposing sight: here scholars like Byron, Churchill and Sheridan studied by the lake designed by Capability Brown.

The Great West Road, the industrial super highway of Middlesex and Britain, is flanked by imposing buildings adorned with many famous company names which are glimpsed as you speed past on the M4 flyover. This is one of the places where Britain became great. Isleworth is now where Sky Television beams its programmes to the world and the original picturesque village on the Thames is worth a visit and a pint. Osterley is a spacious and tranquil park with a delightful National Trust house. As you approach Hounslow watch out for Dick Turpin as this is where he yelled 'stand-and-deliver' to weary and wary travellers on the Great West Road.

Twickenham now beckons to the southwest, said by many to be the birthplace of Middlesex for it was here in 704 that a grant of land was made in 'Tuiccanham in the provincia of Middelseaxan' – the first time Middlesex was officially given a mention in dispatches. A famous Middlesex destination set on the Thames with some of the most beautiful parks and houses in the County: Marble Hill, York House, Strawberry

George Bernard Shaw, Kathleen Ferrier and TS Eliot pass on to a greater life.

HACKNEY Once the resort Londoners went to for fresh air, hence the name Hackney carriage after the trip by horse and cart from London to Hackney. In 1664 Pepys wrote in his diary on June 11th
"with my wife only to take ayre, it being very warm and pleasant . . . thence to Hackney. There light and played at shuffleboard, eat cream and good cherries; and so with good refreshment home."
Now said to be one of Britain's poorest boroughs.

HAMPSTEAD A Middlesex town set in what remains of the Great Middlesex Forest that has always housed the movers and shapers of society along with the great and the good. Queen Boudicca is said to have been buried on Hampstead Hill which is one of the highest points of the County. It is first mentioned by King Edgar in a charter of the 10th century and in the late 17th century Middlesex parliamentary elections were held on the heath. It still retains its separateness from the rest of the relentless metropolitan sprawl.

HANWORTH A small market gardening town with a manor and house Henry VIII used as a hunting lodge. He gave it to his second wife Anne Boleyn. The house was destroyed by fire in 1797. The food grown in the town farm was sold by William Whiteley at his store in Bayswater. Hanworth Airport opened in 1929 and played host to the Graf Zeppelin in 1932 before it closed in 1946.

HARROW Notable Middlesex town and borough famous for its school. First mentioned in a document of AD767 notifying a grant of land from King Offa of Mercia to the Bishop of St Albans. The Hill is a well known Middlesex landmark with the spire of the church of St Mary's soaring skywards and seen for many miles. Henry VIII used the King's Head pub as a hunting lodge and King Charles I watered his horses on the Hill before surrendering to the Scottish Army. The School was founded by John Lyon in 1572.

HEADSTONE A small village but with the only surviving moated manor house in Middlesex. It is said to go back to the 14th century. It now hosts the Harrow

***PERIVALE** The old Hoover factory on the Western Avenue – saved by Tesco!*

Show every year and is being groomed to become the Middlesex County museum.

HENDON A borough which was at the heart of aviation development. Hendon Aerodrome, opened in 1911, was world-famous. Along the western edge of the town motor car and other manufacturing industries developed. Is the centre of the Middlesex née Metropolitan Police training college.

HIGHGATE A genteel village where it is said Dick Whittington heard the message pealed out by Bow Bells: 'Turn again Whittington, Thrice Lord Mayor of London'.

HOUNSLOW Important Middlesex town and now borough. First mentioned as the place the Barons arranged a celebration after signing the Magna Carta at Runnymede. The heath has always been the haunt of highwaymen and soldiers on manoeuvres. Gibbets once lined the Bath Road to Staines.

KENSAL GREEN Small village well known for its cemetery. My own father's shop on the Harrow Road was where bodies were laid out ready for their trip to a greater life. Myth has it that King George V departed via my father's counter.

MILL HILL Well-to-do northern Middlesex town, home to three Lord Mayors of the City of London. At Highwood House lived Sir Stamford Raffles and Celia Fiennes the original 'fine lady on a white horse' from nursery rhyme times. Mill Hill School is one of the finest schools in the country.

MILLWALL One of the most easterly towns in Middlesex so named due to the windmills that stood on the marsh wall on the Isle of Dogs. Brunel built and launched his *Great Eastern* from here in 1859. Millwall dock was closed in 1980. Now more famous for its football club which is situated over the River Thames in Kent and home to the many national newspapers which moved from Fleet Street to the Isle of Dogs in recent times. Newest landmark is the enormous Canary Wharf.

NEASDEN Home to the most spectacular Hindu temple in the western world and the favourite haunt of readers of satirical publication *Private Eye*.

PARK ROYAL Long before Stoneleigh in Warwickshire this area of Middlesex was prepared to be the permanent showground of the Royal Agricultural Society but was unsuccessful. It is now said to be the biggest storage estate in Britain.

PERIVALE Famous for the stunning example of Art Deco in the Hoover building adjacent the A40, said to be Queen Elizabeth II's favourite building.

PICCADILLY Famous street of Westminster. Named after a successful tailor in the Strand had made a fortune out of stiff collars called 'picadils' invested his money in the lands to the north of what is now Piccadilly Circus famous for its statue of Eros, the god of love.

PINNER A popular Middlesex village granted a charter in 1336 by Henry III to John, Archbishop of Canterbury to hold a weekly market and two fairs a year, one of which is still held on the first Wednesday following Whitsun.

POPLAR Originally a fishing village in east Middlesex where the sails were made for Henry VIII's ship, *Henri Grace Dieu*. One of the centres of socialism with Poplar councillors being imprisoned in the 1921 rates dispute leading to the equalization between

Hill and Orleans House. Eel Pie Island is here and features in Charles Dickens's *Nicholas Nickleby*. Kneller Hall is the Military Music school and of course this Middlesex town is synonymous with the game of Rugby Union the world over. Farther along is Sunbury and the Thames which is at its prettiest here as it reaches up from Hampton Court. Who can resist this palace where so much of our history and heritage has been enacted since Cardinal Wolsey and Henry VIII came to a bargain for this illustrious building?

Adjacent to the palace is dreamy Hampton village and along the Sunbury road is Kempton Park, another major Middlesex and national sporting venue. Soon you're in Shepperton with its quaint village centred around the church of St Nicholas. Head to the famous film studios which are actually in Littleton; many a Hollywood star slips out to the shops at Shepperton. Ashford is close to my heart as it's the place since 1996 I am privileged to represent in my official title as 'The Lord of Ashford, Middlesex'.

Staines pocketed in the southwest of the county close to the Buckinghamshire border is a classic Middlesex market town and its Victorian Town Hall is sumptuous architecture. From Staines you're not far from Heathrow as the planes overhead will vouch: Heathrow, once a tiny hamlet bordering Hounslow Heath and now the first glimpse most overseas visitors have of Britain . . . and this is all still in Middlesex. The little villages of Sipson, Longford and Harmondsworth, with its 14th-century Tithe Barn, continues the tradition of real Middlesexness in the middle of international hustle and bustle. North of here is West Drayton, a brewery town for Middlesex Gold beer.

Now hop on the M25 to South Mimms, the most northerly parish in the county, and see where motorway services rub shoulders with the splendid 13th-century church of St Giles where members of my family are at rest. Then on to Potters Bar, the most northerly town of Middlesex, which started life as a small hamlet, possibly as one of the gates or entrances to Enfield Chase. In 1916 a German Zeppelin struck an oak tree and fell in flames. The Football Association has one of its main offices in the town.

LOCAL HISTORY

As the name suggests, Middlesex is caught between Essex, Sussex and Wessex – the various Saxon kingdoms. Though never thought to have been a separate kingdom and more likely to have been a part of the kingdom of the East Saxons, the County was much bigger in territory taking in a large part of Hertfordshire, possibly the region below the River Colne. Surrey is said to have derived from old English for a 'South region', possibly of Middlesex.

So much British history has been acted out on the stage of Middlesex towns and palaces, so many kings and queens have lived and died in Middlesex in her great houses. Her many Saxon churches are a lasting testament to her past; battles that turned the tide of English power have been fought on Middlesex earth. An obelisk to mark the Battle of Barnet in 1471 in the War of the Roses stands in the pretty hamlet of Hadley Green. The decisive battle was actually fought in South Mimms at Gladmore Heath. Barnet itself stands at the crossroads of history. Half in Middlesex and half in Hertfordshire, it was conferred a charter by King John and is known as Chipping Barnet. Elizabeth I was a regular traveller via the town on her way to Hatfield House and Charles I escaped via Barnet to Oxford in the Civil War. Barnet's cattle and horse market was granted by Elizabeth I in 1588 and she founded the Free Grammar School in 1573.

London, of course, oozes history both grand and trivial, but a few choice items are worth recounting. It was known by the Romans as Londinium but also for a brief time, as Augusta. Middlesex and London have always been inseparable. To be a true Londoner you must be born in the City's square mile and the sound of Bow Bells must be heard ringing at your birth – Bow is a parish of east Middlesex. Born without the bells and not in the City and you are from Middlesex, Surrey, Kent or Essex!

Some nice historical twists include Brown's Hotel in Dover Street. Franklin and Eleanor Roosevelt honeymooned here in 1905, King George II of Greece was in exile, and in Room 36 Holland declared war on Japan in World War II. Cecil Rhodes and Rudyard Kipling were among its many patrons. Nearby 17 Bruton Street off Berkeley Square, Mayfair (now demolished) was where Queen Elizabeth II was born. Sheridan, Prime Minister Canning and Norman Hartnell are some of its famous residents.

Nearby to Wembley is the tiny hamlet of Preston which was the 1908 Olympic Games clay pigeon shoot ground at Uxendon Farm, and, in 1586, Anthony Babbington was sheltered by the Bellamy family after his plot to assassinate Queen Elizabeth was discovered.

And then there is Enfield and Hampton Court: Enfield is a Middlesex town and borough to the far north of the county. It existed long before the Domesday survey, in fact by Norman times it was already a village of note. Henry VII's minister and speaker of the House of Commons Sir Thomas Lovell lived here with over a 100 servants at Elsyng House; Mary Tudor and Elizabeth I spent much of their childhoods here. In 1815 a small arms factory was

LORD'S CRICKET GROUND Old Father time on top of the stands.

richer and poorer boroughs. In World War II around half of the town was damaged in the Blitz.

ROXETH Hamlet near Harrow. Due to the name South Harrow being given to the station without thought or sensitivity to the local area, much of the current village's identity has been smothered. A careless error considering the site of the ancient moated manor is said to be where King Stephen stayed during the war with Matilda. Remember in future where you read South Harrow, read also Roxeth.

ST PANCRAS Middlesex town and one-time borough named after its church of the saint who, according to legend, was martyred by Diocletian when only 14. The old church has a Saxon altar dating from 600 AD and a chancel which was rebuilt in 1350. Famous for its station with its 55-ton ribs that spanned 240 feet and 100 feet above the rails said to be one of the wonders of the Victorian engineering world.

ST PAUL'S CATHEDRAL: With its world-famous dome its outline is as instantly recognizable as Big Ben. This is the fourth cathedral to be built on the site where there was once a Roman Temple dedicated to Diana.

SOHO A cosmopolitan district with its own unique flavour, funny to think it was a farming and hunting area; So-ho was once a familiar ancient hunting cry. Charles II's illegimate son, the Duke of Monmouth, lived here along with Anna Clerke, a lewd woman who was bound over to keep the peace. In the permissive '60s the Soho Society was formed to keep a check on the expansion of sex and corruption.

STAINES The Roman Pontes, Staines guarded the River Thames en route to London as it the present day guardian of Middlesex when crossing from Surrey. A pleasant and important Middlesex market town with a cosy 1950s feel but with much modern shopping. The London Stone which rests in Staines has since 1285 marked the limit of the City of London authority over the River Thames. The largest Linoleum works in the world was situated here.

STANMORE Great and Little Stanmore were originally the southern haunt of the Celtic Catuvellauni tribe and it was they who fought against Julius Caesar in 54BC, commemorated by an obelisk in 1754 which stands in the Royal National Orthopaedic Hospital. It is also said that Boudicca was defeated on Stanmore Common after her bloody uprising with a place in Lime's House known traditionally as her grave. Daniel Defoe said in 1720 "a great many very beautiful seats of the nobility and gentry" are in this part of Middlesex like Canons and Bentley Priory. In 1814 the Prince Regent met with Louis XVIII of France at the Abercorn Arms and in the village the finest group of Middlesex 16th-century jettied cottages have to be seen to be believed.

STOKE NEWINGTON An ancient Saxon village on the great Roman thoroughfare of Ermine Street. Home to Daniel Defoe was 95 Church Street, and the area still contains many and varied 18th-century buildings.

TOTTENHAM A Middlesex town and former borough originally in the Domesday Book. Henry VIII hunted here and at Bruce Castle he met his sister Margaret of Scotland in 1516. Known as one of the most prosperous towns of Middlesex in 1600 with notables such as Izaak Walton coming to fish here. However, by the 1840s conditions had deterioated and in 1894 Tottenham was "the most populous town in Middlesex". Now it is the home to the internationally renowned football club the Hotspurs.

TURNHAM GREEN A hamlet between Acton and Chiswick where a crucial battle of the Civil War was fought in 1642. EM Forster lived in the village.

UXBRIDGE The Saxon tribe called the Wixan's gives this major Middlesex town its name although it wasn't until the end of the 12th century it became a major market town and centre for the area; by 1600 it was the principal corn market for west Middlesex and south Bucks. In the Civil War Cromwell established a Roundhead garrison here and in 1645 in the Treaty House right on the river Colne an attempt at peace was made, to no avail. Prosperity continued in the 19th century with the Grand Junction Canal and Great Western Railway all adding to the town's importance. It is the end of the Metropolitan and Piccadilly Lines on the Underground.

WESTMINSTER The main city of Middlesex and due to Edward the Confessor moving his place of residence from the city upstream to the Abbey it was destined to became the centre of government for the UK. Its Abbey is the resting place of the powerful and famous of the nation. It was here William Caxton rented space in the city where he set up the first printing press in England. It wasn't until 1900 that Westminster became a city. Middlesex Guildhall opposite the House of Commons was the centre of county administration until 1965.

***STRAND ON THE GREEN** A pint in the pub in a Middlesex hamlet by the Thames.*

opened, hence the Enfield rifle. Enfield became the centre of the electronics industry at Ponders End in 1880 and Brimsdown in 1903. On the main road to Cambridge, Enfield was always an important Middlesex place, so much industry came in the 1920s. John Keats went to school here and Capel Manor has a rose garden to Bill Bossom, creator of the pretty peach and pink Middlesex County rose. Enfield Chase was a very popular hunting ground for royals and nobles and some of it remains as the glorious Trent Park, now home to Middlesex University. Also in Enfield, it was reputedly at Whitewebbs House that Guy Fawkes and his cronies conspired to blow up Parliament.

Moving south, stop at Chiswick for its exquisite House, a 17th-century villa of distinction, and while you're in town don't forget William Hogarth's house – his 'little country box beside the Thames'.

Hampton Court, one of the shining diamonds in Middlesex's crown, displays some of the finest Tudor architecture in Britain. Cardinal Wolsey bought the site in 1514 and presented it to his envious sovereign King Henry VIII in an attempt to regain favour. The famous zodiac clock was designed in 1540 by Nicholas Oursian. Henry bought five of his six wives to live in the palace, his son King Edward VI spent most of his short life in Hampton Court, and it was here his half-sister Mary received her marriage proposal from Philip of Spain. Elizabeth I lived here in 1559, and kings and queens all made their mark on the palace until Queen Victoria declared it open to the public. In 1986 a fire swept through the palace destroying the south wing of Fountain Court. It is here (and at the Tower of London, she gets around!) that Queen Anne Boleyn is said to walk in ghostly fashion with 'her head tucked underneath her arm'.

For superb country houses Syon House is hard to beat. Since 1594 this has been home to the Percys, the dukes of Northumberland. Originally a Bridgettine monastery founded in 1415 at Twickenham by Henry V, it was moved in 1431 up the Thames to Isleworth. Henry VIII took hold of it in the Reformation and imprisoned his fifth wife Catherine Howard here before her execution in 1542. Syon played its part in British history for it was here that Lady Jane Grey was offered the Crown and began her ill-fated nine days' reign. Inigo Jones was asked to make repairs in 1632, and in 1646 Charles I sent his three children to Syon to escape the plague. Charles II visited the House with John Evelyn in the 1660s.

TOWER BRIDGE *Its twin towers have been Middlesex landmarks for over a century.*

Whitehall lies within the county also. It was at Whitehall Palace that Henry VIII celebrated his marriages to Anne Boleyn and Jane Seymour and it was where he died in 1547. King Charles was beheaded here and Oliver Cromwell governed Britain from Whitehall Palace and died here in 1658. At the Restoration of Charles II, the monarchy returned to Whitehall and the last royal event was when William and Mary were offered the British crown before transferring their court to Kensington Palace. Whitehall is now the centre for many ministries of government.

Another of the county's famous royal residences of course is Buckingham Palace, commissioned by King George IV to replace Buckingham House in St James's. But he never lived to see its completion by architect John Nash. The first monarch to live there was Queen Victoria. And how about Heston once so famous for its wheat that Queen Elizabeth I had her bread made from Middlesex flour ground here, and it was at Heston airport that Neville Chamberlain landed to wave his paper with the so-called Munich agreement with Hitler.

So, though today you might only see the monotony of suburbia remember that just a hundred years ago this was a green and pleasant land and still is, for there are traces in certain places of the old green Middlesex rightly called the 'capital county' bursting with memories and memorials to the history of not just a county but a whole nation too.

WHITECHAPEL A Middlesex village that could be said to have been the first suburb of London. Its chapel was built in the 13th century. Being the first place you reached from the City out on the road to the east it was full of every aspect of life. Metalwork was its main industry with the Whitechapel Bell Foundry and the Gunmakers Company Proof House still going strong. Foreign immigrants have settled in scores from 17th century onwards, and this was seized upon by Sir Oswald Mosley during the war when the Fascists tried to stir up racism, most notoriously at the Battle of Cable Street.

County Rivers: Thames, Brent, Crane, Lea and Colne.

Highest point: High Road, Bushey Heath at 504 feet.

Middlesex's local government: The County of Middlesex's local government needs a lot of understanding! The County is administered mostly by large unitary Boroughs: Brent, Camden, Ealing, Enfield, Hackney, Hammersmith & Fulham, Haringey, Harrow, Hillingdon, Hounslow, Islington, Kensington & Chelsea, Tower Hamlets, City of Westminster. Richmond-upon-Thames is shared with Surrey and Barnet shared with Hertfordshire. Spelthorne and South Mimms with Potters Bar are the only parts of Middlesex under a two-tier structure – Surrey County and Spelthorne Borough Councils for the former and Herts County and Hertsmere District Councils for the latter. The Middlesex village of Poyle and Ridsworth, the Colnbrook side of Middlesex are under the unitary district council of Slough.

◆ The City of London is geographically in the County of Middlesex but has always administered itself through its own Corporation of elected Aldermen and Lord Mayor.

NORFOLK

THE COUNTY LANDSCAPE

◆ "Very flat, Norfolk" is the terse comment awarded to this large county in East Anglia by Noel Coward in his play *Private Lives,* but in fact the land rises steadily from east to west, with an abrupt fall to the fenland bordering Cambridgeshire and Lincolnshire, while reaching its highest point (and that's only a few hundred feet) at Roman Camp at Sheringham.

◆ East of Norwich are the shallow waters of the Norfolk Broads, which resulted from medieval digging for peat.

FAMOUS NAMES

◆ The county's most famous son, Lord Horatio Nelson, was born in the rectory at Burnham Thorpe.

◆ Fanny Burney was born at nearby King's Lynn six years earlier in 1752.

◆ Anna Sewell, author of *Black Beauty*, was born in Great Yarmouth.

◆ Anne Boleyn's childhood home was at Blickling Hall, and the red-brick Jacobean building is said to be haunted by her ghost.

◆ The 17th-century Melton Constable Hall, now divided into several homes, was the setting for the film *The Go-Between*, with other scenes filmed at Norwich's Thorpe Station.

◆ Sandringham contains the country home of the Queen and is the birthplace of Diana, Princess of Wales.

COUNTY CALENDAR

◆ 1st Sunday in August: Blessing of the Broads amid the ruins of St Benet's Abbey at Horning.

◆ Whit Monday: Cromer Fair.

◆ July: lively street carnival in Cromer.

◆ Easter & Christmas: Norwich Fairs.

◆ 4th week in May: Norwich Carnival and Lord Mayor's Procession.

◆ 4th week in June: Royal Norfolk Show at New Costessey.

◆ July: Cottage Horticultural Society Flower Show at Sandringham Estate.

◆ 1st week in September: English Bowling Association Men's Open Tournament at Great Yarmouth.

◆ August: Regatta Week at Oulton Broad.

◆ August: Heacham Lavender Harvest, introduced by the Romans and now the centre of the lavender industry.

◆ Christmas Day: Sponsored Swim at Hunstanton.

CLEY-NEXT-THE-SEA *The windmill stands guard over great expanses of marsh.*

DRIVE UP THE A11, past expansive Thetford, and the minute you reach Norwich the change is quite dramatic. Norwich is one of the most beautiful cities in the whole of the kingdom. Absolutely enchanting. And its county of Norfolk is pure nostalgia – you feel miles and miles away . . . miles from anywhere, in a sense isolated as you sit out on England's eastern edge, but the ambience leaves you at peace and at one with the world.

TOWNS AND VILLAGES

One of the five largest cities in Norman England, the county and university town of Norwich grew out of a Saxon settlement set in a sweeping bend on the Wensum river, and still displays evidence of its important role in history from the Middle Ages through to the Industrial Revolution. Its heart is dominated by the magnificent Norman castle and cathedral, the colourful central market and the soaring 200-foot clock tower of the imposing 1930s City Hall. Local residents claim their city boasts a different church for each week of the year and a pub for every day, and each new vista appears to confirm it (although some of the churches now have a more secular purpose). Lately an important centre for corn, livestock, insurance, mustard and shoe manufacture, Norwich had 30,000 weavers in the 18th century when its textile industry was at its height.

The export of woollen goods was also a major factor in the growth of King's Lynn during the 17th century, when it was the third major port in England. This charming town on the northeast coast has been largely rebuilt since the 1950s, but some of its former strong trading links with the Hanseatic empire are reflected in the architecture of the buildings surrounding the two market places and the country's oldest surviving guildhall, built in 1420.

The nearby Victorian resorts of Cromer and Sheringham no longer attract vast numbers of tourists, but midway round the coast, Great Yarmouth has kept its popularity, although the huge herring fleets and their associated industries, which gave us the renowned smoked 'Yarmouth Bloater', finally petered out in the 1930s, to be replaced by support facilities for the off-shore oil rigs and their workers.

Inland, tourism and agriculture still bring a measure of prosperity to small country towns like Attleborough and Downham Market and to the boating centres of Wroxham, Ranworth, Potter Heigham and Horning on the Norfolk Broads which cater for visitors on the 10,000 craft negotiating these lovely navigable waterways.

LOCAL HISTORY

In ancient times Stone Age people extracted flints from over 300 pits at Grimes Graves in the Breckland. The site became the centre for 'knapping' – breaking flints – an industry that continues to this day next door in Brandon, Suffolk. Later the region was dominated by the Iceni, the tribe led by Queen Boudicca, who unsuccessfully led her people against the Romans.

Christianity was brought to East Anglia by St Felix in AD617, and by the time of the Domesday Book the region was the most heavily populated in Norman England. King John, travelling from Newark to King's Lynn shortly before his death in 1216, lost his baggage train and most of the contents of the royal exchequer while crossing the Wash.

Economic grievances in 1549 led to Kett's Rebellion, with some 20,000 discontented rebels led by Robert and William Kett of Wymondham (pronounced Windham) marching on London. However, the uprising was defeated and its ringleaders executed.

During the Civil War much of the county supported the new parliament, but King's Lynn remained loyal to the crown, and Norwich was one of the first places to welcome King Charles II after the Restoration.

COUNTY FACTS

Origin of name: Anglo-Saxon origin, meaning "the place of the North folk".

Name first recorded: 1043.

County Town: NORWICH

A medieval treasure house, excellent museums – Bridewell, once a prison, houses rural crafts – tea rooms and theatre, and the perfect base to explore the surrounding countryside.

Other towns:

BLAKENEY Attracts yachtsmen and women and has a lively quayside scene.

CLEY-NEXT-THE-SEA Is actually inland from the sea. It has a fabulous windmill dating from 1713.

CROMER A classic Norfolk holiday town with a memorable end-of-pier show.

DOWNHAM MARKET Small market town awash with pubs and inns.

EAST DEREHAM Is in poultry-rearing country and supplies some of the finest turkeys and geese for the Christmas market (Norfolk turkeys rings a bell?).

GREAT WITCHINGHAM Norfolk Wildlife Park founded by Philip Wayre in the grounds of his home.

GREAT YARMOUTH Great rival to Lowestoft over the Suffolk border. Don't miss the Britannia Pier.

KINGS LYNN Once called Bishops' Lynn, the town got its royal accolade because Henry VIII confiscated the bishops' land. St George's Guildhall houses a fascinating history of the town.

SWAFFHAM The lavish church in this market town is said to have been paid for by the so-called Pedlar of Swaffham (John Clapham) who, according to folklore, met a man who told him of a dream in which a treasure had been found in the Pedlar's garden. The Pedlar went home and found riches just as he had been told and built the north side of the church.

THETFORD Once the most important cathedral city in East Anglia. The priory's remains are still worth investigation. The Ancient House Museum shows off flint-knapping: shaping tiny flints for use as firearms. It was the capital of the Saxon kingdom of East Anglia.

WELLS-NEXT-THE-SEA A must for wildlife enthusiasts and walkers. Much of the land is National Trust property and there are seal colonies to see as well as plenty of rare waders.

◆ Attleborough ◆ Diss ◆ Fakenham
◆ Hunstanton ◆ North Walsham ◆ Wymondham

Main rivers: Bure, Yare, Tas, Thet, Waveney, Little Ouse, Wissey, Nat, Ouse, Wensum, Burn, Stiffkey, Chet, Ant.

Highest point: Roman Camp at Sheringham at 336 feet.

Norfolk's local government: The County of Norfolk has a two-tier local government system: Norfolk County Council and the seven district councils of Breckland, Broadland, Great Yarmouth, King's Lynn & West Norfolk, North Norfolk, Norwich and South Norfolk.

NORTHAMPTONSHIRE

THE COUNTY LANDSCAPE

◆ This key county in the East Midlands is located between seven other counties. Geographically the county was favoured after the Norman Conquest as it lay between York and Winchester, then the capital, and half-way between the Welsh border and the east coast. It's fairly easy to traverse, being low-lying country.

◆ When trade was by river the slow and wide waterways of the north part of the county proved useful for barge and boat traffic. Close to the flatlands of Cambridgeshire the land is particularly low and marshy and is known as the Bedford Level.

◆ Getting hillier the land rises from the flat northeast towards Towcester in the south, while the western part of the county encompasses a range of chalk uplands, an extension of the Oxfordshire Cotswolds. Here the towns and villages are stone built and architecture adds much charm to the softly undulating landscape. Very little is cultivated except a few fertile glens and coastal strips, and it is very sparsely populated (except by deer).

FOTHERINGHAY *The church of St Mary and All Saints was a gift from Edward IV.*

BEING VERY FOND of Tudor history I have a soft spot for this county, for Fotheringhay Castle once stood here and in its grounds Mary, Queen of Scots was beheaded. History also resounds in the names of Naseby and Rockingham Castle in this county where countless feet have trudged to the march of time. And shoes – along with agriculture, engineering and paper making – have been a long-term industry here. With traditional footwear from Church's to more mod docs – Dr Marten's – Northants retains its place with plenty of sole! The Central Museum has, appropriately, a large collection of footwear with a section showing the ballet shoes of great dancers from Nijinsky to Ulanova and Fonteyn. Less arcane is the famous Ilchester Hoard of 42,000 ancient coins (mostly of the 3rd century AD) and other local archaeological finds.

WOLLASTON *Griggs' Dr. Marten's factory..*

TOWNS AND VILLAGES

Northampton is the county town and was admired by Daniel Defoe, author of *Robinson Crusoe*. The county seat lost its centre in 1675 when a huge fire destroyed over 600 buildings. However, it is rich in churches and there are several of particular note – one being the central All Saints, a large Norman church with a cupola on its tower, original doorways and a wealth of carving within, while another Norman church of 1110, the Holy Sepulchre, is a rare survival, one of the few round churches in the country of that period. The town hall is a flamboyant Venetian Gothic building with a clock tower and plenty of statuary for perching pigeons. Its lavish sculptured groups show local history scenes.

On the approach to the London Road is a rare survival of an Eleanor Cross (though there is another in the county at Geddington between Kettering and the steel town of Corby). Queen Eleanor, wife of Edward I, died at Harby in Nottinghamshire; and wherever her body rested on its way to burial at Westminster the grieving king erected a cross. Best known is Charing Cross, but it is a Victorian copy – the cross in Northampton is a 13th-century original.

Peterborough is a large conurbation and an important rail link with London. Its cathedral is a great ecclesiastical building in a town now nearly all modernized. It's so little visited however that when the TV *Barchester Towers* was being filmed they used it and its surroundings in preference to Salisbury Cathedral, which has far more visitors. 'A wonderful building,' said Nigel Hawthorne, a member of the cast of the memorable Trollope adaptation. 'It has all the atmosphere and rare beauty you could ask for, and it is often blissfully empty.' The cathedral has an unforgettable facade of three great arches and a central porch, set up as a screen wall before the original Norman front. Tiers of satisfyingly simple round headed stone arches march down the nave beneath a fabulous flat wooden roof, brightly gilded and painted with portraits of saints in its rich pattern of diamonds.

Few of the domestic buildings of the one-time abbey survive, though the abbot's lodgings and several gateways are still there. The cloister walks are gone. The building is set on a wide greensward and is a most impressive sight, especially when floodlit. Mary, Queen of Scots was buried here until her son, James I, removed the body to Westminster Abbey where she lies near her formidable rival, Queen Elizabeth I.

Nearby Oundle is home to famous Oundle Public School. This town is all built of local stone and has a fine mellow appearance. Boughton House, north of Kettering, has been called a Sleeping Beauty, a chateau of the fabled times of Louis XIV transplanted to England in the 17th century. The seat of the Duke of Buccleuch it originated with the 3rd Lord Montagu who was ambassador to France during the Sun King's brightest years and he imported French

COUNTY FACTS

Origin of name: Comes from the Old English North Hamtune meaning northern home town or farm.

Name first recorded: 1011 as Hamtunscir.

County Town:

NORTHAMPTON An ever-expanding, vibrant 'new' town with a long history – it's probably been around since the ancient Brits but does not appear on record until Saxon times. The old town hall dates from 1671. Long before Margaret Thatcher the original poll tax was enacted at a parliament held here in 1380, which led to Wat Tyler's rebellion. In 1459 at the Battle of Northampton Richard Neville, Earl of Warwick, defeated Henry VI.

Other Towns:

BRACKLEY A lovely little town, once a wool centre, with a high street over a mile long flanked by trees. Bartering on the Magna Carta took place at a castle here (no longer standing).

BRIXWORTH A 7th-century Anglo-Saxon church. One of the best of its kind, it was made from abandoned local Roman buildings and included Roman tiles in the arches. A hunting centre also.

CORBY Great iron and steel capital. The workers poured in from Scotland so you could go round the town and never meet an English accent.

DAVENTRY In typical rolling county countryside, this was once a centre for whip making. Automobile works and light engineering took over. Charles I spent several nights here in the Wheatsheaf before the battle of Naseby.

EARLS BARTON One of the finest Anglo-Saxon towers in England is on the Church of All Saints and is decorated with pilasters.

EYE This overgrown village was built on an island before the Fens were drained. A brickmaking centre with an imposing 80-foot windmill well seen from the surrounding flat countryside.

IRTHLINGBOROUGH This small historic town with the remains of a college founded by Edward III is the envy of many big-league sports clubs with its excellent stadium at Nene Park housing Rushden & Diamonds Football Club.

KETTERING A footwear centre with its own Boot and Shoe College.

KINGS CLIFFE Beautiful little village with a 17th-century almshouse, and church with Norman tower and 13th-century spire.

OUNDLE Narrow streets and alleys with tiny cottages and stone-built houses of great character. The church spire rises 280 feet.

RUSHDEN Another Northants shoe town, with a manor that belongs to the sovereign and a beautiful church with a 200-foot spire. Its go-ahead football club plays at Irthlingborough.

PETERBOROUGH "Only one hour from London" as the ads used to say and certainly a thriving new town element with an ancient city to be discovered.

SILVERSTONE This little village in the far south of the county is the magnet for racing men – and women –

all over the world as the venue for the British Grand Prix.

TOWCESTER Once a coaching stop now a race meeting venue. Several old inns including the Saracen's Head featured in Dickens's *Pickwick Papers*. At nearby Weedon Lois, Dame Edith Sitwell is buried with a monument designed by Henry Moore.

WELLINGBOROUGH On the meeting of the Ise and Nene rivers a once old market centre now serves many growing light industries including footwear and clothing.

◆ Bozeat ◆ Brigstock ◆ Broughton ◆ Bugbrooke ◆ Burton Latimer ◆ Desborough ◆ Duston ◆ Finedon ◆ Higham Ferrers ◆ Long Buckby ◆ Middleton Cheney ◆ Moulton ◆ Raunds ◆ Roade ◆Rothwell ◆ Thrapston ◆ Werrington ◆ Wittering ◆ Wollaston ◆ Woodford

County rivers: Nene, Welland, Avon, Swift.

Highest point: Arbury Hill at 734 feet.

Northamptonshire's local government: All of the County of Northamptonshire apart from Peterborough has two tiers of local government service providers: Northamptonshire County Council and seven district councils of Corby, Daventry, East Northamptonshire, Kettering, Northampton, South Northamptonshire, Wellingborough. The City and Soke of Peterborough has its own unitary council.

craftsmen and painters to decorate his mansion. The panelled rooms have splendid French pieces as well as extraordinary late Stuart furnishings. All the boulle, marquetry, gilded gesso and laquerwork cabinets are framed by Mortlake tapestries and Italian paintings, while the floors (he was the first person to import the new Versailles parquet) have fabulous Persian carpets and early English copies. The one-time monastery is recalled now only with the name of the central Fish Court, which monks once stocked with fish for fast-days. The grounds with water gardens, lakes, and broad tree-lined avenues surrounding the house are suitably palatial.

Southwest of Peterborough the county is dotted with important churches – from the Perpendicular St Leonard's at Apethorpe with a massive tomb within, to St Peter's, a church at Great Weldon that is a 'land lighthouse' with an octagonal lantern instead of a spire, a Victorian restoration at Deene and a college church at Fotheringhay. Here Mary, Queen of Scots, after long imprisonment by her cousin Queen Elizabeth, met her sad end by being decapitated at Fotheringhay Castle in 1584.

Kirby Hall off the A43 is a stone-built Elizabethan hall surrounded by gardens currently being restored. Deene Park – a turreted mansion and another of the county's many stately homes – has a racy history. The house has been the home of the Brudenells since Tudor times and the 7th Earl of Cardigan, a choleric, obstinate man, entertained Queen Victoria and her family here to recount his exploits during the Crimean War. (He led the Charge of the Light Brigade at Balaclava.) Later, moral Victoria was upset at Cardigan's open liaison with one Adeline de Horsey – even though he married his mistress after the death of his wife in 1858 – and by royal order the commemorative picture of the Crimea had the queen painted out.

Adeline was a game old girl – after ten years of marriage the earl left her a widow, so she took to other affairs, and eccentric preoccupations such as dressing in a bizarre fashion, cycle riding and eventually, before her death at 91, sporting a blonde wig.

In the northwest lies Naseby battlefield, where the Civil War was effectively ended when Charles I was decisively beaten by Cromwell's New Model Army in 1645. A museum on the site shows models of the battle as well as a collection of vintage farm implements.

NASEBY *A stone column marks the field of the Battle of Naseby, 1645.*

The last stand of the Commonwealth came at Staverton Field near Daventry in the west of the county, when Cromwell's generals were defeated and the monarchy restored.

Nearby Lamport Hall is famous in a county rich in large houses for here the Ishams can claim to be Northampton's oldest landed family, having lived here for four centuries. Designed as a miniature palace by John Webb, a son-in-law of the great Inigo Jones (gardens at Stoke Park south of Northampton are framed with a colonnade and pavilions by Jones), its cool classicism was given a jolt in the High Room when this large chamber was redone with exotic 18th-century plasterwork. One of Sir Charles Isham's famous garden gnomes, made in Nuremburg, can be seen in the house. Southwest is Edgecote House with rococo interiors.

Althorp, west of the county town, has many treasures, not least the pictures that line its long gallery. In the late 18th century Henry Holland, then working on projects for Brighton Pavilion for the Prince of Wales, was brought in and he transformed the house. His walls were removed in the late 1940s, revealing 17th-century panelling. Perhaps the most famous of all the house's many art treasures is the fabled porcelain collection, removed from Spencer House.

LOCAL HISTORY

Peterborough's cathedral began as a Benedictine abbey church and when Peterborough was made a city in 1541, it was given cathedral status as part of Henry VIII's great Tudor privatization plan, the Dissolution of the monasteries. Its site dates from AD655 when the first monastery was built, the present church being commenced in 1118. Built with pale Barnack stone, it is a rare and complete example of the severe Romanesque style.

Houses designed on plans symbolic of the Trinity and Catholicism are one of those odd English things, and Northamptonshire has two, both of them built by Sir Thomas Tresham. One is on the Rushton Hall estate, symbolizing the Trinity, and dates from 1593. Everything is in threes – even the Latin quotations on its frieze are of 33 letters. The triangular lodge, which can't have been a very comfortable place to inhabit, was occupied by Sir Thomas's gamekeeper.

The house that Sir Thomas planned at Lyveden New Bield not far away, this time in cross shape to symbolize the Passion, was started in 1600. However, it was never finished as Sir Thomas's family were caught up in the Gunpowder Plot.

PETERBOROUGH *The cathedral's wooden ceiling.*

FAMOUS NAMES

- ◆ The great poet John Dryden was born in the county and lived at Titchmarsh. The 'Northamptonshire poet' John Clare was born in Helpston, lived most of his life in the county, and published a book of country poems in 1820.
- ◆ George Washington never knew Northampton as he was born in the fledgling USA but his ancestor Lawrence Washington built the ancestral home Sulgrave Manor in 1560 and like Washington Old Hall in Durham it is allowed to fly the stars and stripes.
- ◆ Princess Diana, born a Spencer, spent her girlhood at the stately home of Althorp, the family's home since 1508.
- ◆ Thomas Becket, the martyred Archbishop of Canterbury, was tried at Northampton Castle in 1164.
- ◆ Sir Charles Isham created one of the earliest rockeries in England at Lamport – and dotted it with goblins and elves – the very first garden gnomes to be seen in Britain.

COUNTY CALENDAR

- ◆ July: Organ week at Oundle.
- ◆ Most weekends of the motor racing season: motor racing at Silverstone Circuit, near Towcester. In recent years it has hosted the British Grand Prix.
- ◆ Chestnuts mature in midsummer and Conker championships are held at Kettering.
- ◆ August: Hot-air balloon festival held at Northampton racecourse. Over 200,000 people gather to watch 90 hot-air balloons ascend.
- ◆ Mid-July: Northampton Town Show. Street entertainments in the town, trade stands at Abingdon Park and concerts at the weekend.
- ◆ Early September: County Fair and sheepdog trials at Delapre Park in Northampton.
- ◆ July: East of England Show in Peterborough.

NORTHUMBERLAND

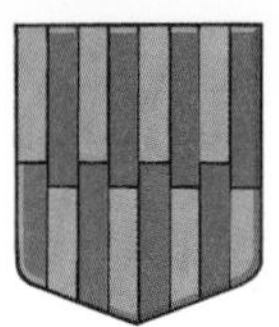

THE COUNTY LANDSCAPE

◆ Richly dramatic scenery is to be found here in England's north country, from an open coast to a wild interior. Northumberland is England's northernmost county. Its border butts against the Scottish Lowlands, and the land can be empty and lonely, even bleak, much of it heathery heights and stony hills.

◆ Against the northern barrier the land softens suddenly and gives way to the undulating Borders of Scotland. Although largely rural the open fields of the county here give a romantic, soft quality and there is a dramatic ending as you cross the high divide of the River Tweed at Berwick.

◆ It may be little populated and savage in its rural heart, yet the county possesses wonderful scenery such as the Cheviots, as well as little oases of sheltered beauty. Small fields and farms cluster round towns like Morpeth and the castled Alnwick.

◆ Along the jagged and stony shore castles finger the air and stand out against the sullen North Sea. This is the land the wild men from Scandinavia invaded, pouring in on their dreaded longships to plunder abbeys and towns, making the name of Viking feared through the land. Fishing ports and resorts are now found on the bays and wide sand beaches of the coast.

LIKE SO MANY of our real counties this most northerly English shire also displays its sharp contrast with the southeast industrial patch harbouring its great shipbuilding towns based around magnificent Newcastle-upon-Tyne and popular seaside 'workers' playground' resorts such as Whitley Bay, Blyth, Amble by the Sea; and then the glorious huntin'-shootin'-fishin' country based around Hexham, Haltwhistle and the Cheviots. To the north lie the mystical Holy and Farne islands and then there is Berwick! I can never think of Berwick as being part of Northumberland. The Tweed is the natural boundary between Northumberland and Berwickshire, so for me Berwick-on-Tweed is in Berwickshire. Berwick Rangers play in the Scottish Football League after all; I rest my case!

TOWNS AND VILLAGES

There's no mistaking your arrival in the city of Newcastle-upon-Tyne. It's a vital, friendly place and the commercial hub of the northeast, a well-planned centre with spreading suburbs and a good deal of local pride. Several bridges stride across the deep ravine of the Tyne River and carry trains and cars into the central city. Crossing the Tyne Bridge by train you enter the station, a notable building in its own right. Opened by Queen Victoria its grandiose portico was part of Newcastle's new town of the early 19th century. Until then Newcastle was a medieval city, and it preserves some ancient buildings, notably remnants of its city wall and a fine castle which dates from the 12th century and has a stone keep. Here the 13th-century Black Gate is approached by steep flights of steps dividing old wooden warehouses. A large parish church until 1882, the city's cathedral, with its distinctive open stonework Scottish style crown spire, St Nicholas is a decorative landmark.

NEWCASTLE *Two of the city's five bridges that cross the Tyne.*

Newcastle has a tight centre, best discovered on foot. Surprisingly much good Georgian architecture survives in the central city from visionary redevelopment. I am especially fond of the Theatre Royal which reminds me of London's Drury Lane Theatre. Down by the river along the old quays Victorian warehouses are being recycled into various uses such as restaurants, museums and ship chandlers' shops. The Guildhall is here, and by Castle Stairs and the Norman South Postern are the Moot Hall and County Hall. Grey and Grainger Streets are handsome late-Georgian thoroughfares, planned as a town centre in the 1830s. Newer developments include a civic centre and university, a library and a number of galleries. What is left of Newcastle's once vital shipping industry can be seen on a ferry trip from the Old Quayside. Newcastle has plenty of parks and open spaces.

At the end of the estuary after Wallsend and North Shields comes Tynemouth, with fine old houses and views over the river. Fed by several tributaries the Tyne Valley to the west attracts fishermen. By the Tyne is Hexham with its square towered Norman abbey. This market town has a comfortable sense of security – due to its age perhaps, for St Wilfrid built his first abbey in 674AD and his Chair is one of the oldest things in this ancient, atmospheric place. Stock markets are held here and on the Market Place before the abbey is a 14th-century towered Moot Hall, with its near neighbour the Manor Office, built of Roman stone. (It's now a local museum.) The town has many Georgian houses.

In the nearby country are a maze of little lanes and rural cul de sacs leading to hamlets. In the Derwent Valley is Blanchlands, with one-time miners' stone cottages around a green and pub. The parish church was once part of an Augustinian abbey. South is Allendale. The dales are quiet places now that lead is no longer mined here and this former mining village has become a centre for skiing and pony trekking. Corbridge has historic houses, many using Roman stones, and there's a complete gateway in the church tower. When the Tyne river is low the foundations of a Roman bridge can be seen.

North from Newcastle the views are a mixture of industrial sites and mining villages, interspersed with green spaces. Inland Ponteland has a fortified manor, now an inn. Morpeth is a market town, surrounded by farms yet within easy reach of the moors and coast. The town hall dates from 1718 and was designed by Vanbrugh. Nearby Mitford gave its name to the Mitford girls whose family began here – unusually it possesses a castle, manor house and mansion, showing the upward progress of the family.

Beyond the pastureland of the coastal plain Cambo with Wallington Hall (its park has stone heads of fabulous beasts from a medieval London gate) and Rothbury are in the open 'forests' before the Cheviot Hills. Here the Coquet

COUNTY FACTS

Origin of name: Comes from the Anglo-Saxon meaning "the place of those north of the Huimber".

Name first recorded: 895 as Norohymbraland.

County Town:
NEWCASTLE-UPON-TYNE Situated in the centre of the once-great collieries which supplied London and elsewhere with its coal, Newcastle once also exported lead, salt, salmon, butter, and tallow. Today it has undergone a renaissance as its restaurants, clubs and nightspots (and thousands of bright young things partying) testify and is cited as one of the Top 10 fashionable European cities.

Other Towns:

ALNWICK Once the county town, it sits on the little river Alne with a fine market square surrounded by piazzas. This is a good centre for exploring the north of the county. Nearby the ancient Alnwick Castle.

BERWICK ON TWEED: see Berwickshire

HALTWHISTLE Fine for seeing some of the best preserved parts of Hadrian's Wall. Nearby Housesteads has the finest stretch of the Roman wall for 72 miles between the Tyne and the Solway Firth built to keep back the barbarians from about AD124.

HEXHAM Beautifully set on the Tyne. The market square has an 18th-century colonnaded shelter.

NEWBIGGIN-BY-THE-SEA Has the world's oldest surviving Methodist chapel dating back to the mid 18th-century. There is also a display of the history of local methodism which many miners here followed.

SEATON DELAVAL Delightful hall built in 1720 by architect Sir John Vanbrugh. The nearby little port of Seaton Sluice is also worth a visit.

TWEEDMOUTH Attached to Berwick by a 15-arched 17th-century bridge. Famous castle founded by King John, sacked by Scots King WIlliam in 1202.

TYNEMOUTH Pleasantly perched on the promontory between the North Sea and Tyne river, there are arresting Benedict priory ruins here and a local maritime museum.

WALLSEND The last outpost of Hadrian's famous wall. There are excavations here amid the shipyards.

WHITLEY BAY Nearby to Newcastle this seaside resort has fine wide sands and amusements.

◆ Ashington ◆ Blyth ◆ Gosforth ◆ North Shields ◆ Prudhoe ◆ Spittal

County Rivers: Tyne, Coquet, Rede, Aln.

Highest point: In the Cheviots at 2,676 feet.

Northumberland's Local Government : Most of the County of Northumberland is governed by a two-tier system - Northumberland County Council and the six Districts of Alnwick, Berwick upon Tweed, Blyth Valley, Castle Morpeth, Tynedale and Wansbeck. The most populous part of the County is administered by the two single-tiered metropolitan boroughs of Newcastle upon Tyne and North Tyneside.

FAMOUS NAMES

◆ The powerful Percy family became Dukes of Northumberland and built castles here, notably Alnwick. The present duke resides mostly at Syon Park in Middlesex.

◆ George Stephenson, railway pioneer, was married not once but twice at Newburn's ancient parish church. His first steam locomotive, *Puffing Billy*, was built here.

◆ Catherine Cookson has portrayed Northumberland frequently in her prolific novels, for example The Mallen Trilogy.

◆ Newcastle provided the gritty backdrop for two classic crime movies: *Get Carter*, starring Michael Caine, and *Stormy Monday* by Mike Figgis.

◆ Police frontman Sting is a native of Newcastle.

◆ Goal-scorer extraordinaire Alan Shearer was born in Newcastle-upon-Tyne.

COUNTY CALENDAR

◆ Castles vye with each other for events in the county. Prudhoe Castle has events of all sorts from beekeeping to archery, Etal Castle presents music, Belsay Castle has flower shows, Chester's Roman Fort has performances.

◆ May: Northumberland County Show at Corbridge.

◆ October: the Newcastle Festival.

◆ Spring; Northumbrian Festival at Morpeth.

◆ Sheepdog trials take place in summer in the fells.

◆ New Year's Day: Allendale Town is alight with fires as blazing tubs are carried to mark the end of the year with the Baal Fire Festival.

◆ September: Great North Run half-marathon from the central motorway at Newcastle to South Shields over the Tyne in County Durham.

◆ Autumn: sea angling festival at Whitley Bay and fishing and boating events at Kielder Water.

CUDDY'S CRAG *Hadrian's manificent Wall.*

river runs down via Coquetdale to the sea by Amble, a sandy beach resort, where seals visit and eider ducks nest on Coquet Island.

Along the shore notable castles include towered Bamburgh, near Holy Island, and Dunstanburgh, and Castle Warkworth. Medieval monasteries on the mainland and the islands close to the shore such as Lindisfarne were easy pickings: having given the area fame and a holy aura they were also known to be very wealthy. From one of the islands the monks carried the body of St Cuthbert to his resting place at Durham.

Fish is landed and prepared at Craster's smokehouses where you can sample the famous kippers. Another local dish is Pan Haggerty, a layered pie of potato, onion and grated cheese, fried on both sides, or browned 'before the fire' (or under the grill!)

LOCAL HISTORY

Northumberland is part of the old kingdom of Northumbria which stretched between Edinburgh right the way down to the Tees. The county's historical roots run deep with many ancient sites. They range from early Iron Age forts (a large example is at Yeavering, where the capital of an Anglo-Saxon king has been discovered, and at Doddington) and Roman occupation (Chew Green Roman camp, the town of Corstopitum at Corbridge, while Hadrian's Wall starts its western progress from Wallsend and marches through Denton in Newcastle) to pele towers (at Staward, Corbridge and Ancroft) and religious foundations along the islands off its coast.

In Newcastle, which started its life as a Roman frontier town, are museums with examples of local antiquities going back to 6000BC, models of Hadrian's Wall, a geological gallery and local natural history exhibits.

In the border lands of the Cheviots where the distinctive breed of sheep with white faces quietly graze, the Scots and English fought for centuries. Norham's great 12th-century keep guarded approaches from the Tweed, and near Branxton is the bloody battle site of Flodden Field. The scene of this border clash in 1513 is in the village of Branxton and a granite cross is supposed to mark the spot on which Scottish King James IV was slain. His body was taken to Berwick where it was embalmed, encased in local lead and then transported to London. This northern part of the county was also reputedly the home to a number of minstrels who attached themselves to different marauding barons and told stories of raids and forays in haunting melodic verses – which were passed on by word of mouth.

NOTTINGHAMSHIRE

SHERWOOD FOREST – ONCE the only Royal forest north of the Trent – and Robin Hood: what could be more evocative of this county or indeed of Englishness? Nottingham is a fine city with an international feel about it, compared to the other towns in this county which are provincial and veer either towards Derbyshire and Yorkshire (as with gritty Mansfield) or head towards Lincolnshire (such as historic Newark).

TOWNS AND VILLAGES

Like its close neighbour, the city of Derby, the county capital of Nottingham sits in the very south of the county. It is a large town, sprawling over the plain, and at first sight not very appealing, but appearances in this case are deceptive. It is a vital centre of trade and has made its money on knitting (it once had a third of Britain's looms), boots and shoes which I always think of, and the famous Nottingham lace (there's a lace centre by the castle). Its historic roots go back to very ancient origins when it was a small settlement around a high rock on which stood a fearsome castle. This stronghold, the scene of many sieges, especially in the Civil War, pre-dated the Norman Conquest and the Normans rebuilt it. Several kings lived here. It is now no more, replaced with a 19th-century mansion (now a museum), though the houses still press up against the rock and old tunnels, such as Mortimer's Hole, bore right into its heart. (A 17th-century pub, the Trip to Jerusalem, is built up against its cliffy height.)

In a park in the suburbs rises the great Tudor pile of Wollaton Hall, described as one of the finest of Elizabethan Renaissance mansions. Its great hall is dramatic, and its otherwise rather drab interior now houses the Nottingham Natural History Museum with collections of exotic butterflies, birds and fossils. Roses are cultivated southeast of the city.

For a place much struggled over in history, the city does not have many monuments although there is an imposing domed Council House, and an ornate Victorian Theatre Royal, as well as the smaller Nottingham Playhouse. Another 'monument' is Nottinghamshire County Cricket Club, founded in 1841, who play at Trent Bridge in the city. It is also one of the five test ground 'homes' of England.

Going from south to north, Nottinghamshire possesses many pretty villages. Ratcliffe on Soar is one such and nearby is Thrumpton Hall, a Jacobean house, once home of the Byrons and with many mementoes of the poet as well as antiques and paintings. The place more associated with Byron is Newstead Abbey, just north of Nottingham, near the village of Papplewick. The mock gothic abbey has

THE COUNTY LANDSCAPE

◆ A long peardrop-shaped county, Nottinghamshire forms with Derbyshire a pair of keystones of the north Midlands, between the south and the borders of Yorkshire. At first glance Nottinghamshire may seem to be an average kind of county. Nevertheless the feeling is purely midlands, open, and though flattish, very fertile, its many fields laced with lanes and county roads connecting ordered settlements.

◆ The River Trent crosses the southern part diagonally, and in the main all land north of this waterway is industrial. The south however is agricultural. Here the pleasantly hilly country is part of the famous hunting country of the rolling Wolds of Leicestershire, its southern neighbour, and its fine open fields flank the River Soar. To the east the hills soften somewhat towards the Vale of Belvoir into some of the best farmland in the country stretching up as far as the market town of Newark-on-Trent.

◆ At Newark the north begins flatly beyond the Trent, where the river enters Lincolnshire.

NOTTINGHAM
The traditional craft of lace-making has been associated with the county town for hundreds of years.

COUNTY FACTS

Origin of name: Nottingham's original name is unfortunate – before the Danes renamed it, the small village was called Snotta, or Snot, from Old English meaning 'a place abounding with caverns or holes dug underground' and certainly prehistoric people left such dwellings at the bottom of a steep rock under this town.

Name first recorded: 1016 as Snotinghamscir.

County Motto: *Sapienter Proficiens* ("Advancing wisely").

County Town: NOTTINGHAM Tower blocks and ring road do their best to disfigure this once great centre for cotton, textiles and lace. Local boy Paul Smith opened his first shop here, continuing the clothes tradition. There is a major TV studio here too.

Other Towns:

BEESTON Home to one Jesse Boot who started work in his mother's herb shop in Nottingham and went on to create a high street phenomenon. The weir here on the Trent is very pretty.

BLIDWORTH Sherwood Forest town linked to Robin Hood lore with Will Scarlet reputedly buried here and home to Maid Marian.

EASTWOOD Birthplace of native son D.H. Lawrence in once-rural peaceful setting amid colliery area.

EDWINSTOWE In the most beautiful part of Sherwood Forest with the grand remains of the Major Oak, supposedly over 1,000 years old and the biggest oak in Britain.

MANSFIELD Cotton and coal were once its staple diet, but it is now a comfortable provincial northern town with a good market and theatre. It was especially famous for its hosiery, footwear and net curtains and doilies.

NEWARK ON TRENT This town is known as the Key to the North and has an interesting connection with Lady Godiva, who presented the town as a gift to the monastery at Stow. Newark was staunchly monarchist in the Civil War, Newark Castle proving impregnable. Gladstone made his first public address from the window of he Clinton Arms. Cobblestoned marketplace and some extremely old pubs.

RETFORD Rich in early and medieval history, this is the main market town in the north of the county. Its east and west sides are joined across the River Idle.

SOUTHWELL Has a famous minster visible from some 20 miles away across the Trent Valley.

WORKSOP Dating back to Saxon times it is the chief town of the area known as the Dukeries. Beautiful parks to the south being the northern reaches of Sherwood Forest.

◆ Arnold ◆ Carlton ◆ Hucknall ◆ Kirkby in Ashfield ◆ Mansfield Woodhouse ◆ Radcliffe-on-Trent ◆ Stapleford ◆ Sutton-in-Ashfield ◆ West Bridgford

Highest point: Strawberry Bank, Huthwaite at 650 feet.

County rivers: Trent, Idle, Maun, Devon.

grounds with rare trees and still contains an impressive ruined façade of the original priory. The poet sold the family home in 1818, to pay debts, but it contains some of his possessions.

Nearby Southwell (pronounced Suthall) has many historical associations, including an inn where Charles I set off for Nottingham to signal the start of the Civil War, as well as charming gardens. It also has a rarity, a spacious, towered Norman church that contains sculpture unique to the British Isles. The early English choir stalls are renowned for their oak carving and there is an elegant chapter house with yet more carving. The marching round arched columns lead to four holding up the tower; the capitals are noted for their sculpted scenes.

Newark-on-Trent possesses one of the great churches of the county. Its tall spire stands over a fine, well-furnished interior and besides a splendid great east window there is other early glass. The castle, a royal stronghold in the Civil War, was reduced to a ruin but this fortress with so many memories still offers much to see. In the town there are old inns and Tudor houses with oversailing storeys, and the Magnus Grammar School now houses a museum with Civil War relics.

Towards the northwest are the coalfields. Across the county are mining villages, marked with ugly slag heaps, still straightforward workaday settlements despite the decline of the pits. There will be local sports events, gardens and many a dog and pigeon fancier here. There's also the chance to try a local delicacy at Mansfield. Mansfield Pudding is a brandy-flavoured suet sponge pudding, served sprinkled with caster sugar. Mines surround Mansfield, which has a local museum and art gallery. Nearby Thoresby Hall is a palatial house with a lake and grounds containing part of Sherwood Forest enclosed by the Earl of Kingston 300 years ago.

In Worksop's town library is a museum of natural and local history. There's also a surprise – a piece of marble sculpture in relief, part of the altar of the Temple of Pergamon, most of which is in the Berlin Museum.

LOCAL HISTORY

Nottinghamshire stands on the important Roman Fosse way which ran from Exeter to Lincoln. Later it was taken by the Vikings who approached it down the Humber, and made it a stronghold against the southern Saxons.

Although the northwest of the county is largely industrial, yet there are patches of quite high country with low folds of hills achieving their heights near Blidworth, the highest being by Sutton in Ashfield, the Robin Hood Hills. These of course take their name from the famous medieval bandit who lived in Sherwood Forest. In the Dukeries (the estates of Clumber, Thoresby and Welbeck) a part of the once vast stretch of trees and heath remains, and there are still impressive remnants, although the Forest once covered a fifth of the county and ran from Nottingham to Worksop.

In the county two fortresses stood long and strong against invaders. Newark's, known as the Key to the North, still broods but of Nottingham's once great citadel where the doomed King Charles I announced the start of the Civil War, only the rock and a much later great house remain from the once stern castle that pre-dated even the Norman invasion.

Newark's museum has two hoards of 17th century coins and part of a Roman helmet, as well as archaeological and local history exhibits. Roman coins have been unearthed at the camp in Mansfield.

From 1350 Nottingham was a centre of alabaster carving and a sample can be seen at the Castle Museum, a virgin and child uncovered at nearby Flawford. Alabaster reliefs from the workshops here were sent all over Europe.

At Laxton is a unique survival of medieval farming. Here the then common custom of farming open fields in long strips which started with the Saxons can still be seen.

Nottinghamshire's local government: Although Nottingham looks after its own affairs the rest of the County of Nottinghamshire *apart* from its capital city is administered by a two-tier system: Nottinghamshire County Council and the seven Districts Councils of Ashfield, Bassetlaw, Broxtowe, Gedling, Mansfield, Newark & Sherwood and Rushcliffe.

FAMOUS NAMES

◆ Robin Hood and his men still retain a romantic appeal. At a time when the Forest Laws were savage and hunting was kept for the king alone, they supposedly robbed the rich to give to the poor.

◆ Without doubt the 'mad, bad and dangerous to know' Lord Byron is one of the most famous sons of Nottingham. He was born at Newstead Abbey.

◆ D.H.Lawrence (*Sons and Lovers*) was born here and wrote novels recalling his childhood in the mining village of Eastwood. His house can still be seen.

COUNTY CALENDAR

◆ The Nottinghamshire County Show takes place each May.

◆ The Nottingham Goose Fair was a trade fair of medieval origin, Now it fills the streets of the city with amusements in the first week of October for three helter-skelter days.

◆ One of the great cricket grounds, Trent Bridge plays host to county and country cricket.

NOTTINGHAM *The annual Goose Fair held in the first week of October is famous.*

Oxfordshire

OXFORD *College spires at dawn from South Hinksey over in Berkshire.*

THE COUNTY LANDSCAPE

◆ Oxfordshire is a gently undulating county which some classify as the South Midlands. I've always deemed it to be a southern county with the notable exception of Banbury which is more of a Midlands town, being closer to Birmingham than London.

◆ Oxfordshire actually lies between the pastoral south and the industrial heart of England and midway between the estuaries of the Thames and the Severn. To the north are the picture-postcard rolling limestone Cotswolds (also mainly in Gloucestershire) rising to a plateau of about 500 feet above sea level; to the south lie the striking chalk hills of the Chilterns which have many beechwood slopes.

◆ Between the two, the basins of the Thames and Cherwell form the central plain of the county with many large arable and livestock farms. The Thames actually becomes the Isis when it passes through the county town of Oxford. This river is also the boundary with Berkshire. Buckinghamshire, Berkshire and Oxfordshire are often described as the Thames Valley.

THERE'S SOMETHING VERY agreeable about Oxfordshire: it's a neat, ordered and very together county. This is the place to escape to from the metropolitan rat race – it's one of those places that's near but far enough away from hell. Although you can't really mention Oxfordshire without mentioning Oxford in the same breath, somehow the multi-spired city and mellifluous county vibrate to different rhythms.

TOWNS AND VILLAGES

Oxford city is out on a limb, somehow quite different from the rest of Oxfordshire. Known as the 'City of Spires' most of which belong to the university, Oxford's colleges lie within fairly easy walking distance and are some of the best-preserved architectural treasures of Britain – some of which you can tour through. It's not surprising that film and television companies seem to be filming here nearly month-on-month. Think of the cultural sleuth *Inspector Morse* played by the excellent John Thaw traipsing around Oxford, in the impressive Randolph Hotel or alongside the beautiful Christchurch Meadows. His TV-based home though wasn't in the city of Oxford but in Ealing in Middlesex! *Shadowlands*, which told the story of the famous Oxford professor C. S. Lewis (who gave us those delightful and ageless stories in *The Chronicles of Narnia*) and the deepening relationship with New

York writer Joy Gresham, was filmed at Magdalen College with its 15th-century chapel, and the Sheldonian Theatre.

A walk through the Botanical Gardens in the city centre – said to be the oldest in Britain – is a must and from here you can try your luck at punting on the river (no blazer or straw hat required). Arnold's view over what this Victorian poet termed "that sweet city with her dreamy spires" is worth a detour 3 miles outside Oxford to Boar's Hill. On a clear day Oxford's spires really do shimmer.

Go to Banbury and you feel a sense of isolation with the Oxford-on-Isis and a closer affinity with Stratford-on-Avon. I have personal memories especially around Banbury (my mother worked there). The nursery rhyme also cannot fail to come to mind:

"Ride a cock-horse to Banbury Cross
To see a fine lady upon a white horse".

But you might be surprised to know that 'fine' doesn't mean in her finery but relates to a member of the Fiennes family (pronounced Fine) who live at nearby Broughton Castle which is open to the public in the summer. As for the cross at Banbury, the original one was destroyed by Puritans in 1602 and was replaced by a Victorian variety. Banbury is also well known for its scrummy Banbury cakes – a 350-year-old recipe for small sponge cakes lined with currants, spice and honey and wrapped in a pastry case.

Today when I think of Oxfordshire I think of the Civil War and Charles I, and those clusters of neat, compact little towns like Chipping Norton, Kidlington, Bloxham along the eastbound A roads. Of course the county is also associated with more modern warfare as the sprinkling of American Air Force bases testifies (though these are closing down now that the Cold War has been put on ice, so to speak).

Witney, 10 miles west of Oxford, on the Windrush, is a mellowed stone-built town on the edge of the rich Cotswold Oxford Down sheep-rearing area. It is world famous for its blanket-making and has attractive Cotswold merchants' houses. Cogges, just outside Witney, is a little hamlet with many strange little twists and turns, and fine old houses with a Benedictine church, manor house and museum. Another wool centre, Burford, 20 miles west of Oxford, is one of the most beautiful Cotswold towns. Its steepish high street is lined with every variety of golden Cotswold stone house sloping down to a fine old bridge over the Windrush. Halfway down the high street is the twin-gabled 15th-century Tolsey House, where the wealthy wool merchants once held their meetings. You can just about picture it as you go inside the museum to find out about the town's bustling past.

COUNTY FACTS

Origin of name: Oxenfordscir from the Old English "Oxenford" meaning a ford over a river (possibly the Isis) for cattle to cross.

Name first recorded: 1010 as Oxenfordscir.

County Motto: *Sapere Aude* ("Dare to be Wise")

County Town:
OXFORD Brilliant covered market selling anything from venison to Versace; visit the Nose Bag for coffee, and explore Broad Street and any of the cobbled streets off it like Turls St. Gloucester Green doubles as the city bus station and a budding piazza Covent-Garden style. All this before you even mention any famous Colleges . . .

Other Towns:

BICESTER A noted hunting centre on the edge of the Cotswolds, now equally well known for its 'Bicester Village' shopping experience.

BURFORD Quintessential Cotswold stone town with the prettiest main high street.

CAVERSHAM Now a northern suburb of Reading, but with its own unique history.

CHIPPING NORTON Chipping means market and this town has a large sloping market place – friendly enough to lure Ronnie Barker to run his antique shop which is not *Open All Hours*!

DORCHESTER On the Thame near its junction with the Thames and dominated by its Abbey Church and nearby walk to Wittenham Clumps with a hill fort and commanding view for miles.

GORING-ON-THAMES Beautifully nestled beside the Thames between the Chilterns and Berkshire Downs. Good setting off point for the Icknield Way and other treks.

HENLEY-ON-THAMES Has a holiday feel about it with many old pubs (excellent local Brakespear brew), a sprinkling of agreeable restaurants, good shopping and relaxing riverside strolls.

THAME A main street of exceptional width and several medieval buildings. Nearby is Raymond Blanc's *Le Manoir Aux Quat' Saisons* restaurant.

WITNEY The Old Blanket Hall, built circa 1720, has a curious one-hand clock on its front.

WOODSTOCK Check out the fascinating ancient chimney pots, one of which was clambered upon by Sir Winston Churchill as a 12-year-old.

◆ Benson ◆ Chinnor ◆ Deddington ◆ Eynsham ◆ Headington ◆ Horspath ◆ Kidlington ◆ Marston ◆ Watlington ◆ Wheatley

Highest point: Portobello in the Chiltern Hills at 836 feet.

County rivers: Thames, Evenlode, Cherwell, Windrush.

Oxfordshire's local government: The County of Oxfordshire apart from Caversham is governed by a two-tier structure with Oxfordshire County Council and the four district councils of Cherwell, Oxford City, South Oxfordshire and West Oxfordshire being the sum of two parts. Caversham comes under the unitary authority of the Berkshire town of Reading.

COUNTY CALENDAR

- ◆ Whitsuntide: The ancient village of Bampton has an all-day Morris Dancing festival.
- ◆ Early June: go to Broughton castle fête if just to see this impressive castle surrounded by a moat of water-lilies.
- ◆ June: the marquees, the blue and white awnings and bunting announce that the annual Royal Henley Regatta, dating back to 1829, is imminent. A firm fixture of the English social season, it climaxes at the beginning of July, often with a spectacular firework display.
- ◆ Late August: the annual Cropedy festival is the annual get-together of local Oxfordshire folk band Fairport Convention, and a marvellous day out with all sorts of stalls and entertainments.
- ◆ Early September: St Giles Fair, Oxford is the 5th largest fair in England, dating back to medieval times. Like other 15th-century fairs it has ceased to be a trading fair but is still held on the original site.
- ◆ Summer Music in Oxford runs classic music in classic venues (such as the Wren-designed Sheldonian Theatre, the grounds of Radley College, and Dorchester Abbey).
- ◆ 1 May: get up at crack of dawn to see foolhardy students jump into the Isis off Magdalen Bridge while choristers greet the sunrise with a hymn at the top of the Magdalen tower – medieval tradition – and Morris Dancers celebrate May morning in more traditional ways.

***BURFORD** The perfect Cotswold market town.*

Woodstock, 8 miles north of Oxford, is well worth a visit and not just for next-door Blenheim Palace. The centre has many lovely old stone houses and an elegant town hall which has a good antiques fair most weekends. It also boasts a pub, the Bear, going back to the 13th century.

If you go to Great Tew, north of Woodstock, you will be rewarded with one of the most traditional pictures of rural England. The village displays delightful cottages of thatch and stone with the old village stocks and the manor house rebuilt in its original gardens. Just around the corner lies Deddington near the river Cherwell. This small town is dominated by its honey-coloured local stone buildings – many rich with Civil War associations.

Henley is perhaps the most famous of Thames resorts thanks to hosting one of the highlights of the English Social Season – the Royal Henley Regatta. The elegant 18th-century bridge linking Oxfordshire to Berkshire has carved masks of Father Thames and the goddess Isis. Beneath the bridge at Regatta time in July fashion and beauty vie with athletic prowess from all over the world as world-class rowers slug it out.

LOCAL HISTORY

A prehistoric reminder of Oxfordshire's past is the Bronze Age stone circle three miles north of Chipping Norton known as the Rollright Stones. Only Stonehenge and Avebury in Wiltshire are more important. The main circle is about 100 feet across and the stones vary from a few inches to 7 feet in height. A place of such antiquity and mystery with names such as the King's Stone and Whispering Knights is naturally steeped in legend.

In Saxon times Dorchester-on-Thames became an impressive cathedral city. The abbey still has a remarkable Jesse window with carved stone figures and richly illustrated glass telling the story of Mary's 'family' and should be visited (as should the Abbey tea house where the local ladies make the finest teas for miles around). Henry VIII visited Binsey Church (off the unglamorous Botley Road, Oxford) to seek a cure from the well there for his leg ulcers (and supposedly his syphilis) as well as at the King's Pool by the pretty watercress-bed stream that run through Ewelme. This village has the oldest primary school in the country attached to some medieval cloisters.

Oxford started life in Saxon times as a frontier town guarding Wessex against Danish attacks. It boasts the oldest university in England. Oxford University developed along with the town from the 12th century. 'Town and gown' did not always get on together however: in fact in 1355 there was a massacre. Fortunately relationships are

OXFORDSHIRE *The prehistoric Rollright Stones are mysterious sentinels.*

somewhat better today. From medieval times wool became a mainstay of the county and Witney has been a blanket-making centre since the 14th century. Local history meets local folklore at Minster Lovell, a charming little Windrush village near Witney. Here lie the peaceful ruins of the ill-fated Lovell family. Francis Lovell was a powerful 15th-century aristocrat who supported King Richard III in the Wars of the Roses but went into hiding when his fortunes fell; he was uncovered in a secret room in 1708 by workmen doing alterations to the house. They were confronted by the sight of a mouldering skeleton at a table with pen and paper.

Oxfordshire featured in the Gunpowder plot of 1605 because at Chastleton, about 4 miles from Moreton-in-the-Marsh, there is a superb Jacobean House where conspirators of the Gunpowder Plot met. During the English Civil War Oxford became the headquarters of King Charles I. It was besieged and finally surrendered to the Roundheads in 1646. Several fierce battles were fought in the county between Roundheads and Cavaliers, including Cropedy Bridge (1644). Chastleton again featured in the county's history as it also has the bible given to Charles I on the day of his execution. Blenheim Palace was built by architect John Vanbrugh for John Churchill, Duke of Marlborough after he won the Battle of Blenheim in 1704. Sir Winston Churchill was born in the palace in 1874. In the 20th century the car industry took off in the county with over 1.5 million Morris Minors made (in Cowley) and the famous MG sportscars (in Abingdon over the border in neighbouring Berkshire).

FAMOUS NAMES

◆ At 46 Leckford Road, Oxford a young, allegedly naïve proto US President Bill Clinton lodged as a student in the late 1960s.

◆ Huntercombe House was home to industrialist and philanthropist William Morris, later Lord Nuffield – the Henry Ford of the British car industry. He brought us the Morris-Oxford of 1913, over 1½ million Morris Minors and the first MG. His stylish pre-World War II period aristocratic home is open on some weekends.

◆ Bladon, a little village just south of Blenheim Palace has quaint cottages with mullioned windows and tall chimneys, but it is also the resting place of Winston Churchill along with his mother, glamorous Lady Randolph Churchill.

◆ Devotees of the book and television series *Inspector Morse* will have lots of interesting sleuthing to do themselves. A visit to the attractive riverside Trout Inn near Oxford is a good start. Or you can take a Morse tour.

◆ Successful jangly pop-rock guitar bands are something of an Oxford speciality with Radiohead, Supergrass, Ride (sadly defunct), Ash to name a few all residing in the vicinity.

◆ CS Lewis taught for many years at Magdalen College and his rooms became the focus for meetings of his close friends known as the inklings, among them JRR Tolkein.

◆ Jerome K Jerome of *Three Men in a Boat* fame is buried at Ewelme Church as is Chaucer's grand-daughter, the Duchess of Suffolk, who started the church there.

◆ Headington Hill Hall, now part of the campus of Oxford Brookes University, was the longtime home of the infamous tycoon Robert Maxwell.

◆ John Wilson buys and sells famous signatures from dead or alive "names" from his office in Eynsham.

RUTLAND

RUTLAND WATER *A reservoir popular with anglers and windsurfers.*

THE COUNTY LANDSCAPE
A mere 15 miles in length and 11 in width, you could be forgiven for saying "oh, have we passed through it?" on your journey from Northamptonshire to Lincolnshire, two adjacent counties.
◆ Nevertheless it is rich pastoral land with picturesque valleys dotted with villages rather than towns and quiet country roads with the odd large manor house suddenly arising surrounded by large parks.
◆ The northern and eastern borders are bounded by Lincolnshire, the southern by Northamptonshire, with Leicestershire to the west. The River Welland runs along most of the southeastern boundary.

FAMOUS NAMES
◆ Sir Everard Digby of Stoke Dry financed Guy Fawkes's Gunpowder Plot.
◆ Titus Oates originator of the Popish Plot was was born at Oakham in 1649.
◆ Sir Isaac Newton lived at Market Overton during his childhood.
◆ 19th-century poet John Clare praised Rutland's beauty and lived at Pickworth.

I'D BE SURPRISED if Rutland ever suffered from the drought conditions of 1995 – it's just that there seems to be so much water in such a small county – and it's man-made at that!

TOWNS AND VILLAGES

If good things come in small packages, as the old adage has it, then the famous local brewery, Ruddles, has milked the county's size to excellent effect for its marketing slogan: 'Much Out Of Little' – regardless of whether the inhabitants are fiercely proud and protective of their heritage in the face of attempts to have it absorbed into its larger neighbours. As for the beer, well, its reputation is nationally established amongst real-ale enthusiasts.

The county town of Oakham is a handsome melange of limestone and ironstone terraces and Georgian buildings interspersed with modern constructions, although the market place with its octagonal Butter Cross and town stocks provides a pleasing focus. The Norman banqueting hall is all that remains of the original town castle built in 1191, its walls decorated with horseshoes donated, under ancient custom, by every monarch and peer of the realm on first visiting the town. Oakham School, founded in 1584, has been refitted as a Shakespearean centre, while the Rutland County Museum, with its mixed exhibits of Iron Age and Roman finds and agricultural tools, occupies the former riding school of the Rutland Fencibles, a volunteer cavalry regiment raised in 1794.

Uppingham, seven miles south, has a more uniform style with its wide sloping high street flanked by bow-fronted shops and ironstone houses of the 18th century. At its west end stands the fortress-like facade of Uppingham School, founded in 1587, which has some of the largest playing fields in England.

The villages of Edith Weston, named after Edward the Confessor's widow, and Empingham stand close to the horse-shoe-shaped Rutland Water (yes, everything is horshoe-shaped here: obviously a lucky place to live!). It boasts the largest surface area (3,100 acres) of any man-made lake in northern Europe. Created by the damming of the River Gwash in 1976, it serves as a leisure and recreation centre, with a string of developments spread around its periphery which cater for assorted watersports and nature enthusiasts. The village of Ketton is particularly noted for the honey-coloured limestone utilized in the building of many of its houses and cottages.

LOCAL HISTORY

The Coritani tribe inhabited the area prior to the Roman conquest. In the 8th century it became part of the kingdom of Mercia. King Ethelred gave Rutland to his queen, Emma, who later became the wife of King Canute. Subsequent monarchs followed suit, bestowing the county on their queens and court favourites, since it offered splendid opportunities for hunting wild boar and deer.

The title of Lord of The Manor of Oakham was granted to his blacksmith by William the Conqueror, leading to the custom of kings and peers presenting horseshoes to the manorial lord when visiting the town. In 1470, during the Wars of the Roses, the battle of Losecoat Field was fought in Rutland, the defeated Lancastrian supporters discarding their coats as they fled. During the Civil War, Rutland was staunchly puritan and supported the Parliamentary cause.

Further to the county's Civil War associations, a dwarf named Jeffrey Hudson was born at Oakham in 1619. Only 18 inches tall by the age of nine (it's fitting he was born in England's smallest county), he was concealed in a pie served to Henrietta, wife of Charles I, during a visit by her to Burley-on-the-Hill. She took him to court, where he served her as a page, but later fought bravely as a Royalist during the Civil War.

COUNTY FACTS

Origin of name: It means Rota's land, a personal possession of Queen Edith, wife of the Edward the Confessor. It was an endowment or dowry for Norman Queens until it became a county. No one knows for sure who Rota was.

Name first recorded: 851 as Dev Fenascir

County Town:
OAKHAM Home to one of the country's most exclusive public schools. L-shaped market place with old town stocks is a treat The Great Hall of the Norman castle houses perhaps the most remarkable collection of horseshoes in the world, including one given by George IV which is seven feet long and made of solid bronze.

Other Towns:
COTTESMORE England's most famous and oldest hunt, the Cottesmore, was established in 1732. In season, the hounds still meet four times a week, on Mondays, Tuesdays, Thursdays and Saturdays.
KETTON One of the largest villages of the county with butter-coloured buildings excavated from its famous local quarry. St Mary's Church is an exceptionally attractive example of this stone.
MARKET OVERTON An historic village with Roman earthworks and a 6th century pagan settlement. Complete with old stocks and whipping post and royal visits by Edwards I and II it had its hey-day.
UPPINGHAM Has a wide sloping high street with bow-fronted shops. Nearby Hallaton is a most pretty village. Rutland's second town.
◆ Ayston ◆ Barrowden ◆ Clipsham ◆ Empingham ◆ Ryhall ◆ Stoke Dry ◆ Whissendine

County rivers: Welland, Eye, Wash, Chater.
Highest point: Ranksborough Hill (625 feet) by Manton near the centre of the county.

Rutland's local government: The County of Rutland is governed by a single Rutland unitary council.

COUNTY CALENDAR

◆ June 29: Rush Strewing Ceremony – Barrowden Church. Rushes from nearby fields are used in keeping with a provision that the field tenant – the Church – keeps up the ceremony each year.
◆ Sunday following June 29th: Hay Strewing Ceremony – Langham Church.
◆ Sunday nearest June 29th: Hay Strewing Ceremony – Braunston Church. Part of a legacy from early Lord of the Manor to the parish clerk as a reward for finding his lost daughter. The East Midlands Gas Board now makes an annual payment in lieu of hay, as the original meadow now lies under the local gasworks.
◆ August: Mayor-making Ceremony – Oakham. Traditional greeting ceremony between new incumbent and predecessor.
◆ May: Oakham Fair – Oakham.
◆ 1st week in August: Rutland Agricultural Fair – Showground, Oakham.
◆ August Bank Holiday: Oakham Horticultural Show.

SHROPSHIRE

THE COUNTY LANDSCAPE

◆ Mountainous and rugged in the southwest, the highest point here being the Stiperstones, the county is more level in the east, although still hilly, with the River Severn winding through lush valleys. North of the Severn are the meres – a sort of Shropshire lake district – for which the county is famous. The Salop plain stretches from Whitchurch in the north to Church Stretton in the southwest, and the Wrekin rises from this plain to around 1200 feet. In the south are the Clee Hills.

◆ Much of this area on the western edge of England is largely hill country, very verdant and deeply sliced with river valleys. It retains a remote, almost cut off atmosphere, even though the county town of Shrewsbury on the Severn was a gateway to the principality of Wales.

YOU CAN STILL soak in the flavour of a medieval border county in Shropshire and imagine how crossing Offa's Dyke for a Welshman might mean losing his right hand, or even his head! Medieval towns such as Shrewsbury and Oswestry are stunning and sport some of the most picturesque black and white timber and plaster houses of the late Middle Ages. Away from the towns this is a county of yeoman farmers and country squires that has changed little since those times of yore.

Shropshire's wondrously mingled and often dramatic scenery is I suppose now forever associated with the poetry of A. E. Housman, a local poet always in love with his county home. In *A Shropshire Lad* he depicts much of this most rural of counties, its splendid lushly green pastures spreading west and up unto the very walls of Wales. The Welsh influence lingers here, with many families claiming Celtic ancestry.

TOWNS AND VILLAGES

Central to its compact county is its capital, Shrewsbury. It's a place that shows its age with great charm – many brick and half-timbered buildings, both black and white and in weathered wood, bulge and lean over picturesque old streets such as Grope Lane. There are other fine examples in Shrewsbury's school and in Abbot's House, Rowley's House, and ancient coaching inns like the Lion. There's an eccentric Georgian circular church and a 12th-century castle of pale sandstone with a garden. A unique aspect of Shropshire's county town is its position, almost encircled by the river Severn.

IRONBRIDGE *The crucible of the Industrial Revolution.*

Nearby is charmingly named Ditherington, where the oldest known iron-framed building is claimed as a prototype of the skyscraper. Atcham Church was first built with stones from Roman Viroconium, now Wroxeter. Haughmond Abbey is a striking Norman ruin.

There's a lot of interest to find in southeastern Shropshire.

Outside the city, towards Wellington, is Attingham Park, a noble porticoed mansion with curving side wings and a notable picture gallery hung with old masters and designed by John Nash. Attingham has grounds laid out by Humpry Repton.

The Wrekin, local legend has it, is a great shovelful of dirt dumped by the devil when he was beguiled into carrying the weight no further. This rocky outcrop certainly thrusts up suddenly out of the plain and there are panoramic views from the summit.

Beyond Wellington and its school is Tong, with a noted church, and Boscobel House with a tree marking the spot where the future Charles II supposedly hid in the Royal Oak. Near here is Weston Park, a Charles II house, and old houses at Shifnal were described by Charles Dickens in *The Old Curiosity Shop*. To the north is Lilleshall Abbey and the new town of Telford, named after the engineer, and a sort-of Shropshire Milton Keynes.

Buildwas Abbey, a Cistercian foundation near Cressage, shows the fine, simple architecture of the order. Coalbrookdale, an early centre of iron smelting, has a museum and ironmaster's cottages while at Blists Hill there is an open-air museum with industrial exhibits. Towards the Staffordshire border is Bridgnorth, an old and inviting town on the Severn divided into two levels, one high up connected by steps and a cliff railway, the other by the river. The high town has a leaning castle keep, steep streets of tall chimneyed houses, and a half-timbered hall that was made from an old barn. There is a church designed by Thomas Telford. Near the town is a cluster of country mansions – Wilderhope's Tudor stone manor, Elizabethan Shipton and Morville, and Acton Round Hall at Aldenham Park, among others.

Between the lovely Clee Hills and Wenlock Edge, two parallel hill ranges, lies the valley of the Corve, known as Corvedale. The beautiful vale is a country of handsome old farmhouses and fertile fields. The Corve runs into the Teme, and this takes you into Ludlow, one of the most memorable of Shropshire's towns. Ludlow's neat and compact centre has many pleasures, from its narrow alleys and fine Georgian and Regency houses to medieval buildings and notably some remarkable old inns; the ornately half-timbered Feathers is 15th century and has many interior details such as elaborate plaster ceilings and wall paintings. Ludlow's claim for the largest parish church in England is disputed by at least three more in other parts of the country, but St Laurence certainly has a grand and elegant 15th-century air.

The northern part of the county is open arable land. It

COUNTY FACTS

Origin of name: Latin: Civitas Scrobbensis, "the city around the scrub folk". The county could easily have followed in the footsteps of Dorset and Somerset and be known as Shropset, but due to the power and influence of Shrewsbury the county name took its form from the town (pronounced "Shro'sbury"), leading the district to be called Shrewsburyshire which was inevitably shortened to Shropshire. Norman clerks found the Shrewsburyshire intolerable to write or pronounce and abbreviated it all to Salop.

Name first recorded: 1006 as Scrobbesbyrigscir.

County Motto: *Floreat Salopia* ("Let Salop Flourish").

County Town: SHREWSBURY Two church spires pierce the skyline of this finely preserved medieval town. St Mary's spire was one of the three tallest in England; St Alkmund's is the other. Its Lord Hill Column is only just shorter than Nelson's column.

Other Towns:

BISHOP'S CASTLE Very pretty off-the-beaten track town clinging to a steep hillside with plenty of interesting pubs (including the Three Tuns, dating back to 1642), restaurants and antique shops to browse through.

BRIDGNORTH Worth seeing alone for the flight of steps and railway with the steepest gradient in England that links the High and Low Towns.

CHURCH STRETTON Said to have the highest golf course in England (much of it over 1,200 feet).

DAWLEY Domesday town which became a constituent part of Telford 'New Town'. Dawley Castle, built in 1361, owned by King Richard II but destroyed in 1645.

DONNINGTON Once an important flax and hemp centre, this town has a cobbled market place with attractive Georgian houses. Matthew Flinders, who discovered that compasses were affected by the iron in ships, died here in 1814.

ELLESMERE Attractive capital of the county's Lakeland with nine meres of its own and many boats jostling for berths.

IRONBRIDGE/COALBROOKDALE Home to probably the most famous bridge in the country, the world's first iron bridge at 196 feet in length. It straddles a gorge across the Severn and is now justifiably a World Heritage Site.

NEWPORT Inland fishing town since Saxon times!

OSWESTRY Unpretentious market town, Welsh in character with Georgian and Victorian buildings standing in harmony. Nearby, the Old Racecourse is a high stretch of common with great views.

TELFORD New, brash and a seemingly endless array of roundabouts and business parks, this was Britain's first new major city for centuries, begun in 1963.

◆ Hadley ◆ Oakengates ◆ Shifnal

Main rivers: Severn, Perry, Roden, Tern, Clun, Onny, Corve, Rea.

Highest point: Brown Clee at 1772 feet.

LONG MYND HILLS *Stunning countryside for miles.*

has many small villages of black and white work, and stately manor houses, reflecting the riches brought to local families by farming these fields. The typical old houses are often built on local sandstone blocks, their upper storeys half timbered in complex patterns, under slate roofs. Aside from these regional aspects the black and white villages are real places to live, such as Hodnet with its Norman church and extensive water gardens at the imposing brick Victorian hall. This is very satisfying countryside, spreading wide to the Cheshire border. Notable places include Whitchurch, with Roman origins and a net of old streets, gaining its name from an early White Church, and Oswestry, with rail and canal links – at nearby Chirk is an aqueduct and a stone viaduct carrying the rails.

The west and southwest of the county is the loveliest, wild and empty with great mysterious hills. The Long Mynd, a wonderful ridge stretching for 10 miles, and the Clun Forest hills are places apart. On the edge of the hill mass the main centre of this sheep-farming area is the pleasant little market town of Church Stretton. It is a good centre for walkers who want to climb these hills.

LOCAL HISTORY

Clun was founded in the Bronze Age and prehistoric relics are kept at the museum. There is a Bronze Age stone circle on a nearby hilltop, and high earthwork walls encircle a fortress at Chapel Lawn. Wroxeter has parts of a Roman town to show and there's a museum of life in Viroconium Cornoviorum. At Quatt the church is deceptive – it looks 18th century but inside it is medieval with a Norman font.

The church at Stokesay has Norman stones, but is largely 17th century with a typical pulpit and sounding board. Nearby Stokesay Castle is a rare example of a fortified moated manor house.

Ludlow is crowned with a looming sandstone castle where Milton's masque *Comus* was first performed, and now a drama festival transforms the fortress every summer. Here the two young sons of Edward 1V were kept before being taken to their death in the Tower of London, and it was the home of the infamous Mortimer who plotted with Queen Isabella to murder Edward II at Berkeley to achieve power through the queen's son.

Shropshire's local government: The County of Shropshire has a two-tier set-up apart from the Wrekin, which controls its own affairs. Shropshire County Council and the five districts of Bridgnorth, North Shropshire, Oswestry, Shrewsbury & Atcham and South Shropshire administer the rest of the County. The towns of Oldbury and Halesowen are Shropshire detached in Worcestershire under the administration of the two unitary councils of Dudley and Sandwell.

FAMOUS NAMES

- ◆ Charles Darwin was born and educated in Shrewsbury. There's a statue in the library gardens.
- ◆ The ashes of A. E. Housman repose in Ludlow churchyard.
- ◆ Clive of India was born in Market Drayton.
- ◆ The composer of Merrie England, Sir Edward German, was born at Whitchurch.
- ◆ Britain's 'first lady' in the early 1990's, Norma Major wife of John, is a Shropshire lass.

COUNTY CALENDAR

- ◆ Shrewsbury's annual Shropshire and West Midlands Show is held in May, and in June there's a regatta and later flower festivals.
- ◆ At Clun there a show and carnival in August, a pageant in May.
- ◆ Ludlow has race meetings and an annual summer festival.
- ◆ Bishop's Castle has a fair in May, and a summer carnival, as well as traction engine rallies.

SOMERSET

BATH *The Royal Crescent with its understated elegance of golden stone graces 30 houses built between 1767 and 1774.*

TO ME THERE are three Somersets – all sharply contrasting. The north, with Bath the southern outskirts of Bristol and the coastline, which takes in the very pleasant resorts of Clevedon, Portishead and Weston-super-Mare with their seaside attractions. The mystical centre with the little city of Wells, the limestoned and caverned Cheddar Gorge and Glastonbury, with its spiritual Tor. Finally and again quite different, the west with Exmoor, Minehead and its common heritage with Devon. It is only when you travel from Minehead to the Devon border that the landscape can be termed spectacular, with great hog-back cliffs created at the point where the hills of Exmoor drop almost perpendicular to the wrinkled sea of the Bristol Channel below. Inland it is a county of superb natural beauty where the hills of Exmoor, the Mendips, the Brendons and the Quantocks rise above rich, mature farmland studded with stone-built towns and quaint villages.

TOWNS AND VILLAGES

Take your pick from the grandeur of the cities of Bath and Wells, more intimate towns like Shepton Mallet and Glastonbury, or the

THE COUNTY LANDSCAPE

◆ Somerset is a rich farming county where cultivation and growing grain took place long before Caesar's arrival. The landscape has an amazing diversity of scenery: there are the high heather-clad hills of Exmoor in the north west with their wild ponies and deer and lovely combes, especially near Oare – Lorna Doone country; the bleak limestone land of the Mendips in the east, and the huge water meadows of the Levels, fed by the rivers Tone, Parrett, Isle and Brue, in between. The Levels have a Fen-like quality about them.

◆ Separating the rivers are ridges of grey and golden limestone, used to good effect for building cities like Bath and Wells.

◆ In the north and east, the deep-cut valley of the River Avon has accentuated the county's isolation from its neighbour, Gloucestershire, encouraging Somerset to look south and west.

◆ All of Bristol south of the Avon is geographically part of Somerset with suburbs dotted right down to Portishead and across to Bath.

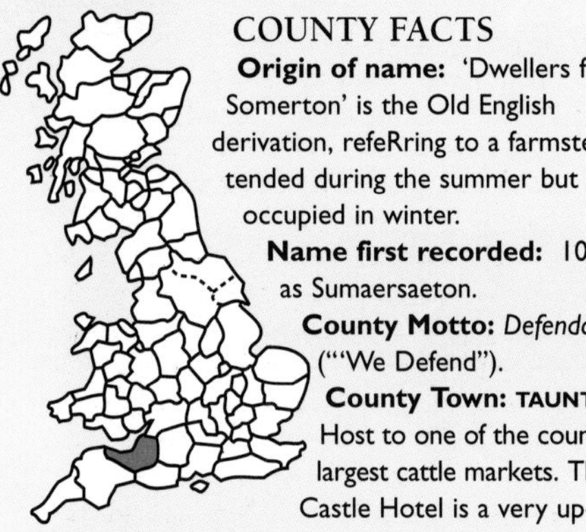

COUNTY FACTS

Origin of name: 'Dwellers from Somerton' is the Old English derivation, refeRring to a farmstead tended during the summer but not occupied in winter.

Name first recorded: 1015 as Sumaersaeton.

County Motto: *Defendamur* ("'We Defend").

County Town: TAUNTON Host to one of the country's largest cattle markets. The Castle Hotel is a very up-market place to stay.

Other Towns:

BATH The city with the best window-shopping in the west takes its name from its unique hot springs.

BRIDGWATER A wide main street, tall spired church and proximity to the civil war battlefield of Sedgemoor put this town on the tour list.

BRISTOL The city's dominance and importance over the centuries has led it to spill both sides of the River Avon and all that area south of the river is within Somerset.

BURNHAM-ON-SEA Miles of sandy beaches attract tourists to this red-brick town facing Bridgwater Bay.

CLEVEDON A quiet resort and residential town on the Severn estuary with a shingle beach and some fine medieval houses.

GLASTONBURY A town associated with Arthur's Avalon and rich in romance and legend; the Abbot's kitchen building at the famous 12th-century Abbey ruins is worth seeing and the nearby sugar-loaf-shaped Tor offers spectacular views over the flats.

MINEHEAD Small-harboured, popular place on the Bristol Channel with picturesque old village and restored old fishermen's chapel (once a salt store).

SHEPTON MALLET Pleasant market town famed for hosting the nearby Glastonbury pop music festival (25 years' worth). There is a market cross and remains of the Shambles of what was once a thriving medieval wool town.

SOMERTON The Saxon capital of Somerset with attractive market place and handsome old Market Cross and late 16th- and 17th-century buildings.

WELLS A gem of a small medieval cathedral city with jousting knights marking the quarter-hour of the superb cathedral clock.

WESTON-SUPER-MARE Highly popular Bristol Channel resort with vast sands stretching into the distance, pier, and lavish entertainment.

YEOVIL Suffered in the air raids of World War II which destroyed many old buildings, but the Ham stone 14th-century church survives. Local history museum in Hendford Manor is well worth a browse.

◆ Bedminster ◆ Bishopsworth ◆ Brislington ◆ Chard ◆ Crewkerne ◆ Frome ◆ Ilminster ◆ Keynsham ◆ Knowle ◆ Long Ashton ◆ Midsomer Norton ◆ Nailsea ◆ Paulton ◆ Porlock ◆ Portishead ◆ Radstock ◆ Street ◆ Watchet ◆ Wincanton

County rivers: Barle, Yeo, Avon, Exe, Tone, Parrett, Brue, Cary and Fortune.

Highest point: Dunkery Beacon at 1,706 feet.

villages of the ancient, eerie Levels, where legends of Joseph of Arimathea, King Arthur and Guinevere abound.

Of all the places in this county, none can compare architecturally with Bath. The city sits in a green fold in the hills, its mellow stone work blending perfectly with the surrounding countryside. Bath, a one-time Roman city, reached its zenith in the late 18th century, when it became the most fashionable spa in Britain thanks almost entirely to the efforts of one man – John Wood.

It was Wood's marvellous talent that led to the creation of one of Britain's greatest architectural masterpieces, the Royal Crescent, a magnificent fan of stone, so unspoilt today that you can almost hear the clop of horses' hooves on the cobbled stones. Over the years Bath has lost none of its charm, despite the huge numbers of visitors who flock to enjoy Bath buns, to the accompaniment of a chamber music, in the Pump Room near the Abbey. Just away from the bustle have a look from Grand Parade at the V-shaped weir that runs just past the Italianate Pulteney Bridge. This city is best visited outside the peak summer season.

After tourism, Somerset has no large-scale industry other than agriculture, now that brick and tile making in and around Bridgwater are declining. But the scenery and the villages remain as compelling as ever. Cheddar has given its name to one of the world's great cheeses, and although little cheese is made here today, visitors do come to admire the limestone caves and the bravest of them indulging themselves in a little pot-holing.

Other places well worth visiting include Dunster, with its wide main street and 17th-century yarn market; Porlock, whose Ship Inn has associations with the poets Southey and Coleridge; and the attractive town of Wellington, close to the Devon border, whose most famous son, the Iron Duke, is commemorated in a conspicuous monument on the highest point of the Blackdown hills. On a 1,000-acre estate at Cricket St Thomas, near Yeovil, there is a wildlife park and the National Heavy Horse Centre.

GLASTONBURY TOR *Rising from the Somerset Levels, this was once an island.*

LOCAL HISTORY

Somerset – 'the old crooked shire in the West' – is believed to have taken its name from the early Saxon settlers who grazed their herds on the county's excellent pastures in summer. Whatever the explanation, the county has a formidable history. Prehistoric man looked out across the Somerset Levels from the Iron Age fort on the isolated hill of Brent Knoll and the Romans established the city of Aquae Sulis above the medicinal waters of what is now Bath. Glastonbury became a great Celtic emporium and it is believed that the massive hill fort at Cadbury could be the site of King Arthur's legendary Camelot. According to the legend, this is the place from which King Arthur set out to find his sword Excalibur.

For those with a taste for something more certain than legend offers, the village of Athelney commemorates the last desperate vigil of King Alfred in the winter of 878, even if it is best remembered as the place where the cakes were burnt rather than the battle at which he defeated the invading Danes. The Isle of Athelney is an island in name only, but in Alfred's time it was surrounded by a waste of trackless marshes which provided the beleaguered king with some security while he regrouped his forces. In subsequent centuries, there were further devastating incursions by the Danes and others – but the gloom was lifted a little when Edmund defeated Canute's army at Penselwood. From then until the Civil War, Somerset prospered; its towns grew, abbeys and monasteries were founded. Montacute House near Yeovil is an example of Tudor domestic architecture at its best. Now in the hands of the National Trust, the house contains an impressive collection of 17th- and 18th-century furniture, as well as Elizabethan and Jacobean portraits.

In the village of Norton St Philip, the George Inn, with its stone floors and timber and plasterwork walls, has the authentic feel of a 15th-century hostelry. It was once a guest house for the now-ruined Hilton Charterhouse Priory. Samuel Pepys once described the tomb of the two ladies at the foot of the priory's tower as having 'two bodies upwards and one stomach.'

Somerset played a considerable part in the Civil War and was staunchly Royalist although Taunton, the county town, was an isolated Parliamentary stronghold. In 1685 Charles II's illegitimate son, the Duke of Monmouth, led a rebellion to overthrow James II and suffered a terrible defeat at Sedgemoor. It was in the Great Hall of the Castle at Taunton, now a museum, that Judge Jeffreys held his Bloody Assizes in the aftermath of that rebellion, hundreds of men being condemned to death in a single day.

Somerset's local government: Apart from the north of the County of Somerset there is two tier local government operating under Somerset County Council and five district councils – Mendip, Sedgemoor, South Somerset, Taunton Deane and West Somerset. North-East Somerset and North-West Somerset & Bath Councils plus that part of the City of Bristol authority south of the River Avon (in 1996 Bristol was made a ceremonial County) are the single-tier structure for the rest of the County. Kilmington is a contiguous part of the County of Somerset under Wiltshire County and Salisbury District Councils. Holwell is Somerset detached in Dorset and administered by both Dorset County and West Dorset District councils.

FAMOUS NAMES

◆ Robert Blake, Cromwell's great admiral, was born in 1599 in Bridgwater where there is a fine museum.
◆ Bristol has developed its own 'happening indie-pop, trip-hop and ambient music scene' with award-winning performers Portishead (named after the suburb of Bristol), Tricky, Massive Attack all playing in each others albums and all achieving critical and commercial success in the mid 1990s.
◆ Parson Woodforde, who wrote *Diary of a Country Parson*, (a classic of 18th century English country life), lived in Castle Cary.
◆ Sir Henry Irving, the first actor to be knighted, was born in the village of Keinton Mandeville.
◆ Television personality Jonathan Dimbleby and his wife, the writer Bel Mooney, live in Swainswick.
◆ The Beatles' film *A Hard Day's Night* was filmed partly on location at Crowcombe and at Minehead.
◆ T. S. Eliot is buried at East Coker, the village from which his ancestors emigrated to the New World.
◆ Leslie Crowther, TV host and enthusiastic Lord's Taverner, lives in Corston.
◆ The town of Wellington gives the Wellesley family its title; its most famous is the Duke of Wellington.

COUNTY CALENDAR

◆ May and June: The internationally acclaimed Bath Music Festival.
◆ May: The Order of British Druids celebrates Beltane, the coming of summer, on Glastonbury Tor.
◆ May: The Royal Bath and West Show takes place near Shepton Mallet.
◆ The last Sunday in May: A Roman Catholic pilgrimage to Glastonbury, followed by a Church of England pilgrimage on the last Saturday in June.
◆ September: A Cheese Festival is held at Frome.
◆ September: There are fairs at Crewkerne and Ilminster
◆ Early November: Bridgwater, Glastonbury and Highbridge hold Guy Fawkes' carnivals.
◆ Wincanton holds race meetings, as does Bath.
◆ The events and venues of Bristol are too numerous to mention here, for this city is Somerset from the moment it spills south across the Avon.

STAFFORDSHIRE

THE COUNTY LANDSCAPE

◆ Staffordshire achieves the geographical feat of very nearly uniting Birmingham and Manchester. It spreads from the northern suburbs of the former almost to Macclesfield, within ten miles of the southern parts of the latter. The open heath and dreary urban wastelands to the northwest of Birmingham are known as the Black Country because of their iron and coal industries. There is a distinctive dialect spoken here. Cannock Chase in the middle, south of Stafford, is wild and ferny heathland, once a medieval hunting forest.

◆ Fast-growing industries in the past two centuries of industrialization and a proliferation of water transport by canal have not urbanized this county. In fact the county and its villages are very rural, and indeed much is still a farming area. Well drained in the north by valleys (notably that of the Trent River and Dovedale) it is a hilly extension of the Derby moors.

◆ Walsall bought the Blackpool Illuminations to bring a little bit of colour to the Stafforshire Black Country.

A CONTRASTING MIXTURE of the very urban and the very rural. Cannock Chase is a great rural spread sandwiched between two different types of industrial area: the Black Country of iron and coal with towns like Wolverhampton and Walsall, and the Potteries with Wedgwood and Spode china manufactured at Stoke-on-Trent and Stafford.

TOWNS AND VILLAGES

Near the county town of Stafford, on the road to Rugeley, is a remarkable great house – Shugborough which has not only a large 18th-century country house to show, but also extensive gardens towards the river. The house lost many of its possessions to a sale by a profligate owner in 1842, but it is still replete with many items of the period, notably porcelains and rare pieces from China and a collection of fabulous French antiques. The formal gardens with clipped shrubs are ornamented with many intriguing temples, architectural follies, monuments and garden statuary. There is a Folk Museum in the old Stable Block.

Lichfield is the county's cathedral city, and has the only English cathedral to preserve three stone spires. The steeples of this compact cathedral are local landmarks, known as the Ladies of the Vale. (The central one was lost in the Civil War and later rebuilt.) Inside you will find a 13th-century choir, transepts and nave, while the multi-tiered west facade, finished about 1300, is like a looming sculpted screen. Lichfield is a pleasing little town which Dr Johnson knew as the son of a local bookseller. The house where he was born is a museum to his memory.

LONGTON *Gladstone Pottery Museum at Longton, one of the Five Towns.*

The bishop's country palace used to be at Eccleshall, originally a castle that has gone through a violent and often odd history. There are lots of porcelain and pottery on view but the family silver went down with the butler when in 1890 the Humber ferry capsized. Not far from Lichfield is Alrewas, which has a Norman church with grotesque carved heads, and Hanbury, whose church has a cross-legged alabaster statue of a

14th-century knight. Hoar Cross Hall, an opulent British Victorian mansion, is in the expansive Tudor style, a country palace of considerable magnificence. Its builder did not live to see it completed however – Henry Meynell was killed in a fox hunting accident in 1871, and the neighbouring church was built by the grieving widow in his memory. The hall was developed for the presentation of 'medieval banquets' in the 1970s.

Newcastle-under-Lyme, Tamworth and Burton upon Trent were in the clothing trade. The latter is famous for brewing, but it also has a local history museum with a gallery of British birds. Tamworth, on the other hand, is known for its pigs.

Wolverhampton is one of the county's best-known towns, famous for engineering works, but originally a wool centre. Nearby Walsall focused on leather and in the 17th century specialized in making locks and keys. There's a unique museum. The two towns sit on the northwestern edge of Birmingham, and while much is depressing suburb there are several fine houses close by. Best known is Weston Park, a red-brick 17th-century house designed by Lady Wilbraham, who as the heiress Elizabeth Mytton owned the original house. She built it in the prevailing style although its interior has been completely altered. Capability Brown laid out the gardens which have many architectural ornaments.

Moseley Old Hall is a rambling half-timbered house on the Stafford road at the edge of the town. It has a fascinating tale to tell of a king's escape as recounted to Samuel Pepys the famous 17th-century diarist by Charles II. After the battle of Worcester the young king, disguised as a a woodcutter, was brought here, leaving after two days and a night to make his secret escape to France.

Just west of Wolverhampton is Wightwick Bank, a rare surviving example of a house built and decorated by the 19th-century movement known as the Pre-Raphaelites. Aside from William Morris tapestries and textiles there are candelabra designed by Holman Hunt and pictures by Rossetti, Ruskin, Burne Jones, Millais, Elizabeth Siddal and Maddox Brown. Even the gardens, with their high clipped yew hedges, are Pre-Raphaelite in style.

To the north Stoke on Trent is the heart of the Five Towns, once crowded with the old bottle-shaped firing kilns. The Five Towns are, with Stoke, actually six – Tunstall, Hanley, Burslem, Fenton and Longton – but that musn't get in the way of a good story. They all display pottery works and you can visit a kiln revamped as a museum at the Gladstone Works, where the packing of the interior for firing is interesting. Be sure to visit the Wedgwood factory at

COUNTY FACTS

Origin of name: Comes from the Old English "ford by the landing place", "steath" being a landing place.

Name first recorded: 1016 as Staeffordscir.

County Town:

STAFFORD Has the large Norman church of St Chad with splendid arcades and arches. The museum holds many special exhibitions throughout the year.

Other Towns:

BURSLEM Another of the Five Towns (as in Arnold Bennett's *Anna of the Five Towns*).

BURTON UPON TRENT The major brewing town of Britain with two brewery museums and brewery tours: what more can you say?

HANLEY One of the Five Towns and full of pottery workshops as well as a city museum, theatre and an art gallery displaying a huge array of ceramics.

LEEK Set in moorland at the southern end of the Peak District and a good set-off point for walkers cyclists and riders. Also plenty of antiques and bric-a-brac to browse through.

LICHFIELD A small city with a splendid 8th-century cathedral with illuminated manuscripts. A Heritage and Treasury Exhibition in St Mary's in the middle of the market square are well worth a visit.

STOKE-ON-TRENT Britain's main pottery and ceramics centre. The sixth town of the famous five.

UTTOXETER Great name! Wotochesede in the Domesday Book or Ucheter to locals today, but it may have derived from Witta which was a man's name and an old word for 'heath'.

WALSALL Came to fame on leather, as in the local soccer team's nickname The Saddlers.

WEST BROMWICH Another Black Country town and home to the famous Albion! The timber-framed Manor House, dating from the early 14 century, became a restaurant.

◆ Aldridge ◆ Biddulph ◆ Bilston ◆ Brierley Hill ◆ Brownhills ◆ Coseley ◆ Darlaston ◆ Great Barr ◆ Harborne ◆ Kisgrove ◆ Rowley Regis ◆ Sedgeley ◆ Smethwick ◆ Streetly ◆ Tamworth ◆ Tipton ◆ Wednesbury ◆ Wednesfield ◆ Willenhall

County rivers: Trent, Penk, Sow, Blithe, Tean, Dove, Churnet, Tame.

Highest point: The Ordnance Station at 1,657 feet.

Staffordshire's local government: A large part of the county is governed on a two-tier basis with Staffordshire County Council and the eight District Councils of Cannock Chase, East Staffordshire, Lichfield, Newcastle-under-Lyme, South Staffordshire, Stafford, Staffordshire Moorlands and Tamworth. The rest of the County has three solely Staffordshire unitary councils, Stoke on Trent, Wolverhampton and Walsall, and three more shared with the Counties of Shropshire, Worcestershire and Warwickshire, namely Birmingham, Dudley and Sandwell. Clent and Broome are both Staffordshire detached in Worcestershire under a two-tier authority of Worcestershire County Council but with Broome in Wyre Forest District and Clent in Bromsgrove District.

COUNTY CALENDAR

◆ June: National craft fair in Stoke.

◆ The folk horn dance, of Norman origin, takes place at Abbots Bromley, near Rugeley, in September (normally on the Monday after the Sunday following 4 September from 8 till 8!). The dancers' attire includes a man on a hobby horse, a maid, a jester, a boy with a bow and arrow, an accordion player and triangle player plus six wearing reindeer antlers.

◆ May: Staffordshire County Show, Stafford.

FAMOUS NAMES.

◆ Reginald Joseph Mitchell was the aircraft designer who created the World War II fighter the Spitfire. He was born in Talke, son a schoolteacher. His life story was made into a biopic produced by and starring Leslie Howard: *First of the Few.*

◆ Arnold Bennett, the Victorian novelist, put Stoke and its neighbours on the map with his famous novels of the Five Towns. He lived in Stoke for seven years.

◆ Doctor Johnson, a famous 18th century literary figure, was born and brought up in Lichfield.

◆ The fisherman's writer (*Compleat Angler*) Izaak Walton was born in Stafford.

◆ Josiah Wedgwood was born in Burslem and founded his pottery in the Five Towns.

◆ Lottery girl Anthea Turner and actor Neil Morrissey (*Men Behaving Badly*) are both from Stoke.

◆ TV's Frank Skinner of Fantasy Football fame is from West Bromwich.

◆ Actress and writer Meera Syal was born in 1963 in Essington not far from Walsall.

nearby Barlaston to see present-day methods of decorating china, and to learn about the processes of pottery and porcelain making. Hanley has a huge collection of pottery in the city museum, from local Staffordshire pieces to South American, Near and Far East and European examples. In Stoke the Arnold Bennett museum shows a collection of the author's possessions.

From here to the Derbyshire border it's open country, with Leek the centre of a web of roads. The town has an art gallery featuring local embroidery.

LOCAL HISTORY

Stafford's Roman origins are illustrated in the one-time posting station of Wall, or Letocetum, near Lichfield. It stood on Watling Street, the principal Roman road from London to North Wales and was originally a place for changing horses – called mutationes, while places where travellers could rest for the night were mansiones. At Wall from the many dated coins found here it's presumed there was a Roman settlement up to the end of the 4th century AD. A set of well-preserved buildings provide what are probably the best surviving example of an extensive Romano-British bath house with many rooms.

Berry Ring is a Iron Age site off the Shrewsbury road from Stafford. Near Wall is the ancient Castle Ring. An Iron Age camp on its hill at Alton Towers has been subsumed by the castle and grounds of a much later 19th-century neo-Gothic mansion. Its famed pleasure gardens are now an amusement park – the most visited attraction charging admission in Britain – beating the likes of Madame Tussaud's and the Tower of London with its Disneyesque rides attracting nearly three million visitors a year.

At Ilam, right on the border with Derbyshire, St Bertram's churchyard has two Saxon crosses. Nearby Ilam Hall preserves the saint's shrine. A local curiosity close to Cheshire is Mow Cop, a steep hill crowned with an exotic 18th-century folly in the shape of a ruined tower, designed to be seen as a landscape ornament from nearby Rode Hall. The Cop is famous as the site of an austere prayer meeting in 1807 which led to the founding of the austere sect of Primitive Methodism.

WEDGWOOD *Firing fine china in the kiln.*

SUFFOLK

EVER SO TRANQUIL, ever so beautiful, Suffolk is a county where few main roads mar the essential peace of the home of the 'Southern people'. No wonder Constable was drawn to the place. It is also a land with a rich wool tradition; wealthy merchants set up shop in the exceptionally pretty small towns of Kersey Lavenham and Long Melford, where many fine timbered houses and large churches testify to the prosperity of this thriving medieval industry. Suffolk is a serene, seductive land of low hills, salty sea and wide open skies where I can commune with the infinite and have done so at Gislingham.

TOWNS AND VILLAGES

There are many remarkable settlements in Suffolk, and anyone getting off the beaten track and onto quiet country roads will stumble across any number of alluring little places, often grouped around a green and with an impressively stone-towered church or a handsome mansion standing in a spreading park. It is small wonder that this bucolic Suffolk scene provided such inspiration to one of Britain's great artists, for John Constable painted his masterpieces around his father's boatyard. Influenced by the French painters Claude and Poussin, Constable's magical views of ordinary English scenes such as *The Corn Field* sum up this heart-warming county of Suffolk.

With its heritage of fine buildings from cottage to castle, it's odd that Suffolk possesses no great town of architectural style and beauty, like Norwich in Norfolk, no real cultural centre of the county. People argue for Bury St Edmund's, once a great centre of pilgrimage and with a fine abbey church, a venerated place that because of its past may be responsible for the soubriquet 'selig' or saintly Suffolk, though this appellation has also been more rudely thought to be the origin of 'silly Suffolk'.

Bury prospered enormously in the medieval period, but it

THE COUNTY LANDSCAPE

- On its North Sea front it is gentle, with shingle shores, sandy beaches or low cliffs, though King Neptune has not always been kind for here the sea can storm in to take away as much as it gives in other parts of Britain. However, birdlife thrives along parts of this coast, especially at Minsmere Bird Sanctuary where avocets and other wading birds seek refuge.
- Inland the softly undulating land is cut into fields and farmsteads, enfolding old, often picturesque villages sunk into flowery meads bordered by slow-flowing streams. The soil base is a soft, friable loam, sometimes clay, over a base of sand. It is a largely agricultural county with belts of woodland; several kinds of crops are produced here alongside cattle farms and smallholdings, with many of the fields still enclosed in low hedges.
- To the west the land breaks up somewhat with high pine-wooded heath around the racing town of Newmarket. There is even some fen. Little dramatic scenery here, but plenty of surprises lie in store in the secrets of Suffolk.

FLATFORD MILL *By the River Stour, featured in many of Constable's paintings.*

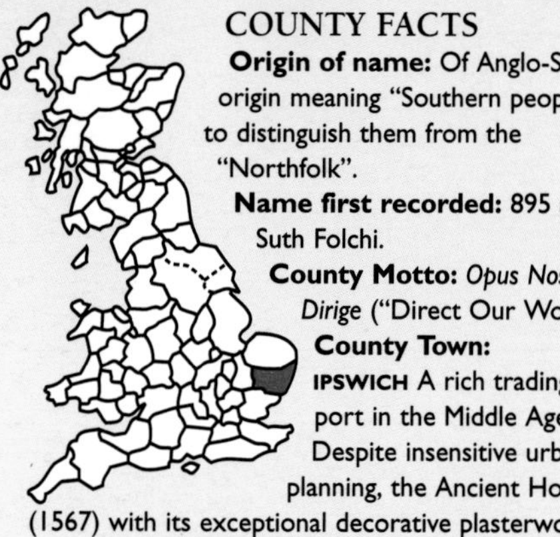

COUNTY FACTS

Origin of name: Of Anglo-Saxon origin meaning "Southern people", to distinguish them from the "Northfolk".

Name first recorded: 895 as Suth Folchi.

County Motto: *Opus Nostrum Dirige* ("Direct Our Work").

County Town:

IPSWICH A rich trading port in the Middle Ages. Despite insensitive urban planning, the Ancient House (1567) with its exceptional decorative plasterwork and Christchurch Mansion are well worth a visit.

Other Towns:

ALDEBURGH Reputedly the best sprats and herring are caught in November and December along its famous long, straight and somewhat desolate shore.

BURY ST EDMUNDS A busy market town manufacturing agricultural instruments.

FELIXSTOWE Seaside resort and container port with Edwardian buildings and a handsome promenade nearly 2 miles long.

FRAMLINGHAM An impressive castle ruin with square towers rather than round ones set in a market town with many attractive buildings centred round the market square. Many film and TV programmes have been shot here.

GORLESTON Seaside resort with a long sandy beach.

HAVERHILL In the far southwest by the border with Essex the centre of Haverhill has been buried by modern development.

LAVENHAM Hardly changed since its heyday as an important Middle Ages wool town, it is one of the most outstanding places in the county. The popular antiques sleuth show *Lovejoy* has been filmed here.

LONG MELFORD A stately village because of all the stately manors and other residences that dot this impressively wealthy area.

LOWESTOFT A centre of fishing from the 14th century and the fleets still unload their catches for the busy fish market. The scores are narrow alleys going down steeply from the High Street to the shore where the herring curing houses stood.

NEWMARKET In a small shepherd's crook of the county, Newmarket offers a handsome and spacious red-brick town that has been a centre of racing for centuries. The Jockey Club's HQ since 1750.

WOODBRIDGE This compact town near Bury was a thriving shipbuilding port, now more famous for antiques and yachts. Along with old houses it has several half-timbered inns.

◆ Bungay ◆ Halesworth ◆ Leiston ◆ Little Yarmouth ◆ Lakenheath ◆ Stowmarket

Main rivers: Deben, Stour, Waveney, Lark.

Highest point: Rede at 420 feet.

Suffolk's local government: A two-tier system of Suffolk County Council and then seven district councils: Babergh, Forest Heath, Ipswich, Mid-Suffolk, St Edmundsbury, Suffolk Coastal and Waveney. Around Suffolk's Gorleston and Little Yarmouth, Norfolk County and Great Yarmouth District Councils take control.

dwindled rapidly in importance after the suppression of the abbeys under Henry VIII. It has wide streets and Georgian houses as well as a period playhouse. The county town of Ipswich may be ancient, and a busy place, but it's hardly worth going in and getting caught up in its crowded streets. Nobody can seriously pretend that workaday Ipswich is on a par with neighbouring Norwich. To be fair to the minster-less Ipswich a dozen medieval churches survived 19th-century redevelopment, in this case destruction, and it does have Christchurch Mansion with a collection of Suffolk antiques and paintings. In the White Horse Inn Dickens provided Mr Pickwick with some adventures.

The busy harbour of Felixstowe is the undisputed king of container cargo and with its ferry services to other European ports and its modern buildings it is in a different league altogether to cliffy Lowestoft, though the latter is also a seaside resort and an ancient place with curiosities to see. From its main street steep alleys called scores go running down to its still used fishing quays and the smokehouses where kippers are made from North Sea herring.

So it is the smaller towns and villages that command attention here, and they richly deserve it. Suffolk has a thick scattering of agricultural settlements, and many of them are worth not just a pause or a passing look, but a stopover to wander round and view their treasures. Wool was a moneymaker here so go to Kersey, a single street dipping down to a ford and up again with thatched and colour-washed houses, its name given to a certain woollen cloth. It's worth warning you: a visit to Suffolk may take much longer than you plan!

Villages begin in the south with a cluster of diamonds. Long Melford is a handsome place with a wide main street, old inns like the Bull and many antique shops as well as two stately homes. Sudbury has a moot hall, medieval houses and a market. It's best known for being the birthplace of painter Thomas Gainsborough, and his house with its imposing doorway can be visited. Clare, a large village in the Stour valley, has many old houses and inns, and it is famed for its pargeting. This is very much a local form of decoration in which panels of plaster on house fronts are raised, mounded and moulded into complicated patterns. Some are white, others colour-washed.

Lavenham would have pride of place in any other county, for it is spectacular. Folded in soft countryside, this group of medieval houses and a grand church is a silvery-grey procession of ancient buildings from guildhall to pub. It merits a long walk of discovery, and best of all it is a living place too.

There are fewer settlements in the high and heathy west, but you should add Glemsford and Wickhambrook to your list. Kentford, Mildenhall and Elveden with Victorian cottages occupy wide open county. The Waveney valley in the north is part of the Broads, since it's a river crowded with pleasure craft. Beccles is an attractive town with several streets of Georgian brick houses. Somerleyton Hall has sumptuous furnishings and there's a maze in the gardens, Fritton has beech trees and a secret lake.

Red-brick and tile Orford has a castle with a circular many-sided keep and ancient church, while at Aldeburgh a small Victorian resort still shows its charms. This is true also of Southwold, and Lowestoft is flanked with beach resorts at Kessingland and Corton. Inland off the main road and across an eerie inlet of tidal flats erupts the surprising church of Blythburgh with its high windows and carved angel roof within.

LOCAL HISTORY

There is an Iron Age encampment near Clare. Ipswich has a good collection of Stone Age and Saxon treasures in its museum, which also contains replicas of the fabled Mildenhall and Luton Hoo treasures which are now in the British Museum. Southwold's museum contains local relics and fossils in a 17th-century house. Brandon, famous for flint knapping, is on the site of an Iceni village.

Along the eastern shore, Dunwich was a prosperous medieval port with a trade in woollen goods to the Low Countries, but after a series of violent storms it was eaten by the greedy North Sea 700 years ago, and bits still keep falling into the water, for the erosion is constant. They say if you stand on the crumbling cliff near the fragment of town that is left you can still hear the lonely tolling of bells under the waves if you listen hard – for Dunwich had eight churches before the storms began their work.

NEWMARKET *The first recorded horse race took place here in 1619.*

FAMOUS NAMES

- Outspoken theatre director Sir Peter Hall is a native of Bury St Edmunds.
- Author and critic V. S. Prichett was born in Ipswich.
- BBC foreign correspondent John Simpson spent much of his childhood in crumbling Dunwich.
- King John was brought to book by the barons at Bury St Edmund's and a butcher's son, later Cardinal Wolsey, from Ipswich achieved the high office of Chancellor under Henry VIII.
- The Merry Monarch, King Charles II, made Newmarket famous, lending his name to events.
- Gregory Peck came to Alpheton and its American air base to star in the film *Twelve O'Clock High*.

COUNTY CALENDAR

- The Suffolk Agricultural Show, the Military Tattoo in Ipswich and the Southwold Fair take place in June.
- Founded by Benjamin Britten (who was born in Lowestoft) in 1947, the Aldeburgh Festival takes place each year for three weeks in June.
- Framlingham Castle hosts events from Civil War battles to Shakespeare plays and dog trials.
- Flat racing at Newmarket in spring and summer.
- Power-boat racing at Oulton Broad and Lowestoft.
- Late August: Felixstowe Fuschia Festival.
- July: Bungay Festival, drama, music, parade. Music and fireworks at Bungay Castle.

SURREY

THE COUNTY LANDSCAPE

◆ Rising steadily up from the floor of the Thames Valley, with the river supplying its northern border, Surrey is crossed from east to west by the rolling chalk slopes of the North Downs – including the popular walking (and skiing if there is snow) area of Box Hill – whose escarpments are sheer to the south.

◆ Further east is a range of sandy hills, which reach their highest point in the outcrop of Leith Hill, a secluded and thickly wooded beauty spot (with a tower dating from 1766) which offers superb views south across the Surrey Weald. It is said that on a clear day you can see Surrey, Sussex, parts of Hampshire, Berkshire, Oxfordshire, Buckinghamshire, Hertfordshire, Middlesex, Essex and Kent – and with the aid of a telescope some of Wiltshire – giving a field of vision of 260 miles!

◆ The Downs are intersected by the River Mole near Dorking, and further west by the Rivers Wey and Eden. The former is linked to the Thames by navigable waterways.

THIS PARADOXICAL COUNTY encompasses the hallowed Centre Court of Wimbledon and the peaceful deer park of Richmond; it also radiates out from familiar-sounding places like Brixton, Barnes, Putney, Battersea and Clapham and sprawls along surburbia. But after you hit the North Downs you enter an unchanged and enchanting land of village greens with cricket games and quaint pubs, wooded hills offering not-too-vigorous hiking – a curious contrast that gives Surrey its uniqueness.

TOWNS AND VILLAGES

Although Surrey lies on the south bank of the Thames, that hasn't appeared to have hindered the rapid expansion of London into its territory, and what a mere 80 years ago were a host of small country towns and villages within 15 miles of the metropolis have now been absorbed into its great, amorphous mass. The much-vaunted Green Belt around London is gradually being squeezed tighter and tighter, and if you want to get an idea of how pleasantly rural and rustic life must have been in most of this county a century ago, you will need to travel some 20-plus miles from the centre of London. Even then, you will still be made aware of what London's proximity has meant to the county when you encounter the concrete swathe of the orbital M25 motorway slicing its path along the North Downs from Kent round to Middlesex at Staines. Within its circumference lies classic commuter-land, which rises up the reverse slope of the North Downs from the Thames Valley. The series of small towns which are positioned along the spring-line on this side of the chalk downs, such as Cheam, Ewell, Epsom, Croydon, as well as Leatherhead and Sutton, have now expanded into one

COMPTON *Idyllic Surrey landscape less than 3 miles from Guildford city centre.*

continuous belt, from whence a fair number of its working population make a stamina-sapping return journey into the capital's centre each working day by road and rail.

If you're observant though, you can still pick out the remnants of the original town centres, even though these vestiges are usually now surrounded by modern offices and shopping developments. Croydon and Sutton, for example, have undergone extensive redevelopment in recent years, with the former's unprepossessing higgledy-piggledy streets giving way to high rise office blocks.

The city of Guildford has been likened to 'the buckle in the stockbroker's belt'. It hasn't escaped redevelopment lightly either, and now boasts a prominent red-brick cathedral, consecrated in 1961, and a modern university. You might not equate the Surrey downs with the Scottish Highlands, but the producers of the hit film *Four Weddings and a Funeral* were happy to let Albury Park, near Guildford, double up as just that (they were strapped for cash) for the wedding of Hamish (Corin Redgrave) and Carrie (Andie Macdowell). Dorking bestrides the gap where the River Mole carves its way through the chalk Downs at the foot of the impressive sheerness of Box Hill at nearly 700 feet. The town has few sights of interest itself but makes an ideal starting point for some of the wonderful walks around.

Chessington's World of Adventure was originally a zoo, but has now been remodelled as a contemporary theme park, like Thorpe Park near Chertsey, while still retaining some of its animal attractions. On the A3 at Wisley are the Royal Horticultural Society's Gardens, a mecca for keen gardeners, and of course the country's most famous botanical gardens, at Kew, also lie within the county. Near Wisley are the National Trust properties of Polesden Lacey (a Regency-style mansion built by Thomas Cubitt housing collections of Chinese porcelain, silver and fine paintings) and Clandon West.

Surrey's only remaining castle stands at Farnham, tucked away on its southwestern border, where the high street exhibits some splendid Georgian buildings.

The county's soil and sheltered climate has also witnessed the growth of viticulture with the Denbies Wine Estate near Dorking comprising 250,000 acres of vineyard – one of the largest in Europe and 300,000 vines planted with 18 different grape varieties. The Romans were growing wine in the region 2,000 years ago and the chalky down soil structure runs on under the Channel to the Champagne region in France so the growers must be on to a good thing. It is open to the public with tours of the vats and other wine-growing activities.

COUNTY FACTS

Origin of name: Surrey derives from the Old English "Suthrige" meaning the region south of the Thames, probably of Middlesex.

Name first recorded: 722 as Suthrige.

County Town:

KINGSTON-UPON-THAMES Several Saxon kings crowned here, hence the name (King's Town).

Other Towns:

CROYDON The palace here has been owned by the archbishops of Canterbury since the Conquest. Fairfield Hall is a Festival Hall-style building comprising a concert hall, smaller theatre (named after Dame Peggy Ashcroft), and art gallery. My great uncle was once Mayor of Croydon.

EPSOM Medicinal purging waters impregnated with alum and discovered in 1618 – otherwise known as Epsom Salts. The racecourse dominates proceedings in this not unattractive market town. The Derby has taken place here since 1780.

FARNHAM End of the road for the Hog's Back, a high ridge of chalk taking the A31 over 500 feet high.

GATWICK London's second-largest airport and main employer for many miles around. Opened in 1958.

GUILDFORD All the modern shops and a fine theatre.

HASELMERE Set in beautiful dense woodland, this is picture postcard Surrey countryside with 17th-century tiled houses surviving. Finely crafted musical instruments continue to be made here.

LEATHERHEAD Another market town another modern theatre (this one is the Sybil Thorndike Theatre). John Wesley preached his last sermon in this Surrey town before he died.

RICHMOND Originally called Shene (Shining or splendour because it was so fine) and became Richmond after Henry VII took a summer residence there (he was earl of Richmond in Normandy before being crowned king, hence the name).

SOUTHWARK The surroundings have undergone massive re-building as Shakespeare's Globe Theatre rises again (thanks to Sam Wanamaker) but the cathedral started life in 1106.

WIMBLEDON Synonymous with tennis and HQ of the All England Lawn Tennis and Croquet Club. There is an attractive heath with two ponds and windmill (1817).

WOKING Once had the biggest mosque in England.

◆ Camberwell ◆ Godalming ◆ Mitcham ◆ Reigate ◆ Streatham ◆ Tooting ◆ Wandsworth

County rivers: Mole, Wey, Thames, Eden.

Highest point: Leith Hill at 965 feet.

Surrey's local government: The southwest of Surrey is two-tier provided by Surrey County Council and the 10 District Councils of Elmbridge, Epsom & Ewell, Guildford, Mole Valley, Reigate & Banstead, Runnymede, Surrey Heath, Tandridge, Waverley and Woking. A small part at Gatwick Airport is also two-tier provided by West Sussex County and Crawley District Councils. The northeast is governed by 8 unitary boroughs: Croydon, Kingston, Lambeth, Merton, Southwark, Sutton, Wandsworth and Richmond-upon-Thames (shared with Middlesex).

FAMOUS NAMES

◆ Three of the Beatles lived on the private St George's Estate during the 1960s.

◆ Other more contemporary artists who reside in the county include members of Squeeze and Soul II Soul and pin-up actors Tim Roth and Gary Oldman.

◆ Aldous Huxley, author of *Brave New World*, was born in Godalming in 1894.

◆ William Cobbett, the writer and social commentator, was born at Farnham in 1762. In his famous book *Rural Rides*, he castigated the influence of London in corrupting and destroying the pastoral beauty of his home county.

◆ John Keats and Robert Louis Stevenson both stayed at the Burford Bridge Hotel at the foot of Box Hill, where the poet John Keats finished writing his epic poem *Endymion*. Now the nearby carpark is a haven for bikers out for the weekend.

◆ George Meredith, the novelist, lived at Flint Cottage on Box Hill for 40 years, and is buried in the cemetery at Dorking.

◆ Lewis Carroll often stayed with his sister at Guildford where he died in 1898.

COUNTY CALENDAR

◆ April: Leith Hill Music Festival at Dorking.

◆ May: Farnham Festival of Youth & Music.

◆ June/July: Polesden Lacey Open Air Theatre Festival at Leatherhead.

◆ October: Croydon Fair.

◆ July: Metropolitan Police Horse Show at Imber Court, Thames Ditton.

◆ 1st week in June: Derby (Oaks) Race Meeting at Epsom.

◆ August/September: Guildford Agricultural Show at Guildford (Stoke Park) while the Surrey County Show, also at Guildford, takes place in May.

◆ July: Annual music festival at Haslemere features medieval music and instruments made locally.

◆ August: Egham & Thorpe Royal Show at Runnymede.

LOCAL HISTORY

In prehistoric times much of the woodland between the downs was used for smelting and there were a number of iron foundries. At Wotton were built the first mills in England for casting brass. Guildford was once the centre of the cloth industry until the Industrial Revolution transferred it 'up north'.

Much of Surrey was handed over to William the Conqueror's nobles after the Conquest, and fortified castles were built as a protection at Farnham, Guildford and at other major points along the routes from the southern coast to London. In later centuries, the beautiful countryside became a favourite hunting ground for royalty, and pockets of these areas still exist at Nonsuch (at Cheam). Herds of deer still run free in these green spaces.

In 1215, King John reluctantly signed and sealed the Magna Carta at a convocation of his barons in a field at Runnymede near Egham. Surrey's subsequent status as a favourite home base for stockbrokers and other wealthy people was initially reflected in the large numbers of prominent individuals who resided here from Tudor times onwards. They included Sir Francis Walsingham, Lord Howard of Effingham, and Cardinal Wolsey who also began the building of Hampton Court Palace in Middlesex.

Surrey is rich in ecclesiastical landmarks: Lambeth Palace, has been a home to the Archbishops of Canterbury for 700 years, and is a splendid Tudor brick residence with white stone facings. Its library has writings from Caxton, Bacon, Gladstone and Elizabeth I. Dulwich has its famous college founded by a rival of Shakespeare, Edward Alleyn. He made his money in the 1600s from his share of the Bear Garden in Southwark, where gambling on bull- and bear-baiting took place. Dulwich also has a famous picture gallery with original portraits of Elizabethan actors.

The forests of the Weald once provided the oak for British ships that saw action in the Napoleonic Wars as well as a flourishing charcoal industry. Today, Surrey's light industry and services have swept away agricultural activities of earlier times, but the demands of London ensure that there is still considerable market gardening.

RICHMOND *The Royal Deer Park is 11 miles in circumference and has 11 gates.*

SUSSEX

THINK OF SUSSEX think of *'Yea, Sussex by the sea!'* – Rudyard Kipling's eulogy to Sussex was written almost 100 years ago, and most of us still think of Sussex as a seaside county. It is, of course, and a jolly lot of fun it gives too, but away from the unconventional razzmatazz of Brighton and the breeziness of the other resorts the county has a calm and beauty which makes it instantly appealing – a sort of Lancashire of the south. I feel a tremendous affinity towards Sussex, especially Eastbourne, where I've been sent on many a happy theatrical assignment.

TOWNS AND VILLAGES

But you must begin in Brighton. The county's largest town is a curious mix of the seedy and the sublime – and the gay in every sense of the word – with a New Age element that only Glastonbury can match. Graham Greene wrote colourfully of the town's vulgar mystique in *Brighton Rock*, but he didn't dwell on the best bits. True, parts of the town can look a little run-down, in the way parts of Nice do, but the overall impression is of a place with a fair degree of style. A good case can be made for suggesting that Brighton is the place for Regency architecture. It has never looked back since, in the 1770s, the lively Prince Regent, later George IV, began patronizing what was then called Brighthelmstone (a sleepy fishing village) in the company of his mistress, thus setting the trend for what is now known as the 'dirty weekend'. In his wake, in the middle of Old Steine, came the edifice that frequently wins the title of England's Most Eccentric Building, the Royal Pavilion, an exotic, eastern-inspired creation by John Nash, designer of London's Regent Street. While in Brighton, also take time out to visit the Lanes, the delightful warren of narrow, pedestrianized streets where you'll find some of the best shops and restaurants in town, and go for a stroll along the promenade, where the Grand Hotel is fully restored to health after the infamous bombing at the Tory Party Conference, and the Palace Pier is the only one still standing after the so-called Great Storm in 1987 when the West Pier went west!

THE COUNTY LANDSCAPE

- ◆ Sussex's spine is the South Downs, the ancient chalk ridge running from east to west, separating the Weald from the English Channel.
- ◆ The South Downs Way footpath runs for 80 scenic miles from Beachy Head to Buriton just over the border in Hampshire, skirting the crests and dipping in and out of the valleys.
- ◆ Much of the Weald, once an ancient forest, is now given over to farming – but some areas, such as Ashdown Forest, are still preserved in more or less their original state.
- ◆ Sussex is drained north to south by a number of rivers, the largest of which are the Adur, Ouse, Rother and Arun, which have cut their way through gaps in the chalk, draining into the English Channel.
- ◆ Cinque Ports: Originally the four Kent ports of Dover, Hythe, New Romney and Sandwich and Sussex's Hastings. Later additions being Rye and Winchelsea. The Cinque Ports were created to defend the south-east coast of England, and until the reign of Henry VII they provided nearly all the ships and sailors of the nation, as a result they enjoyed many special privileges.

BRIGHTON *The most famous exotic building in the country, the Royal Pavilion.*

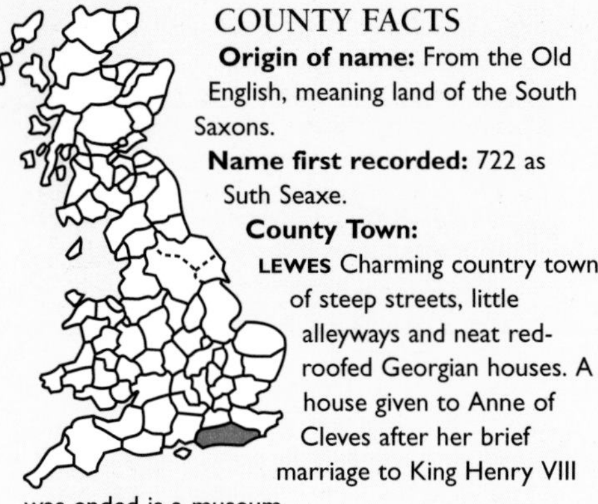

COUNTY FACTS

Origin of name: From the Old English, meaning land of the South Saxons.

Name first recorded: 722 as Suth Seaxe.

County Town:

LEWES Charming country town of steep streets, little alleyways and neat red-roofed Georgian houses. A house given to Anne of Cleves after her brief marriage to King Henry VIII was ended is a museum.

Other Towns:

ARUNDEL A delightful town with steep walks and a medieval castle and church to be proud of.

BATTLE If you can't cross the Channel to see it, there is a replica of the Bayeux Tapestry (1821) in Langton House, which also displays a history of the town.

BEXHILL-ON-SEA Popular seaside town developed by Earl de la Warr after whom the Pavilion is named.

BOGNOR REGIS One of the earliest seaside resorts, known to Queen Victoria as "dear little Bognor".

BRIGHTON Levels of sophistication, accommodation and service matched in few other areas of Britain outside the capital.

CHICHESTER Roman and Georgian influences intermingle in this unpretentious city. The great Norman cathedral has works of art by John Piper and Graham Sutherland.

CRAWLEY A classic 60s New Town but the old high street still retains some 16th-century buildings of note including the George Inn.

EASTBOURNE Being top of the seaside sunshine league year after year no doubt helps this seaside resort thrive as it has since the early 1800s.

HASTINGS The story of 1066 is presented audio-visually inside the ruins of the Norman castle. The Fishermen's Museum is packed with local treasures.

HORSHAM One town that has been tastefully redeveloped with indoor malls and a pedestrianized high street. Several lanes and streets reveal olde-worlde Sussex houses. It is the RSPCA's capital.

MIDHURST A classic small Sussex Weald market town somewhat congested by passing traffic but highly attractive and with famous half-timbered Spread Eagle Hotel as well as nearby Cowdray Park.

RYE Twisting cobbled streets with ancient half-timbered and Georgian buildings all perched high up on a bluff give this town considerable charm.

SOUTHWICK Resort dating back to Roman times. Charles II is said to have hidden at the cottage on the green before escaping to France from Shoreham after the Battle of Worcester.

WORTHING Another pier, another beach, Worthing is a typical Sussex seaside resort and remains popular long after George III descended upon it.

◆ East Grinstead ◆ Haywards Heath ◆ Littlehampton ◆ Newhaven ◆ Selsey ◆ Shoreham ◆ Steyning

Main rivers: Arun, Adur, Cuckmere, Ouse, Rother.

Highest point: Blackdown Hill at 918 feet.

Farther along the coast lies the county's only city, Chichester, famed for its annual middle-brow festival of plays at its excellent theatre-in-the-round, and for nearby 'Glorious' Goodwood Races (second only to Ascot for social prestige). This is a well-heeled place with many uninspiring retirement dwellings sprinkled along the shores. Picturesque Bosham Harbour is a notable exception. Inland Sussex tends to be even more refined. The chalk South Downs separate the coast from the Weald, once a vast forest but now predominantly rich farmland given over to the rearing of cattle and the growing of crops. Today virtually all that remains of significant woodland is Ashdown Forest, thousands of acres of gently undulating woods and heathland which makes excellent walking country.

At the foot of the Downs there is a labyrinth of attractive little towns and villages, many creaking under the weight of formidable history. Lewes, the county town, has a ruined Norman castle and an attractive jumble of medieval streets, and the annual summer opera season at Glyndebourne is now famous the world over. There is, of course, no getting away from the remains of Norman castles in Sussex. In addition to Hastings, you'll come across one, too, in Bramber, now a commuter village but in the days of William the Conqueror a provincial capital and port on the river Adur.

Sussex is awash, too, with fine buildings. In addition to the Royal Pavilion, there are splendid Elizabethan buildings like Glynde Place, near Lewes, and the mainly 17th-century Petworth House at Petworth, which has a number of paintings by Turner and Van Dyck. But in Sussex you will also find more modest hall houses and cottages brick-built on the ground floor with timber on the first floor – a distinctive style, popular in the 18th century and found throughout the South East.

Midhurst and Petworth still retain their old small country town images – and are within easy reach of many of the historic centres of Sussex, such as Arundel, built beneath the massive battlemented walls and keep of Arundel Castle, where international touring teams often have their first warm-up match against the Duke of Norfolk's XI.

LOCAL HISTORY

The Battle of Hastings in 1066 is the date everyone remembers from school history lessons – but the county we now know as Sussex was thriving long before then. On the hilltops of the Downs, prehistoric man left his mark in hill camps, the largest and most important being Cissbury Ring, near Worthing. Later the Romans built one of their principal roads, Stane Street, through Sussex from Regnum

(Chichester) over Bignor Hill to London and signs of their occupation can be seen in the splendid villa at Bignor, which contains some of the best mosaics outside Italy, and the six-acre palace at Fishbourne, near Chichester, with hypocausts (that's Roman central heating to you) and a famous mosaic of a boy and dolphin. The city also boasts one of the finest Norman cathedrals in England.

After defeating King Harold at Hastings – the battle actually took place seven miles outside the town (at Battle!) – William celebrated his victory by building Battle Abbey and then divided Sussex into six 'rapes' (ancient areas of government called hundreds elsewhere), each with its own strip of coast – Chichester, Arundel, Bramber, Lewes, Pevensey and Hastings. In the 14th century, the success of sheep farming on the Downs led to some local prosperity and the Saxon manors flourished into great Tudor estates. Later came ecclesiastical culture from Europe, seen today in medieval wall paintings in churches in West Chiltington and Hardham.

Two of the most impressive large estates in England are those at Cowdray Park, near Midhurst, and Petworth. Cowdray Park is an impressive open space surrounded by beech, oak and chestnut trees, with the ruin of Cowdray House nearby. Polo is a famous pastime in the grounds here. The house was built in 1530, but was burned down in 1793. A week later its then owner, Lord Montagu, drowned in Germany – fulfilling, according to legend, a curse laid on the family by a monk ejected from Battle Abbey by the first owner of Cowdray House after Henry VIII's dissolution of the monasteries.

MIDHURST *Picturesque market town in rural Sussex.*

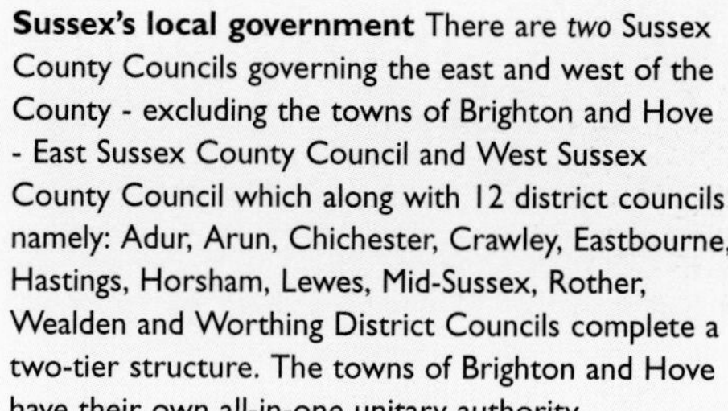

Sussex's local government There are *two* Sussex County Councils governing the east and west of the County - excluding the towns of Brighton and Hove - East Sussex County Council and West Sussex County Council which along with 12 district councils namely: Adur, Arun, Chichester, Crawley, Eastbourne, Hastings, Horsham, Lewes, Mid-Sussex, Rother, Wealden and Worthing District Councils complete a two-tier structure. The towns of Brighton and Hove have their own all-in-one unitary authority.

FAMOUS NAMES

◆ Sussex has always been popular with writers. Rudyard Kipling lived in a Jacobean ironmaster's house, Bateman's, near Burwash.

◆ The American writer Henry James lived for a while at Lamb House, Rye.

◆ Dora Bryan, one of Britain's best-loved actresses, lives in Brighton.

◆ Pop star and former Beatle Paul McCartney and his wife, Linda, live at Peasmarsh.

◆ Some of the location work for the BBC TV sitcom *Waiting for God* was filmed at Eastbourne.

◆ Loadsamoney comedian Harry Enfield was born in and went to school in Horsham. He grew up in Billingshurst and remembers serving actor James Bolam there while working at the chemists.

◆ Worthing and Bognor Regis were the apt locations for the movie *Wish You Were Here* about growing up in a 50s seaside resort. The film launched the career of Emily Lloyd.

◆ The television series Mapp and Lucia - starring Geraldine McEwan, Prunella Scales and Nigel Hawthorne - was filmed at Rye.

COUNTY CALENDAR

◆ May–September: The Chichester drama festival. John Gielgud, Maggie Smith, Keith Michell et al have performed here. Every seat in the six-sided Festival Theatre in Oaklands Park is within 66 feet of the stage. Take a picnic on the lovely grounds beside the modern complex first.

◆ May–September: The Glyndebourne Festival Opera season is held at Glyndebourne near Lewes.

◆ Last Tuesday in July: Goodwood meeting, one of the most important in the racing calendar, opens at the famous South Down course.

◆ August: The International Bird Man Rally, when competitors throw themselves off the end of the pier in Bognor Regis in an attempt to prove they can fly.

◆ November: the London-Brighton veteran car race.

◆ 5–6 June: Corpus Christi Carpet of Flowers takes place at Arundel's Cathedral of Our Lady, built in the grandiose French Gothic style.

◆ June: Eastbourne's International Ladies Tennis Championship serves up Wimbledon hors d'oeuvres.

◆ Each August: Eastbourne United F.C. from Sussex, play Osterly F.C. from Middlesex for the Russell Grant Saxon Shield.

WARWICKSHIRE

THE COUNTY LANDSCAPE

- Not more than 70 miles or so from the coast, Warwickshire is a peaceful place of fertile fields, often with dry stone walls, woods and pastures.
- The hilly edge of the beautiful rolling Cotswolds runs up from neighbouring Oxfordshire and Gloucestershire in the south into Warwick so at the southeastern edges you have chalk hills and typical Cotswold scenery with neat fields and mellow mossed stone houses reminiscent of Oxfordshire villages. Plenty of sheep and cattle too on the extensive farmland of this area.
- The centre is lush and well watered, with the River Avon running right through from Bidford to Rugby. The river valley is a principal contributor to the land formation and serves several towns and villages.
- A second valley threads through the north of the county, that of the Blythe, running between the ever-extending Birmingham and Coventry and entering Staffordshire at Tamworth. The open land adds to the sum of the varied scenery. Here, between the cities, it is pleasantly undulating countryside, with good communications which in part account for Warwickshire's large industrial conurbations being founded here.

YOU COULD ASK for no more typical English countryside than this spectacular rich green spread that is a quilt of quintessential England. An Englishness centred on Stratford-upon-Avon and Warwick itself, though I have a fondness for Birmingham and Coventry, too, where the people are so friendly although there is a city rivalry between the two.

TOWNS AND VILLAGES

Warwickshire's very varied settlements range from the bucolic beauty of villages and towns made rich from agriculture (notably wool) such as Shipston-on-Stour and Stratford by the winding Avon and Stour rivers in the south to elegantly laid out Royal Leamington Spa and Warwick in the centre. In the leafy west towards Worcestershire are characterful towns like Henley-in-Arden and Alcester, old, atmospheric and comfortable. In the far east is the commercial centre of Rugby, famous as the school town where Tom Brown spent his early days. As the county climbs north towards Leicestershire and Staffordshire it becomes more urbanized with busy Coventry city and ever-spreading Birmingham all but elbowing Sutton Coldfield, Atherstone and Nuneaton into the northernmost corner of this exquisite county.

Birmingham is a city not as unwelcoming as its growing urban sprawl might indicate. With its National Exhibition Centre and Symphony Hall it aspires to become the cultural, artistic and commercial centre of the land. In and around Birmingham you have more olde-worlde pleasures such as the 17th-century Aston Hall, once a grand house and now an important local museum of furniture and paintings, while other period rooms can be seen at 16th-century Blakesley Hall with its wall paintings. Birmingham's Anglican cathedral St Philip's is in unusual early Georgian baroque style, and St Chad's, its Catholic cathedral of 1841, was designed by Pugin. The City Museum and Art Gallery has a number of excellent collections (pictures, drawings, ceramics and silver – the city has long had its own assay office). There are several theatres (the Birmingham Royal Ballet is at home here) and a

STRATFORD-UPON-AVON *Shakespeare's gabled Tudor house in Henley Street.*

lively shopping centre as well as many markets of all kinds offering often exotic goods from new settlers. One of the finest of Britain's small museums is the Barber Institute, with a small yet very fine collection of pictures, antique bronzes and ivories in an immaculate suburban setting. Birmingham has a jewellery quarter, and makes many foodstuffs from chocolate to Indian specialities.

Sutton Coldfield is marked by its high television mast, and nearby is a Jacobean castle, Bromwich Hall. At Merevale, near Athelstan, the church was the original gate chapel of a large Cistercian abbey, now lying in scattered ruins. Astley possesses a church with ancient choir stalls, while Nuneaton offers a museum with varied collections from mementoes of George Eliot to local pottery. South of Nuneaton you pass through Bedworth to come to Coventry, which is well worth investigating.

The World War II blitz that destroyed so much of this motor-making town did leave some ancient pockets that are all the more treasured for being survivors – there is an unusually fine Elizabethan hospital, a set of almshouses, and a net of narrow streets around the ruins of the great parish church that became Coventry's cathedral, only to burn at the height of the fiery onslaught. The striking new cathedral by Basil Spence, which seems peculiarly stuck in the 1960s, is built next to the ruins of its precursor. Imagine the old cathedral as it appeared after that blazing night in 1940, its floor littered with charred timbers and thousands of medieval nails freed by the flames. The red stone walls and spired tower, almost 300 feet high, are all that remain. In the city of the famous ride of Lady Godiva you will find a thriving motor museum and the Belgrade Theatre, named after its twin Serbian capital.

A few miles west and you are in the Forest of Arden, used by Shakespeare in his comedy *As You Like It*, though some claim it is the Ardennes of Belgium that is the setting. Berkswell has a famous well, a set of stocks on its green and a cannon from the Crimean War outside the Tudor half-timbering and thatch of the Bear Hotel. There are Victorian almshouses and a church with a rare feature – two crypts.

East you come to Rugby, a major rail junction, via Brinklow and here are the school buildings framed in playing fields. To the southwest Royal Leamington Spa and Warwick are as close as Minneapolis is to St Paul. The former received its prefix from Queen Victoria and it possesses some charming Regency houses, formal gardens, and an art gallery with modern pictures and collections of 18th-century glasses and ceramics.

COUNTY FACTS

Origin of name: Anglo-Saxon, meaning "the farm by a river dam". War means an offshoot from a larger farm; Wic is a weir or dam, constructed for catching fish.

Name first recorded: 1016 as Waeinewiscscr.

County Motto: *Non Sanz Droict* ("Not Without Right").

County Town:
WARWICK At the centre of the county, this old town has picturesque half-timbered houses, including the Elizabethan Oken's House which is a doll museum.

Other Towns:

ASTON Famous football team (Villa). Aston Hall is a great Jacobean house dating from 1635 with a panelled long gallery that is one of the finest in the land.

BIRMINGHAM Ring-road city but if you can navigate through it well worth a visit to the City Museum and Art Gallery and Science & Industry Museum. Bournville, home to Cadbury's chocolate, is an absolutely fascinating garden-suburb-factory estate established by George and Richard Cadbury with their Quaker idealism to provide pleasant and healthy working surroundings for their workers. Cadbury World is a must for any choco-holics!

COVENTRY Known as the city of three spires: the original 303 feet cathedral spire that survived German bombs; Holy Trinity Church at 231 feet; and Christ Church's spire at 204 feet.

EDGBASTON A mere six-minute drive from the city centre, this is home to the famous international cricket ground but there are also fine Botanical Gardens laid out in 1831, and Cardinal Newman's Classical church, the Oratory.

KENILWORTH The castle is its glory with Norman, Plantagenet and Tudor add-ons – Henry I, Henry II, John of Gaunt, Henry VIII and Elizabeth I all had connections with it. Cromwell had it dismantled and it remains the grandest fortress ruin in the country.

NUNEATON Busy manufacturing town with 12th-century Church of St Nicholas.

ROYAL LEAMINGTON SPA Fashionable 19th-century spa town with lovely Georgian, Regency, and early Victorian terraced houses. Napoleon III resided here awhile, and the Duke of Wellington, Sarah Bernhardt and others took its waters.

RUGBY Apart from the obvious - the market dates back to Henry III.

STRATFORD-UPON-AVON There is much to see here, and it is also a lively market and shopping centre for local people. In the many pubs try the local beer.

SUTTON COLDFIELD Saxon ties. Glorious Sutton Park has altered little since Norman times.

◆ Alcester ◆ Bedworth ◆ Coleshill ◆ Knowle ◆ Solihull

Main rivers: Avon, Tame, Anker.

Highest point: Ilmington Downs at 854 feet.

Warwickshire's local government: The County of Warwickshire is an administrative mixture: Warwickshire County Council along with the five districts of North Warwickshire, Nuneaton & Bedworth, Rugby, Stratford-upon-Avon and Warwick complete the two-tier line-up. The City of Coventry and the Borough of Solihull are single-tier authorities exclusively covering Warwickshire land while Birmingham Council provides services for not only parts of Warwickshire's territory but Staffordshire's and Worcestershire's too. Tardebigge and Hewell Grange is Warwickshire detached in Worcestershire under that County and Bromsgrove District Coucils.

FAMOUS NAMES

◆ Comedian Tony Hancock came from Birmingham.

◆ Writer David Lodge teaches English at Birmingham University, which provides the background for many of his wry novels.

◆ Shakespeare, of course, was born in Stratford-upon-Avon.

◆ The 15th-century Earl of Warwick known as the Kingmaker lived at Warwick Castle, now owned and run by Madame Tussaud's.

◆ Francis Galton, who studied heredity and found that everyone's fingerprints are unique, lived in Claverdon.

◆ George Eliot (real name Mary Ann Evans), authoress of the novel on which TV's popular *Middlemarch* was based, was born in 1819 at Arbury near Nuneaton and moved with her family to Griff House in Nuneaton four years later.

◆ The TV soap *Crossroads*, now a cult programme, was set in a fictitious Birmingham suburb called King's Oak, an amalgam of King's Heath and Selly Oak.

Warwick's stern towers are reflected in the Avon. In the unusually complete medieval castle, which preserves curtain walls and immense towers, there is a parade of grand state rooms and a collection of arms and armour. At one end of the steeply sloping main street picturesque Lord Leycester's hospital, built 600 years ago, leans over the street, and contains a half-timbered courtyard.

The huge castle ruins at Kenilworth loom majestically on a hill. This now empty shell has recorded much history since it was built as a vital fortress in 1122. It has seen John of Gaunt's banquets and lavish and legendary entertainments by Queen Elizabeth I's favourite, the Earl of Leicester. Not far off, Claverdon's cluster of brick and timber-framed buildings include a curious forge with an entryway shaped like a horseshoe.

Towards the Worcestershire border, Henley-in-Arden has a wide main street and attractive old shops and Alcester is a lovely old market town with timber-framed medieval buildings: ale was brewed at the old Malt House which was built almost 500 years ago

In the county's deep south Shipston-on-Stour (historically Worcestershire detached) has associations with magic and witchcraft while nearby in pretty Ilmington with its pair of greens you are in a Cotswold village, all cottage gardens and clumped houses twinkling with small-paned windows and sheltering under stone roofs.

Undoubtedly the county's most famous town, Stratford-upon-Avon had the good fortune to be the birthplace of William Shakespeare in 1564. It is a charming place with many old buildings, quite a few associated with the poet, and a plenitude of half-timbering and thatch. Passing under the many arches of the still used medieval Clopton Bridge, the winding Avon with its wildfowl and swans ties the whole place up with a silver ribbon. Shakespeare is buried in the spired church of Holy Trinity and across the way is Hall's Croft, home of his son-in-law, with its garden and Elizabethan pharmacy. You can troop through the Bard's supposed birthplace and wander round the foundations of the grand house he built for himself when a rich man. (The owner in the 18th century got so fed up with tourists gawping at his home he pulled the place down.)

The Memorial Theatre stands by the river, and within it is the handsome Jacobean-style Swan Theatre, while the Other Place is a space used for experimental and new plays. You can get to Stratford easily by train

WARWICK *The castle terrace viewed from below the Avon escarpment.*

now, in two hours from Paddington in London going via Oxford. It means the possibility of seeing a play and getting back after the show. Outside the long spring and summer season these buildings are often used for local events.

The nearby Shottery has a seductive atmosphere and Anne Hathaway's thatched cottage and garden. If you don't mind taking a trip (or a 3-mile walk) you can visit the house of Shakespeare's mother, Mary Arden, in Wilmcote – there is a railway station. It is now a museum of local farming and is probably one of the most genuine of the buildings that are associated with Shakespeare's life.

BIRMINGHAM *The Rotunda dominates the Bull Ring shopping and market centre.*

LOCAL HISTORY

Arguably the finest medieval castle in England is to be found at Warwick, standing proud on the banks of the Avon on a rock which rises 40 feet straight above the river. Richard Neville, Earl of Warwick, resided here till his death in 1471. A supporter of the Yorkists, he was the unseen power behind the throne during the Wars of the Roses and was responsible for the seizure of the throne by Edward I, though he later changed sides and restored Henry VI to the throne. His story is vividly re-created in the walk-through 'Kingmaker Experience'. The first battle of the Civil War, at Edgehill, was fought on 23 October 1642: a stone tower marks the Royalist position at the start of the struggle. Compton Wynyates was a centre for the Royalists. It is an extraordinary survivor of the period, a vast Tudor brick and stone mansion, fortified and moated until Cromwell's forces overtook it. The chapel was destroyed, but later rebuilt in 1665 with handsome box pews. The park is a parade of shrubs with connecting hedges in fantastical clipped shapes.

In the same period Birmingham was already a small industrial town and its Bull Ring was the centre for metal making with 16,000 sword blades tempered for Cromwell's troops in the 1640s. By 1889 it had expanded so rapidly Queen Victoria declared it a city.

COUNTY CALENDAR

◆ Regular performances at three theatres – the Royal Shakespeare Theatre, Swan Theatre and The Other Place – during the long summer season at Stratford. You can see famous plays and works of Shakespeare's contemporaries and even modern plays.

◆ There are celebrations in Stratford-upon-Avon on the Bard's birthday, 23 April – also St George's Day.

◆ June: Stratford Regatta. Boat race on River Avon.

◆ Warwick: Year-round pageants and banquets at Warwick Castle.

◆ The Royal Show is held at Stoneleigh in July.

◆ Birmingham's NEC (National Exhibition Centre) plays host to anything from motor shows to Meatloaf and Cliff Richard concerts. Huge antiques fairs happen here in January and April; Crufts Dog Show is in March, with over 100 breeds competing for the Best in Show title.

◆ Warwickshire County Cricket Club hosts the first test match for overseas visitors at Edgbaston, Birmingham, with County matches throughout the season.

◆ Mid-October: Warwick Mop. Now a funfair but traditionally a hiring fair where people looked for work.

◆ December (first week): Victorian street fayre.

◆ January (second Saturday): Warwick National Race (jump racing).

◆ July: Warwick Folk Festival.

◆ August: Warwickshire and West Midland Game Fair in Alcester.

WESTMORLAND

THE COUNTY LANDSCAPE

◆ Less severe, less dramatic than neighbouring Cumberland, this county lying to the southeast and with only a tiny access to the sea at Morecambe Bay, makes up the centre of the rightly famed Lake District. The mountain scenery is incredibly varied, and here are the two largest lakes – Windermere and Ullswater and the most popular peak, Helvellyn (the latter two sites are shared with Cumberland).

◆ A complex series of geological actions formed the land we know as Lakeland. The valleys we see were formed by glacial action, cutting ravines and scooping paths into great domes of rock. The mountains of Lakeland are dramatic yet they are mere worn-down crags compared to 26 million years ago when the hills first thrust up from below. Now these wide, spacious valleys, containing lovely clear water lakes, left behind when the great glaciers melted 10,000 years ago, are splendid in spring, and make wonderful walks. High Street is a walk along the tops of surprisingly steep hills.

◆ The eastern part bumps against the range of the Pennines, and here are deep narrow valleys.

DRIVE UP THE M6 and you see the peaks in the distance. You are entering one of Britain's most beautiful counties and the gorgeous gateway to the Lakes. Yonder lie heather and bracken-covered fells, hills and moor towering into an ever-changing sky. By contrast, the lower part of the county around Kendal is a completely different kettle of fish to feast your eyes on.

TOWNS AND VILLAGES

This county has two kinds of settlement: those on the tourist track and those that somehow have contrived to remain resolutely hidden. It's hard, nevertheless, to hide away here and much of Westmorland is busy with the curious who come here to enjoy the splendid scenery and the exhilarating air, but who also sadly clog the roads and even crowd the footpaths, especially in spring and summer and on weekends.

Still, some villages such as Kentmere, Bampton and Rosgill have stayed away from the continuous flow but it takes an effort to find them. They also seem to melt into the landscape, for Lakeland houses use local slate and rough lichened stone for walls, though these are often whitewashed. If you want to see conventional Lakeland places then confine your explorations to wandering

GRASMERE *Tranquil waters that have a little island to which Wordsworth rowed and made a cup of tea outdoor-survival style.*

round Kendal and Windermere, or the smaller centres of Grasmere and Troutbeck. They still have much atmosphere to offer and need less effort. However, if your hankering is for the wild places of Lakeland then put on your walking shoes, or climbing boots, for you will need to mount up into the deep green valleys or even clamber up into the hills.

Kendal is a bustling road and rail centre for the area and also a market town and shopping centre. It's excellent for local souvenirs, not least of which is the famous Kendal Mint Cake. There is the excellent Abbot Hall art gallery and museum of local Lakeland life and industry in the adjacent stableblock. The 18th-century house has a collection of antique furniture and paintings by Turner, Reynolds and the Kendal-born society painter Romney as well as modern pictures and sculpture. Why this town should have become a centre for snuff-making may be due to the 14th-century weavers who set up a woollen and dyeing industry here (the green cloth worn by English archers, Kendal Green, got a mention in Shakespeare's *Henry IV*) and exported their wares to America later on in return for tobacco and snuff. The snuff factory is on Lowther Street.

Ambleside is the town most people think of as the middle of the district and it is always crowded with visitors, particularly walkers, for here there are many fellside walks. One will take you up to the waterfall at Stockgill Force. Other walks lead to lonely heights where it's still possible to be on your own with the moorland birds and the sheep.

Bowness-on-Windermere curls comfortably along its long lake, and this handsome town offers good hotels and places to eat as well as Lakeland bread and cakes from local bakeries. There is also a splendid 15th-century church containing fine medieval glass. From here you hire a boat, or make excursions on boats touring the lake, or take a ferry across to Lancashire to see Sawrey, Hawkshead and the clear sheet of Coniston Water. From points around, notably from the top of Orrest Head, are wonderful views of the countryside. As you approach Bowness the views down to Lake Windermere through evergreen trees and rhododendrons are superb.

Grasmere's noted place of literary pilgrimage is Dove Cottage, where Wordsworth lived for nine years. The house and a museum of relics can be visited. He also lived at Rydal Mount and from here are views of Rydal Water. Fell racing to the top of Butter Crags and hound trailing take place during the annual August games called Grasmere Sports, an English version of the Highland games which also features a local form of wrestling. Grasmere specialities include gingerbread. From here it's a

COUNTY FACTS

Origin of name: Westmorland comes from the Old English Westmoringland, meaning "land of the people west of the moors".

Name first recorded: 966 as Westmoringland.

County Town:

APPLEBY A charming and quiet place and this eastern stretch is a lure for anglers in the rivers Eden and Lune. The county town has a fine castle and it's a good centre for walkers. The famous Settle to Carlisle rail line, the highest and most expensive link in England, runs through the valley, providing a ride over dramatic viaducts and through deep tunnels.

Other Towns:

AMBLESIDE Was on the route of the Roman road from Ravenglass and Hardknott to Penrith and the Roman fort of Galava stood between the town and the lake. Today hotels, B&Bs and souvenir shops jostle for space in this popular Lakes centre. The curious 18th-century Bridge House is well worth a stroll by.

BOWNESS-ON-WINDERMERE Sited to the east of the largest natural lake in England (covers 10 ½ miles from north to south) and geared to fell-walking and watersports. Boating and steamer trips nearby.

GRASMERE Has the Wordsworth museum and is a good centre for nearby Easdale Tarn and Grasmere lake.

KENDAL Old town with top-notch shopping centre. it has many grey limestone buildings, noted for its woollen goods since the days of Edward I.

KIRKBY LONSDALE On the extreme southern border this was the 'Lowton' in Charlotte Brontë's Jane Eyre (she went to school close by). It has a Norman church with a fine strong pillared interior, but it's more famous for the view of high fells and the Lune from its churchyard, which was painted by Turner. Along the Lune valley lies the three-arched Devil's Bridge dating back to 1275, when tolls were taken for the privilege of crossing it. Follow the Ruskin Walks (he was smitten with the place).

KIRKBY STEPHEN Set amid the moorland of the Eden valley where the river views really are splendid. The nine cairns of Nine Standards Rigg (2,008 feet) form a dramatic backdrop.

SHAP A much quieter place since the M6 motorway opened; has the easily missed 12th century Shap Abbey beside the Lowther.

◆ Milnthorpe

County rivers: Eden and Rothay.

Highest point: Helvellyn at 3,118 feet (shared with Cumberland).

Westmorland's local government: The County of Westmorland is under the two-tier local government system. Cumbria County Council and the two districts of South Lakeland (shared with the Counties of Lancashire and Yorkshire) and Eden (shared with the County of Cumberland) are the service providers.

FAMOUS NAMES

◆ Beatrix Potter is best known as a writer of children's books and creator of *Peter Rabbit, but locally* she was better known as a breeder of Herdwick sheep. Although her house was in Sawrey, across the border in Lancashire, she owned much land in Westmorland which she left to the National Trust.

◆ The Lake District which Westmorland forms apart of, lured romantic artists and writers 200 years ago,. William Wordsworth is best known, but poets Southey and Coleridge also came here, and the critic and social reformer Ruskin.

◆ Lady Anne Clifford was a redoubtable royalist sympathiser of Civil War times who built and restored many landmarks in and around Appleby.

COUNTY CALENDAR

◆ March and April: Daffodil tours.

◆ Regular shows at Kendal's Abbot Hall Gallery. Also projects at the Brewery Arts Centre.

◆ June: Appleby has a gypsy horse fair and trotting races in spring.

◆ Speedboat races on Windermere on Saturdays.

◆ Rush bearing at Ambleside and Grasmere on two summer Saturdays.

◆ Summer sports days at Grasmere, and at Ambleside.

◆ September: Westmorland County Show at Kendal.

short distance to Chapel Stile and Langdale Valley – the place for serious climbers, with the rock faces of the Pikes providing the challenges. You can take a dramatic walk from Dungeon Gill to the waterfalls and Stickle Tarn.

Kentmere is approached from Windermere along a bridle way which gives views along Troutbeck Valley from Garburn Pass. Kirkston Pass, the road linking Windermere to Patterdale, is a high steep ascent up to the Kirkstone Pass Inn. From Patterdale it's possible to take lake trips on Ullswater and there are many easy lakeside walks, but this village with its holy well of St Patrick is best known as a centre for tackling a trek up to the highest peak here, Helvellyn. Alternatively, you can go from the west along an easier route from Thirlspot, along the east shore of Thirlmere. It's a good hike up to the mile-long ridge of Striding Edge, but the fabulous views take in the whole of Lakeland and beyond on a good day. East of Patterdale is the loneliest lake, Haweswater, which was deepened and enlarged when it was made into a reservoir with a dam, which was built in 1940.

LOCAL HISTORY

At Crosby Ravensworth, near Shap, there are groups of circular huts that were once lived in by Romano-Britons, while at Crosby Garrett there is evidence of Celtic houses, three closely set villages in small square fields and boundary banks are Iron Age survivals. Norsemen settled at Ambleside here in the 10th century. Brough Castle, built on the site of a Roman fort, stands against the sky. It's a ruin now, but was once the stronghold of Baron Clifford, a cruel foe who gave it the name of Castle of the Butcher. You can see local archaeological finds in Kendal's museum, and at nearby Sizergh Castle built around a peel tower, there is a number of fine carved Elizabethan overmantels. Levens Hall is also an ancient peel tower with an Elizabethan mansion. It has famous topiary gardens laid out in the 17th century and a collection of working steam engines. At Townend in Troutbeck you can browse through a 17th-century house showing old domestic implements.

APPLEBY-IN-WESTMORLAND *Washing gypsy horses in the River Eden.*

WILTSHIRE

THE SMOKE AND noise of the once vast rail workshops of Swindon have long gone to be replaced by high-tech Japanese and other trans-global businesses but once you leave this M4 corridor town you find yourself in the northern rolling, smiling country which I always associate with butter and milk ads. This is a dairy and arable farming county and it produces fine butter and cheese or brings it fresh from New Zealand. In fact the expression 'as different as chalk and cheese' originates from this West Country land – the rolling chalk downs lie to the the south and east where Salisbury Cathedral's spire beckons you for miles around.

TOWNS AND VILLAGES

Wiltshire is one of Britain's best-kept secrets and although the north is on the M4 and the Paddington to Bristol rail corridor it can be remote. The feeling of isolation is heightened by the awesome presence of Salisbury Plain, the eerie 100,000 acres of chalk upland, now largely owned by the Ministry of Defence, where man has worshipped since the dawn of history. Wiltshire has few remarkable places, but two it does have are truly remarkable: Stonehenge, the abstruse prehistoric monument in the middle of the plain, with its icon-like image of summer solstice; and one of the nation's finest cathedral cities, glorious Salisbury.

The cathedral spire, at 404 feet the tallest in England, is a graceful centrepiece for a unified city in which a medley of different architectural styles blends in seemingly perfect harmony. The city, where the three rivers the Avon, Bourne and Nadder meet, was the natural capital for the wealth generated by the farming lands stretching out on all sides. Here, in a riverside setting, you'll find medieval gabled houses, old timber-framed inns where you can break your tour of the city for a refreshing pint and elegant Georgian houses.

THE COUNTY LANDSCAPE

- Wiltshire is a land-locked county in central southern England, influenced by both Somerset to the west and Dorset to the south.
- At its heart is Salisbury Plain, the vast expanse of chalk uplands, stretching roughly 20 miles from east to west and 12 miles from north to south. Modern farming has reclaimed much of the historic plain huge fields of corn reaching unbroken to the horizon. The plain is fringed by attractive river valleys, such as those of the Avon, the Bourne and the Wylye.
- In the west the countryside has a rustic feel to it – low-lying agricultural land watered by the Lower Avon – while in the north it reverts back to quiet water meadows fed by streams leading into the Thames.

STONEHENGE *A place of ritual sacrifice or astronomical calculator?*

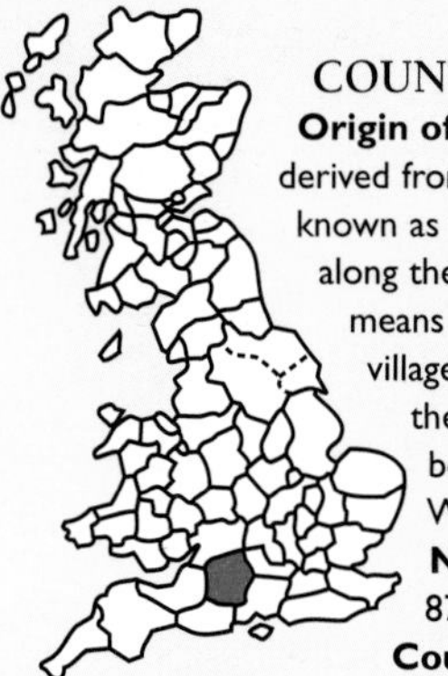

COUNTY FACTS

Origin of name: Anglo-Saxon, derived from West Saxon settlers known as the Wilsaetan who lived along the Wylye valley; Saetan means settlers. Their main village, Wilton, "farmstead on the banks of the Wylye", became the first centre of Wiltshire.

Name first recorded: 878 as Wiltunschir.

County Town:

AMESBURY Ancient town that predates its Roman links by over 1000 years. Legend has it that Queen Guinevere came here when she had been unfaithful with Sir Lancelot.

TROWBRIDGE Attractive stone town that once flourished as a cloth-making centre (check out Fore Street) and still produces for the clothing industry.

Other Towns:

BRADFORD-ON-AVON Exceptionally pretty stone-built town across the Avon with an ancient bridge preserving a rare chapel converted into a small lock-up. With its twisting narrow streets and air of wealthy cloth-making, this is a place to linger.

CHIPPENHAM Before the war Wiltshire bacon was known and prized the whole country over, with Chippenham being a great bacon-curing centre.

DEVIZES Gracious old town where flax-growing and linen-spinning still continue. Ornamental Market Cross and Georgian Bear Hotel of particular note.

LACOCK Has a fascinating museum dedicated to William Henry Fox Talbot, the founding father of photography. A picturesque village, swarming with visitors in the summer.

MALMESBURY Highly attractive hilltop town which grew up around the remains of a 7th-century Benedictine abbey; many of its streets are lined with 17th-century golden Cotswold stone houses.

MARLBOROUGH The Polly Tearooms are wonderfully English, with scones and jam . . . and cream!

SALISBURY Perhaps the most painted spire in the country, but why not see it for yourself in all its Gothic splendour. It is said the steeple was set on fire by lightning the day after it was consecrated (not long after the Norman Conquest in 1066).

SWINDON Biggest town in the county and with much modern development. The old GWR train workshops may be gone but there is a fascinating rail museum; after trains, Swindon is football mad with an ambitious club for its fans to follow.

WILTON Once a county town itself, and a bishopric and a royal residence. Wiltshire is derived from Wilton-shire and Alfred founded an abbey here in 871. You might know the name better if you link it to carpets – perhaps the first place in Britain to manufacture them. The Royal Wilton Factory can be visited.

◆ Calne ◆ Cricklade ◆ Melksham ◆ Mere ◆ Pewsey ◆ Tisbury ◆ Warminster ◆ Wootton Bassett

Main rivers: Avon, Wylye, Kennet, Nadder, Bourne

Highest point: Milk Hill, near Alton Barnes, at 9648 feet.

Even Salisbury's modern shopping centres don't seem too much out of place in a city that is a stepping-stone of time.

Perhaps because of Salisbury Plain and the scarcely picturesque railway workshop town of Swindon, Wiltshire isn't famous for its wild scenic beauty. But, in addition to Stonehenge and Salisbury, there are many other places worth visiting. East of Salisbury, the river Bourne wends its way effortlessly through wooded downs and picturesque villages like Winterbourne Earls and Winterbourne Dauntsey. To the west of the city lie the valleys of the Wylye and the Nadder, both fine fishing rivers. The Wylye delighted Izaak Walton, the 17th-century author of *The Compleat Angler*, and the light reflected from the river's waters provided inspiration for landscape painters, notably John Constable. The town of Wilton, on the Wylye, was once the capital of Saxon Wessex and Wilton House, the home of the earls of Pembroke, stands on the site of an abbey founded by Alfred the Great. Much of the original house was destroyed by fire in 1647, but it was reconstructed by the architect Inigo Jones. Today the house, which is open to the public, contains a fine collection of paintings and furniture, as well as some 7,000 19th-century model soldiers.

Tucked in the gently undulating Marlborough Downs lies Marlborough, with a truly sumptuous main street, partly arcaded and full of Georgian buildings; it is one of the broadest in Britain. Mere, a grey-stone town in the lee of Salisbury Plain, also has a number of fine buildings, including the atmospheric Ship Inn, a 17th-century mansion with a fine early timbered dining room. Just outside Mere are the National Trust mansion and landscaped gardens at Stourhead. The 18th-century house, which faces on to the last slopes of Wiltshire chalk, contains fine furniture and paintings. The gardens, laid out by Henry Hoare in the 18th century, contain a number of rare shrubs and trees. House and gardens are open to the public between April and the end of September. An all-year-round attraction finally must be Castle Combe, frequently voted the prettiest village in England. It has been the setting for many films, notably *Doctor Doolittle*, starring Rex Harrison.

LOCAL HISTORY

Stonehenge on Salisbury Plain is not just at the heart of Wiltshire, it is at the heart of England and civilization, too. The gigantic stones, placed in position some 3,800 years ago, are the country's most potent, yet enigmatic, symbol. Stonehenge has mystified archaeologists and other scholars for centuries, as it did the poet Wordsworth, who described it as 'innate of lonesome Nature's endless year'. The explanation seems to be that it was a temple or perhaps seat of government of a New Stone Age and then Bronze Age kingdom. Companions of the Most Ancient Order of Druids still keep a dawn or midnight vigil at Stonehenge at the time of the Summer Solstice.

To the south of Stonehenge lies Avebury – Old Sarum – which is believed to be even older than its more illustrious neighbour and is regarded by some experts as the most important early Bronze Age monument in Europe. It comprises about 100 great sarsen (local sandstone) stones, standing like a group of old men encircling an area some 450 yards across. Many of the stones weigh more than 40 tons. They are easy to walk around (or were until someone started daubing supposedly New Age symbols on them) and some are in people's gardens! Close by is the attractive village of Avebury, which has a church that partly dates back to Saxon times.

There's no escaping history or mystery here. Malmesbury was a borough before the time of Alfred the Great. In fact, from medieval times until the Industrial Revolution, the county made its money from weaving and many of the fine buildings reflect these prosperous times. Bradford-on-Avon's tithe barn is one of the best preserved in the country. Built in the 14th century by the Abbess of Shaftesbury, it has a massive stone-tiled roof covering a granary more than 167 feet long by 30 feet wide.

A couple of centuries later came Longleat, the home of the marquesses of Bath near Warminster. Set in grounds landscaped by Capability Brown, the magnificent mansion was built between 1559 and 1578 and it is one of our most important Elizabethan buildings. Today history goes alongside public entertainment. Capability Brown's grounds have been re-landscaped to include a famous safari park, through which lions roam. Another concession to modern tastes is the juke box in the old stables.

Wiltshire's local government: A two-tier structure, apart from Thamesdown, a unitary council opting out of Wiltshire County Council control. The two-tier stucture is Wiltshire County Council along with four district councils: Kennet, North Wiltshire, Salisbury and West Wiltshire. Wilshire detached in Berkshire at Wokingham, Twyford and Swallowfield is administered by Wokingham Unitary Council. Parts of Wiltshire which protrude into Hampshire are governed by that county's council and Test Valley or New Forest District Councils.

FAMOUS NAMES

- Pop star Peter Gabriel's recording studio is at Box, and Sting has a home in West Wiltshire.
- Some scenes from *Pride and Prejudice* were filmed in the county at Luckington and Lacock.
- Former prime minister Edward Heath has a house in Cathedral Close, Salisbury.
- Some scenes from the Oscar-winning film *Sense and Sensibility* took place at Mompesson House in Salisbury.
- Sir John Betjeman went to school at Marlborough College and despised it!

COUNTY CALENDAR

- March–June: Salisbury Arts Festival of music, comedy, literature and visual arts.
- July: Bradford-on-Avon regatta.
- Many events at Lord Bath's Longleat throughout the year.

SALISBURY *The highest spire in the land, built over 100 years after the cathedral.*

WORCESTERSHIRE

THE COUNTY LANDSCAPE

◆ A small, generally level county with the northerneastern part now very much Birmingham suburbia.

◆ The hilly, wooded parts in the northwest of the county, bordering Herefordshire and Shropshire, is all that now remains of the once mighty Wyre Forest. Further south, the central plain of the county is bordered by the sharp ridges of the Malvern Hills which are also shared with Herefordshire. North towards the conurbation of Birmingham, are the Clent and Lickey Hills.

◆ The richly fertile vale of the River Severn runs from north to south through the centre of the county, and towards the Gloucestershire border. The Severn is one of the largest rivers in Britain, springing from Plinlimmon in Montgomeryshire, and its two chief tributaries are the Wye and Avon: the River Avon winds across the Vale of Evesham. Bredon Hill (991 feet), described in verse by A. E. Housman, is close to this southern border.

FAMOUS NAMES

◆ Sir Edward Elgar, the famous English composer, was born at Upper Broadheath in 1857, and his works are annually performed as part of the Malvern and Worcester Music festivals.

◆ William Huskisson, MP for the county in the early 19th century, was the first victim of a railway accident, being knocked down and killed at the opening of the line from Manchester to Liverpool in 1830.

◆ Sir Rowland Hill, founder of the penny post, was born at Kidderminster in 1795.

◆ Lucien Bonaparte, the brother of the Emperor Napoleon, lived in exile at Thorngrove for a time.

◆ Stanley Baldwin, three times Prime Minister, was born at Astley Hall at Bewdley in 1867.

COUNTY CALENDAR

◆ Late May: Oak Apple Day Ceremony, Worcester Guildhall.

◆ Late June: Peace & Good Neighbourhood Dinner, Kidderminster.

◆ 2nd week in June: Three Counties Agricultural Show – Malvern.

◆ 3rd week of May to 1st week of June: Malvern Music Festival – Malvern.

◆ Pershore Organ Festival – Pershore (biennially).

◆ 4th week in August: Droitwich Horticultural Show – Droitwich.

◆ August: Three Choirs Festival – held alternately between Worcester, Hereford and Gloucester.

WORCESTER *The cathedral, which dates from 1084, seen from the River Severn.*

THIS IS THE land of apples, plums, and pears: the land of Pershore and Worcester: a centre of market gardening nestling in the abundant Vale of Evesham. Come here in blossom time and see flowery orchards deliver their pinks and whites beneath a clear blue sky and you could be forgiven for thinking it's snowing! Come again in August when all those fruit trees are laden with luscious fruit just waiting to be picked . . .

TOWNS AND VILLAGES

Worcester is a mixture of the sublime and the mundane as it stands on the banks of the smoothly flowing Severn, its glorious 14th-century cathedral and timbered Tudor houses offset by charmless modern buildings. It's perhaps hard to imagine that there was once a deer forest close by, thus making the town the centre of the glove-making industry. Among its other famous local industries are the manufacture of porcelain (Royal Worcester) and Worcestershire sauce, based on a recipe of Sir Marcus Sandys, once Governor of Bengal. The local barley fields provided the brown vinegar but where the other ingredients including walnut ketchup, anchovy essence, soy sauce, cayenne and shallots originated remains a mystery.

To the east lies the richly fertile Vale of Evesham, renowned for its vegetables and fruit, with the market town of Evesham itself still retaining its 15th-century half-timbered Round House, along with 16th-century Town Hall, and pleasant tree-lined walks along the River Avon.

Another pleasing town on the banks of this river is Pershore, which acquired its name as a result of the pear-orchards in the vicinity. The choir and transepts of its original Benedictine Abbey of ancient date are now preserved as part of the parish church.

Just west of Worcester, looking across to the Malvern Hills is the village of Lower Broadheath, birthplace of the Victorian composer Edward Elgar, whose music reflects much of the rural atmosphere of this region. Although Malvern is the generic title for a string of towns extending along the lower slopes of these hills, Great Malvern serves as the main centre. A pretty Victorian spa town, it now exudes a genteel resort atmosphere, with the main attraction being the Norman priory church and its 15th-century stained glass windows. St Ann's Well, on the slopes of the nearby Worcestershire Beacon (1,395 feet), provided the waters on which the spa's popularity was based.

North of Worcester, Kidderminster has the distinction of being the southern terminus of the Severn Valley Railway (operating between April and October and at Christmas), one of the longest and most picturesque steam railways in Britain. It offers a most attractive way to travel to Bewdley, a beautiful Georgian town on the banks of the Severn itself.

The village of Broadway, near Evesham, acts as a gateway to the Cotswolds, but its scenic charms have led to it being permanently swamped with visitors and tourists. Sited above the village is the Broadway Tower, an 18th-century folly which now houses exhibitions on William Morris and the members of the pre-Raphaelite movement.

LOCAL HISTORY

In 1041 the city of Worcester was razed to the ground by Hardicanute in revenge for a tax revolt by the inhabitants. The county also suffered from raids by both the Danish and the Welsh, and the Benedictine monasteries at Evesham and Worcester were fortified. During the 16th and 17th centuries, cloth manufacture grew into a thriving industry in the county. With the coming of the Civil War, the gentry sided with the Royalist cause, while the clothiers supported the Parliamentary forces. Worcester was the first city to declare for the King and was the last to surrender in 1646. In 1651, Charles II marched into Worcester, where he was warmly greeted by the citizens. But Cromwell and his forces took up positions outside the gates, and in a subsequent battle the King's forces were routed and the monarch sought refuge in a room in the cathedral.

COUNTY FACTS

Origin of name: From the Anglicized Latin, meaning "fort of the Wigoran".

Name first recorded: c. 1040 as Wirceastrescir.

County Town:

WORCESTER Walk in meadows by the Severn under the cathedral. New Road cricket ground is said to be the prettiest in the country.

Other Towns:

BROADWAY An extraordinarily pretty place permanently overrun by tourists.

BROMSGROVE An ancient market town with elegant Gothic church. Famous for making buttons and nails.

DROITWICH Famous for its salt spring waters and for the beneficial effects of its brine baths during a cholera outbreak in 1832.

DUDLEY The "Capital of the Black Country"gets its name from a Saxon prince. Has a superb museum

EVESHAM Named after a swineherd called Eoves who had a vision of a monastery which was subsequently built. The town of Eovesham grew up around it.

GREAT MALVERN Inland resort spa now world famous for its spring water.

KIDDERMINSTER Its carpets are famous for durability and brilliant colours, which may stem from properties of the Stour river on which the town stands.

PERSHORE A very ordered, neat Georgian town with pear orchards and a fine abbey.

REDDITCH A town once famous for making bicycles as well as needles and fish hooks.

STOURBRIDGE The school here boasts poet A. E. Housman, who was born at Fockbury in 1859 and educated at Stourbridge School, where he later taught for a time. The lexicographer Samuel Johnson was educated for a time at Stourbridge.

◆ Alvechurch ◆ Bewdley ◆ Hagley ◆ Kempsey ◆ Rednal ◆ Rubery ◆ Stourport-on-Severn ◆ Tenbury Wells ◆ Upton-upon-Severn ◆ Yardley

County rivers: Stour, Severn, Teme, Avon.

Highest point: Bredon Hill at 991 feet.

Worcestershire's local government: The County of Worcestershire is a jigsaw of a local government puzzle! It is primarily two-tier with Worcestershire County Council and the six District Councils of Bromsgrove, Kidderminster, Malvern Hills, Worcester, Wyre Forest and Wychavon.There are three unitary Metropolitan Boroughs of Birmingham, Dudley and Sandwell which are shared with the Counties of Shropshire, Staffordshire and Warwickshire. Alderminster, Shipston on Stour, Tidmington and Tredington are Worcestershire detached in Warwickshire falling under the auspice of Warwickshire County and Stratford upon Avon Councils as does the Worcestershire parish of Oldberrow. Blockley, Cuddesden, Daylesford, Evenlode and Icombe are Worcestershire detached in Gloucestershire with that County's Council and Cotswold District providing the two-tier government for all. Edvin Loach is Worcestershire detached in Herefordshire and under its unitary council.

YORKSHIRE

THE COUNTY LANDSCAPE

◆ The largest county in the land – so large it had to be divided by the Danes for administrative purposes into its ancient divisions called Ridings, or 'thridings' (third parts). Between them the North, East and West Ridings account for roughly an eighth of England's land area and a tenth of its population. In general terms, the North Riding, stretching in a ribbon across the county from the Pennines to the North Sea, can be said to be predominantly pastoral; the West Riding, running from the Pennines southeast, is industrial; and the East Riding, running between them to the Humber Estuary, is given over primarily to arable farming.

◆ The shape of this county, in the north-east of England, is like a ragged square, pulled down a little in its lower left hand corner. Within the boundaries of the three Ridings is amazing scenic variation.

◆ The Pennine mountains, grey-white limestone peaks reaching upwards of 2,000 feet, provide the county's western boundary. In the south can be found millstone grit deposits, fringed with the large coal measures which make up some of Britain's largest coal fields, while in the northeast, the North York Moors composed of the considerable Cleveland Hills provide a bastion against the growing encroachment of the North Sea.

◆ The large central plain, called the Vale of York, in the middle of Yorkshire comprises rich alluvial soil suitable for all kinds of farming.

BOLTON ABBEY. W. R. *Beside the Wharfe.*

BRIDLINGTON.E. R. *Very popular seaside town with a small fishing fleet.*

IF YOU'RE LOOKING for one county that's a Britain-in-miniature, this is it. Think of high fells and rolling moors, mountain torrents and soothing estuaries, wooded dales and spreading plains, criss-crossed with ancient stone walls and drovers' roads – and this is just the *hors d'oeuvres* of this vast place. The ridings are so very different: East is flat and reminds me more of Lincolnshire; the North has some breathtaking scenery along with some of the West but which on the whole is a reflection of Red Rose Lancashire on the other side of the Pennines.

TOWNS AND VILLAGES

It goes without saying that Britain's largest county contains within its borders a rich diversity of character. The frequently hard way of life in both town and countryside has given birth to folk of determined (and dogged) character, but Yorkshire 'grit' has served both the county and the country well. In literature, it has produced writers of the standing of the Brontës, Anne, Charlotte and Emily, JB Priestley and Alan Bennett. Yorkshiremen – and women – have excelled at sport, particularly at cricket. The hallowed turf of the Headingley cricket ground in Leeds echoes with the footsteps of world famous tykes such as Wilfred Rhodes, Herbert Sutcliffe, Len Hutton and, more recently, Geoffrey Boycott and 'Fiery Fred' Trueman. Winners of the Derby and Grand National have been trained at Malton and Middleham and throughout the year you can enjoy horse racing at Redcar, Thirsk, Catterick, Pontefract, Ripon, York, Beverley, Doncaster and Northallerton.

There is a link, of course, between sport and food. In season, the grouse and trout which appear on restaurant menus invariably would have been caught locally. There are also foods which are exclusively Yorkshire in origin. Yorkshire pudding, light as a feather, was supposedly an invention to pad out the Sunday roast when times were hard and portions more meagre. But the county can also offer tasty York ham, Wensleydale cheese, which is made from the milk of cows reared in the dales, and don't forget curd tarts from leftovers of the creamy cheese, and Fat Rascals which are huge scones with lots of fruit and spice and Pontefract cakes made from licorice.

Yorkshire confectionery is also valued. In the medieval city of York, Rowntrees turns out Yorkie bars and other 'naughty but nice' goodies, while Halifax boasts, as well as the world's largest building society, the largest toffee factory – Mackintosh's – the sweet, heavy aroma competing for supremacy in the city centre with the traffic fumes. A century ago the air pollution in Halifax was so bad that smogs descended upon the town for weeks on end. In an attempt to prevent pollution, an eccentric dyer called John Wainhouse conceived a plan to build a chimney on a hill 1,000 feet above his dyeworks. To conceal its purpose the tower was designed in an Italianate style. It never served its purpose, but it still stands today, beside the A646, as arguably the most absurd folly in the West Riding.

This is also a county rich in folklore and superstition. In the cathedral city of Ripon, the deafening blast of an ox's horn can still be heard each evening at 9PM – a throwback to the days when the town wakeman used to guarantee the safety of citizens after dark by sounding a nightly curfew. But the glittering prize in Yorkshire's treasure chest is undoubtedly York itself, a walled, medieval city which can trace its history back for more than 2,000 years.

Although in its minster York possesses the largest medieval church in western Europe, many of its buildings are on a smaller scale. The city centre is a dream for those interested in architecture and history and the beauty of it is that it can easily be explored on foot. Take a stroll down the street known as the Shambles and you really do transport yourself back to medieval times. The buildings on either side of the street, which in the Middle Ages would have been butcher's shops but are now cafés, craft shops and the like, are built so close together that they almost touch at the top.

COUNTY FACTS

Origin of name: York comes originally from the Latinized Celtic Eboracum, meaning the estate of Eburos; to this was added the wic (dwelling) termination by the Angles, producing Eoforwic. This was rendered as Jorvik by the Danes to become York.

Name first recorded: 1050 as Eoferwicucir.

County Motto: *Audi Consilium* ("Heed Council").

County Town:

YORK The Jorvik Viking Centre takes you on slow-moving carts back through time – smells and all. St Williams College is HQ of the York Brass Rubbings Society and a fine half-timbered building you can visit by horse and cart too! It was Charles I's Royal Mint and printing press. A unique city.

Other Towns:

NORTH RIDING: CAPITAL – NORTHALLERTON An old posting town with many staging inns to prove it. The long curving main street broadens into a busy market place with many Georgian buildings in evidence.

HAWES The largest livestock market in the north takes place in this small town. Home to Wensleydale cheese introduced by Cistercian monks but taken over by farmers after the Dissolution of the Monasteries. A cheese-making factory was set up in 1897 which you can visit. The Wensleydale Creamery Museum gives another sort of flavour of rural life in the early 1900s.

HELMSLEY The heart of the moors and one of Yorkshire's fairest market towns on the banks of the Rye. West of the market square lies the gaunt 13th-century ruin of Helmsley Castle and two miles away stands the fabulous 12th-century Rievalux (pronounced Reevo) Abbey.

MIDDLESBROUGH Iron ore was discovered here in 1850 in the Cleveland Hills and this dying village was transformed. Steel-making followed in 1875, then engineering and by the 1970s the largest petro-chemical industry in Europe. Housing estates, shopping centres and factory chimneys predominate.

PICKERING The story goes that a woad-painted warrior lost his ring here and found it in a stomach of a pike, hence 'pick-a-ring'. That's a nice touch. An important staging post between York and Whitby in the 1700s, the White Swan was a resting place before the bone-shaking journey across the moors. Red pantil roofs advertise Smiddy Hill once the old cattle market place. Fantastic 15th-century murals grace the walls of St Peter and St Paul's Church.

SCARBOROUGH "Are you going to Scarborough Fair?" serenaded Simon and Garfunkel, and in medieval times traders came here for the 45-day fair. Mineral waters were discovered in 1620 followed closely by the first seaside resort. Oliver's Mount provides a super view over this 'great fischar toune' as one 7th-century angler put it.

WHITBY Herring still comes in to this port to be sold fresh in markets across moors and dales. 200 years ago it was whale blubber that reeked all over the town.

◆ Bowes ◆ Guisborough ◆ Marske ◆ Yarm

EAST RIDING: CAPITAL – BEVERLEY The sign above the Push Inn shows the market place at around 1800 and really little has changed except for traffic. The Corn Exchange is now the Picture House – the oldest cinema in use in England. St Mary's Church and Beverley Minster are ecclesiastical gems with the world's largest collection of carvings of medieval musical instruments.
KINGSTON-UPON-HULL (otherwise known as Hull) Was badly hit during bombing raids in World War II and has been re-built as a modern and *Great Yorkshire City* as its slogan trumpets. It developed after the war as one of the country's largest ports (running for seven miles down the north side of the Humber) and with the largest fishing operation in the land. The dock and old town have been tastefully redeveloped and there is a fascinating Town Docks Museum highlighting Hull's dockland heritage.
◆ Bridlington ◆ Filey ◆ Hedon ◆ Pocklington

WEST RIDING: CAPITAL – WAKEFIELD Important weaving and dying centre as far back as the 13th century and grain market. The city centre has its Bull Ring with modern shops and the cathedral has the tallest spire in Yorkshire at 247 feet.
HARROGATE Home of the tea room – the first was opened in 1919 by Frederick Belmont and known affectionately as 'Betty's'. Novelist Agatha Christie was discovered here staying incognito (having disappeared for 10 days). A Hollywood film *Agatha* with Dustin Hoffman was filmed on location here.
HUDDERSFIELD Boasts the envy of many sporting clubs with its magnificent new MacAlpine Stadium.
LEEDS Once proud textile centre but still a bustling shopping centre with many grand Victorian buildings. From a market stall here one Michael Marks went on to conquer the high streets of the land with M&S.
PONTEFRACT The liqourice for the famous Pontefract cakes – ½-a-crown-sized pastilles – is no longer grown here, but local firms still produce the tasty treat with the emblem on top.
SHEFFIELD The best indoor swimming pool facilities in the country at Pond's Forge, and the city hosted the World Student Games in a blare of publicity. It is also the home of peerless, stainless British cutlery!
SKIPTON Marvellous medieval castle. Barges can be hired here to travel the canal. Close by are the five-rise locks at Malham and the rare double arch bridge at East Marton – not to be bypassed!
Barnoldswick ◆ Barnsley ◆ Dewsbury ◆ Earby ◆ Goole ◆ Rotherham ◆ Saddleworth ◆ Sedbergh ◆ Selby ◆ Todmorden (partly in Lancashire)
County rivers: The principal rivers – the Ouse and its tributaries the Swale, Ure, Nidd, Wharfe, Aire, Calder, Derwent and Don – flow east into the Humber.
Highest point: Mickle Fell at 2,591 feet.

Yorkshire's local government:
◆ **EAST RIDING:** Is governed by two unitary councils of Kingston upon Hull and East Riding for the main part with a two-tier system operational in the far north where a swathe of the East Riding stretching from Filey to Norton is two-tier by North Yorkshire County Council, with Filey and Hunmanby coming under Scarborough and the rest under Ryedale

A mile and a half from the centre of York is one of Britain's most stylish country house hotels. Middlethorpe Hall is a Grade II listed house built by a Yorkshire industrialist in 1699. It overlooks York racecourse and is sumptuously, if a little formally, furnished – and has a restaurant to satisfy discerning diners.

Yorkshire's largest house, though, is Castle Howard, six miles west of Malton, not so much a stately home, more a palace. The 3rd Earl of Carlisle chose Sir John Vanburgh, who was later responsible for Blenheim Palace, to design the building, to replace Henderskelfe Castle which was burned down in 1693. It took 37 years from 1700 to complete the house and grounds, and the result is a masterpiece which has truly withstood the passing of time. As well as being a treasure house of art (paintings by Rubens, Tintoretto, Canaletto, Reynolds and others), Castle Howard has in its costume gallery the largest private collection of garments from the 18th century to the present day and is a regular television location 'star'.

No other town or city in the county can hold a candle to York – but that's not to say there isn't plenty of interest elsewhere. The great towns of Yorkshire's industrial heartland are rediscovering their past. Bradford, the once-great wool town, has rebuilt itself with an enthusiasm which the Victorians would have admired. Smoke control and stone scrubbing have given a facelift to the Gothic-styled City Hall. Next to it is a new park with a rose garden and the city also boasts the splendid National Museum of Photography, Film and Television, which traces the history of the movies from the first blurred snaps to Britain's biggest cinema screen – IMAX. But some things never change: St Blaise, the patron saint of wool-combers, still overlooks the Market Square from the tower of the Wool Exchange, even if it is now an office block.

But the smaller towns offer greater allure for the visitor – places like Harrogate and Richmond, Settle and Skipton. Unlike that of any other Yorkshire venue, Harrogate's history is as a resort. The town's mineral springs were discovered in 1571 by William Slingsby, but Harrogate didn't really achieve great fame until the late 19th and early 20th centuries, when thousands thronged to take the waters. In 1926 the Royal Pump Room served 1,500 glasses of sulphurous water in one morning and although the demand for spa cures may now be dwindling, the town still thrives on its tourism and conference business.

Richmond is another attractive town, crowned by its castle, sitting high on a cliff, surrounded on three sides by the fast-flowing waters of the River Swale. In Elizabethan times, it was the centre of the home-knitting industry, exporting gloves, caps and stockings to Holland (it's said that the first were sent as a gift to Queen Elizabeth I) – but today it gains greater fame as the northern gateway to the Dales. This is James Herriot country – much of the filming of the popular TV series *All Creatures Great and Small* about the life of a Yorkshire vet took place around Reeth, a village about ten miles away. Richmond makes a good base for exploring not just the Dales, but much of northern Yorkshire – the most strikingly beautiful part of the county.

Fine Pennine mountains, among them Ingleborough and Pen-y-Ghent, make a superb backdrop to the landscape. Swaledale, steep and rocky, and Wensleydale are both extremely lovely. As the North Riding stretches east, it rises into the heather-covered slopes of the North York Moors. In winter, it is a land of pure air, rocky streams, hidden waterfalls and roads which are often impassable after heavy falls of snow. But in summer it presents an altogether softer face to the world, the sun beating down on lonely miles of road, the air heavy with the sweetness of warm grass and the breeze carrying a myriad of different scents from the valleys below. Here can be found lesser-known – and therefore lesser-crowded – dales like Farndale (ablaze with daffodils in early spring), Bilsdale and Rosedale. Over on the coast are picture-book fishing villages such as Staithes and Robin Hood's Bay, and celebrated resorts like Whitby and Scarborough, where around 1660 a Dr Whittie came up with the-then novel idea of sea bathing, thereby allowing the town to steal a march on its rivals and guaranteeing it a place in the history of tourism for all time.

LOCAL HISTORY

Yorkshire is shrouded in the mists of prehistory. The first major development started more than 4,000 years ago when Bronze Age farmers began settling in a region which had previously only supported wandering

Council. In 1996 a new ceremonial county of the East Riding of Yorkshire was created which omitted Filey, Norton and other historic East Riding towns but included the West Riding's Goole!

◆ **NORTH RIDING:** Has two-tier local government for most of its vast lands with North Yorkshire County Council and the five districts of Hambleton, Richmondshire, Ryedale, Scarborough and lastly Teesdale which along with Durham County Council provides local government for the Lune and Stainmore Forests areas of the North Riding. The three unitary authorities of Middlesbrough, Redcar & Cleveland and Stockton on Tees (shared with County Durham) provide services for the heavily populated northeast corner of the North Riding.

◆ **WEST RIDING:** Primarily administered by the nine large Metropolitan Boroughs of Bradford, Barnsley, Calderdale, Doncaster, Kirklees, Leeds, Rotherham, Sheffield and Wakefield. But the northern part of the West Riding is two-tier with North Yorkshire County Council and Craven, Harrogate and part of Richmondshire operating in unison. Sedbergh in the far northwest is administered by Cumbria County and South Lakeland Councils. A large block of Yorkshire called the Forest of Bowland, Earby and Barnoldswick is governed by Lancashire County Council plus the Ribble Valley District Council for the former and Pendle District Council the latter. Saddleworth in the far west of the West Riding is under the unitary Oldham (Lancashire). Metropolitan Borough. Goole is governed by the burghers of the East Riding unitary council.

LEEDS. W. R. *Cross Arcade is one of the many fabulous settings for shop-aholics in this centre.*

FAMOUS NAMES

◆ Legendary literary figures of 19th-century England, the Brontë sisters – Anne, Charlotte and Emily – were born at Thornton, near Bradford. Haworth, the pretty town in the Worth valley where the parsonage home of the sisters is located, is portrayed in the film version of Emily's classic *Wuthering Heights*.

◆ *Emmerdale*, the long-running television series about life in a small Yorkshire town, is shot on location in Esholt and the nearby town of Otley.

◆ *The Secret Garden*, Frances Hodgson Burnett's story about an arrogant orphan girl who is sent to a Yorkshire mansion, was filmed partly at Fountains Abbey, near Ripon, and Allerton Park, outside Knaresborough. The film stars Maggie Smith. Location shooting for the long-running TV series *Last of the Summer Wine* was done in Holmfirth.

◆ Artist David Hockney was raised in Bradford, and there is the 1853 Gallery housing the world's largest collection of his work at Saltaire.

◆ Playwright Alan Bennett was born in Leeds and is one of its most famous sons.

◆ Alan Ayckbourn, has resided in Scarborough for the past 20 years and has premiered 47 of his own plays at the Stephen Joseph Theatre.

◆ Film and stage actor Tom Courtenay was born in Hull as was Amy Johnson, CBE, the British aviator.

◆ Mother Shipton was a seer extraordinaire. Her cave at Knaresborough is really spooky.

◆ Popular chat show host Russell Harty lived up until he died at Giggleswick.

bands of Stone Age hunter-gatherers. They cleared the land for their animals and crops and put their cremated dead in urns, burying them in circular barrows such as the one at Danby Rigg, west of Whitby. Later the British tribes rebelled against the Roman occupation, so the Romans were obliged to send legions to quell the discontent, setting up camps in places like Aldborough (Isurium), Bowes (La Vatræ) Doncaster (Danum) and York (Eboracum). After the Romans, armies of Angles and Saxons, marauding tribes from the other side of the North Sea, invaded. But they did not rule for long, pushed out by the Vikings, who settled and made the country their own.

But the greatest step forward in Yorkshire's development came with the arrival of the Norman barons, who built 22 castles in the county before 1216. Some of these have been destroyed, some have decayed, but an impressive handful at Scarborough, Skipton, Conisbrough, Richmond and Pontefract remain. The Normans also built cathedrals, such as York and Beverley, churches, abbeys and monasteries. Before Henry VIII's Dissolution programme, there were more monasteries in Yorkshire than in any other county in England and two, Fountains and Rievaulx, survive as a reminder of their great beauty and impressive size.

WILTON. N. R *The ICI plant near Redcar has been producing chemicals and polymers since the 1930s.*

Several great battles in the Wars of the Roses (1455-85) were fought in Yorkshire – including the bloodiest at Towton near Tadcaster in 1461 – not for territorial purposes, but for the requirements of their feudal allegiance. It was very different, though, in the Civil War, when the towns of the West Riding, and Hull in the East Riding, were for Parliament, while the rich central belt fought for Charles I. The whole county is littered with places which have played a prominent part in the nation's history. Richard II was incarcerated in Knaresborough Castle on his way to his death at Pontefract in 1400, while Mary, Queen of Scots was imprisoned for six months in Bolton Castle near Skipton in 1568.

Yorkshire's proud industrial record is second to none. The proximity of sheep and streams for washing wool gave rise to the woollen industry, with cloth made by hand in the workers' homes for many centuries and was being exported possibly as early as AD796. Edward III helped fine tune the wool trade in the 14th century by inviting over Flemish weavers, who taught Yorkshire folk how to spin more (and finer) yarn. The Valleys of the Aire and the Calder were nucleus for this blossoming business that turned little villages into the towns of Leeds, Halifax, Bradford and Wakefield to name a few.

The West Riding was at the heart of this trade but other parts of Yorkshire also contributed their share. Helmsley, for example, in the heart of the moors is one of Yorkshire's most attractive market towns lying on the banks of the River Rye, and at the height of its prosperity as a weaving centre its loom operators had a reputation for prodigious thirst, breaking into song and wearing leather breeches. Settle was famous for its sheep fairs with tanning and the sale of raw and spun wool also important as well as its railway line to Carlisle.

The Industrial Revolution transformed the wool trade from hand-power to steam and the West Riding's looms were in their heyday continually weaving cloth on 30,000 looms and exporting £150 million's worth of cloth per annum.

Around the same time the people of Sheffield were making steel in their homes by smelting iron ore by charcoal as long ago as the 14th century. This is confirmed by the Miller in Chaucer's *Canterbury Tales* (written in about 1387), who carried "a Sheffield thwytel in his hose".

In 1801 only a handful of people lived on the spot where that great conurbation of Middlesbrough now lies. Thanks to the discovery of iron ore nearby and its exploitation Middlesbrough make millions of tons of steel and exported it – the girders on Sydney Harbour's famous bridge came from here.

- ◆ Captain Cook sailed from Whitby to discover the east coast of Australia. His statue and m are housed in the town.
- ◆ Cook may not have discovered Australia if it had not been for the invention of the chronometer by another Yorkshireman, John Harrison.
- ◆ Actor Charles Laughton, of many classic black-and-white films from the 1930s-50s including *The Hunchback of Notre Dame,* was born in Scarborough, the son of an hotelier.
- ◆ *Dracula* author Bram Stoker was so inspired by the dramatic setting of the clifftop graveyard at Whitby while on holiday there,that he used it for one of the scenes in his classic horror story.
- ◆ Probably Yorkshire's most extraordinary celebrity wedding ever was when Headingly hero Fred Trueman's son married Hollywood heroine Raquel Welch's daughter at Bolton Priory.

COUNTY CALENDAR

- ◆ January 6: The traditional Haxey Hood Game, which has been played for around 700 years, is held in Haxey, near Doncaster.
- ◆ Mid-February: The Great St Valentine's Fair, Leeds.
- ◆ May: The World Dock Pudding Championships take place at Hebden Bridge at Mytholmroyd Community Centre. The local delicacy is precooked and brought to the competition in a jar or dish. It is made of dock leaves, nettles, oatmeal, onions, butter and seasoning. The dock pudding is then heated through along with bacon and eggs to form part of a traditional Yorkshire breakfast. The dock leaves used are *Polygonum Bistorta* and not the common cow dock.
- ◆ April: Competitors set off the Royal Oak public house in Ossett on a Coal Carrying Championship.
- ◆ April: Harrogate Spring Flower Show. The autumn flower show in September is also worth a visit at the great Yorkshire Showground; plus a competition to find the world's heaviest onion.
- ◆ Late April: Three Peaks Race, Horton-in-Ribblesdale.
- ◆ Mid-May: The old custom of the Planting of the Penny Hedge takes place in Whitby.
- ◆ Mid-June: Harewood Classic Car Show, Harewood House, near Leeds.
- ◆ June: Beverley International Folk Festival.
- ◆ Late June/Early July: Bradford Festival, one of Britain's largest street and community festivals.
- ◆ July: Great Yorkshire Show, Harrogate.
- ◆ Mid-July: Harrogate Cricket Festival, annual festival featuring a county championship match and the Cost Cutter Cup knock-out competition.
- ◆ Late-July: Ryedale Show, full agricultural show at Welburn Park, Kirkbymoorside, near York.
- ◆ Early August: Old Gooseberry Show: held at St Heddas School, Egton Bridge has been going for 150 years and was created to find, surprisingly enough, the heaviest gooseberry, some as large as tennis balls!
- ◆ August 1: Yorkshire Day.
- ◆ Late-September: Scarborough Angling Festival, shore and boating competitions at the North Sea coast resort.
- ◆ Mid October: Autumn Steam Gala on the North York Moors Railway, Pickering station.

THE *REAL*
WELSH COUNTIES

ANGLESEY

YNYS MÔN

THE COUNTY LANDSCAPE

◆ At 276 square miles, Anglesey is the biggest island off the Welsh and English coasts, separated from the mainland by the tidal Menai Strait, which is only a few hundred yards at its narrowest point, between Bangor and Menai Bridge. Its sea-facing shores are a haven for migrating birds; thousands of puffins and guillemots nest on the 600-million-year-old perpendicular cliffs of South Stack. There is a spectacular bird sanctuary here, run by the RSPB.

◆ The north is rocky and wild, and mining has left its scars along Parys Mountain; but to the east and west the shoreline grows gentler, and is dotted with shingle and sand beaches.

◆ Compared with the mountains of the mainland, Anglesey is quite flat, rising no higher than 500 feet and harbouring saltmarshes and wide estuaries at its lowest levels. Its biggest lake, the 777-acre Llyn Alaw, was created by the flooding of northern marshlands.

◆ Seals and porpoises can be seen basking off the north coast of the island.

I KNOW THIS ISLAND SO WELL – in fact on a clear day you can see Anglesey from my home on the Lancashire coast. It is an enchanting isle possessing such magic and variety. The short trip across the Menai Strait from mainland Wales to Anglesey seems like a journey into another world. There is something about this island, known to the Welsh as 'Môn, Mam Cymru' – 'Anglesey, Mother of Wales', that makes it stand out from the rest of the nation. For centuries its lush farmlands fed the barren Welsh highlands; and when white-robed druids were the leaders of Celtic life, Anglesey was their headquarters.

Look at the bridges that carry you to and from the mainland. These were the high-tech marvels of their day: Menai Suspension Bridge, the first iron bridge of its kind in the world, built by engineering genius Thomas Telford in 1818; and Britannia Bridge, whose wrought-iron tubes opened to trains in 1850 – and were rebuilt in 1970 after two boys on a bat-hunt set them on fire.

TOWNS AND VILLAGES

There's a prosperous, holiday atmosphere about the towns strung along the Menai Strait. The Georgian houses and gabled Victorian villas of Beaumaris give this neat sailing town an air of seaside gentility; this is the kind of place where you can take a promenade along the quayside, watch the boats bobbing up and down on the strait and the soak in the fine view across to Snowdonia. Further west along the coast, at the end of the Britannia Bridge, is Anglesey's worst-pronounced village: Llanfairpwllgwyngyll-gogerychwyrndrobwllllan-tysiliogogogoch. The original name was plain old Llanfair-pwllgwyngyll; its extended title was invented by a 19th-century wag, with an eye to the tourist trade. Llanfair PG, as it's known to locals, has two grand monuments to its past glories: Plas Newydd, the 18th-century home of the Marquess of Anglesey, and the 90-foot

LLANDDEUSANT Picking up a few tips of flourmaking at Lynnon Windmill.

The tree-lined road from Beaumaris to Menai Bridge with its bungalows and off-white villas dipping their foundations in the briny is one of the prettiest stretches you'll ever travel down.

LOCAL HISTORY

Even in the most remote reaches of Ynys Môn humans have left their mark for thousands of years. At the Neolithic burial sites of Bryn Celli Ddu or Barclodiad y Gawres ('The Giantess's Apron'), curves, zigzags and spirals carved into the stone chambers add to the air of mystery. The Celts arrived from about 1,000 BC, bringing new ironworking skills and tools so hardy that in 1943 a tractor digging peat near Caergeiliog was found to be using an ancient Celtic chain. This led to the discovery in a nearby lake of a horde of Celtic riches – weapons, shields, chariots, trumpets – all, perhaps, thrown in as offerings to a water-god.

Eventually Anglesey settled down to life as a Roman colony, forming settlements such as Din Lligwy, a 4th-century village in woods west of the Dulas estuary. You can still see the stone outlines of its round huts, huddled in their enclosure – even the doorsteps have survived.

Hardly any trace is left of the island's true golden age, when Aberffraw, now a windswept village, was the base of the glittering royal house of Gwynedd. The last of the dynasty's princes, Llywelyn, ruled all Wales before his defeat by Edward I, the 13th-century English conqueror. Beaumaris Castle is still there – the most impressive of Edward's string of fortresses, with its double walls and squat, symmetrical towers.

The only traditional working windmill survives inland at Llanddeusant. Before leaving this spellbinding isle, take home some healthy stoneground flour!

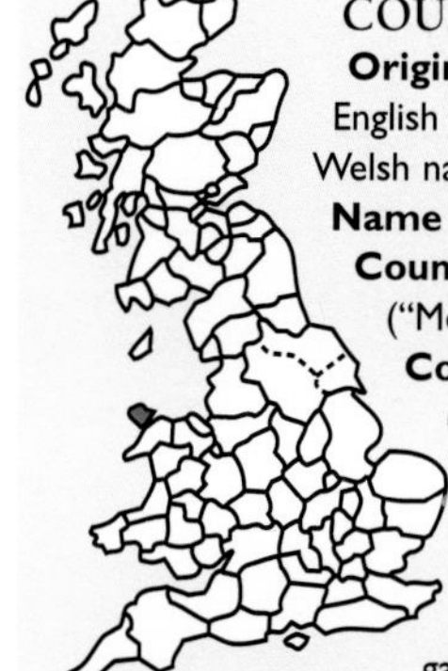

COUNTY FACTS

Origin of name: From the Old English for island of the Angles. (The Welsh name is Sir Môn or Ynys Môn.)
Name first recorded: 1098.
County Motto: *Môn Mam Cymru* ("Mona, Mother of Wales").
County Town: **BEAUMARIS** (Llange Fni) glorious town and Anglesey's one-time capital.
Other Towns:
HOLYHEAD Tremendous transformation for this busy gateway to Ireland. Fine seafood restaurants.
LLANERCHYMEDD Market town with yew tree said to span 40 feet in girth and the island's largest lake.
MENAI BRIDGE Has an Uxbridge Square – so it's home from home for me!
NEWBOROUGH Enclosed by a forest with a lonely beach where you feel the island's wild, windy side.
TREARDDUR BAY A sheltered sandy bay which takes a deep bite out of a rocky, indented shoreline. Activities on offer include sailing, swimming and golf.
◆ Aberffaw ◆Amlwch ◆ Benllech ◆ Bodedern ◆ Bryngwran ◆ Brynsiencyn ◆ Cemaes Bay ◆ Gaerwen ◆ Gwalchmai ◆ Kingsland ◆ Llanfairpwll ◆ Llanfechell ◆ Llangefui ◆ Llangoed ◆ Pentraeth ◆ Rhosneigr ◆ Valley
County rivers: Cefui.
Highest point: Mynydd at 720 feet.

Anglesey's local government: Surely even the pen-pushers couldn't muck up this one up, but they did once, but have got it right now by making the County of Anglesey and its local government one of the same. The unitary authority district is known as Isle of Anglesey/Sir Ynys Mon – which translates as Angleseyshire! Wrong!

FAMOUS NAMES

◆ At Plas Newydd one of the first articulated wooden legs is on display, now separated from its owner, Henry William Paget, who passed the famous remark at Waterloo 'By God, Sir, I've lost my leg'; to which Wellington replied 'By God, Sir, so you have'.
◆ Guests who have put up at Beaumaris's 17th-century posting inn, the Old Bull's Head, include Samuel Johnson and Charles Dickens.
◆ Aled Jones, the former choirboy who shot to international fame with his rendition of Walking in the Air grew up at Llandegfan, northeast of Menai Bridge.
◆ Actor Hugh Griffiths, who appeared in Ben Hur and as Long John Silver in the 1960s TV version of Treasure Island, was born in Marian Glâs and attended Llangefni Grammar School.

COUNTY CALENDAR

◆ Spring Bank Holiday: home-made sea-going vessels of all shapes are launched for the Raft Race between Y Felinheli (Port Dinorwic) and Menai Bridge.
◆ Late July–Early August: the Menai Strait Regattas are held at Beaumaris and Menai Bridge.
◆ 26 December: the fancy-dress Pram Race is a Beaumaris institution on Boxing Day.

BRECONSHIRE

SIR FRYCHEINIOG

BRECON BEACONS *Covers some 500 square miles of glorious Welsh landscape.*

THE COUNTY LANDSCAPE

◆ South Wales ends and Mid-Wales begins with the Brecon Beacons, one of the four mountain ranges stretching from Offa's Dyke on the Welsh-English border to Llandeilo in the west. Breconshire's borders reach down towards the southern valleys and up into the empty centre of Wales, with the mountains at its heart, covering the transition from industrial towns to rural, sheep-grazed hill country.

◆ From the Black Mountains in the east, this band of high land rises to 2,907 feet at Pen y Fan in the central Beacons, then spreads into Fforest Fawr's bare moors and, finally, spills over the border into Carmarthenshire as the (singular) Black Mountain.

◆ The whole region is protected as the Brecon Beacons National Park, and its reservoirs and woods and rounded sandstone hills are a magnet for walkers and outward-bound people. Of the many waterfalls in the area, Henrhyd Falls are among the finest in the country and in a beautiful spot tumbling down nearly 90 feet of deep wooded ravine.

ENTER THE HIGH, beautiful, wild and ever so remote country of the Brecon Beacons. Look out over the pine forests, ravines and waterfalls, as I have done, and you see this predominant burnt ochre tinge – except in winter when frost and snow conspire to white out the landscape.

TOWNS AND VILLAGES

The ancient agricultural town of Brecon sits right in the middle of the county, with the Beacons forming a magnificent backdrop to its busy market and winding streets. In summer, the crowds of backpackers and strollers who swarm in to make use of the shops and cafés can be a distraction from Brecon's real charm, but this is much more than a passing place for trekkers and tourists. At the Bulwark, the main square, several impressive buildings testify to its long history as a strategic centre and prosperous cloth-trading town. A statue of Wellington casts an eye over the Georgian buildings, including the neo-Classical Shire Hall, with its rather grand portico, and the 1770 Guild Hall. The High Street widens out around St Mary's Church, a brooding building with Norman pillars and a 16th-century tower. A stiff climb up the hill away from the shops takes you to what remains of Brecon Castle and the cathedral. Once upon a time the castle was a massive Norman stronghold guarding the confluence of the Honddu and the Usk; now it's split in half and some of the walls are built into the Castle Hotel. The same lord who constructed the castle – Bernard Newmarch – founded Brecon Cathedral, now a lovely, unaffected 14th-century building with 19th-century restoration by Sir Gilbert Scott.

Sitting right on the border where three counties meet – Breconshire, Herefordshire and Radnorshire – is another historic little town of narrow streets and elegant old buildings. Hay-on-Wye is best known today for its second-hand bookshops, a reputation started in the 1960s by the eccentric Richard Booth, otherwise known as the King of Independent Hay, who reigns from a 17th-century mansion in the grounds of the old Norman castle. Books are everywhere – they spill out on to the pavements in boxes, on tables and shelves, and crafts, antiques, prints and paintings have been added to their ranks to attract the browsers crowding into the centre. There are fine black and white half-timbered houses, including the 16th-century Three Tuns pub, serving the pints on Bridge Street.

To the north, you can pick up the old Wells trails, beginning at Llanwrtyd Wells and continuing through Builth Wells and up into Radnorshire. Victorians were very keen on taking the waters to cure all sorts of aches and pains, and wherever mineral springs were discovered, hotels and spas soon popped up. Builth is better known as a lively agricultural town (its Welsh name is Llanfair-ym-Muallt: St Mary's in the Cow Pasture); it gets even livelier in summer with the Royal Welsh Show.

LOCAL HISTORY

Tracks and roads mark out much of Breconshire's history. West of Brecon, Y Gaer was once a huge fort on the Usk; from here the Romans built their roads across the high country as they set out to conquer Wales, and you can still follow parts of their route along Sarn Helen, over the brown-grey brows, crags and moorland of Fforest Fawr. Centuries later the cattle drovers were also plodding over the mountains on their long journeys to the markets of England, driving huge herds of cows, sheep and geese (with tarred feet to ease the way) across miles of remote land.

The 18th-century Welsh version of Robin Hood, Twm Siôn Catti, is said to have laid low in a cave near Llyn Brianne reservoir, on the border with Cardiganshire. A master of disguise, a singer and poet and practical joker, Twm fell for a squire's daughter when he was robbing her on the highway; they married and he ended his days a pillar of the respectable community.

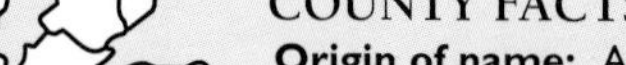

COUNTY FACTS

Origin of name: After a 5th-century British chieftain named Brychan. The county is also known as Brecknockshire.

Name first recorded: 916 as Brycheiniog.

County Motto: *Undeb Hedd Llwyddiant* ("Unity, Peace, Prosperity").

County Town: BRECON Market centre with wide streets and a 1940s feel.

Other Towns:

CRICKHOWELL picturesque base for dramatic mountain walks or caving, canoeing and rock climbing; attractive 300-year-old bridge spans the Usk. The Bear is an excellent pub-restaurant.

HAY-ON-WYE Half-timbered black and white houses in self-styled 2nd-hand book capital of the world.

LLANWRTYD WELLS Its Ffynnon Drewllyd (Stinking Spring) of sulphurous water is a peaceful, if smelly, spot by the river Irfon. Wonderful countryside.

◆ Bronllys ◆ Builth Wells ◆ Brynmawr ◆ Cefn-coed-y-cymmer ◆ Clydach ◆ Coelbren ◆ Gilwern ◆ Gurnos ◆ Llangammarch Wells ◆ Llandewi'r Cwm ◆ Llanfaes ◆ Penrhos ◆ Sennybridge ◆ Talgarth ◆ Upper Cwmtwrch ◆ Ystradgynlais

County rivers: Wye, Usk, Honddu, Irfon, Elan, Claerwen, Taff Tawe.

Highest point: Cadar Arthur at 2,910 feet.

Breconshire's local government: The whole of the County except for some southern places, is governed by Powys unitary authority: Penderyn by Rhondda-Cynon-Taff (Glamorgan) and Vaynor by Merthyr Tydfil (Glamorgan), Brynmawr by Bleanau Gwent (Monmouthshire), and Gilwern, Clydach and Llanelly by Monmouthshire unitary councils.

FAMOUS NAMES

◆ Sarah Siddons, the Glenda Jackson of her day, was born at the Shoulder of Mutton (now the Sarah Siddons) Inn in 1755; her brother, famous actor Charles Kemble, was born in Brecon 20 years later.

◆ TV and theatre actor Gerald James, who appeared in the BBC series *Hadleigh*, was born in Brecon in 1917.

◆ Sir George Everest, the Surveyor-General of India who gave his name to a mountain, lived at Gwernvale, now a hotel, in Crickhowell, in the Usk valley.

◆ *On the Black Hill* (1988), the film of Bruce Chatwin's book, was shot in Hay-on-Wye.

COUNTY CALENDAR

◆ Late May-early June: Top literature festival in Britain takes place in bookworms' paradise, Hay-on-Wye. The town plays host to authors and actors for readings, talks and other literary events.

◆ Early August: Brecon hosts one of the most celebrated jazz festivals in the country, featuring big names from all over the world, as well as local jazz celebrity George Melly, who perform in various venues, including the main square.

◆ Mid July: Royal Welsh Show: Large collection of all things agricultural at Llanelwedd (Radnorshire) over the River Wye from Builth Wells.

CAERNARFONSHIRE

SIR GAERNARFON

THE COUNTY LANDSCAPE

◆ Snowdon rises majestically over the dramatic landscapes of this northern county, its 3,560-foot peak permanently dusted with snow. This and the other mountains of the Snowdonia range – Eryri, or Place of Eagles, in Welsh – are the focus of the Snowdonia National Park, which covers Caernarfonshire's mainland; and to the west, the long arm of the Llyn Peninsula reaches into the sea, with some of the loveliest and loneliest hills and beaches in Wales, as well as popular harbour towns and bays.

◆ Along the northwestern coast is a series of elegant towns, offering powerful medieval architecture at Caernarfon and Conwy (with the dramatic headland of nearby Great Orme's head), an ancient cathedral and modern university at Bangor, and the holiday atmosphere of the seaside at Llandudno.

◆ Bardsey Island lies two miles off the Lleyn Peninsula and has links with pilgrimages and ruins of a 13th century monastery, but most people visit for the wonderful array of screeching seabirds who nest here including fulmars and guillemots.

WHEREVER YOU GO in Caernarfonshire, it is dominated by stunning mountain scenery. To the east are the Carneddau, or 'Cairns', named after great Welsh princes and dramatic landscapes – Pen-Llithrig-y-Wrach, for instance, is The Slippery Head of the Witch, and looks it. Westward are the Glyders and Snowdon (Yr Wyddfa) itself, climbed by hundreds every year, especially via the gentle path from the old quarry town of Llanberis.

TOWNS AND VILLAGES

Mountains form the backdrop for Caernarfonshire's historic towns too, and for a real trip back in time go to Conwy, an almost perfectly preserved walled town on the Conwy estuary at the county's northeastern edge. Its narrow streets are still enclosed by their 4,000 feet of walls, 21 towers and three gates. Huddled within them are wonderful old buildings such as the 14th-century Aberconwy House, part stone, part timber; or Plas Mawr, a grand mansion built in 1576. Thomas Telford's graceful bridge sweeps across the estuary from the castle, and outside the town confines, on the quayside, a red fishermen's cottage, just 10 feet high and 5 feet wide, squeezes between its neighbour and a stone wall. About 12 miles up the river Conwy, the charming greystone town of Betws-y-Coed lines a road deep in the wooded valley which is a springboard for Wales' best-known trail-walking and beauty spots. Salmon and sea-trout swim in the three rivers that meet here – the Conwy, the Lledr and the Llugwy – and west of town the wonderful Swallow Falls tumble and dazzle over the rocks creating at one site instant rainbows in the mist. Nearby is a strange monstrosity known as Ty Hyll (Ugly House), crookedly built of vast round boulders. It might be one of the 'tai unnos' – 'one-night houses' – whose freehold could be claimed as long as they were built between dusk and dawn. Over to the west, the mountains become gentler along the 25-mile Llyn

***CAERNARFON** with its colourful harbour and magnificent 13-towered castle.*

Peninsula, lined with fishing villages and bays up to the claw of land that encloses Porth Neigwl (Hell's Mouth), where the strong currents have wrecked many a ship and the waves eroded the beach-heads. Beach-lovers and sailboat enthusiasts make for the sand and shingle of Pwllheli, Criccieth or the charming holiday resort of Abersoch, but the county's real centre of seaside life is Llandudno, on Caernarfonshire's northeastern hook. Here a long crescent of sand curves round between the two headlands of Great and Little Orme, and Victorian shops and hotels with delicate canopies stretch into the town and away from the cable car and ski slope and promenade clamour of an old-fashioned holiday resort. Nearby a sturdy little coastal resort called Penmaenmawr is fascinating in having Prime Minister Gladstone's holiday home.

LOCAL HISTORY

About 4,000 years ago people were making their homes near the sheltered beaches and fertile seas of the Llyn – and you can still see the traces of their village, Britain's oldest walled community, at Tre'r Ceiri, high on a hill north of Nefyn. Several millennia later, the Romans were in Caernarfonshire on the lookout for strategic bases between sea and inhospitable mountain. They found a spot south of Caernarfon: Segontium Fort housed troops from AD78 until they pulled out of Britain. Later on the Breton missionary, Cadfan, landed on Bardsey Island or Ynys Enlli ('Island of Currents'), off the tip of the Lleyn. His monastery there became a refuge for monks fleeing from the Saxons, and a place of pilgrimage for the faithful (who stopped off for sustenance at Aberdaron's Y Gegin Fawr – Big Kitchen – before tackling the crossing).

Granite and slate were quarried from the hills and made fortunes for a few, including the Pennant family, owners of the Bethesda quarries, whose display of wealth in the luxurious Penrhyn Castle near Llandegai included a solid slate bed (move that if you dare). Tourists arrived in the 19th century and wiped a tear at Beddgelert ('Gelert's Grave') for the faithful hound slain by his master, Prince Llywelyn. The prince had found his son's upturned cradle in a pool of blood and feared the worst. In fact, Gelert the dog had killed a wolf while trying to protect the baby boy, who was lying safe and sound under the cradle.

Actually, the whole thing was dreamed up by a local innkeeper, keen to grab his own share of the sightseeing trade. But the picturesque stone village of Beddgelert by two rivers, near the Aberglaslyn Pass between the Snowdonia peaks, is beautiful enough, with or without its lachrymose legend.

COUNTY FACTS

Origin of name: Comes from the Welsh 'Fort of Arfon' (Arfon being district opposite Anglesey).
Name first recorded: 1196 as Caer'n arfon.
County Motto: *Cadernid Gwynedd* (The Strength of Gwynedd).
County Town:
CAERNARFON Lively, modern, Welsh-speaking community, but you can still get a sense of its medieval past as one of Edward I's prime fortified settlements.
Other Towns:
BANGOR On the breezy Menai Straits, has both a cathedral and university.
BETHESDA Located on the river Ogwen, is named after the biblical pool where the sick came to be treated. Originally called Y Wern Uchaf (the upper marsh).
CONWAY The castle evokes a medieval spirit and has commanding views from the towers of the estuary and nearby Snowdonia mountains. There are 800 years of history to take in on a comfortable day's stroll.
PORTHMADOG Known locally as Port, this resort's name came from an entrepreneur MP named Maddocks who in the 1800s had a harbour constructed to ship slate from Ffestiniog.
◆ Deganwy ◆ Llanfairfechan ◆ Nefyn ◆ Penrhyn Bay ◆ Penygroes ◆ Port Dinorwic ◆ Pwllheli ◆ Tywyn.
County rivers: Conwy, Cadnant, Glaslyn, Gwyrfai, Seiont, Ogwen.
Highest point: Snowdon at 3,560 feet.

Caenarfonshire's local government: The County of Caernarfonshire comes under both Conwy and Gwynedd (shared with Merioneth) unitary authorities.

FAMOUS NAMES

◆ Prime minister and charismatic orator Lloyd George grew up at Llanystumdwy, near Criccieth.
◆ The mountains around Beddgelert and Capel Curig were transformed into hostile Chinese territory for the filming of *The Inn of the Sixth Happiness* in 1958, starring Ingrid Bergman as the real-life missionary who led 100 children to safety in the Chino-Japanese war.
◆ Bryn Terfel, the man with a velvet voice, is a native of Pwllheli, on the southern shore of the Llyn Peninsula.

COUNTY CALENDAR

◆ Late July-early August: Arts and entertainment are celebrated in the five-day Gwyl Conwy, an annual summer festival.
◆ Early July: The Welsh love affair with American music continues at the North Wales Bluegrass Festival, featuring old-time music bands, cajun and appalachian dancing and guitar-pickin' at venues throughout Conwy.
◆ Early August: Sailing, racing, air displays and beach events are all part of the week-long Conwy River Festival on the quay.
◆ Early October: Llandudno's North Wales Theatre on the prom hosts a week of musical events and concerts for the town's October Festival.

CARDIGANSHIRE

SIR ABERTEIFI

THE COUNTY LANDSCAPE

◆ Sweeping up the western coast of Wales, Cardiganshire forms a long crescent between its county town, Cardigan, in the southwest and the mouth of the Dyfi at its northern tip. Here the Irish Sea washes into Cardigan Bay, a shallow, sandy stretch of coast with a series of harbour towns running along the shore and stony reefs lying offshore. Bottlenose dolphins, porpoises and grey seals all enjoy its sheltered waters.

◆ Inland, about 15 miles of the seaside university town of Aberystwyth, is the bleak peak of Plynlimon (Pumlumon), where five rivers have their sources: the Severn, the Wye, the Dulas, the Llyfnant and the Rheidol, the last of which meets the Mynach river in a 300-foot plunge at the Devil's Bridge chasm.

◆ The Cambrian Mountains run down the middle of Wales and form part of Cardiganshire's inland boundary. As you travel away from the sea the land heaves and dips into deep wooded valleys and high grass and moors, grazed by sheep and scattered with farms and tiny villages. The river Teifi is believed to have been the last resort of the British beaver.

◆ Further south, the land broadens out into the protected wetlands of Tregaron marsh, once enclosed by a lake and now enjoyed by a rich variety of birdlife.

COUNTY CALENDAR

◆ Saturday after May bank holiday, August bank holiday weekend: The sport of harness racing has been around since the Roman occupation, when legions drove ponies hitched to their chariots. The modern version is held at Tregaron's Dôl-yr-Ychain racetrack, and attracts entrants from all over Britain.

◆ Mid June: Cattle, sheep, goats, poultry and dogs are on display at the Aberystwyth Agricultural Show in Rhydyfelin, where trotting races are also part of the spectacle.

◆ Late July: Young football teams travel from several corners of the world to compete in the Ian Rush International Soccer Tournament, played over five days on the University playing fields in Aberystwyth.

◆ Late July-early August: The International Music Festival and Summer School at Aberystwyth combines chamber music concerts with an internationally renowned summer course for budding performers.

◆ Late September: Raft races are held on the river Leri at Borth, a few miles south of the Dyfi estuary.

LLECHRYD *Coracle fisherman on the River Teifi.*

I FIRST FOUND opera in Aberystwyth – *The Barber of Seville* – performed by the Welsh National Opera many moons ago. It was also the first time I'd really heard Welsh spoken all the time. Cardiganshire has really hung on to its traditional identity (unlike many Welsh counties, where English influence replaced and divided old Celtic territories) and who can blame it! This is a glorious part of Wales, with coves, beaches and harbours all along Cardigan Bay, and rushing rivers and rolling mountains inland.

TOWNS AND VILLAGES

A trip up the coast takes you to the county's liveliest centre, Aberystwyth, whose promenade and tall, bay-windowed seafront houses still carry a sedate, Victorian air. The University of Wales college, on its modern hillside campus, adds to the town's vivacity in term-time, but this is still essentially a good, old-fashioned seaside resort. Sitting at the southern end of the front is a neo-Gothic oddity, a grand building of towers and mosaics. Now owned by the university, this was originally a hotel, built by businessman Thomas Savin in 1864 to capture the new rail-travelling tourist trade. The scheme foundered when a proposed rail link over the mid-Wales mountains was abandoned, and Savin had to sell his extravagant building for a song.

Cardiganshire's once-thriving 18th-century lead and silver mining industries have been turned over to the leisure trade. The

narrow gauge Vale of Rheidol Railway, which opened in 1902 to carry lead and timber, now pulls tourists up a spectacular 600-foot climb to Devil's Bridge, a lush gorge where the rivers Mynach and Rheidol thunder into a series of waterfalls. Three bridges span the gorge, one over the other: the first is said to be the work of the devil, who built it to rescue an old woman on condition that he could possess the first living soul to cross it (which turned out to be her dog). The second bridge is 18th-century and the third was added early this century.

Some of the forest between Devil's Bridge and Pontrhydygroes was originally planted by 18th-century environmental pioneer Colonel Thomas Johnes. He landscaped his grounds at Hafod and planted acres of oak across the valley slopes. Look out for the neo-classical Bedford Monument, set up in the Hafod estate to commemorate Johnes' friend Francis, 5th Duke of Bedford: from here there's a sweeping view of the hills south towards Ysbyty Ystwyth. To the north, the high wilderness of Plynlimon has a pretty impressive view – in clear weather, it's said you can make out 11 of the 13 Welsh counties.

LOCAL HISTORY

In the 5th century, so the legend goes, the Celtic chief Cunedda came down from Scotland, drove the invading Irish from Wales and divided the lands between his sons. One of these sons was Ceredig: his kingdom, Ceredigion, was the long curve of western land which the English mispronounced as Cardigan.

At the county town, Cardigan – Aberteifi ('mouth of the Teifi') in Welsh – Lord Rhys ap Gruffydd gathered together the bards and musicians of north and south for a competition in his castle in 1176. This was the very first National Eisteddfod – a Welsh-language festival still held every August at alternate venues throughout Wales.

Even the idyllic little village and beach of Tresaith, about eight miles northeast, claims a romantic past: the name, which means 'Town of the Seven', may refer to seven Irish princesses, exiled by their father, who landed and lived here. But a more likely derivation is the river Saith, which tumbles over rocks to the beach and sea.

The same Lord Rhys who started the Eisteddfod founded a Cistercian abbey near the source of the Teifi, where Tregaron marsh meets the Cambrian foothills. This was Strata Florida, the 'Westminster of Wales', where Llywelyn the Great brought together all the Welsh princes in 1238 to pledge their allegiance to him and his descendants. The abbey is now in ruins, but a solitary gateway, decorated with carvings, still stands.

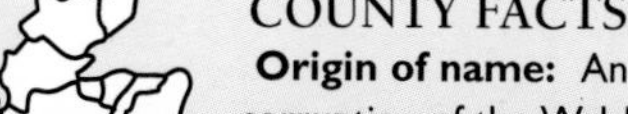

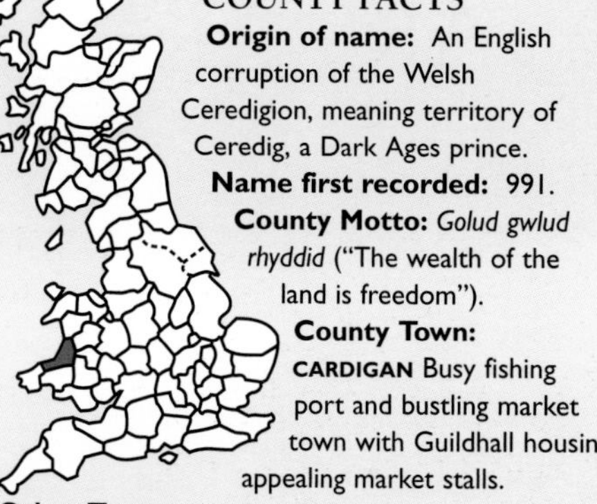

COUNTY FACTS

Origin of name: An English corruption of the Welsh Ceredigion, meaning territory of Ceredig, a Dark Ages prince.

Name first recorded: 991.

County Motto: *Golud gwlud rhyddid* ("The wealth of the land is freedom").

County Town:
CARDIGAN Busy fishing port and bustling market town with Guildhall housing appealing market stalls.

Other Towns:

ABERAERON About 22 miles up the coast from Cardigan is an attractive Georgian port that seems to have roamed into the wrong country. Aberaeron's immaculate, colourful Georgian terraces and elegant streets are more resonant of a prosperous English resort than the usually haphazard towns of rural Wales. It was built from scratch in 1807 to the master plan of the Reverend Alban Thomas Jones-Gwynne, who spent his inheritance on the project. It's said that the great architect John Nash may even have lent a helping hand. The houses have good fan-lights and coloured stucco.

ABERYSTWYTH Splendidly situated with wide sweeping bay and backdrop of hills: a holiday and university town (with National Library of Wales).

LAMPETER Cafés and bistros cater for the students at St David's (the smallest of the colleges that form part of the University of Wales) and passing tourists in this crafts-centred town on the Teifi.

NEW QUAY Resort which grew up around harbour built in 1835 (replacing an earlier smaller one). The Welsh word is Ceinewyydd.

◆ Aberporth ◆ Adpar ◆ Borth ◆ Llandyssul
◆ Penparcau ◆ Talybont ◆ Tregaron

County rivers: Teifi, Towy, Yst, Claerwen, Rhydol, Arth, Ayron, Wirrai, Lery.

Highest point: Plinlimmon at 2,468 feet.

Cardiganshire's local government: The County of Cardiganshire gives its boundaries to its unitary administrative shadow called Sir Ceredigion.

FAMOUS NAMES

◆ Some say Dafydd ap Gwilym was the greatest Welsh poet of all time. Born in the 14th century in Llanbadarn Fawr, near Aberystwyth, he wrote in Welsh about love, lust and the joys of nature. His remains are buried within the monastery precincts at Strata Florida near Pontrhydfendigaich.

◆ Cardigan's bridge is graced with a fine sculpture of an otter, made by Geoffrey Powell and presented to the town by the naturalist and broadcaster David Bellamy.

◆ Roger Rees, the TV and stage actor who starred in *Bouquet of Barbed Wire* and *Nicholas Nickleby*, is a native of Aberystwyth, on the Cardiganshire Coast.

COUNTY CALENDAR

◆ Mid November: Welsh and English feature films, seminars and talks form part of the Welsh International Film Festival in Aberystwyth.

CARMARTHENSHIRE

SIR GAERFYRDDIN

THE COUNTY LANDSCAPE

◆ After the wild cliffs and waves of the southwest, the Welsh coast swings south to enter the gentler waters of Carmarthen Bay, where the Tywi estuary spreads into a star of inlets, wide sands and dunes.

◆ Carmarthenshire is the county that links mid and west Wales with the south, taking in a 25-mile stretch of the southern coast from the 8-mile Pendine Sands in the west to Llanelli in the east.

◆ Part of the northern boundary with Cardiganshire follows the course of the river Teifi, whose turbulent currents are a sharp contrast to the calm waters of the Tywi (Towy), which flows south from Llandovery to Carmarthen Bay and out into the Bristol Channel.

◆ Most of the county is rich farming land, but its northern reaches touch the central Cambrian mountains, and in the west the county boundary loops around the Black Mountain, a long, wide swathe of high moorland at the western end of the Brecon Beacons National Park.

◆ As you head northeast, into the county's upper reaches, the character of the landscape changes from rolling farmland to high moors and the Old Red Sandstone peaks of the Carmarthenshire Fans and Black Mountain, rising to 2,642 feet at Ban Brycheiniog.

CARMARTHENSHIRE CAN CONJURE up images of Dylan Thomas with his quiet boathouse in Laugharne and inspiration for much of *Under Milk Wood;* or Sir Malcolm Campbell roaring along the flat stretches of Pendine Sands in his attempts to break the world land speed record. But one enduring picture of Carmarthenshire for me is Llanelli – at the eastern end of the Carmarthen Bay – the proud home of a champion rugby team.

TOWNS AND VILLAGES

Some people say that Llanelli hasn't got much going for it but I love Llanelli and the people there are really warm and friendly. They are fanatical too about their sport and justly so: in the 1970s, when Wales dominated the game, some of her greatest stars emerged from the town's rugby club, the 'Scarlets' of Stradey Park. Gareth Edwards, Barry John, JPR Williams...all started their rugby days at the pitch with the 'sospans' on the posts – symbols of the local tinplate industry, and subjects of the well-known rugby anthem 'Sospan Fach'.

Llanelli's nickname is Sospans because it's where they make saucepans and lots of kitchenware, but of course the whole town revolves around the rugby club. It's a real working town, more the product of Swansea and the valleys, and yet up the road in direct contrast is Carmarthen with all its sheep and farms. The Tywi flows on through fertile farmlands to Carmarthen. This old but lively market town has always been an important centre.

Salmon and trout are chief among the tastiest delicacies associated with the county, and you can sample a lot more by visiting Carmarthen's covered market. Look out for home-cured ham and organic bread, and especially for the delicious Carmarthenshire cheeses, such as Caws Ffermdy Cenarth, or unpasteurised Llanboidy cheese. The town's Welsh name, Caerfyrddin, means 'Merlin's Fort': the wizard's oak stood near the town for hundreds of years, its stump eventually shored up with concrete, because Merlin had warned that 'when the oak falls down, then falls the town'.

CENARTH *Where salmon leap up the Teifi Falls about five miles from Felindre.*

Traffic convenience won out in the end, and the oak's remains were moved gingerly to the town museum. You can still see traces of Carmarthen's Roman amphitheatre, which dates from the days when this was Caer Maridunum, one of two fortress towns in Wales.

Sitting right on the river and the Cardiganshire border, is Cenarth, where the ancient coracle is still occasionally used to catch salmon. Coracles are little oval boats, made of wooden frames covered with leather and pitch. They were probably used by Stone Age fishermen, and a few craftsmen still produce them at Cenarth's Coracle Centre.

LOCAL HISTORY

Between Laugharne and Pendine, on the shores of Carmarthen Bay, archaeologists made astonishing finds on the floor of Coygen Cave. The bones of extinct wild animals preserved in the stalagmites here are up to 25,000 years old. A few miles inland is Whitland (known in Welsh as Hendy-gwyn), whose history is rather more recent: this was the 10th-century meeting place of Hywel Dda (the Good), the powerful chief who drew up a code of Welsh laws that lasted over 300 years, until the English conquest in the 11th century.

Up in the remote hill country is the mysterious Llyn y Fan Fach, the lake where a beautiful fairy woman rose from the waters and married a mortal, Rhiwallon, on condition that he would not touch her with iron. Poor Rhiwallon managed to touch his wife three times – with the tip of a whip, the buckle of a glove and a ring – and she promptly disappeared into the lake, followed by her hapless husband's sheep and cattle.

One of the most romantic castle ruins in Wales is also found up in the highlands. Carreg Cennen Castle was captured in its time by rebel leader Owain Glyndwr and by Sir Richard Herbert of Raglan, who wanted to flush out the 'nest of robbers' hiding out there. But the dark ruins still stand, perched on a 300-foot limestone rock, and a passage still tunnels into the cliff and emerges in the old well. This ragged fortress, silhouetted against the mountains at sunset, is an unforgettable sight. Another commanding castle perched above the tranquil coast and countryside is the fortress at Llansteffan. Its rough stone walls, dating from 1192, occupy a far older hill-fort from around 600BC.

Into the 14th-century and Carmarthen had cornered the market in wool, exporting to Flanders and beyond. The wool trade has served the county well for many centuries, and 18th-century textile machines are still on display at the Museum of the Welsh Woollen Industry in Drefach, Felindre, near the lovely Teifi valley.

COUNTY FACTS

Origin of name: From the Welsh Caer Mardin referring to a seafort or stronghold of the seaport. The Romans called it Maridunum, also meaning fortress by the sea (môre also means sea in Welsh).

Name first recorded: 1109.

County Motto: *Rhyddid Gwerin Ffniant Gwlud* ("The freedom of the people is the prosperity of the country").

County Town: CARMARTHEN

Site of the Romans most westerly fortress in Britain, Morindunum. The museum houses jewels and other artefacts from the fort.

Other Towns:

KIDWELLY A beautiful, well preserved medieval fortress (and well kept secret) plus an Industrial Museum highlighting the great tin-plate work carried on here.

LLANDEILO Has the remains of the medieval Dryslwyn Castle and the 18th-century Paxton's Tower.

LLANDOVERY Cobbled market square, archways, clock tower and Georgian façades.

LLANSTEFFAN Includes the ruins of an imposing castle built by a Merioneth prince in 1138.

NEWCASTLE EMLYN Flourishing little market town with castle ruins offering super Teifi views and nearby local flourmaking around a working 16th-century watermill with fishing museum and falconry centre.

ST CLEARS Owen Glyndwyr was defeated here in 1406; also a Norman church with striking tower.

◆ Ammanford ◆ Brynamman ◆ Burry Port ◆ Glanamman ◆ Gorseinon ◆ Hendy ◆ Llangennach ◆ Llwynhendry ◆ Pemberton ◆ Pwll ◆ Tumble

County rivers: Towy, Taff, Gwendraeth Fawr, Gwendraeth Fechan, Lloughor.

Highest point: Carmarthen Fau at 2,525 feet.

Carmarthenshire's local government: The County of Carmarthenshire gives its boundaries to Carmarthenshire unitary council.

FAMOUS NAMES

◆ Barry John, who was born in Cefneithin, and his team-mate in the glory days, Gareth Edwards, are the most celebrated products of the Llanelli 'Scarlets'.

◆ Siân Philips, the elegant actress who made such a devious Livia in the BBC's *I Claudius*, hails from Betws.

◆ Actor Hywel Bennett comes from Garnant.

◆ Rachel Roberts, the powerful and emotional actress once married to Rex Harrison, was born in Llanelli.

◆ A museum dedicated to the poet Dylan Thomas is set out in the boathouse at Laugharne, the little town on the Tywi estuary where he spent the last years of his life. His grave is in the local churchyard.

COUNTY CALENDAR

◆ August: in the second week of the month the United Counties Agricultural Show displays the best of west Wales agriculture and features craft stalls and spectator events.

◆ June-July: Welsh Motorsports Day at Pembrey, Llanelli with stalls, children's rides and driving school.

DENBIGHSHIRE

SIR DDINBYCH

PLAS NEWYDD *Fantastic half-timbered home of the eccentric ladies of Llangollen.*

THE COUNTY LANDSCAPE

◆ This is a thoroughly Welsh county in its lively culture and in its multifarious scenery of rivers, waterfalls and lakes, wooded hills and open pastures.

◆ Invaders from the east came up against a formidable natural barrier in this part of Wales. The landscape changes abruptly across the border from England, rising into the Clwydian Hills that sweep down the north coast along the county's eastern boundary and down to Llangollen. Here the river Dee (Dyfrdwy in Welsh) swings round to rush through the town and flow along the county's edge.

◆ Over to the west, the river Conwy marks the approach to Caernarfonshire and the Snowdonia mountains, and in between are several miles of the most popular coastline in Wales.

◆ Near Llanrhaeadr is another wonder of Wales – Pistyll-y-Rhaeadr, a slender 240-foot waterfall that leaps down the rock.

COUNTY CALENDAR

◆ Over 12,000 singers, choristers, dancers and musicians travel from all over the world to compete in Llangollen's International Musical Eisteddfod, a week of dancing and singing first held to celebrate the end of World War II.

THE VALE OF Llangollen is a seamless blending of woodland and river (the Dee), moor and hill, and the higher mountains rising in the background fold upon fold. Nestled in this narrow valley lies Llangollen itself, which to me is the embodiment of a Welsh town. It is also the mecca where over 30 folk cultures and costumes come together for the International Music Eisteddfod which appeals to my Aquarian sense of brotherhood.

TOWNS AND VILLAGES

Despite the steady flow of traffic and visitors that clog up the streets in summer, Llangollen has remained a town with great and genuine Welsh character. Greystone and Victorian buildings straddle the turbulent river Dee, which tumbles through the arches of a 14th-century bridge; the calm Llangollen canal carries passengers in horse-drawn barges along Thomas Telford's soaring 1,000-foot Pontcysyllte aqueduct, high above the river as it flows northwards towards the Horseshoe Falls. Looming over the town are the hilltop ruins of Castell Dinas Brân, a medieval Welsh fortress whose shattered walls still have the haunting air suggested by their name, which means 'Castle of the City of Crows'.

South of the river is a house with a curious past: elaborate half-timbered Plas Newydd, where the notorious Ladies of Llangollen lived from 1780. Lady Eleanor Butler and Miss Sarah Ponsonby 'eloped' here from Ireland with their servant, Mary Carryl, and set up an eccentric household stocked with a collection of wooden objects and curios. Their distinguished callers included Walter Scott, Wordsworth and Wellington.

Sitting at the junction of several main roads from England and from south and north Wales, Wrexham boasts one of the Seven Wonders of Wales – its 136-foot 16th-century tower, decorated with medieval carvings and topped with four turrets. A couple of miles south of town, Erddig Hall is a stately 17th-century mansion, which has been kept almost unchanged since the 1730s. The original owner, county sheriff Joshua Edisbury, borrowed so much money to build his grand new home that he had to move to London to escape his creditors, and never saw Erddig finished.

Deep in the Vale of Clwyd, Ruthin an ancient market town has a delightful stretch of medieval half-timbered buildings. Central St Peter's Square is overlooked by the 1401 courthouse, still with part of its gibbet conveniently sticking out of the eaves for quick dispensation of justice; and the 1500 Exmewe Hall. Maen Huail (Huail's Stone), in the pavement outside the hall, is the spot where Huail's head hit the ground after being cut off by his love-rival – none other than King Arthur. If you get the feeling of being watched here, it's probably not by the ghost of Huail but by the seven 'eyes of Ruthin', three rows of little dormer windows peeking out of the roof of the 17th-century Myddleton Arms.

A totally different Denbighshire sits on the north coast: the county of proms, piers and fairgrounds. Colwyn Bay has three miles of sandy beach, backed by a seafront promenade, and elegant 19th-century houses marking its beginnings as a favourite Victorian resort.

LOCAL HISTORY

At Sycarth, in the southern tail, only a mound remains of the glittering court of Owain Glyndwr, where the renowned bard Iolo Goch sang his master's praises. Prince Madog ap Gruffydd of Powys founded Valle Crucis Abbey, now a graceful ruin at the foot of Horseshoe Pass. This was the last resting place of Iolo Goch, who may lie in one of the damaged tombs near the choir. The abbey had passed its prime long before its decay. A 16th-century abbot, Roger Salisbury, passed his time producing counterfeit money and popping out for the odd spot of highway robbery. At the dark-stoned village of Llanrhaeadr-ym-Mochnant, Bishop William Morgan produced a Welsh version of the Bible in 1588, providing a work of great literary beauty that helped preserve the language in the face of official attempts to stamp it out.

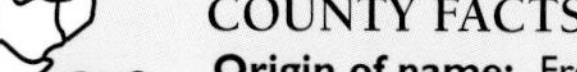

COUNTY FACTS

Origin of name: From the Welsh *din* meaning little, and *bych* which translates as fort.

Name first recorded: c. 1350.

County Town: DENBIGH Has an impressive county museum and its imposing high-walled castle ruin atop a hill.

Other Towns:

ABERGELE A seaside town with limestone outcrops beckoning to the Denbigh Moors. There is a livestock market on Mondays and a general weekend one.

CHIRK Visit here for the famous marcher castle (really a stately home) with glorious gardens and topiary.

COLWYN BAY Victorian flavour thanks to its architecture, set on a sandy coastline overlooked by wooded hills. A Glamorgan cricket venue!

GRESFORD The Parish church rivals Wrexham's St Giles and a yew tree said to be over 1,400 years old.

LLANRWST Attractive little market town in the broad luxuriant vale with thick forest and mountains edged along its boundaries. A famous stone bridge crosses the Conwy – a stretch known since Roman times for its pearl fishing. Excellent walking and touring centre.

WREXHAM Revitalized and utilizing its rich industrial heritage to lure a new wave of sightseers.

◆ Brymbo ◆ Bryn-teg ◆ Coedpoeth ◆ Llay ◆ Rhosllanerchrugog ◆ Ruabon

County rivers: Conway, Clwyd, Dee.

Highest point: Moel Sych and Cader Berwyn at 2,713 feet.

Denbighshire's local government The County of Denbighshire is governed by four unitary councils: Denbighshire, Wrexham, and Conwy (Caernarfonshire) unitary councils. The three communities of Llanrhaeadr-ym-Mochnant (partly in Montgomeryshire), Llansilin and Llangedwyn fall under Powys Council.

FAMOUS NAMES

◆ Broadcaster Mavis Nicholson lives in Llanrhaeadr-ym-Mochnant (partly in Montgomeryshire).

◆ Hugh Grant was *The Englishman who Went up a Hill and Came down a Mountain* in the 1995 film set in the countryside around Llanrhaeadr and the local hotel.

◆ Henry Morton Stanley ('Dr Livingstone, I presume') started life as John Rowlands in Denbigh. After escaping from the workhouse and sailing to America as a cabin boy he was adopted by Stanley Senior and set out on a series of world adventures, before finding Livingstone in Africa in 1871.

COUNTY CALENDAR

◆ Early June: Hundreds of male voice choristers get together for some great Welsh singing at the Llangollen Choral Festival in the International Pavilion.

◆ Mid-October: The British Open Canoe Slalom Championships bring about 200 canoeists to brave the Dee rapids near Llangollen every year; and later in the month teams from all over the UK compete in the National Regional Slalom Finals.

FLINTSHIRE

SIR Y FFLINT

THE COUNTY LANDSCAPE

◆ There are three segments of Flintshire, the smallest county in Wales: the main county, which hugs the northeastern shoulder of Wales and the broad Dee estuary; and a much smaller piece of land, southeast of Wrexham, originally known in Welsh as Maelor Saesneg (English or Saxon Maelor). This was established by Edward I as a detached administrative slice of his conquered territory around Flint, and has a more English character than the intervening towns and villages of Denbighshire. There is a tiny island detached in Denbighshire between Flint major and Flint Maelor centred around the parish of Marford and Hoseley.

◆ The coastal area of the county has a strip of heavy development lining the estuary across the water from the Wirral in Cheshire, and the ruins of a series of castles thrown up as armies followed these flatlands into Wales to avoid the forbidding mountains further south.

◆ To the west, though, are the beaches and bright resorts that have made this such a popular holiday county; and inland are wooded slopes, limestone cliffs, attractive market towns and the picturesque remains of once-formidable fortresses.

HOLY PLACES AND holidays, sandy beaches and saintly atmosphere: this county has marvellous contrasts. Rhyl and Prestatyn are premier Welsh coast resorts offering sun and fun . . . or you can seek a more gentle atmosphere in the lovely little cathedral city of St Asaph. I relish these differing themes which run like a silver thread through the north Welsh coast.

TOWNS AND VILLAGES

Flintshire is the gateway from gloomy industrial development to beaches, buckets and candy floss. The A548 coast road starts the North Wales holiday trail that brings hordes of visitors from northern England every summer and takes them through a string of breezy beach towns. First stop is Prestatyn, right at the top end of Offa's Dyke (you can reach the long-distance footpath from here). No fewer than three beaches are on offer here, along with a prom, holiday camps and caravan parks. Four miles further along the coast there's even more of the same at Rhyl, where guaranteed good weather is laid on at the Sun Centre, and brash amusements, rides and shows compete with the gentler seaside pastimes of crazy golf, boat trips or strolls along the quay where fishermen still manage to ply their trade. A trip to the top of the 240-foot Skytower gives a stupendous view of the coast sweeping away towards Llandudno and the Caernarfonshire mountains behind and beyond the town into distant Anglesey.

All along the points of entry into Wales from the river Dee, ruins of medieval castles recall English conquest and power. Sitting on the invaders' coastal route, right on the edge of the estuary, Flint Castle once overlooked a busy port – now gone. The modern town threatens to crowd its fortress as it lurks behind the main square; but even the reduced walls and towers tell you that this was a magnificent building in its day, designed by Edward I's master architect from Savoy, James of St George, with a squat Great Tower, once surrounded by a moat, standing apart from the main complex and linked by drawbridge.

South of Flint, and only a couple of miles from another Edwardian stronghold, Hawarden, are the imposing ruins of the Welsh Ewloe castle, built by Llywelyn the Great. It still has its D-shaped tower, a favourite feature in Welsh fortresses. This was a base for the last prince of Wales, another Llywelyn, when he set out to impose his rule on Wales in place of the English.

ST ASAPH *Twice destroyed since its foundation in* AD537.

In the eastern crook of Flintshire, between the rivers Clwyd and Elwy, is St Asaph (Llanelwy), the smallest cathedral in Britain, founded back in the 6th century. After the original church was demolished by English armies King Edward announced his intention to build a new version at Rhuddlan, further downriver. But Bishop Anian put his foot down, and even Edward had to bow to the church and allow the new cathedral to built on the same spot. Among the cathedral's treasures are a newspaper announcing the death of Oliver Cromwell and a dictionary of Welsh, Greek and Hebrew, compiled by Dic Aberdaron, a self-taught 19th-century linguist who eventually mastered 35 tongues.

LOCAL HISTORY

When the Romans occupied this area they realized that there was lead in them thar hills, and Halkyn Mountain, north of Mold, became a honeycomb of mines, which burrowed even further into the rock when the 19th-century industrial age brought new machinery and techniques.

The early Middle Ages were a time of religious devotion, when pilgrims flocked to the little town of Holywell, on the slopes of Halkyn, to bathe in the restoring well at St Winefride's Chapel. A mile away are the remains of Basingwerk Abbey, which was admired for its elegance and beautiful windows from 1132 until it was taken apart by reformers in the 16th century.

An even earlier monument stands to the northwest, near Whitford: an 11-foot stone Celtic cross, carved with elaborate patterns copied from Viking artwork. Its Welsh name, Maen Achwynfan, translates as Stone of the Place of Sorrow, or Complaint: maybe it commemorates the loss of a leader or the death of some loved one 1,000 years ago.

The exceptional monument of Flint Castle was where Richard II met his enemy Henry Bolingbroke and agreed to abdicate in his favour in 1399; some 85 years earlier, the feckless Edward II had welcomed his beloved Piers Gaveston here on his return from exile.

One of the most poignant historic sites in Wales is Rhuddlan, another of Edward's castles: this massive stronghold sits on the banks of the river Clwyd, diverted to flow past its walls and give supply ships easy access. It was at Rhuddlan that King Offa was killed in battle in 796, before his dyke had reached the sea; nearly 500 years later the tide had turned, and this was the scene of English victory over the Welsh, where Edward produced the Statute of Rhuddlan, stripping away Welsh government and laws and carving up the princedoms into shires.

COUNTY FACTS

Origin of name: From the Old English for any hard rock or flint.
Name first recorded: 1277.
County Motto: *Gorau Tarian Cifiawnder* ("The Best Shield is Justice").
County Town:
MOLD Unassuming, pleasant centre with impressive modern buildings including Theatr Clwyd, one of Wales's major theatres and concert halls. Nearby Halkyn Mountain offers moorland and superb views across the Dee.
Other Towns:
BODELWYDDAN Beautiful castle housing a National Portrait Gallery outpost and opulent Victorian interiors beckons one to this town.
DYSERTH Two villages of Upper and Lower Dyserth are linked by a plunging 60-foot waterfall.
FLINT The remains of the 13th-century castle are still an imposing sight.
HOLYWELL A fascinating place to walk around the abbey ruins, a farm museum and Holy Well, a place of pilgrimage for centuries at St Winefride's Well – the so-called Lourdes of Wales.
OVERTON A muddle of half-timbered and mellow pink bricked buildings, with churchyard attractively ringed with ancient yew trees.
PRESTATYN Holiday resort renowned for its holiday camp.
RHUDDLAN A stunning castle set by the Clwyd marks this once-thriving Victorian port.
RHYL "Sunny Rhyl" is the Blackpool of North Wales. Good for shopping.
◆ Broughton ◆ Buckley ◆ Caergwrle ◆ Caerwys
◆ Connah's Quay ◆ Hope ◆ Queensferry ◆ Shotton
County rivers: Clwyd, Elwy.
Highest point: Moel Fammau (the Mother of Hills) at 1,820 feet.

Flintshire's local government: The county is governed by three unitary authorities - Flintshire and Denbighshire council which takes in Flintshire's Prestatyn, Rhyl, Rhuddlan and St. Asaph. Maelor and Marford are both Flintshire detached in Denbighshire under Wrexham Council.

FAMOUS NAMES

◆ William Gladstone made his home at Hawarden Castle after marrying the daughter of its owner in 1839, and founded St Deiniol's library in the town.
◆ Footballer Ian Rush was born in St Asaph in 1961.
◆ Emlyn Williams, the actor and playwright, drew on his early Flintshire childhood in Mostyn for his works, including *The Corn is Green*.

COUNTY CALENDAR

◆ Mid-September: St Asaph Cathedral is a perfect venue for the week-long North Wales Festival.
◆ Numerous events centred on Rhyl and Prestatyn throughout the year.

GLAMORGAN  *MORGANNWG*

THE COUNTY LANDSCAPE

◆ Two-thirds of the population of Wales lives in the south, and Glamorgan is the most populous county of all. In the valleys behind Cardiff and Swansea are the undulating terraces and close communities of the ex-colliery towns, built along the Taff, the Rumney, the Daw and the Ogmore. At one time South Wales was as beautiful as North Wales but the development of the coal mines spoiled the scenery of the Rhondda Valley (even if it provided a livelihood for the inhabitants) with pit wheels, slagheaps and tall chimneys lying under a smoky sky. Times have changed and massive reclamation schemes including planting of conifer forests, now lure visitors with industrial heritage trails, and even this most urban and industrial of Welsh counties has landscapes of great natural beauty.

◆ The Vale of Glamorgan, the lowlands stretching westward from the southern coast to Port Talbot, is an unspoilt area of farmland and small villages.

◆ To the north, beyond the coal valleys, are the forests and waterfalls of the hills that eventually become the Brecon Beacons. And along the coast to the west, between Swansea Bay and Carmarthen Bay, are the rugged cliffs, the beaches and marshlands of the lovely Gower Peninsula. The south and west line the Bristol Channel and include the islands of Barry and Sully.

TOGETHER WITH THE western half of Monmouthshire, this *is* the Welsh Valleys, and the warmth and welcome you get from the people of the valleys is just out of this world. I lived in Cardiff and Barry for many years and left my heart there: I adore the cities, especially Cardiff (Caerdydd) and Swansea (Abertawe), which are so different! Cardiff, like Edinburgh, is the most beautiful capital city, far more attractive than London and with terrific shopping. Swansea is much more Welsh in character. Not surprisingly there is a Liverpool-Manchester, Leeds-Bradford sort of rivalry going on between these two great Welsh cities.

Sprawling between the valleys and the coast, this county has seen the best and worst of industrial life, which has left a legacy of grand architecture, derelict coal pits and some of the most outgoing and welcoming communities in the country. It also has the rural plains of the Vale of Glamorgan, where vineyards produce the award-winning Cariad wines; and it has the wild cliffs and quiet beaches of the Gower, jutting out into the Bristol Channel west of Swansea and ending in the islet of Worms Head, accessible only when the tide is out.

TOWNS AND VILLAGES

Today the evidence of Cardiff's heyday as an industrial centre is in the tall Edwardian buildings and canopied shopping arcades; the graceful civic centre, built in White Portland stone around broad avenues and parks; and the exotic castle, refurbished for the 3rd Marquis of Bute by the eccentric architect William Burges. The

RHOSILI BAY *The Land's End of Gower – the furthest point west you can go is Worms Head, unless you're a surfer…*

castle is a real treat. It sits in the city centre, surrounded by traffic, a perfect escape from urban bustle. Peacocks roam the grounds, which extend into the green acres of Bute Park; and the Burges apartment, topped with an ornate clocktower, are an orgy of neo-Gothic romance and whimsy: marble, lapis lazuli and gold, secret switches, fables illustrated in tiles, brightly coloured carvings and murals. Another example of Burges' work can be seen at Castell Coch (Red Castle), two miles from Cardiff at Tongwynlais, where fairytale conical towers perch on a hillside above the motorway.

Cardiff's docks are finding a new identity as a leisure area and marina, and the waterfront is lovely to amble along and see the grandiose red-brick Pier Head Building, with terracotta decoration inspired by India's red Mogul architecture. Look out, too, for the solitary wooden Norwegian church, first built in 1868 for Scandinavian sailors bringing timber for the pits, and moved plank by plank to its present site during the docks' redevelopment. Incidentally, that mischievous children's writer Roald Dahl was a Cardiff-born descendant of one of those Scandinavians.

A few miles north of the capital, at Caerphilly, is the biggest castle in Wales: 30 acres of it, started in 1268 by Norman lord Gilbert de Clare, and then started again in 1271 after his arch-enemy Llywelyn, Prince of Wales had burnt it down. One of its corner towers, ripped down the middle by a cannonball in the civil war, has stuck at a worryingly sharp angle – but it has stayed up so far.

At the head of the valleys, in Merthyr Tydfil, is a battlemented mansion, built in 1825 for ironmaster William Crawshay, overlooking the biggest ironworks in Britain. Today this, too, is a museum – and a reminder of the vast fortunes made by a few from the valley's workforce. It is now the H.Q. for Hoover.

Swansea has a smart new marina in the docks area so badly hit during the Blitz raids. It also has one of the best covered markets in the country, and this is the place to look for Glamorgan's gastronomic offerings. The white, crumbly Caerphilly and other excellent local cheeses are sold here, and so are cockles and mussels, collected at Penclawdd on the Burry Estuary. The sands at Penclawdd stretch for some seven miles and at low tide are two miles wide so there is ample space if you fancy hand-picking them yourself. But the real speciality is laverbread. It's actually seaweed, washed thoroughly and boiled in a large heavy pot for hours until a thick cauldron's-worth is left. It is sold fresh or tinned, to be eaten mixed into an oatmeal cake which is then fried in home-cure bacon fat and preferably served with bacon.

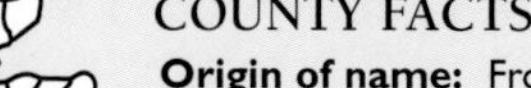

COUNTY FACTS

Origin of name: From the Welsh *Glanna Morgan* meaning Morgan's shore. Several princes named Morgan ruled the area.

Name first recorded: 1242 as *Gwlad Morgan* (the land of Morgan), a 10th-century Welsh prince.

County Motto: *A ddioddetws a orfu* ("He that endureth, overcometh").

County Town: CARDIFF A very elegant city undergoing massive regeneration. Check out the cigar-shaped visitors centre, the scrummy indoor market, the open-air Museum of Welsh Life at nearby St Fagan's and the Welsh Industrial & Maritime Museum of Cardiff Bay to explore the industrial and cultural heritage.

Other Towns:

ABERAVON A seaside resort with extensive sweep of sand and major sports and leisure complex on its lido. Once a borough in its own right.

BARRY Spells seaside fun and I should know – I lived here. In the halcyon years before the Great War it once exported more coal than Cardiff! Now it trades in more bananas than any other port in the UK. Visit the swans on the Knap.

CAERPHILLY A lively town with a massive castle complete with water-filled moat, rivalling Windsor in size. Traditional Caerphilly cheese is still made and boxed at the Old Court restaurant. Nearby, the Universal Colliery Memorial is a symbolic pithead wheel on the site where 439 men and boys died in Britain's worst pit disaster in 1913.

LLANTRISANT Home of the Royal Mint. A quaint hilltop town which once provided warriors for the Black Prince, and a Doctor Price who helped get cremation legalised (by burning his dead boy on an open-air pyre). He also believed in free love and nudism and his statue stands in the town.

MAESTEG Former coal-mining town almost enclosed by high forested slopes. Its town hall gave Richard Burton his first boards to tread on.

MERTHYR TYDFIL Blast furnaces smelted metal round the clock in this now sedate town's 19th-century heyday. It once smelted metal for the trans-Siberian railway and the rail line from here to Abercynon was the first for Trevithick's world's first steam engine.

NEATH A character all of its own despite Swansea close by. Pedestrianized town centre and indoor market. The Castle Hotel was where the inaugural Welsh Rugby Union meeting was held in 1881 and Neath Rugby Club, the Welsh All Black, played an important part in the game's development in Wales. Nearby Aberdulais Falls gush with natural beauty.

PORT TALBOT Steelmaking town named after wealthy Talbot family who developed the docks, and whose ornamental home, Margam Castle, is the centre of a superb country park with Orangery.

SWANSEA Dylan Thomas, who was born here, called it an ugly lovely place. Now its dockside development has made it a happening place. It is still very much a working port too. Nearby oddly named Mumbles is an attractive sailing and watersports centre.

◆ Abercynon ◆ Aberdare ◆ Aberfan ◆ Bargoed ◆ Bridgend ◆ Briton Ferry ◆ Cowbridge ◆ Gorseinon ◆ Hengoed ◆ Hirwaun ◆ Morriston ◆ Mountain Ash ◆ Penarth ◆ Porthcawl ◆ Pontardawe ◆ Pontardulais ◆ Pontypridd ◆ Tonyrefail ◆ Treharris ◆ Treorchy
County rivers: Rumney, Taff, Daw, Ogmore.
Highest point: Craig-y-llyn at 1,969 feet.

Glamorgan's local government: Glamorgan is governed by eight unitary authorities: Swansea, Cardiff, Bridgend, Caerphilly, Merthyr Tydfil, Neath, Port Talbot, Rhondda-Cynon-Taff and Vale of Glamorgan.

FAMOUS NAMES

◆ Oscar-winning Sir Anthony Hopkins was born in Margam, a rural suburb of Port Talbot. Despite the lure of Hollywood, Sir Anthony is actively involved in the conservation of rural Wales as President of the National Trust's Snowdonia Appeal.
◆ Richard Burton came from Pontrhydyfen and honed his acting talents at Port Talbot Secondary School.
◆ BBC's anchorman John Humphry was brought up and cut his teeth in Cardiff as a foreign correspondent and now owns a Welsh farm.
◆ Sir Geraint Evans and the writers of the Welsh national anthem all hail from Pontypridd.
◆ Ex-Goon Sir Harry Secombe has his roots in Swansea.
◆ In Cardiff's old dockland community of Tiger Bay, now demolished, Shirley Bassey exercised her vocal chords while sitting under the kitchen table, away from family bustle. Tiger Bay was the setting and title of the 1959 film that shot young Hayley Mills to stardom.
◆ Ray Milland was born Reginald Alfred Truscott-Jones in Neath. Equipped with his neat new name, he became a Hollywood favourite and won an Oscar for his performance as an alcoholic in *The Lost Weekend.*
◆ The Welsh answer to Noël Coward, Ivor Novello, learned his musical skills in Cardiff and went on to write such evergreens as *Keep the Home Fires Burning.*
◆ Two more musical talents made the most of their training in the Land of Song: Mary Hopkin, angelic singer of *Those Were the Days*, who comes from Pontardawe in the west; and the Voice himself, Tom Jones, born in Treforest south of Pontypridd.
◆ Tennyson said Caerphilly Castle was more like a ruined town than a castle. The makers of the film *Restoration* (1995, starring Robert Downey Jr) used the castle to recreate Cheapside in 1666 London.

COUNTY CALENDAR

◆ February-March: Cardiff Arms Park is one of the venues in Britain and France hosting matches for the International Rugby matches – a perfect opportunity to see and hear Welsh rugby fans in full regalia (giant leeks included) and full voice.
◆ Mid June: Another biennial event has become one of the world's best showcases for operatic singing: the Cardiff Singer of the World competition, which takes place in the modern St David's Concert Hall.
◆ Mid-Late June: Gwyl Ifan is the biggest display of Welsh folk dancing: take your partners in Cardiff and surrounding areas.
◆ Mid-June: The Welsh Longboard Festival with surfing and kite-flying competitions at Llangennith.

LOCAL HISTORY

Cardiff's foundations were laid by the Romans as an important outpost of the Legions based on Caerleon across the border in Monmouthshire. Before that, copper and ore were being shipped from Cornwall and later from overseas to be smelted with Swansea coal. The county's fantastic deposits of coal and iron were exploited especially in thew Rhondda Valleys – narrow and steep-sided and tightly-packed with terraced communities growing up in the boom years of the 18th century.

Roads and railways led to Cardiff which, only 250 years ago, was a swampy village, plagued with pirates. Then the enterprising Bute family built docks there, and before long black gold was being carried by the ton from Pontypridd, Aberdare, Merthyr Tydfil, Tredegar. By the end of the 19th century Cardiff was the world's biggest coal port.

Until the end of 1990 the valleys were black with slag, and their towns lay under a permanent veil of coal dust. Anthracite was in demand around the world. Now the hills are green again and some of the pits are working museums. But there's still a special character to these towns: the grey-stone chapels, the long rows of terraced streets following the hillsides and the Welsh-Italian cafés that have been part of local life since labourers flocked from Europe looking for work earlier this century.

BLAENRHONDDA *Once the great source of 'the black diamond' – coal.*

MERIONETH *MEIRIONNYDD*

MOUNTAINS…LAKES…CASTLES, and Portmeirion, Merioneth is simply gasp after gasp of scenic surprises. It is stunningly beautiful with the majestic Cader Idris, the haunting Lake Bala, and the formidable Harlech Castle. Merioneth is an exquisite county.

TOWNS AND VILLAGES

Up in the northwestern corner of Merioneth are three places that illustrate this county's element of theatre and surprise. First comes Harlech, a tiny town overwhelmed by a white World Heritage castle, which towers over it on a high crag between the Snowdonia mountains and glorious Tremadog Bay. When it was built the huge round towers and fortified stairs were right on the sea's edge: supplies were brought to the doorstep by boat. Today a golf links leads to the long, sandy beach. A few miles northeast and you're in a moonscape. Blaenau Ffestiniog – just Blaenau to locals – was the slate capital of north Wales and behind the town, the mountains are slashed and scarred into a gloomy grey by the old slate quarries, now tourist attractions taking visitors deep into the Llechwedd and Gloddfa Ganol caverns. From here a steam train chugs along the narrow-gauge Ffestiniog Railway – now carrying sightseers instead of carts full of slate – to bright and busy Porthmadog.

Surprise number three lies hidden on a thickly wooded peninsula nearby – the most exotic and unexpected spot in the country. Portmeirion is a folly gone mad, the creation of architect Sir Clough Williams-Ellis, whose 'fancy' was pastel pinks, dusty reds, statues, carvings and piazzas, a campanile, a domed pantheon, a triumphal arch. They all contribute to a bizarre mix he called 'light opera' – and an apt setting for the cult 1960s TV series *The Prisoner*.

FFESTINIOG RAILWAY *Tan Y Bwlch station.*

LOCAL HISTORY

Edward I left his mark on the late 1200s with the massive fortress chain that begins at Harlech. Owain Glyndwr took it in 1404, and made the town his capital until he lost it again in 1408. In the Wars of the Roses it withstood a seven-year siege before falling to the Yorkists in 1468 – a resistance that inspired the rousing anthem *Men of Harlech*.

THE COUNTY LANDSCAPE

◆ The county's southern boundary marks the lower edge of the Snowdonia National Park, and this is where the great transition takes place from rolling green moors to soaring crags and deep chasms.

◆ Its western limits follow the coastline from the Dyfi estuary in the south to close by Porthmadog in Caernarfonshire, just turning the corner into the Llyn Peninsula; along the way, estuaries and inlets bite into the shore, and mountains and sea provide stunning views across to the Mawddach estuary and Tremadog Bay, overlooked by Harlech Castle.

◆ Where the county narrows towards the east is Bala Lake, Llyn Tegid in Welsh, the biggest natural lake in Wales, a four-mile stretch of water with its own unique fish, the gwyniad, a member of the salmon family found nowhere else in the world. The Premier Slalom and Open White Water Race is held here in late May.

COUNTY FACTS

Origin of name: From Meirion, grandson of Cunedda Wledig, who conquered much of northern and eastern Wales in the 5th century.

Name first recorded: 450. **County Motto:** *Tra Mor tra Meirion* ("While the sea lasts, so shall Merioneth").

County Towns: **DOLGELLAU** Beneath the shadow of Cader Idris (2,927 feet) has distinctive granite and slate buildings and handsome square.

Other Towns: **ABERDOVEY** A pretty sea-and-sailing Tywyn estuary resort approached by a soothing road through the lush Wye valley.

BALA A town strung along one very attractive stone-lined street at the foot of its lake. In the 18th century it was the centre of nonconformity.

BARMOUTH Start of the exhausting Three Peaks Yacht Race starts at the Quay in late June.

HARLECH The Plâs tearooms offer superb views of Tremadog Bay and occupy the former family home of Denys Finch-Hatton. His affair with Karen Blixen was described in *Out of Africa*, starring Robert Redford and Meryl Streep as the lovers.

TRAWSFYNYDD Mountain village with tranquil feel and pretty houses. Local shepherd and poet Hedd Wyn's life was recent Oscar-nominated bio-pic.

◆ Corwen ◆ Fairbourne ◆ Penrhyndeudraeth

County rivers: Dee, Mawr, Dovey.

Highest point: Arab Fawddwy at 2,972 feet.

Merioneth's local government: The County of Merioneth is administered by two unitary authorities: Gwynedd (shared with Caernarfonshire) while Corwen comes under Denbighshire council.

MONMOUTHSHIRE

SIR FYNWY

THE COUNTY LANDSCAPE

◆ Monmouthshire sits on the southeastern edge of Wales, where the river Severn begins to widen out into the Bristol Channel, pushing the English and Welsh coasts apart. Spreading along the river Usk, which flows into the mouth of the Severn, is Newport, the third biggest town in Wales; and from here river, road and railway travel up to Pontypool, an industrial centre for hundreds of years, drawing on the mining valleys of the east. Beyond its urban and industrial heart, this becomes a county of deep valleys and remote, haunting ruined abbeys and priories.

FAMOUS NAMES

◆ Charles Stewart Rolls (of Rolls-Royce fame) was a Monmouth boy. His statue in Monmouth shows him holding a model of the bi-plane which carried him in the first non-stop flight to France and back.

◆ Actor and entertainer Victor Spinetti belongs to one of the many Welsh-Italian families who have settled in the South Wales valleys. He comes from Cwm.

◆ Ex-miner and father of the Welfare State Aneurin Bevan served as a member of parliament for Ebbw Vale, an old iron and steel making centre. A monument to 'Nye' stands to the west of town. Michael Foot and Neil Kinnock also served the county.

◆ Snooker champion Ray Reardon, from Tredegar, worked as a miner and a policeman before wielding the cue from 1967.

◆ Leslie Thomas, the best selling author, is from Monmouthshire

THIS COUNTY HAS a dual personality: the historic hub of industry, which has left its mark in the towns and valleys of west Monmouthshire; and the rural idyll, with its romantic ruins and tranquil river valleys to the east. The Monmouthshire valleys are a mirror image of Glamorgan, while the east is the beautiful and verdant countryside of the Usk and Wye Valleys. They come together to make a fascinating county with which I have great empathy – I should do as I lived in the tiny village of Llantilio Crossenny tucked in between Monmouth and Abergavenny.

TOWNS AND VILLAGES

A good deal of the industrial character was formed quite recently – from the 19th century, when the coal, steel and tinplate business really took off and Newport began its urban sprawl along the Usk. A visit to Blaenafon's Big Pit mining museum will give you some idea what it was like to extract the black diamond. Ex-miners will take you on a guided tour via the pit cage (with obligatory helmet of course) 300 feet to the pit bottom. This town still has working coalmines and an ironworks which you can also see in action. But Pontypool, a few miles north, has been forging iron since 1425, and emigrants from this town continued the tradition by building the first forge in America, in 1652. Centres of mass production and hard labour were also centres of unrest, and in 1829 the rebellious Chartists marched from Pontypool to Newport to besiege the Westgate Hotel. You can still see the marks of bullets fired at the rioters by soldiers, in the pillars of the old hotel; and you can trace the whole story in Hans Feibusch's murals in the towered, white 1930s civic centre. Newport's main curiosity is the Transport Bridge, a 242-foot iron construction spanning the Usk, built in 1906 to carry heavy loads (cars, nowadays) across the water on a moveable platform. There are only three other examples in the world: one in Middlesbrough in Yorkshire, two in France.

TINTERN ABBEY *Sits above the river Wye, surrounded by wooded hills; near Chepstow.*

Following the old trade routes from Pontypool's forges and mills to Newport's docks is the Monmouthshire and Brecon Canal, built at the height of the commercial boom between

1797 and 1812, and now used for leisurely sightseeing.

After the noise and clamour of the south, seek the smart border market town of Monmouth for a complete contrast. This is a glimpse of genteel, pre-industrial Monmouthshire, and it preserves its buildings and its history with pride. Agincourt Square, in the middle of town, sets the tone with its neo-Classical 18th-century Shire Hall, its fine old inns and its statues of two Monmouth heroes: Henry V, scourge of the French, who was born in now ruined Monmouth Castle in 1387; and Charles Stewart Rolls, of Rolls-Royce fame. Near the shell of the castle is a stately red-stoned Stuart mansion, Great Castle House, built by a local worthy who wanted his first grandchild raised near the place 'where our great hero Henry the Fifth was born'. Even the ancient fortified Monnow Bridge has developed an air of gentle dignity over the centuries. Traffic crawls through the gateway now, but when it was built in the 13th century this was a formidable defence and it remains reputedly the only one of its kind in Britain.

LOCAL HISTORY

Monmouthshire has always served as a stepping stone from southern England into the western reaches of Wales. For 400 years the Romans used their fortress at Caerleon as a permanent Welsh base, served by the town that eventually grew around it. Their amphitheatre is still there, as are the magnificent baths, three halls making up a legionnaires' leisure centre. And then came the Normans, throwing up castles as they thundered across Offa's Dyke: one of the earliest was at Chepstow, Britain's first stone stronghold and still a forbidding sight on its hill overlooking the Severn and the Wye.

Two superb sites recall the more spiritual side of 12th-century life. In the valley of the river Honddu, Llanthony Priory sits in a grassy hollow, surrounded by gentle hills. There was already a ruined chapel here when landowner William de Lacy took shelter from a storm in 1100 and was so moved by its tranquility that he became a hermit there. The present ruins were bought by poet Walter Savage Landor in 1807. His plans to plant 10,000 cedars and graze a flock of merino sheep didn't appeal to the neighbours and he had to abandon his unusual home.

Tintern Abbey was founded in 1131 by Cistercian monks from Normandy; stripped and looted during the Dissolution; and left to fall into the romantic decay that inspired Wordsworth and Turner. Though roof and windows are gone, the abbey looks almost complete from a distance, protected by the forested Wye valley slopes, and it's one of the most graceful and peaceful spots in Wales.

COUNTY FACTS

Origin of name: From the early Welsh *Aper Mynwy*, meaning mouth of the (river) Monnow.

Name first recorded: 1086 as *Monemude*.

County Motto: *Utrique Fedelis* ("Faithful to Both").

County Town:

MONMOUTH On the rivers Wye and Monnow, this prosperous market town has Nelson memorabilia.

Other Towns:

ABERGAVENNY Cheerful market town strikingly situated where the Usk valley gives the only easy route into Wales. Surprising variety of historical buildings and a town trail to help you as you pass along them.

BLACKWOOD Once dependent on coalmining, this small busy town has a smart pedestrianized shopping centre and lively street markets and is surrounded by open hillsides and mountains.

CHEPSTOW Major port in medieval times and shipbuilding centre in Industrial Revolution. Now handsome Georgian and Victorian buildings prevail.

EBBW VALE New roots to its old iron and steel making days came with the 1992 Garden Festival upon which much regeneration has been based.

RAGLAN Relatively intact fortress-cum-stylish palace for Sir William ap Thomas, Raglan Castle is a medieval must-see.

TREDEGAR Unexpected sites such as a 72-foot clock tower and nearby planned model village.

USK Famous for its salmon fishing, this is another border town based on a Norman stronghold. Victorian times recorded in the Rural Life Museum.

◆ Abertillery ◆ Bedwas ◆ Blaina ◆ Cwmbran ◆ Llanhilleth ◆ Nantyglo ◆ Newbridge ◆ Newport ◆ Pontllanfraith ◆ Pontnewydd ◆ Rhymney ◆ Risca ◆ Rogerstone ◆ Rumney ◆ St Mellons

County rivers: Monnow, Usk, Wye, Ebbw, Rumney.

Highest point: Chwarel-y-Fan at 2,226 feet.

Monmouthshire's local government: The county of Monmouthshire is governed by six unitary authorities: Blaenau Gwent, Monmouthshire, Newport and Torfaen. Glamorgan's Cardiff and Caerphilly take in the rest of Monmouthshire around St Mellons and the valleys stretching from Tredegar to Risca. Welsh Bicknor is Monmouthshire detached in Herefordshire and under that county's unitary council.

COUNTY CALENDAR

◆ Mid-May: A weekend of dance displays, ceilidhs, concerts and crafts is laid on at Tredegar House and Park, Newport, for the town's annual folk festival.

◆ Mid-July: Newport's Welsh Balloon Festival, also staged at Tredegar House and Park.

◆ Late July: A procession of floats travels into Welsh Street for Chepstow's Carnival and Fayre outside the castle, combining with the Chepstow Beer Festival.

◆ Late August: Monmouthshire Agricultural Show with trade stands, side shows and livestock at Monmouth.

MONTGOMERYSHIRE

SIR DREFALDWYN

MONTGOMERY *Graced with pristine red-brick Georgian buildings, and perched where the Severn Valley enters the Welsh hills.*

THE COUNTY LANDSCAPE

◆ From the English border to the Dyfi estuary in Cardigan Bay, Montgomeryshire embraces some of the most tranquil and deserted land in Wales. Its mountains, though not as high or as craggy as the Snowdonia range in the north, have a dramatic beauty of their own: deep river valleys, wooded slopes and heather-covered rocks and ridges that seem to roll on forever.

◆ Wind farms forest some of the higher land, taking advantage of the natural energy blowing in from the sea. And in the county's upper reaches, as the hills begin their climb into the Berwyns and north Wales, 45 million gallons of water fill the Vyrnwy Valley, where the village of Llanwddyn once stood, and have been pumped across country to supply the needs of Liverpool since the reservoir's creation in 1877.

COUNTY CALENDAR

◆ Mid-May: concerts, dances, displays, crafts and comedy are all part of the two-day Mid-Wales May Festival in Newtown.

◆ Late June: a nine-day series of classical concerts is held at Llanfyllin parish church.

◆ Early July: the Mid-Wales Festival of Transport is a weekend rally of all kinds of vehicles from the turn of the century on. Held at unforgettable Powis Castle.

LAURA ASHLEY, COTTAGE industries and little Welsh market towns dotted amid pasture with hoards of sheep spring to my mind with this county…well, Llanidloes certainly fits this bill. But this is also a county where Methodism took a firm hold, and monumental stone chapels appear in town and villages and even on the remote reaches of the mountain slopes.

TOWNS AND VILLAGES

Architectural surprises abound in the middle of the lively market town of Llanidloes, in the south. The half-timbered market hall has been there for over 400 years, held up with sturdy wooden stilts. Markets used to be held under the hall, and locals still gather there for a gossip. This is another town where Tudor buildings meet Georgian and Victorian, as well as the age-old stone farmhouses of the surrounding hills.

The county crosses the divide between south and north, east and west, and several traditions of architecture meet in towns such as Machynlleth, over to the west in the Dyfi Valley. Lining the wide main thoroughfare, Maengwyn Street, which leads up to an ornate Victorian clocktower, are Georgian shops, half-timbered buildings and the local dark grey stone typical of northern villages. One of the most striking buildings is the low, brooding Parliament House, where rebel leader Owain Glyndwr assembled his followers in the early 15th century. This part of Wales has always attracted refugees from the rat race and 'Mach' is just down the road from Britain's best working example of green living. The Centre for Alternative Technology is actually on the far side of the river in Merioneth: its solar-heated houses and energy-saving machines are set up in a derelict quarry, and the community that lives there sells its home-grown products in the wholemeal café in Machynlleth.

East of Llanidloes, the main road travels to Newtown, once known as 'the Leeds of Wales' but now another rural, riverside town with a backdrop of green hills. Elaborate shopfronts such as Pryce-Jones – the biggest department store in mid-Wales – are survivors of Newtown's 19th-century golden age, when houses were transformed into weaving factories, crammed with looms.

Longboats carried supplies and materials to Newtown along the Montgomery Canal, which passes the ancient town of Welshpool (Y Trallwng) en route. There are plenty of gems here, including an 18th-century six-sided cockpit. But the big attraction lies a mile southwest: the pink-stoned Powis Castle, packed with priceless paintings and furnishings. Italianate garden terraces step down the ridge from the castle to its beautiful formal gardens.

LOCAL HISTORY

Over 2,000 years at Caersws, where three rivers meet (the Severn, the Garno and the Trannon), two Roman forts were set up, manned by troops from Spain, to link the major bases of Castell Collen, Y Gaer, Pennal and Chester. It was at a Celtic settlement near Caersws, so the story goes, that Prince Caradog – Caractacus to the Romans – fought his final battle against the invaders.

Two forces hit the county in the 18th and 19th centuries: industry and religion. A statue in Llandinam, a village of 'magpie' houses along the Severn, commemorates David Davies, who built Barry Docks in south Wales and became one of the great coal barons of the 19th century. In Newtown wool and textiles were the business, and local industrial-philanthropist Robert Owen introduced new ideas of profit-sharing and decent working and living conditions. Llanidloes made its money from local silver and lead mines and the flannel trade (and more recently from the designs of Laura Ashley at home in nearby Carno), and was a centre of Chartism, the protest movement calling for political reforms.

A century or so earlier, Methodist preacher John Wesley delivered his sermons from under Llanidloes market hall. Their congregations still sing the hymns of young Ann Griffith, who wrote 70 lovely verses at her home in Llanfyllin, in the Berwyn foothills, before her death in 1805 at the early age of 29.

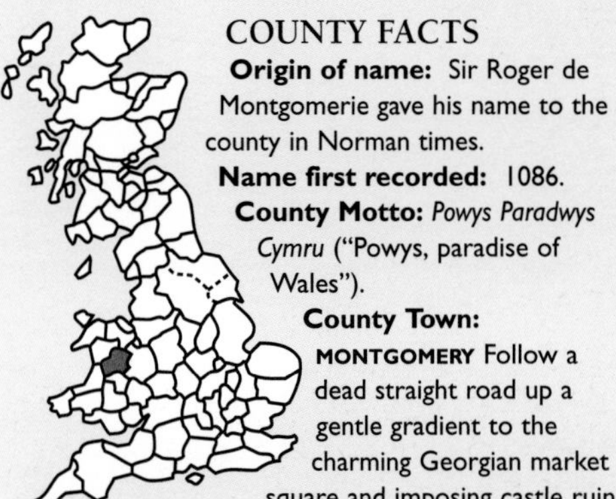

COUNTY FACTS

Origin of name: Sir Roger de Montgomerie gave his name to the county in Norman times.

Name first recorded: 1086.

County Motto: *Powys Paradwys Cymru* ("Powys, paradise of Wales").

County Town:
MONTGOMERY Follow a dead straight road up a gentle gradient to the charming Georgian market square and imposing castle ruin.

Other Towns

CARNO The little town where Laura Ashley launched her sparkling international career.

LLANFYLLIN Typically attractive Welsh market town but with a rare 18th-century brick church.

LLANRHAEDR YM MOCHNANT (partly in Denbighshire) Has low stone buildings and is mainly welsh-speaking. It also boasts the highest waterfalls in Wales nearby.

LLANSANTFFRAID YM MECHAIN This tiny village's football team became Welsh Cup Holders in 1996 and qualified for Europe with Manchester Utd!.

MACHYNLLETH Unpretentious market town.

WELSHPOOL Renovated canal yard and dock (on the Montgomery Canal) with museum, craft centre and boat hire.

◆ Berriew ◆ Caersws ◆ Llanfair Caereinion
◆ Llanidloes

County rivers: Severn, Fyrnwy, Tiannon, Afon, Garno, Mule, Rhiw, Camlet, Wye, Dovey.

Highest point: Mole Sych in the Berwyn Mountains at 2,713 feet.

Montgomeryshire's local government: The County of Montgomeryshire comes under Powys unitary authority.

FAMOUS NAMES

◆ Known as the Father of Socialism, local man Robert Owen had a whole village built to house his workers in New Lanark and was one of the founders of the trade union movement. He lies in St Mary's Church, Newtown, whose gates were a present from his children, and a museum in his name recreates his former home on the upper floor of the Midland Bank.

◆ Indian and Far Eastern art and weapons on display in Powis Castle are heirlooms of Robert, Lord Clive – better known as Clive of India. His family inherited the castle in 1784.

◆ Julie Christie, the leading actress who captured the spirit of the 1960s and starred in such films as *Dr Zhivago* (1965) and *Far from the Madding Crowd* (1967), left the bright lights behind to make her home near the village of Llandyssil.

◆ Llanrhaedr ym Mochnant (partly in Denbighshire) was the setting for the film *The Englishman Who Went Up a Hill and Came Down a Mountain* (1995) based on Welsh folklore about locals who built up their hill to get it classified as a mountain.

◆ Laura Ashley, Montgomeryshire's most famous daughter, was born in the county.

PEMBROKESHIRE

SIR BENFRO

THE COUNTY LANDSCAPE

◆ Picture Wales as an old woman pointing out to sea: Anglesey is her head; the Llyn Peninsula her arm and hand; and Pembrokeshire is the tip of her skirt, with a toe stretching tentatively towards the Atlantic.

◆ The county forms the southwestern corner of Wales: its Welsh name, *Penfro*, means 'Land's End'. The county looks out to sea on three sides, taking in 170 miles of shoreline. Running along the coastal boundary is the long-distance Pembrokeshire Coastal Path, part of Britain's smallest national park. This 225-square-mile area covers the entire coast apart from the urban centres of Fishguard, Milford Haven and Pembroke Dock, as well as two inland regions, the Preseli Hills and the Cleddau estuary, a winding tidal inlet that eats into the southwestern tip of the peninsula.

◆ The Preseli mountains – Bluestone Country – are a southern outreach of the Cambrian range which runs along the spine of Wales. Peppered with prehistoric monuments, they form a stretch of wide, high moorland, partly forested and punctuated with rocky outcrops rising to 1,760 feet, between Cardigan, just over the northeastern county border, and Fishguard, on the north coast.

◆ Islands with the Norse placenames of Skomer and Skokholm lie offshore, and have extensive sea-bird and seal colonies.

TENBY *Or Dinbich y Pysgod, the 'Little Fort of the Fish'.*

NOT WITHOUT CAUSE this county sometimes known as 'Little England Beyond Wales'. It remains very much a divided county in language and culture. However it also boasts some of the most beautiful stretches of British coastline: drive along the A487 coast road or – better still – follow part of the long-distance footpath, and you will be rewarded with mile upon mile of green fields and hillside towns sloping down towards high sea cliffs. Secret, sandy coves nestle among the rocks and scattered groups of tiny islets lie offshore, home to seabirds and seals.

TOWNS AND VILLAGES

People have lived along this coast and on the inland Preseli mountain moors for thousands of years; and the sea still provides a living for working harbours and fishing ports such as Milford Haven, Fishguard and Pembroke. Seafood is naturally a Pembrokeshire speciality: try the fresh oysters, farmed at Carew, near Pembroke, or choose from whiting, dogfish, plaice, crabs and lobsters, all landed at Milford Haven.

Pembrokeshire is a county of little treasures. As well as housing the smallest national park, it boasts Britain's smallest city. The pretty community of St David's, on the western headland, earns its city status from its handsome cathedral, which sits below the shops and houses in a deep hollow next to the ruins of the 13th-century Bishop's Palace. Founded by St David himself, in about 550, the site was originally a monastery, later a cathedral housing his shrine. In 1088 Viking raiders burnt it to the ground, but the pilgrims kept on coming to pay their respects at the site and in 1180 the present cathedral was built – the saint's shrine is still there. The mighty Bishop's Palace was constructed in the 14th century to welcome pilgrims and entertain dignitaries. It went into decline in the 16th century when Bishop Barlow stripped the lead from the great hall roof – to provide the dowries, according to local gossip, for his five daughters, who all made 'good matches' with bishops. In more modern times an annual week-long festival at St David's Cathedral from May to June draws orchestras, soloists and chamber groups to perform a series of classical concerts.

After the serenity and wild beauty of northern and western Pembrokeshire the coast loops round into the Cleddau estuary before turning south, and becomes busier and more industrial. A series of castle ruins ring the southern shore – Carew, Pembroke, Manorbier and finally Tenby, now known for its glorious beaches and pastel-painted Georgian terraces. This has been a popular and prosperous harbour town for centuries; many of its older houses have gone now, but the 15th-century stone Tudor Merchant's House, on a hill overlooking the harbour, gives an idea of the rambling, chimneyed buildings that once crowded along narrow medieval streets. Beatrix Potter enjoyed a holiday in 1900 at No. 2 Croft Terrace, an 1830s balconied house in Tenby. She whiled away her leisure hours painting pictures of the garden and writing letters illustrated with some of her earliest rabbit drawings.

LOCAL HISTORY

The Mabinogion, a collection of Welsh folk legends, relate the adventures of Pwyll, Prince of Dyfed, and his beautiful wife, Rhiannon: this ruler of seven regions had his royal court at Narberth, in the southeastern loop of the county. Narberth sits on an invisible border between south and north Pembrokeshire, established by Norman invaders and called the 'Landsker Line', or frontier. This marked the division between the Welsh-speaking rebels of the north and a colony of English-speakers in the south, and was protected with a string of castles and strongholds. This gave rise to the term of 'Little England Beyond Wales'.

A more distant and mysterious past has left its clues all around the uplands of Preseli. Standing stones, burial chambers and stone circles have survived here since the Neolithic Age; and between 2,000 and 1,500BC quarrymen carved out the 'blue stones' that would end up, after being dragged along an ancient trade route, as part of Stonehenge in Wiltshire.

Legend has it that David, or Dewi, the patron saint of Wales, was born in about 500 to Non, a local chieftain's daughter, at a tranquil spot on the coast near St David's. The site is marked by the ruin of a pre-Norman church and a shrine at the spring still known as Non's Well.

King Arthur and his knights are associated with several remains that may actually have existed 2,000 years before their time. Bedd Arthur (Arthur's Grave), near Crymych, is probably a Bronze Age group of stones; Cerrig Meibion Arthur (Arthur's Sons' Stones), further west, are said to commemorate two of the king's children killed by the giant boar Twrch Trwyth. One of the most evocative sites on the Preseli Hills is Pentre Ifan, a communal tomb about 4,000 years old, where a long slab of rock still balances precariously on the tips of three standing stones.

COUNTY FACTS

Origin of name: From the Welsh *penn bro* meaning head of the district and mutated by the Normans to Penbroc.

Name first recorded: 1180.

County Motto: *Ex Unitate Vires* ("Strength From Unity").

County Town:
HAVERFORDWEST Historic town of steep streets and handsome riverside buildings with a fantastic view atop the 12th-century castle.

Other Towns

FISHGUARD Has a picturesque old quayside with gabled harbourside cottages sheltering beneath gorse-laden headland. Elizabeth Taylor and Richard Burton strolled along it for the 1971 film *Under Milk Wood.*

MILFORD HAVEN Nelson no less thought this to be one of the finest natural harbours in the world. it is certainly treacherous as the oil supertanker disaster in 1996 proved. The 18th century 'new town' is dominated by the giant petro-chemical installations.

NARBERTH Theme park and open farms.

NEWPORT Rocky ridges, ample sands and all!

NEYLAND An old seafaring town and railway port with new marina. Brunel's Great Western Line reached here in 1865 (a section still remains).

PEMBROKE/PEMBROKE DOCK A magnificent castle with museums and galleries to boot. Take a boat from the Dock to see historic docklands, Napoleonic fortifications and the oil refineries.

ST DAVID'S Britain's tiniest, most tranquil city. The cathedral, dating circa 1176, contains the shrine of St David, Wales's Patron Saint.

ST DOGWELL'S Birthplace of Owain Glyndwr, Welsh Prince and patriot.

TENBY Pastel-coloured Georgian houses crowd around the pretty harbourside while the streets above are a medieval muddle: delightful and not to be missed.

◆ Goodwick ◆ St Dogmaels ◆ Saundersfoot

County rivers: Eastern Cleddau, Western Cleddau, Nevern Gwann, Solva.

Highest point: Wadbury Hill at 974 feet

Pembrokeshire's local government: The County of Pembrokeshire gives it boundaries to Pembrokeshire unitary council.

FAMOUS NAMES

◆ Lord Nelson came to stay at East Rock House, Tenby in 1802; as did artists Augustus and Gwen John, whose father lived at 5 Lexden Terrace.

COUNTY CALENDAR

◆ August: over 600 traders attend the Pembrokeshire County Show of livestock, horse-jumping and crafts at Haverfordwest.

◆ Early July: National Water-Ski Races in Milford Haven marina.

◆ May-June: a week-long festival at St David's Cathedral draws orchestras, soloists and chamber groups to perform a series of classical concerts.

◆ June 1st is Pembrokeshire Day.

RADNORSHIRE

SIR FAESYFED

RIVER WYE *Where Radnorshire meets Breconshire.*

COUNTY LANDSCAPE

◆ This roughly diamond-shaped county is at the very heart of Wales. Its eastern border follows Offa's Dyke and the boundary with Shropshire, and boasts the only town on the Dyke – Knighton. To the west are the immense, man-made lakes of Elan Valley, storing water for the big cities of the Midlands; and in the southwest is Llandrindod Wells, a Victorian time capsule sitting incongruously in this wild hill country.

◆ The county is a region of mountains, rivers, sheep and buzzards. Walkers are spoilt for choice of long-distance paths: the Offa's Dyke Path, easily reached from Knighton; the 123-mile Glyndwr Way, which climbs on to Welshpool across the county border; and the Wye Valley Walk, heading south from Rhayader. Whichever route you follow, it will offer a revealing glimpse of the rural 'desert of Wales'.

◆ The vast man-made stretches of water in the Elan Valley are awe-inspiring, and carry water along 73 miles of pipeline to Birmingham. There are five lakes with a water capacity of 22,000 million gallons. But if you prefer to see water in its natural state, there's no finer sight than the thundering cascade of Water-Break-its-Neck, in a wooded gorge near Llanfihangel-nant-Melan and the ancient borough of New Radnor.

ABBEYCWMHIR, ONCE A magnificent Cistercian abbey with the longest nave in the country, is now no more than a scattering of stones in a quiet field beside the Clywedog. But for me it is one of the most mystical places in Britain. From the sublime to the sparkling, the wonderful Victorian spa town of Llandrindod Wells is at the fizzing heart of Radnorshire. I still go to the rock gardens and have home-made cakes and try to avoid drinking the ghastly salted mineral waters!

TOWNS AND VILLAGES

Although it's a good base for trips to the sheep farms and mountains of Radnorshire, Llandrindod Wells is something of an oddity in its surroundings. Less than a hundred years old, the town offers wrought-iron and glass canopies, grand hotels and neat gardens – a classic 19th-century resort town, complete with pump house serving sulphur and magnesium waters. These may not sound appetizing, but they drew a steady stream of Victorian holidaymakers via the new-fangled railway. Unlike the other Welsh spas – Builth and Llanwrtyd (both in Breconshire) – Llandrindod has treasured its heritage and even dresses the part for its annual Victorian Week.

Over to the west, Knighton and Presteigne have a completely different kind of charm. Knighton is known in Welsh as Trefyclo, a corruption of Tref y Clawdd, or Town of the Dyke. Some of the best-preserved remains of King Offa's barrier between Mercia and the Celts are a few miles north at Llanfair Hill. Knighton spreads up a steep hill above the Dyke and river Teme, with a 19th-century clocktower marking its centre, and the site of a vanished Norman castle at the top. In between are some wonderful half-timbered houses, especially in the Narrows, a little street of 17th-century buildings. And Knighton can lay claim to its own healing waters: Jacket's Well, on a Bronze Age burial site half-a-mile from town, gets its name from the Welsh word 'iechyd', meaning 'health'.

More black-and-white architecture lines the streets of Presteigne, whose pillared Shire Hall makes it clear why it is the county town. In the churchyard a grave with two headstones marks the sad fate of Mary Morgan, a teenager who was sentenced to death in 1805 for strangling her newborn illegitimate baby. She had been seduced by a local lord, who sat without a blush on the condemning jury. A reprieve was issued in London and carried hell-for-leather across the hills, but poor Mary had already been hanged. The original gravestone rebukes the girl's 'sin and shame'. The second, added by remorseful townspeople, recalls that only 'he that is without sin' should cast the first stone.

LOCAL HISTORY

Empty spaces mark the sites of Presteigne's and Knighton's castles, once the scenes of fierce battles; Llywelyn the Last, Prince of Wales, did away with Presteigne's fortress in 1262. Llywelyn was killed at Cilmeri and buried at Abbeycwmhir. A later wave of Welsh revolt saw action on the Radnorshire border when Owain Glyndwr, descendant of the Princes of Powys, led his followers against the English in the 15th century. Among his exploits were the sacking of Abbeycwmhir and the destruction of Knucklas Castle, north of Knighton, where King Arthur is said to have lived with Guinevere.

In these remote highlands history has an edge of magic. Wizards practised their arts here, healing animals and people: one of them was Ieuan Ddu – Dr John Dee – who was also a mathematician and astrologer, and tutor to Queen Elizabeth I – the last 'astrologer royal' until this author in 1978! He lived at the aptly named Beguildy, up in the Teme valley. Some say he was the original model for Shakespeare's Prospero.

In the 19th century, as industrial towns sprang up in England, engineers looked to the Welsh mountains for water. From 1892 to 1903, the Elan Valley, fanning out to the west of Rhayader, was flooded to create huge reservoirs. Homes were evacuated and even the dead reburied higher up to make way for the 7-mile string of lakes.

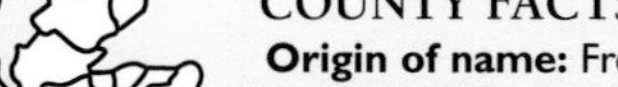

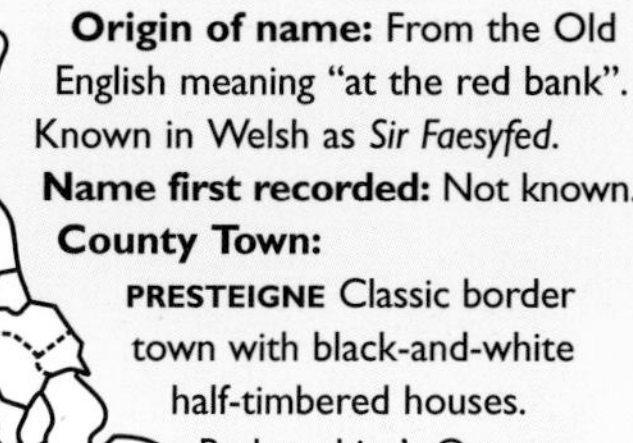

COUNTY FACTS

Origin of name: From the Old English meaning "at the red bank". Known in Welsh as *Sir Faesyfed.*

Name first recorded: Not known.

County Town:

PRESTEIGNE Classic border town with black-and-white half-timbered houses. Radnorshire's Quarter Sessions and Assizes were once conducted at Shire Hall, a grand pillared building (now a museum) built in 1829.

Other Towns:

ABEREDW Amazing rock formations, Llewelyn's Cave and a church with a 14th century screen.

KNIGHTON Medieval town sitting on Offa's Dyke – its Welsh name, Tref-y-Clawdd, means Town of the Dyke. Charming traffic-free Tudor Narrows.

KNUCKLAS The castle was one of the powerful Mortimer family's strongholds and was occupied by Queen Guinevere's father - Cogfrann Gawr.

LLANDRINDOD WELLS Bastion of Victorian Britain, celebrated annually with Victorian festival.

NEW RADNOR Quiet streets and good pubs. A good base for outdoor pursuits.

PAINSCASTLE Important place since the Dark Ages as surrounding defensive sites give testament. The castle - now gone - has links with Maude de St. Valerie who starved herself to death in defiance of King John.

RHAYADER Lovely little crossroads in the heart of the Welsh hills with many unpretentious eating and watering holes. Real farming life here with leading livestock market in ponies, sheep and cattle. Good fishing on the Wye.

◆ Clyro ◆ Llanelwedd ◆ Newbridge on Wye

Main rivers: Wye, Elan, Ithon.

Highest point: Radnor Forest at 2,166 feet.

Radnorshire's local government: The County of Radnorshire is administered by Powys Unitary Council (shared with Breconshire and Montgomeryshire).

FAMOUS NAMES

◆ The Elan Valley did its bit for the war effort when Barnes Wallis used it to calculate the size of his famous Dambusters bouncing bombs.

COUNTY CALENDAR

◆ Late April/Early May: the first of the mid-Wales trotting or harness races takes place at Monaughty Poeth, near Knucklas, featuring sturdy Welsh ponies.

◆ May: Knighton's annual fair, which has a long pedigree: it dates back to the times when Mop or Hiring Fairs were regular events.

◆ Mid-August: for nine days Llandrindod Wells goes back in time for its Victorian Festival.

◆ July: Royal Welsh Show at Llanelwedd.

THE REAL
SCOTTISH COUNTIES

ABERDEENSHIRE

ABERDEEN *Fishing boats and oil industry support boats jostle in the lively harbour.*

THE COUNTY LANDSCAPE

◆ All Aberdeenshire is attractive, but few parts more so than Royal Deeside, around Braemar and Ballater. Apart from the month of October when the stalking season is in full swing, the landowners have no great objection to sensible people walking in the hills, to the top of Lochnagar from where the views are wonderful. Prince Charles's children's book, *The Old Man of Lochnagar,* is set hereabouts.

◆ If time permits, stroll along Glen Muick or around the shores of the loch. Ski lifts have marred the wildness of the hills but they soon fall away and here too the views and the walking are wonderful.

◆ The Grampian Mountains are quite splendid, purple with heather in the autumn, capped with snow for much of the winter, always dramatic, with breathtaking views. The rivers Don and Dee and a host of lesser streams feed the lochs and run noisily through the glens, many of them alive with trout and having an annual run of salmon.

◆ One river viewpoint not to miss is the Linn of Dee near Braemar, where the river is compressed into a narrow gorge, exploding into a cloud of spray after heavy rain.

I know it's a cliché but The Monarch of the Glen stands out a mile when I think of Aberdeenshire. It's a sensationally scenic county with beautiful countryside and, for those who are that way inclined, huntin', shootin' and fishin'. It's one of the largest and most varied of all the Scottish counties, running from the North Sea coast east to the Grampians, and from Kinnairds Head, the northeast tip of Scotland, south and west to the Royal Enclaves around Braemar and beyond. This takes in a plethora of picturesque views and landscapes and some splendid towns, but few are more splendid than the county capital, the granite city of Aberdeen, where I've spent many happy times.

TOWNS AND VILLAGES

Aberdeen used to be described as 'the silver city by the silver sea', a romantic reference to the fact that the houses of Aberdeen are largely built in granite and the city stands on the North Sea coast. The city also stands on the banks of two fine rivers, the Dee and the Don, but that fact often seems to be overlooked by the sheer glory of the granite. Seen on a fine day everything sparkles – the rivers, the sea, the buildings of the city all have a silvery sheen – but it has to be admitted that fine days are not all that common this far up on the North Sea coast. It can rain a fair bit in the Granite City and the visitor should come prepared. On the other hand, the mid 19th-century architecture, a mixture of the Classic and the Gothic, is always appealing and the city fathers have devoted a lot of their recent oil revenues to filling every nook, cranny, garden and park in the city with a dazzling array of flowers.

The harbour area contains fascinating old buildings, like Provost Ross's House, now a museum to the sailing and fishing industry, with more old buildings in the Footdee, the old fisherman's quarter at the mouth of the Dee. Harbours are always worth exploring and Aberdeen's throbs with activity. Finally, a bus ride away from the harbour, there is Old Aberdeen, which contains St Machar's Cathedral, a fine, largely 15th-century church, and the university. This part of town has narrow cobbled streets and quantities of charm, even in the rain. If the sun is shining, a walk around the splendours of the Cruickshank Botanic Gardens, just by the cathedral, would be delightful.

Southwest of Aberdeen lies Drum Castle, open to visitors and well worth a visit, especially for those who like medieval castles. The villages of Ballater and Braemar in the heart of Deeside, further west, are worth closer inspection, not least because most of the village shops seem to carry Royal Warrants from members of the Royal Family, who have been spending their summer holidays here since Queen Victoria and Prince Albert purchased the nearby Balmoral Estate in 1848.

The best way to get from Aberdeen to Braemar is to drive on minor roads, turning off to see the sights en route, which include yet more castles, many of them built in that style called 'Scottish Baronial', though Kildrummy is a ruin and Corgarff hardly looks like a castle. It was erected as late as 1537, just in time for the clan wars. Alford was created during the railway boom of the last century, and is still both the base for the Alford Valley Railway and home to the Grampian Transport Museum. Nearby stands another castle, Craigievar, built in 1626 and a riot of towers and turrets. Deeside is very beautiful, with splendid views over the valley from the nearby hills and mountains.

Moving north towards Banffshire, Huntly is an old town, quite small, and a centre for the whisky trade, with numerous distilleries in the town or nearby. In the Civil War the castle here was held for Charles I by the Earl of Huntly, who was put up against the wall and shot when the Parliamentary forces took the castle. Most of Huntly Castle is in ruins, but Haddo House, the home of the Gordons, is still intact and a very beautiful stately home, a William Adam building dating from 1730 and full of fine things. As for the Aberdeenshire coast, which lies to the north of the city, apart from the floral gardens at Pitmedden and the

COUNTY FACTS

Origin of name: Old Briton word meaning "At the mouth of the Don".

Name first recorded: 1100.

County Town:

ABERDEEN A cultured, lively city. There is a very fine art gallery, a good harbour area, once supporting a large herring fishing fleet, now a depot for the North Sea oil rigs, plenty of pubs and a surprising number of theatres. Aberdeen is just compact enough to explore on foot and the sights to see, apart from the art gallery, include Provost Skene's House in Guestrow, the oldest surviving private house in Britain, occupied continuously since 1545, though now a museum set out as a 17th-century merchant's house. The nearby Marischal College is worth a look, and forms part of the university, and St Nicolas Kirk in Union Street is the largest kirk in Scotland, though it actually achieves that status by being two churches knocked into one. Aberdeen University has that rare and lovely Scottish architectural device, a crown spire.

Other Towns:

BALLATER This neat holiday village is surrounded by beautiful wooded hills.

BRAEMAR Village dedicated to the great outdoors. Book your ticket six months ahead if you want to attend the hugely popular Braemar Gathering in September. Braemar Castle was built in 1628 and has a gloomy underground pit.

DYCE Busy airport contrasts with prehistoric remains on Tyrebagger Hill.

FRASERBURGH One of the busiest fishing ports in the north-east. Fish are sold daily on weekdays in the fish market.

HUNTLY Small town whose chief asset is its proximity to the Malt Whisky Trail around the eight distilleries of the so-called 'Golden Triangle'.

INVERURIE Granite town that makes a good base for exploring castles nearby.

PETERHEAD Pink granite fishing port and oil base which was once Scotland's most important whaling port. At the 400-year-old Ugie Salmon Fish House you can watch the traditional (but smelly) smoking of salmon and trout.

◆ Bucksburn ◆ Cults ◆ Ellon ◆ Kemnay ◆ Kintore ◆ Maud ◆ Mastrick ◆ New Deer ◆ New Pitsligo ◆ Old Meldrum ◆ Peterculter ◆ Rosehearty ◆ Strichen ◆ Turriff

Main rivers: Don, Dee, Ythan, Ugie, Deverton.

Highest point: Ben Macdhui, at 4,296 feet.

Aberdeenshire's local government: The County of Aberdeenshire is currently governed by two unitary councils – Aberdeenshire Council itself and Aberdeen City Council.

THE OLD BRIG' O' DEE *This solid medieval structure spans 400 feet.*

ruins of Slains Castle, only the sands of Cruden Bay and the Salmon Fish House in Peterhead need detain you; the real charm of Aberdeenshire lies in the hinterland.

LOCAL HISTORY

Much of the county's past is linked to the Highland clans but with some unique local touches. The people of Peterhead, for example, still speak Doric, an old Scots dialect not heard anywhere else. Six miles from Inverurie, the Loanhead Stone Circle dates back some 6,000 years and the nearby Maiden Stone carries Pictish runes. Near Inverurie, check out the ruins of Bass Castle, the first 'motte and bailey castle' erected in northeast Scotland, about 1160. Barmekin of Ecte is an Iron Age hillfort, with three ramparts and an internal stone wall, a most unusual example of such an early defence work.

Castles are the most visible historic relics in Aberdeenshire and there are a great many of them, most of which have already been mentioned. Most of them are worth a look, but if time is short then Haddo, Balmoral (if it is open), Slains and Drum Castle are the ones to go for. Even if Balmoral is closed the area is worth a visit if only to see Crathie Church, the place to spot the Royal Family who attend services there every Sunday when in residence at the Castle. Otherwise, the best way to enjoy the history of Aberdeenshire is to stop at any site as you travel around, taking care to visit some of the excellent local museums.

One sight not to miss is Brig' o' Balgownie, a picturesque bridge over the River Don, by Aberdeen. Legend has it that the bridge will fall if it is ever crossed by an only son riding a mare's only foal, which must be a rare event as it has been standing since the 13th century. For more dramatic tales try Kildrummie Castle, where Robert the Bruce sent his family for safe-keeping before going to war with Edward II. An English force captured the castle, which was betrayed into their hands by the castle blacksmith. Bruce's wife and children were made prisoner, his brother was hanged and the entire garrison was hanged drawn and quartered. As for the traitorous blacksmith, the English paid him his gold – but first they melted it and then poured it down his throat.

FAMOUS NAMES

◆ Crathie Church, Balmoral, is the place where Princess Anne married her second husband, Captain Tim Laurence.

◆ Slains Castle, near Peterhead, is said to have given Bram Stoker the idea for Count Dracula. This castle was built in the 16th century but the remodelling in the last century has given it a suitably ghoulish appearance.

◆ The village of Pennan, on the border with Banffshire, was used as the location for David Puttnam's film *Local Hero*, filmed here in 1982.

COUNTY CALENDAR

◆ February: Gordon Art Exhibition, Inverurie.

◆ March: Annual Talent Competition, Inverurie.

◆ June: Oldmeldrum Sports and Highland Games.

◆ June: Alford Cavalcade, a large show of vintage vehicles, with numerous ring activities, Alford.

◆ June: Scottish Pipe Band Championships, Aberdeen.

◆ July: Annual Pipe Band Competition at Aboyne.

◆ August: Lonach Highland Gathering and Games, Strathdon.

◆ August: Aboyne Games, a traditional Highland gathering (always on the first Saturday in August).

◆ September: the Braemar Gathering, with the Royal Family in attendance, takes place on the first Saturday of the month.

◆ October (usually in the second week of the month): Aberdeen Alternative Festival, the north of Scotland's premier arts festival.

ANGUS *FORFARSHIRE*

BROUGHTY FERRY *Fishers Street on the Firth of Tay has a castle and museum right on the shore.*

ANGUS MAY BE relatively small in size – it covers a mere 873 square miles – but what it lacks in magnitude it more than makes up for in variety. I remember a journey from Aberdeen to Dundee in February with snow everywhere. There were four small, neat, towns which I'd always wanted to visit – Brechin, Montrose, Forfar and Arbroath – a dream come true.

TOWNS AND VILLAGES

There is in Angus infinite diversity not just in scenery, but in the character of its towns and villages. When you drive over the Tay Bridge into Dundee, you enter not just one of Scotland's most prosperous cities, but a place steeped in individuality and tradition. In the 19th century, jute, journalism and jam brought prosperity to Dundee – and to a certain extent each industry still does today. The home of bitter orange marmalade, its invention was ascribed to Mr and Mrs James Keiller in the early 1700s who

THE COUNTY LANDSCAPE

◆ On the east coast of Scotland, this most dramatic county slopes down from the immense grandeur of the Grampian mountains, with towering peaks rising above lonely lochs, to the relative calm of the Tay estuary in the south. The county is bounded on the east by the sea, on the south by the Firth of Tay, in the west by Perthshire, and in the north by Aberdeenshire and the Kincardineshire.

◆ Steep-sided glens - the 'Braes of Angus' - cut their way through the hills. The rich farming land of the Vale of Strathmore divides the Grampians from the gentler Sidlaw hills, in the southwest of the county.

◆ On the coast, lie dramatic red sandstone headlands, slowly eroded by the continuous action of sea and weather, interspersed with some truly glorious beaches, and some of the world's finest golf courses.

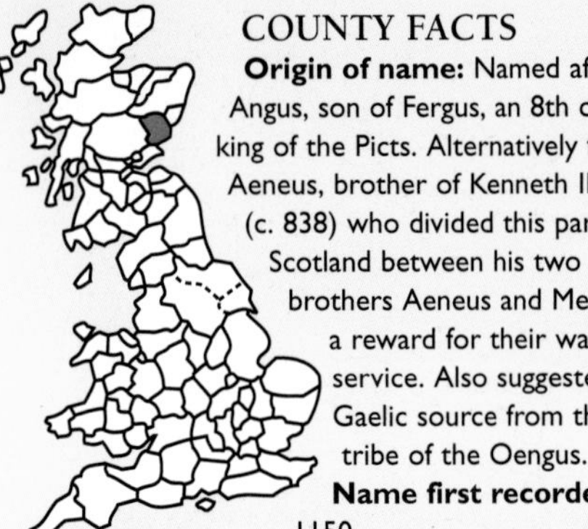

COUNTY FACTS

Origin of name: Named after Angus, son of Fergus, an 8th century king of the Picts. Alternatively from Aeneus, brother of Kenneth II (c. 838) who divided this part of Scotland between his two brothers Aeneus and Mekras as a reward for their wartime service. Also suggested is a Gaelic source from the tribe of the Oengus.

Name first recorded: 1150.

County Motto: *Lippen on Angus* ("Depend on Angus").

County Town:

FORFAR Tourist mecca and once a seat of the Kings of Scotland. Also famous of old for its witches.

Other Towns:

ARBROATH Busy fishing port, resort and industrial town famous for its 'smokies'.

BRECHIN The oldest part of Brechin's cathedral is a 106-foot Round Tower, dating from about 1000, built as protection against Viking raids.

CARNOUSTIE A well-known windswept golfing resort and venue for world-famous Scottish and British Open Championships with Henry Cotton, Ben Hogan and Gary Player among those winning the toughest finishing holes in golf.

DUNDEE The whole of this 'City of Discovery', as it is known, can be seen from the top of Dundee Law, a great plug of volcanic rock, that rises from the heart of the city. Nearby Glamis Castle was rebuilt in the style of a French château in the 16th century. Shakespeare gave Macbeth the title of 'Thane of Glamis' and in 1715 the Old Pretender, the son of James VII of Scotland, stayed at the castle. The beautiful park surrounding the castle is attributed to Capability Brown.

FINTRY A picture-postcard village and regular winner of the 'Best Kept Small Village in Scotland' award.

KIRRIEMUIR Sleepy market town on the south side of the Braes of Angus and celebrated as 'Thrums" by the town's famous son, novelist J M Barrie. Behind his museum is the wash-house where he had his first theatre. He is buried in the local cemetery.

MONTROSE A pleasant fishing port with excellent bathing and sands and an important North Sea oil base. 'Big Peter', the curfew bell which is rung each night at 10PM in Montrose, gets its name from Peter Ostens, the craftsman who cast it in Rotterdam more than 300 years ago.

◆ Broughty Ferry ◆ Downfield ◆ Edzell
◆ Invergowrie ◆ Lochee ◆ Monifieth ◆ Southmuir

County rivers: Isla, Esk (North & South).

Highest point: Glas Maol at 3,502 feet.

Angus's local government: The County of Angus is served by two unitary councils – Angus District and Dundee City Councils. The Bandirrin part of Caputh parish is a tiny enclave of Angus detached in Perthshire and administered by Perth & Kinross unitary council.

bought Seville oranges cheaply and in bulk from a Spanish ship seeking refuge from a storm in the port. Because they were bitter, the Keillers couldn't sell the oranges so, not wishing to waste them, Mrs Keiller made them into a conserve. But alongside Keiller's tasty marmalade has come Dundee cakes, an electronics industry and an all-cargo port. Dundee, the fourth largest city in Scotland, has been a growing base for the North Sea oil industry. It is also the HQ for Biffo the Bear and Korky the Cat – creations of the D.C. Thomson comics publishing empire.

Dundee's love affair with the sea is easy to understand. The Firth of Tay, spanned by both road and rail bridges, is one of the best deep-water harbours on Britain's North Sea coast and the dockyards, in which Scott's exploration ship *Discovery* was built, are still reasonably busy. You wouldn't describe Dundee as an attractive city – most of its old buildings have long since been pulled down – but it does have appealing parts, such as Dunhope Park, where the 13th-century Dunhope Castle, rebuilt in the 16th century, is situated.

Outside Dundee is the 'real' Angus of small towns and pretty villages like Auchmithie and Cortachy. This is the Angus, too, of dramatic glens: you'll find some of the finest scenery in Scotland here, on the southern slopes of the Grampians. In fact, you shouldn't leave Angus without seeing at least something of one of the glens – possibly Glen Esk or Glen Clova, which can be reached quite easily from Brechin and Kirriemuir respectively. Below these dramatic hills is the broad Vale of Strathmore, on whose plump pastureland the distinctive black, horn-less Aberdeen Angus cattle graze – according to many experts providers of the best beef in the world.

An Angus town with an historic past is Forfar, which lent its name to the county. Malcolm III held a parliament in Forfar in 1057. His castle in the town was destroyed by Robert the Bruce, but the site is marked by a 17th-century octagonal turret which was once the town cross. Later Forfar was sacked by Oliver Cromwell's troops during the Civil War and a couple of miles outside Forfar is the ruined Restenneth Priory, where Robert the Bruce's son is buried. Forfar is now virtually given over to tourism. Here you can follow in the footsteps of Malcolm III, and try out the local culinary speciality – the Forfar bridie, a spiced minced-beef pastie. The more active can go sailing on Forfar and Reescobie lochs, go trout fishing or do what many people do when they visit Scotland – play golf.

Talking of golf, down on the Angus coast you can try out the championship course at Carnoustie, considered by many professionals to be one of the finest in the world.

Carnoustie sits comfortably amid a string of Utopian beaches at the mouth of the Tay. If this were the French Riviera, the beaches would be packed in summer. But this is the east coast of Scotland and the cooling influences of North Sea breezes ensure that, even in high summer, you'll never have to struggle for a place on the sand – as you won't at any of the other resorts strung out along this highly peaceful stretch of coastline.

Another coastal town, Arbroath, is best known for its 'smokies' – these are whole haddock, with just the guts and head removed. They are only lightly brined and then smoked until cooked by the heat of an oak chip fire. They can be skinned and eaten as they are, or warmed and served with melted butter. Arbroath has a more notable non-culinary claim to fame: it is the place where, in 1320, Robert the Bruce signed Scotland's Declaration of Independence at Arbroath Abbey.

LOCAL HISTORY

This is one of the most historic corners of the British Isles. There are a number of 'vitrified forts' in Angus: these are actually artificial ramparts of granite that have been fused together by great heat, presumably in pre-historic times. They are a mystery, since though great deciduous forests are known to have been present at one time, and enormous oaks and ashes have been found in peat bogs, even if the entire country had been deforested to supply the fires, there would have been nothing like enough. At the same time, there were no coal-workings at such an early date.

Evidence of Mesolithic Man, a hunter living around 6,000BC, have been found here and the Roman legions were also known to have tramped around the county. A pre-Roman hill fort stands on the Law, the 571-foot volcanic crag on whose lower slopes Dundee is situated.

Dundee, which was made a royal burgh as long ago as 1190, features prominently in Scottish history. In 1288 William Wallace, portrayed in the film *Braveheart* by Mel Gibson, began a lifetime of struggle against the English when he killed the son of the English Constable of Dundee. Wallace is commemorated in Dundee today by a wall plaque in Castlehill – but despite his efforts, the city was seized by the English in the 14th, 16th and 17th centuries.

Scottish history unfolds, too, at Glamis Castle. Glamis (pronounced 'Glahms') is probably the best known rural castle in Scotland after Balmoral. It was the ancestral home of the Earl of Strathmore, father of the Queen Mother. It was her childhood home and the birthplace of Princess Margaret, sister of the current Queen.

DUNDEE *Sailors' Home in Dock Street.*

FAMOUS NAMES

◆ J M Barrie, creator of *Peter Pan*, was born in Kirriemuir in 1860. His home at 9 Brechin Road is now the Barrie Museum.

◆ Olympic athlete Liz McColgan was born in Dundee and still lives in the city.

◆ Princess Margaret was born at Glamis Castle in 1930. The castle is the ancestral home of the Queen Mother's late father, the Earl of Strathmore. The Queen Mother, though born in Hertfordshire, spent much of her childhood at Glamis.

◆ Keiller's have been making jams at Dundee since 1797. The soil in the area around Dundee is particularly good for fruit growing.

COUNTY CALENDAR

◆ Early June: Dundee Rep Jazz Festival sees top artists from the British jazz and blues scene appear at Dundee's Rep Theatre.

◆ Early July: Broughty Ferry Gala Week includes an itinerary of fun events for all ages at the resort.

◆ Early July: Carnoustie Gala Day has a parade of decorated floats through the town.

◆ Mid-July: Kirriemuir Agricultural Show, Kilnhill Farm, Kirriemuir. Agricultural show with craft fair, trade stalls, and Highland dancing and pipe band.

◆ Mid-July: Scottish Transport Extravaganza, Glamis Castle, a display of vintage vehicles with autojumble, antiques and craft stalls.

◆ Early September: Kirriemuir Festival of Traditional Music and Song, a three-day festival of musical events at ceilidhs in Town Hall and various hotels.

◆ Carnoustie Golf Course hosts many national and international events, tournaments and championships.

◆ Lorraine Kelly - Breakfast TV queen is Dundee United crazy.

ARGYLLSHIRE

THE COUNTY LANDSCAPE

◆ The county is bounded in the north by Inverness-shire, in the east by Perthshire, Loch Long, and the Firth of Clyde, elsewhere by the wild Atlantic Ocean. It also includes many offshore islands.

◆ The main offshore islands are Mull, Islay, Jura, Tiree, Coll, Iona and Staffa – places that conjur up images of wandering monks, whiskey making, and windswept solitude.

◆ The countryside of Argyll is quite beautiful and typical of the Western Highlands, narrow glens, plenty of rushing burns and blue lochs, great expanses of open moorland, like the wastes of Rannoch, and a large number of sea lochs poking chilly Atlantic fingers up into the warm heather mixture of the heavily indented land.

◆ The southern part of the mainland includes the long and narrow peninsula of Kintyre – which stretches away from Knapdale to end at the famed rugged headland of the Mull of Kintyre with its lighthouse – and the smaller peninsulas of Cowal which are dotted with resorts. The magnificent scenery remains unscarred by industry.

◆ One of the finest viewpoints on the West Highland Way, that splendid footpath which runs across much of Argyllshire, is Fleming's Cairn on Rannoch Moor, erected to commemorate the traveller and writer Peter Fleming, who died out shooting here in 1971. More fine views and great walking can be found around the well-known 'Rest and Be Thankful' pass, over the hills near Inveraray. The entire county is now well provided with roads, often rather narrow with passing places, but the best way into the glens, like Glen Orchy, Glen Etive and the rest, is probably on foot.

◆ One of the best ways to enjoy the countryside of Argyllshire is on the West Highland Way, from Glasgow along Loch Lomond and into Argyll at Rannochshire, crossing the moor to the foot of Ben Nevis. Less energetic people can do almost equally well with a day out on the West Highland Line. The best time to see it is either in the month of May when the wild flowers are out and the West Highland midge is not yet in action, or in September-October when the purple heather is flaming on the hillsides. Actually Argyllshire is pretty well perfect at any time, though the mountain tops are best avoided in the harsh months of mid-Winter.

GLEN COE *(literally 'Valley of Weeping') is breathtakingly beautiful.*

ARGYLLSHIRE IS WHOLLY Highlands, the home of Clan Campbell and the red deer. It is a country of loch, mountain and seacoast – beautiful, romantic, full of history, extremely large, and almost empty of people outside the summer months. All this combines to make Argyllshire one of the most popular Scottish counties, as visitors are drawn to its stunning scenery.

TOWNS AND VILLAGES

Large towns are few and the capital of the county, Inveraray, home of the Duke of Argyll, who still lives in the castle just outside the centre, is very small indeed. It is just a few streets by the harbour at the head of Loch Fyne, a sea loch famous for herring, wood smoked kippers – my particular favourite – and other seafood. The town has a museum in the old jail, laid out like a 19th-century prison, and the 126-foot high Bell Tower gives splendid views over the surrounding countryside, but the castle is the real attraction, though it is only open two or three times a year. The present castle was started in the late 18th century, and inevitably involved the talents of the Adams family, who seem to have had a hand in most of Scotland's stately homes.

Apart from Inveraray, most of the other places in Argyllshire are at best small villages or scattered hamlets – once clan centres – now largely engaged in tourism or the local sports of stalking and shooting. Some places, like tiny Bridge of Orchy on the edge of Rannoch Moor, exist as stations on the famous and beautiful West Highland Line, just 100 years old and Britain's most frequent entry on the list of Great Train Rides. Oban, one of the terminals on the West Highland Line, is a small fishing and ferry port; a Victorian town, where the old distillery produces a famous whisky and one of the fish shops offers a rare combination, 'haggis and chips'. There is also a glass factory producing a range of paperweights but most visitors will quickly board a ferry and set off for a visit to Mull and the Holy Island of Iona.

One small town of note is Tobermory on Mull, a pretty little port, famous as the place where a Spanish galleon was blown up by a local man in 1588 and rather more useful as the modern site of a fine whisky distillery. Another popular place far to the south of the county is the resort of Dunoon, on the Firth of Clyde, the traditional destination for the people of Glasgow who, on public holidays, would take a Clyde steamer for a day out in Dunoon.

Lacking any great stock of towns and villages the man-made attractions of Argyllshire consist in the main of castles, the ancient fortresses of the clans. Inveraray is a fine sight, but the picture postcard castle is Kilchurn, a romantic ruin today, set in the reflecting waters of Loch Awe. It was built in 1440 by a Campbell lord, Sir Colin Campbell of Glenorchy, founder of the Breadalbane branch of the clan. Other castles well worth a look include Carnasserie Castle, the remains of a fortified manor built by the Bishop of the Isles in the 16th century, just after the Reformation started to add fresh fuel to the ancient feuds between Highland and Lowland. The manor has battlements with cannon loops and a lot of the inside remains intact.

Duntroon is a more modern castle and a good example of the Scots Baronial style. Rather more traditional is another medieval ruin, Ardtornish Castle, once the castle of the Lord of the Isles, a title now held by Prince Charles. This castle faces the Sound of Mull, which has another fine and still inhabited castle at Duart.

Mull has a little settlement at Phainphort, the crossing point for visits to Iona, but otherwise the county is just a litter of country and coastal hamlets, each of which has a pub and some may have a hotel. Argyllshire's attractions remain the simple ones of countryside and solitude, and the places you pass through are just pegs to hang the

COUNTY FACTS

Origin of name: From Gaelic Arregaithel or Argathelane = Coast or boundary of the Gaels.

Name first recorded: 970.

County Town:

INVERARY Perfect little Georgian Royal Burgh, its buildings form a harmonious whole.

Other Towns:

BOWMORE Chief town of Islay. Its church was built circular so the Devil would find no corners to hide in.

CAMPBELTOWN Popular holiday centre whose heyday was as a shipbuilding centre in Victorian times. Distilleries are also in evidence. Flora Macdonald who helped Bonnie Prince Charlie in hiding from the British sailed from this port to America in 1774.

CONNEL Ferry port on Loch Etive with two attractions – one natural, the Falls of Lora – and one man-made, the cantilever rail bridge.

DUNOON Wall-to-wall trinket shops and amusement arcades in Glasgow's favourite playground.

FURNACE Takes its name from iron-smelting which first began in 1745, though granite quarrying now dominates.

KILORAN Little town on Colonsay with exotic plants at Kiloran Gardens.

KINLOCHLEVEN Fascinating example of a new town built in 1906-08 due to its proximity to water power available for aluminium production.

LOCHGILPHEAD A small town and administrative centre close to the Crinan Canal which links Loch Gilp to Loch Fyne.

LOCHGOILHEAD Holiday resort within Argyll National Forest Park.

OBAN Charming town with an air of eccentricity: curiosities include a railway station whose architectural style is part Scots baronial, part Wild West, and a mock Coliseum.

PORT ELLEN Holiday town producing Laphroaig and Islay Mist whiskies.

TARBERT Bustling port. Fish Quay is busy every morning with the day's catch. Village takes fishing seriously and holds seafood festivals.

TIGHNABRUAICH Scenic resort with outstanding views over the Kyles of Bute. Many summer villas built by Glasgow businessmen in the late 19th century.

TOBERMORY Pretty port of bright colour-washed houses. The town also offers golf, pony-trekking and good anchorage. The 16th-century Spanish Armada galleon *Florencia*, treasure and all, was blown up in the Bay.

◆ Ardrishaig ◆ Hunter's Quay ◆ Kames ◆ Sandbank ◆ Taynuilt

County rivers: Urchay, Awe.

Highest point: Bidean nam Bian at 3,766 feet.

Argyllshire's local government: The County of Argyllshire is part of one large unitary council known as Argyll & Bute Council based at Lochgilphead. Two far northern areas of Argyllshire known as Ardnamurchan and Glencoe have their affairs taken care of by Highland Unitary Council.

FAMOUS NAMES
◆ Writer Peter Fleming, author of *News from Tartary* and brother of Ian Fleming, the creator of James Bond, is commemorated by a cairn on the Black Mount above Rannoch moor.
◆ John Smith, late and much lamented leader of the Labour Party, is buried on Iona.
◆ Glencoe is notorious as the site of the massacre of the Macdonalds by the Campbells in 1692.
◆ TV stars Judi Dench and Michael Williams have been known to frequent the Isle of Eriska Hotel north of Oban.
◆ Wings (Paul and Linda McCartney) made Mull of Kintyre famous with the eponymous folksong single which, in 1977, sold 2.5 million copies and was the biggest selling UK single until Band Aid.

COUNTY CALENDAR
◆ May: Neil Munro Festival, Inveraray is a celebration of the life and work of Neil Munro, best known for his *Para Handy* tales, made even more famous by their recent translation on to television, and episodes were filmed hereabouts.
◆ May: Annual Isle of Jura, Scottish Peaks Race involves a sailing and fell running race, including an ascent of Ben More on Mull and the Paps of Jura and Goatfell on Arran in Buteshire.
◆ June: The Annual Highland Festival. A new, hopefully annual, event. A celebration of the traditional and contemporary culture of the Highlands.
◆ August: West Highland Yachting Week. An annual yacht racing festival held around Crinan, Oban and Tobermory.
◆ August: Cowal Highland Gathering, Dunoon.
◆ October: Dunoon Jazz Festival. International jazz festival, featuring trad, mainstream and modern jazz.

IONA *10-century 17-foot-high Celtic Cross fashioned in granite.*

journey on; Kilcrenan, Kilfinan and all the other Kils – it means 'place' or 'village' in Gaelic. This is a county to roam about in, stopping off in one or other of the villages, using the busy Caledonian MacBrayne ferries to get to some of the far-flung, offshore islands.

LOCAL HISTORY

Argyllshire makes up in history for what it lacks in habitation and the history begins in the 6th century on Iona. St Columba, a missionary from Ireland, landed here with 12 followers in 563AD and established a monastery. When the Roman Empire in the West finally collapsed, the remnants of Western civilization hung on here, in the remote islands off the West Coast of Scotland. Iona was ravaged by Viking raids but the monks, and civilization, survived.

One of their number was St Aiden, who was sent on a civilizing mission to England and established the abbey on Lindisfarne in Northumberland. In the 13th century an abbey was built on Iona and this became the burial place for generations of Scots kings, including Macbeth, the real king, not the semi-fictional villain of Shakespeare's play. A more recent burial was that of the leader of the Labour Party, John Smith, whose grave now brings thousands of visitors to the island. The abbey was restored in the early years of this century but many old relics remain, including three of the rare Celtic stone crosses. St John's Cross dates from the 9th century, St Martin's Cross from the 10th century and MacLean's Cross from the 15th century.

The most famous event in the history of Argyllshire took place in February 1692, when a party of the Earl of Argyll's Regiment, most of them Campbells, fell on the Macdonalds of Glencoe and massacred them in their beds. The events of that tragic night are explained in the National Trust for Scotland centre in Glencoe, open to visitors at selected times of the year.

The shock of the massacre lives on to this day, for the tragedy was compounded by the fact that this massacre was 'murder under trust'. The Campbell soldiers had been billeted on the Macdonalds and had been living in perfect amity with their hosts until the orders arrived telling their Captain, Robert Campbell of Glenlyon, to 'fall on the rebels, the Macdonalds of Glencoe and put all to the sword under seventy'. This Glenlyon did and although many of the Macdonalds escaped – only 38 were actually killed – the Macdonalds left Glencoe, never to be repopulated.

AYRSHIRE

ALLOWAY *Robert Burns's old thatched cottage still contains the bed on which he was born and furniture used by Tam O'Shanter.*

THINK OF AYRSHIRE and you think of Rabbie Burns because this is where he came from. Those of a less literary persuasion might prefer to think of delicious Ayrshire bacon, with its unique rolled appearance, as this is a county also noted for its farming.

TOWNS AND VILLAGES

When working at Butlin's I used to walk from Doonfoot all the way into Ayr and it always seemed to be so lovely... so sunny. The town will always be connected with Robert Burns, the poet, who paid it the ultimate in tributes with his dedication:

To Ayr, which ne're a town surpasses,
For honest men, and bonnie lasses.

Ayr is not very large, with a population of around 50,000, but it is still the largest town on the Firth of Clyde and the capital of the county. The town has old roots but most of the present town is Victorian, for in the last century Ayr was one of the great seaside resorts for the people of Glasgow. Indeed it still is, pulling in the crowds with a fine sandy beach, a summer-long series of meetings on the local racecourse, and a quantity of good golf courses along the coast nearby.

THE COUNTY LANDSCAPE

◆ Ayrshire is a great scoop of land, on the western coast of Scotland, looking across the North Channel to Northern Ireland, Arran and the little pyramid of rock called Ailsa Craig.

◆ The county has a fairly gentle landscape, much of it farmland, with forests and moorlands butting in from the south, across the Carrick Forest. The River Ayr is the main central stream and the main scenic attractions are the offshore islands, in particular Ailsa Craig, which is now a bird sanctuary. Visitors cannot go ashore but a visit to the seabird colonies on the soaring cliffs of the island is not something to miss.

◆ The coastline is a mixture of those sandy dunes which came in so useful for links-style golf courses, rocky headlands and long sandy beaches, which in turn do so much to attract tourists to resorts like Largs, Troon and Ayr.

◆ The moors to the south provide the best walking country, Carrick Forest is fine for watching birds.

◆ Cunninghame, Kyle and Carrick are the names of the ancient forerunners of Ayrshire.

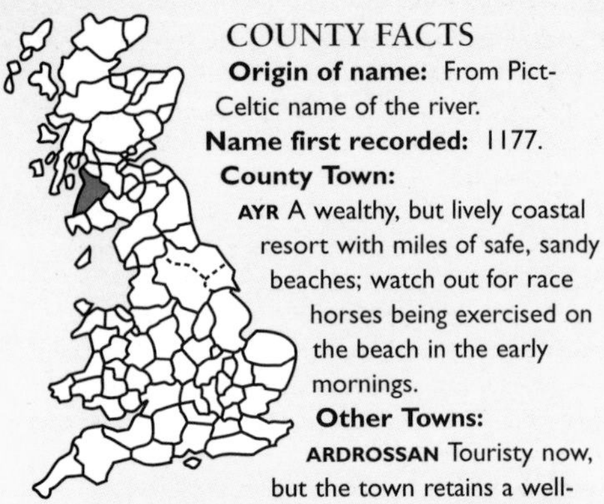

COUNTY FACTS

Origin of name: From Pict-Celtic name of the river.

Name first recorded: 1177.

County Town:

AYR A wealthy, but lively coastal resort with miles of safe, sandy beaches; watch out for race horses being exercised on the beach in the early mornings.

Other Towns:

ARDROSSAN Touristy now, but the town retains a well-planned feel with good, square stone houses. The harbour dates from 1806 and is the ferry point for the Isle of Arran in Buteshire. From here on a clear day you can see the granite peaks of Arran all of 15 miles away.

GIRVAN has a sheltered and colourful harbour and a yard which specializes in building traditional wooden fishing boats.

IRVINE An industrial centre and once the main port for Glasgow which is retold in the Scottish Maritime museum at the old harbour Moored to the museum are a dredger, fishing skiff, lifeboat, tug and 'puffer' boat – the last one used as an inshore supply boat along the Clyde and between the islands.

KILWINNING On the River Garnock, it has a rare example of a wooden cross on top of the Mercat Cross (where proclamations were made or criminals punished).

LARGS The town's long esplanade offers all the fun of the fair: boat trips, amusement arcades and so on. Largs has some of the best sailing to be found in the whole of Britain.

PRESTWICK A neat bright town with good shops, close to Prestwick international airport where so many golfing Americans and Japanese touch down to start their whistle-stop golf tours taking in Troon and Turnberry. Prestwick itself was the site of the first Championship in 1860. Old Tom Morris was beaten by two strokes.

SALTCOATS One of Glasgow's favourite weekend escapes, a busy, cheerful resort with lots to do. The North Ayrshire Museum here illustrates the shipping and coalmining history of the area.

TROON Another 'home to golf' this time the British Open, or Open Championship and a pretty town noted for its towered and turreted red-sandstone Victorian houses.

◆ Auchinleck ◆ Beith ◆ Cumnock ◆ Dalmellington ◆ Dalry ◆ Darvel ◆ Drayton ◆ Galston ◆ Hurlford ◆ Kilbirnie ◆ Kilmaurs ◆ Mauchline ◆ Stevenston ◆ West Kilbride

County rivers: Ayr, Farnock, Irvine, Lugar, Doon, Girvan, Stinchar.

Highest point: Shalloch An Minnoch at 2,520 feet.

Ayrshire's local government: The County of Ayrshire's administration cuts three ways. The unitary councils of North Ayrshire, South Ayrshire and East Ayrshire. At least the county keeps its identity by the use of the County's name in all three authorities.

Ayr stands on the river Ayr, and is in two parts: The old town is notable mainly for the 'Auld Brig', which was put over the river in the 13th century, recorded in a poem by Robbie Burns and saved from collapse by an international appeal at the turn of the century. This bridge connects the old town with the old port and the main attraction there is the Auld Kirk, erected with funds provided by Oliver Cromwell, of all people. Cromwell had pulled the previous town church down to build fortifications around the town and was then smitten with remorse. The church is still full of Cromwellian gloom, and not cheered by the inclusion of a mort safe – a niche where bodies could be kept safe from bodysnatchers before burial – in one of the gateway walls.

The newer, Victorian part of the town, behind the beach, is much more cheerful, with Wellington Square, named after the Great Duke, as the centre of the present tourist led prosperity. Ayr is lively and never livelier than on January 25, Burns Night, when the whisky flows and the haggis is piped in and the guests subjected to Burns's *Ode to the Haggis*…"great chieftain of the puddin race".

The next stop after Ayr has to be the village of Alloway, a ten minute drive to the south. This is where Robert Burns was born, on January 25, 1759, a date known to generations of Scots and their descendants in every corner of the world as 'Burns Night'. Burns moved about Scotland a great deal, and although he never made much money, having been persuaded to hand over most of his copyright fees to his agent, he was already Scotland's most famous poet when he died in 1796, at the early age of 37. The sights to see in Alloway include the Burns Cottage and Museum, a small thatched cottage where the poet was born and, a little way down the road, the Land o' Burns Visitor Centre, which, if not especially attractive and rather too modern for the subject, still gives a good overview of Burns's life and work.

The Centre lies just across the road from the ruins of Alloway Church, where Burns's father is buried. Here too is that 'Brig o' Doon' which features in Burns's liveliest poem, *Tam o' Shanter*, where the drunken Tam flees from the witch Cutty Sark, who pulls off the tail of Tam's horse. (It also gave its name to the Lerner & Loewe musical *Brigadoon*.) From here, real devotees of Scotland's favourite bard can follow the Robert Burns Trail to Dumfries, where he died.

South of Ayr lie the splendid towers of Culzean Castle, and the challenging links courses at Turnberry, one of the great golfing meccas with the classic hole by a lighthouse where you could be buffeted into the sea, but the next large town of Ayrshire lies a little further to the north of Ayr, at Kilmarnock.

Kilmarnock is chiefly famous for the production of Johnny Walker Whisky. The most important and enjoyable thing to do in the town is to tour the distillery, a tour which always ends up in the tasting room. More generally enjoyable is the seaside town of Largs, west of Kilmarnock. Largs is another of those pretty Victorian resorts which has managed to retain its popularity to the present day, thanks to a good beach and a great number of boarding houses and a great ice-cream parlour.

Troon, on the coast further south, is another resort famous for golf and therefore attracting a rather wealthy crowd, though the 'carriage trade' from America and Japan, tend to prefer visiting Turnberry these days. Girvan, the last resort on the way south caters for more popular tastes and pulls in the city folk, though those people who want to visit Ailsa Craig and see the birds, need to come here to catch a boat ride out to the rock.

LOCAL HISTORY

Ayr has that 13th-century bridge and the grim Auld Kirk, while the tiny village of Alloway is a paean to the 'Immortal Memory' of Robbie Burns and tells the visitor as much about Burns as they possibly need to know. The Burns Monument, a neo-Classical temple across the street from the ruins of Alloway church, is well worth a visit though.

Largs can provide a warlike piece of history, in the Battle of Largs which took place here in 1263 when a fleet of Vikings, heading for a raid on Ireland and the Western Isles, were forced ashore on the beach here and brought to battle by the Scots. Both sides claimed victory, but the Norsemen got such a rough handling that they stayed away from this part of Scotland for many years. This battle is commemorated by the Pencil Monument at Largs. This is a modern monument, but one historic site not to miss in Largs is the Skelmorlie Aisle, once part of a larger church but converted in 1636 as the mausoleum of Sir Robert Montgomerie. The mausoleum contains his splendid tomb with lots of coats-of-arms and some marvellous Italianate stonecarving.

One of the most popular historical attractions in the country (let alone county) is Culzean Castle, which was first erected in the 15th century although nothing remains of that medieval fortress and the present building is another of those marvellous creations by the ubiquitous Robert Adam. Adam was commissioned to build Culzean in 1777 by the 10th Earl of Cassillis and the work took 15 years to complete, in the finest Adam Style. The gardens are especially beautiful and are surrounded in their turn by a large country park.

FAMOUS NAMES

- Robert Burns, a native of Ayrshire, is one of the most famous names in Scotland, if not the world. His birthplace in Alloway, and the various places all over the county connected with his life and work are all worth visiting.
- General Dwight D Eisenhower, the American who commanded the Allied Armies in Europe during the Second World War and later became President of the USA, is commemorated by an apartment kept for him in Culzean Castle after the war, a gift from the Kennedy family, the Earls of Cassillis. The General visited the Castle several times and the apartment, which can be rented, is full of photos and Eisenhower memorabilia.
- James Boswell was born at Auchinleck House, an ancestral house since the 1400s.
- Sir Alexander Fleming, the discoverer of penicillin, was born at Darvel.

COUNTY CALENDAR

- January 25: Ayr and Alloway, Burns Night Festivities in the birthplace of the national poet.
- April: Scottish Grand National, Racecourse, Ayr.
- September: Largs Viking Festival, commemorating the Viking past of Ayrshire with concerts, Viking Village, battles, Craft Fair and fireworks, Largs.
- December 26: Boxing Day National Hunt Horse Racing Meeting, Ayr, which is the foremost racecourse in Scotland and beautifully maintained.
- July: Highland gathering at Dam Park Stadium, Ayr.
- Mid-April: The Ayr Agricultural Show.
- August-May: League football played at Ayr and Kilmarnock.

TURNBERRY *Yet another Ayrshire Open venue! The championship links are called the Ailsa.*

BANFFSHIRE

THE COUNTY LANDSCAPE

◆ The county forms a long, narrow inverted triangle, with its base sited on a 30-mile stretch of northern coastline, which tapers southwestwards to a point near Cairngorm at 4,084 feet.

◆ The greater part of the county, apart from the coastal lowlands, lies above 500 feet and a considerable part at more than 1,000 feet. In the south drainage is via the River Avon and the upper Deveron, with the undulating northern lowlands by the Spey and the lower Deveron.

◆ The scenery is typical of a vigorously glaciated highland area, with ice-carved corries (mountain hollows) gouged from the hillsides. Away from the Cairngorm region, with its sub-alpine vegetation, the breeding and fattening of Aberdeen Angus cattle is widespread.

COUNTY CALENDAR

◆ Mid-June: Festival of Ceilidhs at Keith is a traditional event where traditional Scottish musicians perform and other aspects of local culture are celebrated.

◆ July: Highland Games at Tomintoul.

◆ August: Highland Games at Aberlour.

◆ End July: Gala Week at Dufftown.

◆ End July: Sheepdog Trials at Keith.

◆ Mid-August: Flower Show at Banff.

◆ Mid-August: Agricultural Show at Keith.

A NARROW COUNTY perhaps but broadly boasting over 20 whisky distilleries with household names (to whisky tipplers at least) like Glenfiddich and Glenfarclas. Perhaps more than any other industry whisky making relies on, and is vulnerable to, its natural resources; this county provides the barley, wheat, and a plentiful supply of cool clear water coming from the famous Spey river. To me this county also has that marvellous combination of Cairngorm-tinged wilderness to the south and a different sort of tranquillity in the little ports and fishing villages on the southern shore of the Moray Firth. The way of life here is an apt reminder to those who hail technological progress at any price ...

TOWNS AND VILLAGES

Dominated by the mighty wind-blown granite slopes of the Grampians to the south, Banffshire's towns and villages lie scattered along the Highland roads driven through the mountains after the Jacobite risings of the 18th century to transport the garrisons and their supplies. In fact, most of the contemporary roads follow the routes which were pioneered by the military engineers of the time such as Generals Wade and Caulfield or, during the following century, by Thomas Telford.

Back in the 12th century, the county town of Banff was a thriving seaport and a member of the Northern Hanseatic League. Since those halcyon days its herring fisheries have declined, but it remains an elegant town with some impressive 17th- and 18th-century buildings in its upper reaches, while the picturesque sea-front area of Scotstown exudes a scruffier charm. The architectural showpiece is Duff House, designed by William Adam for the local plutocrat William Braco, and presented to the burgh in 1906. It now serves as an outpost for the National Gallery of Scotland's extensive collection. The sister town of Macduff stands on the opposing east bank of the Deveron estuary and is connected to it by a bridge. A mile south, along the A97, is the Colleonard Sculpture Park, the world's only garden of archetypal abstractionism,

BANFF *The harbour on Banff Bay at the mouth of the River Deveron.*

started by Frank Bruce in 1965. Nearby is a noted local beauty spot, the Bridge of Alvah. At the border with Morayshire is the renowned distillery of Glenfarclas, complete with castle, at the tiny village of Ballindalloch. You can see pure malt whisky being made (not perhaps as it was originally over 100 years ago) at the J&G Grant Distillery.

With a total county population of under 50,000 people, most of the other small burghs, such as Keith and Buckie, and the coastal towns of Gardenstown and Whitehills depend for their existence on the local industries of fishing, distilling, farming, boat-building and limestone quarrying. Cullen, 12 miles west of the quaint village of Portsoy whose green marble was once shipped to France for the building of Versailles, is a paradise for devotees of 19th-century railway architecture. The town is overshadowed by a series of graceful, snaking viaducts, and also has a surprisingly ornate 12th-century kirk. Tomintoul, at 1,150 feet, is the highest village in the Scottish Highlands and owes its existence to the stringent population control measures (otherwise known as the clearances) introduced after the 1745 rebellion. Its long, thin street layout is reminiscent of a Wild West frontier town. Queen Victoria described it as "the most tumble-down, poor looking place I ever saw". It achieved some notoriety in the 1990s when the self-styled Laird of Tomintoul turned out to be the ex-accountant of Scotland Yard who had embezzled millions but had invested in several local enterprises.

LOCAL HISTORY

Many of the finest stone-age axes yet found in Scotland come from this area. The county was the scene of numerous conflicts with Danish and Viking raiders who, in 1010, were defeated in the field of Bloody Pots at Gamrie by Malcolm III. A sculptured stone at Mortlach marks the site. Notable medieval relics include the ruined castles of Findlater, Auchindown and Balvenie. Cullen Church had a chaplain supported by Robert the Bruce to serve the parish, in memory of his wife Elizabeth, who died there.

The history of this county is distinctly intertwined with the history of Scottish whisky: the nectar was distilled here for centuries – by anyone who cared to do it. But private distilling was banished in the mid 1700s so smuggling blossomed overnight. Illicit distilling continued in the remote glens with some 200 still operating until 1824. Other bootleggers realized it would be more profitable to legitimize their trade and this led eventually to the start of the growth of the whisky-distilling in the county.

COUNTY FACTS

Origin of name: From the Gaelic Little pig, an affectionate term for the river Deveron.

Name first recorded: 1150.

County Town: BANFF Ancient seaport and resort with fine sands and bathing.

Other Towns:

ABERCHIRDER The smallest Royal Burgh founded in 1764 by the River Deveron.

BUCKIE Good base to see a string of attractive fishing ports nestling in the cliffside on Spey Bay.

CULLEN An 11th-century monument reminds passers by that her Viking invaders were driven back to sea with great slaughter. A culinary claim to fame may be the original kitchens to serve out Cullen Skink a traditional stew soup of the region (Skink comes from the Gaelic meaning essence). You need haddock, onion, milk, butter, mashed potato and salt and pepper. Make it creamy and serve with dry toast.

TOMINTOUL Springboard for the Glenlivet estate with its peat mosses spread across much of the land around the village. The old days of peat-cutting are recalled in an award-winning museum in its centre.

◆ Charlestown of Aberlour ◆ Craigellachie ◆ Dufftown ◆ Findochty ◆ Ianstown ◆ Macduff ◆ Newmill ◆ Portessie ◆ Portgordon ◆ Portnockie ◆ Portsoy ◆ Seatown

County rivers: Deveron, Spey, Avon.

Highest point: Ben Macdhui at 4,296 feet.

Banffshire's local government: The County of Banffshire is carved up between two councils. The bulk of Banffshire loses its identity under a unitary council called Moray. The town that gives the shire its name, Banff, along with the ancient burghs of Aberchirder, Macduff and Portsoy are under the auspice of Aberdeenshire unitary authority. St Fergus is Banffshire detached in Aberdeenshire and comes under that County's unitary authority.

FAMOUS NAMES

◆ James MacPherson, a noted troubadour and footpad who was caught and hanged in 1700, wrote a march while in jail awaiting execution and played it on the way to the gallows. With words by Robert Burns, it remains among the best-loved Scottish marches.

◆ The slopes of the mountain Ben Macdhui are reputedly haunted by an invisible ghost, Ferlas Mor or the Grey Man, whose footsteps can be heard when no-one else is present. The noted climber J. Norman Collie was once inexplicably stricken with panic while climbing here and fled the mountain, never to return.

◆ James Sharp, a Presbyterian divine, converted to the Church of Scotland and became Bishop of St Andrews. He then persecuted the Covenanters and reputedly delayed the news of a reprieve so that 12 were still hanged. He also had 200 others imprisoned in the hold of an unseaworthy ship on the pretext of shipping them to the colonies, but ordered the master to then founder the vessel on rocks. The master escaped the wreck but the passengers all drowned. He was murdered on Magus Moor in 1679.

Berwickshire

THE COUNTY LANDSCAPE

◆ This is varied and pleasing rather than dramatic countryside, but it has its moments and the great asset of solitude. It is an empty land, where crowds are a rarity and rushing about unnecessary. The main features are the valley of the Tweed which marks the southern border and the Lammermuir Hills in the north which divide this county from the Lothians.

◆ In between the two lies the Merse, the great plain of the Tweed, seamed with rivers and streams, perfect farming country. The county is also ideal walking country crossed by that beautiful long distance footpath, the Southern Upland Way, which enters Berwickshire south of Greenlaw and terminates on the North Sea coast at Cockburnspath.

◆ For a splendid view over the Tweed Valley go to Scott's View above Dryburgh, where the poet would go to admire the valley and the distant Eildon Hills. Those who enjoy good walking should visit Lauder and roam up into the Lammermuirs.

◆ The coastline is varied, a mixture of high cliffs and pebble beaches, all washed by the grey and chilly waters of the North Sea. St Abb's Head (a bit of a Land's End) or John o' Groats, dominates the coast hereabouts and is famous for its seabirds, while the hinterland is a mixture of woodlands, moorlands, arable and pasture farmland, much of it well supplied with a great quantity of sheep.

DRYBURGH *The Wallace Statue.*

A BONE OF contention between England and Scotland, the town of Berwick-on-Tweed has been snatched back and forth 13 times – and that was just between 1300 and 1482! So what has all this past enmity resulted in? Today you might expect Berwick-on-Tweed to be in Berwickshire? Wrong. It lies across the river in Northumberland in England. The English claimed it and got it – but I would challenge that: Berwick-on-Tweed has to be in Berwickshire, there's no way it can't be. While I throw down my gauntlet and defend this rather neglected Border county, let me tell you that it is a beautiful, historic, and quite charming place that tends to be rushed through or by-passed as people head for Newcastle or Edinburgh. It's their loss but it can be your gain.

TOWNS AND VILLAGES

The River Tweed is as famous as the town that bears its name, and not just for salmon fishing. It is one of the longest at 100 miles in length and most important in Scotland marking the country's border for some 16 miles of its course. Three bridges span it at Berwick including Robert Stephenson's rail bridge (1850).

While the once important port of Berwick-on-Tweed, which gives its name to the county as a result of history, lies officially just across in England, so the capital of Berwickshire is the little town of Duns, right in the middle of the county. It is famous as the birthplace of the medieval scholar and philosopher, Duns Scotus, born in the town in 1266, a man whose views were so advanced that anyone who believed in them was regarded as crazy and referred to as a 'duns' or 'dunce'. The second famous son of this little market town is motor racing champion Jim Clark, who won 25 Grand Prix before being killed on the Hockenheim circuit in 1968. The Jim Clark Room in the town is filled with his trophies and Jim lies buried at Chirnside, a small village a few miles to the east.

In fact small villages rather than large towns make up the urban parts of Berwickshire and to find another town of comparable size to Duns we must go over to the North Sea coast, to Eyemouth, and its Museum, in the Auld Kirk, which records the Great East Coast Fishing Disaster of the last century in which 189 fishermen were lost in a storm, 129 of them from Eyemouth. The displays also feature the fishing and farming activities of Berwickshire and are the perfect way to get to grips with the real life of this little-known part of Scotland.

On to the banks of the Tweed and the little town of Coldstream. Coldstream is a centre for salmon fishermen. Coldstream also contains the Marriage House on the bridge, the East Coast answer to Gretna Green, where runaway couples could be married until

1856. But the town is best known for its reminders to the founding of the Coldstream Guards, including a plaque in the market place recording details of Colonel Monck raising the regiment here in 1659, and small placards of Guardsmen decorate lamp posts and buildings in the main street.

Among the smaller villages that cannot be missed is Dryburgh, also on the Tweed and best known for Dryburgh Abbey, one of the Border Abbeys built by King David I in 1150 and destroyed by the Earl of Hertford in 1548. Dryburgh is tranquil and very beautiful and contains within its precincts the graves of two famous men, Sir Walter Scott and the controversial Great War commander of the British Armies in France, Field Marshal Haig, founder of the Poppy Day appeal.

Nestling in Lauderdale on the Leader lies Lauder, with the nearby imposing red sandstone. Another place worth visiting in this part of Berwickshire is Mellerstain House, one of the most attractive houses in Scotland, begun by William Adam in 1725 and completed by his son Robert in about 1778. Further to the north, on the road to Edinburgh lies Thirlstane Castle, largely 16th century but containing parts of an earlier medieval fortress, as well as a fine collection of paintings by artists like Lely and Romney.

LOCAL HISTORY

The history of the Scottish Borders is a long and bloody one, which only ended when the accession of James I – and VI of Scotland – to the throne of England, and the later Act of Union, united the two Kingdoms. Previous attempts to coerce the Scots into union had ended in disaster and led to the destruction of many Border Abbeys when Henry VIII wanted the Scots to let his son Edward marry the infant Mary, later Queen of Scots. The Scots Lords preferred a French marriage so, in an attempt to change their minds, the English King, who was not known for subtlety, sent an army to ravage Scotland, which it did with terrible effect. The Earl of Hertford rampaged with his forces in the Borders after sacking Edinburgh in what is called the "rough wooing". Battlefields and ruined abbeys now mark the Border counties and if few abbeys or battlefields actually lie in Berwickshire, they can all be easily visited from places like Duns or Greenlaws.

Coldstream is best known as the place from where, in the uncertain days of 1660, a Parliamentary colonel, George Monck, marched his regiment to London and placed Charles II on the throne of his ancestors. Monck's Regiment of Foot later became the Coldstream Guards, the only regiment of the British Army that can trace its origins back directly to the Cromwellian New Model Army.

COUNTY FACTS

Origin of name: From Old English berewic – barley farm (bere = barley; wic = farm or dwelling).

Name first recorded: 1097.

County Town:

DUNS Delightful Border town with a stone cairn marking 13th century-scholar Duns Scotus's birthplace.

Other Towns:

BERWICK-ON-TWEED Still uses its 17th-century bridge. Its proximity to battlefields – Halidon Hill, Chevy Chase and Flodden Field – would suggests its strategic importance set between a gap in the hills and the sea. Elizabeth I spent a fortune updating the battlements against a French invasion spectre which failed to materialize, but the splendid battlements remain. Today salmon fishing is a main lure. Berwick Rangers FC continues to be the only 'English' club playing in the Scottish League. Berwick Cockles is a quaint name for a mint sweetie.

COLDSTREAM Is a pretty little town in a fine setting by the River Tweed, which can be viewed at its best from the 18th-century bridge. Classic salmon fishing.

EYEMOUTH A fishing port near St Abb's Head, this has various points of interest, including the harbour and some attractive buildings set around the market place.

LAUDER On the southern edge of the Lammermuir Hills is a market town with a fine historic river bridge. Created a Royal Burgh by William the Lion and ratified by James IV's Parliament in 1503.

◆ Ayton ◆ Chirnside ◆ Coldingham ◆ Earlston ◆ Greenlaw ◆ Reston ◆ Swinton

County rivers: Tweed, Eye, Blackadder, Whiteadder, Dye.

Highest point: Meikle Says at 1,749 feet.

Berwickshire's local government: Berwickshire is served by the Scottish Borders unitary council. Berwick-upon-Tweed is administered by an English two-tier system – Berwick upon Tweed district council *and* Northumberland County Council.

◆ Merse, Lammermuir and Lauderdale are the ancient names of the historical districts which preceded Berwickshire.

FAMOUS NAMES

◆ Sir Alec Douglas-Home's home was The Hirsel at Dundock (two miles from Coldstream). It has a very pretty woodland garden noted for its azaleas and rhododendrons and is open to the public. There is a wildfowl sanctuary on the lake here and the grounds boast more species of birds than any other equivalent wood in Britain. True or false, the boast was enough to lure many bird-song broadcasts.

COUNTY CALENDAR.

July: Eyemouth Herring Queen Festival.

August: Thirlstane Castle Scottish Horse Trials, Thirlstane Castle, Lauder.

Early August: Lauder Common Riding is an enactment of riding the bounds of the people's common land on the first Saturday of the month.

BUTESHIRE

THE COUNTY LANDSCAPE

◆ Buteshire offers a vision of the old romantic Scotland. This dramatic natural holiday area is cut up into islands by a great natural inlet of the sea, the Firth of Clyde, which in turn contains sub-inlets like the marvellously picturesque Kyles of Bute.

◆ The county is a collection of islands. The two main ones – Bute and Arran – comprise bleak, savage mountain. On the margins of the old granite mountains are softer hills and valleys. The south of Arran, for example, is almost pastoral in appearance.

◆ As well as Arran and Bute, the county also consists of the islands of Great Cumbrae, Little Cumbrae, Inchmarnock and Pladda. All are formed from ancient cystalline rocks.

SOME PEOPLE SAY Rothesay, on the island of Bute, is like the Southend of Glasgow – holidaymakers flock there. You get the ferry from the mainland and you think you've come a very long way, but you've actually not gone that far at all. In fact, you've just sampled the shortest sea crossing in the western isles. The ferry journey across the beautiful Kyles of Bute from Colintraive on the hilly Cowal peninsula to Rhubodach at the northern tip of Bute takes just five minutes. Before the car ferry was introduced, cattle used to be made to swim the crossing. There are many who consider this narrow stretch of water to be the island's scenic wonder, the rocks are so close you can almost touch them as the ferry boat twists and turns through the Kyles.

TOWNS AND VILLAGES

When you arrive in Buteshire, you find yourself in a different world to that on the mainland. For one thing, although you're quite close to Glasgow – Glaswegians used to talk about going 'doon the watter' to Bute on the old Clyde steamers – the climate is quite different. The presence of the Gulf Stream flowing up the west coast of Scotland is credited with warmer weather here. Although rain frequently drifts in over the mountains, it rarely snows until January. As a result, palm trees wave in the wind and flowers usually associated with warmer climates, such as fuchsia, grow in profusion. It's said that Buteshire strawberries have appeared in the Glasgow shops as early as Eastertime.

BUTE *Once cattle bound for Bute were made to swim the straight at Rhubodach.*

The county is great sailing territory. The Scottish National Watersports Centre is based in Cumbrae; there can be few more agreeable places to improve your skills than in these beautiful surroundings. Agriculture and fishing are still the main industries, but tourism is growing. The northern part of Bute is quite hilly; to the south the land is flatter and more fertile. Rothesay, on the sheltered east coast, is both the county 'capital' and a popular summer resort. This is the place where the old Clyde steamers would put in, discharging visitors for a visit to the moated castle or a chance to sunbathe, if weather permitted, on the fine sand beaches of Etterick Bay and Kilchatten. You can still do these things today, of course – or visit Ardencraig Gardens or Mount Stuart House, one of the most unusual stately homes in Scotland. A Gothic-styled palace in red sandstone, the house is a fantasy of marble and stained glass. It includes a marble hall where the columns soar to a roof painted with stars and lit by stained glass.

Arran, to the south of Bute and reached by car ferry from Ardrossan, is an unashamed holiday island and, like its near neighbour, benefits from the Gulf Streams influences. Mountains, low hills, streams and glens come together here to provide a sort of Scotland in miniature. In the north, the granite ridges are dominated by the appropriately named Goatfell, which rises to 2,866 feet. The scenery may be dramatic, but it's easy enough to get about: a good road runs the 56 miles around the island.

Arran has villages rather than towns. Brodick, on the east coast, is the main holiday village, dominated by a 15th-century castle which was once the home of the Dukes of Hamilton and is now owned by the National Trust for Scotland. Close by, Lamlash Bay, protected by Holy Island, is a popular spot with yachtsmen. The south of Arran is more pastoral than the dramatic north and the island's popular cheese is made here, at Torrylin.

LOCAL HISTORY

The western isles of Buteshire have been inhabited by man since the earliest times. It's believed that, 8,000 years ago after the last Ice Age, Mesolithic men from Ireland, with flint arrows and tools in their reindeer belts, settled on Bute and near Blackwater Bay, on the west coast of Arran, Bronze Age cairns have been found. At Holy Island, also on Arran, is St Molais's cave, the home of a hermit who lived in the days of St Columba in the 6th century. From the 9th to the 13th centuries Arran was a Norse colony and this is evident in many of the place names. In 1263, at the Battle of Largs in Ayrshire, the Norse were defeated. The Macdonalds – the Lords of the Isles – took over and the countryside is strewn with their ruined castles, such as the one at Rothesay, built in 1098. Robert the Bruce also has connections with the area. He sheltered in the King's Caves on the west coast of Arran early in the 14th century and the picturesque cove at Lochranza, in the north of the island, is where he made his landing from Ireland in 1306.

The very first cotton-mill in Scotland was established on the island of Bute in 1788 and lasted 100 years. Shipbuilding and fishing flourished and steamers began to arrive, marking the island as a popular holiday resort.

COUNTY FACTS

Origin of name: Named from the island of Bute in the Firth of Clyde. The word Bute may derive from Both = a cell, or Ey Bhod = Island of corn (Gaelic). Alternatively, its source could be the Old Irish word Bòt meaning a fire or a beacon.

Name first recorded: 1093.

County Town:
ROTHESAY An elegant town with a classic promenade. There are red sandstone remains of Rothesay Castle, one of the most remarkable and important medieval castles in Scotland, distinguished by high curtain walls fortified by projecting drum towers.

Other Towns:
BRODICK Arran's main port has diving and sea-angling centres. The Castle and Gardens lie north of the pier.
LOCHRANZA Its pretty harbour spreads along the shore on both sides of a sea loch, which is guarded by the substantial ruins of a picturesque castle.
MILLPORT On Great Cumbrae, opposite Millport Bay, well known for its sandy beach and good bathing.
WHITING BAY A sandy beach and a ruined castle.
◆ Craigmore ◆ Lamlash ◆ Port Bannatyne

Highest point: Goatfell on Arran at 2,866 feet.

Buteshire's local government: Buteshire is made up of a number of islands, the four main masses being Arran, Bute and the Cumbraes. The County of Buteshire is split in half for local government purposes. The Island of Bute joins up with Argyllshire to form the unitary council of Argyll and Bute, whereas Arran and Great and Little Cumbrae are tied to the unitary North Ayrshire council.

FAMOUS NAMES

◆ The harbour of Lochranza – "the loch of safe anchorage" – is where Robert the Bruce landed on Arran from Ireland in 1306.
◆ Also on Arran, you may rest on Goatfell, experiencing for yourself the emotions described by Robert McLellan in *Sweet Largie Bay*.
◆ Edmund Kean, the famous but hard-drinking tragic actor, maintained a country seat on Bute.
◆ TV presenter Selina Scott worked for the Scottish Tourist Board on Arran.

COUNTY CALENDAR

◆ Early May: West of Scotland Cycle Union Senior & Junior Cycling championships, Rothesay, Isle of Bute.
◆ June: Isle of Arran Folk Festival, Arran.
◆ July: Arran Fleadh festival of Celtic, Scottish and international music, Arran.
◆ Early August: Brodick Highland Games, Brodick, Arran.
◆ Late August: Bute Highland Games, Bute.
◆ September: Isle of Bute Regatta, Rothesay Seafront, Bute.
◆ May: Scottish Peaks Race – Goat Fell on Arran, plus an ascent of Ben More on Mull and the Paps of Jura in Argyllshire.

CAITHNESS

DOUNREAY *The Atomic Power Station has a permanent exhibition on nuclear power.*

THE COUNTY LANDSCAPE

- The natural border between Caithness and Sutherland to the west is the great headland of the Ord. The southern part of Caithness is the mountainous part, and home to considerable numbers of Golden Eagle. Much of the rest is farming, or rather crofting country, supporting sheep and some arable farming.
- Caithness is called 'the Lowlands beyond the Highlands' for beyond the headland of the Ord which is a huge mass of cliffs and heather, the bulk of Caithness is rolling moorland known as the 'Flow Country'. And flow it does for hundreds of square miles of river valleys, trout loch, and a few scattered hills, one of the last great wilderness areas of Europe.
- The 'Flow Country' which straddles the border with Sutherland, north of Forsinard, on either side of Strath Halladale, is a region of moorland dotted with small lochs and threaded by trout streams but the country tends to flatten out in the north and along the coast.
- The East Coast, all the way north from Berriedale is a spectacular mixture of cliffs and sheltered bays, many of the latter supporting a small harbour while the cliffs support large seabird colonies. One of the most spectacular sights on the coast are the 'Stacks', offshore rock pillars and pyramids near Duncansby Head.

CAITHNESS IS AS the last gasp of Scotland, bleak and beautiful, but best known for John o' Groats, supposedly the most northerly part of the British mainland (but not actually!) and the terminal, or starting point, for the Lands End-to-John o' Groats Walk. Caithness is about as remote as you would wish to get.

TOWNS AND VILLAGES

The county could be called underpopulated if there was an abundance of places for people to live. As it is, the total population of Caithness is just 26,000 so, apart from a few small towns and a slightly larger number of villages, the bulk of Caithness is open country, scourged by the relentless wind that swoops in from Norway across the North Sea, and a very inhospitable county indeed when that wind turns chilly.

The county town of Caithness is Wick which lies on the eastern coast and is a place best known for the manufacture of Caithness glass. A factory was established in 1960 and has been producing high-class, hand-blown glassware and famous coloured paperweights ever since. The pretty harbour, once full of fishing boats, is now more often a welcome haven for wandering yachts. The Wick Heritage Centre tell the story of this part of Scotland, ravaged by Vikings and the Highland Clearances of the last century. A sad little history, friendly folk and good walking in the countryside round about is what Wick has to offer, and after that the visitor will have to travel on.

Thurso is larger, or seems larger, quite large anyway for such an out-of-the-way Highland town. There is a whisky museum, a golf course and some fine architecture and the whole place has a pleasing, welcoming atmosphere but here again, nothing that can detain the traveller for long. In the old days it was different, when this was the trading port between Scotland and Norway, with a thriving commerce in hides and beef and fish. The rule for Caithness today is that you have to keep moving.

John o' Groats on Duncansby Head, now owned along with Land's End by a Lancashire entrepreneur living in Jersey, is the place everyone visits if only to say they have been there; but the seabird colonies on the Head itself are worth seeing anyway. This northern coast is very spectacular, with views out to the small island of Stroma and the Orkney Islands, the cliffs rising to the point of Dunnet Head, eight miles to the west, which really is the most northerly spot on the British mainland. The coast road leads through Thurso to Scrabster, the ferry port to Orkney, with a lighthouse and good views across Thurso Bay.

Other locations worth a look in Caithness include Ackergill, where the Northern Viking Centre explores the history of Viking settlements in this region. Watten, set in the east of the county and on the shores of Loch Watten, is another angling centre, and is also very pretty, but that is true of many of these secret Caithness places, especially when the sun is shining.

LOCAL HISTORY

As the prehistoric sites at Ousdale, Langwell, Forse and Camster indicate with huge mysterious cairns, Caithness has been populated since prehistoric times, the then population surviving by subsistence agriculture and the bountiful fish in the North Sea; it is noticeable that all these early settlements are on the East Coast.

The story of the Picts in Caithness is told in Theresa Museum, but in about 500AD the Scots arrived from Ireland and worked their way north until they collided with the Northmen, coming south from Shetland and Orkney. The Vikings kept a foothold in Caithness for centuries and place names ending in 'ick' (like Wick) or 'ster' like Scrabster, or Ulbster, indicate that these places were Viking settlements. Then came the clans, who lived here for half a millennium until the Highland Clearances of the last century when the lairds cleared out the clansmen to make way for sheep, a disaster from which the lands never recovered. Small farmers got back some security and a few people have returned but the emptiness of this lovely land can be traced directly to those savage Clearances.

COUNTY FACTS

Origin of name: At the dawn of British history, Caithness was one of the 7 provinces of Pictland – Cait, probably meaning land of the cat-tribe. It was then one province with Sutherland and the Duke of Sutherland's Gaelic title is still the Great Man of the Cats.
Name first recorded: c. 970 as Cait or Cat.
County Motto: "Commit Thy Work To God".
County Town: **WICK** Boom town in Victorian era with over 1,000 fishing boats and is still a fishing port. Robert Louis Stevenson stopped here while his dad built the breakwater.
Other Towns:
DUNBEATH An ancient place with a 'bluff old castle' precariously perched on a narrow neck of land.
DUNNET Now here lies the real 'John o' Groats' for the Head here juts out three miles from the mainland to become the most northerly point of Britain.
HALKIRK On the river Thurso, the top spot for visiting anglers. The ruins of Braal Castle are close.
JOHN O' GROATS Village that has become a British landmark; once the site of an unusual eight-sided house of the same name now a grassy mound.
LYBSTER The prehistoric Camster Cairns lie near this pretty fishing village set on a wild and rocky stretch of coast (at the head of Amherst Bay), and date back to 3,000BC. Lybster itself has a church built of local distressed flagstones.
MEY Small hamlet with big castle owned by Queen Mum.
SCRABSTER The ferry port for the Orkneys across the turbulent Pentland Firth. This port is sheltered by Holborn Head with curious-shaped chasms.
THURSO A modern boom town of today thanks to Atomic Energy Plant at Dounreay. Splendidly situated on the southern shores of the great sweep of Thurso Bay. The name probably derives from the Norse *Thor's-a* ("the river of the God Thor"). It has a heritage museum and the Old St Peter's Kirk.
County rivers: Thurso, Wick, Oikel.
Highest point: Morven at 2,313 feet.

Caithness's local government: The County of Caithness is governed by Highland unitary council.

FAMOUS NAMES

- Dunbeath is the birthplace of the 20th-century Scots writer, Neil M. Gunn born here in 1891. His books like *Highland River* evoke the county.
- The Gunns are the local clan and there is a Clan Gunn centre in Latherton.
- Watten is the birthplace of Alexander Bain, credited with the invention of the fax machine.
- Wick is the birthplace of Dane Sinclair, who invented the automatic telephone exchange.

COUNTY CALENDAR

- June: Thurso and Wick, Caithness Science Festival.
- July: Thurso has the Caithness Highland Gathering,
- July: Caithness Agricultural Show and Gala Week at Wick.
- September: Thurso, Wick share Northlands Festival.

CLACKMANNANSHIRE

STRATHDEVON

THE COUNTY LANDSCAPE

◆ This is Scotland's (and Britain's) smallest county. It is part of the Central Lowlands geographically yet also sits on the edge of Highland Scotland within sight of the higher hills.

◆ To the north the Highland mountains are anticipated with the spread of low hills, known as the Ochil Hills. This range is split by deep-cut, wooded glens. A walk up any of these glens is very rewarding; the Glen at Dollar leads up to Castle Campbell (Gloom) which stands at its head.

◆ Towards the north the countryside opens out and distances between towns get longer as the population diminishes away from the crowded Glasgow-Edinburgh corridor.

◆ Clackmannan is a countrified county of farms and small settlements, and it nestles close to the heart of Scotland with its neighbour counties of Perthshire, Kinross-shire, Fife and Stirlingshire.

◆ The land is not dramatically scenic – low hills tipped toward the end of the Firth of Forth sea inlet, and pleasingly rural for the most part. The southern part slopes gently through good pasture lands to its border, edged with the river from the Bridge of Allan in Stirlingshire almost to Culross on the River Forth.

CLACKMANNANSHIRE IS THE smallest county in the British Isles, and although tiny, it's got a great deal going for it. I remember driving along the A91 and on one side there'd be tremendous steep-sided ravines and huge peaks, while the other side dropped right the way down to the Forth valley. The north part of Clackmannanshire is very hilly and steep, while the southern part is low-lying country, and industrial. There is so much in so little in this wee county.

TOWNS AND VILLAGES

The town of Clackmannan is situated inland, the county seat being this small town above the narrowing Firth where it becomes the Forth River. Like other burghs in the county it's an unassuming yet pleasant market town. On a western hill beside the town is its main monument, Clackmannan Tower, 80 feet high and built in the 14th century, though with 17th-century amendments. Local legend states it was built by Robert the Bruce at the time of his kingship.

From Clackmannan you pass along the coast through Alloa to come to Cambuskenneth Abbey. It is placed beside the Forth, a striking mid-12th-century stone church built by the Augustinians under King David's rule. Most of the abbey is in ruins but there is a particularly fine bell tower of the early 14th century standing tall above the river.

In the west at Abbey Craig, near Bridge of Allan, stands the prominent Wallace Monument, dedicated to the 13th-century knight who beat the Earl of Surrey's forces to become ruler of Scotland, only to be defeated later and to face execution in London in 1305. The pinnacled Victorian tower beside a crow-stepped gable house, erected on a mound, is a shrine to Sir William Wallace and contains what is said to be his two-handed sword. You can climb a spiral stair to the top for panoramic views of the river valley and Stirling to the south, mountains to the north.

CLACKMANNAN *Castle Campbell stands overlooking the dramatic chasm of Dollar*

Dollar is a neat little place, at the base of the rugged Ochil

Hills. From here you can walk the pretty wooded Dollar Glen to visit imposingly sited Castle Campbell. This ancient pile was also known as Castle Gloom, and as it stands at the confluence of two streams known as the Burn of Sorrow and the Burn of Care, perhaps puns on its name were inevitable.

Dollar is one of the Hillfoot mill towns which made its money from wool production, and it is part of a woollen mill trail. The focal town is Tillicoultry on the A91 route to the west where you will find the Clock Mill Heritage Centre explaining the part the wool trade has played in Clackmannanshire history.

This part of Scotland had enlightened views about the education of children (as at New Lanark). At Dollar, designer William Playfair of Edinburgh built a handsome school named the Dollar Academy, for poor children of the local parish in 1818. The building, with an impressive portico of six Tuscan columns, stands in a large spreading park with the Ochil Hills as a background. Nearby are stone houses of the same period built for the school's teachers and staff.

Just west of the small settlement of Alva (historically detached part of Stirlingshire) is Menstrie Castle, the birthplace (1567) and home of the statesman and poet Sir William Alexander. He was later commissioned by James I (of England) and VI (of Scotland) to be 'lieutenant for the plantations of new Scotland' in North America. This was the reason that many Scots travelled to the provinces of eastern Canada to settle, and Nova Scotia (New Scotland) has still very much a Scottish air. The castle displays the sculpted coats of arms of scores of new baronets created by the money-conscious James to finance the founding of fledgling North American colonies.

LOCAL HISTORY

Scottish kings have made their mark here – notably Robert the Bruce, while King David I founded abbeys and churches in the heartland of his kingdom. As it was situated north of the earthwork known as the Antonine Wall, built to keep out the Picts, and on the edge of the Highlands, this part of Scotland remained Pictish during the Roman occupation and there are some signs of this ancient tribe.

Mary, Queen of Scots, her son James VI, and his son Prince Henry all spent part of their youth in the county at Alloa Tower, once the stronghold of the Earl of Mar.

In Clackmannan's central square are the tower of the Tolbooth, the old Town Cross and the Stone 'Clach' of Mannan or Manae or Manaw.

COUNTY FACTS

Origin of name: From the Gaelic, meaning Stone of Manae, the name of a glacial rock in the town centre.
Name first recorded: 1133.
County Motto: Look about ye.
County Town:
ALLOA The largest town in the smallest county. The oldest building in the town is the 13th Century Alloa Tower, standing 90 feet high with walls 11 feet thick. Mary Queen of Scots stayed at Alloa House as did her son, James I of England and VI of Scotland, when as a child he was educated at Stirling by the Earl of Mar. It is home to Alloa Athletic.

Other Towns:

ALVA A weaving town for over 400 years, Alva was also once known for silver mining.

CLACKMANNAN This ancient town gave its name to the county.

DOLLAR Residential town. The Academy has become one of Scotland's most respected private schools. Might once have been called Dolour as Castle Campbell, standing between the Glen of Care and the Burn of Sorrow, was known as Castle Gloom.

MENSTRIE This small town was once noted for weaving and furniture-making.

TILLICOULTRY Wool town at the heart of the Mill Heritage Trail, which links towns, historic sites and mill shops. Known as the floral burgh. Queen Victoria commented how much the area reminded her of the valleys of Italy and Switzerland when passing through by train in 1879. Bronze-age artefacts have been found here.

◆ Coalnaughton ◆ New Sauchie ◆ Tullibody

County river: Black Devon.
Highest point: Ben Cleugh at 2,363 feet.

Clackmannanshire's local government:
The tiny County of Clackmannanshire is in the rare position, unlike the County of Banffshire for instance, of having a unitary council called Clackmannanshire to look after its local government in downtown Alloa. Here the real county and administrative area are *almost* identical, coming together to conserve history and heritage and to maintain a strong local identity.

FAMOUS NAMES

◆ King Robert the Bruce is commemorated in this small county with a contemporary tower.
◆ The writer Robert Louis Stevenson attempted to help his delicate health at the spa of Airthrey.
◆ The founder of the province of Nova Scotia in Canada, Sir William Alexander, was born at Menstrie Castle in middle of the county.

COUNTY CALENDAR

◆ Early May: Country and Western Show, Tillicoultry.
◆ Mid-May: Clackmannanshire Beer Week, various local breweries.
◆ July: Alva Highland Games.
◆ September: Alloa Flower Show.

DUMFRIESSHIRE

THE COUNTY LANDSCAPE

◆ Dumfriesshire is a predominantly hilly agricultural county in the southwest of Scotland, adjoining Cumberland. The county is bounded in the south by the Solway Firth, in the north by Lanarkshire, Peeblesshire and Selkirkshire, in the east by Roxburghshire and in the west by Kirkcudbrightshire and Ayrshire.

◆ It has a coastline of about 20 miles, running along the north shore of the Solway Firth. Southern Upland hills line the north, west and east boundaries and the county is effectively divided into three north-south areas by the valleys created by the rivers Nith, Annan and Esk.

◆ Lochs Skeen and Urr and the cluster around Lochmaben are the chief lakes – Loch Skeen giving rise to one of Scotland's highest waterfalls, the Grey Mare's Tail, which is almost 200 feet high.

◆ The terrain is largely hilly where it is not actually mountainous, with many lakes 1,300 feet above sea level.

◆ Although many Scottish counties have just one or, sometimes, two ancient names or alternative titles derived from the sherrifdoms or lands stretching back into time; Dumfriesshire wears four historic titles with pride - Nithsdale, Annandale, Eskdale and Ewesdale - the original forerunners of the modern county.

FAMOUS NAMES

◆ Part of the spy thriller *Mission Impossible,* starring Tom Cruise and directed by Brian de Palma, was filmed on the railway lines between Dumfries and Annan and Dumfries and Auldgirth.

◆ Ecclefechan is the hometown of Thomas Carlyle, the famous Victorian historian, essayist, social reformer and visionary. He was born in an attractive white house built by his master-mason family, now in the hands of the National Trust for Scotland.

◆ According to Sir Walter Scott, in his novel *Redgauntlet*, the hills in which the Devil's Beef Tub is situated look "as if they were laying their heads together to shut out the daylight from the dark hollow spaces between them".

◆ Robert Burns lived in Dumfries from 1791 until his death in 1796. He wrote some of his best poetry here, including *Auld Lang Syne*, and is buried in a mausoleum in St.Michael's churchyard. His home in Burns Street (once Mill Street) is a museum containing some of his manuscripts and other Burns memorabilia can also be found in the Town Museum, the Globe Inn and the Hole in the Wa' Tavern.

GRETNA *The blacksmith's shop where, until 1940, many runaways were married.*

LIKE ITS SOUTH of Scotland neighbours, Dumfriesshire is a county people tend to rush through on their way somewhere else – to the Western Isles or Highlands. It's a cross-over county as you come from Carlisle to go to Edinburgh or Glasgow, en route to or from England.

TOWNS AND VILLAGES

Dumfriesshire hasn't always been somewhere to pass through. For one thing, it used to be popular with eloping English couples. An 18th-century English law prevented clandestine marriages from taking place in England – but runaway lovers got over the problem by crossing over into Scotland at Dumfriesshire and marrying at Gretna Green. The first place they came to was the blacksmith's shop where they could marry by declaration. The law was changed in 1940 to prevent the smith from performing the ceremony – you'd have thought they'd have had better things to do with a war on – but memories of those days live on: the shop has been transformed into a museum, with souvenirs of those romantic times.

Dumfriesshire has another romantic connection: the poet Robert Burns lived in Dumfries, the county town, from 1791 until his death in 1796, writing some of his most famous songs here, including *Auld Lang Syne*. Dumfries is a pleasant borderland town with no fewer than five bridges crossing the River Nith, the oldest of which dates back to 1426.

The Nith is one of three main rivers which flow south through

Dumfriesshire to the Solway Firth. Dumfriesshire is full of fine scenery, ranging from the heady heights of the Lowther Hills to the flatlands beside the Solway Firth, a haven for migrating birds escaping the Arctic winter. In the north, a high winding road leads up the Mennock Pass to Wanlockhead, at 1,380 feet Scotland's highest village, and the appropriately named Leadhills. Lead, gold and silver were once found in the surrounding Lowther Hills. To the east, near Moffat, the Devil's Beef Tub is a sheer-sided hollow in the hills which was once used for hiding stolen cattle. On Moffat Water is one of Scotland's highest waterfalls, the Grey Mare's Tail. As one would expect, fishing is important in these parts: the rivers are well stocked with salmon and trout and, in Castle Loch, between Dumfries and Lockerbie, there are good catches of large pike and bream.

Dumfriesshire's traditional industries like textiles and tanning have declined, but the whisky distilling and agriculture live on. The Annandale town of Moffat thrives as a centre for sheep farming – the industry's importance to the area symbolized by the statue of a ram in the wide High Street. Moffat's popularity with tourists grew from a 17th-century discovery that the water from the local wells had curative qualities. Among the many who came to take the waters was Robert Burns, who composed the drinking song *O Willie brew'd a peck o' Maut* there.

LOCAL HISTORY

Historians dispute just how far the Romans penetrated beyond Hadrian's Wall into Dumfriesshire. But a little way north of the village of the rhythmically-named Ecclefechan there are two substantial reminders of Roman occupation – the hill forts at Birrens and Brunswark, which is thought to have been used as a training ground for siege warfare. Ecclefechan is Celtic: the name comes from the church (eaglais) of St Fechan, who was a 6th-century Celtic missionary, and in the church at Ruthwell you'll come across a runic cross bearing the oldest surviving fragment of written English, dating back to around 680AD.

To the north of Dumfries the 13th-century Caerlaverock Castle, sturdy and romantic, has featured on many a television commercial. It's most people's idea of a medieval castle – triangular, with round towers and a double moat. Just outside Thornhill is Drumlanrig Castle, not a castle at all but the stately home of the Duke of Buccleuch and Queensberry which was altered in the 17th century by Sir William Bruce. It has splendid wood panelling, historic portraits and a chandelier given by Charles II to the Duke of Monmouth on his marriage to the Countess of Buccleuch.

COUNTY FACTS

Origin of name: Gaelic meaning the fort (Dun) of the copse or little wood (phreas).

Name first recorded: 1183.

County Town:

DUMFRIES This bustling textile town – nicknamed "Queen of the South" as its football club glorifies – specializes in stockings, tights and knitwear. Rabbie Burns' mausoleum is in the town.

Other Towns:

ANNAN Very pleasant small Victorian red-stone town stands on the River Annan, popular with anglers. Being on the border it was often the point of attack fron the auld enemy.

ECCLEFECHAN Small neat village, with a brilliant name and the birthplace of Thomas Carlyle.

GRETNA At Gretna Hall, built in 1710, over 1,000 runaway marriages were performed between 1825 and 1855 as well as at the well-known smithy in Gretna Green, a little to the north of Gretna.

LOCKERBIE Roman links to this quiet sheep market town forever unfortunately linked with the Pan Am 747 bombing disaster of 1988.

MOFFAT A pretty market town of simple brick cottages and grand Georgian mansions. James Boswell, biographer of Dr Johnson, came to 'wash off the scurvy spots' in Moffat's sulphur springs.

LANGHOLM A stone-built mill town, was once famous for textiles, still into wool manufacturing. Not the place to be on Halloween as this could be classed as the centre of the county's witch country.

◆ Brydekirk ◆ Cummertrees ◆ Dornock ◆ Eastriggs ◆ Hightae ◆ Kirkconnel ◆ Locharbriggs ◆ Lochmaben ◆ Moniaive ◆ Sanquhar ◆Thornhill

County rivers: Nith, Annan, Esk.

Highest point: White Coomb at 2,695 feet.

Dumfriesshire's local government:
The whole of the County of Dumfriesshire is governed by the Dumfries and Galloway unitary council.

COUNTY CALENDAR

◆ Mid-June: Guid Nychburris. Re-enactment of granting of the Royal Burgh charter in Dumfries.

◆ Last Friday in July: Langholm Common Riding and Fair. The Langholm Riding, first held in 1816, begins at 5am with a procession led by a flute band The festivities, which include horse racing, wrestling and highland dancing, continue throughout the day.

◆ Mid-July: Moffat Gala Week – crowning of the queen and other events, Moffat.

◆ August: Dumfries and Lockerbie Agricultural Show, Dumfries.

◆ Mid-August: Sanquhar Riding of the Marches, traditional riding and other events, Sanquhar.

◆ Mid-August: Canonbie Agricultural Show, Canonbie (centenary event in 1996).

◆ End of August: Moffat Agricultural Show.

◆ End of September: Eskdale Agricultural Show, Castleholm, Langholm.

DUNBARTONSHIRE

LENNOX

LOCH LOMOND *This inland loch is 24 miles long and varies between ¾ to 5 miles wide. Take a boat cruise from Luss or Balloch.*

THE COUNTY LANDSCAPE

◆ The southern half of Dunbartonshire is blighted by the factories, ports and submarine bases around the Holy Loch and the Gareloch, and the other, commercial undertakings that have sprawled out of Glasgow, but the countryside improves immensely and becomes far more visible further north. This journey north can be made in two fashions, both excellent, either on foot up the West Highland Way, or by train on the West Highland Line, both of which plough up this way en route for the Highlands.

◆ Glen Douglas, which cuts through the northern half of the county between Loch Lomond and Loch Long, is well worth exploring, offering good walks and a great amount of birdlife in the late Spring. The countryside has not yet opened out but the views across the loch are soon superb.

◆ Loch Lomond and all the western shores and southern shores plus many of the 30 islands lie within the county boundary. It has to be seen at least once from the water. The trek to the summit of Ben Lomond is also worth taking, though this lies in the neighbouring county of Argyllshire; the views are superb.

THE WATERS OF Loch Lomond (shared with Stirlingshire), famed for its bonnie banks and braes, sparkle here as the most precious gem in scenic Scotland. And yet to the south lies one of the most industrialized regions of Britain: the county name is synonymous with shipbuilding on the Clyde, and it plays host to many trans-global corporations including the largest sewing-machine works in the world. And the very first Scottish new town of Cumbernauld presented a show-case of modern architectural town planning to the world.

TOWNS AND VILLAGES

Dunbartonshire has two distinct detached parts jutting up towards the Highlands from the northern suburbs of Glasgow, sandwiched between Loch Lomond and Loch Long. It follows from this that Dunbartonshire is not over-endowed with towns or even villages, but the ones there are provide a good amount of interest – and there is always Glasgow, for those who need a night on the town, though Glasgow lies in the county of Lanarkshire.

*Dun*bartonshire is the county but for some unexplained reason, *Dum*barton is the town. It is a small place on the Clyde, looking across the river to the shores of Renfrewshire. This little town has ancient roots, having been founded in the 5th century AD as one of the western fortresses on the Roman Antonine Wall, but after the World War II the planners got to work and transformed this once pleasant riverside town into a celebration of concrete.

Leave hurriedly, but do not go too far, for Dumbarton Castle is well worth a look, occupying an ancient site on the summit of two extinct volcanoes. This is, or rather was, the site of the original 5th-century Roman fort and these hilltops have been garrisoned, in one form or another, ever since. At the base of the castle rock lies the Governor's House, dating from the middle 1700s and from there two flights of steps, both extremely steep, lead up to the twin peaks which support the Castle. The views over the Clyde Valley from the top are quite superb. Those who like castles should also visit Knockderry, a fine fortress on the east side of Loch Long, which stands on the foundations of a much older fortress called Knock Dunder, which is featured in Sir Walter Scott's *Heart of Midlothian.*

Helensburgh, a little further to the north, is the last gasp of suburbia before the open country begins and is still a rather pleasant town, laid out in regular squares in the best Georgian fashion. It was built in the 18th century as an overspill town for Glasgow and a seaside resort. Apart from those two places the urban charms of Dunbartonshire rest in the little villages along the edges of Loch Lomond, of which Balloch at the south end is the place to visit if you want to try a cruise on the loch. The small village of Luss is also extremely picturesque, though jammed with tourists for most of the summer being where the Scottish TV soap *High Road* is filmed.

LOCAL HISTORY

The history of Dunbartonshire begins with the Roman legions, who came up this way to cow the Picts and tried to do so by building the Antonine Wall, from the Firth of Forth to the Firth of Clyde, with the twin volcanic peaks which now support Dumbarton Castle providing a useful, commanding site for a Roman fort. Bearsden has some of the best-preserved portions of this wall to its north. Dumbarton was the capital of the Kingdom of Strathclyde until that was absorbed into the Kingdom of Scotland in the 11th century. Dumbarton remained a Royal castle, though after the Scots Kings departed for England in the 17th century, it became a fortress guarding the western approaches to Glasgow. Back in the 16th century, the infant Mary, Queen of Scots, sailed from Dumbarton Castle for her marriage to the Dauphin of France in 1548. In 1568, Mary was trying to get back to Dumbarton after her defeat at the Battle of Langside, when she was captured and imprisoned by her lords.

COUNTY FACTS

Origin of name: From the Gaelic Dun Breatton, meaning "the fort of the Strathclyde Britons".

Name first recorded: 1300.

County Town:

DUMBARTON The 240-foot basalt rock which dominates the town has a longer history as a stronghold than any other place in Britain.

Other Towns:

CARDROSS Robert the Bruce died here in 1329 in a castle now vanished. It was visited by poets Wordsworth and Coleridge.

CLYDEBANK From the docks and factories here emerged liners such as *Queen Mary* and *QE2* to name just two! World War II bomb damage was severe.

CUMBERNAULD Overseas visitors have come here to admire this modern integrated new town.

HELENSBURGH On the Clyde near its junction with the Gare Loch, it has been called "the Garden City of the Firth of Clyde". Much Clyde yachting goes on here.

◆ Alexandria ◆ Croy ◆ Garelochhead ◆ Dalmuir ◆ Duntocher ◆ Hardgate ◆ Jamestown ◆ Kirkintilloch ◆ Old Kilpatrick ◆ Rhu ◆ Silverton ◆ Yoker

County Rivers: Clyde, Leven.

Highest point: Ben Vorlich at 3,092 feet.

Dunbartonshire's local government: The northern finger of the county along with the west bank of Loch Lomond and Helensburgh come under the unitary Argyll and Bute council. The main middle section of the county around Dumbarton, Alexandria and Clydebank is administered by West Dunbartonshire unitary council. The East Dunbartonshire unitary council services the rest, chiefly Bearsden, along with the eastern section of Dunbartonshire detached around Kirkintilloch. The Dunbartonshire town of Cumbernauld is governed by North Lanarkshire unitary authority. And Yoker and district form the far northwest limits of the City of Glasgow unitary council.

FAMOUS NAMES

◆ Harry Lauder, the Scots music hall artist is the name that will always be connected with Loch Lomond.

◆ David Byrne, star of the seminal rock band Talking Heads, was born in Dumbarton.

◆ Helensburgh was the birthplace of John Logie Baird, the man who invented television and Art Nouveau designer John Rennie Mackintosh. Hill House in Upper Colquhoun St Helensburg, is a fine example of Rennie Mackintosh's style.

◆ Film and rock stars like Cher, Prince, Clint Eastwood and Russell Grant have stayed at Cameron House Hotel on Loch Lomond.

COUNTY CALENDAR

◆ February: West of Scotland Antiques Fair, Balloch, on Loch Lomond.

◆ July: Balloch Highland Games, Balloch.

◆ July: Luss Highland Games, Luss.

◆ September. Loch Lomond World Invitational Golf Championship, Loch Lomond Golf Club.

EAST LOTHIAN

HADDINGTONSHIRE

THE COUNTY LANDSCAPE

◆ East Lothian's scenery varies from the placid to the dramatic, with the intervening pleasures of the Lammermuir Hills, which divide East Lothian from Berwickshire, the next county to the south. The drama is provided by volcanic outcrops like Berwick Law, which juts up sharply for 613 feet from the surrounding countryside and offers fine views along the coast, and to offshore islands like the Bass Rock, two hills striking enough even without their historical associations.

◆ The coastline is also dramatic, a mixture of cliffs and rocky bays, well supplied with offshore rocks and small islands like Fidra which is said to have given Robert Louis Stevenson the shape for his *Treasure Island*.

◆ The coast and the Lammermuir Hills provide East Lothian with much of its coast and countryside character, and are the places to explore, preferably on foot. The Lammermuirs are seamed with footpaths and the coast can be followed almost all the way close to the shore, looking out to the grey North Sea and the seabird colonies on the offshore islands.

COUNTY CALENDAR

◆ July: Agricultural Show at Haddington.

◆ July: Dunbar's hosts Scotland's premier Bathing Beauty Competition.

◆ August: Veteran Car Rally at Dunbar.

◆ August: East Lothian Highland Games, Prestonpans.

TO HOLIDAY MAKERS escaping the hurly-burly of urban life especially around nearby Edinburgh, East Lothian means an annual holiday in the driest and sunniest part of Scotland with some of the best-kept stretches of beach and the most wonderful walks over the rolling Lammermuir Hills. Though largely a rest and recreation area for the citizens of Edinburgh, the county has much more to offer those who are prepared to delve deeper.

TOWNS AND VILLAGES

East Lothian started life as Haddingtonshire, and Haddington, a pretty place set under the northern slopes of the Lammermuir Hills, therefore reveals much about this county. The county town is an architectural treasure house with no fewer than 284 listed buildings, all blending into a pleasing whole. Most of them are Georgian and as Nash is to Bath so Adams is to Haddington for he was responsible for so much of the delightful architecture in the spacious central street and elsewhere in the town. The tiny town today is a walking centre and has its own 'Town Walk' which is an annotated amble round the historic heart highlighting the principal townscape features. John Knox, the great Reformer, was born here and there is a statue at the Knox Memorial Institute.

North Berwick is a tight, snug little town, overlooked on the landward side by the height of the hill called Berwick Law – a 'law' being a hill in this part of Scotland – and out to sea by another imposing mound, the Bass Rock, which has served as a hermitage, a garrison and a prison before becoming a bird sanctuary, the role

HADDINGTON *Nungate Bridge is a 16th-century angular bridge spanning the Tyne.*

it fills today. Berwick used to be called 'The Biarritz of the North' and was indeed a holiday home for Kings, like Charles I, who came here in the 1640s and King Robert II of Scotland who gave the town its first charter in 1373. One sight not to miss in North Berwick is the Auld Kirk, by the harbour. Though a lot of it has gone this is a place of legend, the spot where the Earl of Bothwell summoned the Scottish witches and urged them to conjure up gales to sink the ships bringing James VI back to Scotland from Denmark. It didn't work, but it's a good story.

North Berwick and Dunbar, small and pretty though they are, virtually exhaust East Lothian's stock of towns with the excellent exception of the county town of Haddington already noted. Otherwise, the attention must now turn to the villages, and those worth a close look include Aberlady, five miles north of Haddington, which is full of well restored 17th to 19th century cottages and places like Gullane, on the north coast, most famous for Muirfield, that classic, championship golf course and a score more besides, all meccas for keen, and preferably well heeled, golfers who flock here from all over the world, most of them staying at the famous Greywalls Hotel, which looks out onto the links and has hosted all the golfing greats, Arnold Palmer, Greg Norman, Nick Faldo and the rest.

LOCAL HISTORY

Those who are not interested in golf can tour around the castles, of which there are a good number, splendid ruined piles for the most part, like Tantallion and Dirleton Castles, near North Berwick, or Hailes Castle near Haddington, or Gosford near Aberlady, home of the Earl of Wemyss which is open to visitors in the summer.

Battlefields provide most of the history of East Lothian. Pinkie Field saw yet another 16th-century defeat for the Scots, a disaster to rival Flodden, while Bonnie Prince Charlie saw one of his few successes when the Highlanders defeated the Redcoats at Prestonpans. Cromwell's victory over the Scots at Dunbar in 1650 is another famous field and after that it becomes important to find some more peaceful memories. King Alexander II of Scotland was born in Haddington as was the reformer Samuel Smiles in 1812, and Jane Walsh, who married the historian Thomas Carlyle.

Finally, at East Linton, six miles east of Haddington, there are more splendid 18th-century houses clustered neatly round this olde-worlde-village square. Take a note of the town clock which the locals still call 'Jessie', after a local lass who met her boyfriend here, years before the clock was put up ... and that was in 1880. They have long memories in East Lothian.

COUNTY FACTS

Origin of name: Possibly named after Loth, the grandfather of St Mungo. It was also known as Haddingtonshire before returning to its ancient Lothian roots.

Name first recorded: 970.

County Town:

HADDINGTON Boasts a fine 14th-century cruciform church with a central tower (now in ruins) and many Georgian houses.

Other Towns:

DUNBAR Was the site of a famous battle in 1650 between Oliver Cromwell and the Covenanters and remains an historic little town, quite pretty, with a good harbour and views out to the rock and island strewn entrance to the Firth of Forth. It is rather more famous, at least in America, as the birthplace of John Muir, the Father of Conservation, who helped to set up the US National Parks.

NORTH BERWICK Once a Royal Burgh, has a museum with medieval relics from the former 12th-century Cistercian monastery and Scottish pottery.

PRESTONPANS Site of one of Bonnie Prince Charlie's victories over the Redcoats and the 17th-century Hamilton House (rebuilt in 1937). Originally called Saltprestoun, the name refers to salt pans near a village called Preston ('Priest's village') laid out by 13th-century monks.

◆ Belhaven ◆ Cockenzie ◆ East Linton ◆ Elphinstone ◆ Longniddry ◆ Macmerry ◆ Ormiston ◆ Port Seton ◆ Tranent ◆ West Barns ◆ Wester Pencaitland

County rivers: Tyne, Coalstone, Whitewater, Fastna, Peffer.

Highest point: in the Lammermuir Hills at 1,733 feet.

East Lothian's local government: The County of East Lothian is almost coterminous with its administrative mirror, East Lothian unitary council. A tiny part between Monynut Edge and Spartleton Edge is taken care of by the Scottish Borders council.

FAMOUS NAMES

◆ Golf is one reason for heading to East Lothian these days. Jack Nicklaus paid the famous links at Muirfield the highest compliment by naming his own international championship course in Ohio, 'Muirfield Village'. The Scottish course has over 160 bunkers. Many famous golfing names and photographs can be found in the Visitors' Book and on the walls of Greywalls Hotel at Gullane.

◆ Haddington was the birthplace of John Knox, the 16th-century preacher and enemy of Mary, Queen of Scots.

◆ Walk the coast of East Lothian and remember that Robert Louis Stevenson set several scenes from *Catriona* here.

◆ At East Linton, take a look at the stone at the east end of the village commemorating the life and work of John Rennie, a famous engineer, who built three of the bridges over the Thames and was born here in 1761 in Phantassien manor house.

FIFE

FORTH RAILWAY BRIDGE *This 150-foot-high rail bridge links Fife with West Lothian.*

THE COUNTY LANDSCAPE

◆ The countryside of Fife is green farming country for the most part, with plenty of beaches and rocky headlands round the coast and along the estuaries of the Forth and Tay. There are good beaches at Elie and Earlsferry and another long sandy strand at St Andrews, as well as the rocks supporting the abbey and the castle.

◆ The north coast, along the Tay, is a region of green hills and woodlands, notably the Tentsmuir Forest near the RAF station at Leuchars. The valley of the river Eden in the south, is a pleasant place to wander when the North wind is blowing (as it usually is) while the landscape around Kirkcaldy has been blighted by industry, though it may soon recover as industry declines.

◆ The countryside is gentle and appealing rather than spectacular; it may not compare with the northern and western counties in terms of mountainous grandeur, but the great appeal of Fife lies in its quiet charm and the old historic towns, unless of course, you play golf.

FAMOUS NAMES

◆ Robert the Bruce's tomb is in Dunfermline Abbey.

◆ Sir Walter Scott used Ravenscraig Castle for a story in his *Lay of the Last Minstrel*.

◆ St Andrew is Scotland's patron saint so his abbey should be visited. The beach was a setting for the runners (Ben Cross, Ian Charleson) in the 1981 film *Chariots of Fire*.

COUNTY CALENDAR

◆ April: The Links Fair in Kirkcaldy, a funfair and market, dates back to 1304.

◆ April: Kate Kennedy Pageant. The annual student 'rag' at St Andrews, in support of local charities, when students parade through the town dressed as characters from the history of the university, including Kate herself, who was niece to one of the 14th-century founders of the university.

◆ Late June: Festival of St Catherine at Newburgh.

◆ July: Burntisland Highland Games. The second oldest Highland Games in the world, first held here in 1652.

◆ July: St Andrews Highland Games.

◆ August: Lammas Fair, St Andrews. The oldest surviving medieval fair in Scotland, where the events are announced to the crowds by the Town Crier.

◆ Mid-September: Scotland's largest International Airshow, RAF Leuchars.

◆ October: Alfred Dunhill Cup, St Andrews. The most prestigious team golf tournament.

UNLIKE MANY OF the other counties of Scotland, Fife is much more than a mere county. Though it is not very large and not well favoured by the weather, Fife is a Kingdom of its own and a very, very charming one. Fife does not intend to let any visitor forget that fact, even if the Kingdom referred to existed in the 4th century AD, in the time of the Picts. Fife remains much as it always has been, green, tranquil, historically interesting, full of sights to see and things to do ... especially golf.

TOWNS AND VILLAGES

Golf is said to have had its origins at St Andrews, that tiny university town on the eastern tip of Fife, and the Royal and Ancient Golf Club of St Andrews certainly occupies a leading position in the golf world, with the links of St Andrews, especially the Old Course, pulling in golfers from all over the world, all paying homage to the spot where their sport began – even if that claim is widely disputed, not least by the Dutch, who declare that golf has its origins in the Low Countries.

St Andrews does have many other claims to fame. It is the seat of Scotland's oldest university, founded in the 14th century and contains a magnificent ruined abbey, once the shrine of Scotland's patron saint. Of more recent date is the fame that came to the town when the beach was used for the opening shots in the Oscar winning movie, *Chariots of Fire*.

Equally historic, but at the other end of the county, is the town of Dunfermline, once the seat of the Scottish monarchy, where the old abbey church contains the tomb of Robert the Bruce and the town basks in the benefits conveyed upon it at the end of the last century by a native son who became a millionaire, Andrew Carnegie. Dunfermline remained Scotland's capital until 1603, and still has the air of a Royal town.

The capital of Fife, Cupar, is another medieval town, set astride the river Eden, a little jewel in the emerald setting of the smooth, surrounding hills. The first Scottish Parliament was held in Cupar in 1276, called by King Alexander III. The town centre, around the Mercat Cross, is well worth a wander, but the main sight in the town today is the Hill of Tarvit, actually a country house with splendid gardens, two miles south of the town centre. A little to the east of that lies the village of Ceres, which has a collection of attractive 17th-century houses set around a green.

Kirkcaldy is more modern and best known for its amazingly long esplanade, more than four miles in length, a promenade built on top of the sea defences. The town is mainly a tourist resort, popular with summer visitors, rather bleak in winter. The architecturally gifted Adams brothers, Robert and John, who designed many of Scotland's great castles-cum-stately homes were born here and it is said that John Buchan used the steps at Ravenscraig Castle as inspiration for *The 39 Steps*.

There are more pretty places around the southeastern tip of Fife, called the East Neuk, including the simple but charming fishing ports of Crail, Anstruther, Elie, Earlsferry, Pittenweem and St Monance.

LOCAL HISTORY

The history of Fife dates back some 1,600 years to the time when this small peninsula was occupied by the Picts. All traces of the Picts have gone but later monarchs have left many memorials. Dunfermline was established as Scotland's capital by Malcolm Canmore in the 11th century, and his wife Margaret, sister of the Saxon exile, Edgar Atheling, built the first priory here. Her son David I founded the abbey where The Bruce was buried in 1329.

Pittencrieff House in Dunfermline used to belong to the local lairds, who forbade the young Andrew Carnegie to play there. Years later, Carnegie now a multi-millionaire, came home from America, bought the estate and turned it into a public park – where anyone could play. Kinghorn, further east, is another place of legend for Alexander III died here in 1286, when his horse ran off the top of the cliffs.

Fife may be best known for golf but the oldest tennis court in Britain can still be seen in the 14th-century stronghold of Falkland Palace, having been installed in 1539 for the entertainment of King James V.

COUNTY FACTS

Origin of name: Named from Fith, and signifying his territory. No one knows who or what Fith was.

Name first recorded: 590.

County Town: CUPAR The Eden river is close by this Royal Burgh with a Parish church tower dating from 1415 but the spire is two centuries later!

Other Towns:

ANSTRUTHER Shortened version of the longest name for a Scottish burgh: Kilrenny, Anstruther Easter and Anstruther Wester. Until 1940 the capital of Scottish herring fishing.

AUCHTERMUCHTY Made famous by ex-*Sunday Express* editor Sir John Junor, father of broadcaster Penny Junor. Royal Burgh noted for its linen, bleach, distilleries and sawmills. Centre of fertile farming area known as Howe of Fife.

CULROSS A remarkably intact medieval town with a Cistercian Abbey dating from 1217 and a palace with exquisite painted ceilings. Under one of those weird quirks of real county history, Culross is actually a part of Perthshire detached.

DUNFERMLINE The Pittencrieff Glen, with its beautiful trees and gardens, given to the town by public benefactor Andrew Carnegie, is well worth a visit

FREUCHIE The Coventry of Scotland because people were banished or sent to Freuchie "Awa tae Freuchie and eat mice". Now a bastion of Scottish club cricket.

LEVEN Miles of golden sand and a central position for touring the rest of Fife attract summer visitors to the caravans, guest houses and shops. There is a curious shell house on the promenade.

KINCARDINE A small port on the estuary of the river Forth spanned here by the Kincardine Bridge – the last bridge before the estuary widens. Like Culross, the town is geographically part of Perthshire detached.

KIRKCALDY Well known for the manufacturing of linoleum and along the main street giving it the name of 'Lang Taun'. Adam Smith author of *Wealth of Nations* was born here. Home to Raith Rovers FC.

ROSYTH Royal Naval Dockyards a major military port buffeted by the winds of change. Old castle attacked by Oliver Cromwell.

ST ANDREWS This is full of old tales, one being that the students in medieval times were obliged to wear red cloaks, as they still do, so that the university proctors could spot them more easily in the brothels. When walking about St Andrews note the stones in the pavement by the castle, marking the spot where John Knox's friend and supporter, George Wishart, was burned at the stake in 1545.

◆ Auchterderran ◆ Ballingry ◆ Buckhaven ◆ Burntisland ◆ Cardenden ◆ Cowdenbeath ◆ Glenrothes ◆ Inverkeithing ◆ Kelty ◆ Kennoway ◆ Leslie ◆ Lochgelly ◆ Methil ◆ Newport-on-Tay ◆ Tayport

County rivers: Eden, Leven, Den.

Highest point: West Lomond at 1,712 feet.

Fife's local government: The County and kingdom of Fife is governed by a Fife unitary council.

INVERNESS-SHIRE

THE COUNTY LANDSCAPE

◆ Inverness-shire forms a wide belt across the Highlands, spanning the North country in a great sea-to-sea swath, from Inverness on the Moray Firth, all the way across to the Sound of Sleat that divides the mainland from the Isle of Skye.

◆ The landscape is pure Highland. Ben Nevis, the highest mountain in Great Britain, bulks up above Fort William. Here are mountain ranges like the Monadhliath Mountains and part of the Cairngorms. Here is Loch Ness and Loch Lochy and great sea lochs like Loch Linnhe and Loch Morar and Loch Hourn. Here are some of the famous glens, not just the Great Glen itself, or Glen Albyn as it used to be called, but Glen Spean and Glen Strathfarrar and Glen Affric each with its loch and rushing trout stream.

◆ The West Highland Way comes in from Rannoch moor and finishes at the foot of Ben Nevis, and there is good walking almost everywhere and at almost any time, outside the stalking and shooting season in the autumn and the more bitter months of winter. Climbing Ben Nevis by the footpath route will take between five and six hours and requires good weather.

◆ One man-made sight worthy of attention is Thomas Telford's Caledonian Canal built in the early 1800s to link the Atlantic with the North Sea. It took 24 years to complete, runs for 22 miles, linking the lochs in the Great Glen and has 24 locks, including the flight of eight locks at Corpach which lifts vessels from sea level to a height of 64 feet.

WILD AND STERN, Inverness-shire with Ben Nevis, Loch Ness and the Isle of Skye lying within its borders you just know you're in Real Scotland. Believe it or not it also takes in all the outer Hebridean Islands (except Lewis) but includes St Kilda some 40 miles even further out to sea and 120 miles from the county town. It's the largest county in Scotland.

TOWNS AND VILLAGES

Though the scenery is the main attraction anywhere in the Highlands, Inverness, the 'Capital of the Highlands', is the star town. With a population of 42,000, it stands on the River Ness and at the head of the Great Glen, that giant rift that runs across the land, southwest to northeast, from the Atlantic to the North Sea. Inverness is dominated by its castle, largely 19th century, but on an older site and still impressive. The town goes back a further 1,000 years, to the time of St Columba, who converted the local Picts to Christianity in the 6th century. Inverness then became a successful trading port. The castle went up in the 10th century and the site is associated with both Robert the Bruce, who threw out the English garrison, and Mary, Queen of Scots, who hanged the Governor for refusing her admittance. The rest of Inverness is an old Highland burgh, a place of narrow streets and squares, with good strolls along the banks of the River Ness and the Caledonian Canal. The town was ravaged by British troops after the Battle of Culloden, on the outskirts of the town, in April, 1746.

The next major town of Inverness-shire is Fort William, at the southern end of the Great Glen. Built in the early 18th century and named after William of Orange, the present town stands on the site of an old castle, Inverlochy, and was built to subdue the Highland clans, especially the Camerons, who had their lands in these parts. The West Highland Museum in Fort William is a splendid place full of fascinating memorabilia of the old Highland way of life, but otherwise the town is modern, a tourist and railway centre, a base for the ascent of Ben Nevis.

BEN NEVIS *The highest mountain in the British Isles dominates Fort William below.*

South of the Great Glen, at the foot of the Monadhliath

Mountains lies the little town of Kingussie, a place all lovers of the Highlands should visit. The setting is beautiful, with mountains on every side, and the town contains the Highland Folk Museum, which shows every facet of the Highland way of life, from the furnishings of a Highland chief to the inside of a crofter's cottage.

Scattered down the Great Glen are other smaller towns, each a former garrison for the Redcoat soldiers, Fort Augustus at the southern end of Loch Ness, and Spean Bridge, where the Commando recruits in the Second World War used to get off the train and start their seven mile march to Achnacarry. This was the training ground for the Second World War Commandos, and the splendid Commando Memorial at Spean Bridge records their exploits.

Further west, on the coast opposite Skye, is the little rail town and port of Mallaig, the departure point for Skye and one of the termini for the West Highland Line.

LOCAL HISTORY

No one really knows if there is a Monster in Loch Ness, but the legend of the Monster goes back at least 1,400 years, to the day in AD 589 when St Columba was being rowed up the loch to what is now Inverness. He was half-way up the loch when the Monster appeared and attacked his boat. Sightings continued down the centuries and flourished in the 1920s and 1930s when hardly a summer went by without someone spotting the Monster. There were 33 sightings in 1933 alone, including one of the Monster on land, crossing the road near Dores. This was very unusual, for the Monster is most usually seen in the waters near Castle Urquhart. As to whether there is a Monster in the lake, who can say? The loch is 24 miles long and up to 800 feet deep, so anything is possible though various scientific expeditions in recent years have failed to come up with any firm evidence for the existence of a Monster in the loch. The village of Ivermoriston on Loch Ness is the place where Dr Samuel Johnson and Boswell spent a couple of days on their *Journey to the Western Isles*.

This is the country of the Catholic, Jacobite clans, the Macdonalds, the Camerons, the Frazers, who supported the Old and Young Pretenders and met their end so gallantly on Culloden Moor, a few miles east of Inverness. The Glenfinnan Monument, beside the railway line on the route to Mallaig and Arisaig, marks the spot where Bonnie Prince Charlie raised his standard in 1745. The monument was erected in 1815 and the figure on top is of a clansman, not the gallant Prince. The battlefield of Culloden is much as it was in 1746 and what happened there is told in detail in the Battlefield Centre.

COUNTY FACTS

Origin of name: From the gaelic-Brittonic meaning the mouth of the Ness.

Name first recorded: c.1300.

County Town: INVERNESS Bustling town overlooked by sandstone castle.

Other Towns:

AVIEMORE The centre of the British Skiing.

BEAULY Has a 13th century Valliscaulian monastery, and is a centre for Highland crystal.

BROADFORD A tourist resort on Skye dominated by Beinn Dearg Mhor.

DUNVEGAN The Castle here on Skye – home to the Chiefs of Clan Macleod since 1200 – was once only accessible from the sea.

FORT WILLIAM A very fine touring centre.

KINGUSSIE Visit the Am Fasgadh (Gaelic for shelter) which has a collection of fine old Highland artefacts.

MALLAIG Ferry-port and gateway to the Isles though the Toll Bridge may change that.

NEWTONMORE Just one of the many centres of the Aviemore ski areas offering ski schools, and après ski.

PORTREE On the Isle of Skye is a pleasant sheltering harbour for steamers and fishing boats.

◆ Ardersier ◆ Castlebay ◆ Fort Augustus

County rivers: Classic trout and salmon fishing rivers too numerous to list here but including Endrick, Feshie, Garry, Ness, Nethy, Spey.

Highest point: Ben Nevis at 4,406 feet.

Inverness-shire's local government: The County of Inverness-shire has Highland unitary council to purvey its local government north and south. The County's Outer Hebrides islands of Harris, Uist, and Barra come under the Western Isles unitary council. Grantown-on-Spey and Cromdale are Inverness-shire detached in Morayshire and governed by Highland unitary council.

FAMOUS NAMES.

◆ Achnacarry is famous in soldiering circles all over the world, as the home of the British Commandos.

◆ Mel Gibson stayed at the Inverlochy Hotel at Fort William while filming scenes from *Braveheart*.

◆ Loch Ness is famous for Nessie, the elusive Monster who may be seen, if at all, near Castle Urquhart. *Cheers* star Ted Danson was on location here in action-hero mode trying to do just that for the 1996 *Loch Ness* movie.

◆ *Whisky Galore!* (1949), one of Ealing Studios best comedies, was filmed entirely on Barra.

COUNTY CALENDAR

◆ February: The annual slalom and giant slalom ski race is on the Nevis Range Ski Area, Fort William.

◆ April: Culloden Commemorative Service with the Laying of wreaths at Culloden battlefield.

◆ July: Inverness Tattoo with Pipes and Drums, with the bands of the Highland regiments, and Highland and Country dancing.

◆ July: Arisaig Highland Games, Arisaig.

KINCARDINESHIRE

MEARNS

KINCARDINE *Dunnotar Castle, captured from the English by William Wallace in 1296.*

THE COUNTY LANDSCAPE

◆ Kincardineshire is basically a coastal county, low-lying rather than mountainous, although there's the odd hill towards the west. Kincardineshire is roughly half-way up the east coast of Scotland. It is bordered in the west by the Grampian mountains which, although little more than foothills here, still offer many peaks in excess of 1,500 feet.

◆ In the central part of the county is the Howe of Mearns, part of the great valley of Strathmore which stretches down into Angus. The name is derived from two Gaelic words, magh and innis, meaning 'plain-of-the-islands', which described the Howe when it was a desolate moorland dotted by ridges. Now it is an area of rich farmland.

◆ The county's northern border is marked by the river Dee – royal Deeside – and the North Sea coast alternates between sweeping bays with sandy dunes and precipitous cliffs.

ALMOST ANYWHERE ALONG the coast of Kincardineshire you can indulge yourself in a little celebrity spotting (well, even I'm not averse to a spot of that!): but these celebs include bottlenose dolphins leaping through the air and, high on cliffs soaring up to 400 feet above the sea, puffins galore and dozens of colonies of kittiwakes, auks and Scotland's only mainland gannet colony. Travel inland to the Grampians and you see golden eagles soaring on the thermals and red deer thrashing through the undergrowth.

TOWNS AND VILLAGES

Dotted throughout the county are some of Scotland's finest castles, towns and villages rich in character and history. Fishing and farming are the traditional industries. Spinning flourished here in the 19th century but has since declined. The weather is what is euphemistically termed 'bracing'. East winds prevail, frequently bringing the damp sea mist known locally as a 'haar.'

Stonehaven, the county town, almost half-way along the Kincardineshire coast is in the line of those winds. It is a clean, breezy little place which has built its reputation primarily as a herring port. Fishing is still important, but tourism is growing. Like Aberdeen to the north and Montrose to the south, it is situated on a stretch of beach between two rivers so, on warm summer days, it attracts its share of visitors. To the south of the town lie the ruins of one of Scotland's largest medieval castles, Dunnottar, dramatically perched on a rock near Stonehaven and joined to the mainland by a path. William Wallace, recently portrayed in the film *Braveheart* by Mel Gibson, captured the castle from the English in 1296. In its long and stormy history, it was subsequently besieged in turn by the armies of Balliol, Bruce, Montrose and Cromwell. From Stonehaven, a road cuts northwards through the heather-covered slopes of the Grampian foothills to Banchory, a pretty village beside the Dee. Lavender is grown here and you can visit the factory where it is distilled into Dee Lavender Water, a product which is greatly valued in the perfume business. Another attraction in Banchory is watching salmon going up the Dee to spawn. Just outside the village, on the Brig o' Feugh, an observation platform has been built from which, in spring, you can watch the fish leaping up the rapids. Edzell is another little inland resort which can be enjoyed for its fishing; you'll find both sea trout and brown trout here in the North Esk, as the river tumbles down off the Grampians and into the North Sea near St Cyrus.

LOCAL HISTORY

Prehistoric man built stone circles in the once-desolate Howe of Mearns, but Kincardineshire is best remembered for its splendid castles of later periods. Some are little more than ruins, recalling turbulent centuries of Scottish history; others survive as massive stone forts still capable of withstanding a siege; a few are simply fairy-tale structures with castellated towers and conically roofed turrets. In the 13th century, King William the Lion built the once almost impregnable bastion of Red Castle to guard the mouth of Lunan Water.

Or you could go for smaller castles like the Jacobean Crathes Castle, which was built in the 16th century. It was originally the home of a Saxon family, the Burnards, who became Normanized after travelling to Scotland with the feudal barons in the 12th century. Today people go to Crathes not so much to see the castle, as the gardens, beautifully laid out and with a yew hedge which is almost 300 years old. In the south of the county, Edzell Castle, of which only the 16th-century tower still stands, has a pleasant walled garden, laid out by Lord Edzell in 1604. There's another historic memento four miles away in Fettercairn. Scots have never been afraid to maintain their independence – even in the matters of measurement. In the square in Fettercairn, the shaft of the town cross is notched to show the width of the 37-inch Scottish measurement, the 'ell'.

COUNTY FACTS

Origin of name: From the Gaelic and Britonic, signifying the end of a copse or a thicket, "wood end".

Name first recorded: 1295 as Cinn Chàrdain.

County Motto: *Laus Deo* ("Praise be to God").

County Town:

STONEHAVEN The bustling Old Town retains the charm and intimacy of an old-fashioned fishing village, with its ancient and picturesque two-basin harbour.

Other Towns:

BANCHORY – meaning "fair hollow" – is a holiday and health resort. The Watch Tower in the churchyard was built as a look-out against body-snatchers.

FETTERCAIRN A handsome stone arch commemorates Queen Victoria and Prince Albert's secret stay here in 1861 as 'wedding guests from Aberdeen'.

INVERBERVIE Became a royal burgh in 1362 after King David II was shipwrecked on the coast and was treated well by local Bervie folk.

KINCARDINE Anciently the county town up until the reign of James VI and still gives its name to the county. Now a decayed village with castle ruins.

LAURENCEKIRK A fine example of the 18th-century planned village once noted for the manufacture of snuff boxes.

ST CYRUS This salmon-fishing village has been completely rebuilt since being destroyed by a tidal wave in 1795. More than 300 varieties of wild flowers are found in the nearby nature reserve.

◆ Gourdon ◆ Inverbervie ◆ Kincorth ◆ Marykirk ◆ Nigg ◆ Torry

County rivers: Dee, North Esk, Dye, Cowie.

Highest point: Mount Battock at 2,555 feet.

Kincardineshire's local government:

The County of Kincardineshire has both unitary councils of Aberdeen city and the Aberdeenshire local authorities governing its area. The main percentage of Kincardineshire comes under the Aberdeenshire council and a tiny per cent, encircling Cove Bay, is ruled by Aberdeen City council.

FAMOUS NAMES

◆ Robert William Thomson, inventor of the pneumatic tyre, fountain pen and dry dock, was born in Stonehaven in 1822.

COUNTY CALENDAR

◆ May: Craft and Design Fair, Crathes Castle, Banchory.

◆ June: Auld Feeing Market, Stonehaven – A market, with highland dancing and country music, celebrating the occasion when, at the end of their term of employment, farm servants gathered to be 'fee-ed.'

◆ June: Veteran Car Rally, Stonehaven, in memory of Robert Thomson, inventor of the pneumatic tyre.

◆ December 31: Fireballs Ceremony, Stonehaven – wire netting bags packed with combustible material are swung around heads to ward off evil spirits.

KINROSS-SHIRE

THE COUNTY LANDSCAPE

◆ Kinross-shire is the second smallest county in Scotland in terms of area after its next-door neighbour, Clackmannanshire. It covers a mere 82 square miles and lies like a shallow saucer, with its main feature, Loch Leven, in the eastern half of the county. Loch Leven's 4,000 acres make it the largest loch in the Scottish Lowlands.

◆ Of all the counties in Britain, probably none is less well known outside its own area than Kinross-shire. Wedged between the glens of Perthshire and the gentle hills of Fife, it covers a mere 82 square miles – and much of that is taken up with the broad expanse of Loch Leven. But what Kinross-shire lacks in size, it more than makes up for in the quality of life it offers. This is Scotland in miniature: lochs, rivers and hills coming together to form a landscape worthy of a place on a poster advertising the country's attractions.

◆ The county is clearly defined geographically, ringed as it is by the Ochil Hills in the north and west, the Cleish Hills and Benarty in the south and the Lomond Hills in the north and east. Between the hills and the lake are rolling hills, fields and woods.

◆ Once the low-lying areas of the county were marshy and therefore unsuitable for farming – but many years of skilful drainage created more fertile land, increased still further when the level of Loch Leven was lowered in the 1830s.

Kinross-shire was anciently a part of the historic area known as Forthryfe.

OUT IN THE loch at Leven the ruins of an island castle hold a special magic; I can imagine Mary, Queen of Scots as she effected a sensational escape across the waters . . .

'On Leven's banks, while free to rove
And tune the rural pipe to love;
I envied not the happiest swain
That ever trod the Arcadian plain.'

It's more than 200 years since Tobias Smollett penned his *Ode to Leven Water* at the heart of Kinross-shire, one of the least-populated counties, but one of the prettiest. Smollett, who was born in Dunbartonshire and studied medicine in Glasgow, was a lover of fine scenery and were he to return to Loch Leven today, he probably wouldn't notice that much difference. The things which caught his attention then – bowers of birch and groves of pine, springing trout and 'salmon, monarch of the tide' – are still very much in evidence. Today the loch is a bird sanctuary of international importance and was declared a nature reserve in 1964. Each autumn around 15,000 geese fly in to winter here – and at dusk the sky is filled with the sight of the birds landing.

TOWNS AND VILLAGES

With excellent road links to other parts of Scotland – the M90 motorway steams past its doorstep – Kinross-shire is now something of a commuter area for cities like Perth, Dundee and Stirling. But it is still predominantly an agricultural county, with a clutch of attractive and intriguingly named villages (Cleish, Crook of Devon and Drum to name but three) and only two places of any size, Milnathort and Kinross. The county town is situated on the shore of Loch Leven and is full of fine buildings, such as the soft, mellow-stoned Kinross House, built in the 17th century, whose gardens are open to the public every afternoon from May to September. The gardens lay neglected for more than a century, but were restored in 1902 by Sir Basil Montgomery and now contain colourful herbaceous borders, smooth lawns and clipped

KINROSS CASTLE ON LOCH LEVEN *The inspiration for Michael Bruce.*

yews. Out in the loch, the ruins of Loch Leven Castle, where Mary, Queen of Scots was once imprisoned, can be reached in summer on a five-minute ferry boat ride from Kirkgate Park.

A road runs for about 15 miles around the loch and if you're feeling energetic you can cycle it (it's recommended that you make the journey in an anti-clockwise direction to avoid having to struggle against the prevailing winds on the South Loch Road!). The road leads you round the lake to the villages of Scotlandwell and Kinnesswood, where you can visit the home of the 'gentle poet' Michael Bruce, and Balgedie, before returning to Kinross via Milnathort, which developed as a community for wool and linen weavers. Flax was widely grown in the county until the First World War; in 1880, there were 129 weavers in the parish of Orwell, which includes Milnathort. West of Loch Leven, the Cleish Hills present a softer face to the world than those in the Highlands, but from their peaks there are delightful views and Cleish village is unspoilt, comprising perhaps a dozen houses, a tiny village hall, a school, and a church where Sir Walter Scott worshipped on several occasions.

LOCAL HISTORY

Two large whinstones in the middle of a field at Orwell suggest that man has been living in Kinross-shire since at least 2000BC. Roman soldiers marching between their camps at Lochore in Fife and Ardoch in Perthshire are believed to have rested at Scotlandwell, drinking the pure, clear water which still bubbles from the spring there to this day. And St Moak, an early Christian missionary probably born about the beginning of the 6th century AD, founded a movement which flourished in the area for centuries. Around the same time, St Serf, a Pict scholar from Culross in Fife established his headquarters on one of the two islands in Loch Leven, but it was not until two centuries later that the Pictish king Brude V, converted to Christianity, founded the abbey on the island and dedicated it to St Serf. During the Reformation, St Serf's community was dispersed and nothing now remains of it apart from the walls of the chapel and the foundations.

There are also seven tower-houses, keeps, in Kinross-shire, each within sight of at least one other so that beacon warnings of approaching enemies could be passed quickly around the county. Many are now in ruins. All that remains of the 15th-century Burleigh Castle, once the home of the Balfour family, barons of Burleigh, is an old four-storey tower joined to a smaller round tower, which was once a gatehouse. Be careful when you visit it. The building is said to be haunted by the ghost of 'Grey Maggie.'

COUNTY FACTS

Origin of name: From the Gaelic, meaning the tip or end of a promontory. Alternatively, it may derive from the word ros, meaning a moor.

Name first recorded: c. 1144.

County Motto: For All Time.

County Town:

KINROSS Known locally as "the Sleepy Hollow of Scotland", this old town is now sadly transformed by the advent of "progress" in the form of the M90 motorway. A lively covered market takes place on Sundays. The leading centre for cashmere and other high-class hosiery it once had a prosperous cutlery trade until competition from Sheffield became too great.

Other Towns:

MILNATHORT Kinross's second - and only other - town. Its name derived apparently from the Gaelic means "mound of the burial". Birthplace of Ochils poet J. Logie Robertson. Small woollen manufacturing town with ruins of Burleigh Castle, still haunted by the broken heart of its lovelorn, lovetorn master. Robert Balfour.

SCOTLANDWELL Wee village which takes its name from springs bubbling up in a parapeted stone cistern west of the main street. It's said that Robert the Bruce took the waters here as a cure for leprosy.

◆ Carnbo ◆ Craigow ◆ Easter Balgedie ◆ Powmill ◆ Wester Balgedie

County rivers: Garney, North Queich, South Queich.

Highest point: Bishop Hill at 1,492 feet.

Kinross-shire's local government:
The County of Kinross-shire joins up with Perthshire to form the unitary council of Perth and Kinross.

FAMOUS NAMES

◆ Mary, Queen of Scots was imprisoned in Leven Castle from June 1567 until her escape the following year. That she was able to escape was due entirely to the 18-year-old nephew of her jailer, Sir William Douglas. "Daft Willie", as the son was known, stole the castle keys from under the nose of his uncle at dinner, smuggled the Queen on board, locked the castle gate on the outside, and rowed her to meet her supporters who were waiting on the shore.

◆ Michael Bruce, the "Gentle Poet of Loch Leven", was born in the Cobbles, Kinnesswood, in 1746. Although he died young, at the age of 21, he wrote many poems including *Ode to the Cuckoo*, *Loch Leven* and *Elegy Written in Spring*.

COUNTY CALENDAR

◆ Late May: National and International Angling Championships are held at Loch Leven.

◆ July: Kinross Golf Week, professional tuition and competitions at The Green Hotel, Kinross.

◆ Mid-August: The Annual Agricutural Show is held in Kinross.

KIRKCUDBRIGHTSHIRE

EAST GALLOWAY

KIRKCUDBRIGHT *The pretty harbour, with its mixture of architectural styles, is overlooked by the imposing McLellan's Castle.*

THE COUNTY LANDSCAPE

◆ There are three distinct regions to the county of Kirkcudbrightshire. In the north, on the borders of Ayrshire and Dumfries, is the wild desolate region known as the Glenkens – full of lochs, waterfalls and jagged mountains reaching more than 2,000 feet.

◆ The mountains give way to rolling pastureland, on which can be found sheep and the hardy Galloway cattle. Finally there is the coast of the Solway Firth – a looping mixture of dramatic headlands, wide bays and river estuaries, giving the area a character all its own. The river estuaries are very much alike - they have wide sandy banks and salt marshes and are ringed by wooded hills.

◆ Inland, nowhere is the scenery or the wildlife more impressive than on the 10-mile "Raiders Road" forest drive between Clatteringshaw Dam, six miles west of New Galloway, and Bennan, five miles south of New Galloway. There's a wildlife centre at Clatteringshaws, with waymarked trails, and indigenous species here include golden eagles, otters and pine martens. Traditional Galloway sheep have disappeared, to be replaced by the coarser-woolled blackface breeds, but Galloway cattle can still be seen in droves!

I AM ALWAYS put in mind of Galloway bulls when I think of Kirkcudbrightshire. I suppose it's because I was presented with a big, woolly, black one by my fan club here. All in all a rather special place because Kirkcudbrightshire is strictly not a county but a stewartry. Once the stronghold of the Stewart clan, it sits comfortably on the north coast of the Solway estuary, a quiet backwater with a distinctive character. Here is the softer side of Scotland, but scenically splendid just the same. Heather-clad hills, gentler than those in the Highlands, sweep down to the rugged peninsulas and estuaries of the Solway coastline, making this whole area a bird-watcher's delight.

TOWNS AND VILLAGES

Along the way are quiet towns like Kirkcudbright, Castle Douglas and Gatehouse of Fleet, a clean, elegant late-18th-century place divided by the estuary known as the Water of Fleet.

The county town Kirkcudbright – pronounced 'Kirkoobree' – sits at the head of the Dee estuary. Once a busy coastal port, the harbour is now used by one or two fishing boats, yachts and occasionally by oil tankers. The name means simply 'the church of St Cuthbert', but what impresses here is the neat lay-out of the town, with its wide streets of terraced two-storey greystone houses and colourful cottages, rising above the banks of the Dee.

Kirkcudbright is Scotland's answer to St Ives, having for years been popular with artists (there's still an internationally famous summer art school here.) Hardly surprising, for the mild climate and soft light make this an ideal town for art. Of the town's principal buildings, the Tolbooth – Scots for Town Hall – is now a memorial to John Paul Jones, an 18th-century slave trader and privateer who later founded the American Navy.

Southwest Scotland's mild climate makes it a great place for gardens – and Kirkcudbrightshire is no exception. Just outside Castle Douglas, the gardens at the Scottish Jacobean mansion Threave House are well worth seeing.

LOCAL HISTORY

Kirkcudbrightshire shares with its neighbour Wigtownshire the distinction of once having been part of the Pictish province of Galloway. Ever since the days of the Picts, the people of Kirkcudbrightshire have maintained a sturdy independence.The mountains lying behind the Solway coast harboured Robert the Bruce during his days on the run. The Covenanters – Scots who in 1581 signed the National Covenant to uphold the Presbyterian religion and to fight Catholicism – died here in their hundreds. Throughout the county you'll find memorials to their martyrdom, some of them the work of Robert Paterson, the wandering stonemason, and the inspiration for the central character in Sir Walter Scott's classic novel, *Old Mortality.*

Dundrennan Abbey was founded in 1142. Mary, Queen of Scots spent her last night on Scottish soil here on 16 May, 1568. She then escaped across the Solway Firth to England – you can still see the stone from which she climbed into the boat to take her across the water – but when she arrived at Cumberland on the other side the fates were not kind. Queen Elizabeth promptly imprisoned her and, after being implicated in the Babington Conspiracy, she was executed on a charge of high treason.

Kirkcudbright also has its own considerable history. Once the Stewarts' most ancient burgh, its old town graveyard contains memorials to three Covenanters, who were among many Scottish Presbyterians executed for refusing to use the *Book of Common Prayer*, and to the tinker king Billy Marshall, who died in 1792 at the age of 120. According to Sir Walter Scott, Marshall fathered four children after he was 100. On the north side of the town is the ruined Tongland Abbey, one of whose abbots, John Damian, attempted to fly from the ramparts of Stirling Castle in front of King James IV, wearing wings of bird feathers. He suffered the indignity of landing in a heap of manure.

COUNTY FACTS

Origin of name: Either from Caer-Cuabrit, the name given by the pre-Roman Novantae, or named from the church of St Cuthbert.

Name first recorded: 1278 as The Church of St Cuberct.

County Town:

KIRKCUDBRIGHT Long years as the county town have given this place some elegant buildings, mostly Georgian and Victorian.

Other Towns:

CASTLE DOUGLAS Cosy market town with 18th-century streets designed by its owner, William Douglas. Originally called Causewayend and then Carlingwark before getting its present name in 1792.

CREETOWN An 18th-century "planned" village which took the place of the original village Creth.

GATEHOUSE OF FLEET A quiet and elegant town, divided in two by the Water of Fleet. Industry once flourished here, making it a treasure trove for industrial archaeologists.

NEW GALLOWAY Little more than one long street lined by neat and attractive stone houses.

Dalry ◆ Dalbeattie ◆ Maxwelltown (continuous with Dumfries to the east) ◆ Minnigaff

County rivers: Dee, Urr.

Highest point: Merrick Mountain at 2,764 feet.

Kirkcudbrightshire's local government: The County of Kirkcudbrightshire is governed by the Dumfries and Galloway unitary council.

FAMOUS NAMES

◆ Mons Meg, the great cannon at Edinburgh Castle, was forged by a Castle Douglas blacksmith called John McKim. The cannon was used by James II in1455 to overcome Threave and its rebellious Douglas defenders.

◆ In 1778 John Paul Jones, the founder of the American Navy, actually attacked the British cutter *Hussar* off the Isle of Man and then St Mary's Isle, at the tip of the Kirkcudbright peninsula, hoping to capture the Earl of Selkirk as a hostage to exchange for American prisoners of war. The Earl was not at home, so Jones took the silver instead, later returning it to the Earl.

COUNTY CALENDAR

◆ Late May, early June: Dumfries & Galloway Arts Festival. Ten-day festival featuring music, dance, crafts, visual arts – some events held in Kirkcudbright, Castle Douglas and Dalbeattie.

◆ End of May: Newton Stewart Trot, grass track horse racing at Newton Stewart.

◆ August: Gala Day in Kirkcudbright.

◆ August: Scottish Borders Enduro-Club race, 20-mile cross-country motor cycle event, Dalbeattie.

◆ October: Classic Motorbike Rally, viewing and scenic drive for old cycle enthusiasts, Clatteringshaws Forest Wildlife Centre, New Galloway.

LANARKSHIRE

CLYDESDALE

NEW LANARK *With its textile mills, this is Scotland's finest showcase of industrial archaeology courtesy of Robert Owen in the 1790s.*

THE COUNTY LANDSCAPE

◆ Lanarkshire's countryside is dominated by the River Clyde and the Clyde valley but it has its share of heather-covered hills, especially around Lanark itself. New Lanark is noted for the Falls of Clyde. There are three in number along a wooded and sometimes rocky stretch of the river. Cora Linn, above Lanark descend 86 feet from an amphitheatre of rocks. The force of these falls are now utilized for hydro-electric power. Those who have only seen the lower tidal Clyde, flowing out towards Dunoon and the Kyles, will find the Clyde gorges filled with the rushing river after rain, a considerable surprise.

◆ To the southeast, Tinto Hill, north of Abington, is a prominent landmark in the flatter part of Clydesdale, and the county is cradled to the south by the green Lowther Hills, which rise to 2,000 feet in some places, and to the east by the Pentland Hills, which rise here and head into Midlothian.

◆ With moors and valleys, Lanarkshire has beautiful countryside, fascinating towns and best of all the splendid city of Glasgow.

LANARKSHIRE IS LIKE three counties rolled into one: start in the south with pleasant rolling uplands and river valleys, a pastoral scene that has changed little, and then head to the centre to the famed orchard country between Lanark and Hamilton, and finally you reach the grittier industrial north based on the immense deposits of iron and coal and centred around the grandeur that is Glasgow, one of the great cities of Europe.

TOWNS AND VILLAGES

With its dark-chocolatey brick buildings Glasgow has a New York architectural feel about it, yet it is a warm-hearted town and perhaps best known today as the city of *Taggart*, that dour Glaswegian TV detective. Glasgow quite rightly was recently enshrined as one of the Cultural Cities of Europe, a fact that will surprise anyone who only knew of the Clyde shipyards, the Gorbals and Sauchihall Street on Saturday nights.

Though Glasgow's heart is in Lanarkshire, a good part of the city spills west into Renfrewshire and north into Dunbartonshire and Stirlingshire. The sights to see are almost too numerous to mention but must include the Burrell Collection, housed in a new museum opened in 1983, containing a fine collection of 19th-century French art, glass, ceramics, furniture and textiles, donated to the City by Sir William and Lady Burrell.

The Botanic Gardens are another of Glasgow's attractions, especially the orchid collection, but for something very special and a chance to meet the real attraction of Glasgow – the people – a visit to the Barras is a must. The Barras is a weekend market, held every Saturday and Sunday near Glasgow Cross. There are now more than 800 covered stalls in the Barras, a market thronged every weekend with thousands of Glaswegians in search of a bargain, their shopping enlivened by buskers and street artists.

Since culture in Glasgow might be a surprising discovery, a visit to the city Art Gallery and Museum may be called for, to see the art collection, with more French Impressionists and works by such Old Masters as Rembrandt. Glasgow is full of good museums, among them those of the Royal Highland Fusiliers, a Museum of Transport, which includes a reproduction of a pre-World War II Glasgow street, and the Museum of Education, in a building designed by George Rennie MacIntosh.

The public buildings are also very fine, especially St Mungo's Cathedral, the most complete Gothic cathedral in Scotland, which has survived centuries of religious strife, and dates in part from the 13th century. Outside, the amazing Victorian Necropolis has Doric columns, catacombs and neo-classical temples of wealthy industrialists. A little way outside the city lies Crookston Castle, build by Robert Croc in the 12th century, though most of what remains dates back only to the early 15th century. That forlorn couple Mary, Queen of Scots and Darnley spent their honeymoon here in 1565.

Lanark, which gives its name to the county, lies some distance to the south, in the beautiful hills above the Clyde. This is an old Scots burgh. Its almost namesake New Lanark, is a place which is not all that new, having been built by David Dale and Richard Arkwright in 1785, partly to harness the Clyde waterfalls for their new mills and partly to house the workers that came to serve the looms.

The village is most attractive and built in the classic Palladian style, put up around 1798 by David Dale's son-in-law, Robert Owen, a social reformer who saw no reason why working-class folk should not be decently paid and decently housed – a revolutionary idea at the time. Some features of that 200-years-ago experiment in working practices, like crèches for the babies and schools for the workers' children have still to gain general acceptance.

Some idea of Owen's intentions can be obtained from the

COUNTY FACTS

Origin of name: From the Brittonic word Llanerch, meaning a glade or forest clearing.

Name first recorded: 1116.

County Motto: *Vigilantia* ("Vigilance").

County Town: GLASGOW One of Britain's great cities, it is full of attractions and very lively, with a sense of humour, which has survived great economic hardship in the present century. Two famous football teams Celtic (at Celtic Park) and Rangers (based at Ibrox) are based in the city.

Other Towns:

BLANTYRE The attraction in this suburb is the David Livingstone Centre (once the tenement block where Livingstone was born) which charts the explorer's life. The Priory here was founded in the 12th century.

BIGGAR Ancestral home of the Gladstones, family of the great Liberal Prime Minister. A market town, with some rather splendid buildings, Biggar is well worth a look with its Moat Park Heritage Centre, which occupies a neo-Romanesque church near the High Street, and for history buffs, the Greenhill Covenanters Museum by the Biggar Burn, the ideal place to learn more about the Covenanters and their 17th-century religious wars.

BOTHWELL The birthplace of James Keir Hardy, father of British Socialism, was at the now defunct village of Legbrannock close by. Castle built possibly around the 13th century for the Lords of Bothwell.

HAMILTON This town is rather fashionable and caters for the Glasgow commuters and 'Accie' football fans.

LANARK This very pretty, small market town is perched high in the hills above the River Clyde and is visible for miles around. The Church of St Nicholas is reputed to have the oldest known bell in the western world, cast in 1130. It became a Royal Burgh back in the 12th century.

MOTHERWELL Best known for its football team but hard hit by the closure of the steel works in 1992. There is also a Roman fort and the town lies on the doorstep of the Strathclyde Country Park complete with its own Loch.

RUTHERGLEN A medieval royal burgh and at one time it excelled in importance to Glasgow, but now it's swallowed up by that city's expanse.

UDDINGSTON Imposingly situated on the banks of the River Clyde lies the ancient castle of Bothwell with a very stormy history. It was the main English base in western Scotland during the Plantagenet occupation. it was finally retaken by the Scots in 1336 and later passed to the Douglasses (who embarked on its reconstruction).

◆ Airdrie ◆ Baillieston ◆ Bellshill ◆ Bishopbriggs ◆ Cambuslang ◆ Carluke ◆ Carstairs ◆ Cathcart ◆ Coatbridge ◆ Douglas ◆ East Kilbride ◆ Govan (shared with Renfrewshire) ◆ Larkhill ◆ Lesmahagow ◆ Newmains ◆ Partick ◆ Pollockshields ◆ Shotts ◆ Strathaven ◆ Wishaw

Main rivers: Clyde, Douglas, Avon, Calder.

Highest point: Culter Fells at 2,454 feet.

Lanarkshire's local government: The County of Lanarkshire has four unitary councils for its local government: the City of Glasgow, North Lanarkshire and South Lanarkshire, while its town of Bishopsbriggs comes under the authority of East Dunbartonshire Council.

◆ The Sheriffdom of Lanarkshire was divided into three wards: Upper, Middle and Lower in 1402. Lanark, a Royal Burgh in the 12th century, became the capital of Upper Ward, and Rutherglen, also a 12th-century Royal Burgh, was the chief town of Nether Ward (until superseded by Glasgow). Hamilton was capital of the Middle Ward of Lanarkshire.

FAMOUS NAMES

◆ The most famous name in Scotland today is the 'Big Yin', Glasgow's own Billy Connolly, born in Glasgow and a shipyard worker, like his fathers before him until he took to the boards.

◆ Television viewers will recall the late Mark McManus, star of that successful, gritty and long-running police TV series *Taggart*, which showed the seamier side of Glasgow life.

◆ David Livingstone made his mark elsewhere, in the lonely and remote parts of Africa, dying there in 1873, exactly 60 years after his birth in Blantyre.

◆ Keir Hardie, the first Socialist MP, and founder of the Labour Movement, was born in Bothwell in 1856, and worked in the local coal pits by the age of 10.

◆ Sixties pop icon Lulu is a Glasgow lass.

◆ Novelists Jeff Torrington and James Kelman are just two of Glasgow's new literary celebrities.

◆ Although the cult film *Shallow Grave* is set in Edinburgh, much of it was actually shot in Glasgow.

COUNTY CALENDAR

◆ January 25: West Sound Burns Night Supper.

◆ May means Mayfest in Glasgow. Glasgow's answer to Edinburgh, a vibrant international festival of theatre, dance, popular music, visual arts and the like.

◆ May: Waterfall Day at the Falls of the Clyde Wildlife Reserve Centre – Scotland's most spectacular waterfalls in full flow as electricity generation stops for the day.

◆ May: Gold Panning demonstrations at the Museum of Lead Mining in Biggar. The library here is the second oldest subscription library in Scotland.

◆ June: Lanark has Lanimer Day, an annual traditional street procession, including the crowning of the Lanimer Queen.

◆ June: Shotts Highland Games with pipe band competition and athletics. Games also at Airdrie and Lesmahagow in June.

◆ July: Glasgow's International Jazz Festival is the largest jazz festival in the UK.

◆ Mid-July: 'T in the Park': (the T stands for a well known Scottish lager) Scotland's premier rock music festival takes place at Strathclyde Country Park between Hamilton and Motherwell.

◆ July/August: International rowing and sailing regattas at Strathclyde Park Loch.

◆ August: The RSAC Veteran Car Run gets into gear for cars built prior to 1973; starts in Glasgow.

◆ September: Victorian Fair at New Lanark.

building which stands in the centre of New Lanark and houses the library and chapel. He named this place the 'Institute for the Formation of Character'.

New Lanark is a fascinating place, Scotland's major contribution to the Enlightenment and the cradle of the Industrial Revolution in many ways. Several of the old mill buildings have been converted into museums showing how life was led hereabouts 200 years ago. For a touch of natural drama there are the Falls of Clyde, where the river plunges more than 90 feet in three sharp stages.

A social reformer of a different stamp was born in Blantyre, a small village which is now a suburb of Hamilton. This is where the missionary and African explorer, David Livingstone (of "Dr Livingstone, I presume" fame) was born in 1813. His birthplace now houses the David Livingstone Centre though 'Blantyre' is perhaps better known today as the capital of Malawi, a country in Central Africa once known as Nyasaland.

Close to Blantyre and well worth a visit is Bothwell Castle, one of the most imposing medieval castles in Scotland, a great red, sandstone tower set on a loop of the Clyde. This was built at the end of the 13th century, by the Earls of Moray to fend off the English King, Edward I, and withstood a good many sieges in the following centuries.

LOCAL HISTORY

Lanarkshire was once part of the ancient kingdom of Strathclyde which covered most of Scotland south of the Forth. The county's past and present is closely linked with the Clyde valley and the river. The Clyde has provided the local people with food and industry, from the mills of New Lanark to the great shipyards that made 'Cloyed built', a mark of excellence among the merchant fleets of the world. Now both the mills and the shipyards have ceased production and the area struggles to make a living in a competitive modern world.

Glasgow has some historic relics, not least St. Mungo's cathedral, the finest Gothic church in Scotland and some of the local castles, Crookston, Bothwell, Craignethan, near Crossford, are all well worth a look, relics of a more violent age. Craignethan was the last real castle to be built in Scotland, a late example of a medieval fortress, built for the King, James V, about 1530, by Sir James Hamilton, who had soldiered in the Italian Wars and returned home with some very definite ideas about castle building in the age of cannon. The castle contains a rare embellishment, a caponier, or redoubt in the castle ditch, from which even the smallest numbers of defenders could fire on the attackers as they assaulted the main walls.

MIDLOTHIAN *EDINBURGHSHIRE*

EDINBURGH *The resplendent Military Tattoo is held on Edinburgh Castle's Esplanade.*

COME IN FROM the south over the verdant Pentland and Moorfoot Hills and you witness Midlothian's magnificent beating heart, Edinburgh. Alongside, tucked in south of the Firth of Forth, are the famous docks of Leith which in Victorian days must have presented a stunning array of mast upon mast. Midlothian is really Edinburgh and it is not surprising that the county's alternative title is Edinburghshire.

TOWNS AND VILLAGES

Midlothian makes up the centre of the three counties that compose the Lothians and is dominated, even more than the other two, by the loom of 'Auld Reekie', the capital city of Edinburgh. North of Edinburgh, Midlothian runs off into the Pentland Hills that curve up into the county from the south. Down there, in the south of Midlothian, notable towns and

THE COUNTY LANDSCAPE

◆ The landscape of Midlothian is a mixture of the pastoral, the coastal and the volcanic. Edinburgh grew up around that core of volcanic rock, which is now crowned by the castle, and there are plenty of other volcanic cones hereabouts to add drama to the natural scene. The hills in the southern suburbs of the city are steep enough to offer good walking.

◆ The estuary of the Firth of Forth is always attractive, especially during one of those long summer evenings, while to the south of the county the green Pentland Hills come running up from Lanarkshire, providing a green background to the gentler country to the west. The Pentland Hills, 18 miles long and some five miles wide, are seamed with footpaths and the main lung for the citizens of the capital.

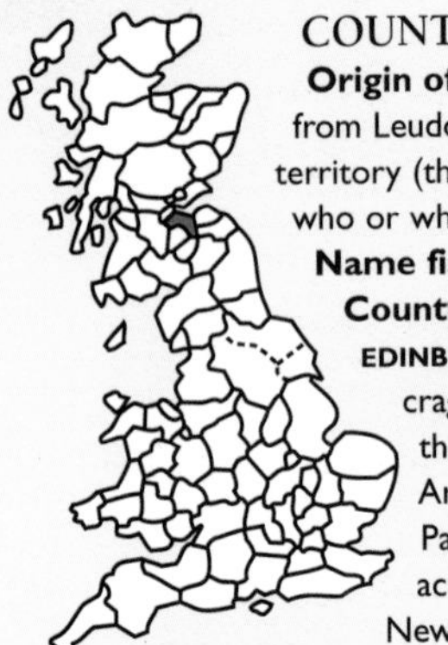

COUNTY FACTS

Origin of name: Lothian derives from Leudonis and signifies his territory (though no one knows who or what Leudonis was).

Name first recorded: 970

County Town:

EDINBURGH Is set atop rocky crags and extinct volcanoes the largest of which, Arthur's Seat in Holyrood Park, offers splendid views across the Old Town, the New Town and across to Leith and the Firth of Forth. Walk the 'Royal Mile' from Edinburgh Castle to the Palace of Holyroodhouse to soak in the atmosphere of this historic city once called Dunedin. New-found fame as the name of a New Zealand city.

Other Towns:

BONNYRIGG Was not named from 'bonny ridge' (a pretty ridge) but from 'bannock ridge' meaning a ridge shaped like a bannock, which is a flat oatmeal cake (see *Selkirkshire*).

DALKEITH Busy shopping centre with wide main street but once a medieval baron's manor under the Douglasses and later the Buccleuchs (whose country park and richly furnished parish church you can visit).

MURRAYFIELD Apparently named after an Archibald Murray who was an landowner in the 1700s; home of Scottish rugby's international matches and ice hockey club. Edinburgh Zoological Park is nearby on the slopes of Corstorphine Hill at 530 feet which, with Robert Louis Stevenson and Sir Walter Scott connections, is well worth the climb.

MUSSELBURGH A famous shellfish-eating centre and has a fine Roman bridge across the River Esk. The links here are famous for horse-racing and archery as well as golf. There is a celebrated chapel where pregnant women sent their bedlinen at childbirth to be consecrated to aid a swift recovery. Mere superstition? – don't be silly!

◆ Arniston ◆ Currie ◆ Easthouses ◆ Eskbank ◆ Gilmerton ◆ Gorebridge ◆ Granton ◆ Lasswade ◆ Liberton ◆ Loanhead ◆ Newtongrange ◆ Penicuik ◆ Portbello

County rivers: Breich, Almond, North Esk, South Esk, Logan.

Highest point: Blackhope Scar at 2,136 feet.

Midlothian's local government: For local government purposes the heart has been ripped out of Midlothian. The County's eastern flank around Musselburgh is governed by East Lothian unitary council. The area known as Gala Water below the Moorfoot Hills takes its orders from the Scottish Borders unitary council. The Calders district – a big finger of Midlothian protruding southwest from Currie – is governed by West Lothian council.

The City of Edinburgh unitary council takes care of northern Midlothian leaving the Midlothian unitary council as a pale imitation of the real County of Midlothian, being almost an uncanny replica in miniature of the County in both shape and form but taking care of the affairs of just a handful of its main towns.

villages are very rare indeed, though little places like Howgate and Penicuik (pronounced Pennycook) are worth inspection. Dalkeith, eight miles south of Edinburgh is largely Victorian, best known today for Dalkeith Palace while Roslin, seven miles south of Edinburgh, is noted for the fine, late-Gothic Rosslyn Chapel.

One place not to be missed on any visit to Midlothian is the old port of Leith, once the trading port for Edinburgh but now largely transformed into the pleasant shopping and dining quarter of the capital, full of well-restored buildings containing boutiques and good restaurants. The older and finer part of Leith lies along 'The Shore' – the front facing the Water of Leith stream just before it pours into the Firth of Forth. Another place well worth a look is the picturesque village of Cramond intruding into West Lothian, on the mouth of the River Almond, five miles north and west of Edinburgh, which has a Roman fort and a medieval tower as well as a fine kirk and an old schoolhouse.

The town of Musselburgh owes its name to a famous mussel bed found at the mouth of the River Esk. It has always been a great mussel-eating centre and mussel-and-onion stew which includes 60 mussels, onions, butter, flour, warm milk, white wine, cream and parsley, is a local recipe. If you like you can substitute oysters, scallops or clams to fire your desires!

Edinburgh however occupies pride of place in Midlothian – the true 'Heart of Midlothian', as famous son Sir Walter Scott might put it and most of the urban attention devoted to Midlothian can be concentrated there. (The original Heart of Midlothian after which the football club was named was the Old Tolbooth jail which used to stand opposite the Royal Exchange.)

Scotland's capital city caters for everyone, the artistic crowd with the annual Edinburgh Festival, the more sporting with the rugby games at Murrayfield, and the hedonistic with the shops of Princes Street. The list of capital attractions in Edinburgh goes on for 20 pages in the official guidebook, and includes many places that are nonetheless worth visiting for being less well known to fame than popular attractions like the Castle, the Royal Mile and the purveyors of Princes Street.

To get a good overview of the city and surrounding countryside climb up the 330-foot summit of Calton Hill in the city centre. This hill which supports a collection of monuments including a reproduction of the Parthenon and a 100-foot-high tower commemorating Lord Nelson. Images of Edinburgh can also be obtained at the Camera Obscura by the Guildhall on the top of the Royal Mile. History lovers must not miss the Canongate Kirk, full of the graves of famous people, and for something to go with the 'Wine of the Country', Crabbie's Historic Winery, where visitors can discover the secrets of Crabbie's Green Ginger Wine, a drop of hot stuff I'm most partial to.

Animal lovers will have to visit Greyfriars Kirk, if only to see the grave and hear the story of 'Greyfriars Bobby' the little terrier that lived for years here, by the remains of its master. Greyfriars is also notable as the place where the National Covenant was signed in 1638. Not far away lies John Knox's house, full of reminders of that furious cleric, and just across the road lies the house of Lady Stair, now a museum dedicated to the life and work of three famous Scots: the writers Robbie Burns, Walter Scott and Robert Louis Stevenson.

LOCAL HISTORY

Edinburgh has almost too much history if that's possible and to take in the city's heritage the best place to begin is the castle because this fortress is still occupied, still the centre for the Edinburgh Festival and still a military garrison. A mile away along the ridge of the Old Town lies Holyroodhouse, at the far end of the Royal Mile. It has seen some bloody events in Scotland's history; here the Italian musician, Riccio, Mary, Queen of Scots's secretary was hacked to death and his bloodstains can still be seen on the floor of the Queen's chamber. Bonnie Prince Charlie held court in 1745 and the way between the Castle and Holyroodhouse passes the exact spot where the Marquis of Montrose was put to death in May 1650.

St Giles Cathedral is one of Edinburgh's two cathedrals (the other being St Mary's Church) and contains the chapel of the Knights of the Thistle and has seen more stirring events in Scotland's long and turbulent history, but the whole city is steeped in history and stories cry out from the stones.

History spills over into places in the countryside of Midlothian that can provide a similar frisson, like Craigmillar Castle, close to Edinburgh, which dates from the middle 15th century and is a fine example of a transitional castle, altered to take account of the development of siege artillery. Something a little earlier in origin, though much altered recently, is Dalhousie Castle, which dates from the 12th century and still has its crenellated walls. Another place of legend is Roslin where the Rosslyn chapel contains a knotted column known as the 'Prentice Pillar', supposedly carved by an apprentice while the Master mason was away. On seeing the work, the Master mason was so consumed with jealousy he killed the apprentice with his mallet. Legends apart, the Pillar is indeed a wonderful piece of work.

FAMOUS NAMES

◆ Lady Stair's house in Edinburgh contains a fine museum to Scott, Burns and Robert Louis Stevenson who was also born in the city. Sir Walter Scott was born in 1771 and trained as an advocate. He met an ageing Burns who encouraged him in his early interest in poetry and folklore. Robert Louis Stevenson was born in 1850 into a family of engineers. Aside from his famous novels such as *Dr Jekyll and Mr Hyde* (made into umpteen films) he also penned *Edinburgh: Picturesque Notes* which unravels the city as he found it warts and all.

◆ Thomas de Quincy is buried in the church of St Cuthberts, the West Kirk, on the Lothian road.

◆ Sir Arthur Conan Doyle, creator of Sherlock Holmes, was born and worked in Edinburgh. He used his tutor, Sir Joseph Bell, a surgeon, as the inspiration for Holmes's remarkable deductive powers. Watson was a self-parody.

◆ Other famous residents in Edinburgh include the Adams brothers, creators of Scotland's finest architecture, and Alexander Graham Bell, inventor of the telephone.

◆ Muriel Spark, whose novel *The Prime of Miss Jean Brodie* is set in the town, was born in Edinburgh.

◆ Author Irvine Welsh is a native of Edinburgh and his novels show the underbelly of that city's life, chiefly around Leith.

◆ Virile Scottish leading actor, and no mean golfer, Sean Connery resided in the Royal Mile of Edinburgh back in the 1930s in his early childhood.

◆ Edinburgh Rock is a candy that has a tradition going back to the 18th century (with the firm of Ferguson).

COUNTY CALENDAR

◆ End August/September: The most significant and lively annual event in the Midlothian calendar is the internationally renowned Edinburgh Festival, a two-week pageant of music and the arts which attracts performers from all over the world, either to main events on the Festival programme or to take their chances at the equally famous 'Fringe'. This alternative festival is now said to be the largest single event of its kind in the world and covers anything from the world's smallest cinema auditorium to the world's finest stand-up comedians (Lee Evans emerged from here as did many other household names). The mainstream Edinburgh Festival was founded in 1947 and attracts one million visitors.

◆ January: The 1st and 2nd of January in Edinburgh are devoted to 'Hogmanay'.

◆ Winter/Spring: International Rugby at Murrayfield.

◆ April: Edinburgh Science Exhibition and Festival

◆ June: Royal Highland Show. Scotland's National Agricultural Show at Ingliston.

◆ August: The Edinburgh Festival and Military Tattoo takes place in the last two weeks in August and is the ultimate spectacle of bagpipes and kilts. Performing animals and gymnastic displays are also part of the programme.

◆ August: Drambuie Edinburgh Film Festival. World's longest-running film festival, which started in 1947.

◆ November: International Storytelling Festival, Netherbow Arts Centre.

◆ End August: Highland Games at Meadowbank.

MORAYSHIRE

ELGINSHIRE

THE COUNTY LANDSCAPE

◆ Morayshire is a maritime county in North East Scotland. It covers an area of 477 square miles and the coastline runs for 32 miles along the south shore of the Moray Firth – an arm of the North Sea extending inland for almost 40 miles.

◆ Morayshire is bordered in the west by Nairnshire, in the east by Banffshire and in the south by Inverness-shire.

◆ In the south, the scenery is mountainous, the lower reaches of the Grampian mountains. Some of the peaks here nudge 2,000 feet – the highest being Carn an Loine (1,795 feet) and Larrig Hill (1,783 feet).

◆ The county's main rivers wend their way off the mountains, through glens and past small lakes. Then they head across the fertile agricultural land of the coastal plain, before ending their journey in the Moray Firth.

◆ At Culbin near Forres, the Forestry Commission has planted trees on a vast area of shifting sand which proved unsatisfactory for farming.

◆ The present-day county of Morayshire is the central division of the ancient province of Moray.

IF YOU'RE FOND of a wee dram and a chunk of juicy salmon then this is the county for you. I don't know if this is what attracted my 'ayn' folk, the clan Grant, here, but settle here they did. Glance at a map of Morayshire and it is peppered with the distinctive red signs of distilleries. This is one of the two classic 'whisky' counties (the other being Banffshire) and there can be no doubt the amber nectar is important to the county's economy – and probably lifestyle, too. But, as a place to visit, Elginshire (as its ancient name attests) offers much more than sampling the mellow malts ... fine scenery, splendid old towns and, not least, some of the best salmon fishing in the land.

The county can thank its rivers for both the whisky and the salmon. It's the peaty waters of the rivers, rushing down from the mountains, that give Scotch whisky in general – and Morayshire whisky in particular – its unique flavour. Likewise, it's in rivers such as the Spey that you find the great salmon which end up on some of the world's best tables – anglers first being called upon to pit their wits against the cunning of the noble fish.

TOWNS AND VILLAGES

The two industries are the backbone of the local economy – but there are also others. Just outside the city of Elgin, at Fochabers, is another name which has found its way around the world – the food manufacturer, Baxters of Speyside. The company has now opened a visitor centre where you can see a large range of Scottish products in varying stages of production including, of course, those famous game soups. After this, you can enjoy a true taste of Scotland in the restaurant, prepared by Enid! Or perhaps pay a visit to the gift shop to buy a deserving jar for friends back home.

CITY OF ELGIN *Ruins of Elgin Cathedral viewed across River Lossie.*

Tourism is growing – not just for people wishing to visit the distilleries or land a salmon on the Spey, but anyone with a longing to explore the wide open spaces – on country roads you're far more likely to meet a sheep than another car – and unspoilt towns and villages. Elgin, which grew up around a low ridge on the river Lossie, is worth half a day of anyone's time ... to trace the layout of the old medieval streets, to see some splendid 18th-century buildings and the cathedral – 'The Lantern of the North' – a ruin, perhaps, but a splendid ruin all the same. The town's museum is one of the oldest in Scotland. It was founded in 1836 by a group of local gentlemen including Dr George Gordon, who used to correspond with eminent scientists of the day such as Charles Darwin. Exhibits include reptile fossils going back 385 million years, found in the same local sandstone of which the museum is built, as well as displays covering local wildlife and history and curios collected from the 19th-century New World.

Grantown-on-Spey (historically Inverness-shire detached), a Georgian development, was attracting visitors 100 years ago sent there by their doctors for a change of air. Today it attracts salmon anglers, golfers, trekkers and skiers. An alternative attraction in the true sense of the word is Findhorn near Elgin. It is a spiritual and an holistic health centre. On the other side of Spey Bay, Lossiemouth is another prosperous fishing port with a second important string to its bow – as home base of three Royal Air Force squadrons. It sits close to the farming area known as Laich of Moray, traditionally known as the 'Granary of the North' because of the fertility of its fields, and offers good walks along the coast where, on calm days, you may even see a group of bottle-nosed dolphins leaping out of the water.

LOCAL HISTORY

Morayshire has its share of prehistoric remains. Throughout the county hill forts and traces of Neolithic villages can be found . The coastal area is particularly rich in antiquities. On the tip of the promontory at Burghead are the remains of a Pictish fort which was partially destroyed in 1805 when the old fishing village was razed to the ground to make way for the present buildings. The old and new stand side by side at Kinloss. A short distance from the ruined abbey which was founded by David I of Scotland in 1150 is an RAF station used by the very latest maritime reconnaissance aircraft.

Inland, Forres is also a place to tempt historians. The Sueno Stone, a shaft of sandstone standing 20 feet high, probably dates from the 10th century. One side of the stone is carved with a cross, the other with warriors. Nearby, the Witches' Stone marks the spot where, in the 17th century, women accused of witchcraft and being in league with the Devil were put to death. And on top of Cluny Hill, overlooking the town, is the 70-foot-high octagonal tower erected in 1806 in honour of Nelson from where, from the top of the tower on a clear day, seven counties are said to be visible.

COUNTY FACTS

Origin of name: From the Gaelic, meaning settlement by the sea.

County Motto: *Sub Spe* ("In Hope").

County Town:

ELGIN A lively market town with an old-fashioned feel. Elgin suffers noise-pollution due to its proximity to RAF Lossiemouth.

Other Towns:

BURGHEAD Once an important grain shipping port, the granaries have now been adapted to other uses.

DUFFUS Quiet picturesque fishing village. Duffus Castle rises above a Norman mound and dates from the 14th century.

FINDHORN Near Elgin is the Findhorn Foundation, spiritual mecca for well-heeled hippies and garden centre with giant vegetables and flowers.

FOCHABERS Has a wealth of elegant 18th-century buildings. A good base for local walks.

GORDONSTOUN Originally called Plewlands House, four miles northwest of Elgin, this world-famous public school is well-known for educating Prince Charles.

LOSSIEMOUTH Busy fishing port, with two excellent sandy beaches and two 18-hole golf courses.

◆ Bishopmill ◆ Cummingstown ◆ Garmouth ◆ Hopeman ◆ Llanbryde ◆ New Elgin ◆ Rothes

County rivers: Spey, Lossie, Findhorn, Divie.

Highest point: Cromdale at 2,329 feet.

Morayshire's local government: The County of Morayshire is administered by Moray unitary council. Two generous detached parts of the County of Morayshire in Inverness-shire centred upon Abernethy Forest and Duthil are governed by Highland Unitary Authority.

FAMOUS NAMES

◆ The name of Wolf the Badenoch, Scotland's 14th-century equivalent of Genghis Khan, will forever be etched in the memory of the people of Elgin. He it was who, in 1390, after a disagreement with the bishop, burned down the town's 'Lantern of the North' cathedral. The cathedral was rebuilt and continued in use until the Reformation.

◆ Ramsay MacDonald, Britain's first Labour prime minister, was born at a house in Gregory Place, Branderburgh in 1866 and spent his childhood here. He died in 1937 and lies buried in Spynie churchyard, east of the Lossiemouth-Elgin road.

◆ The late folk singer Roy Williamson, who wrote among other songs the Scots rugby anthem *Flower of Scotland*, spent most of his life in and around Forres.

COUNTY CALENDAR

◆ Mid-June: Murray Science Festival, Murray College, Elgin.

◆ Mid July: Forres Highland Games, much tartan merry-making in Grant Park.

◆ Late July: Lossiemouth Folk Festival, Lossiemouth.

NAIRNSHIRE

THE COUNTY LANDSCAPE

- ◆ A little wedge of country on the southern shores of the Moray Firth, half of Nairnshire is moorland and all the rest concentrated on the Moray coast.
- ◆ The eastern and southern parts of this minute county are occupied with forests and moors, but it includes a good amount of open farmland, with the hills of the Cairngorms and the valley of the River Spey no distance away to the south.
- ◆ Culbin Sands on the coast is an RSPB reserve, a paradise for overwintering birds and a great place for birdwatchers throughout the year. The same is true of the Cawdor Woods near the Castle, which are full of woodland birds from the early weeks of the Highland spring.
- ◆ The rivers Nairn and Findhorn which flows across the county south of Culloden Moor are quiet and beautiful rivers, in valleys that were home to the first inhabitants.
- ◆ Much of the county formed part of the ancient province of Moray.

ONE OF NAIRNSHIRE'S claims to fame is that it is wee: one of the smallest Scottish counties, with the smallest population in all the Scottish counties. But think of Nairnshire and you think of Cawdor Castle – Shakespeare's setting for that 'Scottish play' where Macbeth kills King Duncan. I don't know if this link is a good or bad thing for the county, but it certainly gives Nairnshire a fatal attraction.

TOWNS AND VILLAGES

The only town is little Nairn itself, which has the reputation of being the driest and sunniest town in all Scotland. Nairn has spent most of its history as a peaceful farming and fishing community and was roused from this historic slumber just once, in April 1746, when the Duke of Cumberland's Army spent the night before the battle of Culloden here, marching out next morning to defeat the clans on Drumossie Moor.

Boasting as it does one of the mildest, driest and sunniest climates in the British Isles, Nairn became popular with visitors in Victorian times, and is still dependent on tourism, especially with

CAWDOR CASTLE *A fairy-tale castle of turrets, dungeons and hidden passageways; best known for its literary associations.*

golfers who come here to play on the Links, one of the finest golf courses in Scotland.

LOCAL HISTORY

Clava Cairns are Scotland's Stonehenge and they lie below Culloden Moor in the valley of the River Nairn. Built around 3,000BC they pose more questions than they answer, not least were they burial mounds or astronomical temples? There are 25 stone circles – a veritable Valley of the Kings – and eight of these are located within a distance of a mile on the plain of Clava (a mile to the south of Culloden battlefield). They are known as Druidical circles or Druid Temples but they are not known to have been burial places, that is, the tombs of great men of the Neolithic Age which in Scotland began about 2,000BC and lasted till around 750BC.

Cawdor, a small village in the centre of Nairnshire is best known for the reference to the Thane of Cawdor in Shakespeare's *Macbeth*. Cawdor Castle is a fine, moated fortress, dating from 1454, with a drawbridge and all the medieval trimmings, the most romantic castle in the Eastern Highlands and open to the public in the summer.

In the 16th century, or so the story goes, Nairn supported two communities, one of fishermen, the other crofters. The fishermen only spoke Gaelic and the crofters only spoke English, so the King, James VI, used to boast that he had a town in his Kingdom so vast that the people living at one end of the High Street could not understand the people who lived at the other. The story of the Fishertown community is told in the Fishertown Museum in Nairn.

Bell towers feature in this county with an unusual double bell tower at the Old Kirk in Auldearn, and one that stands separated from its church atop a hill at Ardlach. This was to allow the sound of the bell to carry throughout the surrounding countryside. As well as calling the locals to worship, the bell also warned of cattle reavers in the neighbourhood.

The county shares with Morayshire a history of witches and witchcraft and five miles east of Nairn just off the A96 you will find the site of the original 'Blasted Heath' at Macbeth's Hillock, where the witches stirred their magical brews. More hubble bubble followed in 1662 at a witch trial in Auldearn, where the witch confessed that she and her coven used to fly to Kempock Stone in Renfrewshire to raise the wind there taking "a rag of cloth [we] wet it in water, and we take a beetle (mallet) and knock on the rag on a stone…". Perhaps golfers the world over have these ladies to thank for the finest wind-free golf in the land.

COUNTY FACTS

Origin of name: Named from the local river, which in Gaelic is Uisage'nEarn, meaning River of the Alder Trees. It is possible however that it derives from the Pre-Celtic language for "flowing water".

Name first recorded: c. 1200.

County Town:
NAIRN Standing on the Moray Firth it is a holiday resort enjoying, according to BBC travel shows, the longest sandy resort beach in Europe. The harbour is a haven for pleasurecraft and there are two 18-hole championship golf courses.

Other Towns:
AULDEARN Has a very fine 17th-century circular dovecote at Boath with a commanding view of the battlefield where Montrose defeated the Covenanters in 1645.
CAWDOR A picturesque medieval castle with a fine drawbridge and gateway and splendid gardens surrounding it. This pleasant village also has a church with an unusual tower and Norman doorway.
FERNESS Close to one of the loveliest reaches of the river Findhorn with woods and high rocky banks culminating in the beauty spot of Dulcie Bridge where the hills rise to 2,000 feet and a rocky gorge spanned by an 18th-century single-arched bridge.

County rivers: Nairn, Findhorn.

Highest point: Carn-Glas-Choire at 2,182 feet.

Nairnshire's local government: The County of Nairnshire comes under the Highland unitary authority. Ferrintosh is a detached part of Nairnshire in Ross-shire and Dunmaglass is Nairnshire in Inverness-shire; both are administered by the unitary Highland District Council. A tiny part of Nairnshire detached in Morayshire around Shenvault on the River Divie comes under Moray District Council.

FAMOUS NAMES

◆ Willie Whitelaw who was a long-standing buttress to Margaret Thatcher's years in office was born and bred in Nairn.
◆ Nairn was a favourite holiday destination of Charlie Chaplin.
◆ Nairn's Newton Hotel has had Harold Macmillan, as well as Hollywood actors Burt Lancaster, Charlton Heston and Larry Hagman as guests.
◆ General Grant who led an expedition to discover the source of the Nile was born in Nairn.

COUNTY CALENDAR

◆ May: Nairn Golf Week combines excellent golfing facilities with tuition provided by famous professionals and a round of social events.
◆ July: Nairn Gala Week includes sheep-dog trials.
◆ Mid-August: Nairn Highland Games.
◆ August: Nairn agricultural show.
◆ August: Nairn Highland Games, The Links, Nairn. First held in 1877 these are traditional games, with caber tossing, piping and Highland dancing.

ORKNEY

THE COUNTY LANDSCAPE

◆ The landscape of the Orkney Islands is not unlike that of the Northern Highlands, with the sea cliffs but without the mountains. The islands have been well described as resembling the backs of sleeping whales, and they present a mixture of soaring cliffs, sandy bays and rocky coves, heather covered moorland, shallow, heavily cultivated valleys, and grassy meadows cloaked with wild flowers in the spring.

◆ The county consists of a group of 73 islands, but some of these become peninsulas at low tide, and most are uninhabited. They are separated from the mainland of Caithness by the Pentland Firth. The largest is called Pomona, or Mainland.

◆ The island of Hoy has dramatic sea cliffs and the soaring challenging column of The Old Man. But taken as a group the islands are gentle rather than rugged, ideal for walks, birdwatching, or observing the seals.

◆ The weather can be a trial, and visitors need to be prepared and dressed for it.

◆ The islands in the west have generally very steep beaches, and are hilly inland. They are quite treeless, owing to the high winds.

◆ Much of the land is peat and moor, but some small-scale, high intensity agriculture, mainly of cattle and poultry, is beginning to encroach.

FAMOUS NAMES

◆ Orkney tends to produce poets including the Booker nominated author and poet George Mackay Brown. Another poet is Edwin Muir, brought up on the island of Wyre.

◆ Local boy Gordon Strachan got a chance to appear alongside Ray MacAnally in the charming film *Venus Peter* (1989). The story of a boy, his grandfather and a whale was shot entirely in Orkney.

◆ Kirkwall is home to the local saint, St Magnus, who provided the reason for the town's remarkable cathedral.

◆ Longhope should be remembered and visited as the home of the crew of the local lifeboat, who went to sea in terrible weather to rescue the crew of a Liberian tanker. The lifeboat overturned and the entire crew drowned, leaving behind seven widows and ten children.

◆ Orkney folk are said to be farmers with boats as opposed to Shetlanders who are fishermen with crofts.

ST MARGARET'S HOPE *The Pink House on South Ronaldsay.*

IT IS EASY to see the Orkney Islands from the cliffs on the north coast of Scotland. They stand out in the sea to the north, flat-topped, bleak, treeless, edged with wave-washed cliffs, the first in a long, stepping-stone series of islands that flows from Scotland towards the coast of Norway. And it's easy to see why so many people from England come here to settle – few places in the British Islands can offer such tranquillity.

TOWNS AND VILLAGES

Of the 70 or so islands in the Orkney group, not counting those wee rocks and skerries, the larger islands are very fertile, a paradise for birdwatchers and botanists, and still greatly underpopulated. Kirkwall, the island's capital is a small town and port, the houses clustered around the bulk of St Magnus Cathedral, the focal point of the town. St Magnus was built from about 1137 by a Viking earl, Kol of Agdir, whose uncle was St Magnus. The cathedral survived the ravages of time and was steadily enlarged over the centuries. Today, although nine centuries of salt sea air have ravaged the soft sandstone, the building is still magnificent and would not look out of place in any of the cathedral cities of Europe. Other sites to see in Kirkwall include the Bishop's Palace, built in the 12th century, though only the walls and tower remain, and the Earl's Palace, which dates from the 1600s but includes such fittings as a medieval lavatory.

One place not to miss in Kirkwall is the Museum of Orkney History, in the Tankerness House, which includes, among other treasures, a set of *ba'* for use in the annual Kirkwall ball-game (of which more anon).

Dounby is a large village and a farming centre, with yet another prehistoric site, Maes Howe, but southeast of here, back on the coast, modernity intrudes again at Stromness, best known for the great bay and anchorage of Scapa Flow, where the German fleet was scuttled in the First World War. Stromness is not very large but it was once the great port of the Orkney Islands, the only 'run-ashore' for generations of British sailors from the Victorian era to the end of the Second World War.

The most dramatic island in the group is Hoy, best known for the great pillar known as the Old Man of Hoy, a challenge to generations of rock climbers. It was here in 1969 that the BBC filmed their ground-breaking live outdoor broadcast. The village of Longhope on Hoy is remembered for the tragic lifeboat disaster of 1969 when the entire crew were drowned.

Most of the Orkney communities are very small and survive on the revenue from the oil refinery on Flotta, crofting, sheep-farming and tourism. The islands are a mix of moorland, some having chambered cairns and prehistoric settlements, with eco tourism and natural history studies attracting visitors to see the large seal colonies and prolific bird life. North Ronaldsay is flat and windswept and scoured by the sea, another good place to see seals. Westray and Papa Westray lie as the name suggests, on the Western, Atlantic side of the group and catch the full fetch of the Atlantic. These islands soar from the sea, sheltered by dramatic cliffs, the two islands connected by the shortest flight in Britain – just two minutes from take-off to landing.

LOCAL HISTORY

Birsay is close to Skara Brae, the most famous prehistoric site on Orkney, the remnants of a Bronze Age fishing and farming community. The peoples here lived by fishing and subsistence agriculture though plagued, as in Shetland and the Western Island, by raiders and sea rovers from Scotland and Norway. The remains of Pictish settlements are found on West Mainland, and the great memorial to the long Viking era is the cathedral of St Magnus. After the Scots kings seized Orkney in 1231, the islands languished under various Earls, and were used as sheep runs, but fishing remained the staple industry, though hundreds of Orcadians, skilled in seal fishing, departed to Canada, recruited as fur-hunters by the Hudson Bay Company.

COUNTY FACTS

Origin of name: From the Old Norse meaning Whale Island (Ork being whale; ay being isles).

Name first recorded: c. 330BC.

County Motto: *Boreas Domus Mar Amicus* ("The North our Home, the Sea our Friend").

County Town:

KIRKWALL Quaint Nordic place with steep-gabled houses line the streets of Mainland's capital. There is a constant coming and going of lobster boats, coasting 'puffers' and ferries in the busy harbour.

Other Towns:

BALFOUR Row of identical cottages built by Balfour family to house estate workers.

PIEROWALL Principal village of the island of Westray. Large Viking cemetery discovered beneath the sand dunes here.

ST MARGARET'S HOPE Lovely group of houses in a sheltered bay on South Ronaldsay. Named after Margaret, 'Maid of Norway', who died here in 1290 on her way to marry the future Edward II.

STROMNESS Consists of one long, narrow street – with several name changes. Many of the seaward houses have their own jetties.

◆ Dounby ◆ Finstown

County rivers: Orkney has no rivers.

Highest point: Ward Hill on Hoy at 1,565 feet.

Orkney's local government: There's not much you can get wrong with Orkney's boundaries as the Orkney Islands unitary authority coincides with those of the County of Orkney.

COUNTY CALENDAR

◆ May: Orkney Country Music Festival including Irish music at various venues.

◆ End May: Orkney Traditional Folk Festival features folk bands from Shetland to Scandinavia, as well as dances, ceilidhs and jamming sessions.

◆ End June: St Magnus Festival, Kirkwall and Stromness. A six-day festival of music, drama, poetry and the visual arts.

◆ July: Stromness Shopping Week. A lively one week programme of events in and around Stromness.

◆ August: Festival of the Horse and Boys. Traditional ploughing match, where boys plough the sand on South Ronaldsay.

◆ June-September: A Taste of Orkney includes exhibitions, demonstrations and competitions throughout Orkney involving much local produce.

◆ August: Orkney Agricultural Show at Bignold Park, Kirkwall.

◆ September: Orkney Science Festival is certainly not for brain-boxes but is hands-on fun with talks, workshops and exhibitions.

◆ Christmas Day: The 200-year-old Boy's and Men's Ba' game, Kirkwall. A mass football game with tussles lasting up to six hours. Not for the soccer purist, or the faint hearted.

PEEBLESSHIRE

TWEEDDALE

THE COUNTY LANDSCAPE

◆ Peeblesshire is a small Scottish county, sandwiched between the Pentland Hills and the Scottish Border county of Selkirkshire. The county is bounded to the north by Midlothian, to the west by Lanarkshire, and to the east and south by Selkirkshire and Dumfriesshire. The ground is high, for a lowland county, and much of the soil is heavy clay.

◆ The countryside of Peeblesshire is not unlike that of the Border. Low hills, forests, green valleys, smooth, open-topped ridges, with the Tweed valley as the central gem.

◆ The River Tweed, famous for salmon fishing, flows through the centre of the county. Some of the loveliest river scenery occurs around Peebles itself.

◆ Glentress Forest is a vast woodland of spruce, Douglas firs, Scots pine and larch and is the oldest State forest in the south of Scotland with golden pheasants and grouse skulking in the undergrowth.

◆ Much of the county is farming land, well supplied with sheep, but there are great forests and the wide stretch of water provided by the Talla reservoir near Tweedsmuir.

◆ The Tweed valley is lined on either side with forested or heather-clad hills. One of these, the Fans Law near Tweedsmuir rises to 1,500 feet. The Tweed valley is fed by smaller streams like the Leithen and Talla Water.

WITH VERY FEW roads, only one or two towns and no great quantity of villages, this is a rural county, of hills and farmland, small streams and winding rivers, the biggest river being the mighty Tweed. This is a borders county, tranquil rather than bustling, but rather pleasant for all that. Although the towns of Peebles and Innerleithen are more-or-less commuter towns for Edinburgh, nevertheless they're both very bijoux and polite … well I had a particularly fine high tea in Peebles I recall.

TOWNS AND VILLAGES

The gentle mood that hangs about the entire county is found in a concentrated form in Peebles, a somewhat swish wee town on the banks of the Tweed. Peebles is a market centre for the Tweeddale valley, a lush farming area, and the town is full of small family-run shops, set about clean, well-ordered streets. The principle attraction for visitors is the Tweeddale Museum in the High Street – Tweeddale is the ancient name of the county – a rather curious place since it contains very few original exhibits but is filled with reproductions of famous things, like part of the Parthenon frieze – better known as the Elgin Marbles – and other famous sculptures.

These reproductions, now less numerous than when donated, were given to the town by William Chambers, a local gentleman who felt that his fellow citizens, while the canniest of Scots in trading matters, needed educating in the finer things of life; what the other citizens thought of this presumption is not on record.

PEEBLES *The place to relax and get fit is the town's Hydro.*

Peebles is a cheerful little town, very popular with fishermen and walkers. The name is curious since it is derived from the Celtic pebyll, which means a tent. The local hills and moors are ideal for walking and there are many places which can serve as walking objectives, including Neidpath Castle, built as a border fortress in the Middle Ages but extensively remodelled in the 17th century. Traquair House, to the east of Peebles, is a very stately stately-home, residence of the Earls of Traquair who have lived here since the 10th century – making it the oldest house in Scotland to have been inhabited continuously by the same family. It is said that 27 monarchs, English or Scots, have stayed or visited Traquair, including Bonnie Prince Charlie, whose visit is commemorated by the ever-open Seekit Yetts, the main gates. The Prince marched out through these gates on his way to England and the Earl vowed that the gates would never be shut until a Stuart King sat on the throne again. That was 250 years ago but the family have kept their promise and the gates stay open. Traquair House is full of fine furniture and relics of the past, including some connected with the Prince.

While in this eastern corner of Peeblesshire, a good place to visit would be the Museum of Woollen Textiles at Walkerburn; interesting for the history of the Border wool trade and good for shopping. Another place well worth a look is Innerleithen, six miles south east of Peebles, a pretty village with pastel-painted houses, mainly because it featured in *St Ronan's Well*, a novel written by Sir Walter Scott in 1823. St Ronan was a Celtic saint and the waters of his well came in useful in the last century when Innerleithen became a spa. The men of Innerleithen were an athletic crowd and they established the annual St Ronan's Games still held here every July, as part of a one-week-long village carnival. The village also has a thriving wool trade, largely in cashmere.

Another pulchritudinous place in this pert county is Stobo, a village in Tweeddale, noted locally for the finely trimmed hedges that line the main street – the 'Stobo Hedges'. Built in local stone, by the local lairds all the houses blend into a pleasing whole, though the church is much earlier and stands on a 6th-century site. Stobo Castle, whose towers can be seen over the trees, is now a popular health farm.

Finally Tweedsmuir, on the road to Moffat and Dumfries, which provided the peerage title for John Buchan, of *The 39 Steps* fame, when he became Lord Tweedsmuir in 1935. Tweedsmuir lies in the narrow part of the Tweed valley and apart from some fine whitewashed houses contains a churchyard full of monuments to local Covenanters, killed here in the wars.

LOCAL HISTORY

The history of Peeblesshire is linked to that of the Border counties, which lie just to the south. The castles were built to buttress the Border peel towers. The Scots Parliament met in Peebles in 1346, the year of Crècy, after King David II had been captured by the English, and the Douglas family, notorious along the Border for their feud with the Northumbrian Percies. Traquair House provides Peeblesshire – and Scotland – with that rarest of historic links, one family with roots in the 10th century, and Innerleithen takes the history further back still, to St Ronan and his well, first mentioned in the 7th century.

COUNTY FACTS

Origin of name: From the Celtic pebyll meaning tent, or shielings. The county was in pre-Roman times the stamping ground of the nomadic Gadeni tribes.

Name first recorded: 1116.

County Motto: Onward Tweeddale.

County Town:

PEEBLES An excellent angling centre and world famous for the manufacture of tweed. Has one of the oldest church remains in Scotland.

Other Towns:

BROUGHTON Village possessed by John Murray, secretary to Prince Charles Edward during 1745. By turning king's evidence he saved its neck. Also a favourite retreat of Lord Tweedsmuir, better known as author John Buchan.

INNERLEITHEN Attractive woollen town, with mineral springs, on the Leithen Water.

TRAQUAIR Once upon a time the village was more important than Innerleithen. .

TWEEDSMUIR Close to the source of three great rivers: the Tweed, Annan and Clyde, and centre of much romantic culture. Historic spired kirk and opposite the ancient Castle of Oliver, the grim guardian of the Upper Tweed, built by Oliver Fraser in the reign of David I. The Frasers were Sheriffs of Tweeddale and the most powerful barons in Peeblesshire.

WEST LINTON Pretty village on the Lyne Water that makes a good base for rambling. Famous for stonemasonry. Linton's stone-carvers became the chief gravestone-carvers of the county.

County rivers: Tweed, Lyne, Manner, Leithen, Quair.

Highest point: Broad Law at 2,754 feet.

Peeblesshire's local government: The County of Peeblesshire is governed by the Scottish Borders unitary council.

FAMOUS NAMES

◆ The most famous local name is John Buchan, later Lord Tweedsmuir, author of *Greenmantle* and *The 39 Steps*, who took his title from the village of Tweedsmuir in the south of the county.

◆ The Marquis of Queensberry, born in Peebles in 1724 was known as Old Q, and famous throughout Britain for his gambling.

COUNTY CALENDAR

◆ April: Innerleithen. The Easter Egg Extravaganza, Traquair House. Over 1,000 Easter Eggs are hidden in the maze and grounds for children under 10 to find.

◆ May: Innerleithen Beer Festival featuring Traquair's own brew.

◆ July: Innerleithen. St Ronan's Games, held here for a week every July, culminating in a torchlight procession to the top of Caerlee hill where the Devil is burned in effigy on a bonfire.

◆ August: The county's agricultural show takes place at Peebles.

PERTHSHIRE

THE COUNTY LANDSCAPE

◆ The county is a large one, roughly circular, with no sea coast at all except in the southeast corner. Its county seat, Perth, is on the beautiful River Tay, close to the widening of Scotland's longest river into the Firth of Tay, a sea inlet.

◆ Perthshire itself has been called the 'Highlands in miniature', a preparation for the looming hills and glens beyond in the range of the Grampians to the north of the county. The clan names include Murrays, Menzies and Stewarts. The scenery in these southern Highlands is lovely, the country rich and prosperous. It is very gentle, lush and green compared with the sterner hills towards Aviemore and Inverness.

◆ The Trossachs are Perth's treasure, a wide mountain range belting the north border of the county, and providing spectacular views down a series of brilliant lochs and rivers. The name itself means 'bristling country' and the Trossachs do indeed surprise with their wild scenery spreading down to the height of Ben Venue, and the Pass of Achray.

◆ Wildlife benefits from the thin population and the undisturbed countryside hosts golden eagles, red and roe deer, wild cats and pine martens. Perth's swift flowing waters are full of freshwater fish and attract many anglers.

FAMOUS NAMES

◆ *Dr Finlay's Casebook* brought fame to Callander as 'Tannochbrae'.

◆ Rob Roy is buried at Balquhidder.

◆ The Duke of Atholl, at his castle in Blair Atholl, is the only person in Britain allowed a private army, the Atholl Highlanders.

◆ The 14th-century original of *The Fair Maid of Perth*, Scott's heroine, was Catherine Glover. She lived in a house in Curfew Terrace (vanished but replaced) in the 14th century.

◆ Neil Gow was born in Little Dunkeld where he composed reels and strathspeys.

COUNTY CALENDAR

◆ April-September: Pitlochry is busy with its season of plays at its Festival Theatre. Highland Games held here in September.

◆ End of July: World Highland Games with heavyweights from around the world tossing the caber and other strongman pursuits – in Callander at end of Callander's week-long festival.

◆ July: Highland Games at Lochearnhead.

◆ August: Highland Games at Crieff.

◆ August: Sheepdog trials held in Callander.

◆ August: Perth agricultural show.

LOCH ACHRAY *This picturesque loch lies in the richly wooded gorge of the Trossachs.*

BEING PLONKED IN the heart of the country gives Perthshire a special quality. This county is almost landlocked, just a teensy-weensy bit in the southeast corner gets its feet wet; but 'land-loch-ed' (!) well that's another matter because this is surely the county of lochs – Tay, Rannoch, Earn, Tummel – not forgetting straths. Perth, fair maid and all, marks the beginning of the most romantic and best known part of Scotland, the Highlands. These are memorable granite mountains set in a country of sea and inland lochs, swift streams, open valleys and heathery heaths. It's not the actual gateway, Stirling is, but it's no anti-climax!

TOWNS AND VILLAGES

In the mountainous west the narrow yet immensely scenic Trossach range is a lure for hikers and climbers, and has attracted many visitors since Scott wrote *Rob Roy*. It still remains essentially as magnificent and wild as it has always been. Here you will find three three lochs – Katrine, once occupied by Ellen Douglas who found fame in Scott's poem *The Lady of the Lake*, Venacher and Achray leading away from the small resort of Callander. Loch Tay is headed by Kenmore, and Fortingal with its thatched houses is at the head of Glen Lyon, Scotland's longest glen.

Perth is a neat little place which has few buildings from its important past, though at St John's Kirk that old blusterer John Knox once fulminated, and the Salutation Hotel once housed Bonnie Prince Charlie. Scone Palace, on the outskirts of the town, is built on the site of an ancient abbey and palace, going back to earliest recorded Scottish history. The present fanciful mansion was constructed in the early 19th century and its state rooms contain good French antiques and a vast collection of fine porcelain.

To the west is Crieff, a pleasant town on the Earn and capital of Strathearn with medieval and market crosses, a toll booth and a set of stocks. Nearby are the ruins of Drummond Castle with 17th-century gardens and a collection of armour in its remaining tower.

For golfers Perthshire is famous for the heather-clad hills at Gleneagles Hotel with its classic King's course (plus two others), and other courses such as hilly Pitlochry. Pitlochry itself is a charming town surrounded by hills, host to a famous annual theatre festival. North of Pitlochry is the white castellated home of the Atholls on the River Garry. Blair Castle is at Blair Atholl and has 32 rooms containing armour, tapestries, lace, china, embroidery, robes and jewellery. To the north is Dunkeld, a charming town with old stone built houses and a part ruined cathedral, now the parish church in a quiet square. East of Dunkeld is Blairgowrie, with Rattray, a useful base for fishermen as the fast flowing River Ericht is a salmon stream, and a place to pause for local sights such as Craighall Rattray standing above a steep river gorge.

LOCAL HISTORY

An ancient geological crack cut through the earth's crust and caused the earth to tremble along the 300 million-year-old Highland Boundary Fault. It still does today. Carved Pictish stones of very early date can be seen at the Meigle museum, and a standing Pictish stone at Fowlis Wester.

In times of recorded history, Perth was fortified by England's Edward I, and later served as capital for a hundred years until James I of Scotland was murdered there, whereupon the grieving queen moved her court and the new young king to Edinburgh for safety. At Scone Palace, the gathering place of the Scottish chieftains, a moot-hill was mounded from the soil of their native heath. Charles II was the last of the Scottish kings to be crowned on the slab of stone brought to Scone by King Kenneth I after defeating the Picts here in the 9th century AD. It was nicked by the English in 1296 and taken to Westminster Abbey, but in 1996 it was announced it will be returned.

COUNTY FACTS

Origin of name: Brittonic, a branch of the Celtic language, for a thicket or copse.

Name first recorded: c.1128.

County Motto: *Pro Lege Et Libertate* ("For Freedom And Liberty").

County Town: PERTH It is a small city, yet famous as having been Scotland's capital in medieval times. It's little St Johnstone football club that play at Perth – St Johnstone being the ancient name for Perth.

Other Towns:

ABERNETHY An erstwhile Pictish capital. It has a notable 74-foot 12th century round tower (one of only two on the Scottish mainland).

BLACKFORD Centre for Highland Spring mineral water.

COUPAR ANGUS Close to the border with Angus, it has a large, famous Cistercian abbey attracting pilgrims.

DOUNE Boasts a magnificent medieval castle on the banks of the Teith, and a vintage motor museum with gardens stretching over 60 acres of shady woods.

CALLANDER A touring centre with fishing on the Teith or pony trekking in the Trossachs. In the town there is a woollen mill and plenty of gift-shop browsing. Home of the World Highland Games too.

DUNBLANE Has a noble cathedral dating back to the 13th century, with a beautiful location overlooking the Water of Allan. James IV's mistress, Margaret Drummond, and her two sisters who were poisoned at Drummond Castle in 1502, are buried here.

KILLIN Delightful little summer and winter sports resort on the very edge of Glen Dochart and Glen Lochav encircled by mountains. Nearby Finlarig castle ruins has what is believed to be the only surviving example of a beheading pit. Views across Loch Tay towards the highest peak in the county are superb as are the nearby Falls of Dochart.

PITLOCHRY Aside from its theatre's drama, music and arts festival, this is a smashing place to buy tweeds, knitwear, rugs and mohair and also to venture to the fabulous Tummel Valley.

SCONE A name synonymous with tea and jam, but more importantly with 'the Stone of Destiny', or Stone of Scone which was the throne appropriated by Edward I in 1296 and, in a glare of publicity, handed back to Scotland 700 years later by John Major.

◆ Aberfeldy ◆ Abernethy ◆ Alyth ◆ Auchterarder ◆ Blairgowrie ◆ Bridge of Earn ◆ Comrie ◆ Errol ◆ Longforgan ◆ Methven ◆ Rattray ◆ Stanley

County rivers: Tay, Garry.

Highest point: Ben Lawers is 4,004 feet.

Perthshire's local government: A great wodge of the southwest part of the County of Perthshire is governed by the unitary Stirling council, the rest of this county forms the major part of the unitary district of Perth and Kinross, apart from the wee villages of the Pool and Yetts of Muckhart in the far south administered by Clackmannanshire unitary authority. Culross and Kincardine are Perthshire detached in Fife and under that County's unitary council.

RENFREWSHIRE

STRATHGRYFE

THE COUNTY LANDSCAPE

◆ Renfrewshire is a butterfly-shaped county on the west side of the Central Lowlands of Scotland, on the southwest side of Glasgow.

◆ The county covers 240 square miles and is bordered to the north and west by Scotland's greatest river, the Clyde. Apart from the Clyde, the principal rivers are the Black Cart and the White Cart, both of which are tributaries of the Clyde.

◆ In the west, above the Clyde estuary, the Renfrew hills consist of a plateau of moorland, with several peaks, such as Creuch Hill (1,446 feet) and, on the southern border with Ayrshire, Hill of Stake (1,711 feet) standing out. Here also are Loch Thom and Gryfe reservoir, an ingenious water system for Glasgow devised in 1827.

◆ East and south of the Renfrew hills are glens. In Shieldhill Glen, the stream known as Kip Water plunges out of the bare moorland into a chasm of birch, ash, rowan and oak – one of the last remaining deciduous woodlands in Renfrew.

FAMOUS NAMES

◆ Fans of Scottish Television's hugely successful crime series *Taggart*, about a dour Glasgow detective, is filmed in and around Paisley and the Clydeside towns.

◆ James Watt, inventor of the steam engine, was born at Greenock.

RENFREWSHIRE HAS BECOME to Glasgow what Middlesex is to London. This is Clyde country, synonymous with shipbuilding, and from the deck of a ship cruising up the Clyde, Renfrewshire unfolds like a painting – the industrial towns of Greenock and Port Glasgow standing out against the Scottish hills. Grey and green are suitable colours for Renfrewshire – the grey of its industrial heartland along the Clyde, the green of some of Scotland's most sparkling landscapes.

TOWNS AND VILLAGES

When Glasgow boomed during the Industrial Revolution, it was natural that Renfrew should do so as well. As it became one of the world's great industrial centres, the city expanded westwards along the south shore of the river. And expand it did: from core industrials including coal mining and shipbuilding to today's sophisticated high technology businesses like computing. There are two faces to the Clyde, with an imaginary line on the Renfrew side at Gourock. To the east of the line are the old industrial towns of Renfrew, which is connected to the north bank of the Clyde with a tunnel to Yoker, Greenock, Port Glasgow and Paisley, which is on the banks of the river Cart, a tributary of the Clyde. To the west lie the Renfrew resorts – villages that grew up out of propensity for wealthy folk to have weekend homes and go sailing on the Clyde. But now that heavy industry is declining, there is an increasing dependence on newer industries like tourism and the line is becoming less well defined.

GREENOCK *The town and the Clyde from the hills.*

It is the Clyde coast which remains foremost in the memory. Gourock itself is built up the side of steep hills around West Bay and Gourock Bay. Although it's close to the industrial Clyde, it's a pleasant resort with many fine, if somewhat unusual features, like Granny Kempock's Stone. This is a huge 6-foot monolith which stands by the cliff and was built to ensure fair weather for fishermen and fertility in marriage. South of Gourock is Wemyss Bay, once an exclusive residential area, with tall cliffs dotted with Victorian red stone mansions – another throwback to the prosperity of 19th-century Glasgow. Below, from the pier on the rocky coast, the car ferry leaves for Rothesay on Bute, the island, and county, on the opposite side of the sheltered Clyde estuary. For centuries, fishing provided the living on this coast – and there is still a significant fish curing industry at Gourock.

Behind the coast, the Renfrewshire hills rise abruptly to moorland and it was here, in 1827, that the civil engineer Robert Thom designed the reservoir to supply Glasgow and Clydeside with water. In this splendid walking country, with views across the Clyde to Loch Lomond and beyond, herons stalk the shallows of Loch Thom and kestrels wheel overhead. On the edges of the moor, deciduous woodlands and farmland stretch down the villages in the valleys below … places like Eaglesham, an 18th-century village built by the Earl of Eglinton. From Eaglesham the B764 road to Kilmarnock climbs to nearly 1,000 feet and in the hills around here that the fleeing Nazi Rudolf Hess landed his aircraft on his bizarre flights to Britain from Germany.

LOCAL HISTORY

The Romans marched this way, settling on the Clyde, but they seldom ventured farther north than Glasgow because they considered the local population was too hostile. Saint Mungo would have been familiar with the area, too, when he established a church in Glasgow in 543AD. The Stewarts inhabited this part of the country in the days when they were still hereditary Stewarts and not yet kings, founding Paisley Abbey in 1163. The abbey is still a massively impressive piece of architecture – the most impressive, in fact, for miles around. It is still in use as the parish church and an effigy in St Mirren's Chapel is believed to be that of Marjorie Bruce, daughter of Robert I. Part of the abbey buildings are incorporated into the 17th-century Palace of Paisley, which has been restored as a war memorial.

Also in Paisley, the town's Museum and Art Gallery contains a priceless collection of the famous Paisley shawls. The shawls, whose oriental peacock design was first introduced from Kashmir in 1770, were traditionally worn by brides when they went out with their husbands for the first time.

The shipbuilding which dominated this county for much of the 20th century was brought about by proximity to Glasgow, Scotland's largest city, and the Clyde, the country's longest river. These two factors helped Renfrewshire develop from being a county which earned its living from fishing and farming at the beginning of the 19th century to a fully industrialized county today. The Clyde provides the northern boundary of Renfrewshire and the history and prosperity of county and river are forever intertwined.

COUNTY FACTS

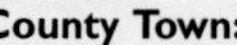

Origin of name: From the ancient British ryhn frwd, meaning "point of current'.

County Motto: *Avito Viret Honore* ("He flourishes by Ancestral Honour").

County Town:

PAISLEY A Roman settlement from AD84, possibly the Vanduara referred to by Ptolemy. A 12th-century monastic settlement was founded here around an abbey. St Mirren was one of three saints it was dedicated to: his name now revered in the town's football club. The town also gave its name to Paisley patterned shawls.

Other Towns:

ABBOTSINCH Astride the two Renfrewshire giants, Renfrew and Paisley, it's the home to Glasgow Airport.

BARRHEAD Once a centre for textile printing.

EAGLESHAM Is an 18th-century experiment in town-planning by the 10th Earl of Eglington. For some reason he favoured a triangular-shaped town.

GOUROCK Centre for steamer trips in the Firth. Head for the lighthouse of Cloch Point.

GREENOCK Site of the first dock on the Clyde, now full of tower blocks and shopping centres. One of Scotland's most ancient towns because of its safe natural anchorage. Free French naval base during World War II hence the Cross of Lorraine Memorial on Lyle Road.

LINWOOD Well-known car manufacturing centre.

NEWTON MEARNS 18th-century church, castle and old hostelry, and also a fine giftshop called Aquarius.

PORT GLASGOW One of the world's greatest shipbuilding towns. The first steamship was built in 1801 and the first service in Britain started-up here in 1812.

RENFREW A centre of what remains of Scotland's once thriving heavy industry, including boilermaking and shipbuilding.

◆ Bishopton ◆ Busby ◆ Elderslie ◆ Giffnock ◆ Inchinnan ◆ Johnstone ◆ Kilbarchan ◆ Kilmalcolm ◆ Neilston

County rivers: Rotten Burn, Black Cart, White Cart.

Highest point: Hill of Stake at 1,711 feet.

Renfrewshire's local government

The County of Renfrewshire's local government is cut into three equal slices with a hefty helping left over. The three main chunks are the unitary authorities of East Renfrewshire, Inverclyde and Renfrewshire. Finally the remnants of Renfrewshire around the populous areas of Pollockshaws, Cathcart and Nitshill fall under the City of Glasgow unitary authority.

COUNTY CALENDAR

◆ May: Kilmacolm and Port Glasgow Agricultural Show held at Knapps, Kilmacolm.

◆ May: Gourock Highland Games – Pipe band, dance competition, track and field athletics and other events.

◆ July: Sma' Shot Day, Paisley. Annual festival (150 years' old) celebrating town's weaving history.

ROSS-SHIRE : CROMARTYSHIRE

THE COUNTY LANDSCAPE

◆ A great sprawl of land running from the Black Isle, just north of Inverness, between the Moray and Cromarty Firths, to the Atlantic coast and, far to the north and west, across Easter Ross and Wester Ross, to the Inner Sound facing the Isle of Skye.

◆ This county is bounded by Sutherland in the north, by the Atlantic in the west, and by Inverness-shire, Morayshire, and the Moray Firth in the south and east. The coastline has many deep lochs. The terrain consists of groups of granite and mica slate mountains divided by glens and ravines. Consequently, there is comparatively little agriculture.

◆ The east coast has the Dornoch, Cromarty, Beauly and Moray Firths, all lovely, some filled today with North Sea oil rigs. The West Coast is glorious, a mixture of sea lochs, bays and offshore islands, like the Summer Islands, Gruinard, and a score beside.

◆ Inland lie the lochs, Loch Vaich, Loch Maree, Loch Orrin and the rest, each with its glen. As for the great glens, the choice is wide and the arguments over which is the loveliest is endless but Glen Oykel or Glen Calvie must be in the first six.

COUNTY CALENDAR

◆ June: The Annual Highland Festival. A celebration of traditional culture in the Highlands and Islands. Various locations.

◆ June: Highland Traditional Music Festival, Dingwall.

◆ July: Dingwall Highland Games has sports, piping and dancing displays.

◆ July: Lochcarron Highland Games.

◆ July: Strathconon Games. Dalbreac, Muir of Ord.

◆ August: Tain Highland Gathering, Tain.

◆ August: Strathpeffer Highland Gathering, Castle Leod, Ross-shire.

◆ August: Invergordon Highland Games.

◆ September: Invercharron Traditional Highland Games, Bonar Bridge, Ross-shire.

FAMOUS NAMES

◆ Sean Connery and Christopher Lambert battled it out with long swords (on film at least) in *Highlander* and *Highlander II* at the beautifully restored Eilan Donan Castle bestride Loch Duich in Wester Ross.

◆ Hector Macdonald of Dingwall, famous as *Fighting Mac*; 30,000 people turned out for his funeral in 1903.

◆ Sir Alexander Mackenzie, explorer of the Mackenzie River in Canada is buried in the churchyard at Avoch.

ULLAPOOL, CROMARTYSHIRE *Whitewashed houses front this busy fishing port.*

ROSS-SHIRE AND CROMARTYSHIRE are so tightly intermingled that it is hard to separate them and so they are usually treated as one county. This is a wonderful stretch of country, very Highland, savagely depopulated in the Highland Clearances (evictions to make way for sheep grazing) of the last century, and now virtually empty of people – but deer, foxes, badgers, weasels and polecats are still common but sadly martens are less so.

TOWNS AND VILLAGES

There are a few small towns and some scattered hamlets, to provide accommodation, or the basis for a tale. A place well worth a visit is Strathpeffer Spa, just west of Dingwall, a rather elegant town, set up in the last century when spas were all the rage. Heading to the northwest, the village of Achiltibuie sits at the foot of Stack Polly, a fine hump of mountain, and is famous for the *Achiltibuie Hydroponicum,* an indoor garden that looks out across the waters of the sound to the Summer Isles (which publishes its own stamps). Tain, which is said to be the bonniest town in Ross-shire and once the capital of the county, can also claim to be Scotland's oldest burgh, with a charter dating back to 1066. In later centuries it became a market town for the people of Clan Ross, who gave their name to this part of the Highlands, as well as a pilgrimage centre, thanks to the shrine of St Duthac, contained in the 12th-century St Duthac's chapel, though this is now a ruin.

On the northeast coast another claim to fame is the picturesque village of Plockton whose alter-ego is the fictional village of Lochdubh, home to the self-styled sheriff *Hamish Macbeth* and the eponymous TV show. Plockton itself does not have a PC Macbeth, the nearest police station being at Kyle of Lochalsh around six miles south of Plockton. Lochalsh is more familiar as the home to the infamous Skye Toll Bridge.

Ullapool is a ferry terminal and most popular port for Russian fish-factory ships, at the entrance to Loch Broom, the departure point for the Western Isles. It has superb coastal and mountain scenery, an arboretum, and the tiny Lochbroom Museum, full of artifacts and relics of the famous, from the Duke of Wellington to Harry Lauder – neither of whom had any connection with Ullapool. The area is also famous for whisky, with the distilleries of Glenmorangie at Tain, Glen Ord at Muir of Ord, Balblair at Edderton, and Dalmore at Alness.

LOCAL HISTORY

The Shandwick Stone near Balintore, one of the sunniest spots hereabouts, is noted for the finest example of Pictish carvings in Scotland. The Picts were well established on the Black Isle and the Groom House Museum at Rosemarkie has fine displays of Pictish life and art.

Kenneth Mackenzie, the Brahan Seer, Scotland's answer to Nostradamus, lived in the first half of the 17th century and made many prophecies about Scotland, some of which are coming true. Unfortunately, he had a vision showing the Earl of Seaforth misbehaving in Paris and passed this on to the Countess; she accused the Seer of witchcraft and he was burned at the stake at Chanonry Point near Fortrose; the spot is marked by a plaque.

The Clearances of the last century when the lairds cleared out the clansmen to make way for sheep (a disaster from which the Highlands have never recovered) cause widespread misery graphically illustrated by the scratches on the glass of the church at Croik: '*Glen Calvie people here, 8 May, 1845*' and '*Glen Calvie people, the wicked generation!*', where the dispossessed clansmen were sheltered after being driven from the glens by their Chief.

The story of *Fighting Mac*, Sir Hector Macdonald, is told in Dingwall's town museum. From Private in the Gordon Highlanders he rose to Sergeant and distinguished himself in the Afghan Wars. He was offered the choice of the VC or a commission; he took the latter and went on to further glory. At the battle of Omdurman, when his battalion was cut off, surrounded by dervishes and ordered to retreat he replied: *Ah'll see them dammed first. We maun just fight it out* … and fight it out they did. But in 1903, when he was stationed in Ceylon he was accused of making homosexual advances and was summoned home for an enquiry and ordered back to Ceylon for court martial. On the way back he shot himself in Paris. He remains, rightly, a local hero, and Dingwall is full of memorials to his gallant career.

COUNTY FACTS

Origin of name: Ross is from the Gaelic, meaning "the high, upsurging rocky moorland where nothing but heather will grow". Cromarty is from the Gaelic, meaning a promontory or bay with a crooked coastline (crom meaning crooked; bàdh meaning bay).

Name first recorded: *ante* 1100.

County Motto: "Dread God and Do Well".

County Towns:

CROMARTY This is the main centre of the Black Isle, and said to be one of the three top seaside towns of Scotland, probably because of the attractive mixture of fisherman's 'cottages' and fine merchants' houses. It's an architectural gem, a rare example of an 18th-century burgh, with a fine Classic style courthouse.

DINGWALL Since 1843 made capital of both Ross-shire and Cromartyshire, this is a fine little town, overlooked by the Fyrish Monument, and built by a local landowner in the last century to provide work for the town's unemployed. Home to Ross County FC.

FORTROSE A Royal Burgh and important religious centre previously called Chanonry where the Bishop had his residence. Like the counties of Ross and Cromarty it has been united with the nearby resort of Rosemarkie - itself a place of great antiquity since it came into being in 1494 courtesy of King James II.

TAIN This charming town with its strong religious connections was the birth place of St. Duthus and is close to the ancient Abbey of Fearn, which must not be missed.

Other Towns:

GAIRLOCH A fishing port and site of the Gairloch Heritage Museum.

INVERGORDON Former naval base with fine harbour.

KYLE OF LOCHALSH Home of the notorious Skye Bridge, opened in 1995, which replaced the ferry as the link to the Isle of Skye.

STORNOWAY Only town of any size in the Hebrides. It's a fishing port.

STRATHPEFFER Victorian spa town where you can sample the sulphur-laden water.

ULLAPOOL Fishing port built on a grid plan. Look out for 'Welcome to Ullapool' sign in Cyrillic script.

◆ Avoch ◆ Balallan ◆ Barras ◆ Carloway ◆ Evanton ◆ Muir of Ord

County rivers: Oikel, Repath (Carron).

Highest point: Càrn Elge on Hoy at 3,877 feet.

Ross-shire & Cromartyshire's local government: Ross-shire so often twinned with Cromartyshire both come under the jurisdiction of the unitary Highland council based at Inverness. The part of Ross-shire in the Outer Hebrides known as the Isle of Lewis is administered by the Western Isles unitary authority. Cromartyshire is made-up of a large number of detached portions within Ross-shire or strewn along the Sutherland border. The differences between them had always been artificial and depended upon which areas were more strongly influenced by the Chieftains of Ross or the Earls of Cromarty. The counties were amalgamated in 1861.

ROXBURGHSHIRE

TEVIOTDALE

THE COUNTY LANDSCAPE

◆ Roxburghshire, which is in the central part of the Scottish borders, is like a steep-sided saucer, with hills in the north and the southeast and fertile valleys in between. With its peaceful rolling landscape, It is perhaps the quintessential border county an inspiration to painters and poets alike.

◆ The valleys are created by the rivers Tweed and Liddel and rising above the valleys are rocky outcrops such as the triple-peak Eildon Hills, so loved by Sir Walter Scott. The hills were formed from volcanic activity millions of years ago. They are a cluster of domes of plutonic rock standing above old red sandstone, which accounts for the colour of the soil in and around Jedburgh. In the southeast, the Cheviots, reach around 2,500 feet on the county's border with Northumberland.

FAMOUS NAMES

◆ Robert the Bruce was so upset at the desecration in 1322 of Melrose Abbey that he voted £2,000 (at that time more than the entire Scots treasury!) for its restoration.

◆ Roxburghshire traditionally produces some of Scotland's finest rugby footballers. Craig Chalmers, Dodie Weir and Brian Redpath all come from Melrose and Gary Armstrong from Jedburgh. The BBC TV rugby commentator Bill Maclaren is a teacher in Hawick.

◆ Yachtsman Chay Blyth, the first man to sail solo around the world against the prevailing winds, was born in Hawick. He worked in a local factory before joining the Army to see and then sail round the world.

◆ James Thomson who wrote the words to *Rule Britannia* was born at Ednam in 1700.

◆ Poet John Leydon was born at Denholm.

COUNTY CALENDAR

◆ Early February: Jedburgh Ba' Games is a traditional event involving an energetic game of handball played with leather balls decorated with coloured streamers.

◆ Early June: Hawick Common Riding has horse riding and other events.

◆ July: Jedburgh Border Games; an athletics meeting at the Riverside Park, Jedburgh.

◆ Late July: Dunedin Dancers' International Folk Dance Festival is a week-long festival at various centres in Kelso and Hawick.

◆ Late July: Border Union Show – the agricultural show in Springwood Park, Kelso.

◆ Mid-August: Melrose Pipe Band Contest with pipe band, drum major and Highland dance competition.

◆ Late September: Kelso races National Hunt meeting at Kelso racecourse.

***JEDBURGH** The Abbey has the only complete Transitional west front in Scotland.*

MY FIRST FAN club was based in Lilliesleaf, Roxburghshire so I have got a natural soft spot for this county. It is a hub of the woollen industry and I've come away from many a main town with some fabulous tops and sweaters. And getting there is as pleasurable as arriving, as they say, for a dramatic entry to a county it's hard to beat travelling along the A68 from Northumberland into Roxburghshire. As the road vaults over the Cheviots at the hill known as Carter Bar, practically the whole of Roxburghshire is laid out at your feet – hill, dale and river coming together in perfect harmony.

TOWNS AND VILLAGES

It's hard getting away from Scott in Roxburghshire. Scotland's best-known writer was born in Edinburgh, but spent much of his life in the Borders, in and around Melrose, a friendly little place sandwiched between the Tweed and the Eildon Hills. Melrose is built around its 12th-century Cistercian abbey – with just a main street and one or two other roads leading off it. This is very much abbey territory, but like its counterparts in Jedburgh and Kelso, Melrose Abbey suffered greatly from the warfare which raged over the centuries in these parts. In Scott's time, these gaunt ruins showed the signs of their battle-scarred past, but although they have been cleaned up they have lost none of their romanticism.

This is also the land of the swirling and sparkling Tweed – and Tweed means cloth. Sheep and clear streams, ideal for washing wool, were the catalysts for the industry and for centuries it was quite literally a cottage industry – the tweeds being woven by hand in the grey whinstone houses in the hill country. Today local wool is considered a little too coarse for the manufacture of top quality garments and so much of the wool for factory use is imported.

Hawick, 12 miles south of the Tweed, is the most important centre for the manufacture of classic sweaters, with notable names like Pringle and Lyle & Scott having factories there. Both these names have even dressed me for my television shows in Britain and America – for these Roxburghshire companies have a cosmopolitan cachet.

Tweed also spells salmon fishing – a sport which makes a significant contribution to the success of local hotels and restaurants. For eating out visitors are assured good cooking from fresh local ingredients – salmon from the Tweed, trout from the streams and beef raised on the plump pastures - what more could you ask.

LOCAL HISTORY

An Iron Age hill fort was established on the Eildon hills and, to the east of Melrose, Newstead is reputed to be the oldest continually inhabited village in the country, having been occupied since the Romans established their fort of Trimontium on the banks of the Tweed. The Romans built a bridge to carry Dere Street north to Edinburgh.

Later came the religious movements, establishing the great abbeys at Melrose, Dryburgh (in Berwickshire), Kelso and Jedburgh – all of them ruined now, their broken masonry standing like ghosts from a vanished past. Melrose was founded in 1136 in the reign of David I (along with the other three Border monasteries) and suffered repeatedly at the hands of invading English armies. It was pillaged and burnt by Edward II in 1322, virtually destroyed again in 1385 by Richard II, and burned yet again in 1546 in Henry VIII's reign.

The decline of the abbeys was followed by the rise of the Reivers, or plunderers, who brought anarchy to the countryside. Only clan loyalties mattered and Jedburgh gave its name to 'Jeddart Justice' – a euphemism for hanging without trial. Later civilization returned, with the building of stately homes, none grander than Floors Castle, home of the Duke and Duchess of Roxburgh, at Kelso. Built by William Adam in 1721, it has a rooftop as magnificent as any in Britain, with superb corner towers, fretting and balustrades. It also has splendid views – out across the Tweed Valley to the distant Cheviots.

COUNTY FACTS

Origin of name: From the Old English, meaning Fortress of Hroc – Hroc being the rook.

Name first recorded: Not known.

County motto: *Ne Cede Malis Sed Contra Audentior Ito* ("Yield Not To Adversity But Oppose It More Boldly").

County Town: **JEDBURGH** The Castle here was the frequent home of royalty from the end of the 11th century. Nearby Hermitage Castle was visited by Mary, Queen of Scots. Scott met Wordsworth in the town – that must have been quite a meeting of minds.

Other Towns:

HAWICK World-wide reputation for its classic knitwear goods. Its Lamb Sales (in August and September) are the oldest mart in Britain.

KELSO The most eye-catching feature of the town (apart from the luxurious Sunlaws House Hotel) is the five-arched bridge modelled in 1800 on London's old Waterloo Bridge. The town square looks like a cross between continental and Scottish architecture and is all the better for that with its cobbled grounds and high-pitched attic windows. Nearby Smailholm Tower is 57 feet high and is an impressive borderland keep built on a rocky outcrop with magnificent panoramic views to the Cheviots.

LIDDESDALE This is one of the ancient names and areas associated with Roxburghshire. It includes Canonbie, Newcastleton, Riccarton and Hermitage Castle – historic communities all well worth a detour. The latter is a famous 13th-century castle, once stronghold of the Douglases, overlooking Hermitage Water and moorland. Mary, Queen of Scots contracted a fever here and nearly died.

MELROSE Unassuming abbey town with the heart of The Bruce buried here. Nearby is Abbotsford house, the last and most famous of Sir Walter Scott's homes, which he designed himself adding gaslight, one of the first owners of country-houses to do so. He died here in 1832. There is a collection of his effects here.

NEWTON ST BOSWELLS Administrative centre; this town is linked to the village of St Boswells by a spacious green, by the River Tweed, where the modernized 16th-century Lessudden House has two very interesting knockers.

ROXBURGH Once ranked on a par with Edinburgh and Stirling but was destroyed by the Scots themselves to avoid it getting into English hands.

TOWN YETHOLM Lies nestled at the foot of the Cheviots and was once the chief base for the Scottish gipsies, known as Gipsy Palace. Marks the end of the Pennine Way, the 250-mile hill-top walk from Derbyshire.

◆ Darnwick ◆ Denholm ◆ Maxwellheugh

County rivers: Tweed, Teviot, Liddel, Jed, Ettrick, Gala, Leader, Eden.

Highest point: Auchop Cairn at 2,422 feet.

Roxburghshire's local government:
Roxburghshire is governed by the Scottish Borders unitary council.

SELKIRKSHIRE

ETTRICK FOREST

THE COUNTY LANDSCAPE

- ◆ Selkirkshire is in southern Scotland, wedged between Peeblesshire to the north and Roxburghshire to the south.
- ◆ Geographically, it is well defined, its boundaries following the valleys of the Tweed and Gala Water in the north and Ettrick Water in the south. The rolling, heather-clad Mount Ettrick and the beautiful valleys of the rivers Yarrow and Ettrick influence the county's landscape. The two rivers head in a northeasterly direction on either side of this mountain until they join together just before the county town of Selkirk. This highly attractive border town was much loved by its Sheriff (for 33 years) Sir Walter Scott.
- ◆ The river valleys are broken up by the smooth mountains of the Southern Uplands, with any number of ruined towers, further evidence of less settled times.
- ◆ Here, too, are formidable stands of forest – Elibank and Traquair to the west and Yair Hill near Selkirk.
- ◆ There are also lakes – the wide expanse of St Mary's Loch in the southwest and Akermoor and Hellmoor in the southeast. The various lochs, lakes and rivers attract trout anglers, as well as coarse fishermen after grayling, perch, pike and eels.
- ◆ Selkirkshire, and Galashiels in particular, is linked to the textiles industry and quality Scottish tweed. There are mills dotted around the landscape to prove this.

A TINY COUNTY I pass through on my way to Edinburgh. Galashiels, or Gala as they call it, is famous for rugby (and tweed), and a town whose name I was already familiar with from the Scottish rugby results. Within its meandering border it contains some of Scotland's most glorious scenery: serpentine rivers ambling between tree-draped banks, hills and heather moorland where, in autumn, grouse fall foul of the marksman's gun. The Ettrick hills, whose beauty coaxed some of the best writing from both Scott and Wordsworth, drop down to St Mary's Loch, which is perhaps the finest expanse of water in southern Scotland.

TOWNS AND VILLAGES

Galashiels is the county's, if not the country's, principal textiles town. It takes its name from the word 'shielings' – the name for summer shelters built by herdsmen to protect their flocks – and the town is the headquarters of the Scottish College of Textiles, which attracts students from all over the world. Spread out for two miles along the banks of the Tweed, Galashiels would never win a beauty contest, but it does have some attractive parts – notably Valley Mill, behind Market Street, which is a fine example of 19th-century architecture. It is principally a workaday town, with one or two unusual features. The town's motto is 'sour plums', proudly displayed on the municipal buildings, a reference to an incident in 1337 when some English soldiers were slain for picking wild (sour) plums. The woollen industry is still important – and tourism increasingly so. The two industries come together in the proliferation of gift and clothes shops selling locally made garments.

SELKIRK BANNOCK *A famous local delicacy since 1859.*

Just outside Galashiels is Sir Walter Scott's old home, Abbotsford, a turreted mansion which is almost as fanciful as some of the writer's fiction and is still in the hands of female descendants, the Maxwell-Scotts. When Scott bought it in 1811 it was just a damp farmhouse called Clartyhole. Rebuilt and enlarged by Scott, it's now one of the most visited homes in the Scottish Borders. The study, with its gallery and writing desk, is little changed since Scott's time and the library contains some 9,000 bound volumes. Mementos like Napoleon's pen case and blotting book, and a lock of Lord Nelson's hair, explain the writer's passion for collecting old and unusual things.

Selkirk, where Sir Walter Scott was Sheriff from 1799 to 1831, is serenely situated on the edge of Ettrick Forest. The town rises on a hill from Ettrick Water, a salmon and trout tributary of the great Border fishing river, the Tweed. In the town centre, a row of 18th-century houses has been converted into an impressive museum – Halliwell's House Museum and Gallery – while the Flodden Monument, put up in 1913 on the 400th anniversary of the Battle of Flodden, is another reminder that there's no getting away from history in this part of the world. Cloth has been woven in Selkirk for almost four centuries – but before that the town was known for its shoes (hence, Selkirk folk are called 'souters', or shoemakers.) Nearby is the bakery where Robert Douglas turned out the original Selkirk bannock – a fruit loaf which found favour with Queen Victoria. Selkirk Bannock is quite unlike the oatcake as it is yeasted bread fruit, round and flat, originally made with only the finest sultanas imported from Turkey. Nowadays a little candied orange peel is also added.

LOCAL HISTORY

Strung out along the river Tweed and its tributaries, Ettrick Water and Gala Water, Selkirkshire reflects the twists and turns of history and fortune in the Scottish Borders. Although the Romans passed through Selkirkshire, the county is best known for the bloody skirmishes which took place in more recent times. Across the river from Selkirk is Philiphaugh where, during the Civil War, royalist forces led by Montrose were defeated in a bloody encounter by Lesley's Covenanting army in 1645. A hundred years later, the Stewart Prince Charles Edward – Bonnie Prince Charlie – passed by, stopping in Selkirk for the souters to fit his men with good shoes for their ill-fated march south into England. And each year the Selkirk Common Riding ceremony remembers a famous battle which took place outside the county – Flodden – said to be the most disastrous event in Scotland's history. At Flodden the Scots were slaughtered by the English in 1513 and each year in Selkirk, at the Common Riding, a banner captured from the English is cast on the cobbles, as allegedly it was done by the only local man to survive the battle.

But between the battles, the county's woollen industry prospered. Galashiels has been a weaving town for more than 700 years, but the present woollen industry can be traced back to 1790, when one George Mercer established the first real factory in Scotland here. This was the home of Scottish Tweed, but not because of the river. Apparently it came about because of a slip of the pen by a clerk. He transcribed the word twill (pronounced 'tweel') and by mistake put a letter 'd' at the end. Little could he have realized at the time that his slip would become a marketing man's dream.

COUNTY FACTS

Origin of name: From the Old English, sele-chyrche, meaning 'blessed church' (built for the king's use while hunting in Ettrick Forest). An alternative suggestion has the name meaning 'hall church' (sele being Old English for hall).

First recorded: 1113.

County Motto: "Leal to the Border".

County Town:

SELKIRK There is a statue of Mungo Park here which is situated in the High Street.

Other Towns:

ETTRICKBRIDGE On the Ettrick Water. The old river bridge was washed away in 1777 but a stone from it bearing the Harden coat-of-arms is built into the new bridge.

GALASHIELS Crowded textile town, known locally as 'Gala'. International reputation for the quality of its tweed. Known for its rugby team.

◆ Ashkirk ◆ Foulshiels

County rivers: Ettrick, Yarrow, Cawder.

Highest point: Ettrick Pen at 2,269 feet.

Selkirkshire's local government: The County of Selkirkshire gets its administrative act together under the Scottish Borders unitary council. Sinton is Selkirkshire detached in Roxburghshire governed under the same unitary authority as the main County.

FAMOUS NAMES

◆ The poet James Hogg, the 'Ettrick Shepherd' lived on the shores of St Mary's Loch. He was a friend of Scott and Wordsworth and there is a memorial to him beside the loch.

◆ Sir David Steel, the former Leader of the Liberal Party, lives in Selkirkshire at Ettrick Bridge. He has been MP for Selkirk, Roxburgh and Peebles which mutated into Tweedsdale, Ettrick and Lauderdale – in area one of the largest and longest titled constituencies in the UK – for more than 25 years.

◆ Mungo Park, the explorer, was born in Selkirkshire in 1771. He drowned in Africa in 1805.

COUNTY CALENDAR

◆ April: Gala Rugby seven-a-side is one of the most important events in Scotland's rugby calendar and is held in Galashiels.

◆ May: Wildlife on your Doorstep: Tweedbank, Galashiels involves a day of activities showing wildlife in and around a typical modern housing estate.

◆ June: Selkirk Common Riding is one of a series of Common Riding events held throughout the Borders.

◆ Late June : The Braw Lads Gathering is a week-long festival in Galashiels.

◆ Late July: Let's Go Fly a Kite with kite-making and an afternoon of fun at Bowhill Visitor Centre, Selkirk.

◆ November: Border Canary Association annual show, Galashiels – second largest annual show of Border canaries in the UK.

SHETLAND

THE COUNTY LANDSCAPE

◆ The county consists of over 100 islands, islets and skerries, of which well under half are inhabited. The largest is Mainland, but of the rest only Yell and Unst are of any size. They are the most northerly group of the British Isles. Their coasts are generally very ragged, with deep bays, or voes, and fjords.

◆ The landscape of the Shetland Islands will amaze, even appal, those who come from more sheltered climes. The islands are virtually treeless. Only in the hollows out of the wind do bushes and shrubs manage to survive; otherwise they are bent and twisted by the wind or scoured out of existence by the salt in the air.

◆ The one exception to this generality is the island of Fetlar, the *Garden of Shetland*, still largely without trees, but a paradise of wild flowers in the spring and early summer, ablaze with purple heather in the autumn.

◆ The coastline is a mixture of rugged cliff and white sand beach, dramatic and attractive, and the whole island group is a seabird paradise. There are nature reserves on Fetlar, Unst, at Spigga Loch on Mainland and on the island of Noss, where the cliffs of the Noup of Noss offer a home to a huge seabird colony. Another island popular with birdwatchers is Papa Stour, famous for its population of puffins. Also worth visiting is St Ninian's Island, which has a *tombolo*, a long sandspit connecting the island to the shore.

COUNTY CALENDAR

◆ January: The big event, almost the only big event in the Shetland year, is the Up-Helly-Aa festival, held in Lerwick on the second Tuesday in January. This is a very lively affair, with the men dressed in Viking costume, complete with shields and winged helmets, culminating in the firing of a Viking longship. In former times this last event took place in the harbour but the presence of oil tankers has made the launching of a blazing ship into the harbour less than sensible so the burning now takes place ashore.

◆ April: Shetland Fold Festival, Lerwick. A three to four day festival of music from the islands.

◆ May: Bergen (in Norway) to Shetland Yacht Race.

◆ New Year's Day: Foula. The inhabitants of Foula, one of the smaller islands, have yet to decide between the Julian and Gregorian calendars. They therefore use a bit of both, celebrating the old Yule-Christmas on January 6 and New Year's Day on January 13.

UNST, SHETLAND *Muckle Flugga lighthouse, the British Isles' most northerly point.*

THE FIRST POINT to make about the Shetland Islands is that they are never to be called *The Shetlands*. For local reasons, calling their home *The Shetlands* drives the islanders frantic, and since the islanders are of Viking stock driving them frantic is best avoided. I remember from my schooldays that the Shetland Islands are on the same latitude as Norway. They're so far north they seem like a foreign land windswept and interesting!

The Shetland Islands are Britain's most northern outpost, a litter of islands scattered across the North Sea. Lerwick, the capital, is closer to Bergen than Edinburgh, and this northern, not to say Norse, connection seems to cast a spell over the whole archipelago.

TOWNS AND VILLAGES

The Shetland islanders have made their living for centuries by fishing and running small crofts. Today, most of their income is derived from tourism – especially birdwatchers, and of course North Sea oil. Lerwick has become rich on the oil boom, and much of the revenue so earned is being re-invested in local developments. Just across the harbour lies Scalloway, the former capital, which retains a castle built in 1600. Scalloway today is just a fishing port, but most of the trawlers have been laid up. One place that should be visited here is the museum which contains, among other exhibits, one relating the story of the *Shetland Bus*, those boats which ferried secret agents and resistance fighters to Norway in the Second World War.

The northern parts of Mainland are noted for the oil terminal at Sullom Voe, though locals prefer to direct visitors to the village of Hillswick, which has the distinction of containing The Booth, the oldest pub in the islands. A small fishing community lives on

Whalsay, one of the most northern islands of the group, but the majority of the islands are uninhabited except by seabirds and visited only by snugly dressed groups of birdwatchers. The rest of the islands, Herma Ness, Yell, Fetlar, the outer skerries, and the especially remote island of Foula are wild, empty, desolate places.

Out on its own, set between the Shetland and Orkney islands, is Fair Isle, which both island counties have claimed over the years, though it now belongs to Shetland. The main centre of population on Fair Isle is Stonybreck and the main occupation knitting those colourful Fair Isle sweaters, and these days, tourism, especially eco-tourism.

Most of the smaller islands are just specks of land in the midst of the ocean, none more so than Unst, which is the last inhabited island before Norway. Beyond that lies Out Stack, the most northerly uninhabited island.

LOCAL HISTORY

At Mousa Broch and the settlement at Jarlshof, the evidence indicates continuous occupation of the site for at least 3,000 years. Close to the centre of Lerwick, in the middle of Clickimin loch, stands a small island containing a stone tower some 10 feet high, the centrepiece of Clickimin broch, which dates back to around 700BC. This tower once reached a height of 50 feet and the whole island would once have contained a large, well-established population.

In medieval times these islands belonged to the Kings of Norway, whose rule was disputed by the lords of Scotland and Orkney, so the islands were constantly raided and fought over. The Scots finally got possession of the islands and held them until the Act of Union in 1707 when, with the rest of Scotland, they became part of Great Britain. The islands maintain strong Nordic links and hardly feel British or Scottish for that matter.

The islands' ability to maintain a viable population depended on the rich fishing available in the North Sea and the Atlantic, but this natural bounty made at least some of the islanders rich; among the treasures excavated on Clickimin is a glass bowl, manufactured in Alexandria, Egypt, about 100BC.

The rest of the islands' story is told, in whole or in part, in the island museums, of which there are a surprising number for a place with just over 20,000 people. The archaeology of the islands and the history of the fishing industry can be studied at the Shetland Library in Lerwick. The Croft House Museum at Boddam explains the crofting industry and local crafts, and the Interpretative Centre on Fetlar explains how life is managed on one of the smaller Shetland Islands.

COUNTY FACTS

Origin of name: From the Old Norse Hjaltland, meaning 'High Land', thence Yealtland, Yetland and Zetland.

Name first recorded: ante 1289.

County Motto: *Med Lögum Skal Land Byggja* ("By Law is The Land Built Up").

County Town:

LERWICK Lies on the main island, Mainland, on the natural harbour of Bressay Sound. It is the main port and the only town of any size in the Shetland Islands. Small, rather attractive and set around a harbour, Lerwick has a fair selection of pubs, shops and hotels, and is the jumping off point for tours around the other islands. It also has the County Museum with exhibits including Stone Age implements, spinning wheels and a traditional Shetland room.

Other Towns:

BALTASOUND on the island of Unst is where you'll find Britain's most northerly pub and post office. Unst has the densest population of Shetland ponies of all the Shetland Isles.

SCALLOWAY On the west of Mainland, this main town is dominated by the ruins of the castle, built in 1600 by Earl Patrick Stewart, using forced labour. Legend has it that the blood of tenants is mixed in the mortar! The castle also features an unusual gun-port in the stair tower. Stewart also forcibly replaced Norse law with Scottish feudal law.

SUMBURGH Village dominated by airport. Until its oil boom of 1971, a man was employed to drive sheep off the airport's single runway. Remains of 3,000 year old settlement of Jarlshof lie just south of the airport.

STONYBRECH Hamlet on Fair Isle where you can see demonstrations of Fair Isle knitting, for which the island is famous.

◆ Burravoe ◆ Hamnavoe ◆ Otterswick

County rivers: There are no rivers.

Highest point: Ronas Hill, Northmaven at 1,475 feet.

Shetland's local government: The local government area for Shetland is the same as that of the County of Shetland, entitled the Shetland Islands unitary council. Both boundaries are one of the same. Mind you, whatever happened to 'Zetland', the official title for Shetland once upon a time? It's now abbreviated into the Islanders' post code – ZE!

FAMOUS NAMES

◆ The most famous name in the islands belongs not to a person but a pony. The Shetland pony, a classic breed, was bred at its best on the island of Bressay, where there was a stud which bred these sturdy little ponies by the thousand, most of them destined for work underground, in the low tunnels of coal mines.

◆ Shetland also has the distinction of having its own breed of sheep dog (15 inches high) and sheep which are also small, or 'peerie' as they say locally.

STIRLINGSHIRE

THE COUNTY LANDSCAPE

◆ Stirlingshire is a snake-like county, running north and west into the Highlands from the Firth of Forth to the eastern shores of Loch Lomond, the furthest tip touching Loch Katrine. The flatter parts, the Carse and the Forth Valley, are given over to farming but it is the rivers, lochs and hills that give this county its character.

◆ Coming up from Edinburgh the first touches of the Highlands arrive with the Ochil Hills and the Campsie Fells. The Campsie Fells are fairly gentle and have a number of small villages. There is also a Campsie Fells Trail which might attract the walkers. The Ochil Hills are rather steeper. The Forth valley is very long, some 40 miles in all, and fed by numerous streams, including the little Bannock burn.

◆ The east, Stirlingshire, bank of Loch Lomond is less developed and more attractive than the western side, though it's more heavily wooded and harder to see.

FAMOUS NAMES

◆ Rob Roy Macgregor, the 'Highland Rogue', used to collect his blackmail from the local lairds at Drymen.

◆ William Wallace, Scottish patriot, is commemorated at the Wallace Memorial, Stirling and at Falkirk and Stirling Bridge.

◆ Mary, Queen of Scots, is remembered in Stirling Castle and at the Church of the Holy Rood in Stirling town, where she was christened.

STIRLINGSHIRE IS FOR me the gateway to the Highlands, and the magnificent setting of Stirling Castle perched high on its lofty crag sticks in mind despite not having seen it for nigh on 20 years. This fortress leaves me with striking memories still. But the county also claims a large slice of Loch Lomond which is absolutely beautiful as well as romantic-sounding Bannockburn stirring historic heartstrings … but then Stirlingshire occupies a central position between the Highlands and the Lowlands and is like a belt around the narrow waist of Scotland, and has held a pivotal position in Scottish history for centuries.

TOWNS AND VILLAGES

Stand on the battlements of Stirling Castle resting as it does some 250 feet high on a great basalt rock and the battlefields of Stirling Bridge (1297) and Bannockburn (1314) are within easy view, while away to the north, beyond the boundary of the river Forth, lies the Highland Line and the country of the clans.

Stirling was a doorway in the 'Highland Line', the frontier with the Lowlands, overlooking the River Forth and 'the Forth bridles the wild Hielaníman', was an old saying of the Lowland Scots. The lock on the door was Stirling Castle, a splendid medieval pile, much rebuilt in the 14th and 15th centuries, which now contains the museum of the Argyll and Sutherland Highlanders. The castle has seen a lot of excitement in its 800-year history.

Stirling town has historic delights including the Church of the Holy Rood – or Rude – built in the 15th century and the place where, in 1543, the baby Mary was crowned Queen of Scots at the age of nine months. The town has a university, and the Smith Art Gallery and Museum contains an eclectic collection, ranging from Japanese samurai swords to the oldest curling stone ever found in Scotland, dating from 1511.

STIRLING *The castle was occupied by the French in the 16th century.*

One of the most popular sights in this close-set town is the Mercat Cross, which is crowned with a small unicorn known locally as 'The Puggie'; nobody seems to know why. Stirling is a place of narrow wynds and winding streets, and contains a good deal of fine architecture from the 17th and 18th centuries.

To the east lies the industrial area around Falkirk with the nearby oil refineries and docks of Grangemouth on the Forth estuary. The town of Falkirk itself has Roman roots and the remains of a Roman fort, as well as some fine architecture. Bridge of Allan, close to Stirling, is a Victorian spa, full of hydro hotels and a popular base for people touring north to Perthshire and the Rob Roy Country or for walks into the Ochil Hills or the Campsie Fells where the little village of Fintry is very picturesque, at the head of the Strathenderick valley.

From Fintry, you can roam north and west, across ever more empty farming country, to the loom of the Highlands. All roads west eventually lead to Drymen on Endrick Water, the gateway to Loch Lomond.

LOCAL HISTORY

The Romans came beyond the frontier of Britain, to build a Wall further north from Hadrian's, part of which included the fort at Falkirk. This was erected by Agricola in about AD80 and it eventually became part of the Antonine Wall (which failed to last as long as the one built by the Emperor Hadrian).

Close to Stirling lie those meccas for battlefield buffs, the sites of Bannockburn, where Robert the Bruce defeated Edward II (but it was another 14 years before the English recognized Bruce as the legitimate King of Scotland); and Stirling Brig, where William Wallace beat the English army but Edward I, known as The Hammer of the Scots, came north and defeated Wallace at Falkirk in 1298. Wallace was eventually captured, and then hanged, drawn and quartered at Smithfield, in 1305.

The story of Wallace is told in the 1995 film *Braveheart* starring and directed by Mel Gibson, but you can get closer to his story at the Wallace Memorial by Stirling, which contains such relics as Wallace's sword. From the Wallace Memorial there is a winding footpath to another local attraction, the ruins of Cabuskenneth Abbey, a mile to the east of Stirling, which was founded in 1147 by David I, the man who built the Border Abbeys. Robert the Bruce held a Parliament here in 1326.

The Battlefield Centre at Bannockburn tells the full story of the battle and the Anglo-Scots wars. There is a splendid mounted statue of Bruce outside the centre, the King carrying the battle-axe he broke in single combat with an English knight, Sir Henry Bohun, before the battle started. The King sank his axe in Sir Henry's skull and cantered back to his cheering troops lamenting, 'I have broken the haft of my good battle-axe.'

COUNTY FACTS

Origin of name: Possibly from Strevelin meaning the dwelling of Velyn – again possibly referring to the name of a river on whose banks the town of Stirling stands.

Name first recorded: 1124.

County Town: STIRLING History abounds around this ancient town on top of a rock. With medieval castle beyond compare and remains of a medieval abbey at Cambuskenneth. Carpets and bacon-curing are the town's industries.

Other Towns: BANNOCKBURN Once a coal-mining village with a heritage centre devoted to the eponymous battlefield.

BONNYBRIDGE On the Clyde Canal with Antonine Wall castle left by the Romans.

BRIDGE OF ALLAN A pleasant touring centre and spa town lying on the Allan Water.

FALKIRK Once important for its cattle droving and coal-mining and the Carron iron works (where guns used in the battle of Waterloo were cast). Canals abound and it's the Forth Valley's commercial centre.

GRANGEMOUTH Forth estuary port and industrial town where the river Carron meets the Forth and Clyde Canal. Interesting industrial heritage museum.

LENNOXTOWN A good base to see the sparse and often misty Campsie moorland and waterfalls.

MILNGAVIE Small town in a pleasant setting with the Mugdock and Craigmaddie reservoirs and woodland to the north and several attractive local castles.

◆ Cowie ◆ Denny ◆ Dunipace ◆ Kilsyth ◆ Larbert ◆ Laurieston ◆ Polmont ◆ Stenhousemuir

County rivers: Bannockburn, Carron, Avon, Teith, Allan, Devon, Enfrick, Kelvin.

Highest point: Ben Lomond in the northwest extremity is 3,192 feet.

Stirlingshire's local government: The main area to the north is governed by Stirling unitary council. But the central belt stretching from Milngavie to Lennoxtown through Kilsyth, Denny and Falkirk until reaching the eastern end of the County at Grangemouth is divided up between the unitary authorities of East Dunbartonshire, North Lanarkshire and Falkirk – although a Stirlingshire town why didn't they call this district East Stirlingshire – if it's good enough for a football club surely it's good enough for a local council! Alva is Stirlingshire detached in Clackmannanshire and under that County's unitary council. Another tiny portion just southeast of Dunblane is Stirlingshire detached in Perthshire administered by Perth & Kinross unitary council.

COUNTY CALENDAR

◆ May: Clackmannan Mayfest Festival. A wide variety of artistic entertainment celebrated in the Trossachs and Stirling.

◆ July: The Stirling Highland Games, Stirling.

◆ July: Highland Games at Airth Northgreens Park, Airth, Falkirk.

◆ August: Highland Games at Bridge of Allan.

SUTHERLAND

THE COUNTY LANDSCAPE

◆ A land of mountain, heath and bog with very little cultivated except a few fertile glens and coastal strips, and very sparsely populated (except for deer).

◆ The county bordered by both the North Sea to the east and the Atlantic Ocean and giant cliffs of Cape Wrath to the northwest. In the northeast lies Caithness, in the west the Minch, and in the south Ross-shire and Cromartyshire.

◆ Most of the county is very broken and wild countryside, and is intersected by deer fences. The ground cover of heather and moorland grasses provides not only food for these animals but also a breeding ground for the notorious midges, which plague holidaymakers and residents alike during the summer months.

FAMOUS NAMES

◆ The last witch in Scotland was burned alive in a barrel of tar at Dornoch in 1772, having failed to accurately quote the Lord's Prayer in Gaelic during her trial, at which she was accused of turning her daughter into a pony. The event is commemorated by the Witches Stone, placed near the town square.

◆ The 3rd Duke of Sutherland was chairman and majority shareholder in the Sutherland Railway Company, aimed at stimulating development of the region, by extending the line from Culrain to Lairg. The third-class fare across the viaduct over the Dornoch Firth from Culrain to Invershin was held at the price of one-halfpenny until 1917, the cheapest ticket in the country.

◆ The county gave its name to the Sutherland Highlanders or 93rd Foot who made history as the 'thin red line' at the battle of Balaclava in the Crimean War.

COUNTY CALENDAR

◆ Early July: Dornoch Festival Week.

◆ Late July: Highland Games at Durness.

◆ Late July: The Sutherland County Show is held at Dornoch.

◆ Early August: Gala Week in Golspie.

◆ Early August: Salmon Queen Week is held at Bonar Bridge when a newly-elected Salmon Queen is ceremonially crowned in the presence of local dignitaries by the bridge at Bonar.

◆ Mid-August: Highland Gathering.

◆ End August: Sutherland has its Sheepdog Trials at Golspie.

LOCHINVER *Highland Games with traditional costumed competition dancing.*

ISOLATED, SOLITARY, LONELY … this county is a grand and savage landscape, with awesome mountain and coastal scenery, which evokes most people's conception of what constitutes the Scottish Highlands. There's something very special about a place where you can roam free, and where the sky, mountains and seas all interlock to satisfy the spirit of the hungriest soul. Sutherland assuages that thirst.

TOWNS AND VILLAGES

People were not always thin on the ground here of course: the 15,000 clansmen who once dwelled here with their kith and kin would have made up a sizeable population. But in the 19th century they were removed to make room for sheep, starting with the order of the Duke of Sutherland in 1811 amid scenes of great brutality and suffering. These so-called clearances forceably re-settled the people into small allotments and crofts on the coast or, in most cases, they were forced to cross the oceans to settle as far afield as Canada and Australia. The clearances are still marked by roofless crofts in the glens and bare patches on the hillsides, while most of the existing settlements are to be found scattered along the coasts.

Blessed with a fairly sunny climate, Dornoch has become a middle-class holiday resort. The cathedral, built in 1224, and surrounded by other sandstone buildings in the spacious square, was the victim of the Countess of Sutherland's 'restoration' work in 1835, but fortunately much of this has now been rectified. Ten miles north of Dornoch is the straggling town of Golspie, its challenging golf course and Dunrobin Castle, modelled on a Loire Château by its architect Sir Charles Barry, who also designed the Houses of Parliament. Now partly used as a boys' school, it is the seat of the infamous Sutherland family whose wealth as one of Europe's biggest landowners was, in part, generated by their role as the principal force behind the Clearances.

The opulence of the interior and its furnishings (including two Canalettos) bears testimony to the fact, along with the macabre host of hunting trophies and other curiosities contained in the museum. A 100-foot monument to the first Duke of Sutherland dominates the nearby summit of Benn a'Bhragaidh (1,293 feet), carrying a saccharine inscription which makes no reference to the fact that he forcibly evicted thousands of tenants from his million-acre estate. There have been several attempts to blow the monument up, and campaigners are still lobbying to have it destroyed.

A scenically splendid route to Cape Wrath is from the westerly village of Kinlochbervie passing along the coast and across the beautiful golden stretch of Sandwood Bay. Six miles east of Durness, and ringed by limestone mountains, are the deep waters of Loch Eriboll, the north coast's most spectacular sea-loch. Servicemen stationed in this isolated spot during the Second World War to protect the Russian convoys nicknamed it 'Loch 'Orrible', but its wild and untamed aspect also offers the prospect of seeing porpoises, otters and minke whales.

LOCAL HISTORY

When travelling here you are travelling over one of the oldest known parts of the world, hundreds, nay thousands of millions of years old. The grandeur of the mountain-scape gives you an inkling of this, or should. Ancient brochs (castles), Celtic crosses, and the ruins and emptiness which relate to the area's 400 years of involvement with the House of Stuart are still visible, including the remains of roads and barracks which were built to enforce the will of government upon the clans.

In 1517, during the minority of James V, and during the absence of Adam, Earl of Sutherland, the MacKays of Strathnaver laid waste to much of the area. The Countess of Sutherland, with the aid of other clans, defeated them decisively at Torran-Dubh. MacKay was subsequently forced to submit to the Earl of Sutherland the following year.

COUNTY FACTS

Origin of name: From the occupation of Caithness by Norsemen to whom these lands were "South Land".

Name first recorded: c. 1040 as Sudrland.

County motto: *Dluth Lean Do Dhuthchas Le Durachd* ("Cling To Thy Heritage With Diligence").

County Town: **DORNOCH** Dates from the 12th century and was established as a Royal Burgh in 1628 and became a county town in 1633. It stands on a headland surrounded by sand dunes. The stained glass windows in the north wall of the cathedral were endowed by the American philanthropist Andrew Carnegie. The 16th-century Bishop's Palace has been transformed into an upmarket hotel, and the old town gaol a bookshop.

Other Towns:

BETTYHILL Hamlet founded by Lady Elizabeth of Stafford as agri-and fishing centre to alleviate hardship of the barbaric Sutherland Clearances of 1810-20.

BRORA Miles of golden sand and a golf course laid out by one of the great early Scottish golfers James Braid who was the first golfer to win five British Open Championships titles (between 1901 and 1910) .

DURNESS The most northwesterly village on the British mainland, and the centre of several crofting communities, the descendants of the few not forced off their land during the 19th-century clearances. It also has the Smoo Cave, a 200-foot long natural wonder formed by the action of the sea and a small local burn which boasts some unusual rock formations. The village is a jumping-off point for a day-long walk to Cape Wrath, the UK mainland's most north-westerly point with its prominent lighthouse built by the novelist Robert Louis Stevenson's father..

HELMSDALE Working fishing harbour once overlooked by a castle but now by a road bridge. Nearby are many foundations of the crofters simple turf houses. Has a ruined castle built in 1488.

GOLSPIE Has magnificent Dunrobin Castle looking like a French château with high sea-view terraces.

KILDONAN Many an archaeological remain and scene of the gold rush of 1868-69.

LAIRG Resort and gateway to the Sutherland glens.

LOCHINVER Crofting and fishing centre with the fantastic sugar-loaf mountain of Suilven rising behind it. This is a great place for touring this rugged area and views of this and Cul Mori, Cul bearg and Stac Polly await the intrepid walker.

MELVICH Great salmon fishing on the Halladale River with the striking Bighouse Rocks at its mouth.

TONGUE Pretty town and coastal walking centre around the lush Kyle of Tongue.

County rivers: Eanack, Carron, Oykill, Cassley, Shin, Fleet, Brora, Helmsdale, Halladale, Strathey, Naver, Torrisdale, Hope to name a few.

Highest point: The peak of Ben More of Assynt at 3,431 feet.

Sutherland's local government: The County of Sutherland is governed by Highland unitary council.

WEST LOTHIAN

LINLITHGOWSHIRE

THE COUNTY LANDSCAPE

◆ West Lothian is green and pleasant where it is not occupied by housing and commercial developments spreading out from Edinburgh and Glasgow.

◆ The lower reaches of the Forth are attractive and there is always the hint of the sea in West Lothian, especially when an east wind is blowing.

◆ Linlithgow Loch is a fine stretch of water and the region is well supplied with streams, mostly flowing north into the tidal waters of the Forth.

◆ Of course, West Lothian must not be confused with the other Lothians: East Lothian and Midlothian, all of them laid out in a rough semi-circle south of Scotland's capital, Edinburgh. West Lothian is the smallest of these three counties and runs, roughly, from the Forth Bridge, up the river towards the town of Falkirk in Stirlingshire, and southwest from the Forth.

COUNTY CALENDAR

◆ June: The most historic event in West Lothian takes place in early June, when at around 0700 hours the villagers of Blackness are woken by the sound of two flute players and a drummer heralding the Riding of the Linlithgow Marches, an event which dates back to the granting of the town's charter in 1389. This now consists of a march around the boundaries of Linlithgow and Blackness and includes the laying of wreaths on the War Memorials and the consumption of a great deal of Blackness Milk. The finale of this event is the enthroning of the Baron Bailie, who is installed or reinstalled at the Barons' Court on Castle Hill.

THE BRIEF STRIP of countryside that makes up West Lothian tends to be dominated by the great swathes of nearby Edinburgh and Glasgow, though this is not to say that the county is without its own architectural or historic interest. Far from it, for who cannot feel the spirit of the famous palace and church at Linlithgow, where the ill-fated Mary, Queen of Scots was born? This town, the name of which was formerly applied to the county as a whole, dominates West Lothian's scenic and historic interest, but South Queensferry also has strong connections to the Scots monarchy, and there are great in-every-sense-of-the-word houses like the Binns, Hopetoun House and Niddery Castle.

TOWNS AND VILLAGES

A gateway erected by James V leads you to the palace, now a romantic ruin which, since 1746, has remained unroofed and uninhabited and stands on a mound overlooking Linlithgow Loch. The church (of St Michael) is one of the finest in Scotland and is exceptionally richly detailed. Though it is best known for these ancient monuments, Linlithgow town itself is worth inspection. It lies 18 miles east of Edinburgh, along the shores of Linlithgow Loch, and although the town is medieval, many of the former houses were replaced by Victorian dwellings in the last century.

The centre of the town is clustered around the Cross, which still contains the Cross Well, dating from 1535, and once the town's only source of fresh water. All the main streets run off the Cross and most of the most memorable houses stand nearby, like the Town House, which dates from about 1660 though it was rebuilt, rather well, after a fire in 1847. Notice, too, the Cross House, in

BLACKNESS *A formidable fortress.*

the corner of the Square, once the home of a passionate Jacobite lady, who in 1745 greeted Bonnie Prince Charlie with flowers and an orchestra and fountains flowing with wine.

Another place well worth a visit hereabouts is Abercorn, 6 miles east of Linlithgow, a tiny place but full of charm, set about a much-restored 12th-century church. This little village lies alongside one of the great houses of the Lothians, Hopetoun House, seat of the Marquis of Linlithgow and dating from 1703, though much enlarged by the Adam family, William, Robert and John, at the latter end of the 18th century. It is a splendid mansion with rich treasures and a museum and stands in a fine park overlooking the estuary of the Forth.

Dalmeny House, close to South Queensferry, was built in 1815 and is the seat of the Earl of Rosebery. The house is Neo-Gothic and full of treasures, including fine French furniture and paintings by Reynolds, Gainsborough and Lawrence.

South Queensferry is overshadowed, in every sense of the word, by the Forth Bridges: the 1890 rail bridge taking trains from Edinburgh to the Fife coasts and the 1964 road bridge spanning the widening Forth Estuary here. But as the name implies, Queensferry had a crossing here long before the rail bridge was opened in the Victorian era. Queen Margaret, wife of Malcolm Canmore, established a ferry here in the early years of the 12th century, so that pilgrims could cross the Forth and visit the shrine of St Andrew in Fife.

As a final place to visit there is pretty Blackness, four miles east of Linlithgow on the banks of the Forth. Blackness was the port of Linlithgow and gained a Royal Charter as long ago as 1389, a fact celebrated with a local drink, Blackness Milk – a mixture of milk and whisky. Blackness Castle was used as a prison for Covenanters in the 17th century.

LOCAL HISTORY

Visitors to West Lothian are most often attracted there by the story of Mary, Queen of Scots, who was born at Linlithgow Palace in 1542. Charles I spent a night in the Palace in 1633 and 'Butcher' Cumberland slept there on his way back from victory at Culloden in 1746, his troops setting the palace alight before leaving. Linlithgow Palace is now a beautiful ruin. The Forth Bridge is 1 mile and 972 yards long, covers an area of 145 acres, contains over 6½ million rivets, and takes 17 tons of special rust-resisting paint to cover the iron of the arch, a task that takes four years to complete.

COUNTY FACTS

Origin of name: Named from Leudonus, and signifying his territory. No one knows who or what Leudonus was. It has been suggested, though with little confidence, that he may have been Loth, grandfather of St Mungo.

Name first recorded: c. 970 as Lothian.

County Town:
LINLITHGOW Medieval town that has suffered from 1960s town-planning madness. Now a centre for the microchips industries. Some of the finest buildings now sadly lost. From here you can walk along the Union Canal all the way to the centre of Edinburgh.

Other Towns:
ARMADALE A mining town standing at over 500 feet.
BLACKNESS 15th-century Blackness Castle, built (if you use a lot of imagination!) in the shape of a galleon.
BO'NESS The name is a contraction of Borrowstounness. Scotland's largest vintage train centre is here. Also a 16th/17th century mansion.
LIVINGSTON Administrative centre and designated new town since 1962, set in Scotland's so-called Silicon Valley. Where you pay your Sky TV subs.
SOUTH QUEENSFERRY The Forth Bridge, completed in 1890, was hailed as one of the wonders of the modern world, but is in fact heavily over-engineered. Now it must be repainted incessantly.
◆ Blackburn ◆ Blackridge ◆ Broxburn ◆ Fauldhouse ◆ Kirkliston ◆ Uphall ◆ Winchburgh

County river: Avon.

Highest point: The Knock at 1,023 feet.

West Lothian's local government: In recent times the cry has gone up with politicians asking for the answer to the West Lothian question! If it is anything to do with the local government of the County it could be quite a time coming. The east of West Lothian around South Queensferry comes under the auspices of Midlothian's City of Edinburgh unitary authority. The west edge around the town of Bo'ness comes under Falkirk's (Stirlingshire) unitary authority. Only the southern part of the County of West Lothian plus a tiny piece on the Forth coast called The Binns is governed by West Lothian unitary council.

FAMOUS NAMES

◆ Mary, Queen of Scots, born at Linlithgow Palace in 1542, must be the first of all the local famous names.
◆ General Sir Tam Dalyell, who founded the Royal Scots Greys cavalry regiment and served in the Civil War as a Royalist commander, is less well known today than his descendant Tam Dalyell, Westminster MP. This MP posed the famous and tricky West Lothian question – can Scots MPs sitting in a devolved Scottish assembly still retain the right to sit in on debates which concern matters affecting England – and harassed Mrs Thatcher over the *Belgrano* affair during the 1982 Falklands War.

WIGTOWNSHIRE

WEST GALLOWAY

THE COUNTY LANDSCAPE

◆ This is the extreme end of Scotland's large and relatively empty southwest corner, a quiet sea girt part of the country, with an exceptionally long coastline, completely bypassed by main routes. A glance at a map will tell you why – apart from taking the ferry at Stranraer to and from Larne in County Antrim, and local journeying, there is little reason to traverse this county in the Irish Sea. There are no big urban centres and the main roads from Carlisle to the south and Ayr to the north are sited well to the east, leaving Wigtown to enjoy its open hilly countryside, the sea that almost surrounds it and the solitude of its unique position.

◆ The forested hills and bleak moors that back up the coasts protect Wigtownshire from cold blasts from the north. The county is therefore blessed with good beaches, some fine gardens, and surprisingly high temperatures for a northerly latitude it shares with Northern Canada and Russia.

◆ The southern part of Scotland is known as the Lowlands, yet there are plenty of hills here. The underlying granite rock supports a diverse array of scenery from high moors to agricultural land in the Machars peninsula, from cliffy bays to river valleys and lochs. There is good salmon and trout angling, and sea fishing in Loch Ryan.

FAMOUS NAMES

◆ Clans associated with the area are the Macdowall and Kennedy.

◆ Sir Walter Scott used the area, notably ruined Baldoon Castle, as a setting for his *Bride of Lammermoor*.

◆ St Ninian, son of a local chieftain who converted to Christianity and brought it to Scotland in AD395, landing on the Isle of Whithorn after journeying from Rome.

◆ The ill-fated Mary, Queen of Scots visited Whithorn's priory in 1563.

COUNTY CALENDAR

◆ June: Stranraer has pipe concerts where competitors come from far and near, including Ireland, as well as and contests and a Scottish Week.

◆ Summer: There are regattas and sailing events at the Isle of Whithorn.

◆ Early July. Newton Stewart hosts a pageant where the Queen of Galloway is crowned annually in front of McMillan Hall.

◆ Early August: Wigtown's annual show takes place.

WIGTOWNSHIRE *Idyllic setting of Tart Water in the southern Lowlands.*

SCOTLAND'S MOST SOUTHERLY county reaches out to Ireland and seems almost to touch it – it's Britain's shortest ferry-crossing to the Emerald Isle and the province of Ulster at Larne in County Antrim. This is the Cornwall of Scotland because it has a coast exposed to the south and the gentle breath of the Gulf Stream. As long as that warm current continues its wide surge across the Atlantic this broad and deeply indented peninsula will enjoy a dulcet climate, especially along the coasts where sub-tropical plants are not unusual.

TOWNS AND VILLAGES

Wigtown gives its name to the county, and it is a pleasant place with a large central square containing not one but two market crosses.There is a monument to the Covenanters at Windyhill above the town. At Bladnoch are the early 19th-century buildings of Scotland's most southerly whisky distillery.

Heading down the eastern shore of Wigtown Bay and the broad fertile finger of The Machars you come to Garlieston, a fishing village with a harbour given over to pleasure craft. This was the home of the earls of Galloway: the 18th-century mansion still stands near the village.Its gardens sloping to the beach contain the inevitable rhododendrons and azaleas, but also a walled garden and spring displays of flowering bulbs.

The peninsula ends with Burrow Head and the Isle of Whithorn, with ruins of an ancient chapel and a tower, with a nearby Iron Age fort.

The neck of land before the hammerheaded peninsular is known as The Rhinns of Galloway. It is a largely agricultural area and within this warm location are several gardens. Here the famous Castle Kennedy Gardens spread around the ruined tower with an old monkey puzzle tree avenue. Glenwhan Gardens were begun quite recently and contain sub-tropical plants in a hilltop site with views down Luce Bay. At Soulseat herbs are grown in a one time abbey precinct at Meadowsweet Herb Gardens.

The A75 ends at Stranraer, the county's largest town and commercial capital, with ferries or a swift catamaran crossing to Ireland. This is a busy town with gardens and parks. In the middle is the 16th-century tower house, the Castle of St John Visitor Centre, a museum devoted to law and order – appropriate for the original town jail. There's also a museum of local history.

A drive south takes you to several fine beaches – notably at Sandhead. At Ardwell is another noted garden. Drummore, Scotland's most southerly village, sits on the northerly point of the double promontory that marks the Mull of Galloway. The other point has a prehistoric fort. There are beaches, cliffs and a lighthouse with views as far as Ireland, England and the Isle of Man. On the western coast is the sheltered seaside village of Portpatrick with a museum of model railways and toy transportation. Nearby Dunskey Castle is an impressive clifftop ruin. At Port Logan are the Botanic Gardens and a tidal pool where cod are so tame they can be fed by hand.

The northern part of the county toward Ayrshire is open hill and moor country, with a road, the A77, continuing along the coast and passing through Cairnryan at the border.

LOCAL HISTORY

The Stones of Torhouse, near Wigtown, are of Bronze Age origin, 19 standing stones in a circle. There are also many ruined castles, relics of the battles of Robert the Bruce and an indication of Wigtownshire's struggles for religious and political freedom. The area also has memorials to early Presbyterians, the martyred Covenanters, of which one of the saddest and grimmest episodes in the sad and grim history of Scotland took place at Wigtown. Two women, Margaret Wilson and Margaret McLachlan, one aged 18 the other a widow of 83, were tied to stakes and drowned in the River Bladnoch for the 'crime' of being Covenanters and attending open-air services (conventacles).

COUNTY FACTS

Origin of name: Wigtown is said to be the Old English for a manor "town". The county was also known as Galloway East.

Name first recorded: 1266 as Wigeton.

County Town:

WIGTOWN Peaceful and homely atmosphere pervades in the county's oldest town which had its first Sheriff in 1264 and was granted a charter as a Royal Burgh by King David II in 1341.

Other Towns:

CAIRNRYAN This simple whitewashed lakeshore town (Loch Ryan is a sea loch) belies its importance as a war time port. Parts of the famous mulberry harbours, vital floating docks used at the Normandy invasions, were made here.

GLENLUCE Set in a broad-bottomed valley with a motor museum of vintage cars and classic bikes and a Cistercian abbey, its noble chapter house alone saved from the ruins. The Tudor battlemented Castle of Park surveys the village from across the river.

PORTPATRICK Tropical plants flourish in this picturesque port and for six months it is a riot of colour. In 1662 it had Stranraer's place as the terminal for the shortest sea-crossing to Ireland.

PORT WILLIAM On the west coast facing Luce Bay is Port William and the 18th-century Monreith House with an ancient Celtic cross. Nearby is the ruined chapel of St Finian on the beach.

NEWTON STEWART This is the first town you encounter crossing the River Cree on a granite bridge from the neighbouring county of Kirkcudbrightshire. The town is small yet lively, with woollen mills making mohair items and a livestock market. Nearby is the Wood of Cree, a bird sanctuary with native birch and oaks.

STRANRAER The most populous town, and the commercial and industrial centre, with the port for Northern Ireland plying ferries for Larne and hovercrafts to Belfast. Back in the 14th century the Knights of St John of Jerusalem had a property here called St John's Croft, and the remains of the Castle of St John bear witness to this heritage. The site later became a police station and prison.

WHITHORN May be the site of the first Christian church in Scotland (and claims to be the birthplace of Christianity in Scotland), for here St Ninian built his White House. (The cave he supposedly lived in is on the opposite coast.) The ruins of the later priory may contain this building. There's an ongoing archaeological dig and visitor centre and in the local museum are early Christian relics. It also has an fine wide harbour. Has the richest history in the county.

◆ Drummore ◆ Garlieston ◆ Kirkcolm ◆ Spittal

County rivers: Cree, Luce, Bladnoch.

Highest point: Craigairie at 1,025 feet.

Wigtownshire's local government: The County of Wigtownshire is administered by the unitary Dumfries and Galloway council.

ACKNOWLEDGEMENTS

◆ Special thanks to Michael Bradford, Chairman of the Association of British Counties.
Laurence Bresh of the British Tourist Association.
The Welsh Tourist Board for all their help.
◆ Much thanks to Louisa Somerville for editing support and Nick Withers for dtp assistance. To Carolyn Price at Virgin for her constant project-editorial encouragement.

CONTRIBUTORS

◆ **Robin Neillands**
Travel and travel-guide writer since 1976. He has authored books on walking through Britain and is a frequent contributor to many publications including *The Times* and *Financial Times.*

◆ **Michael Leech**
Writer of several *AA travel guides* and has a regular travel feature on BBC-BFBS radio.

◆ **Tim Ware**
Contributor to *Reader's Digest Discovering Britain* as well as to many other prominent publications including the *Scotsman, Business Traveller,* and *The Sunday Telegraph.*

◆ **Nia Williams**
Writer-editor on travel books. Contributor to the *Rough Guides, Michelin (Wales)* and *The Eyewitness Guide to Britain.*

◆ **Keith Howell**
Author of several travel books. Has broadcast on LBC and is a contributor to Classic FM.

PICTURE CREDITS

All pictures from Spectrum Colour Library except Edward Kinsey (p93, 94, 95, 96, 99), Welsh Tourist Board (p155, 157, 160, 162, 164, 168, 180), CEPHAS (p80) Dennis Hardley (p218, 230, 238), Collections (p42, 59, 78, 109, 111), Peter Smith Photography - Malton (p57), Philip Nixon (p59), Joseph Wedgewood and Co (p126), Southern Reporter, Selkirk (p244), Poole Pottery (p54).

The coats of arms
England: Bedfordshire (granted 1951), Berkshire (granted 1947), Buckinghamshire (granted pre-1948), Cambridgeshire (granted 1914),Cheshire (granted 1938), Cornwall (granted 1939), Cumberland (granted 1951), Derbyshire (1937), Devon (granted 1926), Dorset (granted 1950), Durham (granted 1961), Essex (granted 1932), Gloucestershire (granted 1935), Hampshire, Herefordshire (granted 1946), Hertfordshire (granted 1925), Huntingdonshire (granted 1937), Kent (granted 1933), Lancashire (granted 1903), Leicestershire (granted 1930), Lincolnshire (granted 1977), Middlesex (granted 1910), Norfolk (granted 1904), Northamptonshire (granted 1939), Northumberland (granted 1951), Nottinghamshire (granted 1937), Oxfordshire (granted 1949), Rutland (granted 1950), Shropshire (granted 1896), Somerset (granted 1911), Staffordshire (granted 1931), Suffolk County Council (granted 1977), Surrey (granted 1934), Sussex, Warwickshire (granted 1931), Westmorland (granted 1926), Wiltshire (granted 1937), Worcestershire (granted 1947), Yorkshire: East Riding (granted 1945), North Riding (granted 1928), West Riding (granted 1927)

Wales: Anglesey (granted 1954), Breconshire (granted 1933), Caernarfonshire (granted 1949), Cardiganshire (granted 1957), Carmarthenshire (granted 1935), Denbighshire (granted 1962), Flintshire (granted 1938), Glamorgan (granted 1950), Merioneth (granted 1952), Monmouthshire (granted 1948), Pembrokeshire (granted 1937), Radnorshire (granted 1950)

Scotland: Aberdeenshire (granted 1890), Angus (granted 1927), Argyllshire (granted 1953), Ayrshire (granted 1931), Banffshire (granted 1951 and 1971), Berwickshire (granted 1890), Buteshire (granted 1927), Caithness (granted 1935), Clackmannanshire (granted 1927), Dumfriesshire (granted 1928), Dumbartonshire (granted 1927), East Lothian (granted 1927), Fife (granted 1927), Inverness-shire (granted 1927), Kincardineshire (1927), Kinross-shire (1927) Kirkcudbrightshire (granted 1951), Lanarkshire (granted 1886), Midlothian (granted 1951), Morayshire (granted 1927), Nairnshire (granted 1927), Orkney (granted 1931), Peebleshire (granted 1931), Perthshire (granted 1800), Renfrewshire (granted 1889), Ross-shire. Cromartyshire (granted 1957), Roxburghshire (granted 1798), Selkirkshire (granted 1927), Shetland (granted 1956), Stirlingshire (granted 1890), Sutherland (granted 1957), West Lothian (granted 1952), Wigtownshire (granted 1955)